D1564170

# The Biblical Interpretation
# of William of Alton

OXFORD STUDIES IN HISTORICAL THEOLOGY

Series Editor
David C. Steinmetz, Duke University
Editorial Board
Irena Backus, Université de Genève
Robert C. Gregg, Stanford University
George M. Marsden, University of Notre Dame
Wayne A. Meeks, Yale University
Gerhard Sauter, Rheinische Friedrich-Wilhelms-Universität Bonn
Susan E. Schreiner, University of Chicago
John Van Engen, University of Notre Dame
Geoffrey Wainwright, Duke University
Robert L. Wilken, University of Virginia

THE UNACCOMMODATED CALVIN
*Studies in the Foundation of a Theological Tradition*
Richard A. Muller

THE CONFESSIONALIZATION OF HUMANISM
IN REFORMATION GERMANY
Erika Rummell

THE PLEASURE OF DISCERNMENT
*Marguerite de Navarre as Theologian*
Carol Thysell

REFORMATION READINGS OF THE
APOCALYPSE
*Geneva, Zurich, and Wittenberg*
Irena Backus

WRITING THE WRONGS
*Women of the Old Testament among Biblical
Commentators from Philo through the Reformation*
John L. Thompson

THE HUNGRY ARE DYING
*Beggars and Bishops in Roman Cappadocia*
Susan R. Holman

RESCUE FOR THE DEAD
*The Posthumous Salvation of Non-Christians in Early
Christianity*
Jeffrey A. Trumbower

AFTER CALVIN
*Studies in the Development of a Theological Tradition*
Richard A. Muller

THE POVERTY OF RICHES
*St. Francis of Assisi Reconsidered*
Kenneth Baxter Wolf

REFORMING MARY
*Changing Images of the Virgin Mary in Lutheran Sermons
of the Sixteenth Century*
Beth Kreitzer

TEACHING THE REFORMATION
*Ministers and Their Message in Basel, 1529–1629*
Amy Nelson Burnett

THE PASSIONS OF CHRIST IN HIGH-MEDIEVAL
THOUGHT
*An Essay on Christological Development*
Kevin Madigan

GOD'S IRISHMEN
*Theological Debates in Cromwellian Ireland*
Crawford Gribben

REFORMING SAINTS
*Saints' Lives and Their Authors in Germany, 1470–1530*
David J. Collins

GREGORY OF NAZIANZUS ON THE TRINITY
AND THE KNOWLEDGE OF GOD
*In Your Light We Shall See Light*
Christopher A. Beeley

THE JUDAIZING CALVIN
*Sixteenth-Century Debates over the Messianic Psalms*
G. Sujin Pak

THE DEATH OF SCRIPTURE AND THE RISE OF
BIBLICAL STUDIES
Michael C. Legaspi

THE FILIOQUE
A. Edward Siecienski

ARE YOU ALONE WISE?
*Debates about Certainty in the Early Modern Church*
Susan E. Schreiner

EMPIRE OF SOULS
*Robert Bellarmine (1542–1621) and the Christian
Commonwealth*
Stefania Tutino

MARTIN BUCER'S DOCTRINE OF
JUSTIFICATION
*Reformation Theology and Early Modern Irenicism*
Brian Lugioyo

CHRISTIAN GRACE AND PAGAN VIRTUE
*The Theological Foundation of Ambrose's Ethics*
J. Warren Smith

KARLSTADT AND THE ORIGINS OF THE
EUCHARISTIC CONTROVERSY
*A Study in the Circulation of Ideas*
Amy Nelson Burnett

READING AUGUSTINE IN THE REFORMATION
*The Flexibility of Intellectual Authority in Europe,
1500–1620*
Arnoud S. Q. Visser

SHAPERS OF ENGLISH CALVINISM, 1660–1714
*Variety, Persistence, and Transformation*
Dewey D. Wallace, Jr.

THE BIBLICAL INTERPRETATION OF WILLIAM
OF ALTON
Timothy Bellamah, O.P.

# The
# Biblical
# Interpretation
# of William
# of Alton

BS
501
W56 B46
2011
web

TIMOTHY BELLAMAH, O.P.

**OXFORD**
UNIVERSITY PRESS

# OXFORD
### UNIVERSITY PRESS

Oxford University Press, Inc., publishes works that further
Oxford University's objective of excellence
in research, scholarship, and education.

Oxford    New York
Auckland    Cape Town    Dar es Salaam    Hong Kong    Karachi
Kuala Lumpur    Madrid    Melbourne    Mexico City    Nairobi
New Delhi    Shanghai    Taipei    Toronto

With offices in
Argentina    Austria    Brazil    Chile    Czech Republic    France    Greece
Guatemala    Hungary    Italy    Japan    Poland    Portugal    Singapore
South Korea    Switzerland    Thailand    Turkey    Ukraine    Vietnam

Copyright © 2011 by Oxford University Press, Inc.

Published by Oxford University Press, Inc.
198 Madison Avenue, New York, New York 10016

www.oup.com

Oxford is a registered trademark of Oxford University Press

All rights reserved. No part of this publication may be reproduced,
stored in a retrieval system, or transmitted, in any form or by any means,
electronic, mechanical, photocopying, recording, or otherwise,
without the prior permission of Oxford University Press.

Library of Congress Cataloging-in-Publication Data
Bellamah, Timothy.
The biblical interpretation of William of Alton / Timothy Bellamah.
    p.    cm. — (Oxford studies in historical theology)
Includes bibliographical references (p.        ).
ISBN 978-0-19-975360-4 (hardcover : alk. paper)
1. William, of Alton, 13th cent. 2. Bible—Criticism, interpretation, etc.—History—
Middle Ages, 600–1500. I. Title.
BS501.W56B46    2011
220.609′022—dc22        2010041096

1  3  5  7  9  8  6  4  2

Printed in the United States of America
on acid-free paper

# Contents

# *Preface*

MOST STUDIES OF medieval biblical interpretation have dwelt on the relevant literature that has appeared in print. This is hardly surprising, but this focus has resulted in the neglect of the vast majority of extant commentaries, which have never been printed. The pioneering work of Beryl Smalley and the more recent studies of Gilbert Dahan have done much to fill this void. Still, much of the history of medieval biblical interpretation as it was shaped during the thirteenth century remains to be written. Writing it will require the authentification, edition, and analysis of the commentaries of those who dominated the field, notably the regent masters in theology at the universities of Paris and Oxford.

William of Alton was a Dominican regent master at Paris during the mid-thirteenth century. As this was a period of rapid methodological development, his commentaries have much to offer for our understanding of medieval biblical studies, both as an endeavor of the schoolroom and as an instrument for preaching. The aim of the present study is to identify William's authentic commentaries and to examine them in comparison with those of other thirteenth-century regent masters, particularly those of Hugh of St. Cher, Bonaventure, Albert the Great, and Thomas Aquinas.

The present study has been made possible by the assistance and support of no small number of people. Over the course of several years, many friends and colleagues have very generously responded to my requests for advice and criticism. Responsibility for any failings in the application of their observations is entirely mine. My gratitude goes out first and foremost to Professor Gilbert Dahan, who approved the project and guided it throughout. From the outset of my reading of medieval manuscripts and my study of medieval exegesis, he has allowed me to benefit from his well-judged advice and criticisms with competence, patience, and kindness. A particular debt is also owed to the late Fr. Louis-Jacques Bataillon, who shared with me his remarkable knowledge of thirteenth-century biblical commentary and passed on to me his own discoveries in the field. With his keen eye for detail and fine judgment, he generously read my monograph as well as my editions of Latin texts. His many judicious suggestions and corrections have been invaluable. Without them, the present study and the accompanying editions would have been less accurate, and for that I extend to him my deepest gratitude. Also to be thanked is Fr. Gilles Berceville, who generously proofread the chapter concerning William's use of patristic and medieval sources and offered several helpful suggestions. Finally, I would like to express my gratitude to the members of the Leonine Commission and to all the brothers of the Dominican Province of St. Joseph and those at Saint-Jacques, Paris. Without their fraternal support and the use of their libraries, this project would not have come to completion. May all of them be assured of my lasting gratitude.

# Abbreviations

| | |
|---|---|
| AFH | *Archivum Franciscanum Historicum.* |
| AFP | *Archivum Fratrum Praedicatorum.* |
| AHDLMA | *Archives d'Histoire Doctrinale et Littéraire du Moyen Age.* |
| ALMA | *Archivum latinitatis medii aevi.* |
| BA | Bibliothèque Augustinienne. |
| BEFAR | Bibliothèque des Ecoles Françaises d'Athènes et de Rome. |
| BIHR | *Bulletin of the Institute of Historical Research.* |
| BJ | *Bible de Jérusalem.* |
| Bon. Opera | *S. Bonaventurae Opera Omnia*, t. VI, Quaracchi, 1893. |
| C | *Biblia sacra iuxta uulgatam Clementinam*, ed. A. Colunga and L. Turrado, Madrid, 4th ed., 2002. |
| CCCM | *Corpus Christianorum*, Continuatio Mediavalis. |
| CCSL | *Corpus Christianorum*, Series Latina. |
| CSEL | *Corpus Scriptorum Ecclesiaticorum Latinorum*, Vienna, 1866 sq. |
| CSLMA | *Clauis Scriptorum Latinorum Medii Aeui*, Turnhout, 1999. |
| CUP | *Chartularium Universitatis Parisiensis*, ed. H. Denifle and É. Chatelain, t. I–II, Paris, 1889–1897. |
| DACL | *Dictionnaire d'Archéologie Chrétienne et de Liturgie*, ed. F. Cabrol, O.S.B., and H. Leclercq, O.S.B., 15 vols., 1907–1953. |
| DHGE | *Dictionnaire d'Histoire et de Géographie Ecclesiastiques*, Paris, since 1912. |
| Dict Sp. | *Dictionnaire de Spiritualité.* |

DS    *Enchiridion symbolorum, definitionum et declatationum de rebus. fidei et morum*, ed. H. Denzinger, Barcelona, 1965.

DTC    *Dictionnaire de Théologie Catholique.*

GCS    Die griechischen christlichen Schriftsteller, Leipzig, 1897ff.

Handlist    R. Sharpe, *A Handlist of the Latin Writers of Great Britain and Ireland Before 1540*, Turnhout, 1997.

HLF    *Histoire littéraire de la France.*

LXX    *Vetus Latina. Die Reste der altlateinischen Bibel*, ed. R. Gryson, Freiburg, currently being published.

MEFRM    *Mélanges de l'École française de Rome*

MiAg    *Miscellanea Agostiniana.*

MOPH    *Monumenta Ordinis Praedicatorum Historica.*

MS    *Medieval Studies.*

NJBC    *The New Jerome Biblical Commentary*, ed. R. Brown, J. Fitzmyer, and R. Murphy, Englewood Cliffs, New Jersey, 1990.

PG    J. P. Migne, *Patrologiae Cursus Completus*, Series Graeca, Paris 1857–1868, 161 volumes.

PL    J. P. Migne, *Patrologiae Cursus Completus*, Series Latina, Paris 1844–1864, 221 volumes.

RAM    *Revue d'ascetique et de mystique* (= *Revue d'histoire de la spiritualité*).

RB    *Revue Biblique.*

Rep. Bibl.    F. Stegmüller, *Repertorium Biblicum Medii Aevi*, Madrid and Barcelona, vols. I–VII, Matriti 1950–1961; VIII–XI, 1976–1980, cura N. Reinhardt.

Réportoire    P. Glorieux, *Réportoire des maîtres en théologie de Paris au XIIIe siècle*, Paris, 1933.

RHE    *Revue d'Histoire Ecclésiastique.*

RSPT    *Revue des Sciences Philosophiques et Théologiques.*

RSV    *Revised Standard Version.*

RT    *Revue thomiste.*

RTAM    *Rechearches de Théologie ancienne et médiévale.*

"Sapiential Books I"    B. Smalley, « Some Thirteenth-Century Commentaries on the Sapiential Books », *Dominican Studies*, 2 (1949), 318–355; 3 (1950), 41–77, 236–274.

| | |
|---|---|
| "Sapiential Books II" | B. Smalley, « Some Latin Commentaries on the Sapiential Books in the Late Thirteenth and Early Fourteenth Centuries », *Archives d'histoire doctrinale et littéraire du Moyen Âge*, 18 (1950), 103–128. |
| SC | Sources Chrétiennes. |
| *SOP* | J. Quetif and J. Echard, *Scriptores Ordinis Praedicatorum*, Paris, 1719–1721. |
| *SOPMA* | T. Kaeppeli, *Scriptores Ordinis Praedicatorum Medii Aevi*, Rome, 1970–1993, 4 vols. (vol. 4: T. Kaeppeli and E. Panella). |
| SPM | Stromata Patristica et Mediaevalia. |
| *W* | *Biblia sacra iuxta uulgatam uersionem*, ed. R. Weber, 4th ed., Stuttgart, 1994. |

# Notes on Style

UNLESS OTHERWISE INDICATED, all translations are my own. Though the excerpts presented contain many quotations of earlier works that have long been available in modern editions and English translations, I have refrained from using them for the sake of following William's mode of expression as closely as possible. His texts of the writings of authors such as Jerome, Augustine, and Chrysostom often vary from modern editions and diverge considerably from English translations, while his own reading of them is verbatim. The same holds true for lemmata and citations of other biblical texts: his analysis of them is much too close to permit their substitution with modern translations, to which they seldom correspond precisely. They have therefore been translated with a view to expressing his understanding of them. However, to the extent possible Scriptural translations have been guided by the Douay-Rheims American edition of 1899, as it is largely based on the Vulgate. For all translations, the editions of the Latin originals have been presented in the notes, including references to the best available editions of any texts cited therein. Biblical references have been recorded according to the titles of books, abbreviations of titles, and numbering of chapters and verses as they appear in *Biblia sacra iuxta uulgatam uersionem* (ed. R. Weber, 4th ed., Stuttgart, 1994). Lemmata have been placed in italicized small capitals, and other biblical passages have been placed in italics.

*The Biblical Interpretation
of William of Alton*

# Introduction

"SACRED SCRIPTURE IS a sea because it is the origin from which all writings arise."[1] Such is one of several interpretations proposed in a thirteenth-century commentary on Ecclesiastes 1:7: *All streams run to the sea, but the sea is not full; to the place where the streams flow, there they flow again.* The remark says much about the frame of mind within which exegetes of the period read and commented upon the Bible. Whatever one may make of its claim concerning "all writings," it holds true for those to be considered here, the biblical commentaries of William of Alton and other university masters of the thirteenth century. All of them take the Bible as their inspiration and wellspring, and all of them are oriented toward the proclamation of the biblical narrative.

A Dominican regent master at the University of Paris, William of Alton was an important representative of university exegesis at a time of remarkable intellectual development—the third quarter of the thirteenth century. With varying degrees of probability, modern scholars have attributed to him no fewer than twenty-five biblical commentaries, few of which have been studied since the Middle Ages. And yet, this literature is of great interest to the history of biblical interpretation.

Chapter 1 provides a brief survey of the available information concerning William's life and works, as well as an account of the several obstacles to exploring them. By contrast with Bonaventure, Albert the Great, and Thomas Aquinas, each one recognized as a saint and doctor of the church, William has remained in the shadows.[2] Only rarely since the Middle Ages has he been cited or discussed by other authors, and apart from his recently edited postill *Super Threnos*,[3] none of his known works has been reproduced. Put another way, for several centuries he had virtually no literary history.[4] Another problem is that the commentaries ascribed to him pose numerous problems of attribution—most copies of the writings believed to be his are anonymous, and the fragmentary evidence left by medieval scribes is often contradictory. Further, the near absence of editions of any authenticated writings and the lack of any known theological treatises by him make it difficult to establish a basis for evaluating works of uncertain authenticity.

Chapter 2 is concerned with methodology. It considers the necessary procedures for determining which works are authentically William's. Figuring prominently here is the assessment of a kind of evidence not previously taken into account—the indications of each commentary's own methodology, exegetical concerns, and style. Though such an approach cannot be counted on to settle all questions concerning every commentary's authorship, it can be expected to supplement the available external manuscript evidence for establishing a credible bibliography.

A group of four commentaries—on Isaiah, Jeremiah, Lamentations, and John—constitutes a basis from which to identify a few distinctive features, or markers, of William's work. For each, we have uncontradicted firsthand manuscript ascriptions. As none presents methodological or stylistic traits absent from the commentaries of other authors of the same genre, university biblical exegesis, this study does not benefit from the identification of any particular methodological or stylistic marker proper to William. Still, they provide a basis for a typology of William's methodology and style. This typology is employed as a measure against which to evaluate each of the remaining twenty-one commentaries associated with William, henceforth Group B. Toward the end of supplying a background for measuring the distinctiveness of the traits found in Group A, we examine a substantial number of commentaries by several of William's near contemporaries—Simon of Hinton, William of Middleton, Bonaventure, Albert the Great, Peter of Tarantaise, Thomas Aquinas, William of Luxi, Nicolas of Gorran, and John of Varzy.

Toward the end of delineating a typology of William's style and methodology, the study attempts to identify a set of traits that distinguish William's language. Analysis is organized around four key elements of the genre of university commentary—the prologue, the *diuisio textus*, the exposition and the *questio*. A working assumption of this study is that extensive correspondence, and nothing less, to the typology of the commentaries of Group A adds up to clear evidence of authenticity. Guided by the principle that attributions are not to be multiplied without clear evidence, we apply a razor of sorts to the list of the other twenty-one works attributed to William. Of these, seventeen are set aside, and one is shown to be the same as another. Only three are accepted as authentic: commentaries on Ecclesiastes, Wisdom, and Ezekiel. Despite the attributions' varying degrees of certitude, it is remarkable that only three of twenty-one works were authenticated. Much of the explanation lies in the manner by which these commentaries were associated with William. Several were ascribed to him by librarians of later generations or even centuries. Others were connected with him by more recent scholars by virtue of their appearance in a codex containing other works thought to be his. Yet both sorts of judgments take for granted that a given commentary's authorship was a controlling concern for its inclusion in thirteenth-century manuscripts. The manuscripts themselves, however, suggest that the authorship of individual commentaries mattered far less to the original bookmakers than to scholars of later generations. For this reason, this study does not take as evidence of authenticity the mere fact of a commentary's inclusion in a manuscript containing authentic works. This, as well as the examination the commentaries' style and methodology, accounts for the exclusion of seventeen of the twenty-one works under consideration.

Chapter 3 considers William's exegesis, which is decidedly representative of the university genre. By William's time, biblical exegesis and theology had become scientific, not in the sense that they employed methods of testing hypotheses by experiment, but in the sense that they incorporated sustained and rigorous reflections upon methodology and made use of specialized analytic techniques. William's work may be called scientific insofar as it manifests these developments. This is not to say that it is nonconfessional. Many of its participants were Franciscan and Dominican commentators who made use of this genre of commentary for the specific objective of preparing friars for their task of preaching.

Thirteenth-century biblical interpretation was marked by an increasing interest in the literal sense and a progressive tendency to identify it with the author's intention. In both his methodological reflections and interpretations, William designates this sense as the intention of the divine author, which he in turn identifies with that of the human author. He was particularly keen to discern it, even by the standards of university scholarship. Toward this end, he used an array of procedures for textual, linguistic, and rhetorical analysis. All of this afforded him a very broad scope for expounding the literal sense—for him, it embraced a wide variety of rhetorical figures, as well as prophecy.

At the same time, our author realized that a given verse's full significance comes to light only within its assorted contexts, immediate and remote. By means of the *divisio textus*, the exposition of the prophetic literal sense, the *questio*, and the study of biblical history, he endeavored to take stock of the individual verse's context within its passage, its chapter, its book, and the Bible as a whole. All of this is consistent with a comprehensive view of history. William viewed biblical history as a continuing reality encompassing even the present.

It would be a mistake, however, to suppose that such concern for the literal sense came at the expense of interest in the spiritual ones. To be sure, scholars of the time generally proceeded to a given passage's allegorical and tropological interpretations only after having provided a literal one. But this was because they understood the spiritual senses to derive from the literal one, not because they imagined the two modes of interpretation to be at odds with one another. Spiritual commentary was central to William's exegetical project—within his work, there is no better place to look for indications of his exegetical purposes and his intended audience. By contrast with their counterparts in the monasteries, commentators of the mendicant orders worked primarily for the sake of preaching. Their commentaries were often used by other friars as resources for the preparation of their sermons, and several manuscripts containing William's works provide indications that his were put to such use. Yet his allegorical and tropological expositions reveal a more proximate purpose—the preparation of his students for preaching and exercising ecclesiastical authority. In his allegories, the Bible's assorted saints and sinners usually typify ecclesiastical figures, especially prelates, good and bad. In his tropologies, the saints tend to prefigure the virtues one would hope to see in a preacher or a prelate, while the sinners prefigure the vices that one often finds in them. But the functioning of such expositions was hardly limited to supplying moral examples, positive or negative. By presenting biblical images to the student's imagination, they furnished matter for contemplation and so facilitated preaching.

Chapter 4 examines William's critical use of sources. Throughout the Middle Ages, biblical interpretation necessarily took place within the additional context of the church's commentatorial tradition. Extensive borrowing from the works of earlier writers was therefore a hallmark of medieval commentary generally. More specific to university commentary was the use of broader ranges of sources and the application of specialized dialectical procedures for integrating them into original and coherent expositions. William often incorporated several of them at a time, and the assortment he drew upon was highly complex. Some were intermediaries containing pervasive borrowings from earlier writers. Others were the original texts of these same writers. Some were considered authoritative. Others were not. Because the pedagogy of the time was wholly dependent upon the use of authoritative texts, university commentators devoted considerable effort to reconciling them with each other, as well as with the church's doctrine. In this endeavor, William made use of several dialectical techniques. But neither he nor his contemporaries adopted the practice of obscuring the identities or meanings of various authorities to disguise their disagreements. Even more than his contemporaries, William tended to discuss such discrepancies openly, sometimes adjudicating between authoritative interpretations, but more often putting all of them forward as alternatives. Here, too, we find a concern for maintaining the broadest possible scope for literal interpretation.

Chapter 5 considers a few of William's theological concerns. As no theological treatise of his has yet come to light, any attempt to elaborate his theology systematically would be inescapably artificial. And yet it should come as no surprise that his biblical interpretation says much about his theological perspectives. Conspicuous among these is a comprehensive view of divine revelation, which is entirely consistent with his comprehensive view of biblical history. For him, the prophets, apostles, and evangelists were complemented as channels of revelation by the church's doctors and even the preachers of his own time. All of them formed a whole. The salient respect in which they differed from each other was chronological, as each had a specific historical connection to Jesus Christ, the object of revelation, as well as the primary agent of it.

If the exegetical setting within which William worked was highly structured, it was not stifling. Though undeniably traditional, it was also resourceful and dynamic. Filled with borrowings from previous writers, his expositions usually also include his own remarks, suited to his own purposes. This, too, is consistent with the comprehensive perspective within which he worked. Without presuming to have *auctoritas*, he viewed his own work as a commentator as instrumental in revelation. By restating, organizing, and synthesizing the texts of previous writers and by complementing them with his own remarks, William ventured to become one of them and to contribute to the work in which they had taken part.

# William of Alton:
# An Englishman in Paris

## Life

THOUGH OUR INFORMATION concerning him is meager, we can be reasonably confident that William was originally from Alton, near Southampton, England; that he joined the Dominicans at their priory in Winchester, established around 1235; and that sometime afterward he was sent to Saint-Jacques, the Dominican *studium generale* in Paris.[1] It was likely there that he served as a bachelor of Peter Lombard's *Sentences* before succeeding Thomas Aquinas as the holder of one of the Dominicans' two regents' chairs at the University of Paris in the academic year 1259.[2] Jean Destrez has suggested that Thomas's designated successor was not William but Gerard Reveri, an otherwise unheard-of secular master who had recently taken the Dominican habit and who died in February 1260. In this case, William would have filled the vacancy left by Gerard upon his death in February 1260.[3] Though this possibility cannot be discounted, evidence to the contrary is presented by William's appearance on a list of Dominicans who had taught as masters at Paris (*legentes in sacra pagina Parisius*) up to 1259.[4] This list, compiled by the contemporary Dominican Gerard of Frachet, provides no precise dates for William's tenure, but it does give reason to suppose that it lasted only one or two years.[5] The order regularly rotated its two chairs at Paris, most likely because it was in the process of implementing a program of studies similar to university formation, which required the allocation of a substantial number of masters in theology to its various provinces.[6] It is possible that William held this regency once again during his career, which, according to the earliest evidence, extended to approximately 1270.[7] Upon his inception as master, William's Dominican colleague was Peter of Tarentaise, later to become Pope Innocent V.[8]

Unless he was an exception to the University of Paris's regulations, William would have lectured at Saint-Jacques at an introductory level, first as a *cursor biblicus* and subsequently as a *cursor Sententiarum*, before holding the title of *magister in sacra pagina.*[9] And unless he was an exception to the Dominican Order's normal practices, his studies as a Dominican would have begun with perhaps three years as a theology student, followed by a few years as a conventual lector, and then by at least two more years as a *cursor biblicus*, either in one of the Dominicans' provincial *studia* or in the *studium generale* of Saint-Jacques. Subsequently, he would have taught at Saint-Jacques as a *cursor Sententiarum*.

Let us consider briefly what our evidence will allow us to say about which of Thomas Aquinas's lectures William could have heard. We do not know whether William arrived in Paris before or after Thomas Aquinas became regent master, which occurred sometime between March 3 and June 17 of 1256. If before, he probably heard Thomas deliver his inaugural lectures, or *principia*, during two separate phases of the ceremony of his *inceptio*. Much of the interest of these discourses, *Rigans montes de superioribus* and *Hic est liber mandatorum Dei*, lies in the methodological considerations they contain, specifically, a *commendatio* of Scripture and a subsequent taxonomy of the books of the Bible.[10] In such a case, William would have also heard at least a few of Thomas's lectures on Peter Lombard's *Sentences*. Far less likely is the possibility that he heard his cursory lectures on Isaiah and Jeremiah, given that they were delivered several years earlier, while Thomas was still a biblical bachelor. Should we assume that William arrived soon after Thomas's inception, we must allow that he could have heard his disputed question *De veritate* and his questions *De quodlibet VII–XII*. While we may speculate about the possibility that he heard at least some part of whatever biblical lectures Thomas delivered during his first regency, none of the available evidence tells us what they were. Thomas's other surviving commentaries have now been assigned with some certainty to other periods.[11] In any case, none of William's commentaries shows signs of dependence on Thomas's biblical commentaries, or any of his other works.

And yet, it is possible that William was never a bachelor of the *Sentences* under Thomas's direction and that he never had extensive exposure to his instruction. In view of a personal friendship and likeness of thought between Thomas and Annibald de Annibaldis, M.-M. Dufeil has raised the possibility that it was Annibald, and not William, who was Thomas's bachelor before he vacated his master's chair, and that William was nonetheless inserted into that chair by the order.[12] While the University of Paris's regulations would seem to argue against this, we shall see that there is good reason to doubt that William was ever a student of Thomas. All the same, at some point along the way, he must have distinguished himself, since the Dominican theology students who made it as far as the position of *Sententiarus* at a *studium generale* such as Saint-Jacques were relatively very few.[13]

## *Works*

All the known surviving works attributed to William are either sermons or biblical commentaries.[14] The latter are line-by-line commentaries of a specific type belonging to the circles of the thirteenth-century universities, named alternatively *expositio*, *lectura*, or *postilla* (sometimes *postille*, even in reference to an individual work). More than a half century ago, Beryl Smalley observed that the precise shade of difference between these terms remained to be satisfactorily worked out.[15] Though this is still the case, we shall use the term lecture to designate a commentary's oral presentation and postill to designate its written form. Since *expositio* was also used to designate a particular part of the postill, namely, the line-by-line explanation, we shall apply the term exposition according to this more specific meaning.[16]

A Paris taxation list indicates that in 1275 William's *Postille Super Isaiam* and *Postille Super Mattheum* were among those placed at the disposal of booksellers for copying.[17] From the early fourteenth century, there appears the following witness of the Stam's Catalogue: *Fr. Guillelmus de Haltona, natione Anglicus, magister in theologia, scripsit postillas super Mattheum, de decem virginibus; item super ecclesiasticum.*[18] Known only by this single notation, the work *De decem uirginibus* either belonged to William's commentary on Matthew or has been lost.[19] In addition, a library catalogue of the Franciscan convent of Todi (c. 1340) credits William with a postill on Luke, though no such work is known to have survived.[20]

With respect to more recent secondary sources, a total of twenty-five surviving biblical commentaries are variously attributed to William by Palémon Glorieux,[21] Friedrich Stegmüller,[22] Thomas Kaeppeli,[23] and Richard Sharpe.[24] For an indication of the complexity of bibliographical problems lying in store for students of this literature, let us look briefly at Kaeppeli's classification. Listed without qualification under William's name are postills on Ecclesiastes, Isaiah, Jeremiah, Lamentations, Ezekiel, and John; listed as questionable are postills on Job, Proverbs, and the Canticle; listed as doubtful are postills on Matthew and the Apocalypse. Excluded from his inventory is a series of postills on the books from Genesis to Ruth, as well as a commentary on Wisdom, all of which appear under William's name in the lists of Glorieux, Stegmüller, and Sharpe. The last, it must be said, qualifies them as "very doubtful." Still another postill, on Daniel, is listed by Stegmüller and excluded by the others.

On the basis of its inclusion in a manuscript containing several anonymous postills suspected of being William's (about which we shall have more to say), Kaeppeli also lists as possibly belonging to him an anonymous *Sermo de Maria Magdalena*.[25] Less questionable is his attribution of a series of twelve sermons contained in another codex with ascriptions in the hand of the copyist pointing to our author. Eleven have been assigned dates falling within the period of his known activity, ranging from December 1261 to February 1264.[26]

Before William's exegesis and thought can be studied, the writings belonging to his authentic bibliography must be determined. Without such a basis, it will be impossible to see where he follows or departs from the conventions of his genre, namely, university biblical exegesis.[27] While his sermons lie beyond our scope, this inquiry will begin with an attempt to determine which of the biblical commentaries may be called his.

## *Problems of Attribution*

Since William appears to have been a master for about a decade before his death, the constraint of time argues against the ascription to him of twenty-five postills. But there are other reasons for caution. To begin, no explicit internal evidence of William's authorship of any of these texts has yet been found. In none of the texts examined for this work has William been found referring to anyone, anything, any event, or to himself in such a way as to betray his authorship. Moreover, until the present, few explicit references to William and his work in premodern literature have been identified. Further, there is no evidence of textual transmission for any of William's works between the Middle Ages and the present, by contrast with the writings of three of William's more famous near contemporaries, Bonaventure, Albert the Great, and Thomas Aquinas. Put another way, up until recently, none of William's works has been printed, and none has been explicitly cited by postmedieval exegetes. The near absence of editions of his writings, as well as the lack of any known theological works by him, makes it difficult to compare his known works with those of uncertain authorship.[28]

Another difficulty lies in the anonymity of most copies of the writings believed to be his. The evidence left by medieval scribes is fragmentary and often contradictory. William's authorship is supported by contemporary manuscript attributions for only six postills: on Ecclesiastes, MSS Basel, Univ. B III 20; Madrid, Biblioteca Nacional, 493; Paris, BnF lat. 14429, and Tarragona, Bibl. Publica 83; on Isaiah, Jeremiah, and Lamentations, all on MS BnF lat. 573; and on John, MS Saint-Omer 260. Moreover, it is hardly likely that William is responsible for each of two postills on Wisdom listed under his name by Stegmüller.[29] Still another source of confusion is that several of the twenty-five have been ascribed to other authors by medieval copyists. From all this results a pervasive uncertainty in modern repertories and studies.[30] Indeed, neither Glorieux, Stegmüller, Kaeppeli, nor Sharpe was unaware of these problems, and none failed to qualify his listings with varying degrees of certitude.[31]

## Manuscript Evidence

The likelihood of William's authorship of the twenty-five commentaries in question must be considered on a case-by-case basis. In the absence of explicit internal evidence, the only place to begin is with the several kinds of information presented by the manuscripts believed to contain William's work. Though imperfect, the kind to be given priority over all others is the evidence of attributions left by the original copyists, before or after the commentaries. Far less weighty, yet significant, are manuscript ascriptions left by subsequent scribes. To be rejected as evidence is the inclusion of a given work in a manuscript containing other works believed to be his. As with other exegetes of the period, William's works are too often interspersed with those of other authors for this criterion to be given credence. Except for a few containing only a single work, none of the manuscripts consulted for this investigation contains William's works exclusively. Separate cases are presented by two manuscripts containing several works that are in all likelihood his and that contain posterior ascriptions of the entire contents to him, namely, MS Paris, BnF lat. 573 and MS Madrid, Bibl. Nac. 493. For reasons to be discussed shortly, there is good reason to question the accuracy of these attributions. All the same, they will be taken into consideration. A final category of evidence to be considered is the independent witness of separate literature. We shall see that three of William's works appear on a thirteenth-century stationer's list and that several appear in catalogues of medieval libraries.

On such evidence, four commentaries are conspicuous—on Isaiah, Jeremiah, Lamentations, and John. For each, we have uncontradicted manuscript ascriptions in the hand of the copyist, who in the occurrence is the same for copies of all four, the first three in MS Paris, BnF lat. 573,[32] the last in MS Saint-Omer 260.[33] This scribe, moreover, has left us an indication that he was quite likely a Dominican: a supplication he has inscribed at the top of the first folio of the Saint-Omer codex is taken from the Dominican formula of religious profession: *Dominus qui incepit, ipse perficiat.* While this may tell us little or nothing about the probability that the works he copied were authored by Dominicans, it does say something about the likelihood that he erred in his ascriptions to William. It is reasonable to expect a member of the same order to be less likely than a professional copyist to be mistaken in this respect. For the commentaries on Isaiah and Jeremiah, we have the additional support of their inclusion in the aforementioned MS Madrid Bibl. Nac. 493, the contents of which have been attributed to William en bloc by a later scribe. The Isaiah commentary has still further corroboration in a posterior medieval attribution accompanying a copy in MS Saint-Omer 155. To this may be added an independent witness to the existence of such a work by him in the aforementioned stationer's list of 1275.[34]

Though certainly the indispensable basis of any sound approach to the compilation of William's complete bibliography, the available external evidence is of itself inadequate to the task. The uncertainty explicitly indicated in the repertories and the manifold discrepancies between them suggest as much.

## Literary Evidence

Moving beyond this ambiguity requires consideration of yet unexamined sources of information. Among the surest approaches would be an investigation of verbal correspondences between dubious works and those of known authenticity.[35] Unfortunately, this is made problematic by the near absence of editions of William's writings. Yet there remains for us another approach. Headway can be made by supplementing available external evidence with internal evidence that is in no respect explicit—each commentary's methodology, exegetical concerns, and style. With what follows, we shall consider such evidence in order to establish a provisional catalogue of William's commentaries. Rather than pretending to make definitive determinations with respect to every postill's authorship, this inquiry will have the more modest goal of constituting a list of works, the authenticity of which can be a matter of reasonable confidence. This, in turn, will provide a basis for studying his exegesis and theology. A work's exclusion from the listing will reflect a lack of evidence for William's authorship, not a definitive judgment to the contrary.

The four aforementioned postills constitute a basis from which to identify a few distinctive features, or markers, of William's methodology and style. To be sure, none presents traits entirely absent from the commentaries of other authors of the same genre, university biblical exegesis. There can be no question here of any particular methodological or even stylistic marker proper to William. All the same, examination of the four commentaries shows that they constitute a group for reasons other than the aforementioned external evidence of authorship. With the sole exception of the prologue and first four chapters of the commentary on Isaiah, they are homogeneous in virtually every significant characteristic of methodology and style. Though they share no particular trait, or signature, setting them apart from the works of other writers, their exegetical methods and style can be described as virtually identical. What distinguishes them is an ensemble of common literary markers rather than just one. For this reason, the focus of the present inquiry is to compile these markers into a list of criteria against which to evaluate the texts of questionable authorship, as well as the aforementioned opening of the Isaiah commentary.

The authenticity of the commentaries on Isaiah, Jeremiah, Lamentations, and John, Group A, is presumed. They are taken to represent William's methodology and style and will serve as the basis of a typology of his postills. Each of the remaining twenty-one postills associated with William, Group B, is evaluated against this typology. Toward the end of evaluating the distinctiveness of the traits found in Group A, the following postills of a few of William's near contemporaries serve as a background for comparison: Simon of Hinton, *Super* XII *prophetas, Super Mattheum*;[36] William of Middleton, *Super Iob*,[37] *Super Ecclesiasticum*,[38] *Super* XII *prophetas*;[39] Bonaventure, *Super Ecclesiasten, Super Iohannem*;[40] Albert the Great, *Super Iohannem*;[41] Peter of Tarentaise, *Super I Epistolam ad Corinthios* (7:10–10:33);[42] Thomas Aquinas, *Super Iohannem*;[43] William of Luxi, *Super Threnos*,[44] *Super Baruch* and *Super Ionam*;[45] Nicolas of Gorran, *Super Mattheum*;[46] and, finally, a group of postills associated with John of Varzy, *Super Proverbiis*,[47] *Super Ecclesiasten*,[48] and *Super Canticum Canticorum*.[49] (As we shall see, it is clear neither that these works are by the same author nor that John of Varzy is responsible for any one of them.)

Here it would be worthwhile to address a possible objection. It could be protested that the likenesses of the base texts are explainable by the kinship shared by Isaiah, Jeremiah, and Lamentations as all of the same kind of biblical literature, at least according to the classification of the Medieval Latin West. In reply, it will be observed that in this respect the commentary on John serves as a control. By any medieval classification or any modern one, John's Gospel belongs to another genre. Worth noting here is that while the commentaries of Thomas Aquinas on Isaiah and Jeremiah have been classified by scholars as the works of a biblical bachelor, this on the grounds of their simplicity of methodology and style, his commentary on John is widely considered one of his weightiest and most refined.[50] On the other hand, the considerable differences between Thomas's diverse commentaries serve to warn us of the limitations of the present inquiry's methodology by reminding us of the remarkable heterogeneity of which some authors are capable, even while writing within the confines of a particular genre, such as university biblical commentary.

# 2

# *Toward a Bibliography*

## A FEW KEY FEATURES OF WILLIAM'S
## METHODOLOGY AND STYLE

IN THE FIELD of linguistics, few terms have been the subject of more controversy than style.[1] It lies within the scope and purpose of this inquiry neither to enter into such debates by attempting to reconcile the multifarious definitions advanced by specialists, nor to defend any one of them. We shall therefore adopt Rei Nogu-chi's broad functional definition of *style* "as a recurrent or characteristic selection from a set of expressive possibilities in language."[2] While Noguchi himself acknowledges shortcomings in his definition, he observes that it has the benefit of subsuming several definitions previously advanced by Nils Enkvist. Particularly germane to the present study's purposes is Enkvist's view of style "as a set of indi-vidual characteristics, as a selection of features that mark a person's language as idiosyncratic."[3] What follows is an attempt to identify a set of individual charac-teristics, a selection of features that mark William's language as idiosyncratic.

The identification of traits as either methodological or stylistic is in no way intended to reflect a judgment that these two categories are unavoidably separate. Several traits could just as easily be placed in one category as the other. As we shall have occasion to observe, for example, the diverse features of William's *divisio* could be described alternatively as matters of methodology or of style. All the same, this selection of terms is employed here as a heuristic device for identifying the various kinds of evidence of authorship presented by the texts.

## *The* Prologus

With the exception of the postill on Isaiah (about which more will be said in the next chapter), the Group A commentaries are introduced by well-developed pro-logues that correspond in all significant respects to this genre's typology (also to be discussed later). Normally, the prologues of postills open with a biblical verse, generally from a book other than the one commented on, which serves as a theme for what follows. In the prologues to Jeremiah, Lamentations, and John, William supplies their references with a formula not used for this purpose in the afore-mentioned works of William's contemporaries: *"Hec uerba scripta sunt. . . ."*

Another important feature of the prologues of university commentaries is their orchestration around Aristotle's four causes. Whereas exegetes of preceding generations organized their prologues around various combinations of *auctor, modus agendi, titulus, intentio,* and *utilitas,* by William's time, regent masters had assimilated these categories to Aristotle's efficient, formal, material, and final causes, usually in that order.

## *The* Divisio Textus

Among the postill's most conspicuous characteristics is a high level of organization or structuring.[4] Its basic component is the individual lesson (or *lectio*), which itself comprises a few distinct components. First among these is the *divisio textus* (or simply *divisio*), wherein the text commented on is divided into component parts, not according to any preexisting set of principles, but according to the interpreter's own exegetical interests. By his selection and application of the principles governing the division, the postillator provides an exegetical perspective for approaching the text and situates the diverse elements resulting from the divisions with respect to each other and with respect to the entire lesson, chapter, and book.[5] Usually, one of the elements resulting from the initial division is subdivided into another series of elements, and so forth, in a potentially indefinite process. In the following example, the *divisio* is followed by five successive subdivisions. Taken from the opening of the third chapter of William's *Super Threnos,* this selection presents several features typical of William:

> [3:1]*I AM THE MAN WHO SEES.* Here he bewails the affliction of his people, as was said above at the beginning of the book. And first he bewails principally the affliction that occurred after the captivity; second principally the affliction of the people that preceded it, in the first part of chapter four. In the first, first he sympathizes with his own people; second he calls down punishment upon the adversary: [60]*YOU HAVE SEEN ALL <THEIR FURY>.* In the first, first he commemorates the manifold affliction of the people and himself; second he calls upon God to be merciful in the said affliction: [19]*REMEMBERING <MY POVERTY AND TRANSGRESSIONS>*; third he invites the people to penance that they might obtain mercy: [40]*LET US EXAMINE <OUR WAYS>*; fourth he reiterates the people's affliction to augment it: [43]*YOU HAVE CLOTHED <YOURSELF IN*

*FURY>*. In the first, first he commemorates the affliction wrought by the Chaldeans; second he commemorates another wrought by those being deported: [14]*I HAVE BECOME A LAUGHINGSTOCK*; third, he retells it to add to the sorrows inflicted by the Chaldeans: [11]*HE HAS BROKEN <ME TO PIECES>*. In the first, first he shows that the recalled punishments were many; second that he could not avoid them: [5]*HE HAS BESIEGED <ME>*. In the first, first he says that it was by scourgings that he and the people became aware of their miseries; second he shows that <God> permitted the said punishments in order to scourge the people: [2]*HE HAS DRIVEN ME*; third <he shows> that their enemies were conspicuous in their concern to scourge: [3]*ONLY AGAINST ME HAS HE TURNED*; fourth he shows that by the vehemence of the scourge a sign has appeared to the people: [4]*<HE HAS MADE MY SKIN> OLD.*[6]

## Vocabulary

Throughout William's postills, divisions and subdivisions of this sort are characterized by a specific vocabulary. To begin at the beginning, William's *divisio* systematically opens with an excerpt of the text commented upon, or lemma, which is regularly followed by *hic*.[7] True, the same may be said of other commentators active at the time, such as Thomas Aquinas and Albert the Great. Yet in the works of several others, such as William of Middleton and William of Luxi, the usage of *hic* is far less regular. While the latter makes frequent use of the term in the opening line of his *divisio*, it is often for some word other than the first. An example is the following introduction to his comments on the third chapter of Lamentations:

> [3:1]*I AM THE MAN WHO SEES POVERTY* etc. Above he deplored the affliction of his people and the destruction of the habitable places. Here he comes back to deploring the affliction of the people. And first. . . . [8]

What is more, William of Alton's initial divisions are normally indicated by the terms, *primo . . . secundo . . . tertio*, and so on, and his subdivisions by *in prima primo . . . secundo . . . tertio*, and so forth. Though the formula *in prima primo* is employed regularly by William of Middleton and still more so by Peter of Tarentaise and William of Luxi, its application in William of Alton's work is particularly systematic. It appears thirty-five times in his *Super Threnos* and eighty-three times in the first ten chapters of his *Super Iohannem*. In his postills on Isaiah (after Is 5:8) and Jeremiah, it appears at least once in the *divisio* at the head of every chapter. By contrast, it appears irregularly in the commentaries of Bonaventure and Simon of Hinton and infrequently in a commentary of Nicolas of Gorran.[9] It makes only six appearances in the all the writings of Thomas Aquinas (according to the editions), all in his biblical commentaries.[10] When William subdivides the last element of the series, his preferred introduction is *ubi primo*.

His vocabulary is also marked by the absence of a few terms. Employed occasionally by William of Middleton[11] and Nicolas of Gorran,[12] and all but ubiquitous in the *divisio* of Bonaventure, Albert the Great, and Thomas Aquinas, *dividitur* in its various forms is generally so used by William only at the postill's beginning and rarely afterward.[13] In addition, whereas other expositors regularly employ the term *ibi* to introduce the lemmata of the *divisio*, William systematically presents lemmata without any introduction. To indicate the transition from the *divisio* to the ensuing *expositio*, he often employs the formula *dicit ergo* and occasionally *continua* or *continuat*. He avoids using both formulae in combination.

A problem with employing terminology and formulae as criteria for authorship is the difficulty of establishing that they are attributable to the author rather than to a reporter or even to a copyist.[14] Given the fragmentary character of the information available concerning the reporting and copying of postills, both possibilities must be taken seriously. Nevertheless, this line of inquiry is pursued, and this for two reasons. First, it must be considered unlikely that a single reporter should be responsible for all four of the lectures of the works of Group A, which were probably delivered over the course of several years. It is much more likely that several reporters were involved, which would make it difficult to explain how these works' shared terminological idiosyncrasies resulted from reporting. Second, the relevant manuscripts present clear indications that copyists normally refrained from imposing their own terms and formulae upon the texts they copied. The seven postills of MS Paris, BnF lat. 526 (1–7 of Group B), contain usages of terminology and formulae markedly different from those of Group A, though all of them have been written by the same scribe. What is more, in copies of these same seven postills appearing in another hand in another manuscript, Vendôme 116, the usage is virtually the same as in the aforesaid codex. A similar stability of vocabulary appears in two copies of a postill on Job, to be discussed later, in MSS BnF lat 573 and Madrid, Bibl. Nac. 493. In these cases, the scribes clearly respected the terminology of the texts they copied and avoided inserting their own words into them.[15] With due reservations, then, it seems reasonable to adopt recurrent terms and formulae of the Group A postills as provisional criteria for authenticity.[16] As well as those mentioned before, these will include terms used for introducing citations of the exposition, to be mentioned later. Wherever possible, the value of such criteria will be evaluated by reference to multiple copies of the postill in question.

## Structure

The vocabulary of William's *divisio* says much about its structure. As do other postillators, William normally subdivides the first element of the preceding division, though he occasionally subdivides the last. He systematically closes each element except the first with a lemma. Since, as a general rule, his *divisio* is reprised point by point in the literal commentary, its divisions and subdivisions correspond to those of the *expositio* such that all its lemmata, including the first, are systematically repeated there. What is more, the major *divisiones*, such as those at the heads of chapters, normally correspond point by point to subsequent minor *divisiones* situated throughout the following commentary according to their location in the biblical text. Put another way, whenever one of the elements of a series is subdivided, the remaining elements (those normally introduced by *secundo, tertio, quarto*, and so forth) are typically subjected to subdivision in a later *divisio* of smaller scale. So for example, in the excerpt above the lemma [3:19]*REMEMBER* is not subdivided, as it closes the second element of its subdivision. Yet further along, it reappears after the exposition of Lamentations 3:18 as the subject of another *divisio*, and once again afterward to introduce the exposition of Lamentations 3:19:

> [19]*REMEMBER*. Here he first puts forward his misery, or that of the people; second, he preaches divine mercy: [22]*THE MERCIES OF THE LORD*; third, he promises kindness, lest they despair: [31]*<THE LORD> WILL NOT SPURN US <FOREVER>*; fourth, he shows that to be merciful belongs to the one who has inflicted punishment: [37]*WHO IS HE*. In the first, first heasks that being compassionate, he recall his mercy; second, he shows that <their misery> is so great that unless he show mercy the people will fail: [20]*MINDFULLY I REMEMBER*; third, he says that recalling his own misery, he does not despair of <the Lord's> kindness: [21]*RECALLING THIS*.
>
> Therefore he says: [19]*ZAY: REMEMBER* for the sake of being merciful *MY POVERTY*, from the taking away of goods. . . . [17]

This technique is applied regularly throughout the commentaries of Group A. With occasional exceptions, the only elements left without subdivision are those of the final series, that is, those resulting from the final division. In sum, William's *divisio* serves as an accurate guide to a highly organized exposition.

## Perspective

Also characteristic of William is the perspective of the *divisio*, which is normally clearly focused on the purposes of the biblical text's human author. While typical of the expositions of Bonaventure, Albert the Great, and Thomas Aquinas, this trait is nonetheless often missing from those William of Middleton, as well as several of those of Group B.

## Rhyming

In university commentary, the diverse elements of a *divisio* are often linked one to another by words that rhyme. William is remarkably regular in applying this device, almost invariably to the last words of each element. So for example, in the previous *divisio*, the initial division results in four elements, the final terms of which are *miseriam, misericordiam, ueniam*, and *penam*. The ensuing subdivision of the first element produces three elements whose final terms are *reuocet, deficiet*, and *desperat*. Though uneven, rhyming of this sort appears in virtually every *divisio* of all the works of Group A. It is far less regular in the commentaries of Bonaventure, William of Middleton, and Albert the Great[18] and rare in those of Thomas Aquinas.

## Function

The last observation to be made of William's *divisio* is that from the outset of every chapter, it remains in the service of the subsequent literal exposition. Each chapter is systematically introduced by a well-developed initial *divisio*, in combination with which an ensuing series of subordinate *divisiones* serve to organize the commentary. Though frequent in its occurrence, the *divisio* is normally of moderate length by comparison with the following line-by-line commentary, with which it is generally consistent. We shall see that in a few of the postills of Group B, the *divisio* appears to be an end in itself, occupying far more space on the page than the line-by-line exposition, and often having little or no relation to it. On the other hand, William of Alton's *divisio* is normally longer than William of Middleton's.

Taken together, the preceding traits serve to distinguish the *divisio* of the works of Group A from many of those of Group B, as well as from those of Simon of Hinton, William of Middleton, Bonaventure, Albert the Great, and Thomas Aquinas. They are, however, of no help in differentiating William's *divisio* from William of Luxi's, where all of them appear regularly and where there is no appreciable difference in length or complexity.[19]

## *The* Expositio
### Line-by-Line Commentary

Among the postill's defining features is a focus on individual lines of the biblical text rather than on larger sections. In this respect, William's commentaries could hardly be more typical; in the commentaries of Group A, each line is generally given at least a brief exposition. Put simply, William does not make a practice of skipping lines.

## Brevity

William's expositions are normally concise and free of lengthy excursus. Lemmata are seldom followed by more than a few lines of commentary, often by only a few words. Neither *exempla* nor *distinctiones* appear with any regularity. The most discursive of the Group A postills, his *Super Iohannem* is nonetheless brief by comparison with the commentaries on the same book by Bonaventure and Aquinas. We shall see that he regularly borrows material from the former's postill, all the while abridging it.

## Literal Interpretation

Hardly proper to William, interest in the literal sense is nonetheless marked in his commentaries, even by the standards of the thirteenth century.[20] After presenting a lemma, he usually comments on the literal sense before adding either references or questions. Moreover, only very rarely does he put forward a spiritual exposition of a given passage without having first advanced a literal one. Seldom does he content himself either with mere compilations of citations or with mere moralities. In other words, William is neither a mere compiler nor a mere moralizer. His controlling concern is the clarification of the literal sense for the classroom instruction of students of modest formation.

## Spiritual Interpretation

Notwithstanding the primacy of the literal sense, spiritual exegesis was in no way peripheral to William's exegetical project. Under the headings *allegorice, mistice,* or *moraliter,* he supplied most verses of Lamentations and many verses of Isaiah and Jeremiah with allegorical or tropological interpretations, often both.[21] In John's Gospel, he gave fewer verses such treatment, yet it was normal for scholars to be less discursive in their spiritual comments on the New Testament than in those on the Old.[22] In William's work, spiritual commentary is absent from the *divisio*, is placed after the literal exposition, is clearly distinguished from it, and is normally preceded by a restatement of the lemma. To be sure, remarks concerning Jesus Christ show up with considerable frequency in his literal interpretations of Old Testament passages. These, however, are comments on prophecies William construes as intended by the human author, and are therefore properly part of the literal exposition. On the other hand, usage of the terms *ecclesia* and *anima* in their various forms is restricted to comments explicitly designated as spiritual. In sum, William separates the senses clearly.

## Presentation of Citations

Methodically succinct, the biblical and nonbiblical citations of Group A are seldom longer than a single line. References to the texts cited are normally placed before the cited material. While most other commentators follow this practice, some do not. Further distinguishing William's manner of citation is a set of terms he does not normally use for introducing references—*ibi, unde,* and *illud.* Rare in the works of Group A, such usage is widespread in several of the commentaries of Group B, as well as those of Bonaventure, William of Middleton, and Thomas Aquinas.[23] On the other hand, with unusual frequency William introduces references with the term *simile.*[24] The last two traits are particularly noteworthy, as they are among the few that differentiate William from his Dominican near contemporary, William of Luxi. Whereas *unde* regularly introduces references in the latter William's commentaries on Lamentations and on Baruch, *simile* does not.

## Sources

While William is no mere compiler of authoritative citations, he does borrow heavily from nonbiblical sources, especially the *Glossa Ordinaria.* He also cites the Fathers unreservedly, particularly Augustine, Jerome, Gregory the Great, and Isidore. Ubiquitous in his postill *Super Iohannem,* references to Chrysostom are rare elsewhere. (In a subsequent chapter, we shall see why this is so.) Earlier medieval authors such as Bede, Alcuin, and Rabanus Maurus are normally cited by name, as are twelfth-century figures such as Andrew and Hugh of St. Victor. Borrowings from thirteenth-century authors such as Hugh of St. Cher and Bonaventure are frequent and invariably without attribution. References to pagan authors such as Seneca and Aristotle are not rare.

## *The* Questio

With rare exceptions, William's questions are simple and arise directly from the biblical text.[25] Most often introduced by *contra,* they typically consist of the mere citation of a biblical verse or of an authoritative text apparently at odds with the line at hand. At times, there is instead the mention of a problem presented directly by the text itself. This is followed by a succinct clarification, introduced by the term *responsio* and supported by a biblical citation. Normally limited in scope to the text's literal sense, William's questions seldom go afield. Finally, they are situated within the exposition of the verse at hand. They appear neither in the *divisio* nor in clusters following the expositions.[26]

## Conclusion

In the preceding survey of the salient features of the methodology and style of the four postills assumed to be William's, we have seen that every one of them falls squarely within the typology of thirteenth-century university biblical commentary. Few of the features of the texts of Group A are altogether absent from the aforementioned works of William's near contemporaries Bonaventure, William of Middleton, Albert the Great, Thomas Aquinas, or William of Luxi. Taken individually, none could be called a signature. Several could be called clichés. Each, however, is missing from at least one of the works of Group B, and when taken together, they mark William's work as idiosyncratic. For this reason, their presence in a postill is considered a necessary condition for authenticity but not a sufficient one. While the presence of any one of them is taken as small corroboration of William's authorship, the absence of all or even any one of them is considered evidence to the contrary. Thus, the ensemble of markers proper to William is employed as a set of criteria against which to evaluate the twenty-one postills of questionable authorship and the commentary on Isaiah before 5:8.

Appendix I presents a listing of relevant bibliographical information for each postill of Groups A and B. The entries for *Super Isaiam* and every postill of Group B are followed by a comparison with the typology described here. Toward the end of avoiding needless repetition, the discussions mention only briefly the many likenesses between these works and those of Group A and dwell mainly on differences. The listings of manuscripts include only those consulted for this study and do not pretend to be exhaustive.

The purpose of these discussions is not to have the last word on the authorship of the twenty-one postills of Group B, but to identify the ones that can be attributed to William with confidence. It is assumed that extensive correspondence, and nothing less, to the typology of the postills of Group A amounts to clear evidence of authenticity. Of the twenty-one works under consideration, seventeen are set aside and one is identified with another (*Super Ecclesiasten*, inc.: *Vidi in omnibus uanitatem* is identified with *Super Ecclesiasten*, inc.: *Aspexi terram*, thus reducing Group B to twenty different works). The last and only two others are authenticated: *Super Sapientiam* (inc.: *Fons sapientie uerbum Dei in excelsis*) and *Super Ezechielem* (inc.: *Vidi et audiui uocem unius aquile uolantis per medium celi*).

Though none of the compilers of the repertories serving as the basis of Group B failed to qualify his listings with varying degrees of assurance, the result is nonetheless striking, and one may wonder why only three works are authenticated out of a collection of effectively twenty under examination. By way of explanation, it will be noted that several of the seventeen discarded works have been associated with William in the ascriptions of librarians often removed from him and his contemporaries by many generations.[27] Of the others, all have been associated with him by modern cataloguers on the basis of mere inclusion in a manuscript containing works believed to be his.

Yet a questionable assumption would appear to underlie the judgments of both the late medieval librarians and those of more recent cataloguers, to wit—that authorship was a salient consideration in the inclusion of postills in thirteenth-century manuscripts. Beryl Smalley seems to have assumed as much in her considerations of a few of these same works, as she was attentive to their manuscript associations with postills of known authorship.[28] Her comment concerning the likelihood of Bonaventure's authorship of the postill *Super Sapientiam*—which we have authenticated as William's—is telling:

> Had Bonaventure expounded all of the sapiential books, his works would have been transcribed together as a set. Since he only expounded one or at most two, if the postill on Wisdom be genuine, those scholars or religious who wanted to have a complete sequence of postills were forced to use a miscellany; they had to combine Bonaventure with other commentators.[29]

If by "miscellany," we are to understand a book containing the commentaries of more than one author, then it is worth noting that every manuscript consulted for this inquiry has the appearance of a miscellany (apart from a few containing only one work, such as MSS Basel, Univ. Bibl. B III 25 and B VIII 28). Most have no appearance of having been dedicated to the commentaries of any particular author, and it would seem that the scholars and religious for whose use they were made were thoroughly accustomed to the use of miscellanies. Manuscripts containing more than one postill on the same book suggest as much, since they could hardly have been intended to contain only the works of any particular author.[30] A lack of preoccupation with authorship is also suggested by the inscriptions accompanying the postills in most of the relevant manuscripts. Whereas the names of the biblical books commented upon typically appear in clear writing at the incipits and excipits and often in running titles in the upper margins of every folio, firsthand ascriptions to authors show up infrequently and then normally at the explicit.

All of this suggests that in the execution of these manuscripts, authorship was not a controlling concern, but an afterthought. What appears to have mattered most to those who first used these books is what the scribes wrote out boldly at the beginnings and endings of the postills, and often on every page in between, namely, the title of the biblical book subjected to commentary. Further, selection of works for inclusion in manuscripts according to their subject matter rather than their authorship would have been much more in keeping with the postills' immediate purpose, specifically, to serve as tools for the classroom instruction of Franciscan and Dominican friars of modest preparation (about which we will have more to say). Because scholars of William's time were less preoccupied than those of subsequent generations with the authorship of individual postills, it hardly seems reasonable to take as evidence of authenticity the mere fact of a postill's inclusion in a manuscript containing authentic works. In addition to the analysis of each postill's style and methodology, the dismissal of this sort of evidence says much about why seventeen of twenty possible postills are set aside.

# 3

# *William as Exegete*

THE FOREGOING DISCUSSIONS and an earlier study of his commentary on Lamentations[1] present a broad picture of William's work as falling squarely within the genre of university exegesis, the typology of which has now been well studied and documented.[2] By the time he became a master, the development of this genre and the separation of biblical exegesis from theology as a distinct field of study had been well under way for more than a generation. Insofar as they integrated sustained and rigorous reflections upon methodology and systematic applications of specialized procedures for textual and literary analysis, both had become scientific.[3] But it should come as no surprise that biblical interpretation remained throughout an entirely confessional enterprise. It is worth keeping in mind that the genre was developed (under the heavy influence of Dominican and Franciscan commentators, particularly those at Paris and Oxford) for the specific objective of preparing clerics for the work of preaching.[4] What follows is an overview of the main features of university commentary as they appear in William's commentaries and those of his contemporaries.

## *Approaching the Text: The Prologue*

Within the corpus of the seven commentaries we have identified as William's, there is probably no better place to begin our consideration of his exegesis than with the prologues by which he introduces them. As do his contemporaries, William makes use of them for setting forth explicit methodological considerations and for introducing the diverse analytical techniques to be employed throughout the commentaries. We shall see that he also employs them to identify the salient themes of the biblical text at hand.

Though a detailed discussion of the prologue's complex provenance need not detain us,[5] a few significant points are worth noting. To begin, though this form of introduction to the author and his work, or *accessus*, originated in the transmission of profane literature, by the late eleventh century it had become a stock feature of biblical commentaries. During the twelfth century, the prologue was standardized in accordance with a framework normally comprising the aforementioned elements: *intentio, utilitas, modus agendi*, and *titulus*. The addition of a biblical verse to introduce and sometimes to organize the prologue came with the so-called biblical moral school, particularly in the commentaries of Peter Comestor (d. 1179), Peter the Chanter (d. 1197), and Stephen Langton (d. 1228).[6] By William's time, changing philosophical currents and the emergence of university exegesis had entailed the assimilation of the aforementioned elements into the framework of Aristotle's efficient, material, formal, and final causes. We shall see that the introduction of Aristotle's thought into the Latin West had several important consequences for late-medieval exegesis, notably in the development of innovative understandings of authority and authorship.[7]

William normally relates each of the four causes to the various terms of the introductory biblical verse, which he thus develops into a theme for the entire prologue. At the outset of his prologue to *Super Iohannem*, he identifies the opening verse's subject with the Gospel's efficient cause, namely, John the Evangelist:

> *An understanding servant is acceptable to the king.* These words are written in Proverbs 14 (35), in which principally the scribe of this Gospel is commended, and consequently the Gospel itself, since the commendation of an author redounds upon his work, as in Ecclesiasticus 9 (24): *Works will be praised for the hands of the artisans.* Moreover, the fourfold cause of this work is implied.[8]

In this fashion, William suggests that he will study the various terms of the verse from Proverbs to find each of the Gospel's four causes implied therein. Yet he then serves notice that he will first employ the verse to make St. John the subject of a *commendatio*:

> He is commended on three points; first with respect to his life: *servant*; second with respect to his knowledge: *intelligent*; third with respect to the approbation of both, or with respect to his special familiarity with Christ: *is acceptable to the king.*[9]

Comprising a study of each of the verse's terms, the following commendation occupies the better part of the prologue. Afterward, we find each of the four causes mentioned explicitly. Implied by the term *king*, the material cause is the book's subject matter, Christ. The formal cause (*ordo* or *modus agendi* in the previous model) is the form imparted to the matter by the author. Implied by the term *understanding*, it is in this case the understanding of the divine nature and the extolling of the human nature united to it in Christ. Previously discussed, the efficient cause, identified with *servant*, is restated without comment. Related to *acceptable*, the final cause (or *utilitas*) is that we should be accepted by God in the present by faith and in the future by glory:

> What is noted secondarily in these words is the fourfold cause of this work. The material, by the saying *to the king*, because this book is about Christ, who is the king of kings with respect to both natures in him. . . . Efficient: *servant*. Final: *acceptable*. He writes so that in the present we may be acceptable to God by faith, below 20 (31): *These things are written that you may believe*, and in the future by glory, thus it continues, *and that believing you may have life*.[10]

## Material Causality: The Consideration of Context

Its lengthy *commendatio* notwithstanding, the previous example is relatively simple. In his prologue to Lamentations, William provides an overview of his conception of the literal, allegorical, and moral (tropological) senses of Lamentations by designating the material cause of each. We shall see that he does the same for the formal and final causes. Corresponding to the history of Jerusalem, the life of the church and that of the soul are three material causes, each of which is itself threefold.

The matter of the literal sense is a threefold desolation and destruction: first, of the land and the city (Israel and Jerusalem), second, of the people, and third, of the temple. Worth noting, however, is William's explicit placement of all of this in a twofold historical context, either the sacking of Jerusalem by the Babylonians during Jeremiah's time or the one by the Romans almost six centuries later.

> The material cause is implied by the following words: . . . *water* . . . *a fountain of tears that I may weep for the slain*. The matter of this book is the vehement lament by which Jeremiah mourns the desolation, or if you will, the devastation of his land, the destruction of its city and temple, the affliction of his people, especially of King Josiah, and the slaying of the temple carried out by the Chaldeans, or then to be carried out by Titus and Vespasian, i.e., by the Romans, according to the historical sense.[11]

So it is that he, in a stroke, leaves virtually any passage of Lamentations open to either context for literal interpretation. The matter of the allegorical sense is a threefold falling away of the church, specifically, from the fervor of charity, from the light of truth, and from the constancy of solidity. As for the moral sense, it is the soul's lament for having fallen away from the state of justice by sins of thought, word, or deed. Should anyone wonder whose soul is doing the lamenting, William once again leaves open more than a single interpretative possibility, mentioning that it could be either the ruined soul or simply the lapsed one.[12]

Nearly as elaborate is his view of the Book of Jeremiah's various kinds of subject matter. Similarly threefold, the book's material cause is Jeremiah's manifestation to the people of their wrongdoing (particularly their idolatry), his weeping and lamentation, and finally, his intercession on their behalf.[13] Again, for the Book of Ezekiel, William designates a threefold literal material cause in accordance with the woes of three groups of people: Jerusalem's exiles who were murmuring, those left behind who were deriding the exiles for being molested by foreigners, and the foreigners molesting the exiles. For the spiritual senses the subject matters are two, the people of God and those of the Devil.[14]

This brief outline provides an indication of William's capacity for recognizing complexity in the biblical text's subject matter. It now remains for us to consider this same capacity at work in his analysis of the twofold character of its authorship (its efficient cause) and then in his understanding of the author's *modus agendi* (the formal cause) and purposes for writing (the final cause).

## Efficient Causality: The Consideration of Authorial Roles

Largely due to the influence of the pseudo-Aristotelian *Liber de causis*,[15] university exegetes typically accounted for the biblical text's divine and human origins by appealing to a distinction between its primary and secondary efficient causes— God and the human author. Put simply, they found in this work a framework for accounting for the divine authority and authorship of Scripture, on the one hand, without prejudice to the integrity of the human author, on the other.[16] On their view, both the human and divine authors understood and intended the literal sense and, as we shall see, sometimes multiple literal senses. Precisely because they had clearly identified divine authorship with primary causality, they could take it for granted and subject human authorship to unfettered analysis. This understanding of efficient causality allowed exegetes to take stock of differences between the perspectives of human authors of Scripture without compromising the unity of revealed truth. In the prologue to his postill *Super Threnos*, William illustrates the distinctiveness of Jeremiah's point of view with respect to those of a number of other prophets:

The title: The Book of Lamentations of Jeremiah, and just as the Canticle
of Solomon is called the Canticle of Canticles, so this is called the Lamentation of Lamentations, because it excels all others. The others are particular: Jacob's sons wept for their father, Samuel for Saul, David for Saul and
Jonathan and Absalom, Hezekiah for his own imminent death predicted
to him. But this one is made for every temporal and spiritual loss; indeed
it exceeds the others in quantity, as is evident, and indeed in the mode of
weeping. Therefore in the first chapter (12) it says: *Oh all of you who pass
by the way* etc.[17]

As for divine authorship, William occasionally assigns responsibility to particular members of the Trinity. Whereas for the Book of Lamentations, it is the
Holy Spirit,[18] for the Book of Wisdom, it is the Word of God *per modum inspirationis* (in the prologue *Fons sapientie*). This fits well with the Latin West's classical
attribution of wisdom to the second of the Trinity. Less traditional is a further
distinction within the secondary efficient cause (in both versions of the prologue)
between remote and proximate human authors, namely, Solomon and Philo.[19]
Whereas the church's liturgy testified to Solomon's authorship (readings from
Wisdom were introduced by attributions to him), a somewhat vague attribution
to Philo had been initiated by no less an authority than Jerome[20] and had been
perpetuated by Rabanus Maurus.[21] William attempts to resolve the conflict by
differentiating between the role of an author and that of a compiler, the first
being Solomon *per modum inuentionis*, the second Philo *per modum compilationis*. After discussing both figures at some length, William mentions in passing
that this conception of multiple human authorship applies as well to Proverbs,
whose author was Solomon and whose compilers were unnamed subordinates
of Hezekiah.[22]

## Formal and Final Causality: The Analysis of Style

The interest William takes in the human authors of the texts on which he comments is keen indeed—the larger parts of his prologues are consecrated to
remarks concerning them. If the framework of this scrutiny is Aristotle's efficient
cause, its broader methodological implications appear in his analysis of the
author's form or *modus agendi* (sometimes *modus procedendi*). In the background
here is the larger thirteenth-century controversy over the question of whether
theology is a science. Alisdair Minnis has drawn attention to the stimulus this
debate provided to exegetes' analyses of the stylistic complexities of biblical
texts.[23] While a complete account of this history lies beyond our purposes, it
will be noted that Alexander of Hales (d. 1245), one of the earliest and most

significant thinkers to take up the question, described a variety of biblical modes of exposition and set them in marked contrast to the scientific mode. He effectively separated the sciences from biblical exegesis by drawing a sharp distinction between human and divine science. On his view, the first appeals to the *intellectus*, or faculty of intellection, and the second appeals to the *affectus*, that is, the mind's faculty of desire. What is more, whereas the *intellectus* operates by division, definition, and ratiocination, the *affectus* functions by precept, example, exhortation, revelation, and oration. The Bible, as he would have it, is not a scientific work because it operates by stimulating pious affections and by treating of realities having to do with salvation.[24]

This bifurcation of knowledge won a very substantial following. Among others, the Dominicans Richard Fichacre and Robert Kilwardby and the Franciscans Robert Grosseteste, William of Middleton, and Bonaventure largely adopted it, though generally substituting the term *aspectus* for *intellectus*. Notwithstanding the differences between their positions, all emphasized the primacy of the *affectus*.[25] We shall see that William, too, makes frequent use of the distinction between *affectus* and *aspectus*, yet his own view of whether theology is a science must on the present evidence remain a matter of speculation—he has yet to be found addressing the question. The point to be made here is that his work bears witness to a rigorous reflection upon biblical modes of exposition.[26]

To return to the prologue to the postill on Lamentations, William identifies as the literal formal cause (or *modus*) a threefold lament over the three aforementioned subjects of desolation and destruction: the homeland, the people, and the temple. Though we need not weigh up all of his distinctions, we would do well to note that they involve William's attribution to Jeremiah of four laments (chapters 1 through 4) corresponding to the four corners of the world to which the Jewish people were scattered by the Babylonians and the Romans.[27]

Lamentation is the form of the allegorical and tropological senses as well.[28] Allegorically, the book is a lament over the church's fourfold ruin in those falling away from the four (cardinal) virtues.[29] Tropologically, it is a lament over the ruin of the faithful soul by the disorder of the four passions[30] and over the encumbrance of the human body composed of the four elements.[31] All of this is of a piece with the final causes, or authorial purposes, behind the literal, allegorical, and moral senses, namely, to bring about lamentation on the part of the synagogue, the church, and the soul.[32] About final causality more will be said shortly. Here it will be observed that there is a conspicuous absence of any mention on William's part of the human author Jeremiah in connection with the formal and final causes of the spiritual senses. For the postillators of the period, the spiritual senses were defined by the very fact that they lay beyond the human author's intention and as such were attributable only to God's. As a lexicographical clarification, it should be noted that the term *intention* here designates the author's meaning, as well as his aim or purpose in writing. Such is the sense of *intentio* in the lexicon of the medieval schools.

As for the Book of Jeremiah, the formal cause, William tells us, is the ease and clarity of Jeremiah's expression. This, in turn, comprises three components: his prophecy (especially at the beginning), his recounting of history (especially toward the middle), and his lamentation (especially at the end, presumably in the Book of Lamentations).[33] Lest anyone fail to grasp or believe such determinations, William typically illustrates and corroborates each of them with one or more biblical references.

Before concluding this section, let us return briefly to William's consideration of the *modus* of John's Gospel, which would appear to be at odds with the certitude necessary for the book's purpose, the generation of faith. Certitude, it would seem, can result only from demonstration, but the mode by which the book proceeds is narrative, not ratiocinative. William solves the problem by distinguishing between two kinds of certitude, one produced by demonstration, the other by authority. Leaving unquestioned the usefulness of demonstration in the human sciences, he remarks that it nullifies faith. Then he observes that while authority is flimsy in the other sciences where the authorities are human, it is irreproachable in the science at hand, inspired as it is by the Holy Spirit. For corroboration, he cites Augustine to the effect that we owe to authority what we believe and to reason what we understand: *Quod credimus debemus auctoritati.*[34] This citation, as well as much of his solution, he has lifted from Bonaventure,[35] but there is nothing in any of these remarks at odds with the thought of Thomas, who at the outset of his *Super Boetium De Trinitate* (a prolonged reflection upon what the human mind can know about God) employs the same text of Augustine to the same effect.[36] By virtue of his formal distinction between knowledge by faith and that by reason, Thomas, too, consistently relates the virtue of faith to divine authority,[37] all the while remaining unequivocal with respect to the scientific character of theology.[38]

## The Evolving Consideration of Authorial Intention

In his exposition of Jerome's prologue to the Book of Ecclesiastes, William has the following to say about a few key roles of literary production:

> It is to be noted that a commentator, a writer, a compiler, and an author differ from one another. A commentator is someone who writes what is his and what is from others, but what is from others principally, and what is his as something adjoined, as it were. A scribe is someone who writes

only what is from others, adding or changing nothing of it. A compiler is someone who writes what is from others, making additions from the sayings of others. An author is someone who writes what is his principally and what is from others as something adjoined.[39]

The defining mark of the author is that what he writes is principally his. In his own prologue to Ecclesiastes, William leaves little reason to doubt that this is what the author, in this case Solomon, intends to show:

> The author shows in this book that creatures, especially sensate ones, are vain. Hence vanity is properly a passion which he intends to show with respect to the subject.[40]

The author's work then proceeds from his own intention; whatever he borrows from others is merely adjoined (*aliena tanquam adnexa*).[41] William's understanding of authorial intention is not without relevance to an important, though hardly unique, feature of his commentaries, specifically, the explicit separation of the literal and spiritual senses. By his time, the problem of establishing a methodology for differentiating between Scripture's diverse levels of meaning had been the object of considerable attention for more than a century. Principally under the influence of Hugh (d. 1142) and Andrew (d. 1175) of St. Victor, literal interpretation had begun to attract renewed interest on the part of exegetes, and its scope had been enlarged to incorporate figurative expressions. No longer a superficial reading of the text's letter, it had evolved into a studied reflection upon the human author's intention.[42] By the second half of the thirteenth century, this tendency had resulted in the application of a reasoned methodology wherein the literal sense was identified with the inspired human author's intention. All of this appears readily in the works of Bonaventure, Albert the Great, Guerric of St. Quentin, Thomas Aquinas, and William of Alton.[43]

Closely related to this was the development of specialized procedures for citing diverse authoritative sources and reconciling their apparent contradictions. Early in the preceding century, Peter Abelard (d. 1142) had brought to the fore problems surrounding the reconciliation of discordant texts and had announced the need to bring the philosophy of language to bear on the interpretation of authoritative writings.[44] Toward this end, university exegetes had brought an array of principles to bear in exegesis, among the most important of which was attentiveness to the author's way of speaking (*modus loquendi*). This process, involving the consideration of the author's literary genre and historical background, had proved particularly helpful for sorting through the Platonic styles of Augustine and Dionysius, which were foreign to dialectical modes of expression. All of this had as its end the *intentio auctoris* from which the authority's historical meaning was to be had.[45]

An important consequence was a development of interest in the psychology of the human authors of biblical texts, an endeavor essential to the discernment of their intentions. Here, too, Aristotle's influence was decisive—the study of his anthropology produced a thorough transformation of psychological presuppositions. Worth recalling here is that in the Neoplatonic perspective, the soul is an integral entity inhabiting the body, and knowledge is had by enlightenment, not sense perception.[46] Such was the paradigm of most pre-thirteenth-century exegesis. Owing to the influence of patristic authors, especially Origen, Augustine, and Gregory the Great, the spiritual senses were usually considered the primary medium of revelation, and the literal or historical sense was normally taken as less important.[47] Inspired, on the other hand, by Aristotle's *De anima* and equipped with his theory of knowledge, university exegetes reassessed traditional anthropological assumptions and recognized the importance of the human faculties of perception. Especially relevant to exegetical methodology was the central place assigned to the imagination. It is worth recalling that for Aristotle and his medieval followers, the soul was the form of the body and was thus dependent upon the mediation of the senses and the imagination for acquiring knowledge. Biblical exegetes were not long in recognizing in this doctrine a basis for the priority of the literal sense with respect to the spiritual ones. To the literal sense, Scripture's "body," they conferred a status commensurate with the body's place in Aristotle's anthropology.[48] True, exegetes of earlier periods did not ignore the literal sense, but they were not preoccupied with it. Instead, they tended to focus on some level of meaning beyond the "body" of the text. University commentators, by contrast, typically had as their primary objective the literal sense intended and expressed by the human authors.[49]

What is more, they found in Aristotle's thought a rationale for a broader understanding of the literal sense itself. More clearly than their predecessors, they recognized the human author's imagination as the provenance of prophecies and rhetorical devices such as metaphor, hyperbole, and irony. Thus disposed to attribute prophetic and figurative passages to the author's intention, they were less inclined than exegetes of earlier periods to resolve textual difficulties by resorting to spiritual interpretations. For this they were more apt to resort to linguistic analysis, about which we shall have more to say.

Relevant to the present discussion is that commentators of William's period were no longer content to focus merely on the biblical text's *auctoritas* to the neglect of consideration of the human *auctor*. This new interest in the human author, divinely inspired yet having his own theological, moral, and literary purposes and limitations, is not difficult to recognize in William's preoccupation with figures such as Solomon, Philo, Jeremiah, Ezekiel, and John in the prologues to his various commentaries. A good example of his method appears in his account of Solomon's authorship of Ecclesiastes. Though generally taken for granted during the Middle Ages, attribution of the book to Solomon was nonetheless problematic.[50] A. J. Minnis has observed that medieval commentators discussed Solomon's moral and literary qualities much more freely than those of other authors, particularly the Evangelists, because their authority was diminished by the sapiential books' absence from the Hebrew Scriptures.[51] Yet William focuses on another difficulty—the scriptural record of Solomon's own personal history, conspicuously at odds with the book's subject matter.

The same problem had been discussed by Bonaventure, William's principal source for his commentary on Ecclesiastes. But the Franciscan master mentions Solomon only toward the end of the prologue to his postill, whereas William is preoccupied with him from the outset. After opening his prologue with a lengthy encomium in which he represents the king by no less a figure than Jeremiah and qualifies him as most wise (*sapientissimus*) and peaceful (*pacifus*), he takes up a series of problems concerning his fitness for the task of writing the book at hand. To Bonaventure, William owes the substance of these objections but not all the replies.[52] First, it is objected that whereas the Book of Ecclesiastes is all about contempt for the world (the world's vanity is the book's *materia*, the teaching of contempt for this vanity its *finis*), Solomon was altogether worldly. In reply, William proposes that Solomon was repentant when he composed the book and that in any case the Holy Spirit is able to speak through bad people as well as good ones. Both responses are from Bonaventure; the first originated with Jerome.[53] A second difficulty arises from Solomon's carnality—it has been objected that since the book is about spiritual matters, Solomon's instruction was scandalous.[54] In his reply to this one, William is on his own. After pointing out that even the words of a carnal preacher are often edifying, William acknowledges that the indignity of a preacher is scandalous and thus implicitly concedes that Solomon's instruction may be so qualified:

> To the second, it is to be said that two things are to be considered in the preaching of someone carnal: the preaching itself, which frequently edifies, and the indignity of the preacher, which scandalizes.[55]

No less irreverent is his reply to a third objection, this one arising from Solomon's sinfulness. It has been protested that whereas the work at hand is about wisdom, Solomon, being a sinner, could not have been wise and was therefore unable to teach wisdom. Texts from the Book of Wisdom and Augustine have been adduced to show the incompatibility of sinfulness and wisdom. Not surprisingly, William's solution lies in a distinction between narrow and broad understandings of "wisdom," the first being knowledge of divine things, along with an appropriate savor and love of them (*diuinorum cognitionem et diuine cognitionis saporem debitum et amorem*), the second being raw knowledge devoid of love (*nudam sine amore cognitionem*).[56] As William would have it, sinfulness precludes only the first. The reader is left to conclude that Ecclesiastes concerns only the second, loveless wisdom. Put another way, the wisdom of Ecclesiastes is not what Augustine had in mind. More explicitly than Bonaventure, William is willing to come to terms with the ambiguity of Solomon's character and acknowledge the limits this imposed on his authorial capacities, divine inspiration notwithstanding.[57]

Then again, in his reply to a fourth and final objection, William claims that for his dubious character Solomon is a *better* author. An objector has pointed out that deeds are more credible than words and has claimed that Solomon is not to be believed because he did the contrary of what he taught. William begins by limiting the scope of the rule (the objector's major premise) to exclude words inspired by the Holy Spirit. This much he has taken from Bonaventure.[58] The concluding remark is his own. Solomon's checkered past, he tells us, was wholly suited to the book's purpose—he was all the better able to teach contempt for pleasures, riches, honors, and curiosity, since he was an expert in all of them.[59]

Solomon isn't the only author to attract William's studied attention. Jeremiah appears in virtually every remark of the prologues to his postills *Super Ieremiam* and *Super Threnos* and is integral to every component of his elaborate accounts of the four causes of both books.[60] Let us return briefly to the first work. At the opening of the prologue, he says that Jeremiah's intended audience is the people of Jerusalem (the "two tribes," as William often calls them). His account of the book's final cause comprises three elements, each of which involves the prophet: that the people quit sinning, serve God, and get to heaven. Toward these ends, William says, Jeremiah composed the book by his preaching, threats, and lamentation.[61] Having placed the figure of Jeremiah so conspicuously at the center of his exegetical project, our author understandably takes an interest in his character and personal history. In the context of his discussion of the book's efficient cause, he remarks that Jeremiah surpassed the other prophets in prefiguring Christ by his holiness and goes on to mention his chastity of mind and body, as well as his humility. He finds it germane to bring up Jeremiah's sanctification in his mother's womb, his virginity, his captivity, and finally his death:

> *The man clothed in linen*, Jeremiah, who was a virgin, and who came forth, below chapter 16 (2),[62] and who was sanctified in his mother's womb, below chapter 1 (5), *was over the waters of the river*. Because he was present

in the captivity, he saw it with his own eyes. . . . Also, Jeremiah was holy, below chapter 1 (5): *Before you came forth from the womb, I sanctified you.* This is clear from the interpretation of his name—it is interpreted "elevated." Also, this is clear from his signification, because more than the others he would appear to prefigure the holy one, i.e., Christ. Also, this is clear from his chastity of mind and body, below chapter 15 (17): *I did not sit in the company of those playing around.* Also, this is clear from his humility, below chapter 1 (6): *I do not know how to speak, for I am a youth.* Also, this is clear from his endurance of evils for the Lord—he was stoned by the Jews in Taphnis.[63]

For all of this, we have an interesting point of comparison in Thomas Aquinas's commentary on the same book.[64] Though earlier than William's work, it was probably not a source for it.[65] In the prologue, Thomas makes many of the same points, but his main interest is the role (*officium*) of prophecy, not Jeremiah himself. Rather than to Aristotle's four causes, Thomas connects his introductory verse to the book's author, matter, mode, and purpose. If discursiveness is any indication of interest, his main interest is the first, to which he devotes better than half the prologue. Yet this is largely a consideration of prophecy in general.[66] Remarks concerning the particularities of Jeremiah's prophecy are occasional, and most of his discussion could apply to any of the canonical prophets as easily as to the one at hand. His commendation of Jeremiah rests upon his having three characteristics necessary to any prophet: prophetic dignity, fraternal charity, and piety of compassion.[67] The *modus*, Thomas tells us, is "to proceed by likenesses and figures," which, he adds, is "the proper mode of prophets."[68] The book's end—not even implicitly limited in scope to the people of Jerusalem—is "to live well and to arrive at immortal glory."[69] Not until the closing line, where he specifies the *materia* as the captivity that inspired Jeremiah's compassionate prayer, does Thomas explicitly limit his perspective to the concrete history experienced by Jeremiah: "According to the historical sense the matter is the captivity of the people, which incited his prayer of compassion."[70]

While all of this suggests that Thomas is less preoccupied than William with the identities of the Bible's human authors, it does not mean that he is uninterested in the human dimension of biblical authorship. Far from it, as we see in his consideration of the author of the Fourth Gospel. Bonaventure, William, Albert the Great, and Thomas are all preoccupied with the Evangelist, and each presents his prologue as a *commendatio* of him.[71] But here, too, Thomas's focus is speculative, William's historical. Thomas introduces John as a contemplative and proceeds to expatiate upon various aspects of his contemplation and its object, Christ's divinity.

*I saw also the Lord sitting upon a throne, high and lifted up* (Is 6:1). . . . The words proposed are those of a contemplative. . . . In the words proposed John's contemplation is described in a threefold manner, just as the Lord Jesus is contemplated in a threefold manner. It is described as high, broad and perfect. . . . Concerning the first, it is to be understood that the height and sublimity of contemplation consists mainly in the contemplation and knowledge of God.[72]

For Thomas, John is a fitting instrument of divine revelation by virtue of his contemplation. Everything he finds commendable in the Evangelist is a function of this. The prologue, in fact, is concerned far less with his own history than with the dynamics of his contemplation. For Thomas, John became an instrument for communicating the Divine Word because he had first been elevated to its contemplation.[73] All of this is in perfect keeping with his understanding of the Gospel's subject matter. No less than Bonaventure and Albert the Great, Thomas follows Augustine in asserting that whereas the first three Gospels were principally about Christ's humanity, this one is mainly about his divinity.[74] It is little wonder, then, that he has little to say about John the Galilean fisherman who accompanied Jesus in his travels. Considerations of this sort are of small importance to his methodology. The only remark Thomas makes in his prologue about John's involvement in any biblical event is a passing allusion to John's reclining upon Jesus' chest at the Cena.[75] (In the prologue to his *Expositio super Iob*, Thomas is similarly uninterested in Job's identity, though his commentary is avowedly literal.)[76]

In his own prologue, William expatiates upon such matters. He finds it revealing that John left his father and his boat, as this bears witness to his being Christ's servant.[77] Also telling for William is an account of the wedding feast at Cana contained in a pseudo-Jerominian prologue to the Gospel.[78] As the story goes, John was the groom, who upon being called by Jesus, left his bride and followed him. Bonaventure, Albert, and Thomas save their remarks on the episode for their expositions of Pseudo-Jerome's prologue. There and in his remarks on the Cana episode, Bonaventure takes the account at face value by virtue of its authority (*quia maior auctoritas in hoc concurrit*).[79] Albert the Great notes the account's lack of a textual basis (*expresse non legitur*), qualifies it as an opinion (*opinio est quorumdam*), and then replies to a few possible objections to it.[80] Thomas discusses it briefly, mainly to point out that it was the occasion of John's reception of a special grace of contemplation.[81] William, for his part, takes it up in three places: in his own prologue, in his exposition of the pseudo-Jerominian prologue, and in his comments on the Cana pericope (Io 2:1–11). In the last, he takes care to call the account a conjecture (*conicitur quod fuerit Iohannes euangelista*), this notwithstanding its acceptance by his principal source, Bonaventure, to say nothing of Jerome's authority. William's reservations, however, don't deter him from employing the account in his prologue to call attention to several of John's virtues, specifically, his readiness to imitate Christ, the excellence of his love, his mortification, and his fidelity.[82] More, when William commends the Evangelist as *intelligens*, it is not in connection with what he has contemplated (though his prologue does touch upon the matter), but because of what he has made manifest—in preaching useful matters in his epistles, revealing secrets in the Apocalypse, and thundering sublime matters in the Gospel.[83] Put simply, throughout the prologue, William expresses an interest in who John is. He makes much of his familiarity with Jesus, with explicit reference to their intimate conversation at the Last Supper (Io 13:25), Jesus' charging of John with the custody of his mother (Io 19, 27), and again, John's forgoing of marriage.

True, Thomas, no less than William, discusses all but the last of these episodes during the course of his commentary. Yet the differences between the two prologues are telling. William's attentiveness to the human author's identity is a matter of methodology. He is therefore careful to draw out the implications of any biographical information available. Here, too, his interest corresponds to his understanding of the text's subject matter. Declining to follow Augustine's remark that the Gospel mainly has to do with Christ's divine nature, William asserts that it is equally about both:

> The formal cause: *understanding*, by his incomparable understanding of the divine nature, to extol the human nature and the existence of both in Christ. First it is about the divine nature; afterwards it is about the human. It deals with both sublimely.[84]

Reading the book as revelatory of both natures, he takes a lively interest in the interactions of Jesus and John as they knew each other in Galilee and Jerusalem at specific times and places, such as the Last Supper and Calvary:

> To the authority of this king, therefore, blessed John was *acceptable*, which is clear from the fact that as being more familiar *at the supper he leaned on his breast*, John 13 (21, 20). Also, from the fact he took into his custody the most precious treasure, John 19 (27): *He took her into his own* custody, or *his own* obligation (*officia*).[85]

In his prologues, Thomas generally refrains from such remarks, but he never loses sight of Scripture's human character. In the prologues to *Super Matthaeum* and

*Super Iohannem*, he identifies both Evangelists as *auctores*, and throughout his biblical commentaries, he searches for the meanings of the human authors, as well as the divine one. All the same, his consideration of the origins of the texts of Jeremiah and John are, finally, investigations into God's actions and purposes. In keeping his gaze fixed on the human *auctor* as a contemplative, Thomas considers him as elevated and illumined by God. That his inquiry into the text's origin is, in the end, a consideration of God's initiative and agency should come as no surprise to anyone familiar with his thought. Anyone looking for such a perspective in William's exegesis will be disappointed, but his approach is not without its own interest. In the following chapters, we shall see a few of the consequences of the historical curiosity that allows William to find significance in John's abandonment of a bride at a wedding banquet.[86]

## *The Literal Sense: Textual and Contextual Studies*

Much of the foregoing discussion of the methodology at work in William's prologues has focused on his understanding of the literal sense; it remains for us to examine his actual literal exegesis. Something must be said, in particular, about the techniques he brings to bear in his analysis of the text and its context. They are in the main typical of medieval methods of literal interpretation,[87] but William's application of them says much about his own reading of the Bible.

### Textual Criticism

As did thirteenth-century exegetes generally, William understood that no text can be studied before having been established. He also knew that the biblical texts he used were imperfect representations of Jerome's Vulgate and that this was itself a translation from the Hebrew and Greek originals. An examination of the lemmata of William's postill on Lamentations shows that for that work, at least, his base text was not far removed from the so-called Paris Bible,[88] a version of the Vulgate better described as a common tradition than as a strictly homogeneous text.[89] Even before it attracted the disparagement of Roger Bacon (c. 1214–c. 1292)[90] for its inadequacies, it prompted both the Franciscans and Dominicans to engage teams of scholars in systematic critical projects that produced several *correctoria*. Their main purpose was not to replace the Paris Bible but to equip commentators with a reliable text. William probably made use of them, though not for the sake of settling textual questions. He generally appears to have had the more modest purpose of supplying alternative readings to better serve his exegesis, without pretending to determine which is preferable.[91] One may surmise as much from his use of the term *or* (*uel*) in the following examples from his exposition of the third chapter of Lamentations:

> [3:18] *GIMEL: AND WHEN I WILL CRY AND PLEAD*, or (*uel*) *WOULD CRY*, i.e., with a cry I will have pled.
> [3:10] *DELETH: A BEAR LYING IN WAIT HE HAS BECOME TO ME. . . . A LION IN A SECRET PLACE*, or (*uel*) *A SECRET PLACE*, i.e., more cruel, by means of Vespasian.
> [3:22] *THE MERCY* or (*uel*) *MERCIES OF THE LORD*. Here he first preaches the magnitude of God's mercies.[92]

Elsewhere, variants are usually introduced by the expression "another letter" (*alia littera*) or "another translation" (*alia translatio*); otherwise, the procedure is the same. In the following example from the aforementioned pseudo-Jerominian prologue to John, William presents two versions of the author's explanation of his purpose in writing:

> " . . . so that having established the desire for knowing"; another letter (*alia littera*): " . . . so that the desire of inquiring may be established in the ignorant."[93]

Normally, "another letter" (*alia littera*) designates an Old Latin text, such as the following citation of Leviticus 25:44 in the exposition of John 8:33:

> [8:33] *AND WE HAVE NEVER SERVED ANYONE*. They lied, because they had served the Babylonians for seventy years, Deuteronomy XVI (cf. Dt 28:48). Yet they understood this much, that by nature they ought to have been free and that by law <they ought> not to serve, Deuteronomy XXV (44): *Let your male and female slaves be of the nations that are round about you*[94] etc. Another letter (*Alia littera*): *The tribute will not be pending in Israel.*[95]

Though implicit, William's point in these cases is clear—the various texts complement one another. A similar case is the following presentation of an *alia translatio* of Ecclesiastes 1:4, which corresponds more closely than the Vulgate to the subsequent biblical reference:

> Hence it follows: [1:4] *A GENERATION PASSES AWAY*, by dying, of course. Another translation (*Alia tranlatio*): <*A GENERATION*> *GOES TO DEATH*, 2 Samuel 14 (14): *We all die, and like waters that return no more, we sink into the earth.*[96]

Another common designation for an Old Latin text is *LXX*. The following clarification of Ambrose's citation of Jeremiah 22:29 appears in his exposition of John 8:6:

> [8:6]*BUT JESUS BOWING DOWN WROTE WITH HIS FINGER IN THE EARTH.* According to Ambrose: *O earth, devour these men rejected,* i.e., deserving to be judged, and this is taken from Jeremiah 22 (29) according to the letter of the LXX.[97]

Examples of this sort are not rare in the commentary on Jeremiah. The following one is taken from the opening exposition:

> "These are," supplied, [1]*THE WORDS OF JEREMIAH; LXX: THE WORD OF JEREMIAH,* and then the letter is plain, *THE SON OF HELCHIAH.*[98]

Immediately following this line is one of William's rare references to a Hebrew text. It is derivative—William himself indicates that he has taken it from Andrew of St. Victor:

> Andrew: Reflect on this, i.e., on the sense of the Hebrews, that the name of Helchiah is expressed in the title of the prophecy, as if Helchiah himself were a prophet.[99]

His occasional references to the "Hebrew truth" (*Hebraica ueritas*) are to the "Hebrew Psalter" (Jerome's translation of the Psalms from the Hebrew), as opposed to the then current "Gallican Psalter" (Jerome's earlier translation based upon Origen's Hexaplaric text of the Septuagint).[100] The following example is from the prologue to *Super Ieremiam*:

> ... in the Psalm where we have: *A hymn, O God, becomes you in Zion,* the Hebrew truth has: *Praise awaits you, O God, in Zion* (Ps 64:2).[101]

William's citations correspond to R. Weber's critical editions of Jerome's Gallican and Hebrew Psalters, though more recent Latin translations of the Psalms from the original Hebrew existed during his own time.[102] None of these cases offers us any reason to suppose that he consulted Hebrew texts directly.[103]

It is no more likely that he made direct use of Greek versions. Similarly derivative are his occasional references to the translation of Symmachus,[104] such as the following one from his commentary on Ecclesiastes:

<¹¹⁶*THE SPIRIT (SPIRITUS) GOES FORTH > AND RETURNS IN CIRCLES*, i.e., through circles. Symmachus says: *THE WIND (VENTUS) GOES MAKING ROUNDS*, and Hugh expatiates upon the wind.¹⁰⁵

For the alternative translation, William has found a corresponding interpretation in Hugh of St. Victor's commentary on the verse, which begins: *If we take "spirit" as wind (Si per spiritum, aerem accepimus)....*¹⁰⁶ Notwithstanding his interpretation of *spiritus* as wind, Hugh did not use Symmachus's version. William probably took it from Jerome, whose Latin translation is identical:

> Symmachus thus interpreted this passage: <It> goes to the south, and returns to the north; *THE WIND GOES MAKING ITS ROUNDS*, and whence it circled the wind returns.¹⁰⁷

Though he usually doesn't name his sources for them, William is normally careful to designate variants of lemmata as such. He is less assiduous with citations of other biblical texts, notwithstanding the aforementioned example. A case in point is the following citation of Isaiah 7:9 in his exposition of John 1:39:

> ¹³⁹*HE SAYS TO THEM: COME AND SEE*, believing, loving, doing good, understanding, Isaiah 7 (9): *Unless you believe, you will not understand (Nisi creditis, non intelligetis).*¹⁰⁸

As it appears in the Vulgate, the text William has presented is: *Si non credideritis non permanebitis.*¹⁰⁹ He has cited an Old Latin version, in all likelihood from memory. He has not found this version in any of his principal sources (the *Glossa ordinaria*, Hugh of St. Cher, Bonaventure), but this does not mean that he has drawn it directly from an Old Latin Bible. Several Fathers, particularly Augustine, had made this line a commonplace, and it had continued as such well up until his own time.¹¹⁰

In none of these cases does William express a preference for one text over another. He puts them forward as alternatives. It would be easy to multiply similar examples of his proffering of biblical variants, yet this inquiry came across only one instance of textual criticism that could be described as negative, that is, intended to rid the text of errors accumulated over the course of time.¹¹¹ What follows is his exposition of a "prothemata," which often introduced the Vulgate text of Lamentations.

> He says therefore: *AND IT HAPPENED*, i.e., all that happened in the preceding book, *AFTER ISRAEL WAS LED INTO CAPTIVITY, JERUSALEM*

*WAS DESERTED* or *DESTROYED, JEREMIAH SAT . . . THE PROPHET . . .*
*WEEPING AND <HE> WAILED THIS LAMENTATION*, or *IN THIS LAMEN-*
*TATION IN JERUSALEM.* Some books have *WITH A BITTER SOUL SIGH-*
*ING AND MOANING*, but this is neither the letter of Jerome nor of
Paschasius; it has been added from the glosses for expressing exagger-
ated sorrow.[112]

After proposing a simple variant of the sort listed here (*uel LAMENTATIONE*
*HAC*), William identifies the concluding phrase (*amaro animo suspirans et*
*eiulans*) as an interpolation. The same, however, could have been said about the
entire prothemata—it is included neither in modern critical editions of the
Vulgate[113] nor in Paschasius Radbertus's *Expositio in Lamentationes*.[114] By the
first half of the twelfth century, however, the text had come to enjoy some
measure of acceptance, and with exception of the phrase William has described
as inauthentic, it became the subject of commentary.[115] By the end of the twelfth
century, the phrase William cast doubt upon had also won inclusion, and for
much of the thirteenth century, the entire passage was a standard feature of
Bibles and commentaries.[116] It appears in three Bibles listed as "Parisian" in the
*Editio Maior* of the editors of St. Jerome.[117] It was probably one or the other of
these Parisian Bibles that William had in mind when referring to *aliqui libri*.
For all that, his base text (which presumably contained the passage yet lacked
the phrase he qualified as inauthentic) was probably no rarity—several such
Bibles have been identified in the *Editio maior*.

## Linguistic Analysis: Etymology, Rhetoric, Semantics

Many times to this point, we have had the occasion to observe that William's
work is characterized by the primacy of literal exegesis systematically applied to
the biblical text's every line. Put another way, upon having established the text,
William makes a priority of unfolding its *littera*, an undertaking bound to bring
textual problems to the fore. For working through them, he makes particularly
free use of the techniques of grammatical and linguistic analysis typical of
his period.

At its most basic, this is simply the explanation of terms he suspects may be
unclear to his audience, often with reference to authorities, particularly Jerome
or Isidore of Seville (c. 560–636). An example appears in his commentary on
Ezekiel, where he pauses at the relatively rare term *electrum*, of which the Vulgate contains only three occurrences in any form, all in Ezekiel. William draws
his explanation from three sources. From Isidore, he borrows the remark that
it is a brilliant stone; from Jerome, that it is as precious as gold or silver; and

from Gregory the Great, that it is made of gold and silver. While he resolves the apparent contradiction between the authorities he cites by distinguishing between three kinds of electrum, William declines to specify which one of them Ezekiel had in mind:

> [1:4] *. . . AND FROM ITS MIDST SOMETHING THAT LOOKED LIKE ELEC-TRUM*, i.e., in the manner of fire, i.e., in the midst of persecution, the radi-ance of the people purged by turmoil. According to the *Etymologies*, book 16, electrum is some sort of stone like the rays of the sun, more radiant than gold and silver,[118] and according to Jerome in the *Glossa*, it is more precious than gold and silver.[119] And yet, Gregory says in the *Glossa* that electrum is of gold and silver.[120] But when they are mixed, silver increases in radiance, while gold pales in its brilliance. Here it is replied that there are three kinds of electrum. One flows from trees and is a good kind of gum; another is a metal which is made artificially from three parts of gold and four of silver; the third is some kind of stone, which is the best, and this is the one of which Isidore and Jerome speak; Gregory speaks of the second.[121]

Only rarely does William refer simultaneously to Isidore and Jerome. Normally, he cites one or the other of them according to two distinct methods for explain-ing words: Isidore for etymologies and Jerome for interpretations. As university exegetes often employed both sorts of explanations to introduce spiritual exe-gesis, we will examine interpretations in the following section dealing with spiri-tual exegesis. Yet because William often uses etymologies in a straightforward manner to clarify the literal sense, we will take a closer at look the procedure here.

In modern lexicography, etymology is terminological history, the study of a term's origin and change. During the Middle Ages, history had little to do with the matter. When studying a term's etymology, William considers a word's origin only for the sake of accounting for its intrinsic force.[122] His perspective is basically the same as Isidore's, whose *Etymologiarum* was throughout the Middle Ages the standard reference for etymological inquiries. However fanciful the results of such inquiries may appear to the modern reader, they could occasionally fall near the mark. So for example, when commenting on Lamentations 4:5, William pauses to explain the fairly rare term saffron (*croceis*), here making one of only two appearances anywhere in any form in the Vulgate:

> [4:5]*THOSE WHO WERE NOURISHED ON SAFFRON*, i.e., on food seasoned and colored with saffron. Saffron indeed has a reddish color, Isidore, book XVII.[123]

To Isidore, William owes the observation that saffron flowers are reddish in color, but it is he who comments that being fed on saffron (*in crocies*) means dining on food seasoned with them. The remark hardly squares with modern translations, which generally take the text to refer to the purple clothing of a luxurious upbringing.[124] And yet it isn't farfetched either—saffron, a species of crocus, was often used for seasoning food in antiquity, as it still is today. No less acceptable is the definition of *stadia* he proposes when attempting to specify the distance Jesus' disciples had rowed on the evening when he came to them walking on the water, as recounted in John 6:19:

> [*Super Io.* 6:19] WHEN THEY HAD ROWED ABOUT TWENTY-FIVE OR THIRTY STADIA. This is said because of the uncertainty of the distance.[125] As Isidore says, book XV, "A stadium is one eighth of a miliarius, given that it is one hundred and twenty-five paces.[126]

A *stadium* was in fact a distance of 125 paces, one eighth of a Roman mile, or *milliarium*.[127]

Grammatical analysis in William's work normally involves little more than a perfunctory remark concerning a basic point. One such case appears in his exposition of the narrative of the wedding banquet at Cana in John's Gospel, where he offers the following clarification of the word *first* (*primum*) in connection with the chief steward's remark that good wine is ordinarily served first. In the Vulgate text, the term is susceptible of an adjectival construal—"Every man serves the first good wine...," so William specifies that it is to be taken adverbially—"Every man serves the good wine first...":

> [2:10]AND (THE CHIEF STEWARD) SAID TO HIM: EVERY MAN . . . FIRST, adverbially, i.e., in the first part of the meal, SERVES GOOD WINE, AND WHEN PEOPLE HAVE DRUNK, THEN THAT WHICH IS WORSE. That was the custom then, and is even now among some people.[128]

Yet he is also capable of entering into more involved grammatical discussions. These often serve for sorting through various possibilities for interpretation of ambiguous passages, such as the final clause of Ecclesiastes 12:13. Appearing in the Vulgate as HOC EST OMNIS HOMO, it will be rendered here as THIS IS EVERY MAN. By introducing the ambiguous THIS (HOC) with the prepositions to (*ad*) and through (*per*), each according to two meanings, William exploits several senses of the Latin term OMNIS—translatable into English as every, all, and all of—to provide four alternatives:

*[12:13]FEAR GOD . . . AND KEEP HIS COMMANDMENTS* doing good. And he adds the reason: *THIS IS*, i.e.: This is to *EVERY MAN*, i.e., made by God. Or *THIS IS*, i.e.: To this is held *EVERY MAN*. Or *THIS*, i.e.: Through this, so that it be in the ablative case, *EVERY MAN*, with respect to spiritual being, 1 Corinthians 15 (10): *By the grace of God I am what I am.* Also, *THIS*, i.e.: Through this *IS EVERY MAN*, i.e., the perfect man, because both are required, specifically, turning away from evil and doing good, to this end, that a man be perfect.[129]

What follows is an attempt at an English paraphrase: With respect to the injunctions of fearing God and keeping his commands, first, every man has been made by God for this purpose; second, every man is held to this; third, from this man is made whole in his spiritual being; and fourth, through this man is made perfect. It is by solecism that William employs *through this (per hoc)* in an ablative sense. While unusual, this usage serves his purpose well by providing an additional avenue for interpretation. It is worth noting here that while several of the possibilities William has explored are particular to the Vulgate text, there has been little unanimity among modern translators on the rendering of this verse.[130]

A more common procedure is semantic analysis, the differentiation between various levels of meaning for particular words. A typical case appears in the first chapter of John's Gospel in connection with Jesus' greeting of Nathanael as *a true Israelite in whom there is no guile (uere Israelita in quo dolus non est)*. To an objector who has implied that this line would make Nathanael sinless, William replies with a simple distinction between common and proper meanings of a key term. As he would have it, Nathanael was subject to a generic sort of guile but was free of the more particular one that Jesus had in mind:

*[1:47] . . . IN WHOM THERE IS NO GUILE.* To the contrary: Every sin is guile. Response: "Guile" may be used commonly or properly, and so it is taken here.[131]

Later in the same commentary, he provides another such semantic clarification in connection with Jesus' citation of a passage of the Psalms (Ps 81:6) as "law"—the term can refer variously to the Old Testament either in its entirety, lacking the Psalms, or lacking both the Psalms and the Prophets:

*[10:34]JESUS ANSWERED THEM: IS IT NOT WRITTEN IN YOUR LAW: I SAID, YOU ARE GODS?* Note that "law" can be applied in three ways. Sometimes it designates all the books of the Old Testament, as here. Sometimes it designates all of them but the prophets, as in Matthew 11 (13): *For all the*

*prophets and the law prophesied until John.* And so it includes the psalms in the law. Sometimes it separates the prophets and psalms from the law, as in Luke 24 (44): *All these things must be fulfilled which are written about me in the law of Moses and the prophets and the psalms.*[132]

Notwithstanding his heavy dependence on both Hugh of St. Cher and Bonaventure throughout *Super Iohannem*, when considering textual problems, William is remarkably independent; each of the preceding formulations is his own. Even where his main sources provide him solutions to such questions, he usually puts his own mark on them. A typical example is his parsing of the term *god* (*deus*) in his exposition of John 10:35: *If he called them gods to whom the word of God was spoken.* Most conspicuous among William's sources here is Hugh of St. Cher, who, citing Gregory the Great, differentiates between three applications of the term: to designate a (divine) nature, to designate adoption by God, or simply to serve as a name: "The term 'god' is said according to three modes . . . by nature . . . by adoption . . . by appellation."[133] The distinction appears, in fact, to have originated with Hilary of Poitiers.[134] Borrowing it from Hugh, Bonaventure modifies it, if only slightly: "since this name 'god' may be used in a threefold manner: by nature, participation, and appellation."[135] If the Franciscan master's substitution of "participation" (*participatione*) for "adoption" (*adoptione*) betrays his Neoplatonic tendencies, William's modifications bespeak a dialectical mind-set. Following Hugh, he inserts a few technical terms to set the discussion within the framework of varying degrees of propriety of signification:

> [10:35] "God" is sometimes said properly, i.e., by nature; sometimes largely, as by adoption and participation; sometimes very largely, as only by appellation.[136]

True, "properly" (*proprie*) and "largely" (*large*) were scholastic commonplaces.[137] Less common in the commentary of the time was the more technical term *li* (occasionally *le*), a definite article that served to draw attention to a word pointed out for study.[138] Not easily translatable into English, it will be rendered here "the term." William is particularly fond of it, and his use of it is generally independent of his sources. In the following case, he employs it to focus on the multivalent Latin conjunction *ut*, translated here "that." Though the latter term often expresses manner or consequence, in this case, he specifies its functioning as expressing causality:

> [9:3-4]*JESUS ANSWERED: NEITHER HAS THIS MAN SINNED, NOR HIS PARENTS, BUT THAT THE WORKS OF GOD MIGHT BE MADE MANIFEST IN*

*HIM*, and he is the direct cause, because *I MUST MUST WORK THE WORKS OF HIM WHO SENT ME*. Thus the term (*li*) "that" (*ut*) is employed causatively.[139]

By this minor exercise, William endeavors to show that the man's blindness has fallen within the scope of divine providence—no accident, God has intended it as a means of manifesting his glory. Later in the same chapter, he embarks on a similar analysis to point out that the acquisition of sight by believers is caused by Jesus' coming into the world. On the other hand, with respect to the loss of sight, presumably by nonbelievers, William is intent upon excluding divine causality:

> [9:39] *...SO THAT THOSE WHO DO NOT SEE MAY SEE*, the term (*li*) "that" (*ut*) here is causal; but afterwards where it is added: *AND THOSE WHO SEE MAY BECOME BLIND*, it is only consecutive.[140]

As he would have it, blindness of the sort Jesus is talking about is merely the consequence of his coming into the world; it is not caused by it. William's interest in accounting for God's permissive will and human freedom are matters about which we shall have more to say.

In these cases, our author has set for himself the modest goal of making a basic point of grammar. Yet he is also capable of engaging in such exercises to emphasize a point of theology. What follows are a few borrowings from Bonaventure into which he has inserted his own lexicographical remarks. In the first case, William focuses upon the term *in* to explain that the Father's life is not an extrinsic possession, but an attribute (the remarks independent of Bonaventure have been placed in bold):

> [5:26] *FOR AS THE FATHER HAS LIFE IN HIMSELF*, i.e., by essence, **hence the term (*li*) "in" is not a note of transition, as if the Father and his life were not one and the same,** *SO HE HAS GIVEN TO THE SON* **begetting him** *TO HAVE LIFE IN HIMSELF*, not by participation.[141]

In the following example, he dwells upon the word 'truly' (*uere*) to develop an apologetic for Catholic Eucharistic doctrine:

> And truly, whoever eats my flesh has eternal life, because [6:56]*MY FLESH IS TRULY FOOD*, not fancifully, as only corporeal food, which nourishes and soon passes away. **Or *TRULY*, not only figuratively, as manna, not only existing there as a sign, as a some heretics said. The term (*li*) "truly" excludes figure, parable, signification, fantasy and passing away.**[142]

He composed this commentary at a time of dramatic growth in Eucharistic piety during which Pope Urban IV (1261–1264) instituted the Feast of Corpus Christi (1264). By naming heretics who held that Christ's body was present only by signification, William probably had in mind Berengar of Tours (d. 1088), who had won fame for his opposition to the doctrine of the Real Presence. Berengar's retraction of this opinion before his death did not prevent him from becoming an enduring target for medieval polemic.[143]

## Rhetorical Analysis

It has already been noted that commentators of the period tended to attribute rhetorical figures to the human author's intention and for this reason to discuss them within the context of literal commentary.[144] The variety of tropes William mentions (generally independently of his sources) is rich. As well as metaphors, he points out instances of hyperbole,[145] metaplasm,[146] irony,[147] emphasis,[148] litotes, antiphrasis,[149] antiptosis,[150] antonomasia, and hendiadys. A basic example appears in his exposition of Jeremiah 2:12, which requires him to explain what Jeremiah meant in telling the heavens to be appalled and shudder in terror. William identifies Jeremiah's metaphor and then puts forward one of his own— that of a man standing in a gateway confronted by something enormous, having to decide whether to take refuge in the house or to close the gate (presumably from the outside):

> [2:12]*AND YOU GATES OF HEAVEN, BE UTTERLY DESOLATE, SAYS THE LORD* ... and note the metaphor here—it is just as a good man who stands in a gateway and sees something enormous would either withdraw and return to the house, or close the gate.[151]

On occasion, he draws on the support of a relevant authority to explain the functioning of the device in question, as in the following comment on Ecclesiastes 4:15:

> [4:15]*I SAW ALL THE LIVING WHO WALK UNDER THE SUN*, i.e., \<those he saw were\> many and innumerable, so that this should be taken as hyperbole. Hyperbole, according to Donatus, is a saying that surpasses belief by augmenting or diminishing force.[152]

Then again, the remarks of authorities are themselves susceptible to this sort of scrutiny. In the following comment on Ecclesiastes 5:11, William finds the biblical text's remark about the sleeplessness of the rich clear enough to be taken at face value, yet qualifies Boethius's manner of speaking about the splendor of wealth as ironic:

[5:11]*THE FULLNESS OF THE RICH DOES NOT LET HIM SLEEP . . .* Thus Boethius in book 2 of *The Consolation* ironically says: "O splendid happiness of noble wealth! Once you have acquired it, you are no longer secure."[153]

When describing less conventional figures, he usually provides a brief explanation for his students. Commenting on a statement of Ecclesiastes (8:8) that the wickedness of the wicked cannot save, William notes that the author's use of understatement for the sake of emphasis is a an example of litotes:

[8:8]*NOR WILL WICKEDNESS SAVE THE WICKED*, specifically, from damnation in hell, but it will damn them all the more. Hence this is litotes, saying less and signifying more.[154]

Less easily translated is the antonomasia he points out in the opening of John's Gospel. Turning on the capacity of the Latin *principium* to mean either beginning or principle, it refers the term to the Father:

[11]*IN THE BEGINNING (IN PRINCIPIO)* etc., i.e., in the Father, according to the *Glossa*. Granted that the term "principle" (*principium*) as applied to creatures designates priority, it nevertheless does not when applied to the divine persons. Hence, it pertains to the Father by antonomasia, because the Father is the principle of the Son and the Holy Spirit and the existence of creatures, whereas the Holy Spirit is the principle only of the existence of creatures.[155]

The identification of the name *Patre* with *principio* had originated with Augustine and had been restated by Alcuin before appearing in William's immediate source, the *Glossa ordinaria*.[156] His own contribution is to provide a few needed precisions, as well as to supply the appropriate technical term, *antonomastice*, to designate the Evangelist's substitution of the descriptive word *principio* for the proper name *Patre*.[157]

On the other hand, further along in the commentary on Ecclesiastes, William seems to presume that his students know what he is talking about when he finds in the words "youth and pleasure" an instance of hendiadys, a figure consisting in the use of a coordinating conjunction instead of subordinating one to unite two interrelated terms, with the result that a single concept is expressed by two separate terms. By the expression "pleasurable youth," William suggests to his students that at least in the present context the two terms constitute a single concept, since the former effects the latter:

<sup></sup>¹¹:¹⁰*FOR YOUTH AND PLEASURE*, i.e., pleasurable youth, for it to be hendiadys, or effective, *ARE VAIN. . . .*¹⁵⁸

Similar considerations concern figures of style. In the following examples, William employs the technical term gemination (*geminatio*) to explain what the author intends to signify by the reduplication of certain biblical terms:¹⁵⁹

¹:²*WEEPING SHE WEPT*, much, i.e., because the gemination designates abundance.¹⁶⁰
³:¹³*JESUS ANSWERED AND SAID TO HIM: AMEN, AMEN.* The gemination is an indication of firmness. John uses such gemination in this Gospel because he wrote it to edify the faithful and to confute heretics.¹⁶¹
⁵:¹⁸⁻¹⁹*THEN JESUS ANSWERED AND SAID TO THEM: AMEN, AMEN*, this gemination is an affirmation of what is to be said.¹⁶²

To this collection may be added "abusive comparison," namely, the juxtaposition of two apparently similar realities, one of which is good and the other bad, so as to place them in contrast. William finds the following two cases in the Book of Ecclesiastes:

⁴:¹⁷*OBEDIENCE IS MUCH BETTER THAN THE SACRIFICES OF FOOLS. . . .*
Note that this is an abusive comparison, because obedience is good and pleasing to God, but in Proverbs 15 (8): *The victims of the wicked are abominable to the Lord.*¹⁶³
    On the other hand, Prouerbs 14 (3): *In the mouth of the fool is the rod of pride.* And this is well said, because: ⁷:⁶*IT IS BETTER TO BE REBUKED BY A WISE MAN THAN TO BE DECEIVED BY THE FLATTERY OF FOOLS*, and this is an abusive comparison, since the latter is evil.¹⁶⁴

## *The* Divisio Textus

Commentators of William's time knew that grasping any text's literal sense presupposes an appraisal of its context.¹⁶⁵ For this, William made use of several procedures. In the previous chapter, we observed in some detail his most important means of situating individual passages within the framework of the biblical book at hand and the whole of the Bible, the *divisio textus*. We have seen that in the *divisio* he employs a coherent series of interrelated primary and subordinate textual divisions to organize his exposition with rigor and coherence, such that smaller sections are placed in the service of larger ones, and larger ones in the service of the whole book. It will be recalled that the present study considers this kind of coherence a key feature of his authenticated works and makes it an important criterion for the consideration of unauthenticated ones—the lack thereof is taken as strong evidence against his authorship. If the technique appears strange to modern eyes, university exegetes such as William viewed such organization as the mark of erudition and found in it several pedagogical advantages. Requiring arduous effort as well as competence, the coherent division of a text was at the time considered an indication of mastery.

Yet the *divisio* also served practical purposes, both for the master and his students. It is reasonable to assume that the *divisiones* of written versions of university commentaries correspond at some level to the lectures presented in the classroom. Hence, it provided a basis for organizing the subject matter. To masters, it offered the possibility of presenting an inherently unsystematic subject matter—the biblical text and its commentatorial tradition—in a coherent fashion. To students, it offered a means of approaching, apprehending, and retaining the matter at hand. In a period when learning typically involved committing substantial parts of the Bible to memory, students probably considered the *divisio* a mnemonic device, with its high level of internal organization combined with rhyming.[166] Moreover, to teachers and students alike, it facilitated access to the biblical text and its commentary by providing an elaborate system of cross-reference.

We have had the occasion to observe that a general feature of the *divisio* is its presentation of the commentator's own exegetical concerns rather than a preconceived formula. Relevant to the present discussion is William's primary concern there, the author's intention.[167] In this, he is hardly unique, but he is remarkably explicit. Terms that show up with considerable regularity in the *divisio* are the names of authors, often in tandem with words expressing purpose, such as *introducit* and *insinuat*. This is normally for the sake of introducing William's explanation of their intention. The following explanation of Jeremiah's motives is typical:

> [1:11]*SEE, LORD, AND CONSIDER FOR I HAVE BECOME VILE.* Here, as was said in the beginning of the book, Jeremiah introduces the mourning people in his own person; and first he shows his own misery; second he shows it to have been justly inflicted: [1:18]*YOU ARE JUST, LORD*; third he mourns his disappointment in vain hope: [1:19]*I CALLED TO MY FRIENDS, BUT THEY FAILED ME.*[168]

Yet in the *divisio*, as in his prologues, William recognizes the complexity of biblical authorship, albeit in a manner that by modern standards could be judged naive. This is conspicuous in his commentary on John's Gospel, where he regularly passes blithely from the Evangelist's perspective to Jesus.' At the outset of the *divisio* introducing chapter 7, for example, he assumes the perspective of the Evangelist:

> [7:1]*AFTER THIS JESUS WALKED IN GALILEE.* After recounting that many of Christ's disciples left him because of the perfection of his doctrine, here the Evangelist recounts that the Jews openly persecuted him because of envy. So Chrysostom continues. And first the persecution of the Jews is implied by what Jesus does; second by what the Jews do: [7:1]*THE JEWS THEREFORE SOUGHT HIM.*

Then, without notice, he adopts Jesus' point of view and proceeds to divide the text according to his intentions, not the Evangelist's:

> Christ implies this persecution, first by his withdrawal from the Jews; second by his difficult return to them: [7:2]*NOW THE JEWISH FEAST OF TABERNACLES WAS AT HAND.* In the first, first the withdrawal of Christ is noted; second its cause is added, specifically, the intent of the Jews to malign him: '*HE WOULD NOT WALK IN JUDEA.*[169]

William simply takes for granted both John's and Jesus' authorship of the text at hand. Bonaventure, on the other hand, assumes the perspective of Jesus throughout his exposition of this passage. Keeping his focus on Jesus' actions, he says nothing of the Evangelist's concerns:

> [7:1]*AFTER THIS JESUS WALKED IN GALILEE.* Above the Lord showed himself the overseer and keeper. Here he begins the third part, in which he manifests himself and shows himself the director and illuminator. . . . [170]

William provides a similar example in the *divisio* introducing chapter 10, where he again alternates seamlessly between the perspectives of Jesus and the Evangelist. Beginning his *divisio* from Jesus' point of view, he remarks that the Lord has made use of a similitude to describe the enemy's entrance into the sheepfold. Then he observes that it is the Evangelist who shows the similitude and takes note of its necessity. Finally, he returns to the perspective of Jesus. In his view, the authorial roles of the two are of a piece:

> [10:1]*AMEN, AMEN, I SAY TO YOU.* Here the Lord shows them to be sinners, showing that neither observances of the law nor a good life suffice without him in whom they refuse to believe. And this he shows by the similitude

of the gate allowing entrance into the sheepfold. First, therefore, the similitude is put forward; second, the Evangelist's manifestation that it is a similitude is put forward: *⁶THIS PROVERB JESUS SPOKE TO THEM*; third, the necessity of the exposition is noted: *⁶BUT THEY DID NOT UNDERSTAND WHAT HE SAID TO THEM*; fourth is the similitude's exposition: *⁷JESUS THEREFORE SAID TO THEM AGAIN*. In the first, first he shows that the one not entering through the gate is not the shepherd; second that the one entering through the gate is the shepherd: *²BUT THE ONE WHO ENTERS THROUGH THE GATE IS THE SHEPHERD OF THE SHEEP.*[171]

There is no awareness here of any distance between the perspectives of Jesus and John (to say nothing of the three stages of development of the Gospel described by modern scholars). If such assimilation of authorial roles may seem unsophisticated to the modern reader, William may be credited with respecting ambiguities inherent in the biblical text itself—the Evangelist's manner of having Jesus speak in the first person has the effect of conflating the perspectives of the two, with the result that it is not always clear who the speaker is.[172]

Then again, where he finds a textual warrant for doing so, William is capable of differentiating between the intentions of Jesus and the Evangelist. An example is his exposition of John 18:8–9, where Jesus' remark to the cohort arresting him—*I have told you that I am he. If therefore you seek me, let these go their way*—is followed by the Evangelist's aside, which includes a quotation of Jesus—*This was to fulfill the word which he had spoken, "Of those whom you gave me, I have not lost anyone."* Not without reason, William takes the quoted remark to mean one thing for Jesus and another for the Evangelist. Though modern scholars usually take it to refer to 6:37 and 17:12, William mentions only the latter, in which Jesus would appear to be speaking about eternal perdition—*Those whom you gave me I have kept, and none of them is lost*. Yet in John's remark in the passage at hand, being "lost" would appear to mean being arrested and killed with Jesus. Once again, William seeks his solution along the lines of authorial intention. As he would have it, in his quotation of Jesus, the Evangelist had in mind both kinds of death—being lost means being arrested and killed, which in the event entails eternal death, given the apostles' lack of faith. Put another way, William understands John to appropriate the Lord's words by setting them within a new context, without doing violence to their original meaning. What follows is the *divisio* and the subsequent exposition:

¹⁸:⁸*IF THEREFORE <YOU SEEK ME, LET THESE GO>*. Here, by his dismissal of the apostles by his mere command, it is shown that he was able to resist. And first his command is noted; second the fulfillment of Scripture by it is shown: ¹⁸:⁹*THIS WAS TO FULFILL THE WORD*.

[18:8]*IF THEREFORE YOU SEEK ME, LET THESE GO*, i.e., let my disciples first run away. Chrysostom, "In other words: I command that there be nothing in common between you and them. In this statement one notes Christ's extreme devotion to and consummate charity for his apostles." Above chapter 13 (1): *He loved them to the end.* [18:9]*THIS WAS TO FULFILL THE WORD WHICH HE HAD SPOKEN*, as if to say: by this was fulfilled the saying above in chapter 17 (12), *OF THOSE WHOM YOU GAVE ME, I HAVE NOT LOST ANYONE.* In fact, above he [Jesus] spoke of eternal death, whereas here the Evangelist wants us to understand corporeal death. And this is true. Indeed, he knew that if they had been captured and killed along with the Lord, they would have been damned because they did not then have faith, and there would have been no fulfillment of the Lord's word: *I HAVE NOT LOST ANYONE*, because he wanted to suffer alone, Isaiah 63 (3): *I have trodden the winepress alone.* If the case of Judas should be brought forward as an objection, it is to be said that he lost himself.[173]

Having distinct perspectives, both Jesus and John are authors of the literal sense. But no incoherence results because the Evangelist's intention respects and embraces the Lord's.

One result of this understanding is that in the course of the exposition, Jesus' words are subject to the same sorts of analysis as those of any other author. A case in point is his prediction that those in tombs will hear the voice of the Son of Man and rise again (John 5:28), a statement easily susceptible of an interpretation at odds with the general belief that before the Last Judgment, the souls of the dead experience either the beatitude of heaven, the torments of purgatory, or those of hell.[174] William clarifies the matter by commenting on Jesus' *modus loquendi*. His point is that Jesus has referred to the part—the body—in order to designate the whole—the person:

> [5:28]*DO NOT WONDER AT THIS*, specifically, that the Son of Man has the power of judgment, *BECAUSE THE HOUR IS COMING* at the end of the age *IN WHICH ALL*, i.e., all bodies—according to this mode of speaking, the whole is indicated by the part, *WHO ARE IN TOMBS WILL HEAR THE VOICE OF THE SON OF GOD.*[175]

## The Prophetic Literal Sense

If in the *divisio* William is particularly independent of his sources, the same can be said of a notable procedure for contextual study already mentioned in connection with William's prologues, namely, the exposition of certain passages according to multiple literal senses. Throughout the Middle Ages, the presentation of several alternative literal interpretations (normally introduced by the term *uel*) was an exegetical commonplace. William was particularly fond of them. But what we are considering here is the attribution to the inspired author of more than one intention, often in a perspective simultaneously encompassing past, present, and future realities. With respect to the prologue to *Super Threnos*, we have seen that on William's view, Jeremiah speaks literally about the Babylonian and Roman invasions. He is equally clear on the matter in the prologue to his commentary on Jeremiah:

> Some of the prophets spoke of this captivity as in the future, such as Isaiah and Hosea; others in the past, such as Daniel, Malachi and Haggai. But this one and Ezekiel at once (*simul*) predicted the future, saw the present, and grieved over the past.[176]

Though hardly what one would expect to find in a modern commentary, this sort of remark was not unheard of at the time. Examples of thirteenth-century scholars ascribing prophecy to the human author's intention could be multiplied.[177] One could wonder, however, about the theoretical framework for such interpretations. Even should we take William's "at once" (*simul*) as referring to Jeremiah and Ezekiel (rather than to the rest of the sentence), on the face of it, he appears to claim for the two prophets the capacity for intending and expressing multiple realities simultaneously. As William would have it, apart from the spiritual senses, virtually any passage penned by Jeremiah is capable of expressing several literal senses. He doesn't specify just exactly how Jeremiah envisioned the future events he wrote about, nor does he seem to be concerned that this mode of interpretation appears to give rise to what is now known as the fallacy of double meaning.

Thomas Aquinas has traditionally been credited with such a doctrine, though his modern commentators have tended to argue otherwise, precisely because of the equivocation this would entail.[178] While settling the debate lies beyond our purposes, it will be noted that he does occasionally find a prophetic literal sense in his Old Testament commentaries. To be sure, it is usually as alternatives that he presents a plurality of literal senses (introducing them by *uel*), but on occasion he puts all of them forward as intended by the human author.[179] Concerning Thomas's theoretical framework, A. J. Minnis has drawn attention to the importance of the case of Theodore of Mopsuestia.[180] In opposition to the allegorizing interpretations of the school of Alexandria, Theodore had asserted that no more than five of the Psalms refer directly to Christ, though he allowed that others could be applied to him by adaptation. For this, he was posthumously accused of denying that anything in the Old Testament referred explicitly to Christ. This mode of Old Testament interpretation was condemned at the Second Council of Constantinople in 553, with the result that Thomas took the prophetic literal sense as a matter of doctrine and the denial of it as a matter of heresy.[181] To avoid Theodore's pitfall, he appropriated Jerome's theory of prefiguration.[182] On this view, when the sages of the Old Testament described realities present to them, they recognized them as *figurae* or *typoi* of future ones; all the while aiming to provide an account of things or events at hand, they primarily intended to describe what remained to be fulfilled.[183]

Whether William was influenced by the Mopsuestia case must, on the available evidence, remain a matter of conjecture. All the same, prophetic literal interpretations appear throughout his commentary on Lamentations.[184] These he often proposes as alternatives (usually introducing them by *uel*) to the immediate historical sense, such as in the following cases:

> [1:5]*FOR THE MULTITUDE OF HER INIQUITIES, HER CHILDREN ARE LED INTO CAPTIVITY BEFORE THE FACE OF THE OPPRESSOR*, specifically, the army of either the Chaldean or the Roman people. . . .
> [1:10]*THE ENEMY*, Chaldean or Roman, *HAS PUT HIS HAND ON ALL HER DESIRABLE THINGS*. . . .
> [1:16]*MY CHILDREN ARE LOST*, as they have been killed, led into captivity, or devoured by their mothers, *BECAUSE THE ENEMY*, Chaldean or Roman, *HAS PREVAILED*. . . . [185]

Yet almost as often, he advances such interpretations as additional literal meanings (typically introducing them by *et*) belonging to the human author's intention. What follows are few examples:

> [1:4]*ALL HER GATES*, i.e., of the city and the temple, *ARE DESTROYED* by the Chaldeans and the Romans.
> [1:7]*HER ENEMIES*, Babylonian and Roman, *SAW HER* and mocked her Sabbaths, i.e., her solemnities, literally.
> [1:15]*AS IN A WINEPRESS THE LORD HAS CRUSHED THE VIRGIN DAUGHTER OF JUDAH*, i.e., as grapes in a winepress he has crushed the two tribes by the Chaldeans and Romans.[186]

Both sets of examples serve to illustrate William's application of prophetic literal interpretation as a means of expanding his scope for literal interpretation. Occasionally, he employs the method to change the historical context altogether, particularly where the original one presents difficulties. In the following example, a strictly historical reading would require explaining how Jerusalem was left without anyone to console it, despite the activity of no fewer than three of the major prophets. William avoids the problem by reading the passage against the backdrop of the Roman wars that followed more than six centuries after its composition:

> [112]*AMONG ALL THOSE DEAR TO HER*, earlier allies, *THERE IS NO ONE TO CONSOLE HER*. This more properly pertains to the Roman captivity, when they had neither prophets nor princes to console them. In the Babylonian captivity they certainly had prophets, namely, Jeremiah, Ezekiel and Daniel.[187]

We may conclude that apart from meeting the demands of avoiding Mopsuestia's error, the prophetic literal sense allows William to claim the broadest possible context for literal interpretation. Put another way, he employs the method to dramatically expand the conceptual map within which to comment on the texts at hand.

## The Questio

Facilitating the task of forming this conceptual map into a coherent whole was an additional procedure for contextual study, the *questio*. In our consideration of William's methodology and style, we saw that his questions are generally simple and closely related to the text. More properly exegetical than the complex questions that often appear in medieval theology in the form of a disputation, they show no relation to any actual oral debate. Disputations of elaborate questions had been customary in school lectures of earlier periods, but long before William arrived at the University of Paris, the *disputatio* had become separated from its parent *lectio*, with the result that only cursory questions remained an integral part of commentaries.[188]

   In the forthcoming consideration of William's sources, we shall see that in his commentary on John, his normal practice is to take his questions, if not necessarily his replies, from Bonaventure, or less frequently from Hugh of St. Cher. Reflecting no actual discussion accompanying the lecture, borrowings of this sort show the *questio* employed as a literary device. A typical case appears in his exposition of John 4:7–8, where he takes up the question of how Jesus could have requested a drink from the Samaritan at the well, which would appear to violate dietary laws. The query originated with Chrysostom, from whom Hugh of St. Cher borrowed it, as well as a reply. From Hugh's exposition, William takes the question, the reply Hugh borrowed from Chrysostom, and one of Hugh's own replies. William inserts his own remarks (in bold) before the borrowings, in the middle of them, and after them. First, he advances his own sensible observation that Jesus could have been thirsty and that there was no one else there to give him a drink. Then he inserts a comment from the *Glossa ordinaria* that bears on the question only indirectly, and finally he proffers two explanations for Jesus' not having brought anything to drink with him: his humility or his interest in giving the woman the opportunity to speak with him:[189]

> **Perhaps he was thirsty, literally, and there was no one there to serve him. Hence it follows:** [4:8]*FOR HIS DISCIPLES HAD GONE INTO THE CITY.* But how is it that he asked this of her, since the Jews consider the Samaritans unclean? Chrysostom: "He was indifferent to the keeping of these observances." **Hence Matthew 15 (11):** *Nothing from without defiles a man.* In fact, he knew that she would not give it to him, but he asked her so that from her response he would have occasion to admonish her and incite her to faith, **as is apparent from the** *Glossa*: "<*THE WOMAN SAID TO HIM*>, not knowing which drink he asked from her" etc. Also, he did not ask this of his disciples because they had gone into the city before he arrived at the well. **It was out of humility that he kept no one with him. Or perhaps this was to give the woman the opportunity to speak with him.**[190]

William takes the passage in much the same way as Hugh, yet by borrowing selectively from him and the *Glossa* and by adding a few of his own remarks, he produces his own synthesis.

Many of William's queries are borrowed from neither Bonaventure nor Hugh of St. Cher. Yet even in such cases, the *questio* has the appearance of a formality. An example appears shortly after the previous exposition, where he attempts to explain the Samaritan woman's motives for asking Jesus for a drink of his own water. Whereas Bonaventure and Hugh—following Augustine, Alcuin, and ultimately the *Glossa ordinaria*—have said that she had in mind only material water and merely wanted to quench her bodily thirst, Chrysostom has suggested that she had already acquired spiritual learning and sought spiritual refreshment. Faced with a choice between the two readings, both Bonaventure and Hugh have omitted Chrysostom's. Yet William includes it and attempts to synthesize it with the *Glossa*'s. This he does, first by presenting an objection concerning the disagreement, then by replying that the Samaritan woman sought to quench both her spiritual and corporeal thirsts (the question is in bold):

4:15*THE WOMAN SAID TO HIM*, according to the *Glossa*, she was still attracted by the carnal desire to thirst no longer; according to Chrysostom, she was in a certain way spiritually learned, hence he says she is wiser than Nichodemus, who did not ask for the water of baptism, above chapter 3 (12); *LORD*. In this she exhibits reverence and confesses the power of the giver. *GIVE ME THIS WATER THAT I MAY NOT THIRST*. Observe one cause of her request, specifically, avoiding thirst, or passing away. *NOR COME HERE TO DRAW*. Observe another, specifically, the cessation of labor. **From this it would appear that she was thinking only of material water, which contradicts Chrysostom. Response: This objection is without merit, because she thought that the water he promised would quench even her bodily thirst.**[191]

Having nothing to do with any spontaneous discussion, both the question and its reply show William's deliberate endeavor to synthesize two disparate lines of interpretation. Also worth noting here is the method by which the synthesis is achieved. No attempt is made to "bend" or retouch either the *Glossa*'s interpretation or Chrysostom's. Instead, it is by way of a dialectical procedure that the two are reconciled. Supporting the objection is the implied premise that the woman expected either that Jesus' water would satisfy her bodily thirst or that it would satisfy her spiritual thirst. The objector has assumed that the two expectations were mutually exclusive. The solution lies in denying this premise, not in smoothing over differences. About this more will be said shortly.

At times William formulates a question merely for the sake of restating a point made by one of his sources. A case in point appears in his comments on John 9:35, where Jesus asks the man whose blindness he cured whether he believes in the Son of God. Since this inquisitiveness seems at odds with the faith the man previously displayed when interrogated by the Pharisees (John 9:15–17), Chrysostom has posed and answered a question to explain that Jesus did this to pay tribute to the man's faith.[192] William borrows the remark and presents it in the form of a *questio*:

9:35*DO YOU BELIEVE IN THE SON OF GOD?* By asking he excites him. Chryosotom: "How is it that he so questions him after he had spoken so many words of faith to the Jews?" Response: Not in ignorance, but praise.[193]

Hardly the record of a classroom dispute, the *questio* functions here as a literary form. It would be easy to multiply examples of such formal usage of the *questio*, but this case is transparent. William had no intention of taking anyone in by it.

## Biblical History

As had so many of his predecessors (Jerome, Bede, Hugh of St. Victor, Peter Comestor, and Stephen Langton, to name only a few), William took for granted that the study of history was integral to biblical interpretation. His investigations into the various books' diverse causes, their authors' intentions and modes of exposition, and their textual evolutions demonstrate an awareness that they dealt with historical events and had their own histories. University commentators generally knew that such considerations were crucial to the understanding of any text's meaning, that is to say, to its interpretation. Yet even by that standard, our author's concern for historical inquiry is conspicuous. Ever reluctant to take the historical accounts of his sources at face value, he regularly reworks them to his own satisfaction.

In the preceding examination of William's prologues, and again in the consideration of his exegesis according to the prophetic literal sense, we have already observed his efforts to come to terms with his text's historical setting. But it would be wide of the mark to suppose that he was "historicist" in any modern sense. He did not regard biblical texts as radically historically contingent—he did not see them as mere products of history. To the contrary, he understood them to result from all the diverse causes he elaborated in his prologues. True, he normally described the material cause in terms of historical events, and as a consequence, he considered a given text's prehistory an indispensable context for its interpretation. But he never considered the historical context the only one worth keeping in mind. For him, the study of history was never an all-consuming enterprise.

Still, his historical interest shows itself periodically throughout his work, even where its absence would be understandable, such as in his commentaries on Ecclesiastes and Wisdom. Yet within the corpus of his known commentaries, a particularly good place to observe the functioning of his historical methodology is his commentary *Super Iohannem*, where he is repeatedly compelled to address discrepancies between the Johannine narrative and the Synoptic one.

A relatively simple case appears at the end of the fourth chapter, where the healing of the royal official's son is called Jesus' *second sign*, though several other signs are recounted by the "other evangelists." For William, the solution is simply a matter of pointing out that with respect to those other "signs," the other three evangelists were more discursive than John:

[4:54] *THIS WAS NOW THE SECOND SIGN THAT JESUS DID* etc. It is asked, since there were many other signs that Jesus did that year before John's death, why does he mention only these? Response: The other evangelists said more about the others.[194]

William owes neither the query nor its reply to his sources. Nowhere is he more independent of them than in his consideration of historical matters. All the same, it is worth recalling that he is not working within a vacuum, but a tradition. In formulating his replies to questions, he must take stock of the solutions of no small number of other commentators, including authorities in the strict sense (Augustine, Jerome, Chrysostom, et al.), as well as more recent figures who generally go unnamed (Hugh of St. Cher, Bonaventure, et al.). Looming large here is the figure of Peter Comestor, whose *Historia Scholastica* was the basic reference for most such considerations.[195] During William's time, he was known simply as the *Magister* and this one of his works as the *Historie*.

On less weighty matters, William is occasionally content to present alternative views without proposing his own. One such case presents itself in his exposition of John 4:3: *Reliquit Iudaeam et abiit iterum in Galilaeam.* In the Johannine narrative, Jesus' return to Galilee is preceded by three discourses: of Jesus with Nicodemus (3:1–15), of the Evangelist on God's sending of the Son (3:16–21), and of John the Baptist on Jesus in connection with their simultaneous ministries of baptism (3:25–35). What follows is Jesus' encounter with the Samaritan woman at a well (4:4–42) and the healing of a royal official's son (4:46–54). Whereas Chrysostom has closely followed the text's sequence of events, Peter Comestor has attempted to harmonize it with the Synoptic account. William gives voice to the views of each without presuming to adjudicate:

> [4:3]According to Chrysostom, these things happened immediately after the instruction of Nicodemus, and the aforesaid baptizing by the disciples of Christ.[196] And yet, in the *Histories* the Master interposes the healings of the royal official's son and Peter's mother-in-law (cf. Mt 8:14–15; Mc 1:30–31; Lc 4:38–39).[197]

Soon afterward, however, we find him disregarding his sources' conclusions and supplying his own timetable for the harvest Jesus mentions in John 4:35. Peter Comestor,[198] Hugh of St. Cher,[199] and Thomas Aquinas[200] place the scene in winter; Bonaventure situates it just before summer.[201] Without mentioning any of these views, William puts it just before Passover:

> [4:35]*DO YOU NOT SAY THAT THERE ARE YET FOUR MONTHS*, specifically, to be completed, *AND THEN THE HARVEST COMES?* From this it is clear that this happened before the Passover, since in those regions the harvests are at the time of Passover.[202]

He is not always so discreet. Subsequently, when considering a somewhat obscure reference by the Evangelist to one of Jesus' feats performed on a certain feast day in Jerusalem,[203] William considers himself able enough as an historian to cast doubt on the chronology of the *Historia scholastica*. The Comestor has presumed that the feast is Passover and on that basis has set aside the chronology suggested by the pericope's context. Correcting him, William points out that there are other possibilities:

> [4:45]*AND WHEN HE CAME INTO GALILEE, THE GALILEANS RECEIVED HIM, SINCE THEY HAD SEEN ALL HE HAD DONE IN JERUSALEM ON THE DAY OF THE FEAST ... FOR THEY TOO HAD GONE TO THE FEAST. ...* From this the Master in the *Histories* took this miracle to have been done around the Passover, not four months before, as the preceding letter seems to say. But this is not necessary, because it could have been a feast other than Passover, specifically, the feast of Tabernacles, which is in September.[204]

A more important and more complicated problem is the reconciliation of the disparate chronologies of the Last Supper, Passion, and Passover presented by Matthew, Mark, and Luke on the one hand and John on the other. At the heart of the matter is the timing of the Passover meal. Whereas in the Synoptic Gospels it appears to coincide with the Last Supper (Mt 26:18; Mc 14:14; Lc 22:11–15), in the Fourth Gospel it follows the Last Supper and the Passion—on John's account Jesus died on the Day of Preparation (18:28) at about the time of the slaughtering of the paschal lambs (19:24).[205] As do his contemporaries, William takes up the problem in his exposition of a verse that brings the matter directly to the fore (13:1): *Now before the feast of the Passover, when Jesus knew that his hour had come. . . .*

Two of the matters at stake here are particularly weighty. First is the credibility of the Gospel narratives, which on this point more conspicuously than on any other appear to contradict one another. More concretely, the trustworthiness of the first three has apparently been called into question by certain *Greci* who hold that John corrected them on this point.[206] This brings us to the second matter, specifically, the character of the Last Supper as a Passover meal. As William's exposition makes clear, this bears directly on the Latin Church's liturgical practice. Taken at face value, the Johannine chronology implies that the Last Supper was celebrated with leavened bread, with the obvious consequence that the Latin Church's celebration of the mass with unleavened bread is questionable.[207] Two contemporary developments sharpened the matter further. As we have already had the occasion to observe, William's period was characterized by a general rise in Eucharistic piety and the institution of the Feast of Corpus Christi, in which the Eucharist is publicly exposed for adoration. But it was also a time of renewed concern for the reunion of the Greek and Latin churches, a major obstacle to which was the divergence in their uses of bread, leavened and unleavened.[208] The implications of the text's interpretation for the church's liturgy were lost on none of William's contemporaries, and it is hardly likely that any of them regarded the problem as merely academic.[209]

William's exposition, worth presenting at some length, is a rare instance of his considering several questions at once. Apart from the opening query, taken from Bonaventure, his style resembles that of Thomas Aquinas, who normally lists all questions consecutively before replying to each one. Not in question here is the dating of the Easter celebration. In addition to Bonaventure's commentary, William appears to have had his eye on the *Glossa ordinaria* and on Peter Comestor's *Historia Scholastica*:

BEFORE THE DAY OF THE FEAST DAY OF PASSOVER. From this it would appear that the Lord confected with leavened bread, but the other evangelists say that he ate according to the common custom of eating the Passover (*pascha*).

Response: It does not say here, "the day of Passover (*pasche*) of the immolation of the lamb," but the first of the days of unleavened bread, on the preceding evening of which the lamb was immolated.

(1) Also, from this the Greeks argue that those events which happened then, namely, the meal and the eating of the lamb, would have happened on the fourteenth day of the month, when the paschal lamb (*agnus paschalis*) was immolated, as is prescribed in Exodus 12 (6).

(2) Also, below in chapter 18 (28): *They did not enter the praetorium, that they might not be defiled, but might eat the Passover* (*pascha*), specifically, the lamb. This was therefore on the fourteenth day of the month. But he celebrated the Passover (*pascha*) one day earlier. It was therefore on the thirteenth day of the month.

(3) Also, the Jews did not want to kill him on the fifteenth day of the month, Matthew 26 (5): *Not on the feast day....* Therefore, he was killed on the fourteenth and he celebrated the meal before. This was therefore on the thirteenth of the month.

(4) Also, the lamb was immolated on the fourteenth of the month, and the truth must have corresponded to the shadow. Therefore, Christ was also killed on the fourteenth of the month and celebrated the meal before. Therefore, as above.

To the contrary, Luke says expressly (22:7): *The day of the unleavened bread came, on which it was necessary that the pasch* (*pascha*) *should be killed.* But the pasch (*pascha*) was killed on the fourteenth of the month. Therefore, they then ate unleavened bread.

To the first it is to be said that here "pasch" (*pascha*) means the solemnity of the fifteenth of the month.

To the second, it is to be said that "pasch" (*pascha*) there means paschal foods, such as loaves of unleavened bread, not the lamb itself, which could be eaten only by the pure.

To the third it is to be said that the Jews, frustrated in their purpose, killed him on that day for the reason that they did not believe.

To the fourth it is to be said that the truth corresponds to the shadow because on the fourteenth day of the month he was captured and his passion began. According to Ambrose, "pasch" (*pascha*) in Greek is "passion" (*passio*) in Latin. According to the Hebrew language, "pasch" (*pascha*) means "passed over" (*transitus*).[210]

It is unlike William to subscribe to readings that run counter to the letter of his text, even where they are supported by his sources. And yet, he simply could not have set aside the Synoptics' chronology in favor of John's. Nor could he have concluded that the two accounts are incompatible. For no Latin scholar of the time was either position tenable. Certainly, his convoluted and somewhat forced interpretation owes much to the necessity of saving the Fourth Gospel's coherence with the other three, but it points as well to the demand of maintaining its cohesiveness with the Latin Church's liturgical practice.[211] The influence of the liturgy on William's work is a matter to which we now turn our attention.

## The Backdrop of the Liturgy

The liturgy has long been recognized as a general context and source of monastic theology, inasmuch as it governed the day-to-day lives of monks and provided the purpose for their work.[212] The same may also be said of university theology and exegesis, most of whose practitioners were Dominican or Franciscan friars, and it is worth recalling that university biblical commentary was largely for the sake of preaching, much of which was liturgical. While the liturgy may not be counted as one of William's principal concerns, its influence in his expositions is often noticeable.

The aforementioned case of the timing of the Last Supper isn't the only such example to be found in the commentary on John. Two recent studies have drawn attention to interesting differences between the chronologies assigned to the wedding feast at Cana by thirteenth-century commentators and by those of earlier periods.[213] For the purposes of the present question, the exegetical point of departure is the pericope's opening phrase: *And on the third day there was a marriage* . . . (2:1). Earlier medieval commentators, such as Bede (d.

735)[214] and Alcuin (d. 804),[215] and twelfth-century ones, such as Rupert of Deutz (d. 1129),[216] discussed whether this was to be counted from the time of Jesus' encounter with Andrew (1:40–42) or his meeting the following day with Philip and Nathanael (1:43–51). Otherwise, they took the text's chronology in a straightforward manner. By the thirteenth century, interpretations had changed under the influence of the liturgical practice of grouping three events into the Feast of the Epiphany: the visit of the Magi, Jesus' baptism, and the wedding feast at Cana. What had originated in a theological reflection upon the initial manifestations of Christ's divinity evolved into a fixed chronology by which the three events fell on the same day, albeit in different years. Bonaventure defends the plausibility of both chronologies,[217] but Albert,[218] Thomas,[219] and William subscribe to the liturgical one. Defending it with a *questio* lifted from Bonaventure (in bold), William identifies it by the formula "according to the common opinion":

> [2:11]*AND ON THE THIRD DAY*, i.e., from the day Jesus went to Galilee and called Philip,[220] as is apparent in the *Glossa*: "Galilee is called transmigration" etc. According to the common opinion, this was the thirteenth day of Christ's thirty-first year, because on the thirteenth day after his birth the Magi appeared, and on the same day of his thirtieth year he was baptized, and on the same day a year later this miracle was worked. **And should it be objected that after this miracle he went down to Capharnaum, as below, and that the Passover was then near, so that it could not have been on this day, it is to be said that he did not go down to Capharnaum immediately after this miracle, but after an intervening period.** *THERE WAS A MARRIAGE. . . .* [221]

William subsequently closes his discussion of the narrative by restating the interpretation, again invoking the "common opinion" as an authority of sorts, this time connecting it to the church's custom:

> [2:12]*AFTER THIS*, not immediately, but according to the opinion of those holding the Church's custom, which appears to hold that the aforesaid miracle was worked on the thirteenth day of Christ's thirty-first year . . . *HE WENT DOWN TO CAPHARNAUM.* [222]

Chronological changes of this sort are uncommon. More often the liturgy informs William's exegesis by way of allusions and occasionally by textual variants. One such case appears in his treatment of Jesus' instruction to Nicodemus concerning his divine origin and destiny in John 3:13. After borrowing from

Bonaventure to explain the passage in terms of Jesus' divinity and Incarnation, he proffers his own ecclesiological reading (introduced by "Or"—*Vel*):

> [3:13]*AND NO ONE HAS ASCENDED TO HEAVEN*, specifically, by one's own virtue, *EXCEPT THE ONE WHO HAS DESCENDED FROM HEAVEN*, by the assumption of his humanity, *THE SON OF MAN WHO IS IN HEAVEN* by his essence and the immensity of his divinity. Or, . . . *EXCEPT THE SON OF MAN*, i.e., the head with his members, Psalm (67:19): *Ascending on high, Christ . . . (Ascendens Christus in altum).*[223]

The citation of Psalm 67:19 is an allusion to the office of the Ascension, where a variant of this section of the verse appears more than once each day for the entire octave. Whereas the Vulgate's "Gallican Psalter" reads: *You went up on high and took captivity captive (Ascendisti in altum cepisti captivitatem)*, William has instead cited a liturgical variant of the breviary, which reads as follows: *Ascending on high, Christ took captivity captive (Ascendens Christus in altum . . . captiuam duxit captiuitatem).*[224] Even if he and his students knew the words by heart, it seems unlikely that this selection was purely accidental.

Since all of William's other commentaries are on books of the Old Testament, exploring their liturgical connections necessarily entails a passage into spiritual exegesis. At the expense of anticipating a forthcoming discussion, let us briefly consider a few instances of expositions bearing witness to a liturgical context.

Among the more obvious places to look is in the postill *Super Threnos*—the commentatorial tradition to which it belongs was in all likelihood inspired by the liturgy of *Tenebrae*, the office of matins and lauds for Holy Thursday, Good Friday, and Holy Saturday.[225] Characterized by a ritual of extinguishing candles, this liturgy in many respects resembled a funeral rite recalling the death of Christ. In this context, the Book of Lamentations was read specifically in reference to the Passion.[226] We have already had several occasions to observe that William's main interest in this postill, as in his others, is the literal sense. But he is not content to explain Jerusalem's history and leave it at that. In several places, he takes the opportunity to present the sacked Jerusalem as a type either of the crucified Christ or of the believer's soul mourning him as a widow would her spouse. The biblical passage of the following example was heard in the first lecture of the first nocturn of matins on Holy Thursday. Applied in the biblical text to the sacked Jerusalem, the image of the destitute widow is taken by William to represent the worldly soul left a widow by Christ, either by falling from grace into sin or by dying while in a sinful state:

> Morally. [1:1]*THE CITY*, the soul, *SITS*, having spurned celestial things, she is inclined to worldly ones, *ALONE*, destitute of spiritual goods. *THE MISTRESS*

OF THE NATIONS, i.e., of vices in the state of grace, HAS BECOME AS A WIDOW, from Christ her husband, or for having been separated in a state of guilt.[227]

The following verse was heard in the third reading of the second nocturn of matins on Good Friday. By connecting the rejected altar of the temple to Christ in his Passion, William evokes the darkness that surrounded the altar of the church at the moment his students heard this verse read aloud:

> Allegorically. [2:7]THE LORD, the Father, HAS SPURNED, i.e., appeared to spurn, HIS ALTAR, Christ in his passion. HE HAS CURSED HIS SANCTUARY, i.e., he has sentenced Christ to the evil of punishment.[228]

Neither of these examples refers to the Paschal liturgy explicitly. In William's work, liturgical influence usually takes the form of some sort of association, such as a reference to one of its rites or an allusion to one of its prayers. So, for example, he situates within a penitential perspective the time for uprooting plants described in Ecclesiastes 3:2, first by way of mentioning the sacraments of baptism and penance, then by borrowing a phrase from the principal prayer of the Mass's penitential rite, the *Confiteor*:

> Morally. . . . [3:2]A TIME TO UPROOT original sin by baptism, and actual (sin) by the sacrament of penance . . . also, everything superfluous in thought, word and deed.[229]

If associations of this sort seem opaque to modern sensibilities, they would have been pellucidly clear to William's students.

## Modes of Spiritual Interpretation

The preceding examples suggest that for all the importance William attached to the literal sense, it would be a mistake to imagine that spiritual interpretation was peripheral to his exegetical project.[230] As did his contemporaries, he subordinated the spiritual interpretation to the literal because he understood the spiritual senses to be dependent upon and derivative from the literal sense.[231] In order to see how, we would do well to consider the understanding of signification Augustine imparted to medieval commentators.[232] On Augustine's view, the literal sense is conveyed by the signification of specific realities by biblical words, and the spiritual sense is conveyed by the signification of one reality by way of another—which itself has been signified by words. As we have seen, the first level of signification is intended by both the divine and human *auctores*, and the second only by the divine one, in whose providence alone lies the capacity to employ contingent events to signify other realities. Therefore, no sense of any reality at a spiritual level can be had before the first, that is, literal, signification is apprehended.

Making allowance for the particularities of his style, William's spiritual interpretation corresponds well to the typology of medieval exegesis, which by now has been well described and documented.[233] All the same, it will be worth our while to examine a few examples for the sake of illustrating the purposes to which he puts it.

## Interpretations

Under consideration here is a kind of word study concerned with Hebrew terms. Taking as their basis the inspired character of the Hebrew text, medieval exegetes often studied such words in search of their intrinsic meanings, and this in order to mediate a passage from the text's letter to its spiritual sense.[234] Two sources, both by Jerome, were the origins of most of William's interpretations: for the interpretation of proper names, his *Liber Interpretationis Hebraicorum Nominum*, and for the interpretation of the letters of the Hebrew alphabet, his "Epistle 30" to Paula.[235] William's immediate source for both was usually the *Glossa ordinaria*, whose compilers, in turn, drew them from the works of early medieval commentators, such as Paschasius Radbertus for those connected to Lamentations[236] and Alcuin for those connected to John's Gospel.[237]

Their functioning may be illustrated by the following interpretation of *gimel* in *Super Threnos*. Like most of Jerome's interpretations, it originally appeared as a simple translation of the Hebrew term consisting of only one word: GIMEL, *fullness*.[238] In William's exposition, it is developed according to three senses: literally, to explain that Judah was forced to migrate because of the fullness of its sins; allegorically, to explain that the church has migrated from affliction to affliction because of the multitude of its tormenters or, alternatively, because of the multitude of sinners; and tropologically, to designate the soul migrating from sin to sin. Worth noticing here is William's additional borrowing from Jerome of the interpretation of *Judah* as "confessing," which he refers to the afflicted Church:

> [113]GIMEL is interpreted "fullness," as if to say: because of a multitude of sins, *JUDAH HAS MIGRATED*, indeed, from her own land to Chaldea. Allegorically. *JUDAH*, the confessing Church, *HAS MIGRATED* from affliction to affliction; because of affliction and slavery, and because of the multitude of those afflicting her, struggling to lead her back into slavery; or

because of the multitude of her pursuers enslaved to sin. . . . Morally. *JUDAH*, the previously confessing soul, *HAS MIGRATED* from sin to sin.[239]

In the following example, William presents Jesus himself as the author of the derivative meaning of the term *devil* as "flowing downwards." While this device serves the immediate purpose of allowing him to explain what Jesus could have meant by referring to Judas as a devil, it also allows him to pass beyond the letter of his text to discuss other realities not mentioned there, specifically, Judas's inclination to worldliness, which results from his care of the purse:

> [6:71]*AND ONE OF YOU IS A DEVIL*, not by nature, but by interpretation of the name. The Devil is, in fact, interpreted "flowing downwards," and perhaps he was inclined to lower things because he had the purse, below chapter 12 (6).[240]

## Allegory

At its most basic, allegorical interpretation takes realities described by the literal sense as figures for Christ, the Blessed Virgin, the Church, its members, or its enemies.[241] William provides a typical example in his exposition of Ecclesiastes 1:5–6, where he takes the sun's rising, setting, and rising again as types of the birth, death, and resurrection of Christ:

> Mystically. [1:5–6]*THE SUN RISES*, i.e., Christ in his nativity . . . *AND GOES DOWN* in his passion . . . *AND RETURNS TO ITS PLACE* in his ascension . . . *AND THERE*, i.e., in heaven, *RISING AGAIN*, i.e., coming in judgment. *HE MAKES HIS ROUNDS THROUGH THE SOUTH* considering those who are good and their works, who are understood by the noun "south" for their virtue and the splendor of their honest way of life, *AND TURNS TO THE NORTH* considering the wicked and their works, who are designated by the term "north" for the coldness of their malice.[242]

Whatever the limitations of this approach, it may be credited for having the advantage of transparence. The reader always knows which of the senses William is expounding and is never seduced into a sublime disregard for the letter. Preceding the comments just cited are elaborate and distinct literal expositions. Yet his methodological clarity may be further illustrated by his diverse explanations of a single term, *spiritus*—literally, it means wind (those taking the term to refer to celestial bodies err), yet mystically it refers to the Holy Spirit, sometimes by way of metaphors—the sun, the wind, and the air. Even the untrained student realizes which mode of interpretation is at work at any given moment:

> [1:6]*SURVEYING ALL THINGS, THE SPIRIT (SPIRITUS) GOES FORWARD AND RETURNS TO ITS ROUNDS*, the wind, i.e., goes around inspecting all things. "The spirit" (*spiritus*) is in fact the wind ... from this passage some have erred in saying that the sun and other celestial bodies are spirits (*spiritus*). By the noun "spirit" (*spiritus*), others understand not the sun itself, but the spirit (*spiritum*) presiding over it. . . . . Mystically, [1:6]*SURVEYING ALL THINGS, THE SPIRIT (SPIRITUS) GOES FORWARD AND RETURNS TO ITS ROUNDS*. What is first shown here is the diverse naming of the Holy Spirit (*spiritus*). Understood here by "spirit" (*spiritum*), are the sun, the wind, and the air: the sun for the fervor of his charity, for the sun is the fountain of heat, Gregory, "The Holy Spirit is love." Hence, he is also called "fire," Luke 12 (49): *I came to cast fire on the earth . . .* ; the wind for the speed and swiftness of his motion, or work . . . ; the air for his gentleness—the Holy Spirit is indeed gentle. . . . [243]

Even if medieval allegory is not often designated as explicitly as it is here, this example corresponds well to the classical norms of Christian allegorical interpretation, wherein realities indicated by the literal sense of the Old Testament are taken as figures of realities revealed in the New.[244] If the most frequent and imaginative allegory is in Old Testament commentaries, the New Testament books were also susceptible of such treatment. In his comments on Nicodemus's visit to Jesus in John's Gospel, William begins by providing three possibilities as literal explanations for its taking place at night—Nicodemus's shame, his fear, and the quiet of night to facilitate learning. Then he explains, mystically, that the night signifies Nicodemus's ignorance:

> [3:2]*HE CAME TO JESUS AT NIGHT*, *Glossa*: "Because as a master in Israel he is ashamed to learn openly, or out of fear." . . . *AT NIGHT*, perhaps so that he could learn more quietly. Or mystically, for signifying that the darkness of ignorance was still in his heart.[245]

Hardly original, this treatment of *nocte* was transmitted by Augustine to Alcuin and, subsequently, to the *Glossa ordinaria*.[246] On the other hand, William appears to be on his own in his interpretations of various realities of the subsequent narrative of Jesus' encounter with the Samaritan woman at the well. Taking the well as a figure for the profundity of sacred Scripture, he sees in the bucket an image of all the virtues one would hope to find in a friar—humility, purity, goodness, assiduousness in prayer, and austerity. He goes on to liken the patriarch Jacob to fighters, his sons to subordinate clerics, and his livestock to simple folk:

> [4:12]*ARE YOU GREATER THAN OUR FATHER JACOB*, in fact, giving something greater, *WHO GAVE US THIS WELL?* Mystically. The deep well is sacred scripture, Ecclesiasticus 7 (25): *It is a great depth, who can find it out?* The bucket is humility, purity, or goodness in life, assiduity in prayer, austerity. The water of this well is wisdom, Ecclesiasticus 15 (3): *She will give him the water of wholesome wisdom to drink. JACOB*—fighters, *AND HIS SONS*— understanding subjects, *AND HIS CATTLE*—i.e., simple ones.[247]

Occasionally, the roles are reversed so that New Testament realities become figures of Old Testament ones. In John's account of the feeding of the five thousand, the boy who presents five barley loaves becomes a figure for Moses, and his loaves become a figure for his five books:

> Allegorically. [6:9]*THERE IS A BOY HERE*, Moses, Hebrews 3 (5): *Moses indeed was faithful in all his house as a servant, in testimony to those things that were to be said; WHO HAD FIVE LOAVES*, his five books, according to Jerome, about which 1 Corinthians 14 (19): *I would rather speak five words with my mind.*[248]

This is another stock interpretation, drawn from the same set of sources as the preceding example (though not from Jerome).[249] More original is William's reading of the account of the wind confronting the disciples in a boat at sea, which he takes as a figure for the breath of the Devil. Though hardly extraordinary, the following remark doesn't show up in any of his known sources:

> [6:21]*THEY WISHED TO TAKE HIM INTO THE BOAT.* . . . Spiritually: The Devil's breath ceases at Christ's word, Ecclesiaticus 43 (25): *At his word the wind is still.*[250]

All of William's known postills contain allegorical interpretations, yet none presents them more consistently and imaginatively than *Super Threnos*. Here we find the sacked Jerusalem taken as a figure of the church or, more particularly, of the religious state, and its various sorts of inhabitants as varied ecclesiastical figures, such as prelates and doctors, who more often than not are referred to unfavorably, typically as corrupting influences. In the following example, we may observe William's creative use of sources, about which more will be said shortly. (See table 3.1)

Table 3.1 Lamentations 1:19: *COPH.* [119] *I CALLED TO MY FRIENDS, BUT THEY FAILED ME. MY PRIESTS AND MY ELDERS WERE CONSUMED IN THE CITY AS THEY SOUGHT THEIR FOOD TO REVIVE THEIR SOULS.*

| Paschasius Radbertus (CCCM 85, 64–65) | *Glossa* int. (ed. Rusch, vol. 3, p. 190a) | Stephan Langton (MS Paris, Arsenal 87, f. 208rb) | William of Alton (ed. cit, 240) |
|---|---|---|---|
| And what is worse, such enemies raged against us more cruelly when the *PRIESTS AND ELDERS*, whom the Greeks call aged, labor among us *CONSUMED* by famine for the word of God. This is especially because in pursuing the riches of the carnal life, they seek the food with which to revive their miserable lives. . . . | What is worse, they raged more cruelly when the *PRIESTS AND ELDERS* were consumed by famine for the word of God. Pursuing the riches of the carnal life, they sought the food of animal life (*animalis vite*) more than heavenly food. | Rightly am I afflicted, because *MY PRIESTS AND ELDERS* who ought to have fed me spiritually *WERE CONSUMED IN THE CITY* by famine for the divine word. *They have become like rams finding no pasture* (Lamentations 1:6), as was said above, *BECAUSE THEY SOUGHT THEIR FOOD*, not spiritual but temporal, *TO REVIVE THEIR SOULS* (ANIMA SUA), i.e., their animality (*animalitatem*) which was discussed above. | Allegorically. The Church's friends are prelates, *AND THEY DECEIVED ME* corrupting by their bad example. *MY PRIESTS*, i.e., the doctors, *AND ELDERS*, those more wise, *IN THE CITY*, i.e., in the Church or in the religious state, *WERE CONSUMED* by the absence of doctrine, *because they are dumb dogs, unable to bark* (Isaiah 56:10), and because *THEY SOUGHT THEIR FOOD*, not spiritual, but carnal, temporal riches *TO REVIVE THEIR SOULS* (ANIMAS SUAS), i.e., their carnal desires. |

The usage of the biblical text's graphic depiction of famine in Jerusalem as a figure for ignorance of doctrine is a theme that originated with Paschasius Radbertus. The contrast between spiritual and temporal food was introduced by Stephen Langton.[251]

## Tropology

Tropology involves the prefiguration of realities having to do with the life of the soul; otherwise, the exegetical procedure is the same as with allegory. In his comments on the Johannine narrative of the healing of the man born blind (9:7), William finds occasion to take up a few of his favorite themes, likening the man's washing to repentance and his seeing to contemplation: "Morally. [9:7]*HE WENT*, doing penance he washes, contemplating he sees."[252] Returning to Lamentations, we find him working with a few of his other preferred themes, namely, the virtues and vices. He likens Jerusalem's faithless friends to the soul's deceitful affections and its priests to the virtues proper to priests—not the ones Jeremiah knew, but those of his own time and place. Associating Jerusalem's elderly to judgment and counsel, he remarks that they are consumed by vices, which, he tells us, are depraved desires:

> Morally. The soul's [1:19]*FRIENDS* are said to be sweet affections which fail the soul intent upon them. The *PRIESTS* are the virtues belonging to the priesthood, *AND ELDERS* those belonging to judgment and counsel, *WERE CONSUMED* by vices, *BECAUSE THEY*, specifically, the soul's affections, *SOUGHT THEIR FOOD*, i.e., depraved desires.[253]

## Distinctions

In the preceding examples, various "literal" realities are taken as figures for one or perhaps two spiritual ones, typically according to allegory and tropology. These are expositions either of individual verses or of combinations of them, with the result that the various spiritual realities signified are related to each other in coherent sentences. Yet in medieval exegesis, individual terms became the subjects of extensive spiritual expositions, resulting in lists of *distinctiones*, or figures signified, which normally had little or no connection with each other. Toward the end of the twelfth century, independent written collections of various allegorical renderings of biblical terms had emerged for use in preaching, as well as exegesis. During the thirteenth, the *distinctio* appeared as an integral feature, a simple form, within commentaries.[254] What follows is William's distinction of *mare* situated within his exposition of Ecclesiastes 1:7: *All rivers run into the sea, yet the sea does not overflow* . . . :

> [1:7] *The sea* (*mare*) is water for having been gathered, Genesis 1 (10): *And the gathering of the waters he called the sea.*
>
> Also, death for its bitterness, 2 Samuel 14 (14): *We all die, and like water we sink into the earth.*
>
> Also, hell for its expanse, Habakkuk 2 (5): *Like hell, he has expanded his soul.*
>
> Also, the world for its restlessness, Psalm (103:25): *This is the sea great and wide, teeming with creeping things without number, little and great.*
>
> Also, the meeting of the wicked for its fervor, Isaiah 57 (20): *The wicked are like the raging sea.*
>
> Also, sacred Scripture, for its being the origin from which all writings arise, Isaiah 11 (9): *The earth is filled with the knowledge of the Lord, as the covering waters of the sea.*
>
> Or the Blessed Virgin for the fullness of its virtue, *Hail, full of grace,* Luke 1 (28). With respect to this sea, on this same passage, ALL RIVERS RUN INTO THE SEA, i.e., all streams of grace, YET THE SEA DOES NOT OVER-FLOW, i.e., does not swell with pride. Indeed, she said: *Behold the hand-maid of the Lord* etc. (Luke 1:38).[255]

Variation of this sort between negative, positive, and ambiguous interpretations is typical of the form, as is the lack of continuity between the various elements—each is distinct and incapable of being connected to the others in a continuous sentence. In the final sequence, several nonliteral realities are so connected (the Blessed Virgin, grace, and humility), yet these are not introduced by the subject of the distinction, sea (*mare*), but by other lemmata. Their appearance signals the end of the *distinctio* and a transition to the more common approach examined in the previous examples.

The functioning of the *distinctio* becomes clearer upon examination of a few of its key features. Conspicuous among these is mobility. Because its various elements are explicitly related only to a single term, it is susceptible of being situated within a commentary or sermon on any biblical text where the term appears. There is nothing about this one to prevent it from being applied to any text containing the term *mare*. Whether William drew it from a separate collection or composed it himself for his immediate purposes must, on the present evidence, remain a matter of conjecture.

However this may be, his intention to make this distinction a part of his exposition of Ecl 1:7 brings us to another of this form's important features, namely, its remarkable capacity for appealing to the imagination. In the preceding example, the individual elements, as well as the biblical references that complement them, place before the mind's eye images of death, hell, the world, sea monsters, sacred Scripture, and the Blessed Virgin, and this in just a few lines. In a subsequent chapter, we shall see that our author had several exegetical purposes for using distinctions and spiritual expositions to deploy elaborate arrays of images. Here we will observe that such vividness would have made them very attractive to preachers.[256] Worth noting here is that William often introduces allegory, tropology, and distinctions by the single term *nota*.[257] No attempt will be made here to provide a complete account of its functioning in medieval exegesis, but it would appear that in William's work, it served to draw the cursory reader's attention to particular expositions, and this often for the sake of designating those particularly well suited to sermons. One may surmise as much from the manuscripts containing postills—in many of them, the term is regularly inscribed in the margins wherever it appears in the exposition. Such is the case with both of the manuscripts consulted for the following selection from his exposition of Ecclesiastes 7:3: *It is better to go to the house of mourning than to the house of feasting*. Independently of Hugh of St. Cher and Bonaventure, William presents both allegorical and tropological comments in the form of *distinctiones*:

Note that [7:3]*THE HOUSE OF MOURNING* is the mind grieving insults to God, present miseries, its own offenses, and those of others.

Also, [7:3]*THE HOUSE OF MOURNING* is the Church mourning her dead children, Jeremiah 31 (15): *Rachel weeping for her children*.

Also, her sojourning in misery, Psalm (119:5): *Woe is me, that my sojourning is prolonged*.

Also, her longing for her homeland, Psalm (136:1): *By the rivers of Babylon, there we sat and wept* etc.

Also, [7:3]*THE HOUSE OF MOURNING* is hell, where *there will be weeping and gnashing of teeth*. (cf. Mt 8:12; Lc 13:28)

Also, [7:3]*THE HOUSE OF FEASTING* is the mind rashly secure in its goods, Proverbs 15 (15): *A secure mind is like a continual feast*.

Also, the synagogue of sinners who gather the flesh of others to feed upon it, Micah 3 (5): *They bite with their teeth and preach peace* etc., Galatians 5 (15): *But if you bite and devour one another, take heed that you not be consumed by one another*.

Also, this world in which the worldly rejoice, Isaiah 22 (13): *Behold joy and gladness, killing calves, and slaying rams, eating flesh, and drinking wine*. Also, note (*nota*) that remembering death avails for avoiding sin,

Ecclesiasticus 7 (40): *In all your works, remember your end, and you will never sin.*

Also, for spurning earthly things, Jerome: "The one who always ponders his own mortality easily spurns all things."

Also, for taming the desires of the flesh, Gregory: "Nothing avails as well for taming the desires of the flesh as pondering the death to come, and this to desire heavenly things."[258]

## Overview

All of the themes of the preceding excerpts appear regularly in William's work, and they say much about his purposes as a commentator. True, meditation upon Scripture, contemplation, purity of life, and manual labor were classic monastic ideals and commonplaces in medieval tropology. But a few themes are more particularly evocative of a mendicant setting—the emphasis on action ("the urgency of action") in the commentary on Ecl 9:7–10 and the references to priests, doctors, and prelates in the preceding ones. As did other university commentators, William composed his postills for the sake of preaching, and in all likelihood, they served as aids to the composition of sermons. It is clear that exhortation was one of his guiding exegetical purposes. This aim would have been well served by his spiritual expositions. Beryl Smalley has drawn attention to the popularization of spiritual exegesis in the preaching of the masters of the biblical moral school during the late twelfth century and of the mendicant orders during the thirteenth.[259] No longer the exclusive domain of a spiritual elite (i.e., monks), spiritual exegesis by William's time had long been a standard feature of preaching to clerical as well as to lay audiences.

But William used them for more than providing material for sermons. His exegetical project had more personal and more proximate ends—it found its primary object in his own audience of student brothers. In this connection, two points are worth keeping in mind. First, more than a few of the student brothers William addressed at Saint-Jacques were destined to hold positions of authority. Neither he nor they were unaware that the University of Paris was a fast track to advancement, and he intended to prepare them for their responsibilities.[260] This much is suggested by his particularly frequent discussion of *prelati*, occasionally in positive contexts but much more often in negative ones, evidently for the sake of providing positive and negative examples to his students. A typical example appears in his exposition of Ecclesiastes 10:16, where he takes Solomon's warning about child kings and gluttonous princes as justification for mentioning the disorder caused by bad and foolish prelates as well as the disorder caused by carnal and effeminate ones:

> [10:16] *WOE TO YOU, O LAND, WHOSE KING IS A CHILD AND WHOSE PRINCES EAT IN THE MORNING.* Above he gave a remedy for the disorder that comes from a bad and foolish prelate. Here (he gives one) for the disorder that comes from a carnal and effeminate prelate, showing that such a one is not to be promoted.[261]

Here as elsewhere, it is difficult to determine exactly whom William means to designate by the term prelate, yet there can be little doubt that he has clerical authorities of various sorts in mind.[262] Admonitions concerning the dangers of ecclesiastical office are one of his favorite themes. In the next chapter, we shall have occasion to observe that William consecrates a particularly discursive question to a matter specifically concerning clerics.

Second, in William's time, the ideal of preaching was understood—particularly among Dominicans—to have contemplation as its antecedent and wellspring.[263] *Contemplatio* is a matter to which he often returns, normally in comments not borrowed from his sources. More generally, the ideal of contemplative preaching provides a context for understanding the exegetical purposes of his spiritual expositions. By proposing images of biblical realities to the imagination, they provided the subject matter for the preacher's contemplation and served as mnemonic devices for their preaching.[264] These, too, are matters to which we shall have occasion to return.

## Conclusion

Even by the norms of his period, William was particularly attentive to authorial intention. Toward the end of grasping it, he made use of an elaborate range of techniques for textual, linguistic, and rhetorical analysis, as well as careful historical inquiries. Such procedures are now considered part of the historical-critical method. But the similarities between thirteenth-century university methods and modern ones should not be exaggerated. If William was concerned to come to terms with all of the Bible's literary complexity, its various authors and modes of exposition, and this to find each line's literal sense, he had no historical consciousness in the modern sense—he did not believe the Bible to be constituted by its history. This is why he had no interest in subjecting it to a reductionist fragmentation into isolated elements. He and other scholars of his time studied the various historical conditions of the books on which they commented for the sake of grasping their meaning. But this is not to say that they considered such conditions the primary source of meaning. This source, it will be recalled, was for them none other than the primary efficient cause—God. Hence, they saw no need to "reconstruct" historical conditions, as modern scholars often do.

This brings us to another difference between medieval methods and modern ones. It hardly needs to be said that none of the expositions examined shows any tendency remotely resembling a hermeneutic of suspicion. If William's investigations arise from genuine curiosity, they also serve the important purpose of organizing his expositions and providing context for them. But it should be pointed out that historical contextualization of this sort is wholly unlike the historicism characteristic of some kinds of modern biblical scholarship. For William, a given text's essential context is not its isolated prehistory, but rather its proper place within a unified history of revelation. Because he saw no need to reconstruct the historical narrative, he saw no need to deconstruct the traditional one. To point out that this was no part of William's project is to state the obvious.

In his historical inquiries, more is at stake, therefore, than the establishment of a cohesive historical narrative for its own sake. As did his contemporaries, William saw biblical history as encompassing even the present. For all of them, revelation was an enduring reality, constantly expressing itself, as we have seen, in *sacra doctrina* and the liturgy, and as we shall see, in contemplation and preaching. Even if scholars of the period showed less reverence for their predecessors than is often supposed, their purpose in putting forward their own solutions was inherently constructive. Oriented toward synthesis, William's use of dialectic in the questions he took up usually allowed him to save some element of each of the diverse positions in play. The *divisio textus* and the constant recourse to citations drawn from the entirety of the Bible leave little doubt about the thoroughly synthetic nature of his enterprise. Never losing sight of the importance of the individual verse's own meaning, he believed that its true significance emerged only within its various contexts—the book's successive divisions and subdivisions and the Bible as a whole.

Then again, the Bible was not for him an isolated artifact. His frequent appeal to the interpretations of his predecessors leaves little doubt that they, too provided context for interpretation and that they, too, called for synthesis.

# 4

# *Sources*

ON THE EVIDENCE of his surviving literary production, William probably had other writers in mind when he described an *auctor* as someone who writes principally what is his own and complements it by what belongs to others.[1] Even a brief examination of his use of sources is enough to show that an ample portion of his literary production has been borrowed. Such replication was typical of medieval biblical commentary, and particularly of university commentary.[2] On the other hand, William was no mere *compilator* of other writers' work either (*qui scribit tantum aliena*). Rather, he carefully synthesized his own comments with those of his sources, weaving them into coherent expositions. Most likely he considered himself a *commentator*, whom, it will be recalled, he defined as someone who writes principally what belongs to others (*principaliter aliena*), complementing these selections with what is his own (*sua tanquam annexa*).

## *Procedures for Employing Authoritative Traditions*

For any given postill, William's selection of sources owed less to his own predilection for certain authors than to the particular book's own commentatorial tradition, which neither he nor any of his contemporaries could disregard. This is recognizable in the marked variation in his selection of sources from one commentary to the next. Whereas the names of Augustine and John Chrysostom appear continuously in *Super Iohannem*, each appears only once in *Super Threnos*, the latter by way of a false attribution.[3] In no other postill does William appear to have borrowed from Chrysostom. Similarly, whereas Paschasius Radbertus figures as the principal source of *Super Threnos* (albeit by way of the *Glossa ordinaria*), he has had no appreciable effect on William's other postills. Examples could be multiplied, but the cases of Lamentations and John are enough to show that William's choice of sources was governed by the exegetical history of the book at hand. To return to *Super Iohannem*, the ubiquity of borrowings from Augustine is typical of the entire Latin commentatorial tradition subsequent to his *Tractatus in Iohannem*.[4] Chrysostom had no appreciable influence until the late twelfth century, when Burgundio of Pisa translated his *Homilies* on John's Gospel (c. 1171–1173).[5] Yet by William's time, he, too, had become a standard reference for commentary on that book. In his own postill on John's Gospel, Thomas Aquinas cited only Augustine more frequently.[6] On the other hand, when William set about composing his other six known postills, there were no commentaries by Chrysostom available for him to consult. While each of his other postills concern books of the Old Testament, all of Chrysostom's biblical commentaries are on books of the New. The case of Paschasius Radbertus is similarly illustrative. During the centuries preceding the composition of his *Expositio in Lamentationes*, the Book of Lamentations had gone virtually without commentary in the Latin West.[7] While this work became a principal source for virtually all subsequent commentaries, including William's, Paschasius left no expositions of the other books on which William is known to have commented.

What is more, as a look at the sources of either *Super Threnos* or *Super Iohannem* will suggest, the lines of influence on William's exegesis are remarkably complex. Setting aside for the moment pagan authors, most of his borrowings involve multiple sources, several of which are often separated from each other by many centuries. While Jerome figures largely among the sources of *Super Threnos*, his influence is generally anonymous and mediated by the *Glossa ordinaria*. In *Super Iohannem*, on the other hand, his name appears with reference to a broad range of writings, and in *Super Ecclesiasten* he is cited regularly, sometimes by way of the *Glossa ordinaria* but often with the qualification *in originali*.[8]

Perhaps the best way to consider the various causal relationships between the authors whose work William borrowed is to begin with a chronological ordering. Without pretending to settle historiographical questions concerning the dating of the various periods of the Middle Ages, we can classify the Christian sources according to four periods: the Fathers, the Early Middle Ages, the twelfth century, and the thirteenth century. Whatever one makes of such distinctions, they have the advantage of corresponding to categories William himself recognized, at least implicitly. Unreservedly, he appeals to the authority of early Christian writers, such as Jerome and Gregory the Great, and particularly in *Super Iohannem*, Augustine and Chrysostom. Noticeably less frequently, he cites early medieval authors such as Isidore, Bede, Alcuin, and Rabanus Maurus, and still less frequently, twelfth-century figures such as Andrew and Hugh of St. Victor, Peter Comestor, and Bernard. Particularly conspicuous among sources of this period is the *Glossa ordinaria*. It is the one reference that appears consistently throughout the corpus of his commentaries. A product of the schools of the twelfth century, as we shall see, it had an authority deriving from the Patristic and early medieval writings it contained. On the other hand, William's borrowings from thirteenth-century authors such as Hugh of St. Cher and Bonaventure,[9] though frequent and often verbatim, are generally without attribution. What is more, by contrast with the aforementioned references, they are easily susceptible to modification on William's part.

While one could wonder about the importance of William's protocols for citing authors of various sorts, these correspond to differences in his methods of employing their texts. To be sure, he seldom qualifies his sources explicitly as members of distinct classes. On the rare occasions where he refers to patristic figures as a group, in keeping with the typical practice of his time, he calls them saints (*sancti*) rather than fathers (*patres*).[10] Considerably broader is another collective reference he employs sparingly, authorities (*auctoritates*). We shall see that in his lexicon this term could designate even non-Christian figures. With what follows, each of the prominent kinds of sources will be considered in approximate chronological order.

## *Profane Writers*

Commonplace in William's prologues, references to non-Christian authors show up less frequently in his expositions. In either case, these are appeals to figures whose authority is limited to a specific field, such as Josephus for the history of the Old Testament,[11] Aristotle for philosophy,[12] or Donatus for grammar.[13] In such cases, they had real weight, and there can be no question that their qualification as *auctoritates* had clear implications for the expositions in which they were cited.[14] What follows is an illustration from the seventh chapter of William's commentary on Ecclesiastes:

> Therefore it says [7:8] CALUMNY, which is, of course, the imposition of a false accusation, DISTURBS THE WISE, specifically, the reformed. To the contrary, Seneca says: "No disturbance falls upon the wise." And Proverbs 12 (21) says: *Whatsoever shall befall the just man shall not make him sad.* Response: These authorities speak of the perfect wise man, whereas this passage speaks of the imperfect one.[15]

Both the question and its solution have been taken from Bonaventure, yet he mentions only Proverbs 12:21. The citation of Seneca and the combined reference to him and the author of the Proverbs text as *auctoritates* are William's additions. Though he has not defined the term, his usage of it in this case is telling.

A problem has been created by Seneca's remark that the wise man cannot be perturbed, an assertion that would appear to contradict the biblical text. Though a pagan, Seneca is an *auctoritas* on the matter at hand, wisdom, with the consequence that his pronouncements must be interpreted according to the principle of *concordia auctoritatum*. On this dictum, no authority can be understood to be in basic disagreement with any other one on the same matter.[16] We have already had the occasion to observe that in addressing questions of this sort, university exegetes normally made use of the tools of dialectic to describe the intentions of authors. The previous solution rests on a distinction between two different senses of *sapientem*—whereas Seneca was talking about the perfect wise man, Solomon had in mind the imperfect one. The king's wisdom, exposed in the prologue to this postill as loveless and imperfect by comparison with Augustine's, appears here as inferior even to the sagacity of a pagan.

## *Sancti*

Veiling authorities in anonymity was not William's way of getting around discrepancies between them.[17] Nor did he presume to substitute his own words for those of a given author in trying to express what the author "wished to say." It has been said that when referring to authorities, medieval theologians submitted them to just this sort of *expositio reverentialis*, leading them around by a "wax nose."[18] If we are to understand the "reverential exposition" to be a method of subordinating the meanings of authoritative sources to the systematic requirements of homogeneous thought constructions, then we may say that William avoids the practice. Much more characteristic of him is his exposition of John 1:19, where he considers the motives of the priests and Levites sent to ask John the Baptist who he was. He offers a clear choice between the views of the *Glossa ordinaria* and Chrysostom: according to the former, they simply wanted to know who he was; for the latter, they were hoping that he would call himself Christ:

> [1:19] *WHO ARE YOU?* so that by his confession they would know who he is, according to the interlinear *Glossa*.[19] Or, according to Chrysostom, so that he would declare himself to be the Christ.[20] Yet they knew who he was since they had been baptized by him, Luke 3 (16).[21]

Presenting them in a straightforward manner, William avoids leading his sources anywhere. He is content to present both as plausible alternatives. His meaning intact, Chrysostom stands in place.

Elsewhere, William occasionally sharpens the opposition between authorities by drawing explicit attention to their disagreements. A case in point appears in his exposition of Jesus' encounter with Nicodemus (John 3:8), where we find him once again interested in the term *spiritus*. According to Chrysostom, Jesus' statement *The spirit blows where it wills and you hear its voice* (*Spiritus ubi uult spirat et vocem eius audis*) refers to the motion of the wind directly and to God's action metaphorically. For Augustine, it refers directly to the action of the Holy Spirit. The disagreement is lost on none of William's contemporaries. Hugh of St. Cher,[22] Albert the Great,[23] and Thomas Aquinas[24] mention both views and present them as alternatives. Whereas Hugh and Thomas discreetly refrain from connecting the latter interpretation with Augustine, Bonaventure explicitly opposes the two.[25] William follows suit, saying that Augustine contradicts Chrysostom:

> [3:18]*THE WIND (SPIRITUS) BLOWS (SPIRAT) WHERE IT WILLS AND YOU HEAR ITS VOICE.* Chrisostom relates this to the wind, which is said to blow where it wills because it naturally has unhindered gusts. Its sound is called its *VOICE (VOX)*. Nevertheless, Augustine contradicts this exposition, saying *THE WIND (SPIRITUS) BLOWS (SPIRAT) WHERE IT WILLS* because it has in its power the heart of anyone it illuminates.[26]

A similar case appears in William's consideration of the identity of the "other disciple" who, with Peter, followed Jesus after his arrest (John 18:15). In view of the biblical text's silence on the matter, Augustine refuses to take a definite position, yet acknowledges a custom of taking the text to indicate John.[27] Chrysostom affirms that it was, in fact, John.[28] Neither Bonaventure, Thomas Aquinas, nor Albert the Great finds it worthwhile to bring up the disagreement. Bonaventure follows Augustine without naming him, citing instead the *Glossa ordinaria*, where Augustine's interpretation is repeated verbatim.[29] The only other source Bonaventure mentions is a commentator known only as Victor, whose view on the matter would appear to be the same.[30] Albert agrees with Chrysostom and cites him to that effect, without, however, mentioning any other interpretation.[31] Thomas similarly takes Chrysostom's view, yet with reference neither to him nor to anyone else.[32] William, for his part, openly connects the two authors to the two interpretations and juxtaposes them for the sake of expressing his agreement with Chrysostom:

> [18:15]*AND THE OTHER DISCIPLE.* Interlinear *Glossa*, Augustine: "Who this could be should not be determined rashly." Nevertheless, Chrysostom says openly that it was John, and that he withheld his name out of humility.[33]

When he deems it necessary, William is capable of doing the contradicting himself. In his comments on Jesus' encounter with the Samaritan woman at the well

(John 4:20), he mentions Chrysostom's contention that the mountain to which she referred (*patres nostri in monte hoc adoraverunt*) was the same as the one on which Abraham was to sacrifice Isaac. Hugh of St. Cher,[34] Albert the Great,[35] and Thomas Aquinas[36] also mention the interpretation. Presenting it as one of several alternatives, they leave it unchallenged. Bonaventure leaves it unmentioned. William calls it false:

> [4:20]*OUR FATHERS*, namely, Abraham, Isaac and Jacob, *WORSHIPPED ON THIS MOUNTAIN*. According to some, with whom Chrysostom would appear to agree, the woman pointed to the mountain on which Abraham intended to sacrifice his son. But this is false, because that was Mount Moria, as Genesis 22 (2) makes clear.[37]

Chrysostom's authority affords him no pious exposition, even if William's reason for gainsaying him is not supported by the Vulgate of the passage he cites as evidence. In modern translations of Genesis 22:2, the mountain of Abraham's sacrifice is generally named Moriah, but in the Vulgate it is simply *the land of vision* (*terram uisionis*). William's source for the remark is probably Jerome, who so identifies the mountain in his *Book of Hebrew Questions on Genesis*, as well as in his *Commentary on Jeremiah*.[38] Obviously, there can be no question here, either for William or for any of his contemporaries, of *auctoritas* understood as a law in itself that had to be accepted.[39] On the other hand, authoritative texts constituted a body of knowledge, recourse to which was integral to thirteenth-century pedagogy. It remains for us, then, to further consider William's methods for citing them.

He is not unprincipled in this respect. When commenting on John the Evangelist's remark (John 11:2) that Lazarus's sister Mary was the one who anointed Jesus' feet (John 12:3), he lays down a clear rule and demonstrates its application. In question here is whether this Mary is to be identified with the unnamed woman who wiped Jesus' head with perfume in Matthew's Gospel (26:7) and, further, with the unnamed sinful woman who washed Jesus' feet with her tears, dried them with her hair, and then anointed them with oil in Luke's Gospel (7:37–38). William presents the views of four authorities, no two of which agree. First, he quotes Chrysostom as asserting that each of the three narratives concerns a different event and a different woman. Next, he cites Jerome to the effect that the events described by John and Luke are the same, yet different from the one described by Matthew. Then he mentions the further complication that the woman mentioned by Luke is commonly said to be (*dicitur*) Mary Magdalene. Despite the difficulty this presents for identifying her with the Mary John says is from Bethany, William finds three glosses from the *Glossa ordinaria* asserting that all three Gospel accounts concern the same woman, though not necessarily the same event. Finally, he quotes Augustine as tentatively identifying the Mary of John's narrative with the sinful woman of Luke's and suggesting that there were two anointings. Augustine says nothing here of Matthew's account. William sorts through all of this by appealing to still another authority—the church:

> [11:2]*IT WAS MARY WHO ANOINTED THE LORD WITH OINTMENT AND WIPED HIS FEET WITH HER HAIR*, below chapter 12 (3) and Matthew 26 (7), *WHOSE BROTHER LAZARUS WAS SICK*. It is asked whether this would be she who figures in Matthew 26 (7) and Luke 7 (37). Chrysostom, "First it is necessary to say that this was neither the prostitute of Matthew 26 nor the one of Luke 7. They were full of wickedness, but this one is honorable and devoted." Therefore, according to him, there were three women. Commenting on Matthew, Jerome says, "Let no one think them to be the same who poured oil on his head and on his feet. The former washed with her tears and wiped with her tresses and is manifestly called a prostitute. Of the latter nothing of the sort has been written." And so, according to Jerome, there were two women. Also, the one who appears in Luke 7 is called Magdalene, from the village of Magdalo. This one is from Bethany. To the contrary, the *Glossa*: "This sinner anointed . . ." etc., and nearly the same is said in the *Glossa* on Matthew 26 and the *Glossa* on Luke 7, "Mary the sister" etc. Augustine seems to hesitate, saying "Behold, the sister of Lazarus (if, indeed, it was she who anointed the Lord's feet with ointment, and wiped with her hair what she had washed with her tears)." Response: It is to be said that the saints are very capable of disagreeing on matters pertaining to fact, but not in those pertaining to faith. Nevertheless, the Church holds that they were the same, and that what Jerome and Chrysostom say to the effect that they are not the same is to be understood with respect to the identity of status, because she was changed from one status to another.[40]

In a stroke, William settles a question left open by no less an authority than Augustine, and corrects Chrysostom and Jerome. Hardly reckless, he has limited their authority according to a principle—the inerrancy of the saints (*sancti*) encompasses matters of faith, not questions of fact. Over and against them, he invokes the authority of the church (*Ecclesia tamen tenet . . .*), and this in a manner considerably more forceful than in his earlier reference to "common opinion" (*secundum opinionem tenentium morem ecclesie, que uidetur tenere . . .*).[41] He has opted for the view expressed by the *Glossa*, the main source of which, in the event, is Bede.[42] To be sure, Bonaventure, Albert the Great, and Thomas Aquinas arrive at the same conclusion, though with greater discretion.[43] For once less discursive than William, Bonaventure leaves unmentioned the interpretations of Jerome and Augustine and contradicts only Chrysostom; in discussing the possibility of disagreements, he refers to the authors in question as *expositores*.[44] As well as the figures William names, Albert and Thomas include Origen, Ambrose, and Gregory; yet passing over their other differences, both classify these authors according to a single criterion—whether they identify Mary of Bethany with the sinner of Luke's Gospel. Bonaventure, Albert, and Thomas all leave unmentioned the question of identifying Mary of Bethany with the woman of Matthew's version, and only Albert brings up the question of her identification with Mary Magdalene. As does William, Albert invokes the church's authority to settle the question.[45] Thomas leaves the impression of preferring Augustine's interpretation, though he refrains from resolving the matter explicitly and provides no general rule for interpreting the *sancti*.[46] In none of these cases do our masters try to homogenize the thought of their predecessors. Still, William is noticeably more explicit than the others in calling attention to differences between authoritative interpretations. This leaves the impression that he finds such differences interesting.

In the closing comment of the preceding excerpt, his interest in differences shows itself even in an attempt at synthesis. In his own display of an *expositio reverentialis*, William brings two of the *sancti* around to his own conclusion without in any way trying to bend the thought of either one—immediately preceding his conclusion is an unambiguous acknowledgment that neither Jerome nor Chrysostom agrees with it. His reconciliation rests on the retrieval of an element of each one's interpretation that can be squared with his own—he allows that they are correct in holding that the two biblical narratives concerned two different women, insofar as they concerned one woman in two different states (as a sinner and as a penitent). By drawing a distinction and not by forcing the texts, he attempts to save something of the two interpretations and avoid having to set either one aside entirely. Whatever one may make of his solution, it cannot be called a retouching or redressing of sources. Betraying little interest in cosmetics, it is a transparent exercise in dialectic.

## *The* Glossa ordinaria

For gaining access to the interpretations of the *sancti*, university exegetes made use of a standard reference they normally called the *Glossa* (occasionally the *interlinearia* or *marginalia*). This has since come to be known as the as the *Glossa ordinaria*.[47] In fact, it is a collection of texts that resulted from an extensive shift in the prerogatives of biblical commentators during the early twelfth century.

While there is no place here for a detailed account of this work's complex provenance, a few of its key features are worth keeping in mind.[48] As the monasteries were gradually displaced by numerous cathedral schools as Europe's principal centers of biblical exegesis, a premium was placed on the organization of the vast and disordered corpus of exegetical writings left by earlier generations of authors, particularly the Fathers and the authors of the Carolingian period. The schools developed distinct methods and tools for exegesis largely because they had a distinct set of objectives in interpreting the Bible. Whereas the monks viewed the Bible before all else as a source of spiritual nourishment, the school masters approached it primarily as an object of study and as a subject matter of teaching.[49] It became for them the basis from which to pursue the church's pastoral concerns, specifically by expounding the church's doctrines and moral teachings in preaching to the laity. Common to all medieval exegesis, monastic or scholastic, was development within the larger context of an authoritative interpretative tradition. Particular to scholastic exegesis was its fundamental orientation toward the systematization of the Latin West's vast collection of texts. More acutely than the monks, the school masters faced the basic pedagogical requirement of lending coherence to an enormously disparate body of literature. Such is the background of the emergence of this collection of compilations.

Probably with a view to training clergy competent for the task of preaching to the laity, Anselm of Laon (d. 1117) led a group of scholars at that town's cathedral school in a massive project of compilation into one work both the biblical text and the glosses of virtually each line of each book, composed principally of selections from the Fathers and Carolingian authors. They didn't manage to complete the task, but subsequent compilers eventually did, and before the middle of the twelfth century, a standard version of the work emerged in Paris.

As each biblical book had its own exegetical tradition, the sources employed by the *Glossa's* compilers varied from one book to the next—Gregory the Great's *Moralia in Iob* predominates among the sources of the *Glossa* on that book, as does Paschasius Radbertus's *Expositio in Lamentationes* in the *Glossa* on that one, Augustine's *Tractatus in Iohannem* in the *Glossa* on that one, and so on.[50] And yet, the influence exercised on the *Glossa* by authoritative texts was remarkably complex. It was not uncommon for patristic commentaries to shape it by way of an assortment of intermediate compositions, the authors of which normally remained unnamed. Shortly, we shall have occasion to observe that Augustine's *Tractatus* on John's Gospel is one such case.[51] Here it will be noted that such anonymous interventions generally didn't stand in the way of the *Glossa's* acquisition of authoritative status in its own right.[52] With rare exceptions (about which more shortly), its comments on virtually any verse were presumed to be worthy of juxtaposition with those of the most revered commentators.

Though William turns to Chrysostom as one of his principal sources for his comments on Jesus' encounter with the Samaritan woman at the well (John 3:5–42), he doesn't hesitate to place one of his remarks on equal terms with an alternative from the *Glossa*:

> [4:9] *THE SAMARITAN WOMAN SAID TO HIM*, taunting, according to Chrysostom, because Jews were odious to Samaritans, *HOW IS IT THAT YOU, A JEW*, according to Chrysostom, she recognized him by the tassels on his garments, about which Numbers 15 (38), *ASK A DRINK OF ME, A SAMARITAN WOMAN? FOR JEWS DO NOT ASSOCIATE WITH SAMARITANS.* According to Chrysostom, the latter remark was spoken by the woman. According to the *Glossa*, it was spoken by the Evangelist.[53]

The biblical text does not make clear who it is that says that Jews have no dealings with Samaritans, and Chrysostom is not alone in taking these words as coming from the Samaritan woman; Alcuin does so as well.[54] Still, William presents the reading of the *Glossa* (generally favored in modern translations) and refrains from expressing a preference.

By the same measure, the *Glossa*'s ubiquitous authority could easily lend itself to the posing of questions. If the interpretations of biblical passages concerning wisdom had to be squared with Seneca's remarks on that subject, any exegete's reading of virtually any verse had to be measured against the *Glossa*. Put simply, it was a standard against which apparent contradictions had to be resolved. William addresses such a difficulty in connection with Jesus' remark that anyone entering the sheepfold otherwise than by the gate is a thief (John 10:1). This would seem to be at odds with a distinction made by the *Glossa* between a thief and a mercenary—whereas both seek their own good (rather than Christ's), the thief plunders the flock (by perverse preaching), while the mercenary doesn't, contenting himself with the pursuit of comfort. So it is that the *Glossa* proposes that the thief is to be feared, and the mercenary tolerated. An objector, however, has pointed to the impossibility of a mercenary entering the sheepfold through the gate, who in the parable is none other than Christ:

> [10:1] *AMEN, AMEN, I SAY TO YOU: WHOEVER DOES NOT ENTER THE SHEEPFOLD THROUGH THE GATE*, i.e., through me . . . *BUT CLIMBS IN BY ANOTHER WAY . . . IS A THIEF AND A ROBBER.* . . . To the contrary: A mercenary does not enter through Christ, and is nonetheless not a thief because he is to be tolerated, whereas the former is not, according to the *Glossa* on the passage below (10:2). Response: The term "thief" is taken broadly here for anyone who seeks his own interest, but nonetheless does

not teach perversely. In the passage below, where it is said that a thief is not to be tolerated, a thief is said to be someone who seeks his own interest and perverts teaching.[55]

Resting on a semantic distinction allowing the term *thief* to encompass *mercenary* (*Fur sumitur large*), William's reply is a typical exercise in dialectic. But two other features of this *questio* are worth noting. First, at least on the face of it, the words of the *Glossa* are employed as a criterion for evaluating those of Jesus, not the other way around. This is understandable if one keeps in mind that in university exegesis the *questio* is a literary form sometimes placed in the service of word studies, and this for the sake of a rhetorical purpose.[56] The foregoing discussion shows an authentic reflection on the various degrees of clerical decadence known at the time, but we need not take it to represent an actual classroom debate. Second, though the gloss in question has originated in no less an authority than Augustine, his name appears nowhere in it. Here the *Glossa* has an authority all its own.

Then again, sometimes the *Glossa* had no authority at all. In his comments on Isaiah 6:1, William sets aside a gloss, and thus an objection arising from it, merely by identifying it as nonauthoritative:[57] "What the *Glossa* says below on chapter 38 is to be called magisterial."[58] More will be said about this gloss in the following chapter.

## *Magistri*

As the preceding case suggests, many sources were not authoritative in the sense on display earlier, either for William or for his contemporaries. We have seen that he was capable of rectifying an interpretation of Peter Comestor, albeit with an explanation. There was nothing unusual about this. As a *magister*, Peter was accorded the respect of being cited by name, most often favorably. Such was equally the case with figures such as Peter Lombard or the Victorine masters Hugh, Andrew, and as in the following case, Richard:

> [*Super Ecl.* 1:16] I HAVE SURPASSED IN WISDOM ALL WHO WERE BEFORE ME IN JERUSALEM. . . . And this is understood to be the "wisdom" that is the bare cognition of things, which is of little profit. Hence Richard on Daniel: "What is bare human knowledge lacking the affection of sanctity, other than a vain statue lacking mobility and sense?"[59]

William cites Richard to lend support to the point he makes. But this doesn't mean that the Victorine weighs in on the subject of wisdom with the authority of

Seneca. Sayings by authors of his kind were generally not considered determinative, and William normally doesn't attempt to reconcile them to authoritative texts by way of the *questio*.[60]

## Moderni

Less authoritative in university exegesis, yet for that not less influential, were the comments of more recent university masters. In William's work, two predominate: Hugh of St. Cher and Bonaventure. Though he names them neither individually nor collectively, we have placed them in a single category, under the heading of *moderni*.[61] This is not to obscure the distinctiveness of their commentaries—they could be said to belong to two different genres—but to show that William makes use of the works of both in much the same way.

At the time William became regent master, both were men of considerable stature. Hugh was a titular cardinal and former prior provincial of the Dominican Province of France;[62] Bonaventure was the minister general of the Franciscans;[63] both exercised influence at the highest levels of the church. None of this accorded either of them *auctoritas* in the aforementioned sense. Yet for their anonymity and lack of authoritative status, their comments were all the more easily susceptible to alteration. Bonaventure adapted Hugh of St. Cher's work freely and without explaining his reasons for doing so.[64] We shall see that William did the same to the commentaries of both.[65] Much could be said about the exegesis of both Hugh and Bonaventure. Here it will only be noted that their heavy use of the *Glossa ordinaria* was effectively an extension of the twelfth-century project of systematization from which that compilation derived. Albeit with important differences, the commentaries of Hugh and of Bonaventure were similarly oriented toward organization.

## Hugh of St. Cher

Nowhere in the literature of thirteenth-century exegesis is the movement toward organization more conspicuous than in the *Postille in totam bibliam*, compiled at the Dominican convent of Saint-Jacques at Paris during the 1230s by a team of scholars working under the direction of Hugh of St. Cher.[66] Throughout, citations from the *Glossa* and the Fathers are juxtaposed to the anonymous comments of more recent writers. That his project largely succeeded in unifying a vast array of disparate texts is attested by the frequent use made of it by later commentators. But this doesn't mean that his *Postille* resulted from a rigorous attempt at synthesis. Rarely found in them is anything like the coherence of subsequent university commentaries or even of Raymond of Penyafort's contemporary compilation of law, *Liber extra*, intended as a supplement to Gratian's *Decretum*. As Robert Lerner puts it, "The *Liber extra* is a feat of systematic organization while Hugh of St. Cher's *liber* is a great bulging duffel bag."[67] In fact, Hugh worked largely within the earlier genre of scholastic commentary, notwithstanding his becoming a master at the University of Paris a generation after its emergence. All the same, the work that bears his name points to the genre that subsequently emerged in that environment.

## Bonaventure

Of all the commentaries figuring among William's varied sources, none resembles his own work as closely as those of Bonaventure.[68] It will be recalled that two of them (on Ecclesiastes and John) served to provide context for the establishment of a typology of William's commentaries, for no other reason than that they typify university exegesis. While we need not revisit what has been said about the similarities and differences between the two scholars, it will be worth our while to take a closer look at Bonaventure's influence on William. To begin, by contrast with Hugh of St. Cher, who left a postill on every biblical book on which William commented, Bonaventure's influence was confined to a limited number of lectures—the authenticated ones are on Ecclesiastes, Luke's Gospel, and John's. This leaves only two (the first and third) as possible sources for William's known works.[69] It is hardly suprising, then, that William borrowed repeatededly from Hugh and never from Bonaventure when commenting on Lamentations,[70] while he drew freely from both throughout his comments on Ecclesiastes and John.

As the following excerpts suggest, William integrates Bonaventure's comments into his own expositions well enough to avoid giving the reader reason to suspect that they have been borrowed. In his comments on Ecclesiastes's remark that he saw a poor wise man save a small city besieged by a mighty king (9:13–15), he draws from Bonaventure a distinction between three types of wisdom—the great, the greater, and the greatest, by which are vanquished three types of enemies—the strong, the stronger, and the strongest. As is typical of him, William lifts a comment almost verbatim (in bold) and inserts it seamlessly within a few of his own:

Therefore he says: $^{9:13}$*THIS WISDOM*, specifically, this which follows, *I HAVE ALSO SEEN UNDER THE SUN* by the experience of cognition, and *AND IT SEEMED TO ME THE GREATEST*, **because there is great wisdom in vanquishing an inferior enemy, greater in vanquishing an equal, and the greatest in vanquishing a stronger one, which is the case here.** Or, that by which the world is vanquished is great; that by which the carnal appetite (is vanquished) is greater, because the enemy is closer; that by which the Devil is vanquished is the greatest.[71]

Beginning with a clarification, he describes Ecclesiastes's vision as intellectual—it owes to the experience of cognition. (More will be said about William's interest in the prophets' diverse modes of perception.) Then, having presented the distinction, he synthesizes it with the classic theme of man's three enemies: the world, the flesh, and the Devil. Though it had emerged in monastic literature, by William's time this topos had become popular among preachers, and one may easily imagine how his application of it here could have been useful in a sermon.[72]

Our next case appears in William's comments on John's account of the calling of Simon (1:42), where he asks why Jesus conferred a new name on him. (See table 4.1.) Both Bonaventure and Hugh had considered the same question, and both replied that it was a sign of the primacy Peter was to receive. Despite their use of Augustine elsewhere in their own expositions of this narrative, it was from Chrysostom that they drew this explanation. William follows suit (his borrowings from them are in bold), yet not before he puts forward another answer that he has taken independently from Chrysostom—Jesus changed Simon's name as a sign that he was the maker of the Old Testament, wherein the names of ancients such as Abraham were changed. As has Bonaventure, William turns to Chrysostom for his comments concerning the common name of Christians, yet he does so independently, directly lifting the remark that all have been named sons of God.[73]

Into a fairly coherent exposition, William has woven the interpretations of an ancient exegete and two near contemporaries. Though this selection is composed entirely of the remarks of others (*tantum aliena*, as he put it), the method it illustrates consists not in compiling disparate excerpts for scholastic pedantry, but rather in critical synthesis, resulting in a reasoned exposition suited to his own pedagogical purposes. In a real sense, then, this may be called his own text. Worth noting here is that this abridgment of Bonaventure's exposition has considerably understated its relative lengthiness.

Still, a casual look at the sources of *Super Iohannem* could give the impression that William's access to Patristic and early medieval writings was normally by way of Bonaventure, Hugh of St. Cher, and the *Glossa ordinaria*. Closer examination shows that he frequently borrowed from these authors directly. A typical case is the following consideration of what Jesus could have meant by apparently disowning his own doctrine with the statement in John 7:16: *My teaching is not mine, but his who sent me.* (See table 4.2.) Chrysostom had posed the question and expounded it at some length. Bonaventure presented it as a *questio* and borrowed a portion of Chrysostom's reply (in bold). William, for his part, borrowed

Table 4.1  John 1:42: *And be brought him to Jesus. And Jesus looking upon him, said: You are Simon the son of Jona.*
*You will be called Cephas, which is interpreted Peter.*

| Hugh of St. Cher | Bonaventure | William of Alton |
|---|---|---|
| But it is asked, why did the Lord change this one's name, rather than Andrew's or any one else's? To this it is to be replied that the change of the name is a sign of a future change concerning Peter. Indeed, he was the future prince of the apostles, which cannot be said of the others. Hence, the name of a pope is still changed upon his ordination, which does not happen to other bishops. | Also, it is asked, why did the Lord put a name upon Peter in his calling rather than upon the others? It would appear that he is a respector of persons (cf. 1 Peter 1:17), because he conferred the dignity of the name without merit. . . . To this it is to be replied that God sees not only what is exterior, but even what is interior, not only those things which are, but those which lie in the future. It was therefore as a sign that he was the future pastor of the Church that the name was put upon him. . . . But why do those entering religious life not have their names changed, or even those who convert to Christianity? To this Chrysostom replies that the change of a name happened as a stimulus to virtue. Because we now have one name, greater than any other, which is especially an inducement to virtue. We should therefore be content with that name, and this name is Christianity, because we are all called Christians. Nevertheless, the Roman Church still preserves the change of name for the Supreme Pontiff. | **It is asked, why did he change his name?** Response, Chrysostom: To signify that it was he who gave the Old Testament, in which the names of some of the ancients were changed, such as Abraham. This he did because of the excellence of grace they were to receive. **He changed Peter's name rather than Andrew's because he was to have a greater excellence. Hence the name of the pope is still changed.** According to Chrysostom, the names of saints are not changed now as they were in the Old Testament because we all have one excellent name by which we are called sons of God. (cf. 1 John 3:1).[i] |

[i] Cf. CHRYSOSTOM, In Io. hom., XIX (PG 59, 122).

the framework of his discussion almost verbatim from Bonaventure (underlined), yet took different remarks from the same exposition of Chrysostom (in bold) and added a few of his own.[74]

Such creative borrowing from Hugh and Bonaventure is common throughout *Super Iohannem*. William often lifted their citations of authorities, all the while maintaining his independence by making substitutions. The same may be said of the most common of all procedures for contextualizing a given lemma, the

Table 4.2  John 7:16: *My teaching is not mine, but his who sent me.*

| Bonaventure (*Opera*, t. VI, 344a–b) | William of Alton (MS Saint-Omer, Bibl. mun. 260, f. 131vb) |
|---|---|
| MY TEACHING IS NOT MINE. As he removed it from himself, it would therefore appear to be false. Chrysostom responds **that his teaching is not his own invention, but is from the Father. Hence the sense is:** MY TEACHING, **specifically, which I teach,** IS NOT MINE, **but is from the Father.** And in this he satisfies their question, sending them to the Father, and calms their fury by humility. Hence it was his teaching because he is in essence Wisdom itself, but he did not say it was his because he received it from another.... But it was not discretely of Christ alone because it was also of the Father and from the Father. | MY TEACHING IS NOT MINE. Here the same is removed from himself. Therefore the statement is false. Response: Formally and effectively it was his, but by primary authority it was not his, but the Father's. And in this he satisfies their question, sending them to the Father, and calms their fury by humility. Christ said, however, that he was the Father's Wisdom itself and that he had this from another, **showing himself to be from another. Also, this was to show himself not to be contrary to God. Also, this was to show himself to be a true man. Also, this was because of the imbecility of his listeners. Also, this was for teaching humility. Nevertheless, below in chapter 8 (58), he spoke highly of himself to show the height of his nature.**[i] Or, IS NOT MINE, i.e., for vain glory. Or, MINE, specifically, discretely, i.e., mine alone, BUT HIS WHO SENT ME, i.e., the Father's, or from the Father, above chapter 5 (30): *I cannot do anything of myself.* |

[i] Cf. CHRYSOSTOM, In Io. hom., XLIX (PG 59, 275).

presentation of biblical citations. Many of his are independent, but others are the same as Hugh's, Bonaventure's, or those of both. Then again, many of them differ, all the while displaying similarities that suggest borrowing. An example appears in the comments of Hugh and William on John 1:10: *He was in the world. . . .* Hugh expounds it with the support of Wisdom 8:1: *She reaches from end to end mightily and arranges all things sweetly.*[75] Rather than restate the citation, William makes use of a similar verse appearing a few lines earlier in the same book, Wisdom 7:24: *She reaches everywhere by reason of her purity.*[76] Again, when commenting on John 1:13: *. . . but are born of God*, Hugh turns to 1 John 5:4: *Whoever is born of God overcomes the world.*[77] For the same purpose, William cites 1 John 5:1: *Whoever is born of God believes that Jesus is the Son of God.*[78] It is no less common to find Bonaventure's biblical references subjected to the same sort of creative borrowing. Among the books he cites in his exposition of John 10:3 are Proverbs, Isaiah, Ezekiel, 2 Timothy, and the Letter to the Hebrews. (See table 4.3.) In his exposition of the same verse, William makes use of the same books, albeit differently. While content to lift Bonaventure's citations of Proverbs and Isaiah, for the other three books William cites different verses.[79]

In the preceding examples, William's contributions largely concern the construal of the text's letter. Often, they are more properly theological. A simple example appears in his consideration of Jesus' remark in John 6:37: *ALL THAT THE FATHER GIVES TO ME WILL COME TO ME.* In explaining how all that the Father gives to Jesus will come to him, William begins with Bonaventure's comment that this is by eternal election and temporal calling; then he borrows Hugh's remark that this is by an infusion of grace, attributed to the Father in view of his authority, yet indeed from the Trinity. Whereas Bonaventure (underlined) and Hugh (in bold) are concerned to explain the divine initiative in the process, William adds a few comments concerning the human role—those given by the Father are believers who come freely, cooperating with grace:

> [6:37]*ALL THAT THE FATHER GIVES TO ME,* <u>by eternal election and temporal calling</u>, by **pouring forth grace, which is said to be from the Father, because authority resides with him, although the entire Trinity pours forth grace**, Psalm (2:8): *I will give you the nations for your inheritance; WILL COME TO ME* by faith and love. It belongs to the Father to give the first grace by pouring it forth; it belongs to believers to come by cooperating with grace. A good work originates with God as the principal mover, from free will as being elicited, and from grace as disposing free will.[80]

Without referring to the postills of Hugh and Bonaventure, one would have no reason to suspect that this exposition is an amalgamation of the remarks of three

**Table 4.3** John 10:3: *To him the gatekeeper opens, and his sheep hear his voice, and he calls his own sheep by name and leads them out.*

| Bonaventure (*Opera*, t. VI, 383b–384a) | William of Alton (v. II, 203–04) |
|---|---|
| *TO HIM THE GATEKEEPER OPENS* . . . The gatekeeper is Christ, who has the key, hence Isaiah 22 (22): *I will lay the key of the house of David upon his shoulder; and he will open, and no one will shut; and he will shut, and no one will open.* And his sheep hear his voice because they willingly obey a good pastor, Hebrews 13 (17): *Obey your elders and be subject to them, for they watch as having to render an account for your souls. . . . AND HE CALLS HIS OWN BY NAME*, i.e., Christ, 2 Timothy 2 (19): *The Lord knows who are his* and who imitate him; Proverbs 12 (10): *The just knows the souls of his beasts; AND LEADS THEM OUT* to pasture, that is Christ; Ezekiel 34 (13): *I will lead them out from the peoples and I will gather them from the lands and I will lead them into their own land,* which indeed was flowing with milk and honey. So the imitator of Christ is like Moses and Aaron, Psalm (76:21) *You led your people like sheep by the hand of Moses and Aaron.* | [3]*TO HIM THE GATEKEEPER*, that is Christ, who has the key, Isaiah 22 (22), *OPENS*, introducing to the charge of governance, Hebrews 5 (4): *No one takes this honor upon himself*. Or *OPENS* for himself the understanding of the Scriptures. Or the hearts of listeners, so that they would submit to him. *AND HIS SHEEP HEAR HIS VOICE* willingly obeying his precepts, admonitions and counsels—an argument that he ought not to be silent. Exodus 28 (34–35) says that there were bells in the robe of the priest, lest he enter the tabernacle without a sound and die, Ezekiel 3 (18): *If you do not announce it to him and speak to warn him from his wicked way, in order to save his life, that wicked man shall die in his iniquity; but his blood I will require at your hand;* 2 Timothy 4 (2): *Preach the word. AND HE CALLS HIS OWN SHEEP BY NAME.* This calling is nothing other than the knowledge by which he distinguishes his own from the others by the administration of the sacraments, preaching, visitation and counsel, Proverbs 27 (23): *Know diligently the state of your herds. AND LEADS THEM OUT of darkness and the shadow of death* (Psalm 106:14), of the darkness of ignorance and guilt, Exodus 3 (10): *I will send you to lead my people from Egypt.* |

different commentators. Here William is less interested in dialectic than in the employment of their texts to produce his own exposition.

It would be easy to multiply similar examples, yet the preceding selections are enough to show that William considered Hugh and Bonaventure peers to be respected, not authorities to be revered. The liberties he took with the interpretations of both leave the impression that he had no doubts about his capacity for improving on their commentaries by incorporating them into his own synthesis. In view of the brevity of his commentary by comparison with either one of theirs, this may seem strange, yet William's abridgment of earlier works was consistent with his larger purpose of bringing order to the unwieldy body of commentatorial literature he had before him. Given the constraints of a classroom setting and the modest background of his students, it is not difficult to imagine why he would have considered brevity an advantage—it probably made for effective pedagogy.

But his tendency was not always synthetic. When dealing with the authorities he cites by name, his primary interest is their *intentio*. We have already seen that when he disagrees with masters such as Peter Comestor, he corrects them without hesitation, rather than attempting to bend their meaning. This is hardly remarkable. Such *dicta magistrorum* generally had no binding authority and could easily be set aside.[81] We shall see that even when dealing with weightier figures, William regularly presents alternative interpretations as such, leaving it to his students to choose between them.

## quidam

If the views of neither the *magistri* nor the *moderni* were determinative in resolving questions, they were normally cited favorably. In this, both may be contrasted with those designated by one of William's few collective references— "some" (*quidam*)—to designate those whose interpretations he generally opposed. M.-D. Chenu has observed that Thomas Aquinas used the term to recall the controversies of contemporary masters without having to name them.[82] William more often employed it to designate stock misinterpretations he presented only for the sake of setting them aside. So, for example, when commenting on the narrative of the royal official of John 4:6 who asks Jesus to heal his son, William tells us that "some" hold him to be the same as the centurion of Matthew's Gospel (8:5). Citing Chrysostom to the contrary, he makes two points: first, while John's royal official asks Jesus to come to his house, Matthew's centurion asks him not to for the reason of his own unworthiness; second, whereas John's supplicant intercedes for a son, Matthew's does so for a servant:

*4:46AND THERE WAS A CERTAIN RULER....* According to Chrysostom, this was not the centurion who figures in Matthew 8 (5), as some (*quidam*) wish to say, because that one did not want Christ to go into his house, this one did. Also, here it was a son, there it was a servant.[83]

Though the citation of Chrysostom is indirect, it includes the reference to *quidam*.[84] As it turns out, Augustine also holds that the two figures are different and discusses the differences between them.[85] None of William's known sources proposes that they are the same. In all likelihood, *quidam* here serves as a foil and not as a pseudonym for discreetly designating anonymous commentators known to William who actually proposed that the royal official and the centurion were one and the same.

Another example appears in William's comments on the narrative of the healing of the cripple at the pool of Bethsaida. He mentions that *quidam* say that the pool's healing power came from a certain piece of wood from which the Cross was later made:[86]

*5:4AN ANGEL OF THE LORD DESCENDED AT CERTAIN TIMES INTO THE POOL . . . AND MOVED THE WATERS . . . AND WHOEVER FIRST DESCENDED INTO THE POOL AFTER THE MOVEMENT OF THE WATERS WAS HEALED OF WHATEVER INFIRMITY AFFLICTED HIM.* Note, some (*quidam*) say that this virtue of healing in this way was by some piece of wood from which the cross was later made, which was in that water.[87]

Though hardly justified by the letter of the text, this is the kind of remark that could offer a preacher several possibilities for developing a sermon. William does not endorse it, but neither does he discard it. Before him Bonaventure,[88] Hugh of St. Cher,[89] and Peter Comestor[90] also mentioned it and attributed it to *quidam* before unambiguously rejecting it. None of William's known sources can be identified with the *quidam* cited here, and it would appear that these writers mention the story for rhetorical effect, not because it stood in need of refutation.[91] Capable of stimulating the imagination and eliciting an emotional response, it is the sort of tale an exegete or preacher could exploit, all the while refraining from attesting to its accuracy. One may surmise as much from the term by which William (though not the others) introduces it—*nota*. In medieval commentary, this was a simple form for introducing just this sort of digression from the text's letter. As employed by university exegetes, it was frequently a means of presenting remarks subsequently to be set aside.[92]

On the other hand, William does at times employ *quidam* to designate identifiable commentators, albeit discreetly. A case in point appears in his treatment of the question of whether the miracle of Jesus' walking on the water as recounted by John is the same as the one described by Matthew. He points out that while some say that it is the same, others say that it is not:

> [6:18-19]*AND THE SEA AROSE BECAUSE A STRONG WIND WAS BLOWING. . . . WHEN THEY HAD ROWED ABOUT TWENTY-FIVE OR THIRTY STADIA . . . THEY SAW JESUS WALKING ON THE SEA. . . .* Some (*quidam*) say that this was the same miracle as the one of Matthew 14 (26), but that John does not include everything. Others (*alii*) say that it was another, because there the storm did not cease until after Christ's word, here it did so immediately; further, there it is recounted that Peter almost sank, here it is not.[93]

Among those whom William could have had in mind when referring to the *quidam* who identify the two events are Bonaventure, Hugh of St. Cher, Peter Comestor, and Augustine.[94] Then again, only one of his known sources belongs to the category of *alii* who say they are different, namely, Chrysostom.[95]

## Thomas Aquinas

The list of William's thirteenth-century sources is notable for a name missing from it—Thomas Aquinas. As the Angelic Doctor commented on neither Ecclesiastes, Wisdom, nor Ezekiel, William's independence in his commentaries on these books calls for no explanation. But one could wonder why he composed postills on Isaiah, Jeremiah, Lamentations, and John without bothering to consult any one of his predecessor's postills on these same books. With respect to Isaiah and Jeremiah, it may be noted that for these books Thomas left only cursory lectures from his period as a biblical bachelor, with the consequence that scholars would not necessarily have considered them valuable sources. While the postill on Lamentations often printed under Thomas's name could well be the work of a master, it is questionable that the master was he.[96] As for John's Gospel, Thomas's commentary is probably later than William's. And in any event, none of his biblical commentaries was published until after his death in 1274, by which time William had probably also died.[97]

More notable, however, is the lack of evidence that William was influenced by any of Thomas's other works. Masters at the University of Paris were supposedly succeeded by their own bachelors,[98] yet we have no clear indication that William was ever a student of Thomas. To the contrary, several of his expositions suggest that he was not. One of them appears in a discussion concerning the church's set of doctrines on the afterlife, specifically, purgatory and the general and particular judgments. These matters had attracted relatively little attention from the Fathers and early medieval thinkers, at least by comparison with questions concerning Christology, the Trinity, the sacraments, and grace. Yet they were of considerable interest in William's time, in part because the Albigensians and Waldensians denied the existence of purgatory, and in part because the Greek Church hesitated to accept the Latin Church's more precise language concerning the particular judgment. Also of consequence was the entrance into the Latin West of the thought of Averroës and, more particularly, of monopsychism, the doctrine of the unicity of the intellectual soul for all people, which came to be known, wrongly, as "Averroist."[99] A result of all of this was a growing willingness on the part of the Latin Church to affirm its doctrines explicitly. In 1270, the bishop of Paris, Stephen Tempier, issued a condemnation of thirteen propositions associated with Averroës, three of which concerned the afterlife.[100] What is more, the existence of purgatory, the efficacy of suffrages for the souls there, and the particular and general judgments were all set forward as doctrines at the Council of Lyons.[101]

In his comments on Ecclesiastes, William confronts these matters without drawing much support from that book's commentatorial tradition. Solomon's apparently pessimistic remark that the dead will never have part in anything done under the sun (Ecl 9:6) has called for some explanation with respect to heaven, purgatory, and hell. William begins with a succinct clarification, the implication of which is that the verse, in fact, affirms the doctrines of the particular judgment (i.e., the judgment of each individual soul at death, with admittance to either heaven, purgatory, or hell), purgatory, and of the efficacy of works (i.e., suffrages) for the souls there.[102] Then he entertains the question of whether the damned, too, may benefit from them:

> [9:6]*NOR HAVE THEY ANY PART IN THIS WORLD . . . AND IN THE WORK THAT IS DONE UNDER THE SUN*, similarly, they have no part in it. This is certain of those who are in glory. Those, however, who are in purgatory have no part in worldly things, yet they have part in the works which are done here. The damned similarly have no use of temporal things. But there is a question of whether suffrages benefit them. It is commonly held that they offer no benefit. Nevertheless, others have said that they benefit for some alleviation, not for full liberation. According to them, the letter may be given the following exposition: *THEY HAVE NO PART IN THIS WORLD*, i.e., with respect to full liberation. Nevertheless, it is commonly held that suffrages would be of no benefit to them.[103]

William apparently leaves open the possibility of interpreting Solomon as saying only that the damned cannot be freed completely. Against an unnamed group (*qui*) who propose that the damned benefit from suffrages, he mentions the "common opinion" to the contrary, among whose adherents were such *sancti* as Augustine[104] and Gregory the Great[105] and more recent figures such as Peter Lombard,[106] Hugh of St. Cher,[107] Bonaventure,[108] and Thomas Aquinas. The last, it will be noted, took up the question in a text anterior to William's regency, his commentary on Book IV of Lombard's *Sentences*.[109] And yet, whereas all of the others were unequivocal on the point, William was ambiguous. It will be recalled that for him the common opinion had an authority of sorts, yet nothing like that of the *sancti* or the church, either of which he could have invoked but did not. In effect, he stopped short of completely ruling out the possibility that the damned can be helped by suffrages.

One is also struck by his manner of referring to a widely read pseudo-Augustinian work, *De spiritu et anima*. Though doubt had been cast on its authenticity as early as 1240, this short text was still ascribed to Augustine during the following decades, notably by Bonaventure, who cited it often and in connection with important matters.[110] Thomas Aquinas, for his part, changed his mind on the matter. After citing it as Augustine's several times in his commentary on the *Sentences* and up to the thirteenth disputed question *De veritate*,[111] he unequivocally rejected its authenticity—and so its authority—in the fifteenth.[112] While continuing to refer to the *De spiritu et anima* in the *De veritate*,[113] the contemporary *Super Boetium De Trinitate*,[114] and numerous subsequent works,[115] he never again credited it to Augustine. Worth noting here is that both *De veritate* and *Super Boetium De Trinitate* belong to his first Paris regency, the period immediately preceding William's inception there as regent master.[116] None of this prevented William from citing the work as Augustine's, independently of Bonaventure, in his comments on Ecclesiastes 12:1:

> Hence, [121]*REMEMBER YOUR CREATOR* so that you fear him, withdrawing from evil . . . Augustine, *On the Spirit and the Soul*: "I am a wretched man, we ought to love my God who made me when I was not, and redeemed me when I was perishing. I was not, and from nothing he made me, not a stone, not a bird, not a tree, nor did he want me to be any of the animals, but a man to his own image."[117]

To these examples may be added a few of William's remarks in *Super Iohannem* concerning Trinitarian relations. Taking the Gospel's opening verse as an occasion for making a few doctrinal points, he finds in the phrase *And the Word was with God* the refutation of a heresy. After remarking that the preposition *with* (*apud*) is transitive, he points out that it signifies a distinction between the Father and the Son, thereby confuting Sabellius, whose error, he reminds us, was to deny that any such distinction exists. To make the point still more forcefully, he adds that with (*apud*) denotes "subauthority" (*subauctoritatem*) in the Son with respect to the Father. While his meaning is not entirely clear, it would appear that he employs the term to propose that the Son's authority is distinct from and in some sense subordinate to the Father's:

> So therefore the Word was from eternity in the Father, nevertheless, the Father and the Son are not the same person. Hence the following: [11]*AND THE WORD WAS WITH GOD.* Since prepositions are transitive, this preposition "with" along with its object implies a distinction, which is against Sabellius, who says that the Father and the Son are one person because they are one principle. Also, by reason of its special signification this preposition denotes subauthority (*subauctoritatem*) in the Son with respect to the Father.[118]

It is hardly likely that William had any concerns about the orthodoxy of the interpretation—he lifted it directly from the exposition of the same verse by Bonaventure,[119] whose source could have been William of Auxerre, who held the same view.[120] In subsequent chapters, he returned to the concept of the Son's *sub-auctoritas* with respect to the Father, on one occasion independently of Bonaventure.[121] But had he been familiar with Thomas's commentary on Book I of Peter Lombard's *Sentences* (Lombard does not employ the term),[122] he would have known that his predecessor had unequivocally excluded the term *subauctoritas* from acceptable Trinitarian language. On one occasion, to an interlocutor who has pointed out that *subauctoritas* has been attributed to the Son (*Sed in filio dicitur esse subauctoritas. Ergo etc.*), Thomas points out that no differences either of grade or of dignity may be said to exist *in divinis* and adds discreetly that none of the *sanctis* applied the term to the Son.[123] Later in the same commentary, he makes the same point with respect to the Holy Spirit, this time remarking that the term's application to him by certain *quidam* implies causal activity between the members of the Trinity, a proposition he is ever concerned to deny.[124]

The *quidam* Thomas has in mind are likely to be William of Auxerre and, more particularly, Bonaventure,[125] and in his critique, there is certainly more at stake than quibbling over semantics. Under the influence of Pseudo-Dionysius, the Franciscan master had adopted the schema of hierarchy so as to encompass all of reality, divine as well as created. Hierarchy for him was a principle of order for the diffusion and communication of the good, not only from the Godhead to angels and worldly realities but also even within the Trinity itself. By applying the schema of hierarchy to the processions of the Son and the Holy Spirit, Bonaventure had, at least in Thomas's view, introduced the concepts of causality and subordination into his account of Trinitarian relations.[126] His usage of the term *subauctoritas* suggests as much. Setting aside such reasoning is the justification Thomas himself offers for setting aside the term.[127] Whether William was familiar with Thomas's commentary on the *Sentences*, either as an oral lecture or as a redacted text, must remain a matter of conjecture. Still, given the capital importance of Trinitarian theology in the thought of both Bonaventure and Thomas, William's apparent unawareness of this discussion is remarkable.

What is more, in the following chapter, we shall see that William did not espouse an important position concerning the virtue of faith put forward by Thomas in two of his early works, the commentary *In III Sententiarum* and the disputed question *De veritate*. Perhaps William deliberately rejected Thomas's view on this matter and the aforementioned ones, but this seems unlikely. We have seen and will see again that William did not hesitate to mention positions with which he disagreed, even authoritative ones. Yet in these cases, he betrayed no awareness of Thomas's views. The most likely explanation is that he was simply unfamiliar with them.

On the other hand, we shall also see that a few of William's theological options are nearer to Thomas's thought than to Bonaventure's. Here it will be noted that if William in fact had any exposure to Thomas's thought during the years before his inception as regent master, it was limited.[128]

## Conclusion

By contrast with patristic exegetes (Augustine or Chrysostom), as well as modern ones (Rudolf Bultmann or Raymond Brown), William was not an author, if this means writing principally what is one's own. In writing, or compiling, mainly what belonged to others, William could hardly have been more typically medieval. Even if literature of the sort he produced can and often does strike modern readers as archaic in style, as well as content, the writers who produced it, as Alisdair Minnis puts it, "saw themselves as being on the very cusp of intellectual change and development."[129] Requiring arduous labor and considerable editorial ability, *compilatio* of the sort William engaged in was an enterprise highly regarded in its own right. It presupposed a mastery of the biblical text, as well as its entire commentatorial tradition, and was intended to result in compositions surpassing the originals in both complexity and organization. We have seen that William compiled not only originals (such as those from Augustine or Chrysostom) but also earlier compilations (the *Glossa ordinaria* or Hugh's *Postille*). In compiling compilations, he retained his freedom, not only in his selections of certain texts and his setting aside of others but also in the choices he made in modifying them, rearranging them, and supplementing them with independent borrowings.

On the other hand, William's compilation did not exclude his proper contributions. If his own comments are seldom a predominant component of his expositions, neither are they often absent from them. Far from setting compilation in opposition to authorship, he made it his project to integrate the two endeavors. This he most often did inconspicuously, seamlessly. Without closely examining his sources, it is generally impossible to differentiate between the comments he borrowed and those he authored. One of William's Dominican contemporaries, Vincent of Beauvais (c. 1190–1264), aggrandized the practice of compilation by introducing his *Speculum maius* with an apologetic discourse entitled *Libellus apologeticus*.[130] Recent research has shown that such discourses were not exclusive to texts that described themselves as compilations.[131] William, however, has left us no such discourse. As a result, our only basis for making judgments about his own self-understanding is his actual exegesis. His engagement in the practice of *compilatio*, so clearly in evidence in the foregoing chapter, did not make of him a *compilator* as he defined the term. By complementing his compilations with what was his own, he met his own definition of a *commentator*. In the forthcoming chapter, we shall have occasion to take a closer look at what was William's own.

# 5

# *Theological Considerations*

AT THE CENTER of William's project as *magister in sacra pagina* was the instruction of ecclesiastics in the recounting of the biblical narrative and the proclamation of the gospel. In that respect, he was a theologian. And yet, his known works offer us nothing that could be properly described as a theological treatise, to say nothing of a theological synthesis. There can be no question, then, of providing a systematic account of his theology after the fashion of studies often given to figures such as Bonaventure, Albert the Great, and Thomas Aquinas. This chapter has the more modest goal of examining a few of the ways in which William's theological concerns show themselves in his exegesis. Before considering his thoughts on a concern that was particularly important in his own time, religious poverty, we shall explore his views of a few matters that fall under a heading whose theological interest could hardly be more general, divine revelation.

If the latter may be understood as God's activity of self-communication, then it may rightly be considered the subject matter of the entirety of William's exegetical writings. To be examined in the following discussions are a few passages wherein he offers explicit reflections on the salient aspects of revelation as it involves the prophets, Jesus Christ, preachers, and finally, individual believers.

## *Prophecy*

We have already seen a few aspects of William's understanding of prophecy in his literal exegesis, notably his use of the prophetic literal sense to broaden the context for the interpretation of specific passages. To be considered here is his conception of the prophet's status and of the object or content of prophetic vision. William was obliged to address several exegetical and theological problems presented by the claims of various prophets to have seen God. A case in point is Ezekiel's introductory assertion that he had seen visions of God:

> [1]*THE HEAVENS WERE OPENED*, according to Origen's interpretation, to the eyes of the flesh, *AND I SAW*, literally, by a corporeal vision, perhaps as Stephen or Paul. Or as the languishing see visions, as Peter saw a vision of animals in a sphere (cf. Acts 11:5). Or *THE HEAVENS WERE OPENED*, according to Jerome, not by a division of the firmament, but by the revelation of some hidden secrets. Or some splendor appeared to him, as if the firmament were opened, just as now sometimes happens in a flash of lightning. Origen therefore understood it to be a corporeal vision, Jerome an intellectual one. *AND I SAW VISIONS* in the plural, not one only, *OF GOD*, i.e., about God, or from God, showing everything.[1]

Briefly proposed here are three basic options for understanding Ezekiel's vision. According to the first, inspired by Origen,[2] the revelation was in corporeal form and was visible to Ezekiel's bodily eyes; on the second, it was imaginary and so bypassed his bodily sensation and appealed directly to his imagination; and on the third, borrowed from Jerome,[3] it was purely intellectual and so bypassed both his senses and his imagination to impress itself directly on his intellect. Also worth noting here is William's concern to show that Ezekiel's *visiones Dei* were of something other than the divine nature. Each of these points calls for consideration.

While reflections on prophecy show up throughout the corpus of his biblical commentary, the most prolonged one appears in his commentary on Isaiah, specifically, in his exposition of the account of the prophet's vision in the sixth chapter. His exegetical interests in this passage are several. Primary among them is to make sense of Isaiah's claim to have seen the Lord (*Vidi Dominum*) without prejudice to the understanding, generally held by Jews and Christians alike, that no flesh may see God, at least not this side of the grave.[4] More broadly, he tries to provide a general framework for prophecy capable of accounting for the various theophanies experienced by the patriarchs, prophets, and, notably, St. Paul (cf. 2 Cor 12:2–4). Then, he situates his account between two opposing erroneous propositions, first, that Isaiah (and by implication the other prophets) saw the divine nature, and second, that the angels and the blessed in heaven do not. Put another way, while asserting that the prophets normally had no beatific vision while living in this world, William is concerned to avoid implying that the same holds true for the blessed *in patria*:

> Therefore he says [6:1]*IN THE YEAR THAT KING UZZIAH DIED, I SAW THE LORD SITTING* etc. Note that according to the *Glossa* on 2 Corinthians 12

(4), concerning the rapture of Paul, there are three kinds of vision. One of them, evidently, is corporeal, by which God is seen in a created subject by corporeal eyes. So it was that Abraham, Isaac, Jacob, and Moses saw him, as Jerome explains in the original of his exposition of this passage.[5] Another is imaginary, by which God is seen by the eyes of the heart under an imaginary figure, just as Isaiah saw him in this passage, Daniel in chapter 7, and Ezekiel in chapter 1. The third is intellectual, by which God and spiritual creatures are seen in a wondrous revelation by the gaze of the pure mind. So it was that Paul saw him in 2 Corinthians 12 (4). In heaven (*in patria*) this vision will be perfect, on the way (*in via*) imperfect and only in a few. Therefore, the *Glossa*'s statement here that Isaiah saw God is to be explained as by the eyes of the heart, i.e., it happened by an imaginary vision, which was by the eyes of the heart, not those of the flesh. Concerning what the *Glossa* says below in chapter 38 (1), it should be said that this is magisterial. Or that reading in the Book of Foreknowledge is seeing God not in his substance, but in an illumination or in a locution from spirit to spirit. Concerning Chrysostom's statement: "Not even an angel can see God in his nature," one is to understand—as fully as the Son.[6]

In evidence here is a more explicit formulation of the same threefold typology wherein God manifests himself variously by way of corporeal creatures, imaginary representations, and direct intellectual contact. William evidently regards the second mode as the most common. Here, it is Isaiah, Daniel, and Ezekiel whom he credits with such perception of imaginary representations by the "eye of the heart." Elsewhere, he describes the visions of Jeremiah[7] and Abraham[8] in similar terms.

It was a classic schema, most likely originating in Augustine's *De Genesi ad litteram libri XII*.[9] While it appears repeatedly in the *Glossa*, William cites it here in connection with the glosses on 2 Corinthians 12 and the passage at hand.[10] It provides him a means of accounting for the privileged, that is to say, infallible, status of prophetic knowledge without equating it with the beatific vision.[11] On the last point, to be sure, he allows for rare exceptions, notably for the apostle Paul. But this is hardly remarkable—that Paul enjoyed the beatific vision was another notion whose widespread acceptance can be credited to Augustine.[12] In this case, William's more proximate source is likely Hugh of St. Cher, who similarly described such rapture as an imperfect and rare parallel to the experience of the blessed.[13]

Returning to the exposition of Isaiah 6:1, we find that a problem has arisen from a discrepancy between this schema and a gloss on Isaiah 38:1, which suggests that Isaiah (and by implication the other prophets) generally beheld the divine nature. In connection with an Isaian prophecy that did not come to pass (specifically, that Hezekiah would die), the *Glossa* has explained that in this case Isaiah had not read the event in the Book of Life, to which it also refers as the Book of God.[14] Since both metaphors designate the beatific vision, the comment implies that this mode of prophetic perception was normal. William's initial response is simply to disqualify it by pointing out that it was magisterial. Then, employing the equivalent expression Book of Foreknowledge, he suggests that the gloss does not really refer to the vision of the divine nature after all, but to an enlightenment or spiritual locution. While in the main following Hugh of St. Cher's exposition of the same passage, he subscribes to a reinterpretation of expressions whose common meaning had previously been well established.[15] The principle that God is without complexity had led earlier theologians to equate the "book" read by the prophets with the divine nature, with the consequence that exegetes no longer had any clear principle for differentiating their vision from that of the angels and the blessed. While the source of the gloss must, on the present evidence, remain a matter of conjecture,[16] we know the names of two influential early-thirteenth-century masters who held the same view, William of Auxerre (d. 1231) and Philip the Chancellor (d. 1236).[17] As a notable corollary, they took the gift of prophecy to be a stable disposition (*habitus*) of the soul.

William attempts to escape this framework by providing an account for prophecy as a passing experience distinct from the beatitude enjoyed by the angels and saints. He is only partially successful. Toward the end of distinguishing reading in the Book of Foreknowledge from the vision of the divine nature, he describes the first as either an enlightenment or a spiritual locution. Hugh of St. Cher employs the same expressions to describe the third and highest form of prophetic experience, the rare intellectual vision enjoyed by Paul in his rapture.[18] It will be recalled that both Hugh and William considered this the beatific vision, albeit in an imperfect mode. Yet here William implies that enlightenment and spiritual locution are the normal modes of prophecy, which he opposes to the beatific vision. Moreover, according to the gloss to which he refers, Isaiah's prophecy of Hezekiah's death was exceptional not only because it did not come to pass but also because it did not originate in the Book of Life. William rightly takes the *Glossa* to mean that reading in the Book of Life was normal for prophets. This is why he sets such reading in opposition to the beatific vision. On his terms, enlightenment and spiritual locution belong to one mode of experience, and intellectual vision to another. On Hugh's terms, all these expressions refer to only one mode of experience—the vision of God.

If in his search for a coherent account of prophetic experience William is not entirely beholden to Hugh, he nonetheless largely aligns himself with him, as well with Thomas Aquinas.[19] Beyond their shared aim of differentiating between prophetic and beatific vision, all three are concerned to avoid describing prophecy as resulting from the prophet's own capacities.[20] It is worth noting that despite their brevity, each of William's descriptions of the three modes of vision makes clear that the initiative is entirely God's.

It is worth remarking that in his subsequent comments on Isaiah 6:1, William indicates that the three modes are not mutually exclusive. Pointing out that Isaiah's vision was imaginary according to Andrew of St. Victor and intellectual according to Jerome, he allows both of them to be right by proposing that Isaiah's imaginary vision was accompanied by an intellectual visualization of the reality it signified:

> [6:1]*I SAW THE LORD*, specifically in human form, and this vision, according to Andrew, was imaginary. According to Jerome, however, it is to be called intellectual. But it may be said that the vision was imaginary, while he saw what it signified in an intellectual vision.[21]

At work here is a distinction, often invoked in William's time, between the mode by which a reality is signified (*modus significandi*) and the reality itself (*res significatum*). In thirteenth-century discourse on theological language, the former—as creaturely and imperfect—was to be denied, and the latter—as divine—was to be affirmed.[22] In the present case, it provides William a means for synthesizing the interpretations of Andrew and Jerome, yet it also allows him to affirm the truth of the content of Isaiah's vision, all the while drawing attention to the imperfection of his human mode of conception and expression, according to which God sits.

Let us turn now to the second proposition framing William's discussion, which in his own time was no less topical than the first, namely, the denial of the beatific vision even with respect to the angels and the elect. This view had previously gained a certain currency in the Latin West with the diffusion of Dionysius the Areopagite's thought in the translations and commentaries of John Scotus Eriugena.[23] In the more proximate background here is Burgundio of Pisa's translation of the *Homelies* of John Chrysostom.[24] Official opprobrium had fallen upon a few of his comments on John 1:18, to which William refers in the preceding excerpt. It is worth presenting at some length:

> [1:18]*NO ONE HAS EVER SEEN GOD*. What, therefore, will we say to the grandiloquent Isaiah saying: *I saw the Lord sitting on a throne, lofty and elevated*? And what, then, will we say to John attesting to him that he said this when he saw his glory? (cf. John 12:41). What, then, to Ezekiel? And indeed he saw him sitting among the Cherubim (cf. Ezekiel 10). What,

then, to Moses saying: *Show me your glory that I may see you recognizably* (Ex 33:13)? From this Jacob received his name, earlier he was called Israel (cf. Gn 35:10). For Israel is the one who sees God. And yet others saw him. How then did John say: *No one has ever seen God?* He said this to show that the preceding were instances of condescension, not the uncovered vision of his substance. If they had seen the nature itself, they would never have beheld it differently. For it is simple and beyond figuration, composition and circumscription. It neither sits, nor stands, nor walks. All of these belong to bodies. Because he is altogether God, not only have the prophets not seen him, but neither have the angels, nor even the archangels.[25]

The original compilers of Hugh of St. Cher's *Postille* took all of these remarks at face value. William accepted all but the last. To see why, we need look no further than a censure issued in 1241 by William of Auvergne, bishop of Paris, condemning ten propositions, the first of which is as follows: *The divine essence in itself will be seen by neither man nor angel.*[26] The condemnations were ostensibly directed at a certain *frater Stephanus*, but the doctrine rejected in this instance was undeniably held by Chrysostom and John Scotus Eriugena.[27] As a result, the relevant section of Hugh's *Postille* on John was corrected in accordance with the Latin Church's increasingly explicit affirmations concerning the beatific vision.[28] (No such rectification was imposed upon the relevant section of Chrysostom's commentary.) William qualifies the problematic remark to have it say that no one sees the Divine nature as fully as the Son. This solution, borrowed from Hugh of St. Cher,[29] amounts to a rebuttal, yet William is uncharacteristically discreet in dealing with the remark's author.

In refraining from an explicit contradiction, William follows the example of the University of Paris's censure, which leaves the saint unnamed. But it is likely that his restraint is also motivated by sympathy for the Antiochene's broader exegetical interests, which are similar to his own. William's understanding of prophecy comprises elements of Chrysostom's framework, as well as Augustine's.

Let us consider briefly the Antiochene's objectives in the preceding excerpt. Certainly, the apophaticism he displays is typical of much of Greek theology, yet his refutation of naive interpretations of prophetic visions was most likely aimed at the exegesis of two specific groups with which he had direct contact, the Anomoean Arians and the Manicheans.

As for the Anomoeans, a key problem presented to Christian doctrine is their denial of the incomprehensibility of God.[30] With respect to the exegesis of the Arians in general and of the Anomoeans in particular, the evidence available to us is fragmentary. Still, it seems clear that whereas Arius was in basic agreement with orthodox Christians on divine incomprehensibility, the Anomoeans held that the totalities of all essences, including the divine one, are conveyed by their names. On their view, by revealing his name, God rendered himself entirely intelligible, allowing himself to be known to believers as thoroughly as he is to himself. Much could be said about this teaching's many implications for biblical interpretation. Here it will be noted that it provided the context for Chrysostom's denial of the vision of the divine nature to the prophets, angels, and archangels.[31]

But Chrysostom also took issue with a notable feature of the Manicheans' exegesis, specifically, their tendency to read the Old Testament's anthropomorphic depictions of the Godhead in such a grossly literalistic manner as to cast doubt upon the Bible's coherence. Though we need not go into a detailed account of the system produced by the preacher and founder Mani, consideration of a few of its basic doctrines will shed light on Chrysostom's response to it. Originating in third-century Babylon and incorporating elements of Zoroastrianism, Buddhism, and Christianity, Manichaeism was an elaborate body of Gnosticism, radically dualistic and certain of the possession of esoteric truths. Predicated on a supposed primordial contest between the spiritual realm of light, ruled by God, and the material realm of darkness, ruled by Satan, it taught that the human condition was the result of Satan's theft of particles of light, which he imprisoned in bodies. On this view, religion's purpose was to effect these particles' release and return to the realm of light. It was toward this end that Buddha, Jesus, and Manes had been sent. Believers, for their part, were to strive to accomplish their liberation from corporeality by the practice of extreme asceticism, which often took the forms of vegetarianism and sexual abstinence. Since matter was, according to them, uncreated, evil, and opposed to the spiritual realm, the human body could have no place in salvation.[32] As they would have it, the differences between the theophanies of the Old Testament and the revelation of the New were to be explained with reference to two different deities, one material and the other pure light.

Particularly relevant to the present discussion are their attributions of the Old and New Testaments to two different deities. On their terms, the Lord who appeared sitting on a throne before Isaiah was not at all the same as the one who left St. Paul speechless. So disposed to read the New Testament, they found in John 1:18 a refutation of all the theophanies of the Old Testament.[33] Worth keeping in mind here is that Chrysostom's commentary on the verse probably originated in a homily preached to an audience living in a world where the Manicheans were a force to be reckoned with.[34] When telling his audience that God does not sit, he was in all likelihood speaking to people who had heard that the one spoken of in the Old Testament does, in fact, sit.

## Divine Condescension

In his exposition of Isaiah's vision, Chrysostom provides an illustration of his manner of addressing questions raised by the Manicheans by invoking divine "condescension."[35] While a complete account of this concept's functioning in his exegesis lies beyond our scope, a few points should be kept in mind.[36] In a broad sense, the notion of condescension describes God's self-communication to humankind. The very fact of revelation, then, warrants the claim that God has condescended to a level beneath his own to adapt his own infinite and transcendent self-knowledge to those belonging to the finite and feeble human condition. This is how the concept functions in ancient Greek literature[37] and, with greater frequency, in the Old Testament.[38] In the work of Christian thinkers such as Origen, Athanasius, and Chrysostom, the notion is Christological in its orientation. It expresses the doctrine that the transcendent, immutable, and incomprehensible God is none other than the One who has communicated himself to humankind in Scripture and in the person of Jesus Christ.

More concretely, Chrysostom speaks of divine condescension to respond to two intimately related problems that can be expressed by the following questions: First, may anthropomorphic passages of the Old Testament be attributed to an immutable spiritual Being, and if so, how? And second, how can Christ, whose human weaknesses and sufferings the New Testament amply describes, be of the same substance as the eternal Father? The first problem arose from the claims of the Manicheans, who, by subscribing to strictly literal interpretations of the Old Testament's anthropomorphic language, denied the identity of the God who created the world and spoke through the prophets with the God who revealed himself in Jesus Christ.[39] The second difficulty came from the New Testament interpretations of the Arians, particularly the Anomoeans, who asserted that the Son is altogether "unlike" the Father by nature. Common to both propositions is the bifurcation of the Godhead and the correlative bifurcation of revelation.

In his exposition of John 1:18, Chrysostom provides an example of his manner of invoking God's condescension to oppose Manichean claims that the divine of the Old Testament differed from the one of the New. In this case, he sets out to show that the differences between the contemplation of figures such as John on the one hand and Isaiah on the other derive not from a plurality of godheads, but from a plurality of the one God's modes of condescending to the human condition. The principle serves as a device for explaining prophetic anthropomorphisms as divine accommodations to the rudeness of the human condition. So equipped, Chrysostom is able to account for the entire range of biblical prophecies without compromising either the absolute unity and simplicity of the Godhead or the unity of the biblical narrative.

The preceding is an exegetical and theological principle, the importance of which is not lost on William, whose interests are similar to Chrysostom's. Shortly, we shall consider his own occasional employment of the principle of *condescensio*; here we will note that he was repeatedly preoccupied with certain so-called *Manichei*, whom he often identified simply as *heretici*. Though we may safely assume that he had the Cathars in mind, it is also reasonable to suppose that if he and his contemporaries called them *Manichei*, it was because they saw actual parallels between the two movements.[40] William's account of their doctrines corresponds closely to what we know of the movement familiar to Chrysostom. Commenting on the prologue to John's Gospel, he doesn't hesitate to find a refutation of their understanding of creation:

> [1:3] *ALL THINGS WERE MADE BY HIM*, i.e., every work of creation, whether it be corporal or spiritual, against the Manicheans, who say that corporeal realities are from an evil principle.[41]

And in his comments on the wedding at Cana, he explains that Jesus used water in his miraculous production of wine to show the goodness of creation, and this in order to confound the Manichean:

> [2:7] *JESUS SAID TO THEM*, i.e., to his ministers, *FILL THE JARS WITH WATER* . . . to confound the Manichean, who says that everything visible was created by an evil god.[42]

Later, when commenting on Jesus' remark that the Devil was a murderer from the beginning, he makes the following points: that the "beginning" in question did not precede creation, but followed it, that the Devil himself was created, that he was originally good, and that his fall was voluntary:

> [8:44] *HE WAS A MURDERER . . . FROM THE BEGINNING*, i.e., after the human race's beginning, or his, or the world's, *AND IN TRUTH*, specifically, of natural realities and original innocence, *HE DID NOT STAND*, because he fell, Isaiah 14 (12): *How you have fallen, Lucifer. BECAUSE THE TRUTH IS NOT IN HIM*. After his fall and loss of truth he was unwilling to seek it, Ezekiel 28 (19): You have been brought to nothing and you will be no more. Or *THE TRUTH*, i.e., Christ, *IS NOT IN HIM* by grace *WHEN HE SPEAKS A LIE*. In other words, not only has he lost the truth, not only does he not seek it, but what is more, *WHEN HE SPEAKS A LIE, HE SPEAKS OF HIS OWN*, specifically, from his own contrivances, because he does not have anyone suggesting this to him. Hence it follows: *BECAUSE HE IS A*

*LIAR AND THE FATHER THEREOF*, i.e., the father of lies, i.e., their cause, and because he spoke the first lie, Genesis 3 (5): *You will be as gods*. It does not mean, therefore, that evil cannot come from anyone other than the Devil, but that his evil was the first.[43]

An example more directly concerned with revelation appears in his comments on Ezekiel's calling. In the prophet's identification as the son of Buzi, William finds a parallel with Christ's sonship with respect to the Father. His warrant is an interpretation of Jerome, who has taken "Buzi" to signify "despised" or "contemptible."[44] For William, Buzi is a figure of the Father, and those who hold him in contempt are certain heretics who reject the Old Testament:

> [1:3]*THE SON OF BUZI*, i.e., despised and disdained. The Father of Christ is disdained by heretics who do not accept the Old Testament.[45]

Both Chrysostom and William see the Manicheans' grossly literal interpretations as the cause of their rejection of the Old Testament, but they also recognize that such construals can mislead even Jesus' disciples in their understanding of the New Testament. Our author presents an example in his treatment of Jesus' farewell discourse to his disciples in John's Gospel. As the biblical narrative itself makes clear, Philip went wrong in asking Jesus to show them the Father (John 14:8). As it is difficult to find fault with the disciple's basic desire to see God, Jesus' subsequent rebuke calls for an explanation. William offers three. The first is an anti-Arian reading taken from Augustine, according to which Philip erred by implying that the Father is different from and greater than the Son. The second is an anonymous position (*Secundum quosdam*), according to which Philip believed the Father and Son to be alike but failed to turn his desire for rapture into a longing for future glory. And the third is Chrysostom's interpretation to the effect that Philip erred in supposing that God could be seen corporeally, and this because of vague recollections that Isaiah and Micaiah had so seen him. In other words, Jesus admonishes Philip for falling prey to the Manichean misreading of the Old Testament. What follows is William's exposition of John 14:8:

> [14:8]*PHILIP SAID TO HIM, "LORD, SHOW US THE FATHER,"* suggesting that he did not at all believe him (the Father) to be like the Son, *AND THIS WILL SUFFICE*, implying that he (the Father) is greater than the Son, according to Augustine, *FOR US*, implying that he was not alone in this error. Was he not therefore unfaithful? According to some, he believed the Father to be like the Son, but did not convert his desire for rapture into longing for future glory. According to Chrysostom, he asked to see

him corporeally, indistinctly recalling that Isaiah saw him, Isaiah 6 (1), as did Micaiah, 1 Kings 22 (19).[46]

Common to each of these three solutions is the finding of fault not in Philip's desire for the beatific vision, but in his way of desiring it.

Whatever one makes of the parallels between the beliefs of the heretics of William's own time and those of Chrysostom's, it is worth observing that both exegetes display similar understandings of prophetic experience. By way of illustration, let us consider William's own exposition of John 1:18:

> [1:18]*No one*, i.e., no mere man with carnal eyes, *has ever seen god*. To the contrary, Genesis 32 (30): *I have seen God face to face* (Gn 32:30). Response: These visions and others like them were in some subject creature. Should Paul's rapture be mentioned in objection, it should be said that that vision was above man (*supra hominem*). *The only begotten son who is in the bosom of the father, he has made him known*, because *No one knows the Father but the Son, and anyone to whom the Son chooses to reveal him*, Matthew 11 (27). He makes known to his own what should be sensed about the Trinity as well as how to reach it, and he introduces it.[47]

Drawn from the *Glossa*,[48] the initial remark that no "mere man" and no " carnal-eyes" can see God was a commonplace in both Greek and Latin theology. In the writings of Chrysostom, it is a recurring theme. In his exposition of the passage, shortly after the comments just excerpted, he remarks: *Therefore, only the Son and the Holy Spirit see him*.[49] To be sure, behind the verbal similarity of the two exegetes' comments lies an important difference of meaning—whereas Chrysostom evidently speaks of the eternal Son's vision of the Father, the proposition William borrowed from the *Glossa* serves to make an exception for Christ in his humanity and, implicitly, for the blessed in heaven, as the subsequent remark concerning Paul makes clear.[50] All of that is foreign to the Antiochene's purposes, but both exegetes share a few of the same concerns, namely, to differentiate sharply between the object of the prophets' visions and the divine nature, and to account for the variety of prophetic experiences by attributing them to a variety of divine modes of revelation. Also common to both exegetes is a keen interest in the narrative concerns of Jesus. In an earlier chapter, we saw that William regards Jesus as an author whose language is to be submitted to the same analysis as any other's. Here, prompted by the Johannine text, he recognizes Jesus as a narrator who explains to his listeners how to think about and attain to the Trinity, and who in so doing introduces them to it. In William's perspective, the Son, as one who sees the Father and shares his life, does what none of the prophets of the Old Testament could do—communicate the Trinity to his listeners.

Albeit with less frequency than Thomas Aquinas,[51] William occasionally invokes the principle of condescension explicitly.[52] Let us consider two examples. The first appears in his comments on Jesus' prayer to the Father as he raises Lazarus from the dead. For the initial remarks he is independent; the rest (in bold) he has borrowed from Chrysostom:

> [11:42]*BUT*, as if to say: so I give thanks; not however as if dubious, because *I KNEW*, with the knowledge of certitude, *THAT YOU ALWAYS HEAR ME*, not sometimes, as (you hear) other saints. Or *HEAR*, as if to say: you hear me as a man, Hebrews 5 (7): *Who in the days of his flesh, with a strong cry and tears, offering up prayers and supplications to him who was able to save him from death, was heard for his reverence.* **Therefore, not as if needy have I asked or given thanks,** according to Chrysostom, *BUT BECAUSE OF THE PEOPLE WHO STAND AROUND HAVE I SAID THIS, THAT THEY MAY BELIEVE THAT YOU HAVE SENT ME,* **and thus, that I am not opposed to you, but concurring in all things, above chapter 8 (29):** *For I always do the things that please him.* Chrysostom: **"It belongs to his wisdom to show condescension in words, power in deeds."**[53]

By drawing out the implications of the text on which he comments, William pursues his goal of dispelling any notion of minority or subordination on Jesus' part—while Lazarus is still in the tomb, he gives thanks in knowledge, not doubt. His knowledge, William adds, is certain because, by contrast with everyone else, he is always heard. As the subsequent lines taken from Chrysostom suggest, both exegetes share the aim of showing that the biblical narrative poses no threat to the doctrine of Jesus' oneness with the Father—Jesus' prayer and gratitude imply no indigence on his part, and certainly no opposition, as the Manicheans would have it. William then draws on the Antiochene's understanding of divine revelation to address the central problem presented by the passage, namely, the apparent contradiction between Jesus' oneness with the Father and his status as one who prays—his words attest to his condescension while his deed bears witness to his power.

Then again, our author is capable of employing the concept independently of Chrysostom. A case in point appears in his comments on Jesus' remark to his disciples that the Holy Spirit will speak whatever he hears:

> [16:13]*BUT WHEN HE COMES, THE SPIRIT OF TRUTH, HE WILL TEACH YOU ALL TRUTH. . . . FOR HE WILL NOT SPEAK OF HIMSELF . . . BUT WHATEVER*

*HE HEARS HE WILL SPEAK.* Note that these are words of condescension, because there is no future in God. But to hear is his existence and his hearing is his essence. Nevertheless, "existence from another" adds to the meaning of "essence." Chrysostom: "By this he means nothing other than 'in a fallacy of the Holy Spirit.'"[54]

William's immediate concern is to show that Jesus' use of the future tense when speaking of the Holy Spirit implies no mutability or temporality in the Godhead. His source here is Augustine, who takes up the same matter in his own exposition of the passage. In his preoccupation for affirming divine immutability, Augustine in all probability has his sights set on the Arian doctrines that the Son and Holy Spirit proceeded from the Father in time. His solution, borrowed by William, lies in identifying the Holy Spirit's "hearing" with the divine essence, the procession of which is eternal.[55] Chrysostom, for his part, is primarily concerned with upholding Jesus' equality to the Holy Spirit. While William's purpose in citing him is not entirely clear, he seems to take him to say that the Holy Spirit cannot contradict Jesus. In any case, neither Augustine nor Chrysostom explicitly mentions Jesus' manner of speaking to his disciples. It is William's contribution to allude to the mutability of the human condition by setting the entire discussion within the context of divine condescension. The result is a brief yet fairly coherent synthesis of the comments of the three exegetes, who despite their many differences, approach this Johannine text with a few common interests.

## The Works of Christ

With what has preceded, we have had some impression of William's approach to revelatory language, whether of the Old Testament prophets or of Jesus Christ. Yet theologians of the thirteenth century generally did not regard revelation as a purely external affair, and even when considering the external dimension of Jesus' life and mission, they normally did not restrict their perspective to his verbal instruction. To the contrary, William's period of activity was characterized by a renewal of interest in the visible deeds of Christ as a source of revelation.[56] It is worth considering, then, how William understood Jesus' actions as salvific.

It generally went undisputed at the time that the object of faith is unseen. Subject to less agreement was the matter of the efficacy of Jesus' visible works, particularly his supernatural ones, as causes of faith. If William and his contemporaries had difficulty in appreciating the fullness of the meaning of the term *signum* in John's Gospel—they generally referred to Jesus' wonders as recounted in any of the four Gospels as *miracula*—they were nonetheless able to recognize the ambiguity of *signa* as evidence of Christ's divinity.[57] One place where we often find such a recognition in evidence is in commentaries on Jesus' reproach, in John 6:26–36, to a crowd of people who have seen a sign without coming to belief. Having benefited from a multiplication of loaves, they have followed him in the hope of having another free meal, with the result that Jesus issues a reproof to the effect that their vision should have led them to belief. The problem this presents is not lost on William, who gives voice to an objector who points to Hebrews 11:1 as evidence that Jesus was mistaken:

> So therefore it is good to believe in me, [6:36]*BUT*, nevertheless, *I SAID TO YOU*, above chapter 3 (11): *We testify to what we have seen, and you do not accept our testimony; THAT YOU ALSO HAVE SEEN ME, AND YOU HAVE NOT BELIEVED*, and so you do not accept this bread. . . . But it would appear that he argues badly because they saw and did not believe, since faith is of things not seen (cf. Hebrews 11:1). Response: He understands not the vision of (his) mere humanity, which does not help faith, but the vision of (his) virtue and power in effect. Concerning the statement that vision is opposed to faith, this is to be understood of the vision that is face to face, not that which is in a mirror (cf. 1 Corinthians 13:12).[58]

If faith has to do with what is unseen, then it would seem that the crowds can hardly be blamed for not believing. William's solution lies in a distinction between three kinds of vision: of Jesus' mere humanity, of the effect of his power, and of his divinity. Whereas the first is of no use to faith and the third precludes it, the second helps it. A key feature of this solution is the ambiguity of the second kind of vision (*adiuuat fidem*)—it is this that lends moral status to the witnesses' belief, or lack thereof. Its importance was lost neither on our author nor on his sources, Bonaventure and Hugh of St. Cher.[59] All three imply that the crowd's unbelief was blameworthy because it was voluntary. Throughout his exposition of this pericope, as well as elsewhere, William is particularly explicit on the element of free choice in belief. We shall have occasion to return to this aspect of his thought.

True, it was not only Christ's supernatural deeds that biblical commentators considered revelatory. No less than at any other period, during the thirteenth century Jesus remained the model for Christian comportment, and exegetes generally remained well aware of the importance of his example.[60] William invokes it repeatedly and explicitly throughout his postill on John. As a reason for Jesus' departure from Judea (4:3), our author follows Augustine and Bonaventure in explaining that he did this to give us an example showing the legitimacy of eluding the furor of persecutors.[61] Later, he makes a similar point in connection with Jesus' departure from the temple (8:59), this time citing Gregory the Great as his source.[62] Usually, however, his invocations of Jesus' example show up in the *divisio textus*, where, it will be recalled, he is generally independent of his sources. A case in point is a *divisio* introducing the parable of the Good Shepherd (10:1–16). Taking the Shepherd's entrance through the sheep gate as a metaphor for elevation to ecclesiastical office, William presents Jesus as the ideal pastor under four headings: his mode of assuming his charge and his authority for assuming it, the obedience of his flock, his honest execution of the duties of his office, and finally, his subjects' imitation of him.

> [10:2]*BUT HE WHO ENTERS BY THE GATE.* Here he shows the one entering through the gate to be the true pastor. And first he says this; second he declares: [10:3]*TO HIM THE GATEKEEPER OPENS.* Here this is shown, first by the proper mode and authority of entering; second by the proper obedience of the flock committed (to his care): [10:3]*AND THE SHEEP HEAR HIS VOICE*; third by the honest execution of the pastoral office: [10:3]*AND HE CALLS HIS OWN SHEEP*—the first regards God, the second subjects, the third himself; fourth by their imitation of his example, his subjects: [10:4]*AND THE SHEEP FOLLOW HIM.*

In a subsequent division, William offers a few specifications with respect to the obligations of office, noting the true pastor's knowledge of his sheep, his withdrawing them from evil and leading them to good. Further specifying the latter point, he finds an obligation of clerical office in Jesus' very example of giving a good example:

> [10:3]*AND HE CALLS HIS OWN SHEEP.* Here he shows himself to be such a true pastor by the duties of his office, which are threefold, specifically, to know his sheep; to draw them away from evil: [10:3]*HE LEADS THEM OUT*; and to draw them to good: [10:4]*HE GOES BEFORE THEM.* Regarding the last, note, first, the attraction of good example; and second, the usefulness and efficacy of good example for subjects, namely, the imitation of the good: [10:4]*AND THE SHEEP FOLLOW HIM*, and the rejection of evil: [10:5]*BUT A STRANGER THEY WILL NOT FOLLOW.*[63]

Again, in his comments on the Last Discourse, William dedicates the better part of a *divisio* to show that Jesus arms his disciples with his own example to equip them for enduring the hatred of the world:

> [15:18]*IF THE WORLD.* After talking about their confirmation in the love of God and neighbor, discussing this love in several ways, here he addresses

impediments to this love, specifically, by arming them against persecutions and the world's hatred. And first he arms them against the intrinsic evil of the worldly, specifically, hatred of the heart; second against their extrinsic evil, specifically, persecutions in works: [20]*IF THEY PERSECUTED ME*. In the first, first he arms them with his example for enduring the world's hatred; second he shows that in this his example will be powerful: [20]*REMEMBER MY WORD*. In the first, first hatred of the world is proposed; second the example of Christ bearing this hatred is remembered: [18]*KNOW THAT IT HATED ME BEFORE YOU*; third the cause of this hatred is manifested, namely, their dissimilarity from the worldly: [19]*IF YOU WERE OF THE WORLD.*[64]

For all that, medieval exegetes generally did not regard the salvific efficacy of Jesus' example as unlimited. Franciscan, Dominican, or secular, all of them were heirs to the tradition of Augustine, with its insistence upon the inadequacy of the external aspects of Christ's mission—his verbal teaching and his visible actions and sufferings—as causes of faith. Figuring largely in the background here is the Pelagian controversy. Without entering into the details of the early-fifth-century dispute on grace and its aftermath, we may note that Pelagius and his followers tended to reduce the salvific efficacy of Christ's life and mission to the power of his good example. By contrast, Augustine and the mainstream of subsequent Latin theology insisted on the primacy of the supernatural order and the interiority of divine grace. To see this interest at work in William's exegesis, one need look no further than his frequent usage of the term *interius* in connection with divine pedagogy. In the first chapter of *Super Iohannem*, he borrows a line from the *Glossa* mentioning that John the Baptist saw Jesus drawing near not only in his bodily footsteps (1:29) but also as the object of interior contemplation who makes himself known in his divinity, as well as his humanity.[65] Subsequently, he remarks that when the disciples first met Jesus, they were not foolish in following him so blithely (1:49) because they had benefited from an interior enlightenment.[66] Later, he indicates that the dead who will come to life upon hearing the voice of the Son of God (5:25) are the guilty who will hear him interiorly, inspiring them to believe and obey by grace.[67] What is more, where William places the term *interius* in apposition to *exterius*, it is usually to designate some sort of superiority. With respect to baptism, John's—in water—is merely external (1:26), yet Jesus'—in the Holy Spirit—is internal.[68] Jesus' honorific welcome upon entering Galilee (4:44), he tells us, involved no real honor because the Galileans received him only externally, not internally.[69] And so forth. In none of these cases are William's remarks original—he has drawn them all from his primary Latin sources, Augustine, the *Glossa ordinaria*, Hugh of St. Cher, and especially

Bonaventure. Yet this list is telling, pointing as it does to the general medieval concern for underscoring the interior dimension of revelation.

An anti-Pelagian interest also shows up in discussions concerning prayer. Pelagius's denial of the efficacy of praying for others figured largely in his contest with Augustine, whose own doctrine of predestination did not prevent him from arguing forcefully to the contrary. Subsequent Latin writers did the same. In the following excerpt of his commentary on John 17:9, *Ego pro eis rogo*, William follows Bonaventure in presenting a *questio* defending the usefulness of Jesus' prayer. Notably, their source here is not the *Tractatus*, but one of Augustine's writings concerned with interlocutors who later came to be known as semi-Pelagians:

> Therefore it says: [17:9] *I PRAY FOR THEM*. . . . Also, it is evident that he prayed only for the predestined, but it would appear that he prayed for them to no purpose. Response, Augustine, *On the predestination of the saints*: "For such people we do not pray in vain, because perhaps they are predestined to be the beneficiaries of our prayers."[70]

Such is the background for an interesting thirteenth-century evolution in the construal of Christ's actions, a development that may be observed in the changing understanding of one of the period's common axioms: *Omnis Christi actio nostra est instructio*. Probably originating in Cassiodorus's commentary on Psalm 85, it gained currency with its restatement in the *Glossa ordinaria* and Peter Lombard's *Magna glossatura*.[71] By the latter part of the twelfth century, when Alan of Lille invoked it in his *Summa de arte praedicatoria*, it had acquired its final form:

> There are three kinds of preaching. One is in word, with respect to which it is said: *Go, preach the Gospel to every creature* etc. (Mark 16:15). Another is in writing, hence the Apostle says that he has preached to the Corinthians because he wrote them epistles (cf. 1 Corinthians 5:9). Another is in deed, hence it says: Christ's every action is our instruction (*Omnis Christi actio nostra est instructio*).[72]

Here at the outset of his guide to preachers, Alan employs the axiom to propose Jesus' preaching activity as a model to be followed. In evidence here is the adage's general functioning to highlight the revelatory character of Jesus' works. Yet this case also illustrates that its use epitomized presuppositions about the extent to which Jesus' actions were to be taken literally as models for imitation. Richard Schenk has shown that toward the middle of the thirteenth century, theologians became wary of taking the saying too literally, particularly with respect to Jesus' submission to the precepts of the old law, such as those concerning circumcision.

While they never called into question the basic pedagogical value of Jesus' actions, they tended to dissociate his pedagogy from superficial moral exemplarity. This was often to draw attention to some other lesson to be had from the biblical narrative. Put another way, they proposed Jesus' actions as matters for reflection, not mere imitation. As a result, they frequently invoked the axiom in connection with some action not proposed for imitation.[73]

William is no exception. In the following example, he employs the saying in connection with an example of Jesus' that he pointedly sets in contrast to his own proposed course of action:

[1:49]NATHANAEL ANSWERED: RABBI, YOU ARE THE SON OF GOD. To the contrary: Many prophets revealed past and secret things, yet they were not sons of God by nature. Response: He does not call him the Son of God by nature, but by excellence of grace, and this is why his confession is not blessed, as is Peter's, Matthew 16 (17), according to Chrysostom. Nevertheless, it could be said that he confessed him to be the true Son of God because he knew that God alone knows the thoughts of men (cf. Psalm 93:11; 1 Corinthians 3:20). Yet he was not blessed because he did not confess with as much firmness as Peter. Note, though Nathanael was so eminent, he was still not called to the apostolate, and this for the reason that he was an expert in the law, lest his preaching seem to proceed from the subtlety of human reason. Nor is there any validity in the objection concerning Paul, because he was an open enemy beforehand and was chosen by Christ already glorified. And Christ's every action is our instruction. Nevertheless, idiots are not to be chosen now, because Christ chose such men and made them wise, which we cannot do.[74]

Nathanael is a paradox. He has identified Jesus as the Son of God, though he has seen no more of his works than had many of the prophets. What is more, his confession has won him no blessing, such as the one accorded Peter. Chrysostom introduces his considerations of these difficulties by posing them as questions, while William presents them in the form of a *questio*. In addition to Chrysostom's reply to the effect that Nathanael's confession was not really of Christ's divinity,[75] William presents another—Nathanael recognized Jesus' divinity in the effects of his virtue and power, that is, in his ability to read the thoughts of others. While this solution is essentially the same as the one offered in connection with Jesus' rebuke to those following him merely for bread (John 6:26–36), in this case William has borrowed neither from Hugh of St. Cher, nor from Bonaventure, but from the *Glossa ordinaria*.[76] All of this is of a piece with what follows—a discussion about why Nathanael was passed over for the apostolate. If it is broadly dependent on Augustine and Bonaventure, William's explanation has a few elements of his own. Augustine asserts that Jesus passed over Nathanael lest his preaching be ascribed to the subtlety of human reason,[77] a remark perfectly in keeping with his characteristic insistence upon humility as a prerequisite for receiving the Word of God.[78] In plain agreement, William adds two reasons for setting aside an objection based on Jesus' calling of another learned man, Paul of Tarsus—the latter's open enmity with Christ and his being chosen after the Resurrection. William's point is that Paul's calling serves not as point of comparison with Nathanael's, but as a point of contrast. A few verses earlier (in connection with the calling of Philip), William cited Paul's admonition to the Corinthians that God chooses the foolish and the weak to shame the wise and the strong (1 Cor 1:27).[79] Here he implies that Paul exemplifies his own remark. And it is here that he presents the expression, *Omnis Christi actio* . . .—one could expect, to invoke Jesus' choice as an example for the church. But such is not the case. As does Bonaventure, William employs it to draw attention to a difference: whereas Jesus can take simpletons and make them wise, no such possibility lies in store for anyone else. By the first-person plural, *we cannot*, our author refers pointedly to himself and his fellow Dominicans—theologians though they may be, they cannot hope to do for future preachers what Jesus did for his band of Galilean fishermen. They are not, therefore, to accept the ignorant among their ranks. Undoubtedly, Jesus' exclusion of a highly qualified candidate is instructive but not as an example to be imitated. Its pedagogy lies elsewhere. Pointing as it does to something unseen, his action functions as a sign of his divinity.

## Preaching

In our earlier consideration of the prologue to *Super Iohannem*, we saw that William commended John the Evangelist as a model preacher, specifically in connection with his role as an agent of revelation.[80] Yet our author's identification of the true ideal of the preacher appears afterward, in his exposition of a text preoccupied with revelation, the prologue to John's Gospel:

> Hence it follows: *AND THE LIGHT*, i.e., the Son of God, *IN THE DARKNESS*, i.e., in people darkened by guilt and ignorance, *SHINES* by preaching and the working of miracles.[81]

The archetype of the preacher, in this perspective, is the one who is himself the subject of revelation. Exegetes have long recognized in the Fourth Gospel a virtually exclusive focus on the person of Jesus Christ as both the subject and principal agent of revelation.[82]

Albeit with the succinctness that is typical of him, William returns to this point a few verses later, identifying Christ, first as the subject of revelation, then as the agent of it, in his divinity as well as his humanity:

> [1:7]*THIS SAME CAME . . . IN TESTIMONY . . . TO GIVE TESTIMONY TO THE LIGHT*, (the Evangelist) specifies to what purpose he (the Baptist) came. Note, so that the truth of Christ be declared, first it was attested by Moses, Deuteronomy 32 (1–44); second by the prophets, Isaiah 43 (10): *Truly, you are my witnesses*; third by John, who was a witness by sight and hearing; fourth by the apostles and other preachers, Acts 1 (8): *You will be my witnesses; TO THE LIGHT.* Christ is called the light (*lux*) because he is God, a lamp (*lumen*) because he is man, 1 Peter 2 (9): *Who called you out of darkness into his marvelous light.*[83]

Worth observing here is the comprehensive perspective within which William approaches the matter at hand. That revelation encompasses the activity of the church—and of preachers in particular—was axiomatic for him, as indeed it was for his contemporaries. Here he betrays a view of his own work, and that of his students, as forming a part of this larger divine project. Albeit implicitly, he inserts himself and the aspiring preachers in his charge into the company of Moses, the prophets, John the Baptist, the apostles, and Christ himself. The proclamations of the luminaries of old are of a piece with those of the "other preachers" of more recent times. The essential differences between the various witnesses are temporal—each is historically situated in a particular way with respect to the principal agent of revelation and the subject revealed, Jesus Christ.

This same perspective is discernible throughout William's commentaries, even in his expositions of passages less directly concerned with revelation. It is conspicuous, for example, in the prominent place occupied by preachers in the spiritual commentary of his postill on Lamentations. There he tells us that the roads to Zion mourning for the lack of pilgrims coming to its feasts (1:4) prefigure preachers whose lives and preaching lead to heaven, while they mourn for themselves and others because there are so few who come by the steps of faith and morals to the feast of the triumphant church. And Zion's ruined gates portend the patriarchs, apostles, and prophets who are destroyed in the opinion of the church's persecutors, presumably the Manicheans.[84] Then, he mentions that Jerusalem's filthy feet (1:9) are the church's prelates, doctors, and preachers sullied by vainglory.[85] Jeremiah's lament that the Lord has sent fire down from heaven into his bones and cast a net beneath his feet (1:13), William proposes, is the church's cry that God the Father has sent the Holy Spirit into the apostles and cast the net of preaching before preachers that the church would follow in Christ's footsteps.[86] What is more, William likens the Lord's forgotten footstool (2:1) to the church, and his feet to the apostles and preachers. Though they should be situated above the church, they sit.[87] In his commentary on Ecclesiastes, he tells us that the clouds returning after the rain while the sun and the moon are darkened (12:2) are preachers returning from their preaching, which has had no effect upon the old, who lie rotting in their own filth.[88]

Other such figurative remarks could be supplied, but for William's more precise statements on preaching, we will return to his commentary on John. There he gives the matter more direct attention, particularly in connection with the preaching of Jesus. In the narrative of the Samaritan woman at the well, the matter of testimony figures prominently. We have already seen that neither William nor any of his main sources failed to expatiate upon Jesus' testimony to the woman (4:7–26). It may be added that they noticed the peculiarity of her own testimony—despite her manifestly imperfect understanding, she was effective in bringing other Samaritans to faith (4:39). Yet medieval exegetes put forward some of their most telling reflections on the subject of revelation in connection with the intervening lesson involving the images of sowers, reapers, and a harvest. There Jesus tells his disciples that he sends them to harvest where others have labored (4:35–38). Augustine and others after him (e.g., Alcuin, Hugh of St. Cher, Bonaventure) find here the opportunity for drawing two sets of comparisons: first, between the patriarchs and prophets of the Old Testament and their successors of the New, whom they generally call apostles; and second, between the order of grace and glory. In the former, the harvestors are the apostles; in the latter, they are the angels.[89] William is unquestionably beholden to the aforementioned commentators, yet in his exposition, it is the preachers who are most conspicuously placed in apposition, first to the prophets, then to the angels:

> [4:36]*SO THAT THE ONE WHO SOWS*, as a prophet, *REJOICES TOGETHER WITH THE ONE WHO REAPS*, as preachers who are reapers of the harvest of grace, as the angels are the reapers of the harvest of glory.... Preachers and prophets both sow and reap by preaching, yet for the aforesaid reason, sowing is attributed more to prophets and harvesting to preachers.[90]

To be sure, our author elsewhere follows the general medieval practice of using the term *apostoli* as a proper name for those whom the Johannine text usually identifies as *discipuli*.[91] Still, such occurrences are relatively rare and usually confined to his borrowings. Where he is independent of his sources, he is more apt than his contemporaries to call them *discipuli*, or *predicatores*, as in the preceding comments. The result is an impression of assimilation between Jesus' followers, on the one hand, and the preachers of his own time, on the other. The remarks of the excerpt are as easily applicable to one group as to the other.

In this respect, William differs from Thomas Aquinas, who more explicitly than any of the aforementioned commentators sets the apostles apart from the prophets and underscores the uniqueness of their knowledge.[92] In particular, he remarks that they revealed what their predecessors could not and accomplished what they did not, and this by bringing people to Christ. When Thomas mentions preaching and preachers, he generally avoids conflating the identities of Jesus' first disciples with those of their thirteenth-century counterparts. What follows is from Thomas's exposition of John 4:36–37:

> According to Chrysostom and Augustine, the sowers of the spiritual seed are the fathers and prophets of the Old Testament, as is said in Luke 8 (11): *The seed is the word of God*, which Moses and the prophets sowed in Judea, but the apostles harvested, because the former were not able to effect what they intended, specifically, to lead people to Christ, which the apostles nevertheless did. . . . The sowers are the prophets because they handed on many things concerning divine matters. The harvesters are the apostles, who by their preaching and teaching revealed what the prophets did not make known. . . . Then, when it says [4:37] *FOR IN THIS THE SAYING IS TRUE* etc., a proverb is introduced, as if to say: in this, i.e., in this fact, the saying is true, i.e., the proverb common among the Jews is fulfilled, that is, "One sows and another reaps."[93]

William, by contrast, suggests that his students look upon the disciples as peers, but he is unambiguous about whom they should take as their model. In explaining Jesus' claim to keep the Father's word (8:55), he distinguishes the various elements of his fidelity with reference to actions of the heart, mouth, and hand—love, preaching, and works, which are, presumably, miracles. In William's order of priority, Jesus' preaching is second only to his love and before all of his works:

> [8:55]*BUT I KNOW HIM.* This he repeats in order to add something, hence it follows: *AND I KEEP HIS WORD*, in the heart by love, in the mouth by preaching, and in the hand by work.[94]

Jesus is the ideal preacher, but even his identity is susceptible of a certain conflation with those of less than ideal ones. His preaching can be assimilated by other preachers, even contemporary ones, as we see in William's exposition of the parable of the Good Shepherd. The one who calls his sheep by name is none other than the narrator, Jesus. Yet his calling, in William's perspective, involves not only preaching but also the administration of sacraments, visitation and counsel:

> [10:3]*AND HE CALLS HIS OWN SHEEP BY NAME.* This calling is nothing other than the knowledge by which he distinguishes his own from the others by the administration of the sacraments, preaching, visitation, and counsel.[95]

William questions neither the historicity of Jesus' institution of the sacraments nor his agency in his disciples' baptismal ministry. In that respect, his comment can be taken at face value, that is, as an account of Jesus' own pastoral activity as recounted in the biblical narrative. Still, William's remark is more evocative of the activity of a thirteenth-century friar than of Jesus of Nazareth, and in that sense, it may be taken as his transposition of the image of the Good Shepherd to make of it an ideal for his students. In other words, he would have them emulate the Good Shepherd in their own sacramental ministry, preaching, visiting, and counseling. By this exposition of the Good Shepherd's calling, William could have in mind the former historical reading, the latter moral one, or perhaps both. Yet his controlling concern is most likely neither. It would appear that his main purpose is more properly theological, specifically, to underscore Christ's agency in the pastoral work of the church's ministers. He actualizes the parable to present the Good Shepherd to his students as the principal agent of their preaching and other pastoral labors. William tells his students that it is Jesus who is at work in their sacramental work, preaching, visiting, and counseling. By implication, their role is secondary, that is, instrumental. William has previously appealed to such an explanation to account for the Gospel's seemingly contradictory assertions that Jesus baptized (3:22; 4:1), yet did not baptize (4:2)[96]—while he baptized internally, his disciples performed the sacrament externally (by pouring water, etc.).[97]

Recognizable in all of this is an understanding of twofold efficient causality not unlike the one we encountered in William's discussions of biblical authorship. Much like the prophets and evangelists, the first disciples and their successors are, in William's view, God's instruments, albeit perfectly free ones. Without going into an account of Thomas Aquinas's sacramental theology, we may note that if William had followed his lectures on the fourth book of Lombard's *Sentences*, he would have known that Christ's humanity is there described as an instrument of his divinity and that the sacraments and their ministers are likewise described as instruments.[98]

Let us turn now to our author's exposition of Jesus' oration in chapter 17. Often called Jesus' "high priestly prayer" (or, more recently, his "farewell prayer"),[99] this pericope is arguably the New Testament's most prolonged reflection on the role Jesus accords his disciples and their successors in extending his mission. Within it, modern scholars often identify three sections: first, Jesus' prayer for himself (1–5); second, his prayer for his disciples (6–19); and third, his prayer for all who will believe through their word (20–26).[100] Overlooking none of these elements, William sets them within a different framework. As his initial *divisio* makes clear, he understands Jesus' oration to comprise two elements, namely, an intercession for himself and one for his disciples:

> [17:1]*JESUS SPOKE THESE WORDS*. From chapter 14 up to this point, he endeavored to confirm his disciples by a solicitous exhortation, here by a devout prayer for them. Or, first he instructed them by exhortation, here by prayer. According to Chrysostom, it may be said that after admonishing them to have confidence amidst hardships, here he teaches them the way to this confidence, namely, to take refuge in prayer. And because he prayed not out of need but for our example, he prayed for himself first, and for them second, thereby teaching the order or mode of praying: [6]*I HAVE MANIFESTED YOUR NAME....*[101]

Only later, in the context of Jesus' prayer for his disciples, does William mention the category of people who will believe through their word. But here, too, his categories are fluid. By his intervening comments, William suggests that he views himself and his students as belonging to the first group of disciples, as well as the second. After noting that Jesus' preceding discourse was for the instruction of his disciples, he remarks that by his prayer *we* are instructed to pray after preaching:

> Therefore it says: [17:1]*JESUS SPOKE THESE WORDS*, for the instruction of the disciples, *AND LIFTING UP HIS EYES TO HEAVEN*. In this, too, we are instructed to pray after preaching.[102]

Soon afterward, he returns to his presentation of Jesus as the archetype of the preacher, proposing three ways of understanding his glorification of the Father: by his preaching, way of life, working of miracles; by his mandate to preachers; and by his presence to the preaching of the apostles:

> [17:4]*I HAVE GLORIFIED YOU ON EARTH* by my preaching, way of life, working of miracles. Chrysostom: "Rightly does he say *on earth*, because in heaven it had already been glorified and adored by the angels." *THE WORK THAT YOU GAVE ME TO DO*, which is the enlightenment of the peoples, Isaiah 49 (6): *I have given you as a light to the nations; I HAVE*

*FINISHED*, i.e., I will soon finish. Hence, according to Chrysostom, he was finishing what he had already begun. Or, literally, he had already ordered that it be preached. Also, he spoke of this as past to show that he would be present in the preaching of the apostles and the conversion of the peoples.[103]

Worth noting here is William's presupposition of a basic continuity and unity between the knowledge of the various subjects—the Father, Jesus, the disciples immediately present, subsequent disciples, and finally, all other believers.

At the *divisio* introducing the commentary on Jesus' prayer for his disciples, we are once again in a perspective of continuity:

> [17:6]*I HAVE MANIFESTED*. After having prayed for himself, here he prays for his own. And first for his own already believing; second for his own who through the former will believe: [17:20]*NOT FOR THEM ONLY*; third for both, i.e., the latter as well as the former: [17:24]*FATHER, I WILL THAT WHERE I AM, THEY ALSO WHOM YOU HAVE GIVEN ME MAY BE WITH ME.*[104]

Instead of contrasting Jesus' manifestations to his immediate disciples with those to later believers, William passes seamlessly from the first to the second, and then to both. Rather than leaving the impression of a disparity between the disciples and future believers, he suggests that the knowledge of those who accompanied Jesus at the Last Supper is of a piece with the knowledge of his other followers. In the subsequent *divisio* and its aftermath, William explains why this is so:

> [17:20]*NOT FOR THEM ONLY*. After having prayed for his own already existing disciples, here (he prays) for his future ones and those to believe through them. And first he asks as a man; second he implies that he will grant himself the petition as God: [17:22]*AND THE GLORY THAT YOU HAVE GIVEN TO ME, I HAVE GIVEN TO THEM*. In the first, first he shows for whom he asks; second for what he asks: [17:21]*THAT ALL MAY BE ONE*. So it continues: I ask for them, and [17:20]*NOT FOR THEM ONLY DO I ASK*, though first and foremost for them, *BUT ALSO FOR THOSE WHO WILL BELIEVE IN ME THROUGH THEIR WORD*. The word is said to be theirs by utterance, but the Holy Spirit's by inspiration.[105]

If this exposition is not strikingly original, it is notable for what it leaves without emphasis. A passage directly concerned with the mediation of the first disciples could be expected to invite commentary dwelling on the uniqueness of their knowledge, their mediatorial function, and their authority. While such considerations are not entirely absent from his exposition, they are understated by comparison with Bonaventure's[106] and especially with Thomas Aquinas's.[107] In William's perspective, the disciples' role is not negligible, but it is merely verbal; as such, it stands in apposition to the agency of the Holy Spirit. This is not to say that he sets these two dimensions of the divine pedagogy in opposition to one another. To the contrary, he presents them as complementary—the Holy Spirit inspires the word that leads to belief, while the disciples announce it.

Our author's conception of the relationship between the two activities is noticeable in his exposition of an earlier passage, where he further specifies what this involves:

> [14:25]*THESE THINGS I HAVE SPOKEN TO YOU.* Here he promises the confirmation of his sayings by the mission of the Holy Spirit. And first he brings to memory that he has said these things; second he promises that the Holy Spirit will come and teach them more fully: [14:26]*BUT THE PARACLETE. . . .* [14:26]*HE WILL TEACH YOU ALL THINGS,* with respect to the intellect (*intellectum*), which he will enlighten, *AND WILL SUGGEST TO YOU ALL THINGS,* with respect to the affections (*affectum*), which he will set aflame, *WHATEVER I HAVE SAID TO YOU,* indeed, all that is necessary for your salvation.[108]

The Holy Spirit teaches the disciples more fully, not by pouring content into their minds, but by affecting them in two other ways—by elevating both their intellectual and affective capacities. Enlightening their minds and inflaming their hearts, he allows them to understand and love what Christ has revealed to them.[109]

It is clear, then, that if William sees the evangelists and disciples as instruments of divine revelation, he does not consider them puppets. Though merely external, or verbal, their participation proceeds from their knowledge of and free engagement with the subject revealed. William's view of the preachers of his own time is effectively the same—historical differences aside, their knowledge of what they communicate is essentially the same as John the Baptist's and John the Evangelist's, and this because of the identity of the subject they communicate. In this perspective, any differences between the understandings of various disciples or evangelists are circumstantial and, as such, of secondary importance.

## Contemplation

To disciples of any age, William proposes, the proper response to revelation is contemplation. In our earlier comparison of his prologue to John's Gospel with Thomas Aquinas's, we saw that of the two exegetes he is considerably more interested in the details of the Evangelist's biography and less interested in the various aspects of his contemplation. This owes to no general lack of interest on his part in contemplation. It would appear to derive from his highly unified view of revelation—he seems to take for granted that the object of John's contemplation is identical with that of every other believer's. Hardly inconsequential, contemplation is in his perspective both a vital predisposition to revelation and the apposite response to it. This view had a long history in medieval exegesis.[110] More characteristic of thirteenth-century commentary is the description of contemplation as a prerequisite to preaching. Albert the Great does so in his commentary on Luke,[111] as does Bonaventure in a few of his sermons.[112] In the work of Thomas Aquinas, this is a recurring theme.[113]

William frequently relates the two activities, describing contemplation not only as the prelude to the preacher's efforts but also as the sequel. In the following spiritual exposition of the initial verses of Ezekiel's vision, he presents the four evangelists as engaged in contemplation before, during, and after their work. Identifying each with one of the prophecy's four animals, William proposes that they shared a common vision. Likened to the object of that vision, namely, Christ, as William tells us, the evangelists are alike in their holiness:

[115]*AND FROM ITS MIDST THE LIKENESS OF FOUR LIVING CREATURES*, i.e., the four evangelists, who would not have been saints unless they had the likeness of Christ, and first they are described in common, then in particular: *And this was their appearance* etc. And first, it is said that [115]*THE LIKENESS OF A MAN*, both simply and antonomastically, i.e., of Christ, was in them by faith, hope, and charity. Second, that each had a fourfold face. Through the face, by which a person is known, faith: [116]*EACH* then *HAD FOUR FACES* because in all the evangelists there was one announcement of faith with respect to the mystery of the incarnation, passion, resurrection, and ascension. Through the wing, contemplation: [116]*EACH* then *HAD FOUR WINGS* because what they contemplated of the divinity of Christ was the same, namely, the unity of essence and the Trinity of persons. [117]*THEIR FEET WERE STRAIGHT* through the ordering of intentions and affections, Hebrews 12 (13): *Make straight steps with your feet*. [117]*THE SOLE OF THEIR FOOT* through discretion and maturity *SPARKLED* through the instruction and preaching of good example. [118]*THEY HAD THE HANDS OF A MAN UNDER THEIR WINGS* through careful work with contemplation *ON FOUR SIDES*, i.e., the four cardinal virtues. [118]*THEY HAD FOUR FACES AND WINGS ON FOUR SIDES* because they preached Christ's humanity and divinity in the four parts of the world. [119]*THEIR WINGS WERE JOINED TO EACH OTHER* because they had concord and unity in contemplation. [119]*THEY DID NOT TURN WHEN THEY WALKED* in caring for

and recovering temporal things, *BUT EACH ONE WENT STRAIGHT AHEAD* in the quest for heavenly things.[114]

By antonomasia, William explains, the "likeness of a man" in their appearance refers to the likeness of Christ in them by faith, hope, and charity. Further, each one's four faces indicate the unity of each one's awareness of the four central mysteries of the life of Christ—his incarnation, passion, resurrection, and ascension. Similarly, each one's four wings indicate the four realities known by the contemplation of Christ's divinity—the unity of the divine essence, as well as each of the persons of the Trinity. Put simply, the four evangelists' awareness of the central mysteries of Christian faith is one and the same. Whatever one may make of his interpretations, William leaves little room for doubt about his unified conception of the four evangelists' contact with revelation. What is more, as he subtly shifts the mode of exposition from allegory to tropology (at 1:7), he seamlessly extends this same conception to embrace his audience of aspiring preachers—in contemplating the very same mysteries of Christ, they are endowed with virtue and are united with each other. So disposed, they are able to preach to the four corners of the world.

It is clear, then, that in William's understanding of the life of a preacher, a prominent place is occupied by *contemplatio*, which he understands to be the mind's gaze upon God.[115] Yet one may wonder, given the impossibility of seeing God in this life, what precisely this activity involves and how one goes about it. Soon after the exposition just presented, William offers a few precisions. After remarking that it is by the labor of preaching that each of the four animals has the face of an ox, he adds that it is by their contemplation that they have the face of an eagle:

> [1:10]*AND AS FOR THE LIKENESS OF THEIR FACES, THERE WAS THE FACE OF AN OX* through the labor of preaching, Isaiah 2 (4): *They shall beat their swords into plowshears*; Hosea 10 (11): *Judah shall plow and Jacob shall break furrows for himself*; of which there are four wings, touched upon in 2 Timothy 3 (16): *All* Scripture, *divinely inspired, is useful in correcting, in instructing, in teaching, in arguing; AND THE FACE OF AN EAGLE* through the contemplation of the highest things, of which there are four wings, namely, reading, prayer, meditation, and the foretasting of divine sweetness. Reading seeks, prayer knocks, meditation enters, and foretasting finds (cf. Matthew 7:7; Luke 11:9).[116]

The eagle's four wings designate four means to the end of contemplation. All except the last belong to the classical monastic formula: reading, prayer, meditation, and contemplation."[117] While the schema was freely adopted by mendicant friars such as Bonaventure,[118] William's proximate source is most likely Hugh of St. Victor, who also closely associates contemplation with the foretasting of divine sweetness.[119] It will be noted that for Hugh and William, sensory engagement of this sort stands in contrast to the other exercises, which do not strictly belong to contemplation, but are dispositive to it. Thomas Aquinas is of the same view.[120] Shortly we shall see that William is apt to describe contemplation in sensory language. Here it will be noted that he refers to the previous verse in his prologue to *Super Iohannem* specifically to corroborate a remark that John the Evangelist's association with the eagle owes to the height of its flight and the acuity of its vision.[121] It would appear, then, that William's tendency to assimilate the experiences of diverse contemplatives is limited—though all four evangelists and presumably all contemplatives behold the same object, they do so with varying degrees of clarity.

Though the imagery employed in this excerpt might lead us to anticipate an esoteric project, William takes for granted that what he proposes is attainable generally. Shortly we shall see that he considers even the last element, foretasting, to belong to a widely available range of experience. Here we will observe that he understands contemplation to be the clearer vision of previously known truths, not the acquisition of secret mysteries set aside for a privileged few. In his exposition of the pericope of the raising of Lazarus (John 11:33), he says as much in connection with the most famous figure of the contemplative, Mary of Bethany:[122]

> [11:33]*WHEN JESUS SAW HER WEEPING AND THE JEWS WHO CAME WITH HER ALSO WEEPING* out of compassion *HE GROANED IN SPIRIT*, i.e., he was truly sorrowful and disturbed by compassion. . . . Here it is asked why he earlier asked Martha about her faith, but here does not ask Mary about hers. Response: Because (Martha) so became more fervant in faith. Also, according to Chrysostom, in this case many Jews were there; such was not the case earlier. Also, by this he signified that contemplatives see more clearly, hence Leah was bleary eyed, whereas Rachel had a beautiful face and was lovely in appearance (Genesis 29:17).[123]

Following Chrysostom and Bonaventure, William addresses the question of why Jesus did not question Mary about her faith as he had Martha. The problem has been crystallized by a curious difference between the two as they appear here— whereas the paradigmatic contemplative has given no evidence of her faith, Martha, the embodiment of the active life, has just brought forth a confession that medieval exegetes, William included, took to be a model of perfection

(John 11:27).[124] As we shall see in a subsequent examination of this exposition, the source of the first reply is Bonaventure, who explains that Jesus questioned Martha to confirm her faith; presumably, this was unnecessary in Mary's case.[125] The second solution, taken from Chrysostom, explains that the circumstances of the moment made it impossible for Jesus and Mary to have any such conversation.[126] More directly relevant to the present discussion is the third reply, for which William is independent. On this account, Jesus questioned only Martha in order to teach a lesson on the contemplative life, specifically, that it allows for clearer vision. By exempting Mary from inquiry, Jesus indicated that his true identity was already clearly visible to her. By contrast with her more active sister, Mary saw it in her contemplation. To corroborate all of this, William turns to the Book of Genesis, where there appear two other sisters famous for prefiguring activity and contemplation, Laban's daughters Leah and Rachel. For her fatigued eyes and fertility Leah typified the active life, and for her beauty and sterility Rachel typified the contemplative.[127]

True, William imputes neither physical blindness to Leah, nor spiritual blindness to Martha. Nor does he suggest that the active life is shadowy. His point is that contemplation leads to a more acute perception of what is already known, not that it reveals what cannot otherwise be known. All of this underscores two features of his understanding of contemplation that should be kept firmly in mind throughout the following section: he neither considers this mode of perception an alternative to the virtue of faith, nor calls into question the axiom that faith has as its object what is not seen.[128]

## Spiritual Sensation

Independently of his sources, notably Bonaventure, William frequently describes this heightened clarity of perception by employing the language of sensation. In the previous example, it was Mary's superior vision that allowed her to know Jesus well enough to escape inquiry about her faith. And in his account of Ezekiel's vision of four animals, the last of the eagle's four wings is the foretaste of divine sweetness (*diuine dulcedinis pregustatio*). Such language is not rare in his other postills. In the following tropological exposition of Ecclesiastes 9:7–10, presented in the form of a *divisio*, he employs a nearly identical expression to relate tasting to contemplation. After taking Ecclesiastes's command to eat bread and drink wine as an exhortation to contemplation, he divides it into four activities, the last of which is, once again, tasting divine sweetness. Introducing a few variations to the familiar schema for the contemplative life, he combines the first and third elements, reading and meditation, and adds purity of life and cheerfulness of conscience:

*9:7 GO THEN* etc. Up to this point this is to be explained as something good, such that first he exhorts to the joy of contemplation, second to the urgency of action: *9:10 IN WHATEVER YOUR HAND IS ABLE TO DO, WORK URGENTLY.* With respect to the first, he touches upon four points: first, meditation upon Scripture: *9:7 AND EAT YOUR BREAD WITH JOY AND DRINK YOUR WINE WITH GLADNESS;* second, purity of life: *9:8 AT ALL TIMES LET YOUR GARMENTS BE WHITE;* third, cheerfulness of conscience: *9:8 LET NOT OIL FOR YOUR HEAD BE LACKING;* fourth, tasting divine sweetness: *9:9 ENJOY LIFE WITH THE WIFE WHOM YOU LOVE;* fifth, as if concluding he adds a commendation of this state: *9:9 THIS IS YOUR PORTION.* And note the order. The first, in fact, generates the second, Jerome: "Love the study of letters and you will not love the vices of the flesh." The second generates the third, 2 Corinthians 1 (12): *Our glory is this, the testimony of our conscience.* The third generates the fourth, Proverbs 15 (15): *A secure mind is like a continual feast.* With respect to action, he teaches three things, specifically, to work usefully: *9:10 IN WHATEVER,* because James 2 (10): *Whoever keeps the whole law but offends in one point has become guilty of all of it;* and corporeally, through oneself, not through others: *9:10 YOUR HAND,* Psalm (80:7): *His hands had served in baskets;* and also to *9:10 WORK URGENTLY* and quickly, Galatians 6 (9): *Let us not grow weary of doing good.*[129]

While this exposition contains elements proper to William, in its broader perspective it has much in common with the aforementioned monastic prescription. As do his predecessors, William situates contemplation within the context of a way of life comprising specific activities and finds a biblical basis for each of them. He is also on familiar ground in describing contemplation with the language of seeing and tasting God. Though he has borrowed these remarks from no one, he has a biblical basis for them, as well as abundant precedent in the Latin commentatorial tradition.[130] All the same, in view of what has been said about the impossibility of seeing God, one could wonder whether he uses such terms as mere metaphors for the knowledge of faith or for describing some sort of quasi-sensory experience. On the face of it, the texts cited are susceptible of either interpretation—while William would appear to have real experiences in mind, he relates seeing and tasting to faith closely enough to suggest that they are metaphors for it. Of course, more than a few biblical passages warrant such interpretations. That William realizes as much is evident in his comments on Jesus' remark that the world cannot receive the Holy Spirit because it cannot see him. William takes the world's blindness as a metaphor for its lack of faith—it cannot see because it does not believe:

*14:17THE SPIRIT OF TRUTH . . . WHOM THE WORLD*, i.e., the lovers of the world as long as they are such, because they have been filled from another source, *CANNOT RECEIVE, BECAUSE IT NEITHER SEES HIM* within by faith *NOR KNOWS HIM* without by works.[131]

It was not unusual at the time to describe faith as a kind of interior vision.[132] Yet in his comments on the rest of the verse, William seems intent on describing the disciples' knowledge of God as involving something more than the assent of belief. He explains their knowledge of the Holy Spirit as a kind of sensory experience—by an interior sense they are able to savor him:

> *14:17BUT YOU WILL KNOW HIM*, specifically, within by an interior sense and a certain experiential taste, and without by visible signs, *BECAUSE HE WILL ABIDE WITH YOU*, regarding his exterior effect, *AND WILL BE IN YOU*, regarding his interior one.[133]

William describes two analogous kinds of sensation: with respect to the third of the Trinity, the disciples enjoy two parallel perceptive capacities providing two kinds of experience, one external and the other internal. Thus he accounts for the disciples' experience of each of the two modes of the Holy Spirit's mission to the created order, visibly—such as on the day of Pentecost—and invisibly, in the daily inspiration of the minds of believers.[134]

The Spirit is not the only member of the Trinity subject to spiritual perception. In connection with John the Baptist's claim to have seen and testified that Jesus is the Son of God, our author remarks that this vision was twofold, engaging a bodily eye and a spiritual one:

> *1:34AND I SAW* by a corporeal eye and a spiritual one *AND GAVE TESTIMONY . . . THAT THIS IS THE SON OF GOD*, the only one, hence he is able to baptize with authority.[135]

It is no coincidence that this double vision corresponds to the two missions of the Son, one visible, by the incarnation—and the other invisible, by his entrance into the souls of believers.[136]

But sight is not the only sense involved. Hearing is the operative mode of spiritual sensation in William's exposition of Jesus' remark that all who hear and learn from the Father come to him (John 6:45)—those who come to Jesus have heard the Father in a way that would seem not to be merely metaphorical. Lest anyone wonder how the various spiritual senses differ from and relate to one another, William offers a clarification in his comment on the following verse's affirmation that no one but the Son has seen God:

And note that he says: [6:45]*EVERYONE WHO HEARS*, and afterwards: [6:46]*NOT THAT ANYONE HAS SEEN* . . . because even though spiritual vision and hearing do not differ from one another, vision properly regards the speaker, while hearing regards the speech of the speaker. And even though someone who perceives the Father's inspiration sees as well as hears it, he does not see the one inspiring because hearing does not regard him, but his effect.[137]

He makes clear that spiritual hearing and vision (and presumably the other spiritual senses as well) indicate the same reality—a certain perception of God—while they differ in their connotations. On his account, the Gospel denies the possibility of seeing God because vision implies direct perception, while it affirms the possibility of hearing him because this implies the perception of his effect.

Still, one could wonder whether perception of this sort really differs from faith, and if so, how. For William, the difference is clear. In the following exposition of John 12:45, he takes Jesus' remarks about seeing the Father as a description of spiritual vision, not as a metaphor for faith. He also explains how they differ—spiritual vision is fixed directly upon its object, namely, God, whereas faith has to do with tangential matters:

> [12:45]*WHOEVER SEES ME* spiritually *SEES HIM WHO SENT ME*. The reason is the unity of essence, below chapter 14 (9): *Whoever sees me sees the Father*. And it should be noted that spiritual vision differs from faith, because vision is directed properly to a substance, and faith to the condition or circumstance of a substance (*circumstantiam substantie*). Hence spiritual vision is fixed on God, faith on what is about God.[138]

Conspicuous here is a difference between William's understanding of faith and Thomas Aquinas's. By *circumstantiam substantie*, our author in all likelihood refers to matters such as Scripture and the church's doctrinal formulations, which call for the believer's faithful assent. According to Thomas, such matters are the virtue's secondary material object, while its primary material object and formal object are none other than God. Though Thomas treats the matter at some length in a few of his earlier works,[139] no awareness of these positions is in evidence here.

The prior excerpt makes clear that William regards spiritual sensation as a means of perceiving God. It is worth considering, then, how he understands this to occur. This question is not without important implications for biblical interpretation, as the preceding examples of his discussions of contemplation suggest. As well as illustrating his conception of the spiritual senses, they provide context for understanding a few aspects of his exegetical method. In particular, they afford us a framework within which to explore his use of biblical citations in his spiritual expositions. No mere proof texts, these verses are generally well selected for the purpose of exciting the imaginations of his students, who, from the liturgy as well as their studies, would likely have been quite familiar with them.

Also in evidence in the previous excerpt is a close correspondence between William's conception of the experiences of prophets on the one hand and those of contemplatives on the other. In each case, he employs the language of sensation, all the while drawing attention to the interiority of the experience. It should be noted that he does not always treat the two categories as inescapably separate. While repeatedly referring to John the Baptist as a prophet, he mentions that it was in his contemplation that he saw Jesus' two natures. Then again, the spiritual eyes with which John the Baptist, John the Evangelist, and Martha saw Jesus' divinity bring to mind the eyes of the heart (*occulis cordis*) at work in the prophetic visions of Abraham, Isaiah, Jeremiah, and Ezekiel. In all of these cases, the operative perceptive faculty is the imagination, which suggests that for our author, prophecy and spiritual sensation are very much alike.

And yet there are a few important differences. With respect to prophecy, William occasionally leaves open the possibility of perception by nonimaginary modes, that is, physical sensation and direct intellection, and he invariably assumes that the initiative is entirely God's. Spiritual sensation, on the other hand, he generally associates with contemplation, an endeavor he understands to presuppose certain human initiatives, such as reading and meditation. Among his various purposes for idealizing such activities, one is particularly germane to the matter at hand—to propose them as a means of transforming and elevating the mind's grasp of the imagination.

Neither William nor his contemporaries provided a theoretical account for spiritual sensation that would permit a detailed comparison of their thoughts on the matter. Yet William and Thomas appear to differ on a key point—the means to the attainment of such sensation. Whereas William discusses perception of this kind with reference to the visible missions of both the Son and the Spirit, and occasionally without explicit reference to either, Thomas mentions it exclusively in connection with Jesus Christ. On his view, it is only through the Incarnate Word that there is any seeing, hearing, smelling, tasting, or touching of the Divine Essence or any of the members of the Trinity. What follows is an example from his prologue to John's Gospel, where he depicts the Evangelist's vision of the First and Second of the Trinity by the eyes of the heart and of the mind:

> Flying like an eagle above the cloud of human weakness, John gazes upon the light of immutable Truth with the acutest and firmest eyes of the heart. And looking upon the divinity itself of our Lord Jesus Christ, by

which he is equal to the Father, he has endeavored principally to commend this in his Gospel, to the extent that he believed sufficient for people. And about this flight of John it says in Job 39 (27): *Will the eagle,* i.e., John, *soar up at your command?* And below (29): *His eyes watch from far away* because the Word of God himself is seen in the bosom of the Father by the eye of the mind.[140]

To be sure, both Thomas and William understand spiritual sensation to involve the imagination, and both limit the imagination to the realm of the corporeal— *Nothing except a body can fall into the imagination*, as Thomas puts it.[141] Their understanding of this kind of perception is not that it allows the imagination to grasp any reality that is essentially incorporeal, but that it provides images to the graced mind, thus allowing it to know God. By contrast with William, however, Thomas understands all sensation of God to begin with some image of Christ's humanity.

Still, the common features of their understandings are worth keeping in mind. Both refrain from describing the spiritual senses as new powers of the soul, while both regard spiritual sensation as a mode of perception different from faith on the one hand and bodily sensation on the other. Both, moreover, dwell on it in their biblical exegesis to come to terms with a basic conundrum presented by the Old and New Testaments, to wit, explaining how believers, formed as they are by sense and imagination, can aspire to union with the God who utterly transcends the sensate world.

During the twentieth century, a renewal of interest in theological aesthetics brought this problem considerable attention, notably in the thought of Hans Urs von Balthasar[142] and Karl Rahner.[143] Even if their methods differ too greatly from William's, and from each other's, to permit a detailed discussion of their work, a brief look at their views on spiritual sensation may help us to determine whether William shares common ground with them, and if so, where.[144]

Let us begin with Balthasar. Central to his theological project is the reaffirmation of the religious significance of sensation and imagination. He claims that Christian thought has generally tended to depreciate these two faculties as media of divine revelation out of favoritism for a Platonic anthropology, and this notwithstanding the corrective influences of Aristotle and scholasticism. On his view, the influence of Platonism may be blamed for the adoption of a generalized dualism between sense and spirit, which has led to a negation of sensation and imagination. All of this, he observes, is foreign to the biblical image of man as a single organism.[145] He proposes that if the senses are the medium of all knowledge, they must be spiritualized in faith to mediate transcendent reality. In other words, he calls for thinking of religious experience as perceiving the nonsensible sensibly. Toward the end of providing such an account of sensation, he develops a theological anthropology wherein the believer is radically reconstituted by faith in harmony with its object, Jesus Christ, the humanly visible form of God's decisive self-revelation. Human nature is so transformed in faith, on his view, that the intellect is capacitated to receive the forms of grace, with the result that the intellect's subordinate powers of willing, imagining, and sensing are similarly transformed.[146] His purpose in explaining faith as an experience that engages all the believer's faculties is to save religious experience from the inhuman extreme of the purely spiritual, which would negate sensation, without falling into the opposite extreme of reducing religious experience to pure sensation, which on his view would make of it a myth. As he would have it, faith manifests its divine object to sensation by elevating human nature in all its capacities.[147]

Balthasar's relevance to our discussion lies in his understanding of the Latin tradition of biblical exegesis. While he contends that even the Aristotelian and scholastic correctives to Platonism are dominated by the silent a priori of the Platonic image of the human person, he asserts that the church's great theologians, such as Augustine and Thomas Aquinas, accept as a fact without fully understanding speculatively "something like a certain center" between the two extremes of spiritual experience he mentions. This "center" he describes as the result of a "Christianization" of devout bodily senses in conformity with the sensibility of Jesus and Mary.[148] To this effect, he cites two texts, one from Augustine's *Confessiones*[149] and the other from Aquinas's *Expositio super ad Philippenses* (2:2).[150] In the first, Augustine describes his own spiritual sensation of Christ, and in the second, Thomas expatiates on Paul's exhortation to the Philippians to sense and experience after the fashion of Christ. For Balthasar, both expositions stand as examples of theology well practiced. He proposes that Augustine and Thomas, despite their philosophical commitments, have subscribed to the biblical view of man as a concrete and indivisible reality, not a soul wed to a body.[151]

Markedly different from the preceding is the perspective of Karl Rahner, who considers any solution elaborated along such lines empirically untenable.[152] Rahner, moreover, understands the world of sensate being to belong to the realm of grace. Nature, in his view, is a moment within the concretely existing world of grace. Accordingly, he sees no essential difference between the assent to general revelation (the "natural" method of philosophy, in other words, metaphysics as it studies being) and the explicit act of faith assenting to categorical revelation (expressed in the Old and New Testaments). Because he understands both metaphysics and faith to belong to the realm of grace, he sees no need for faith to reconstitute sensation to allow it to aspire to the realm of the transcendent.[153] Hence, he understands the spiritual senses as acts of the graced intellect and will independent of the body, not as acts of devout bodily senses transformed by grace. Independent as it is from corporeal reality, spiritual sensation, as he conceives of it, need not be elaborated along the lines of the five bodily senses and can be described more clearly in other language. As a consequence, he tells us, even when the metaphors used to describe it are drawn from the ambit of the senses, spiritual sensation fails to provide any new understanding.[154]

The diverse conceptions of Balthasar and Rahner, briefly outlined here, have much to recommend them, and it lies beyond our purposes either to defend or to reconcile them. Ours is the more limited project of determining how, if at all, they coincide with William's thought on the matter. Toward this end, we would do well to consider what the available evidence tells us about his understanding of the intellective soul's capacity for spiritual sensation.

Perhaps the best way to begin is by recalling that in his remarks on the spiritual senses William sets the bodily and spiritual modes of sensation in opposition to one another, making clear that the former cannot attain to God while the latter can. Though such claims cannot be taken to represent a systematic development of the matter, they suffice to show that he does not have in mind the elevation of an indivisible capacity for sensation, but the use of two different capacities. Not found in his work is any suggestion that any bodily capacity can either be the subject of grace or be elevated by it. To the contrary, he views the infusion and operation of grace as an altogether nonphysical and spiritual affair.

At work here are anthropological presuppositions that are neither Platonic nor Aristotelian. One place where William reveals his thoughts on what it means to be human is his commentary on the prologue to John's Gospel, where he succinctly sets aside several heretical understandings of the Incarnation:

> *AND THE WORD WAS MADE FLESH,* i.e., united to the flesh by the approach of the flesh to him. He is said to be united to flesh rather than to the soul to show his great humility and tenderness. Also, because of heretics denying this. It does not say "man," but *flesh,* because "man" resonates "person" more than *flesh* does. It says *Word* rather than "Son" to exclude a carnal understanding (cf. John 8:5). *AND DWELT AMONG US (in nobis),* in our nature. Or, in our midst (*inter nobis,* cf. Acts 1:21). Or, with us (*nobiscum,* cf. Matthew 1:23), in us by faith and grace.[155]

Though the appearance of the terms *flesh* (*carni*) and *soul* (*anime*) may suggest otherwise, William is not proposing here a Platonic doctrine of body and soul as formally integral substances. To the contrary, he is preoccupied to show that they are not two entities, but two aspects of one entity—man (*homo*)—as is evident in his successive confutations of various Christological errors.

First among them is monophysitism. Implicit in the opening statement that the Word was united to flesh is the denial that he was metamorphosed into it. Absurd in view of God's immutability, such a transformation would do violence to the integrity of Christ's humanity. During the Middle Ages, this doctrine was generally assigned to the fifth-century figure Eutyches.[156] Without naming him, William here contradicts him by affirming, albeit implicitly, the doctrine that the Incarnation left Christ's divine and human natures unaltered and distinct.

The immediate target of his next remark would appear to be either Arius or Apollinarius, whose names have traditionally been associated with the denial of Christ's human soul.[157] Against them, William explains that the Word is said to be made flesh not for the sake of denying the completeness of the humanity assumed, but for better expressing the humility and piety of the Incarnation.

Then he makes use of the same term by pointing out that it precludes another misreading—the denial of his corporality by certain heretics. Numerous heretical groups have at various times been associated with such a doctrine, and this reference could apply to any one of them or to all of them generally. Yet William most likely has in mind here the same group to which he usually refers when mentioning *hereticos*, the Manicheans.[158]

Then, setting his sights on a fourth heresy, he explains that the Evangelist has not said that the Word became man (*homo*) because this would have suggested that the second of the Trinity assumed a person (*personam*). By this remark, William intends to refute the teaching of Nestorius, to whom the doctrine of a twofold personhood in Christ has generally been credited.[159] Worth noting here is what this account presupposes—the understanding that with respect to everyone other than Christ, the unity of body and soul designated by the term *homo* is a person. As employed by William, *persona* is no mere term of convenience signifying a vague commonality between the members of the Trinity on the one hand and members of the human race on the other. By making the point that the Word did not assume a person, William takes for granted that with respect to both of these classes, the term designates an individual subject.

Even as restricted to mere mortals, such a concept of *persona* (or its Greek counterpart πρόσωπον) lies in uncharted territory for Aristotle, as well as Plato.[160] What is more, though his usage of the terms *soul* and *flesh* is of a sort that has often been qualified as dualist, this characterization scarcely does justice to the true wellspring of his thought. Positively considered, his anthropology conforms neither to Plato's nor to Aristotle's, but to the one that resulted from the Christological controversies—the humanity assumed by the Word is a unity of body and soul, which for every member of the human race save this one constitutes a person. It would appear, then, that however enthusiastic his appropriation of Greek thought may have been, William's speculations on the human condition are marked by a deliberate fidelity to his received tradition, namely, the thought of the Christian Latin West.

But there remains another observation to be made from the last example. In his final proposals for understanding the Word's dwelling among believers, William puts forward three alternatives corresponding to three modes of his presence: first, his assumption of a human nature; second, his living of a human life with other human beings; and third, his interior presence to the individual believer—by faith and grace. His close association of the two suggests that William understands grace to result in belief, not experience. Support for this view is not difficult to find elsewhere. To return once again to his exposition of Jesus' encounter with the woman at the well (John 4:10), he tells us that the living water Jesus offers is the grace of the Holy Spirit, which cleanses from sin and vivifies spiritually:

> [4:10] *JESUS ANSWERED AND SAID TO HER*, humbly, not in exasperation, *IF YOU KNEW THE GIFT OF GOD*, i.e., the grace worked in the world in this time . . . *AND WHO IT IS THAT SAYS TO YOU: GIVE ME A DRINK*, i.e., me, through whom this grace is worked and the Holy Spirit given, *PERHAPS YOU WOULD HAVE ASKED HIM*, suggesting freedom of choice, *AND HE WOULD HAVE GIVEN YOU LIVING WATER*, the grace of the Holy Spirit washing away sins and vivifying spiritually.[161]

Implied by this commentary, as well as by the biblical text itself, is an opposition between the effects of the water spoken of by Jesus and those of the water the woman has in mind. The vivification and purification worked by the grace of the Holy Spirit is altogether spiritual. The same is true of the liberty given by grace:

> [4:14] *BUT THE WATER I WILL GIVE HIM WILL BECOME IN HIM A FOUNTAIN OF WATER SPRINGING UP*, i.e., making spring up, *INTO ETERNAL LIFE*. Grace, in fact, moves freedom of choice to meritorious works through which eternal life is had.[162]

There is no suggestion here that grace has any liberating effect with respect to any sort of physical limitation—it moves the capacity for choice. And so forth. William considers the believer's assimilation to God by grace a spiritual affair, not a corporeal one. From all of this it seems reasonable to conclude that if "spiritual sensation" is taken to signify the acts of the bodily senses elevated by grace, then no such doctrine is to be found in the thought of William.[163]

If, however, by "spiritual sense" we mean the spiritual dimension of an act of a body-soul unity, then our author does indeed have something to say. He views *homo* as a single entity, albeit a multifaceted one (as we see, for example, in his frequent recourse to the opposition between what is external and what is internal, or between what is corporeal and what is spiritual). Put another way, he understands human complexity to involve no real multiplicity, notwithstanding the real distinctions he sees between the body and the soul, and within the soul, between the intellect and the will.

Though he has left us no comprehensive epistemology, William has given us good reason to conclude that he was no empiricist, at least in the strict sense—he did not question the knowability of purely immaterial realities. One place where he discusses the human capacity for knowing spiritual realities is his exposition of Ecclesiastes's remark (Ecclesiastes 1:8) that all things are difficult and inexplicable. Differentiating between three classes of realities—corporeal, spiritual, and divine—he qualifies their perceptibility as difficult, more difficult, and most difficult:

> [1:8]*ALL THINGS ARE DIFFICULT* to know, Wisdom 9 (16): *With difficulty we guess what is on earth, and with labor we find what is before us, but who will search out what is in heaven?* Corporeal things are difficult; spiritual things more difficult, because in 1 Corinthinans 2 (14): *The natural man does not perceive the things that are of the Spirit of God*; and divine things most difficult, Romans 11 (33): *O the depth of the riches of the wisdom and knowledge of God!* To the contrary: Some things are easy to know, such as sensible things, about which the senses are infallible. Response: It is easy to know these things imperfectly with respect to their species and shape, yet it is difficult to know them perfectly with respect to their substance, virtue, operation and cause, because our cognition begins in sensation, from which a thing's virtue and cause are remote. Hence in Wisdom 9 (16) it says: *With difficulty we guess* etc. And because they are difficult, *MAN CANNOT EXPLAIN THEM IN WORDS*, Ecclesiasticus 18 (2): *Who is able to declare his works?* To speak of them is in some way possible, but to explain them, i.e., to express their hidden reasons (*latentes eorum rationes*), is possible only to those who understand them perfectly, and they are few.[164]

Recognizable here is the influence of Aristotle, notably, in the remarks concerning the infallibility of the senses,[165] the origin of all knowledge in the senses,[166] and the increasing difficulty of knowing realities that are increasingly removed from the senses.[167] Broadly similar passages are not rare in the work of Thomas Aquinas,[168] yet William's proximate source here is Bonaventure, as may be surmised by the final remark concerning the understanding of difficult realities by way of the understanding and expression of "their hidden reasons."[169] In this perspective, the sensation of material realities involves more than a simple physical reaction; it has an intentional dimension as well. What these comments will not allow us to determine is how our author understands the soul to be related to the body and, more concretely, whether he understands the power of sensation to reside in the body,[170] the soul,[171] or the composite of body and soul.[172]

Still, it seems clear that William's understanding of spiritual sensation does not presuppose devout bodily senses that have been transformed to resemble the sensitivity of Jesus and of Mary. Certainly, in his accounts of contemplation, he calls for a transformation, and in so doing refers to sensation. Yet this is the sensation—analogically understood—of a transformed mind. It is the elevation of the intellect and will by grace. It is also safe to say that he is not describing distinct intellectual capacities that correspond analogically to the corporeal senses. His approach, therefore, is to be confused neither with Balthasar's nor with Rahner's.

On the other hand, a few important questions must for the moment be left open. The present evidence provides no sure grounds for determining whether William's understanding of the role of sensory images in perception is more akin to Bonaventure's or to Thomas Aquinas's. It will be recalled that that for the Franciscan they serve as mnemonic devices in the service of the reminiscence of innate ideas,[173] whereas for the Dominican they are indispensable to all intellection this side of the grave (about which we shall have more to say).[174] Nothing in the excerpts presented here is patently irreconcilable with either view. While the previous citation points toward Bonaventure, William's remarks on spiritual sensation and contemplation generally have not been borrowed from him and do not appear to derive from his thought.

Then again, we are not without a few indications pointing toward the position of Thomas. William at times leaves the impression that he regards images as revelatory, albeit imperfectly and indirectly. A case in point appears in his exposition of Jesus' remark that the Father will show him greater deeds (John 5:20). A difficulty has arisen from the implication that any such demonstration must involve temporality, as well as nescience, within the Trinity. Augustine recognized the problem and discussed it at length, explaining this demonstration, first, as the Father's eternal generation of the Son; second, as his demonstration to Christ's members; and third, as his demonstration to Christ in his humanity.[175] Passing over most of Augustine's exposition, William offers two brief replies, the first of which rests on an implied distinction between divine agency within the Trinity (*ad intra*) and without (*ad extra*), the former being eternal in every respect, the latter involving causality and temporality. He explains, first, that the implication of succession refers not to the Father's self-communication to the Son, but to his works (in the created order). His second solution is basically a synopsis of Augustine's latter two—Christ will be the mediator of the Father's demonstration to the audience at hand, and this so that all may wonder:

> [5:20] *AND GREATER WORKS THAN THESE . . . WILL HE SHOW HIM.* Therefore the Father shows some things successively to the Son. Response: With respect to the Father there is no succession, but there is with respect to his works, of which one precedes another. Or, *HIM*, i.e., you through him, *THAT YOU MAY WONDER* at their magnitude, Chrysostom: "Wonder is stupor before a great phantasm."[176]

William has inserted an interesting definition: wonder (*admiratio*) is stupor brought on by a great phantasm, that is, an apparition. His attribution of it to Chrysostom was mistaken; it originated in Nemesius of Emesa's *De natura hominis*[177] and was restated in John Damascene's *De fide orthodoxa*.[178] Since both works circulated widely at the time (the former under the name of Gregory of Nyssa), either could have been William's source. Yet the confusion is understandable. All three writers were Syrians (Chrysostom and Nemesius were near contemporaries), and their works took similar paths into the Latin West. As had Chrysostom's *Homilies* on John, the *De natura hominis* and the *De fide orthodoxa* won wide influence there after having been translated from Greek into Latin by Burgundio of Pisa.[179] What is more, all three writers represented a school of thought (despite Nemesius's Neoplatonism), to be called here "Antiochene," whose understanding of contemplation (or *theoria*) diverged from the Augustinian tradition represented by Bonaventure. While a complete account of this divergence lies beyond our purposes, a few key points are worth keeping in mind. To begin, in the Antiochene perspective, the divine nature, as transcendent and infinite, is formless and objectively invisible. Hence, there can be no question of the beatific vision, even for the angels and saints. Further, in this life and in the next, divine revelation takes place by way of sensory images, the reception of which takes place in contemplation, or *theoria*. For Chrysostom and Damascene alike, *theoria* usually denotes the visual grasp of divinely revealed reality.[180] As such, it is the correlative of divine condescension to the human condition—it effects the contemplative's ascent (*anabasis*) to the divine.[181]

   It hardly needs to be said that Thomas Aquinas does not subscribe to the whole of this doctrine—in the aftermath of the condemnations of 1241, no right-thinking theologian could. But then he does not discard the whole of it, either. Leaving no doubt about the impossibility of an image containing the divine nature, and making clear that human intellection does not terminate in a sense image (i.e., phantasm), he holds that sensible images manifest God's existence and, analogically, his nature.[182] In advancing his famous explanation that this is by causality, excess, and remotion, Thomas cites an authority whose background is not without relevance to the matter at hand—Dionysius the Areopagite. Making allowance for the other influences at work in the latter's thought, on this point he may also be considered a representative of the Antiochene view.[183] To return to Damascene, specifically in connection with human perception, Thomas invokes his definition of wonder in several writings, two of which are anterior to William's regency.[184]

Whatever one may make of this as evidence for William's kinship with Thomas on the role of the imagination in contemplation, it is reasonable to conclude that he consistently relates spiritual sensation and contemplation to various salutary activities, particularly *lectio, meditatio*, and *predicatio*, in order to have his readers employ their imaginations to call forth images upon which their minds may dwell. It would appear that he understands the imagination to serve the same end as biblical metaphor—to signify to the mind elevated by grace the divine essence that can neither be seen, nor imagined, nor comprehended. This construal finds support in his predilection for the biblical text's literal sense—if the images expressed therein are inherently revelatory, one need not search for their meaning in other realities prefigured by them. Even his pervasive citation of biblical references suggests as much. Whether in the service of literal or spiritual interpretations, they often convey vivid images. More than to score points in arguments, these references serve to animate the imaginations of his students. While he offers no theoretical justification for his use of such sensory metaphors, William takes for granted that sensation is indispensable to knowledge of the material realm, which he seems to consider the medium of divine revelation. By applying such language to God, he acknowledges that theological language can ultimately be drawn from no source other than the senses.

None of this is to say that William favors metaphorical language over literal—both modes of speaking about God are constant features of his exegesis. Showing no general preference for one over the other, he employs each as a valid, albeit analogical, mode of signification. As he indicates in the final remark of his exposition of Ecclesiastes 1:8, he does not view entrance into the mystery of God as presupposing a transition from literal to metaphorical speech, or vice versa. For William, it is a movement beyond language entirely.

## Evangelical Poverty

One would expect to find William particularly revealing of his own theological interests when discussing matters that were controversial during his own time. So it is with his comments on the ideal of evangelical poverty, which during the period emerged as a subject of such sharp dispute that differing attitudes toward it became emblematic of the differences between the Franciscan and Dominican orders. The issue had been brought to the fore by the antimendicant quarrel of the 1250s, when a number of secular masters at the University of Paris, notably William of Saint-Amour, launched a series of attacks on the mendicant orders' prerogatives to teach and exercise pastoral care within the university.[185] At the heart of the charges was the claim that the mendicant poverty practiced by the two orders was incompatible with the Gospel. Faced with this accusation, Franciscans and Dominicans alike were compelled to reflect on the ideal of poverty and to elaborate a defense of it. Making allowance for the inevitable differences between the views of various individuals, each order's response was largely a collective enterprise. Bonaventure was the principal exponent of the Franciscans' cause,[186] Thomas Aquinas of the Dominicans."[187]

Though the details of the initial dispute need not detain us, it is worth pointing out that by the time William of Alton incepted as regent master, three years had passed since papal intervention had decided the matter in the favor of the friars.[188] It had been settled, temporarily, only to return in another phase in 1269.[189] In the meantime, evangelical poverty remained a matter of debate, with the Franciscans and Dominicans becoming ever more entrenched in their positions, which became increasingly distant from each other. It has been observed that the divisions between the two orders' positions were sharpest whenever the question of poverty had ecclesiological or Christological implications.[190] Such implications are conspicuous in the discussions of Bonaventure, Thomas Aquinas, and William of Alton. All of them related the matter to the three evangelical counsels, then as now generally understood to be the basis of religious life, and this because they were ordered toward the imitation and following of Christ.

For Bonaventure, poverty took clear precedence over the other two counsels, chastity and obedience. A key feature of the approach he and his fellow Franciscans pursued was the tendency to view evangelical poverty, both individual and communal, as inherently good and perfective. As encapsulated by the Franciscan ideal of *altissima paupertas*, the poverty of Christ and his disciples was taken by them as an absolute ideal to be embraced by anyone seeking Christian perfection. The more extreme exponents of this view espoused it in such a manner as to exclude from the *uia perfectionis* not only the laity but also bishops and monks.

Similarly excluded by the Franciscan ideal were the Dominicans, whose practices placed them in a particular situation with respect to all the controversy's other parties. Whereas both mendicant orders differed from bishops, secular clergy, and laity in renouncing individual wealth, and from monks in renouncing revenue-bearing communal property, Dominicans parted company with Franciscans by refusing to renounce the corporate ownership of their convents. As a result, they were obliged to defend their way of life on several fronts. Also relevant to the Dominicans' approach to the problem was their formula of profession—it makes explicit mention only of obedience, taking poverty and chastity as implied therein.[191] Given this state of affairs, espousing poverty as an absolute ideal was for them all but impossible, theoretically as well as practically. Taking the Franciscan position would have involved conceding that their own way of life was defective, that is, incompatible with the *uia perfectionis*. It would have required their consigning themselves to mediocrity.

Epitomizing the Dominicans' response, Thomas Aquinas parts company with Bonaventure by holding that poverty is perfective only insofar as it is animated by charity.[192] He ranks obedience as the most important of the three counsels, and poverty as the least.[193] True, it would be easy to assess this position as a sign of partisanship in the rivalry between the orders of the two theologians, but Thomas's rationale for it cannot be dismissed as artificial. While he offers several reasons in his various works, his primary one rests on the nature of what is offered to God by obedience—that which is most interior, namely, the will. By chastity, he says, what is offered is less interior, namely, the body; and by poverty, what is offered is altogether exterior, namely, possessions. On his view, evangelical perfection essentially consists in the following of Christ, not in poverty. As a consequence, he holds poverty to be conducive to perfection only insofar as it removes impediments to virtue, notable among which is anxiety for worldly goods (*sollicitudo temporalium*). As a further consequence, he asserts that an order given to contemplation and preaching, after the fashion of Christ and his disciples, fittingly holds in common such modest possessions as are necessary for their way of life.[194]

The preceding sketches of the divergent Franciscan and Dominican positions were only a part of much larger debate, in which both orders occupied common ground in holding to a way of life distinct from that of the monks, on the one hand, and that of the secular masters, on the other. The prolonged dispute's ecclesial, political, economic, and social dimensions have by now been well documented. More germane to the present inquiry is the matter of biblical interpretation. Not surpisingly, every party involved sought a biblical basis for its position and took for granted that it could find one. Much of the debate turned on the construal of a few key verses, yet context for comments on evangelical poverty could be provided by a remarkably broad range of passages. This may be illustrated by the polemical interest discernible in William's comments on Lamentations 5:2, where he takes a passing shot at the extravagance of monks. Judah's lost inheritance, he tells us, may be taken as an image of monks who squander their inheritance by their immoderate spending:

⁵¹²*OUR INHERITANCE . . . HAS BEEN TURNED OVER TO STRANGERS*, i.e., to Chaldeans, *OUR HOMES TO FOREIGNERS*, i.e., to Romans. Morally: This is about monks by way of their excessive expenses.¹⁹⁵

It hardly needs to be said that monks, friars, and seculars alike found the perfection and ideal of Christian life in Christ. Little agreement, however, surrounded the questions of whether Christ could be described as poor, and if so, how. This issue eventually became a point of departure between seculars and mendicants, Dominicans and Franciscans, and most particularly, between Conventual and Spiritual Franciscans. In the exegesis of Bonaventure, William, and Thomas Aquinas alike, it is not uncommon to find an eagerness to show that Christ was poor. Their comments on the multiplication of loaves in John's Gospel will serve to illustrate. The *Glossa* is silent about the matter here, as are Hugh of St. Cher and Albert the Great, yet Bonaventure finds evidence of Jesus' poverty in Phillip's remark to Jesus that two hundred *denarii* would not buy enough food to feed the crowd (John 6:7). (See table 5.1.) William follows suit, as does Thomas Aquinas, perhaps after having glanced at William's commentary (boldface has been applied to show literary correspondence).¹⁹⁶

This example reflects the debate in a fairly early stage. One notices what the three commentators have in common—a lively concern to draw attention to the poverty of Christ. If at the time Franciscans and Dominicans were ideologically

Table 5.1  John 6:7: *PHILIP ANSWERED HIM: TWO HUNDRED DENARII OF BREAD IS NOT ENOUGH FOR EACH OF THEM TO GET A LITTLE.*

| Bonaventure (*Opera*, t. VI, 319a–b) | William of Alton (MS Saint-Omer 260, f. 131vb) | Thomas Aquinas (ed. Parma, t. X, 403a) |
| --- | --- | --- |
| *PHILIP ANSWERED HIM: TWO HUNDRED DENARII OF BREAD IS NOT ENOUGH FOR EACH OF THEM TO GET A LITTLE*, **and so a great sum was necessary, and they were poor and did not even have a little**; they had left everything. . . . | *PHILIP ANSWERED HIM: TWO HUNDRED DENARII OF BREAD*, i.e.: how many can be had for two hundred denarii? *IS NOT ENOUGH* for eating *FOR EACH OF THEM TO GET A LITTLE*. **In this Philip suggests that he does not have that many denarii; he also suggests the poverty of Christ.** | *TWO HUNDRED DENARII OF BREAD IS NOT ENOUGH FOR EACH OF THEM*, which we do not have, and therefore we are not able to give them anything to eat. **In this is suggested the poverty of Christ, who did not even have two hundred denarii.** |

opposed over the matter, one would never know it from these comments. In evidence here is William's tendency to lift relevant comments from Bonaventure, all the while retaining his freedom to modify them.

Further illustration appears in William's handling of a few of Solomon's remarks about wealth—the lover of riches reaps no fruit from them; they attract those who would devour them; they serve only to delight the eyes (Ecclesiastes 5:9–10). The passage would seem to invite comments in keeping with a radical point of view, yet his construal is evenhanded, as is that of his immediate source, Bonaventure. William borrows from the Franciscan the substance of a question and its reply, yet not before specifying that Solomon is not talking about just any lover of riches, but the one who loves them in a disordered manner. By contrast with his Franciscan mentor, he is concerned to point out that wealth can be loved in a good way. Further, whereas Bonaventure allows that riches are useful to the one who uses them well,[197] William does not hesitate to call them good:

> [5:9]*THE ONE WHO LOVES RICHES* inordinately *WILL REAP NO FRUIT* understand that he will not even sustain himself for doing good *FROM THEM*, i.e., wrongly acquired, wrongly owned, and wrongly spent, because such a one has his soul up for sale (cf. Sirach 10:10). . . . *AND THIS ALSO*, i.e., to love riches inordinately, *IS VANITY*. . . . [5:10]*AND WHAT DOES IT PROFIT ITS OWNER*, i.e., to have many riches, *OTHER THAN TO SEE THE RICHES WITH HIS OWN EYES* and this sight is of no profit, since it does not satisfy. To the contrary, below chapter 7 (12): *Wisdom is more useful with riches* than without, i.e. Response: These temporal things in and of themselves are neither good nor bad for the one who has them, but the abuse of them is bad, solicitude for them is worse, and the quest for them is the worst. They are therefore bad for those who use them badly, yet good for those who use them well, for the redemption of guilt. . . . Also, for the increase of grace. . . . Also, for the attainment of glory.[198]

Subsequently, he adds a few qualifications, specifically in connection with Solomon's remark that wisdom is made more useful by riches (Ecclesiastes 7:12). Understandably, an objector has seized upon the verse to argue against the notion that poverty belongs to the state of perfection.[199] He has asked how wealth could make wisdom more useful if poverty is inherently good. Beginning with a distinction between three ways of being poor—with pleasure, tolerance, or impatience—William replies that wisdom and riches are better than the latter two only. Indicating that Solomon was not thinking of the perfect form of poverty joyfully embraced, our author implies that such evangelical poverty, unknown to the king, is not made better by riches:

7:12*WISDOM IS MORE USEFUL WITH RICHES*, understand, than alone without them, *AND IS OF GREATER PROFIT TO THOSE WHO SEE THE SUN*. . . . To the contrary: To be poor belongs to the state of perfection, Matthew 19 (21): *If you want to be perfect* etc., where the Lord prefers poverty simply, supposing that one in any case be wise. Response: There is a certain kind of poverty accompanied by pleasure, and this is good and better than riches. Yet there is another accompanied by tolerance, which is good, but imperfect; and a third kind is accompanied by impatience. Wisdom with riches is better than either of the latter two.[200]

Without compromise to the ideal of evangelical poverty, this account allows that wisdom is compatible with the use of wealth. Franciscans of a more radical bent eventually became famous for holding less balanced views. Yet these remarks may hardly serve as an example of the moderation of the Preachers over and against the extremism of the Minors—William has taken the entire discussion from Bonaventure.[201] We shall see that he was not always so irenic with respect to the Franciscans.

Not surprisingly, the best place within William's work to observe the controversy's Christological implications is his commentary on John. Apart from this Gospel's singular preoccupation with the person of Jesus Christ, it is here more explicitly than anywhere else in the New Testament that Jesus and his disciples are described as the stewards of money. Diverging ways of accounting for this stewardship eventually defined the differences between the positions generally held by Dominicans and Franciscans and, more particularly, between Conventual and Spiritual Franciscans. According to Bonaventure, Jesus and his disciples were mere custodians of the purse (*loculus*) in their keeping, and its contents were destined for the poor. By contrast, Thomas Aquinas eventually developed the view that their ownership of the purse was real. In a few works dating to his second Paris regency (1268–1272), he holds that as poor men, Jesus and his disciples were included among those for whose use it was intended. It may be added that Thomas is explicit about the implications of this interpretation for religious life.[202]

The first place William takes up the matter is his exposition of the pericope of Jesus' conversation with the Samaritan woman at the well. The disciples' excursion to buy food, presumably from Samaritans, was for Hugh of Saint-Cher the occasion to take up questions concerning Jewish dietary laws.[203] Mentioning these only in passing, William instead turns his focus to a question not raised by Hugh: Why did the disciples have the means for making purchases? He offers two solutions. In the first, he notes that the disciples had not yet been sent out to preach and work miracles. Presumably, it was only at that point that Jesus commanded them to be poor (cf. Matthew 10:9). Implied by William's conclusion is that Jesus' command applies not just to the disciples present at the time, but to all preachers. In his second solution, he remarks that carrying money was made necessary by the uncertainty that begging could provide sustenance in a hostile foreign environment. In other words, carrying money was permissible because it was necessary.[204] By relating mendicancy to preaching and by excepting cases of necessity, William embraces significant qualifications to the ideal of evangelical poverty. Yet there is nothing typically Dominican about any of this. Here, too, he has lifted his remarks from Bonaventure.[205]

None of the preceding examples shows him displaying a view of evangelical poverty radically different from Bonaventure's. Then again, none of them shows him addressing a key question on which he is more independent—whether Jesus or his disciples owned money. The matter presents itself in each of the Johannine text's two references to a purse (*loculos*). The first of these is the pericope of Mary of Bethany's anointing of Jesus' feet with precious ointment and, more precisely, in the Evangelist's remark that Judas's objection to this extravagance owed not to any concern of his for the poor, but to his being a thief and the keeper of the purse (12:6). The second reference appears in the Last Supper narrative, specifically, in the Evangelist's remark that Jesus' admonition to Judas was taken by the others as a request to use the purse to buy what was necessary for the forthcoming feast, or to give alms to the poor (13:29).

The first passage prompted Augustine to ask why the one who was served by angels had a purse. Posing the same question, both Bonaventure and William reply, with reference to Augustine, that this was to confound certain heretics who held that the church ought not to own property. Augustine, it should be noted, says that this was to show that the church was to have a purse, yet he says nothing of heretics.[206] Presumably, Bonaventure and William have in mind the Manicheans of the fourth and fifth centuries, as well as the Cathars and Waldensians of the twelfth and thirteenth. Both exegetes cite Jerome to the effect that Jesus and his disciples held the purse not for their own use, but for the needs of the poor.[207] Then William dissociates himself from Bonaventure's position, and as we have seen in previous cases, his heavy borrowing from the Franciscan master underscores the significance of his departures from him. Whereas Bonaventure remarks that the Lord was in extreme poverty and that he forbade his disciples to receive money,[208] William says nothing of the sort. To the contrary, appealing to Matthew 6:31 and Luke 12:11 (*Do not be anxious*), he asserts that while Jesus forbade his disciples to be anxious over money, he did not forbid them to have it (William's independent remarks are in bold):

[12:6] *HE SAID THIS NOT BECAUSE THE POOR CONCERNED HIM*, and so he is devoid of compassion. Though they did concern him by the order of his office, by which he had the charge of dispensation, they did not (concern him) by compassion of the heart and piety. *BUT* he said this *BECAUSE HE WAS A THIEF*. Behold the corruption of his mind! **And he was very well able to steal because** HE HAD THE PURSE, Interlinear *Glossa*: "i.e., keeper of the Lord's purses." *AND HE CARRIED* **as one having the charge of dispensation, and it was presumed that he had the money and gave it to the poor, Psalm (108:9):** *May his children be orphans*; WHAT WAS PUT INTO IT **by the Lord and his disciples.** It is asked why the one to whom angels ministered wanted to have a purse. Response: According to Augustine, this was to confuse heretics asserting that the Church ought to have nothing. According to Jerome, he had the purse not for his own use, but for the use of the poor. Hence, when he paid the drachma for Peter and himself, he cast into the sea, Matthew 17 (26), because he did not want to turn to his own use what had been given to the poor. **If one should oppose to the foregoing the passage in Matthew 6 (31–34) and Luke 12 (11–22):** *Do not be anxious*, **it should be said that he does not prohibit their having, but their being anxious.** Also, how is it that the Lord wanted to commit what he had to a thief? Response: For our instruction he put little stock in riches. Also, he did this lest Judas have occasion to sell him out because of destitution. Also, why did he not correct him? Response: Because he knew that he would not become better, but worse. Nor did he take away his office, lest he reveal his crime and invite him to a greater one.[209]

Drawing attention to the importance of avoiding anxiety, rather than to the goodness of extreme poverty, William here puts forward a line of reasoning that was a centerpiece of Thomas's consideration of the matter. True, there is an important difference between the position outlined here and the one developed by Thomas in his later writings, which, as we have seen, included the proposition that Jesus and his disciples put the purse to their own use. Yet in the following chapter, at the Last Supper where Judas is once again mentioned as the holder of the purse, William returns to the question of why Jesus wanted to have money. He recalls Jerome's comment and refers to a similar one by Chrysostom, who in his own exposition of the passage raised the same question and similarly concluded that the purse was for almsgiving only.[210] Here William borrows nothing from Bonaventure and makes clear that neither Jerome's comment nor Chrysostom's represents his own interpretation:

[13:29]*FOR SOME THOUGHT, BECAUSE JUDAS HAD THE PURSE* in which donations were placed. Perhaps the Lord wanted to have them for the needs of himself, those close to him, and others. According to Augustine, he did this to show by example that the Church would be permitted to have such. Nor did he have them out of greed, which is prohibited in Matthew 10 (9), but for the aforesaid purposes. According to Chrysostom and Jerome, it was only for the needs of the poor that he had them, as has been explained more fully above. They nevertheless appear to be contradicted by this text: THAT JESUS HAD SAID TO HIM: BUY WHAT WE NEED etc.[211]

Invoking neither the church's authority nor anyone else's, William in a stroke sets aside an interpretation put forward by two *sancti*, not to mention Bonaventure. Lying in the background are Franciscan authors who had introduced convoluted exegetical and legal distinctions to account for Jesus' "ownership" of the purse in such a way as to evacuate the term of any real meaning.[212]

While it is certainly possible to understand William's exposition as a mere partisan gesture, as a typically Dominican reply to a typically Franciscan interpretation of a sharply disputed text, a few considerations argue for a more nuanced perspective. First, it will be recalled that it was not until his second Paris regency that Thomas Aquinas first expressed the view that Jesus and the disciples lived from the purse. The works belonging to this period are probably posterior to William's *Super Iohannem*. Also worth recalling is that William was not strongly influenced even by the works of Thomas that were anterior to his own writings. It would therefore seem unlikely that his interpretations of the passages about the purse were intended merely to advance the conventional "Dominican" position as put forward by Thomas. Moreover, on several occasions, we have seen that he was disinclined to subscribe to authoritative interpretations at the expense of what he considered the text's literal sense. His preference in the preceding case for a straightforward reading of the Johannine text over and against the interpretations of authorities—even *sancti* of the stature of Jerome and Chrysostom—was typical of him. William viewed the traditional explanation of the purse as unfaithful to the literal meaning of the Johannine text. Perhaps he also saw it as conducive to an unrealistic and impracticable view of religious life. While we have no reason to suppose that he was immune to the dynamics of the heated polemics in which his order was engaged, neither have we any warrant for discounting his interpretation of these passages as the result of the influence of other Dominicans, such as Thomas Aquinas.

## Conclusion

We have seen that in William's view each verse's true significance emerged only within its diverse contexts—the book's assorted divisions and subdivisions, the

Bible, and the exegetical tradition of the Christian Latin West. All of these elements provided background for interpretation and called for synthesis. However objectionable all of this may appear to exegetes of a more strictly historical-critical mind-set, it is wholly consistent with the comprehensive perspective of revelation within which exegetes of his period went about their work. Notwithstanding their sharply varying degrees of authority, the writings of the prophets, evangelists, *sancti*, and more recent figures were considered by William instruments of divine revelation and, as such, constitutive of a whole.

It would, however, be a mistake to imagine that this exegetical framework was suffocating. Beholden to tradition, it was at the same time inventive. For all of their dependence on source material, William's expositions generally make use of more recent techniques and contain his own interpretations. This, too, is consistent with the comprehensive perspective within which he worked. Though he had no authority, our author nonetheless considered his own engagement with the Word of God as an exegete and preacher an instrument of revelation and, as such, part of the same whole. By compiling and complementing the diverse elements of the tradition before which he stood, William endeavored to become a part of it.

To what extent did he succeed? While a comprehensive reply must await the edition of his works and those of his successors, it is clear that his influence cannot be compared with that of any of his three more famous contemporaries, Bonaventure, Albert the Great, and Thomas Aquinas. Still, we are not without evidence to the effect that he did enjoy a measure of success. Two centuries after his death, remarks in his postill on Ecclesiastes on the conception of the Blessed Virgin caused him to be cited as an authority by Vincent Bandellus, later to become the Dominican master general, albeit in opposition to a doctrine that was destined to be defined as a matter of Catholic faith. Also to be counted as an influence of sorts is the reproduction of his postill on Wisdom in numerous printings, albeit under the name of Bonaventure. In addition, Louis-Jacques Bataillon has shown that the slightly later Dominican regent master at Paris, William of Luxi, borrowed substantially from his postill *Super Threnos* for his own commentary on the same book,[213] and we have seen a few indications that Thomas Aquinas borrowed an occasional line from his postill on John's Gospel.

To this may be added another indication of William's success in inserting himself into the church's exegetical tradition. In their 1893 edition of Bonaventure's commentary on John, the editors of Quaracchi noticed a close correspondence between a fairly lengthy *questio* in the Franciscan master's commentary on John 20:21 and Albert the Great's exposition of the same passage. Concerning the efficacy of the sacramental absolution given by bad priests, the question arises in connection with the risen Jesus' gift of the Holy Spirit to his disciples and his instruction concerning the remission of sins. Certain *heretici* have objected that only priests having the Holy Spirit can forgive sins, with the consequence that the efficacy of sacramental absolution of sins can never be a matter of certainty. The substance of Albert's reply is that the power of remitting sins resides not in the holiness of the priest, but in that of the church, whose minister he is. The Quaracchi editors noted that Albert ascribed his reply to a certain Magister Wilhelmus (Gulielmus in the Borgnet edition of Albert's commentary), yet they were unable to identify him.[214] A more recent effort was made by Beryl Smalley, who noted that "his opinion is not to be found in William of Auxerre or William of Auvergne."[215] The present inquiry has confirmed her finding.[216] No corresponding discussions appear in the commentaries of Hugh of St. Cher or Thomas Aquinas, either. There is good reason to suppose, however, that the William in question has gone unidentified because he has been sought as the discussion's source rather than as its intermediary. As it so happens, William of Alton has presented the same *questio* and its solution in his exposition of the same passage, albeit in his typically truncated form. What follows in table 5.2 are the discussions of the three scholars, presented in chronological order (Literary correspondence between all three commentaries is indicated by boldface, and that between William and Albert by underlining; otherwise, the formatting of the editions has been preserved.)

It should be noticed that despite its brevity, William's discussion contains all the elements common to the more discursive ones of Bonaventure and Albert. Put another way, there is nothing in Albert's borrowing that would exclude William as his immediate source. To the contrary, there is one small element missing from Bonaventure's discussion yet common to the replies of William and Albert: both mention that the gift of the power of remitting sins was preceded by a *collatio* of the Holy Spirit. Even if Bonaventure's *prius dat Spiritum sanctum* is substantially the same, William's and Albert's shared use of a different term may be taken as evidence, though indeed not proof, of literary dependence between the two. It is worth mentioning in this connection that Bonaventure does not figure among Albert's sources for this commentary.[217]

On the other hand, any supposition that Albert cited William of Alton in this case presents a few difficulties. One of them concerns chronology: Albert's regency at St. Jacques (1245–1248) preceded William's by more than two decades. On the face of it, this would make it seem unlikely that he drew on William as a source. To this, it may be said that it was not until the latter part of his life, which was long (d. 1280), that Albert produced the final redactions of his lectures on the Gospels.[218] The first of the four, on Matthew, has been approximately dated to the period between 1257 and 1264.[219] While the commentary on John has yet to be assigned a precise time frame, we know that he commented on the four Gospels

Table 5.2 Io 20:22–23: *Accipite Spiritum Sanctum quorum remiseritis peccata remittuntur eis quorum retinueritis detenta sunt.*

| Bonaventure (*Opera*, t. VI, 515a–b) | William of Alton (MS Saint-Omer 260, f. 174ra–rb) | Albert the Great (ed. Borgnet, t. XXIV, 687b–688a) |
|---|---|---|
| Item obiiciunt haeretici de hoc quod prius dicitur: *Accipite Spiritum sanctum*; et post: *Quorum remiseritis peccata* etc., quod nullus sacerdos habet potestatem ligandi et solvendi, nisi habeat Spiritum sanctum inhabitantem; ergo mali sacerdotes non absolvunt, nec etiam summus Pontifex, si malus est. Quodsi hoc, tunc in periculo est nostra salus. | Item, arguunt heretici hic quod malus sacerdos et etiam papa non habet potestatem soluendi, quia preponitur: *ACCIPITE SPIRITUM SANCTUM,* et sequitur: *QUORUM REMISERITIS PECCATA.* | Adhuc ulterius objicitur pro errore haereticorum, qui Manichaei dicuntur. Dicitur enim hic primo: « *Accipite Spiritum sanctum,* ». Et postea subinfertur: « *Quorum remiseritis peccata* ». Ex quo ordine videtur, quod peccata non dimittit qui Spiritum sanctum non habet. Et cum nemo sciat se habere Spiritum sanctum, videtur quod factum Ecclesiae totum sub dubio sit. |
| Ad hoc multipliciter respondetur. Quidam enim dicunt, quod prius datur Spiritus sanctus, et post exsecutio potestatis solvendi, quia solutio vel remissio non fit nisi in caritate Ecclesiae; unde dicunt, quod non est necesse, quod sacerdos habeat caritatem, sed sufficit, quod saltem sit in Ecclesia. | Responsio: Quidam / dicunt quod acceptatio Spiritus sancti premittitur non quia oporteat quod absoluens sit in caritate, set quia oportet quod sit in caritate ecclesie, id est de ecclesia. | Ad hoc respondet Magister Gulielmus, quod collatio praecedens Spiritus sancti, non significat sanctitatem ministri, in qua sanctitate peccata remittuntur, sed potius sanctitate Ecclesiae cujus ipse sacerdos minister est: quia non nisi in sanctitate Ecclesiae peccata remittuntur. Et haec solutio est vera…. |

Aliter respondetur, quod dupliciter est solv-ere, scilicet *merito et officio et officio tantum.* Ad hoc, quod *merito* solvat, necesse est, quod habeat Spiritum sanctum; sed ad hoc, quod solvat *officio*, non oportet. Quod ergo Dominus prius dat Spiritum sanctum, hoc est, ut *digne* exsequatur, vel ad significandum, quod sine gratia Spiritus sancti non datur remissio peccatorum. Sed non oportet, quod illa gratia sit in sacerdote, sed in Sacramentis.

Potest autem et aliter dici, quod Spiritus sanc-tus dicitur dari, quando dantur dona sua. Sunt igitur quaedam dona, quae sunt *a* Spiritu sancto et *cum* Spiritu sancto et nunquam *sine*, ut *caritas*. Sunt et alia, quae sunt *a* Spiritu sancto et nunquam cum Spiritu sancto, ut timor servilis. Sunt et alia, quae sunt et a Spiritu sancto et possunt esse *cum* Spiritu sancto et *sine*, et talia sunt *charac-teres*. Et quia potestas conficiendi et ligandi et solvendi sunt tales, manent et in iustis et in iniustis; et hoc divina dispensatione actum est, ut peccatum praelati subdito non praeiudicet.

Secundum alios, ad hoc quod aliquis absoluat merito, necesse est quod habeat gratiam Spiritus Sancti. Ad hoc quod absoluat officio, non oportet. Premittitur ergo collatio Spiritus Sancti ad significan-dum quod sine gratia non datur remissio peccatorum, set non oportet quod illa gratia sit in sacerdote, set in sacramentis.

Secundum alios, quedam dona sunt ita a Spiritu sancto quod non sine eo, ut caritas; quedam ab eo et nunquam cum ipso, ut timor seruilis; quedam ab ipso que possunt esse et cum ipso et sine ipso, ut caracteres et potestas confi-ciendi et ligandi et soluendi.

Alii tamen dicunt, quod est remissio ex ministerio, et est remissio ex vitae merito. Prima quidem non exigit quod minister habeat Spiritum sanctum per inhabitantem gratiam. Secunda autem exigit. Haec solutio penitus nihil facit ad propositum, et nihil continet nisi verba: quia nulla est remissio ex vitae merito: quia sic etiam vetula posset remittere pec-cata magis quam Papa.

Alii iterum dicunt, quod quaedam sunt dona, quae sunt a Spiritu sancto, et semper sine ipso, ut timor servilis: quaedam ab ipso, et cum ipso aliquando, et aliquando sine ipso, ut characteres sacramentales. Dicunt ergo, quod potestas ligandi et solvendi, quae in charactere ordinis existit, est una de donis illis. Et haec solutio continet vera. Sed nihil est ad propositum, quia non solvit dubitationem. Prima autem est vera, et Sanctorum solutio.

in canonical order. Thus, the present evidence points to a *terminus ad quem* sometime after 1264, that is, at least five years after William became a regent master.[220]

Then again, one could wonder why Albert would fail to consult Bonaventure's commentary, all the while employing one by a scholar of lesser stature. While any reply must remain speculative, it is worth noting that during this period Albert was busy establishing and teaching in new Dominican *studia* in Germany, any one of which may well have had a copy of William's commentary but not a copy of Bonaventure's. It is not farfetched to suppose that the library at Albert's disposition was less well equipped than the one at St. Jacques and that his selection of sources was governed by this state of affairs.

A more serious difficulty is presented by Albert's very mention of the name Gulielmus—commentators of the period normally did not name contemporaries, especially not while they were still living. Nowhere does William of Alton do so in any of his works, notwithstanding his nearly constant recourse to the commentaries of Bonaventure and Hugh of St. Cher. To this, it may be said that such citations, though exceedingly rare, were not entirely unheard of. In Guerric of St. Quentin's commentary on Isaiah, Beryl Smalley identified several explicit citations of Hugh of St. Cher,[221] and in John Peckam's commentary on John, she found references to a certain Hugo who may have been Hugh of St. Cher.[222] It may be added that William was quite possibly no longer living when Albert made the reference.[223]

However that may be, comparison of this *questio* as it appears in the commentaries on John 20:22–23 of Bonaventure, William of Alton, and Albert suggests that until a similar text by some other Master William comes to light, it would seem reasonable to consider William of Alton the most likely object of Albert's reference and the most likely proximate source of his exposition.

# *Epilogue*

THIS INQUIRY WILL be concluded with an acknowledgment of the provisional nature of its findings. Having employed four commentaries of known authenticity to establish a typology of William's methodology and style, we examined what amounted to twenty works of uncertain authorship (two of the original twenty-one showed themselves to be the same). Three of them we accepted on the grounds that their extensive conformity with this typology presents solid evidence of their authenticity. The remaining seventeen we set aside on the grounds that their lack of such conformity is tantamount to a lack of evidence in favor of William's authorship. The extent to which such nonconformity presents evidence *against* William's authorship is a matter we did not address. It is worth recalling that the main focus of the discussions was not to settle all questions surrounding the authorship of these works, but to establish a sound basis for studying William's biblical interpretation. Perhaps one could argue that it would have been desirable to have applied to the seventeen rejected works a scale of varying degrees of probability after the fashion of the repertories of Friedrich Stegmüller and Thomas Kaeppeli. Our reasons for not doing so are two. First, since each of the seventeen failed on multiple counts rather than just one, any such classification would have been impossible to justify with objective reasoning and verifiable demonstration. Though extensive conformity with William's style was required for acceptance, no postill, in fact, was rejected for failing to meet just a single criterion. As a consequence, any judgment that one postill is more "probable" than another would have been inescapably subjective and arbitrary. A second reason is that nothing is to be gained from such a classification. Given the present state of our evidence, there is no reason to attribute these postills to anyone, however tentatively. Even if such a classification could offer a measure of satisfaction to bibliographers, it would have been useless to the present inquiry. Until we have clear reasons for crediting these works to William or anyone else, the most accurate and helpful qualification we can assign them is "anonymous."

And yet, it would be a mistake to presume that no additions remain to be made to William's bibliography. Though we have made every effort to consult as many of the relevant manuscripts as possible, our selection of them represents only an infinitesimal portion of the total number available to historians of thirteenth-century biblical commentary. Other works, as well as other evidence concerning those studied here, may await discovery. Among the purposes of this inquiry has been to facilitate such discoveries.

Also awaiting examination is an important part of William's known bibliography that promises to offer much to our understanding of his thought and exegesis, namely, his sermons. William understood his own reading and interpretation of the Bible to be ordered toward the end of preaching. Composed and read for the formation of preachers, his commentaries also served as material for the preparation of sermons. It would be an interesting work to explore the treatments of particular passages or themes in these sermons and compare them with similar discussions in his postills, but that would be another endeavor.

With their elaborate structures, rigorous methodological reflections, and scientific applications of specialized analytic techniques, William's commentaries are fine examples of university commentary. If his work is a product of its time, William was nonetheless a free man. His exegesis was not at all impersonal, generic, or indistinguishable from that of his contemporaries. Even by the norms of university exegesis, his attentiveness to the literal sense was keen. To discern it, he made full use of a broad range of techniques for textual, linguistic, and rhetorical analysis. He also went about his exegetical project with a corresponding attentiveness to the demands of assimilating the diverse elements of the exegetical and theological tradition in which he stood. But the former undertaking was not merely a matter of analysis, nor the latter merely a matter of synthesis. William's pursuit of the literal and spiritual senses and his theological reflection upon them manifest all the techniques of analysis and synthesis with which his university formation had equipped him. The *divisio textus* and the constant recourse to citations of the entirety of the diverse biblical books leave little doubt about the thoroughly synthetic nature of his search for each verse's meaning. It was for the sake of grasping the individual verse's particularity—and not to escape it—that he studied its contexts within the book at hand, the Bible, biblical history, the church's commentatorial and theological traditions, and even profane learning.

An authoritative interpretative tradition provided context for virtually all medieval exegesis, whether of the monasteries, the schools, or the universities. And certainly William's most frequently cited source, the *Glossa ordinaria*, was the product of the basic orientation of the twelfth-century schools toward the systematization of the Christian Latin West's vast collection of highly varied texts. By William's time, this collection had grown enormously, with the result that the *Glossa ordinaria* could no longer be considered as comprehensive as its compilers had intended it to be. Several factors contributed to this development: the influence upon Christian exegesis exercised by the thought of Aristotle; the translation into Latin of the writings of the Greek Fathers, notably the homilies of Chrysostom; and the intervening commentaries produced over the course of more than a century, notably those of Hugh, Andrew, and Richard of St. Victor; subsequently those of Peter Comestor and Stephen Langton; and finally those of thirteenth-century masters such as Hugh of St. Cher and Bonaventure. Such is the background of William's work as a synthesizer.

For any given postill, his selection of sources owed less to his own preference for certain authors over others than to the particular book's own commentatorial tradition. This is apparent in the conspicuous variation in his selection of sources from one commentary to the next. Neither arbitrary nor pedantic, his selection and use of sources was a work of critical synthesis resulting in reasoned expositions suited to his own pedagogical purposes. By contrast with the *Glossa ordinaria* and Hugh of St. Cher's *Postille*, his commentaries incorporated material from diverse sources into original expositions. And yet, we have seen that William was no mere compiler. Even if his own comments seldom predominate in his expositions, they are seldom absent from them. Far from opposing the tasks of compilation and authorship, he made it his project to integrate the two. Some indication of the extent to which he succeeded appears in the coherence of his expositions, which often show no sign of deriving from multiple sources. Making allowance for his explicit citations, the unsuspecting reader has no indication that they are composites of borrowed and original remarks.

William and his contemporaries were indebted to tradition, but they were not enslaved to it. They considered their work innovative and scientific, and not without reason. By his free use of an assortment of procedures for textual criticism, as well as linguistic and rhetorical analysis, William sought to master the texts he interpreted. The synthetic orientation of his exegesis presupposed such analysis. If he applied a certain *expositio reverentialis* to bring the *sancti* around to his own intended conclusions, this was a dialectic procedure, not an aesthetic one. It was mainly by drawing distinctions, and not by doing violence to his various sources' meanings, that he endeavored to save elements of various competing interpretations in order to avoid having to set them aside entirely, and this in order to offer his students the broadest possible range of valid interpretations.

While the absence of anything that could properly be described as a theological treatise makes it impossible to provide a systematic account of his theology, William's postills betray a comprehensive perspective of revelation that is wholly consistent with his synthetic use of sources. If he viewed the writings of the prophets, evangelists, *sancti*, and more recent figures as having sharply varying degrees of *auctoritas*, he saw them all as instruments of divine revelation and therefore as constitutive of a whole. And if he viewed himself and his own work as having no *auctoritas*, our author also saw his own work as an instrument of revelation and, as such, as part of the same whole. By compiling and complementing the diverse elements of the tradition in which he stood, William endeavored to immerse himself in it, to swim in the same sea. His success in doing so never won him the fame of Bonaventure, Albert the Great, or Thomas Aquinas, but it was not insignificant, either.

Finally, the extracts from William's commentaries presented here are intended to serve only as a sampling of his work, not as a complete representation of it. One need not look far in the rest of his writings to realize that they offer perspectives on his exegesis not found in these passages, rich though they may be. A more thorough account of his work must await the edition of a more substantial portion of his literature. In the meantime, it is to be hoped that the texts already presented will facilitate our reading of this interesting commentator who offers much to our understanding of the history of Christian biblical interpretation.

# APPENDIX I

# Consideration of Works Variously Attributed to William

IN THE EARLIER survey of the salient features of the methodology and style of the four postills assumed to be William's, we have seen that every one of them falls within the typology of thirteenth-century university biblical exegesis. Few of the features of the texts of Group A are altogether absent from the aforementioned works of William's near contemporaries Bonaventure, William of Middleton, Albert the Great, Thomas Aquinas, or William of Luxi. Taken individually, none of them could be called a signature. Several could be called clichés. Each, however, is missing from at least one of the works of Group B now under consideration, and when taken together, they mark William's work as idiosyncratic. For this reason, their presence in a postill is considered a necessary condition for authenticity but not a sufficient one. While the presence of any one of them is taken as a small corroboration of William's authorship, the absence of all or even any one of them is considered evidence to the contrary. In this manner, the ensemble of markers proper to William is employed as a set of criteria against which to evaluate the twenty-one postills of questionable authorship and the commentary on Isaiah before 5:8.

What follows is a listing of relevant bibliographical information for each postill of Groups A and B. The listings of *Super Isaiam* and every postill of Group B are followed by a comparison with the typology described. Toward the end of avoiding needless repetition, the following discussions mention only briefly the many likenesses between these works and those of Group A and focus mainly on differences. The listings of manuscripts include only those consulted for this inquiry and make no pretense of being exhaustive.

## A. THE POSTILLS OF GROUP A

1. *Super Isaiam*; inc.: *Nemo cum prophetas.*
*Handlist* 749; *SOPMA* 1432; *Rep. Bibl.* 2787–2789, 5765 (Nicolas de Gorran); *Répertoire* I, 114–115; *SOP* I, 245a.

Manuscripts: Paris, BnF lat. 573, f. 1ra–85vb; Madrid, Bibl. Nac. 493, f. 170r–265v; Saint-Omer, Bibl. mun. 155, f. 76r–120v.

Bibliography: BRADY, I., "Sacred Scripture in the Early Franciscan School," 65–82 (73); DAHAN, G., *L'exégèse chrétienne*, 381; MURANO, G., *Opere diffuse per exempla et pecia*, Turnhout, 2005, 86, 182, 475–476; SMALLEY, B., "Sapiential Books I," 41–77 (62–64); "A Commentary on Isaias by Guerric of Saint-Quentin, O.P.," *Studi e Testi*, 122 (1946), 383–397.

This postill has been ascribed to William in the first hand in the manuscript at Paris and by later scribes in the other two. The incipit *Nemo cum prophetis* has been rendered erroneously *Venio cum prophetas* by Quetif and Echard and, subsequently, by Glorieux. It opens an exposition of Jerome's prologue found in the copies at Paris and Madrid. In the Paris codex, this is followed by a brief prologue to the biblical text. Based on the four causes, it is introduced by Ecclesiasticus 48:25–27: *Ysayas propheta spiritu magno uidit ultima et consolatus est lug⟨entes⟩ in Syon.*[1] The copy at Saint-Omer begins incomplete at Isaiah 28:1. The cross reference in the *Repertorium Biblicum* to Nicolas of Gorran results from the attribution to him of another postill *Super Isaiam* having the same incipit.

Before Isaiah 5:7, the texts of the Madrid and Paris manuscripts vary from the typology of Group A, as well as from each other. In neither manuscript is there a change of copyist. For the exposition of Jerome's prologue, as well as for the *divisio* and *expositio* of the commentary, the two manuscripts present common texts interspersed with different ones. From Is 5:7 to the end, both copies are alike and in keeping with the typology of Group A.[2]

Departures from William's methodology and style before Is 5:7 can be summed up as follows. In the Paris copy the exposition of Jerome's prologue precedes the author's prologue. Filling exactly one column of text, the latter is far shorter than the three known to be William's.[3] The term *ibi* appears frequently before lemmata, eight times in the author's prologue alone. In the *divisio*, the term *dividitur* shows up regularly, and subdivisions are generally not indicated by *in prima primo*.[4] More significant is the presentation of spiritual commentary. Seldom introduced by *allegorice*, *mistice*, or *moraliter*, it is often muddled with the literal exposition and occasionally precedes it. A case in point appears at Isaiah 4:6, where, without alerting us to the beginning of a spiritual exposition, the author tells us that the biblical text's *tabernaculum* is the church and that the storm and rain from which it provides shelter are the suggestions of demons and temptations of the flesh. Lest we imagine that the commentator takes this as Isaiah's prophecy, that is, as his literal meaning, he subsequently restates the lemmata and interprets it literally.[5] Again, at Isaiah 5:6, the commentator tells us at a stroke that the clouds forbidden by the Lord to send rain upon his vineyard are prophets and preachers.[6] To be sure, William is apt to talk about preachers, but only after literal expositions in comments clearly designated as allegorical. Finally, it will be noted that nonbiblical citations are largely confined to the *Glossa Ordinaria*.

Beryl Smalley has observed that the author's prologue of the Paris copy owes its opening line and other material to Guerric of St. Quentin's prologue to Isaiah. This she took as evidence of a Dominican provenance.[7] However this may be, it does little to settle the question of William's authorship. Moreover, the parallels between the two are far too fragmentary to show that Guerric's prologue was the immediate source of this one. No less than the expositions of Jerome's prologue and of Isaiah 1:1–5:7, this prologue appears to be from another author. William's appears to have been lost. Lacking an author's prologue, the corresponding text of the Madrid copy is no less at odds with William's style.

Given the apparent instability of this text, neither the exposition of Jerome's prologue, nor the author's prologue, nor the commentary on Isaiah 1:1–5:7 will be considered authentic.

2. *Super Ieremiam*; inc.: *Direxit opera eorum in manibus prophete sancti.*
*Handlist* 749; *SOPMA* 1433; *Rep. Bibl.* 2790, 2679 (Guerric of San Quentin), 5767
   (Nicolas of Gorran), 2906 (William of Luxi); *Répertoire* I, 114; *SOP* I, 245a.
Manuscripts: Paris, BnF lat. 573, f. 87ra–145ra; Madrid, Bibl. nac. 493, f. 266r–381v.
Bibliography: SMALLEY, B., "Sapiential Books I," 64.

The cross-references in the *Repertorium Biblicum* to Guerric of San Quentin, Nicolas of Gorran, and William of Luxi are due to the attribution to them of another postill *Super Ieremiam* having the same incipit.

3. *Super Threnos*; inc.: *Quis dabit capiti meo aquam et oculis meis fontem lacrimarum.*
*Handlist* 749; *SOPMA* 1434; *Rep. Bibl.* 2791, 2680 (Guerric of San Quentin), 5768
   (Nicolas of Gorran), 2907 (William of Luxi); *Répertoire* I, 114; *SOP* I, 245a.
Manuscript: Paris, BnF lat. 573, f. 145rb–156ra.
Edition: BELLAMAH, T., "William of Alton's Commentary on the Book of Lamenta-
   tions," *AHDLMA* 73 (2006), 203–281 (233–281).
Bibliography: SMALLEY, B., "Sapiential Books I," 64.

As before, the cross-references in the *Repertorium Biblicum* to Guerric of San Quentin, Nicolas of Gorran, and William of Luxi are due to various attributions to them of another postill *Super Threnos* having the same incipit. William of Luxi's authorship of the latter work has been established by Louis-Jacques Bataillon.[8]

4. *Super Iohannem*; inc.: *Acceptus est regi minister et intelligens.*
*Handlist* 750; *SOPMA* 1437; *Rep. Bibl.* 2795; *Répertoire* I, 116.
Manuscripts: Assisi, Biblioteca Com. 49, f. 1ra–88rb; Saint-Omer, Bibliothèque mun.
   260, f. 110ra–177vb.
Bibliography: SMALLEY, B., "Sapiential Books I," 65–69.

This postill has been ascribed to William in the first hand in the manuscript at Saint-Omer (= *S*) and is anonymous in the one at Assisi (= *A*). The incipit *Acceptus est regi minister et intelligens*, common to both, has disguised the difference between these closely related texts. One is a variant of the other. It has previously been said that the authenticity of *S* will be assumed, this on the evidence of its attribution and its stylistic and methodological conformity with the other postills of Group A. Still, this state of affairs raises a few questions relevant to our present concerns. One has to do with the role of reporters—do the two versions result from a double reporting of the same lecture? If not, we can ask about the authorship of *A*—did William compose it? Should we assume that it was someone else, we could wonder about the relationship between the two versions—which is the anterior, which the posterior?

Worth noting here is that some biblical commentaries, as well as sermons and other kinds of medieval texts, are known to have been transmitted by more than one *reportatio*.[9] What is more, others show signs of posterior interventions, either by editors or the authors themselves.[10] Since we have no reason to exclude any of these possibilities a priori with respect to the case at hand, let us consider them one at a time.

Comparison of the two texts argues against the possibility that each results from a different report of the same commentary. Two separate recordings of the same lecture could be expected to produce two substantially similar versions, with frequent differences of expression, as well as occasional differences of ideas owing to an omission or addition in one version or the other.[11] Here this is not the case. With respect to the prologues, they are basically the same on the main points (the four causes), yet *A* is more discursive throughout and is much longer overall. As for the exposition, *A* often contains remarks not found in *S*; otherwise, most lines of both are virtually identical. It is in the *divisio textus* that the differences are most conspicuous. The *divisio* of *A* occasionally differs in its basic organization (its principles of division, its numbers of *divisiones*, and its lemmata); often, it is virtually the same, yet with longer lemmata and additional *divisiones*. The *divisio* introducing chapter 11 is typical. The text placed in bold is proper to *A*; the remaining material is virtually the same in *S*:

[11:1]*ERAT AUTEM QUIDAM LANGUENS.* Postquam manifestauit suam potentiam et misericordiam uitam habitam quantum ad esse et quantum ad bene esse conseruando, hic uitam amissam restituendo. Primo ergo narrantur **quedam pertinentia** ad hoc miraculum antecedentia; secundo operatio ipsius miraculi: [43]*HEC CUM DIXISSET UOCE MAGNA CLAM⟨AUIT⟩*; tertio **quedam** ad talem operationem contingentia: [45]*MULTI ERGO EX IUDEIS CUM UENERUNT AD MARTHAM.* In prima, primo ponuntur **siue narrantur** antecedentia magis remota; secundo magis propinqua, scilicet ad ipsum **faciendum** incitantia: [18]*ERAT AUTEM BETHANIA IUXTA IEROSOLEM*; tertio antecedentia quasi proxima, scilicet ut ipsum miraculum faceret preparatoria: [38]*IHESUS IGITUR RURSUS FREMENS IN SEMETIPSO.* **In prima, primo narratur quendam qui describitur infirmum extitisse; secundo hoc ipso denuntiatum esse:** [3]*MISERANT ERGO SORORES EIUS*; **tertio Christum denuntiantes dilexisse:** [5]*DILIGEBAT*; **quarto consequenter eum illuc aduenisse:** [6]*UT AUTEM AUDIUIT QUIA.* In

**prima, primo describitur a nomine; secundo ab infirmitatis conditione:**
**¹*LANGUENS*; tertio a patria uel uilla uel habitatione: ¹*A BETHANNIA*; quarto**
*** ¹*DE CASTELLO*; quinto Maria notificatur ex quadam magnifica opera-**
**tione: ²*MARIA AUTEM*.¹²**

None of this points toward a twofold reporting of the same lecture. The systematic appearance of virtually identical material in both versions is difficult to explain as the work
of two independent reporters, however skilled. Moreover, the regular appearance of substantial sections of material in only one version (*A*) argues against the involvement of two
different reporters recording the same lecture, however unskilled. In sum, neither the
lines that are virtually identical in both texts nor those proper to *A* may be easily explained
as the result of a double reporting of a single lecture. While such a possibility cannot be
entirely eliminated, a far more likely explanation is that one text is a revision of the other.
It would appear either that *S* is an abbreviation of *A*, or that *A* is a prolongation of *S*.

It remains for us to set these lines and others like them against the background of
William's other writings to try to determine whether this reviser was William himself.
Evident in this excerpt is the commonality of the first section (of two divisions) to
both versions, and the propriety to *A* of the latter (also of two divisions). Both seg-
ments contain a few features worth noticing. To begin, even in the first, there appear
several terms proper to *A* that add nothing of substance to the text: *quedam pertinentia . . . quedam . . . siue narrantur . . . faciendum.* Whatever one makes of the author's
style, the functioning of these words must be judged aesthetic. Equally cosmetic is the
lengthier presentation in *A* of two lemmata (John 11:45 and 11:18). As for the second
segment, there is no significant change of vocabulary: subdivisions are introduced by
the usage of William's stock formula, *in prima, primo,* and *ibi* is not used to introduce
lemmata. Similarly in conformity with William's style are a few structural traits: each
element save the first is closed with a lemma, and subdivisions are of the first element
resulting from the preceding division. Also worth noting is the application of the technique of rhyming to the final terms of the various elements: *extitisse, esse, dilexisse,* and
*aduenisse* in the first subdivision of the lines proper to *A*, and *nomine, conditione, habitatione,* and *operatione* in the second. Further in keeping with William's style is a close
correspondence between the *divisio* and the subsequent commentary, where each
lemma is subsequently restated, and (apart from those of the final division) each
lemma left without subdivision subsequently becomes the subject of its own smaller
*divisio.* That is, the second, third, and fourth elements of the penultimate division
(closed by the lemmata: ³*ERGO SORORES EIUS,* ⁵*DILIGEBAT,* and ⁶*VT AUTEM AUDIUIT
QUIA*) become the subjects of subordinate *divisiones* in their own places in the commentary. On the face of it, there is no reason to suspect a change in authorship from
one version to the other. Similar examples of the *divisio* could easily be multiplied—
each of these traits shows up throughout *A*.

Still, on further examination, two notable departures from the methodology and
style of William's known works become recognizable. First, since it is especially

within the *divisio* that the material proper to *A* appears, the importance of the *divisio* relative to the exposition is much greater in *A* than in *S* and the other works of Group A. Second, the work as a whole is considerably more discursive, notwithstanding its containing little of substance missing from *S*. It has none of the brevity and concision characteristic of William's known works. To be sure, none of this permits us to conclude that someone other than William is the author of *A*. Yet given its anonymity, these two points suffice to exclude it from the list of William's authenticated works.

Here it remains to be determined whether *A* served as the basis of *S* or resulted from a revision of it. To judge by our example, neither possibility can be eliminated. So it is generally. Given that the differences between the two are normally superficial and that both texts are copies, it is ordinarily impossible to determine which came first. Differences can almost always be plausibly explained as resulting from the stylistic preferences of one or the other author or from faults of copy. Even in the rare instances in which the remarks proper to one or the other version are substantive, it is generally impossible to determine who has borrowed from whom.

What would, however, betray the secondary author is a difference resulting from a misunderstanding rather than a deliberate change. An instance of one author's failure to grasp the other's meaning would expose him as the borrower. Such cases are rare. The two versions' substantial agreement virtually throughout is enough to show that the posterior author has, on the whole, well understood what he has borrowed. And yet, telling remarks show up occasionally. One such case appears at John 11:7, where Jesus, upon learning of the sickness of his friend Lazarus, has waited two days before saying anything about going to visit him: *Deinde post hec dicit discipulis suis: Eamus in Iudaeam iterum.* The apparent redundancy of *Deinde* and *post hec* has called for explanation. Table A 1.1 shows two different replies, neither of which appears in William's principal sources (the commentaries of Bonaventure, Hugh of St. Cher, and the *Glossa ordinaria*).

The difference here is more than aesthetic. While there can be no excluding the possibility that it resulted from a copyist's error, a more likely cause is a basic textual misunderstanding. William has provided a coherent solution for the Vulgate's apparent

### Table Appendix 1.1

| William of Alton (MS Saint-Omer 260, f. 143rb) | Anon. (MS Assisi 49, f. 49vb) |
|---|---|
| [7]*DEINDE POST HEC DIXIT IHESUS DIS⟨CIPULIS⟩ S⟨UIS⟩*. 'Deinde' potest referri ad tempus, 'post hec' autem ad res gestas, et ita non est nugatio. | [7]*DEINDE POST HEC DIXIT IHESUS DISCIPULIS SUIS*. 'Deinde' potest referri ad tempus 'post hec,' id est ad res ante gestas, et ita non est nugatio. |

redundancy by designating separate referents for *deinde* and *post hec*. The former he refers to the previous two days, and the latter to previous events, which he identifies as *res gestas*. This is a classical expression whose meaning appears to have been lost on the anonymous author of *A*.

Overlooking the pair of referents William has assigned to *Deinde* and *post hec*, the author of *A* refers the former to the latter. To the extent that his explanation is coherent, it may be paraphrased as follows: *Deinde* refers to the subsequent time (*post hec*), that is, to events (*res*) that preceded Jesus' deeds (*gestas*). Though the language of *A* is often more polished that of *S*, this case suggests that William was really the better Latinist.

Further illustration presents itself later in the same pericope in connection with Jesus' encounter with Martha's sister Mary: *Ihesus ergo ut uidit eam plorantem* (John 11:33). William asks why Jesus refrained from questioning Mary about her faith as he had Martha (cf. John 11:23). He supplies three answers, from Bonaventure, Chrysostom, and himself, but only the first will concern us here. William, as is typical of him, condenses Bonaventure's reply, yet in this case his brevity results in a misunderstanding. Table A 1.2 shows the remarks of the three.

### Table Appendix 1.2

| Bonaventure (Opera, t. VI, 402a–b) | William of Alton (MS Saint-Omer 260, f. 144vb) | Anon. (MS Assisi 49, f. 51va) |
|---|---|---|
| Sed quaeritur hic: quare Dominus ita diligenter quaerit confessionem Marthae de fide resurrectionis, cum sciret, eam fideliter credere? Et quae necessitas erat? Dicendum, quod fides sororum Lazari impetravit eius resurrectionem; et quia tunc fides est certior et firmior, quando ore confitemur: ideo oris petiit confessionem (cf. Romans 10:10). | Hic queritur quare supra quesierit de fide Marthe, non hic de fide Marie. Responsio: Quia ita fuit feruentior in fide. | Hic queritur quare tantum inquisierit de fide Martha et nichel de fide Marie. Responsio: Forsitan non fuit ita firma in fide. |

By alluding to St. Paul (Romans 10:10: *ore autem confessio fit in salutem*), Bonaventure draws attention to the salvific efficacy of oral confession and remarks that both sisters' faith obtained (*impetravit*) Lazarus's resurrection. He makes no suggestion that Martha's faith was weak, nor does he compare her faith to Mary's. As he would have it, Jesus elicited her confession for the sake of confirming her faith. In William's succinct encapsulation, the term *ita* expresses the manner or purpose ("so as to") of Jesus' questions, and the comparative *feruentior* points to a difference between Martha's faith before and after her confession: Jesus questioned her about her faith so as to strengthen it by eliciting her confession. This has escaped the author of *A*, for whom *ita* denotes a degree of comparison ("so much"), the two points of which are the faiths of Martha and Mary. He seems to have interpreted William's reply as follows: "Because she (Martha) was so much stronger in faith (than Mary)." Seeing the implausibility of it, he has supplied the term *non* to reverse the order of comparison and proposed: "Perhaps she (Martha) was not so strong in faith (as Mary)." Nowhere to be found here is the basis of Bonaventure's solution, the efficacy of oral confession. Whereas William has captured the substance of Bonaventure's thought, albeit in truncated form, the author of *A*, by misreading William's text, has come to a different conclusion. These examples offer evidence to the effect that *A* is dependent on *S*, rather than the other way around, and they support the earlier determination that its author is someone other than William. More is said about this exposition in chapter 5.

Objections could be raised against the preceding line of reasoning. Here we shall mention two. First, one could argue that the differences mentioned may be explained as faults of copy. While this is certainly possible, it must be judged unlikely. In neither of the two cases has the Assisi manuscript been corrected, nor is there any other evidence to suggest that its text is corrupt. While neither manuscript is free of inaccuracies, these are generally normal errors of copy that reflect no intent on the part of either scribe to alter the text. During the course of editing the commentary, I have never had the impression that the copyists of either codex intervened deliberately.

Less easily set aside is a second possible objection. One could point out that differences of the sort illustrated may owe to differences of reporting. Even someone willing to assume that the two versions result from two different lectures could point to the possibility that the errors of *A* result from the misunderstandings of the reporter rather than the author, who could have been William. This hypothesis is certainly plausible, but it and the previous one it run up against *A*'s failure to correspond thoroughly to the typology of William's known works. Moreover, we have seen that the differences between the two versions can hardly be explained as resulting from two reports. Still, attempting to disprove the authenticity of A would require asserting more than the available evidence will support. It seems reasonable to conclude, then, that while the authenticity of *S* may be assumed, that of *A* must be left undetermined. It is considered a witness to the text of William's postill *Super Iohannem* only where *S* is manifestly defective.

## B. THE POSTILLS OF GROUP B

1. *Super Genesim*; inc.: *Transite ad me omnes. Handlist* 750; *Rep. Bibl.* 2771; *Répertoire* I, 113; *SOP* I, 244b.

Manuscripts: Paris, BnF lat. 526 , f. 1ra–50ra; Vendôme 116, f. 1ra–46vb.

Bibliography: BRADY, I., "Sacred Scripture in the Early Franciscan School," 65–82 (80–81, n. 34); DAHAN, G., "L'Exégèse de l'Histoire de Cain et Abel Du XIIe au XIVe Siècle en Occident," *RTAM* 49 (1982), 21–89; 50 (1983), 5–68; *L'exégèse chrétienne*, 273; "Nommer les êtres: exégèse et théories du langage dans les commentaires médiévaux de Gen. 2, 19–20," in *Sprachtheorien in Spätantike und Mittelalter*, ed. S. Ebbesen, Tübingen, 1995, 55–74 (55–56); "Genèse 2, 23–24 dans l'exégèse chrétienne du Moyen Age occidental," in *"Ils seront deux en une seule chair," Scénographie du couple humain dans le texte occidental*, ed. P. Legendre, Bruxelles, 2004, 69–105; DOUCET, V., "Commentaires sur les Sentences. Supplément au Répertoire de M. Frédéric Stegmüller," *Archivum Franciscanum Historicum* 27 (1934), 542–543; SMALLEY, B., "Sapiential Books I," 57–61; "William of Middleton and Guibert of Nogent," *RTAM* 16 (1949), 281–291 (282).

This is the first of five postills associated with William by virtue of a posterior ascription in MS Paris, BnF lat. 526.[13] The texts are left without attribution by the copyist, who happens to be the one who left the four works of Group A and attributed each to William of Alton. None shows evidence of William's authorship. They are identified as a series on the Heptateuch by Beryl Smalley[14] and as a series on the Pentateuch by Ignatius Brady.[15] Both scholars observe that the postill on Genesis consists of extracts from a work contained in MS Quaracchi 24 and that the postills on Exodus and Leviticus have identical counterparts in the same manuscript. With strong evidence, both associate the series in the Quaracchi manuscript with William of Middleton. Largely on the basis of the ascription in the Paris manuscript, Beryl Smalley speculates that William of Alton made extracts from William of Middleton's postill on Genesis, copied his postills on Exodus and Leviticus, and garnished the group with his own prologues.[16] Ignatius Brady credits William of Middleton with postills on Genesis, Leviticus, and Numbers, as well as another on Deuteronomy. Without producing further evidence, he ascribes to William of Alton the abridged version of the postill on Genesis, as well as the postill on Leviticus. He leaves open the question of whether either William authored the postill on Exodus.[17] While it lies beyond our scope to settle questions about William of Middleton's involvement, the likelihood of William of Alton's authorship will be considered case by case.

*Super Genesim* is introduced by an exposition of Jerome's prologue, as well as by two examples of a *principium biblicum*, that is, a prologue to the entire Bible.[18] On the other hand, it lacks a prologue to Genesis. Otherwise, it is similar in methodology and in many points of style to William's works. The *divisio* is normally introduced by *hic* and the *expositio* is focused on the literal sense.

Differences of style, however, are apparent. Seldom found in the *divisio* is William's familiar formula *in prima primo*. In its place, we find the regular application of *diuiditur*, a term William normally avoids for this purpose. The *divisio* following Genesis 1:3, *Dixitque Deus*, is typical. The first division is introduced by *Et diuiditur in duas*; the second by *Item prima diuiditur in duas*; the third by *Item prima pars diuiditur in tres*.[19] Though the technique of rhyming is often applied to the last elements of each division, this is with considerably less regularity than in William's postills. For example, in the *divisio* at Genesis 7:10, *Cumque transissent*, the last terms of the elements of the first division are *fieri, esse, effectum,* and *durationem*; of the second, *cause* and *progressum*; of the third, *ingressus* and *inuentio*. A still more easily recognizable departure from William's style is the recurrent application of *ibi* for the introduction of citations. It is common to find several instances in a single column of text.[20] Further, the elements of the *divisio* left without subdivision (introduced by *secundo, tertio, quarto,* etc.) are only irregularly subjected to subdivision in a subsequent smaller scale *divisio*. Whereas William normally employs this method so that each chapter's initial *divisio* is integrally related to each of a series of subsequent smaller scale *divisiones*, here we find that the various instances of the *divisio* correspond neither to each other nor to the exposition. What is more, the lemmata of the *divisio* are often left without restatement in the *expositio*.[21]

Nowhere to be found is the brevity characteristic of William. Instead, we often find fairly extensive digressions from the literal sense. A case in point appears at Genesis 18:5, where the story of Abraham and Sarah's hospitality toward three mysterious visitors serves to introduce the outline of a sermon for Holy Thursday: *Thema in die cena. . . .*[22] Still more significant is the author's tendency to leave lines of the biblical text unrepresented by a lemma and without an explicit line-by-line commentary. Even when making allowance for his unawareness of our standard verse divisions, we see that he regularly groups several lines into a single exposition. A typical example appears at Genesis 36:39, where the lemma, [36:39]*REGNAUIT PRO EO ADAD*, is followed by an extensive commentary occupying more than half the column, which is itself followed by a lemma several lines further along in the biblical text: [36:43]*EGO SUM DEUS BETHEL*.[23] This is wholly unlike William. Finally, spiritual interpretations often appear without having been introduced by terms such as *allegorice, mistice,* or *moraliter*.[24]

In sum, neither the style nor the methodology of this work argues for its authenticity. In view of the lack of any other clear evidence in favor of it, we see no reason for following Beryl Smalley and Ignatius Brady in attributing this work to him, and we decline to include this postill among his authenticated works.

2. *Super Exodum*; inc.: *Hec sunt nomina.*
*Handlist* 750; *Rep. Bibl.* 2772; *Répertoire* I, 113; *SOP* I, 244b.
Manuscripts: Paris, BnF lat. 526, f. 50rb–117va; Vendôme 116, f. 48ra–104va.
Bibliography: BRADY, I., "Sacred Scripture in the Early Franciscan School," 65–82
    (80–81, n. 34); DOUCET, V., "Commentaires sur les Sentences. Supplément au
    Répertoire de M. Frédéric Stegmüller," *Archivum Franciscanum Historicum* 27

(1934), 543; SMALLEY, B., "Sapiential Books I," 57–61; "William of Middleton and Guibert of Nogent," 282.

Lacking a prologue, the work is introduced by an extended *divisio* beginning with the word *hic* and indicating the first subdivision with the formula *in prima primo*. The first trait appears regularly thereafter, the second less so. Yet several consistent practices at odds with William's style may be observed in the following excerpt taken from the exposition of Ex 1:6:

> [1:6]*QUO MORTUO*. Hic insinuatur eorum múltiplicatio, et primo a multiplicatione diuitiarum; secundo personarum, ibi: [1:7]*ET QUASI GERMINANTES*, id est ex simili simile in natura simile producentes; germinare enim est ex simili in natura simile producere; tertio uirtutis siue roboris, ibi: [1:7]*AC ROBORATI*; quarto ab habundantia istorum, scilicet diuitiarum, personarum et uirtutus, siue roboris, ibi: [1:7]*NIMIS INPLEUERUNT TERRAM*.
>
> [1:6]*QUO MORTUO, Glossa*: "Morientibus uice uitiis uirtutes augentur." Ergo simile sunt uitia et uirtutes, nam quando augentur sunt. Responsio: Vitia dicuntur mori ratione pronitatis ad peccatum que est ex fomitate.
>
> [1:8]*SURREXIT INTEREA REX NOUUS*. Hic narratur afflictio Israel illata ab Egiptiis. . . . Dicit igitur: [1:8]*SURREXIT INTEREA REX*. Andre: "Alii reges. . . ."[25]

The introduction of lemmata by *ibi* is typical of the commentary, as well as the *divisio textus*. As elsewhere, rhyming of last words is irregular: *diuitiarum, personarum, roboris*, and *roboris*. Also worth noting is that the second element ends with no lemma, whereas those in William's work almost invariably do. Occasionally, a lemma is attached to the first element of a division, and at times two lemmata in combination are added to a single element.[26] More significant is the status of the *divisio*. Rather than serving the literal exposition, in this work it frequently appears as an end in itself. Apart from the disproportion between its length and that of the following commentary, the elements resulting from its divisions often appear nowhere in it. The second, third, and fourth elements of this selection, for example, are supplemented with lemmata that are altogether absent from the following exposition. We find no such omissions in William's postills. This brings us to another important difference already noticed in the preceding work. The expositor at hand has left the entirety of Exodus 1:7 unrepresented by a lemma and without an explicit line-by-line commentary. Throughout the postill, he has often grouped several lines into a single exposition. This is a method absent from William's known work. A final observation concerns the question he has attached to Exodus 1:6. Having to do with vices, virtues, and sin, it arises from the citation of the *Glossa*, rather than the literal sense of the biblical text, to which it has no bearing.[27] While typical of this postill, this could hardly be less typical of William.

    Since this work presents no more evidence in favor of its authenticity than the previous, we decline to include it among William's works.

3. *Super Leuiticum*; inc.: *Vocauit autem.*

*Handlist* 750; *Rep. Bibl.* 2773; *Répertoire* I, 113; *SOP* I, 245a.

Manuscripts: Paris, BnF lat. 526 , f. 117va–166rb; Vendôme, 116, f. 104va–139ra.

Bibliography: BRADY, I., "Sacred Scripture in the Early Franciscan School," 65–82 (80–
81, n. 34); DOUCET, V., "Commentaires sur les Sentences. Supplément au Répertoire de M. Frédéric Stegmüller," *Archivum Franciscanum Historicum* 27 (1934), 543;
SMALLEY, B., "Sapiential Books I," 57–61; "William of Middleton and Guibert of
Nogent," 282.

Though similar in style and methodology to the two previous ones, this postill differs
from them in a few significant respects. As with the previous works, in place of a prologue based on the four causes, there is a general introduction in the form of a protracted *divisio*, occupying slightly more than the first two columns of text, replete with
several citations and questions. Once again, this is unlike William. While usage of *hic* as
the opening word of the *divisio* is as consistent as it is in William's work, rhyming is far
less so. Introduction of lemmata by the term *ibi* is systematic. Further, it is common to
find either a lemma attached to the first element of a division or a comment following a
lemma, such as in the following example introducing the first chapter:

> [1:1]*VOCAUIT AUTEM* etc. In hoc capitulo primo agitur de holocausto duplicis
> gressibilis, scilicet armenti et gregis, quod notatur ibi: [1:10]*QUOD SI DE PECORI-
> BUS*; secundo uolatilium, ibi: [1:14]*SIN AUTEM DE AUIBUS*, usque in finem capituli.
> Vbi autem de holocausto armenti, primo de oblatione. . . .[28]

Still more telling is the lack of any restatement of the lemmata of the *divisio* in the *expositio*.[29] On the other hand, the commentary seems to follow each line of the biblical text
more closely than in the two preceding postills, inasmuch as most lines are represented
by lemmata. Moreover, the formula *in prima primo* appears more frequently than in the
previous postills, though considerably less systematically than in William's known
works. Questions are occasionally employed for the clarification of the literal sense.[30]

All in all, this evidence provides no support for William's authorship. With no other
clear supporting evidence, we see no reason to include this postill among his works.

4. *Super Numeros*; inc.: *Locutus est Dominus.*

*Handlist* 750; *Rep. Bibl.* 2774; *Répertoire* I, 113; *SOP* I, 245a.

Manuscripts: Paris, BnF lat. 526, f. 166va–209vb; Vendôme 116, f. 139ra–170vb.

Bibliography: BRADY, I., "Sacred Scripture in the Early Franciscan School," 65–82 (80–
81, n. 34); DOUCET, V., "Commentaires sur les Sentences. Supplément au Répertoire de M. Frédéric Stegmüller," *Archivum Franciscanum Historicum* 27 (1934), 543;
SMALLEY, B., "Sapiential Books I," 57–61; "William of Middleton and Guibert of
Nogent," 282.

In methodology and style, this postill is similar to the preceding works. As before, instead of a prologue based on the four causes, there is a general introduction in the form of a prolonged *divisio*, replete with citations and questions. Throughout, the *divisio* is marked by the systematic application of *ibi* for the introduction of lemmata. William's stock formula *in prima primo* is applied infrequently. The term *diuiditur* is occasionally employed for the same purpose.[31] Rhyming is highly irregular. More significant is the irregularity with which lemmata of the *divisio* are restated in the exposition.[32] Moreover, the commentary seldom proceeds in a line-by-line fashion. One often finds a lemma introducing a protracted exposition occupying the better part of a column, with the following lemma more than ten verses further along in the biblical text. In other words, the expositor's focus normally falls on sizable sections of text rather than on individual lines.[33] This is decidedly uncharacteristic of William.

Neither the style nor the methodology of this work argues in favor of its authenticity. In view of the lack of any other clear evidence in favor of it, we decline to include it among William's authenticated works.

5. *Super Iosue*; inc.: *Fortis in bello*.
*Handlist* 750; *Rep. Bibl.* 2775; *Répertoire* I, 113; *SOP* I, 245a.
Manuscripts: Paris, BnF lat. 526, f. 210ra–224ra; Vendôme 116, 172ra–184vb.

Though written in the hand of the same copyist, this postill differs markedly from the four preceding ones. It is introduced by a prologue based on Aristotle's four causes corresponding to William's style in all significant respects. The introductory biblical verse is followed by the formula *Hec uerba scripta sunt, Eccli* XLV. . . . The order in which the four causes are presented corresponds to that of the prologue to William's *Super Threnos*, while differing from that of his commentaries *Super Ieremiam* and *Super Iohannem*. This is followed by an exposition of Jerome's prologue. Further, the vocabulary of the *divisio* is much like William's. As regularly as in William's work, the formula *in prima primo* is applied, and where it is missing, it is often replaced by *ubi primo*. With similar regularity, *hic* is employed as an introduction, and *dicit ergo* is used to indicate transitions to the *expositio*.

Notwithstanding such likenesses, the *divisio* differs noticeably from what we have come to expect from William. Though it appears occasionally, the technique of rhyming is applied irregularly; lemmata are occasionally introduced by the term *ibi*.[34] Less systematic than in the Group A postills is the practice of closing with a lemma all elements except the first of each division. More important, the elements of the *divisio* frequently correspond to nothing in the *expositio*. In other words, the *divisio* at times appears as its own end.[35] Moreover, the *divisio* often contains questions.[36] Another important point of departure from the typology of the Group A postills is the application of spiritual exegesis. Allegorical and tropological expositions frequently lack any designation as such, as well as any preceding literal commentary.[37]

In sum, neither the style nor the methodology of this work argues in favor of its authenticity. In view of the lack of any other clear supporting evidence, we see no reason to ascribe this postill to William.

6. *Super lib. Iudicum*; inc.: *Iudicabit Dominus populum suum.*
*Handlist* 750; *Rep. Bibl.* 2776; *Répertoire* I, 113; *SOP* I, 245a.
Manuscripts: Paris, BnF lat. 526, f. 224rb–239rb; Vendôme 116, f. 185ra–198ra.
Bibliography: DAHAN, G., "Samson et Dalila: le chapitre 16 des Juges dans l'exégèse chrétienne du XIIe et du XIIIe siècle," in *Samson et Dalila = Graphè* 13 (2004), 97–118 (113).

Introduced by a prologue based on Aristotle's four causes, this work corresponds in all respects to the description of the previous one. The introductory biblical verse is followed by the formula *Hec uerba scripta sunt, Daniel* XXIIII. . . . In the *divisio*, we find the systematic usage of the formulae characteristic of William, yet no systematic application of rhyming. Here again, the practice of closing all elements of each division except the first with a lemma is less regular than in the Group A postills.[38] More important, as in the preceding postill, the elements of the divisions often correspond to nothing in the exposition.[39]

With respect to the *expositio*, the commentary seems to closely follow each line of the biblical text, as most of them are represented by lemmata. Still, many lines are skipped.[40] Moreover, spiritual expositions are only irregularly preceded by literal ones and often appear without being designated as such by terms such as *mistice* or *moraliter*.[41]

While all of this suggests that the author is the same as the one of the preceding postill, it does nothing to suggest that William is he. No more than in the preceding case do we find reason to list this commentary as authentic.

7. *Super Ruth*; inc.: *Breuis in uolatilibus.*
*Handlist* 750; *Rep. Bibl.* 2777; *Répertoire* I, 114; *SOP* I, 245a.
Manuscripts: Paris, BnF lat. 526, f. 239rb–241va; Vendôme 116, f. 198ra–199vb.

As do the two preceding postills, this one opens with a prologue based on Aristotle's four causes. Its introductory biblical verse, *Breuis in uolatilibus ⟨est⟩ apis et initium dulcoris habet fructus illius*,[42] is followed by the formula *Hec uerba scripta sunt, Eccli.* XI.

There are only four occurrences of the *divisio*, one at the head of each chapter, and these are relatively simple. The first two have no subdivisions, the third has one, and the fourth has three. The technique of rhyming is applied in each. As in the two previous works, the vocabulary of the *divisio* is similar to William's. Once again, the lemmata of the *divisio* are often missing from the exposition and correspond to nothing therein.[43]

What is more, we find once again the telling fact that in the *expositio*, the exegete repeatedly skips lines, sometimes several at once.[44] Also worth noting is the spiritual exposition, which on occasion is applied to verses with no preceding literal commentary, such as Rt 41:

[4:1]*ASCENDIT ERGO BOOZ AD PORTAM . . . ET SEDIT IBI.* Mistice. Christus ad beatam Virginem, de qua Ez. XLIIII: *Porta he⟨c⟩ clausa erit*[45] etc. Contra: Descendit, Ysa. LXIIII (1), *Vtinam disrumperes celos et descenderes.* Responsio: Quod apparet in notitiam ascendit, cum prius non apparuit, Ysa. XIX (1): *Ascendet Dominus super nubem leuem* etc.[46]

This brings us to a final trait uncharacteristic of the Group A postills. The question attached to this verse concerns the Incarnation—whether it involved the Lord's descent or ascent. Arising from the spiritual exposition, it has no bearing on the literal sense of the lemma. In view of such evidence we find no reason to list this postill among William's authenticated works.

8. *Super* I–IV *Regum*; inc.: *Ad uos ergo o reges.*
*Rep. Bibl.* 2778; *Répertoire* I, 116.
Manuscript: Saint-Omer, Bibl. mun. 260, f. 178ra–206ra (ends incomplete at 3 Rg 2, 27).
Bibliography: SMALLEY, B., "Sapiential Books I," 65, 69.

Though on a different manuscript, this postill is written in the same hand as the seven previous, as well as all those of Group A. It opens with a prologue based on Aristotle's four causes; its initial biblical citation, *Ad uos ergo reges sunt hii seromnes mei ut discatis sapientiam et non excedatis*,[47] is followed by the familiar formula *Hec uerba scripta sunt. . . .*

Once again, the vocabulary is similar to William's. Nonetheless, departures from the typology of Group A are easily recognizable. Only sporadically is the *divisio* introduced by *hic*. While subdivisions are regularly signaled by *in prima primo*,[48] almost as often they are introduced by a variant such as *in prima adhuc primo*[49] and occasionally by a term virtually absent from the Group A postills, *diuiditur*.[50] Rhyming is less regular than in William's known works, and lemmata only irregularly terminate the elements subsequent to the first.[51]

Still more revealing is the inconsistency with which lemmata of the *divisio* are restated in the exposition. In fact, the divisions often correspond to nothing in the expositions.[52] What is more, a few chapters have no *divisio* other than a highly truncated introduction, and numerous others have none at all.[53] Among the few notable similarities between this work and those of Group A is the usage of questions to clarify the literal sense and the placement of them within the *expositio*.[54] Another is the clear designation of spiritual exegesis by terms such as *mistice* and *moraliter*. The similarity ends there. By contrast with William, the author of this postill at times expounds the spiritual senses before having expounded the literal.[55] Finally, in the *expositio*, lines are skipped regularly, sometimes several at a time.[56] In view of this, we find no reason to list this postill among William's works.

9. *Super Iob*; inc.: *Consumpta est caro eius a suppliciis.*
*Handlist* 748, 790 (William of Middleton); *Rep. Bibl.* 2932 (William of Middleton).
Manuscript: Troyes, Bibl. mun. 487.

The first part of the incipit to the prologue is the same as that of a postill on Job listed by Stegmüller under William of Middleton's name. Above the incipit in a posterior hand, this work is ascribed to *Guillelmus de Melitona, Ord. Predicatorum*. The last term was subsequently crossed out and replaced by *Minorum*, and there is a separate posterior ascription to the Franciscan William in the lower margin. Richard Sharpe listed this work under William of Alton's name apparently because the incipit to the commentary is the same as that of another postill on Job variously attributed to him, to be discussed next. Yet this is a different work.[57] Apart from its having another prologue (also based on Aristotle's four causes), it is considerably longer. Its *divisio* often comprises the same elements, though it is generally worded differently and at times arranged differently. Though Friedrich Stegmüller lists this work only under William of Middleton's name, it also differs from still another postill *Super Iob* he has included in the same listing, found in MS Paris, BnF lat. 14250.[58]

This postill's terminology is consistently different from William's. The *divisio* often begins with a term other than *hic*, and subdivisions are seldom indicated by *in prima primo*. Only sporadically are the elements of the *divisio* after the first closed with lemmata. Further, lemmata, biblical references, and nonbiblical references are often introduced by *ibi*.[59] On the other hand, a point in common with the commentaries of Group A is the regular rhyming of the elements of the *divisio*.[60]

Though the exposition normally follows the biblical text closely, it occasionally skips lines.[61] Perhaps the most easily recognizable departure from the typology of Group A is the length and discursiveness of the *expositio*. In place of the succinctness characteristic of William, we normally find in this work comments on a single verse extending to an entire column of text or more.[62] Finally, spiritual interpretations often appear without being designated as such and seldom follow literal interpretations.[63]

None of this argues in favor of this postill's authenticity. In view of the complete lack of any evidence supporting it, we decline to attribute this work to William.

10. *Super Iob*; inc.: *Surgite postquam sederitis.*
*Handlist* 747–748, 614 (Simon of Hinton); *SOPMA* 1427; *Rep. Bibl.* 2779, 7655 (Simon of Hinton).
Manuscripts: Basel, Univ. Bibl. B III 25, f. 1ra–105rb; Madrid, Bibl. Nac. 493, f. 6v–73r; Paris, BnF lat. 573, f. 199ra–282rb.
Bibliography: SMALLEY, B., *Study of the Bible*, 319; "Some More Exegetical Works of Simon of Hinton," *RTAM* 15 (1948), 97–106 (99–104); "Sapiential Books I," 338; SHARPE, R., *Titulus*, 177–183.

In the three manuscripts consulted for this inquiry, as well as in the two other known copies (mss. Roma, Bibl. Casanatensis 454 and Toledo, Bibl. Capitular 5–5), this work lacks any firsthand ascription to William or anyone else. The copy of the Paris manuscript is written in the same hand as all the first eight of the postills discussed previously, as well as those of Group A; at the explicit, an ascription to William has been added in a late medieval hand.[64] In this manuscript and in the one at Madrid, it is accompanied by works known to be William's. In the latter, the commentary is placed in the margins, as well as between the lines of the biblical text, in a format like that of the *Glossa Ordinaria*.

The work opens with an unusually lengthy prologue based on Aristotle's four causes, whose initial biblical citation, *Surgite postquam sederitis qui man⟨ducatis⟩ pa⟨nem⟩ do⟨loris⟩*,[65] is followed by the formula *In hiis uerbis primo et principaliter*.... Of the three copies examined, no two present the same text reliably. By comparison with the copies at Madrid and Paris, the one at Basel is particularly different and considerably longer.

Having examined this work in the manuscripts at Basel and Rome, Beryl Smalley concluded that "there seems to be a strong probability" that it should be added to the list of commentaries of a slightly earlier English Dominican, Simon of Hinton.[66] Her reasoning may be summarized as follows: she found it significant that one of the existing copies should be bound up with a work of the Franciscan William of Middleton (MS Casanatensis 454), just as Simon's postill on the Minor Prophets is bound up with William of Middleton's postill on Ecclesiasticus (MS Paris, BnF lat. 468). Further, she found external evidence of a Dominican provenance in the postill's appearance in the manuscript at Basel, which belonged to the Dominicans of that city, and internal evidence to the same effect in the following note at Job 1:3 (*eratque uir ille magnus inter omnes Orientales*): *Thema de sancto Dominico*.[67] She went on to note an absence of traces of borrowing from Hugh of St. Cher and remarked that while this is consistent with Simon's two known commentaries, this would not be expected of a Dominican of the second half of the thirteenth century. In addition, she observed that a verse given by the sixteenth-century bibliographer John Bale as the incipit to a no longer extant copy of a postill on Job by Simon of Hinton (Ecclesiasticus 1:29: *Vsque ad tempus sustinebit patiens*) appears about midway through this work's prologue. Since she had seen that the great length of a few of Simon's other works had resulted in their being truncated in transmission, and since the prologue to this work is indeed long, she surmised that John Bale's description was based on a copy lacking the first part of its prologue. So taken, Bale's report would amount to an attribution to Simon of the postill beginning *Surgite postquam sederitis*. She saw further evidence in a system of cross-reference to specific columns and lines in the exemplar, now lost. Since line numbering is characteristic of some thirteenth-century English scholastic manuscripts, and since she had previously come across such cross-references in Simon's works, she took this as evidence, first, of an English provenance and, more specifically, of Simon's authorship. She did recognize, however, a feature that contrasts with Simon's postills, namely, that its questions "are few and brief."[68]

Let us briefly consider each of these points. This work's inclusion in a manuscript containing a work by William of Middleton tells us little and hardly provides evidence for Simon of Hinton's authorship, even if another manuscript contains postills by both authors. Though Smalley was unaware of it when she made her inquiry, two manuscripts (at Madrid and Paris mentioned previously) present much more direct evidence of this sort pointing to another Dominican, namely, William of Alton. Both contain several of his known works, as well as this postill. All the same, we have previously decided to exclude such manuscript associations as evidence of authorship. (In the conclusion to chapter 2, more is said about our reasons for doing so.) Nor do we learn much from this work's apparent lack of borrowings from Hugh of St. Cher. Whereas much of the fifth chapter of William's *Super Threnos* has been taken directly from Hugh, in the first four borrowings from him are scarce. Similarly, while a few chapters of his *Super Iohannem* are heavily dependent on Hugh, others are virtually devoid of borrowings from him.[69] With respect to the incipit of the postill ascribed to Simon by John Bale, as Richard Sharpe has pointed out, it does not, in fact, correspond to the prologue to this work, notwithstanding the coinciding reference to Ecclesiasticus 1:29.[70] Finally, the system of cross-reference she found in the manuscripts at Basel and Rome is missing from the copies at Madrid and Paris. In its place, we find an expression commonly put to this use by commentators of the period, including William: *ut dictum est supra*.[71] It is therefore unclear whether the cross-reference appearing in the manuscripts at Basel and Rome is the work of the author. Even were we to assume that it is, we would have no reason to conclude that Simon of Hinton is he.

To the contrary, this work's style provides clear indications that its author is someone other than Simon. In several respects, it contrasts with his postills on the Minor Prophets and on Matthew[72] and is in many respects in keeping with the style of William's known works. In all copies consulted, we find all of William's characteristic terminology, though only after the early chapters, as it appears inconsistently in the first four and is largely absent from the first two.[73] And yet, there appears to have been no change of authorship; all other aspects of the postill's methodology and style are consistent throughout, and its initial *divisio* is explicitly coherent with one near the end:

[*Super Iob* 1:1] *VIR ERAT* etc. Iste liber totalis scilicet Iob in duas partes primo diuidi potest. In quarum prima agitur de ipsius perfectione; in secunda de perfectionis remuneratione. . . .

[*Super Iob* 42:10] *DOMINUS QUOQUE*. Terminata totali prima parte huius libri in qua agitur de ipsius Iob perfectione, hic secundo de ipsius perfectionis remuneratione. . . .[74]

Subdivisions are most often indicated by *in prima primo* and in most of the remaining cases by *ubi primo*. In Simon's known postills, the first formula is virtually absent, and the second is rare. The *expositio* systematically restates the elements of the *divisio*, is concise, and avoids skipping lines. Further, the technique of rhyming is regularly applied to the *divisio*, and lemmata are rarely introduced by *ibi*. In Simon's postills, by contrast, rhyming is far less consistent, and lemmata are regularly introduced by *ibi*. In *Super Iob*, neither *unde* nor *ibi* is employed to introduce citations, while *simile* is frequently put to this use. Questions are brief, related to the literal sense, and placed within the *expositio*.[75] Except for the prologue, the postill is generally free of lengthy digressions. In Simon's works, on the other hand, questions tend to be lengthy and often go far beyond the elucidation of the literal sense. Moreover, by contrast with William, Simon at times places questions, as well as digressions, within the *divisio*.[76] Simon's style of presenting spiritual expositions is, unfortunately, difficult to assess, since his commentary on the Minor Prophets survives only in two incomplete versions, one containing the spiritual commentary, the other the literal.[77] It is nonetheless worth noting that the spiritual expositions of *Super Iob* are occasionally in keeping with William's style. They are at times placed after literal comments and are indicated by terms such as *allegorice, moraliter*,[78] or *mistice*.[79]

To the present author, such considerations at first appeared sufficient grounds for ascribing this work to William, notwithstanding its terminological inconsistencies. On subsequent reading, however, considerable evidence to the contrary came into view. It may be summed up as follows: though shorter than the preceding postill *Super Iob* and more concise than Simon of Hinton's known works, this commentary is still far more discursive than any of William's known works.[80] More important, substantial sections of the biblical text are left without any literal commentary, while they are given lengthy allegorical or tropological expositions. These, it may be added, are explicitly identified as such only sporadically. A typical case appears in the exposition of Job's lamentation of his birth in 3:9: *obtenebrentur stellae caligine eius expectet lucem et non videat nec ortum surgentis aurorae (W)*.

> [3:9]*NEC ORTUM*, id est gloriam resurrectionis, que est ortus ad uitam beatam, *SURGENTIS AURORE*, id est militantis ecclesie, que lucem habet quodammodo cum tenebris.[81]

The commentator has nothing to say about the literal sense of this verse. This postill contains expositions extending to well over a column of text that betray little effort on the exegete's part to account for the text's literal meaning. This is not what we have come to expect from William.

In sum, this postill's methodology and style, clearly unlike Simon's, cannot be said to correspond to William's, either. Therefore, we decline to include this postill among his authenticated works.

11. *Super Proverbiis*; inc.: *Sapiens in uerbis producet seipsum.*
*Handlist* 748; *SOPMA* 1428; *Rep. Bibl.* 2780; *Répertoire* I, 116.
Manuscripts: Madrid, Bibl. Nac. 493, f. 73v–130v (ends incomplete at end of ch. 17);
    Saint-Omer 260, f. 219ra–249rb (ends incomplete at end of ch. 17).
Bibliography: SMALLEY, B., "Sapiential Books I," 66, 75.

Save for differences of copy, the texts of the two manuscripts known to contain this work are the same. Both are anonymous. In the Madrid manuscript, the missing chapters (18–31) are replaced by the corresponding chapters of Hugh of St. Cher's postill on Proverbs. As we have seen, the Madrid codex contains two works belonging to Group A; the one at Paris contains one. The postill opens with a well-developed prologue based on Aristotle's four causes, followed by an exposition of Jerome's prologue. Beryl

Smalley provisionally added this to the list of William's works, apparently as a result of its inclusion in MS Saint-Omer 260.[82]

Perhaps owing to the nature of the text commented upon (Proverbs is a collection of succinct two-line adages), the *divisio* of this postill appears with less frequency and complexity than in the works of Group A. It generally appears only at the beginning of each chapter, and in more than half the cases examined, it involves nothing more than a simple binary division with no ensuing subdivisions.[83] Its vocabulary is therefore difficult to classify as either typical or atypical of William. It is regularly opened by *supra*, a term infrequently put to this purpose in the Group A postills. *Hic* is so employed only once.[84] Subdivisions often appear without the formula *in prima primo*. The technique of rhyming is applied regularly to the elements of the *divisio*, yet less methodically than in the postills of Group A. Elements excluded from subdivision (introduced by *secundo, tertio, quarto*, etc.) are only sporadically subjected to subdivision in a subsequent smaller scale *divisio*.

Also differing from what we know of William's style is the exposition's discursiveness: comments on a single verse occasionally occupy more than a column of text.[85] Further, the author of this work tends to expound the spiritual senses without designating them as such and without having first given a literal interpretation of the verse at hand. An example appears at Proverbs 9:1 (*Sapientia aedificavit sibi domum, excidit columnas septem*), where he opens with the comment that the wisdom spoken of is Christ, who by his divine nature has built as his dwelling his body and soul. Without indicating that he is interpreting spiritually, he then identifies the house of wisdom with the church and then with the Blessed Virgin.[86] Again at Proverbs 9:3 (*Misit ancillas suas*), without first providing a literal interpretation and without indicating which sense he is expounding, he identifies the maidens sent out by wisdom as apostles and preachers.[87] Elsewhere, he often confuses the allegorical and moral senses. Rather than treat them separately under the distinct headings *allegorice* and *moraliter*, the author repeatedly places both allegorical and moral interpretations under a single heading (usually *mistice*, occasionally *moraliter*) and passes from one to another indiscriminately.[88] By contrast with the aforesaid scarcity and simplicity of the *divisio*, this departure from William's style and methodology cannot be explained by the particularity of the text commented upon. On the other hand, as with William's known postills, questions are short and related to the literal sense.[89]

Notwithstanding this last point of similarity, neither the style nor the methodology of this work corresponds to the typology of Group A in such a way as to provide clear evidence of its authenticity. Since there is no evidence in favor of it, we decline to list this postill among William's authenticated works.

12. *Super Ecclesiasten*; inc.: *Vidi in omnibus uanitatem et afflictionem.*
*Handlist* 748; *SOPMA* 1430; *Rep. Bibl.* 2782.
Manuscript: Tarragona, Bibl. Publ. 83, f. 47ra–76vb.

This postill is, in fact, the same as the next one, *Aspexi terram et ecce uacua erat*. Because its identity has been concealed by a different author's prologue (f. 47ra–49rb), Stegmüller, Kaeppeli, and Sharpe have taken this to be a distinct work and listed it separately. Yet apart from differences of copy, the exposition of Jerome's prologue (49vb–50va) and the entire commentary are identical with those of the following work and will therefore be considered in the discussion of it.

As for the prologue itself, its association with only one of eight known copies of this work argues strongly against its being part of the original composition. Also worth noting is that its author has taken the introductory verse (Ecclesiastes 2:11) from the book of the Bible to be commented upon. This is unlike William, who has done this in none of his known works. We see no reason to consider this prologue William's.

13. *Super Ecclesiasten*; inc.: *Aspexi terram et ecce uacua erat*.
*Handlist* 748; *SOPMA* 1429; *Rep. Bibl.* 2781; *Répertoire* I, 115; *SOP* I, 245b, 246a.
Manuscripts: Basel, Univ. Bibl. B III 20, f. 93ra–113ra; Paris, BnF lat. 14429, f. 119ra–154ra; 15592, f. 191ra–213rb; Madrid, Bibl. Nac. 493, f. 131r–165r; Tarragona, Bibl. Publ. 83, f. 47ra–76vb.
Bibliography: DAHAN, G., "L'Ecclésiaste contre Aristote? Les Commentaires de Eccl 1, 13 et 17–18 au XII<sup>e</sup> et XIII<sup>e</sup> siècles," in *Itinéraires de la raison. Études de philosophie médiévale offertes à Maria Cândida Pacheco*, Louvain-La-Neuve, 2005, 205–229; *L'exégèse chrétienne*, 128, 282, 355; GRABMANN, M., "Ungedrukte exegetische Schriften von Dominikanertheologen des 13. Jahrhunderts," *Angelicum* 20 (1943), 204–218 (206–208); SMALLEY, B., "Sapiential Books I," 71–75, 272–273; "Sapiential Books II," 104; COLLEGIUM SANCTI BONAVENTURAE, "Prolegomena," *Bon. Opera*, t. VI, xix–xxi.

This postill is credited to Thomas Aquinas in posterior hands in two manuscripts.[90] In another, two separate posterior attributions to William of Middleton have been altered (by different hands) to read "Altona."[91] All the repertories indicated include a text under this heading that is ascribed to Bonaventure.[92] It has been excluded from the previous list and will be ignored here because it is altogether different from the work now under consideration and appears to be an abridgment of the Franciscan's postill on Ecclesiastes. If not for these scarcely plausible ascriptions to a few of William's contemporaries, *Aspexi terram*'s authenticity would have been assumed, and it would have been included in Group A, so weighty is the external evidence in favor of his authenticity—it has been attributed to him by the original scribes of no fewer than four manuscripts.[93] Two of these four offer evidence for a *terminus ad quem* of 1267 for the date of this work's composition.[94]

Supporting William's authorship, we have a rare, albeit late, external reference that would appear to connect him to this work. He is cited—favorably—in a diatribe against the Immaculate Conception that first appeared in 1475 under the title *De veritate conceptionis Beatae Virginis Mariae.* The author of this treatise was Vincent Bandellus, a Dominican friar who became master of the order in 1501. Under the heading of 250 "very famous" doctors who held that the Blessed Virgin was conceived in original sin, Vincent cited William with reference to chapter 7 of a commentary on Ecclesiastes:

> Beatam uirginem in originali peccato fuisse concepta ducentiquinquaginta doctores tenent famosissimi. . . . Idem tenet Magister Gulielmus de Alcono doctor Parisien⟨sis⟩, super Ecclesiasten, c. 7.[95]

To be sure, nowhere in the postill in question does there appear anything remotely resembling a developed exposition of the question. Still, in the comments on Ecclesiastes 7:21 (*Non est enim homo iustus in terra qui faciat bonum et non peccet*), the author maintains that the Blessed Virgin was capable of venial sin before the Annunciation, yet not afterward:

> Contra, Iob XVII (Iob 17:2): *Non peccaui.* Responsio: Multi sunt sine mortali, sine ueniali nullus utens li⟨bero⟩ ar⟨bitrio⟩, nisi Christus, et hoc creditur de Beata Virgine. Potuit tamen peccasse uenialiter ante susceptionem Filii Dei, post non.[96]

Soon afterward, in the comments on Ecclesiastes 7:29 (*Et non inueni uirum de mille unum repperi mulierem ex omnibus non inueni*), he mentions original sin. Making an exception for Christ, he refrains from making one for any woman:

> [7:29]*ET NON INUENI*, supra parum: *Alta profunditas quis inueniet eam* (Ecl 7:25); et specificat generalitatem huius concupiscentie, quia fere in omnibus dominatur, dicens: *UIRUM DE MILLE UNUM REPERI*, id est Christum in quo non fuit hec concupiscentia, quia nec originale nec inclinatio ad actuale, *MULIERUM EX OMNIBUS NON INUENI*, in qua, scilicet non fuerit originale.[97]

Even if neither remark amounts to an explicit assertion that Mary was conceived in original sin, given the highly polemical and tendentious tenor of the *De veritate conceptionis*, it may reasonably be assumed that when referring to chapter 7 of William of Alton's commentary on Ecclesiastes, it was these passing remarks that Vincent had in mind.

Palémon Glorieux qualified this postill as doubtful, yet apparently following a suggestion of the editors of Quaracchi,[98] he raised the possibility that it is a *reportatio* of Bonaventure's commentary on Ecclesiastes, perhaps due to a likeness between the openings of the two commentaries, as well as to the aforementioned ascription.[99]

Bonaventure:

> *Verba Ecclesiastae* etc. Iste totalis liber dividitur in tres partes: in *titulum* sive prooemium et *tractatum*, qui incipit ibi: *Vanitas vanitatum* etc.; et *epilogum*, qui incipit ibi: *Cumque esset sapientissimus Ecclesiastesi.*[100]

MS Madrid, Bibl. Nac. 493, f. 132r:

⟨*V*⟩*ERBA ECCLESIASTES* etc. Iste liber diuiditur in titulum, siue proemium, et tractatum, qui secundum Hebreos incipit ibi: [113]*QUID HABET ANPLIUS HOMO*; secundum Ieronimum ibi: [112]*VANITAS UANITATUM.*

In fact, the two are otherwise altogether different, notwithstanding a close correspondence. As we shall have occasion to observe, William borrowed extensively from Bonaventure when commenting on John's Gospel.

There is nothing about this postill to lead us to doubt its authenticity. Every important aspect of its methodology and style falls within the typology of Group A. Specifically, it opens with a lengthy prologue (lacking in MS Paris, BnF lat. 14429) organized around Aristotle's four causes. *Hic* methodically introduces the *divisio*. Subdivisions are usually indicated by the formula *in prima primo*, and apart from the last example, *diuiditur* is virtually absent, as is *ibi* for the introduction of either lemmata or citations.[101] With rare exceptions, the technique of rhyming is applied to the final words of the elements of the *divisio*, and all these except the first are closed with a lemma. Subdivisions are of the first element, and subsequent elements are normally subdivided further along in the exposition. The lemmata of all elements are restated in the *expositio*. This, in turn, is generally concise, focused on the literal sense, and line-by-line. It is usually introduced by *dicit ergo*, occasionally by *continua*.[102] Questions are simple and closely related to the literal sense. They are, moreover, situated within the *expositio*. They do not appear clustered afterward, as they are in Bonaventure's authenticated commentaries.[103] Spiritual expositions are brief, placed after the literal commentary, preceded by a restatement of the lemma, and introduced by *allegorice, mistice*, or *moraliter*.[104] Finally, the entire work is relatively brief. Comparison with Bonaventure's commentary on Ecclesiastes is facilitated by the appearance of a copy of each in MS Paris, BnF lat. 14429. There, Bonaventure's work occupies approximately 40 percent more space, though it is written in columns of the same number of lines and of virtually the same dimensions.[105]

In sum, this postill's correspondence to the typology of Group A is extensive and consistent. In view of such evidence, as well as the four firsthand ascriptions to William, this work will be listed as authentic.

14. *Super Ecclesiasten*; inc.: *Si annis multis uixerit homo.*
*Rep. Bibl.* 2783; *Répertoire* I, 114.
Manuscript: Paris, BnF lat. 14260, f. 59–126v ("Expliciunt scripta fratris Guillelmi de Tornay super Ecclesiasten").
Bibliography: SMALLEY, B., "Sapiential Books I," 48–49.

This work has been ascribed to William of Tournai in the hand of the copyist. Beryl Smalley noted that Palémon Glorieux probably listed this and a postill *Super Sapientiam* (inc.: *Beati serui tui*) among William of Alton's doubtful works by association with a preceding postill on the Canticle, *Funiculus triplex* (to be discussed next), that is generally attributed to him. She also pointed out that there is no reason for questioning the ascription to William of Tournai, since it is nearly contemporary and is uncontradicted.[106]

While the likelihood of William of Tournai's authorship does not concern us, we may sum up the evidence for William of Alton's as follows: the work is preceded by a lengthy prologue based on Aristotle's four causes. Notwithstanding a few similarities, the vocabulary of the *divisio* differs from that of William's known works. As with the works of Group A, the *divisio* is regularly introduced by *hic* or *supra*, the final words of the elements resulting from the *divisio* rhyme regularly, and lemmata are applied to all elements save the first. Questions, moreover, are situated within the expositio and generally concern the literal sense.[107]

On the other hand, there are several departures from William's typology. The lemmata of the *divisio* are regularly introduced by *ibi*, and subdivisions are seldom indicated by the formula *in prima primo*. In its place, we often find *diuiditur* or *prima in duo, tres*, and so on, neither of which William of Alton employs regularly.[108] Further, by comparison with William of Alton's known works, the amount of text given to the *divisio* relative to the *expositio* is disproportionate. *Divisiones* occasionally occupy the larger part of a column of text and follow each other in close succession, with only a few lines of the *expositio* intervening. In consequence, those elements not subdivided in a major division (introduced by *secundo, tertio, quarto*, etc.) are often not subsequently subdivided in a smaller scale division, as they are in William's known works. One result is that the *divisio* appears as an end in itself, rather than as a guide to the *expositio*. Another difference is the work's discursiveness. Failing to show the brevity characteristic of William, it is far longer than either of the two preceding postills on Ecclesiastes. Finally, the author makes no effort to distinguish between the literal and spiritual senses by the use of terms such as *litteraliter* or *moraliter*. So, for example, at Ecl 7:27 (*et inveni amariorem morte*), he remarks that concupiscence is more bitter than death because it separates the soul from God, disturbs the conscience, and accumulates temporal and eternal punishments.[109] Whether this is the biblical text's literal or spiritual sense, the reader must decide for himself.

Since this postill's style hardly bears witness to William of Alton's authorship, we find no reason for listing it among his authenticated works.

15. *Super Canticum Canticorum*; inc.: *Funiculus triplex difficile rumpitur.*
*Handlist* 749; *SOPMA* 1431; *Rep. Bibl.* 2784; *Répertoire* I, 114.
Manuscripts: Madrid, Bibl. Nac. 53; f. 160ra–182rb; Paris, BnF lat. 472, f. 34ra–69vb; 14260, 1ra–58rb; 15571, f. 27ra–38rb; 15592, f. 214ra–251rb; 15960, f. 166ra–240ra; Troyes, Bibl. mun. 1861, 171ra–219va.
Bibliography: BALE, J., *Index Brittaniae Scriptorum*, ed. R. Poole and Mary Bateson, Oxford, 1902 (reprinted with additional material, C. Brett and J. P. Carley, Woodbridge, 1990), 113; DAHAN, G., *L'exégèse chrétienne*, 270; RIEDLINGER, H., *Die*

*Makellosigkeit der Kirche in Den Lateinischen Hoheliedkommentaren Des Mittelalters*, Munster, 1958, 285–287; SMALLEY, B., "Sapiential Books I," 70–71.

This postill is believed to survive in sixteen manuscripts. Its single prologue, based on Aristotle's four causes, is the same in all the copies consulted. At the explicit of the Madrid manuscript, the work is ascribed in the hand of the original scribe to Nicolas of Gorran.[110] In each of the Paris manuscripts, this work is anonymous. All copies consulted have the same explicit.[111] Similarly anonymous are two copies at Cambridge. The attribution to William apparently owes to the explicit of a copy at Bordeaux, whose catalogue entry is as follows: "Expliciunt scripta fratris Guilelmi de (mot effacé) super Canticum." This, however, could just as easily be a slightly later Dominican named William, to whom the same work is ascribed in a manuscript at Siena: "fr. Guillelmus de Tornaco." None of the preceding four manuscripts was consulted for this inquiry.[112] Of the seven examined, the text of the commentary varies from one copy to another, yet none is sufficiently independent to call for a separate assessment.

In no copy does the terminology of the *divisio* correspond to the typology of Group A. Examination of the initial *divisio* of each of the eight chapters of each copy shows that none begins with *hic*.[113] The expression *in prima primo* is altogether absent, and in its place, there often appears a formula not found in William's known commentaries: *in primo dicuntur....*[114] In all copies, *ibi* regularly introduces the lemmata of the *divisio*, and it occasionally precedes biblical citations.[115] The technique of rhyming is applied less regularly than in the postills of Group A. Still more telling is the opening of the *expositio*. As in the postills of Group A, it is generally indicated by the formula *dicit ergo*, followed by a restatement of the initial lemma of the preceding *divisio*. Then there appears something new. The term *continuatur* systematically follows immediately to introduce another lemma, generally taken from a verse preceding the previous *divisio*. The following example taken from the opening of the second chapter is typical:

> [2:1]*EGO FLOS CAMPI.* Secundum capitulum et secunda pars, ubi sponsus reuocat sponsam ad laborem actionis. Et dicuntur quatuor: primo sponsus reuocat sponsam ad laborem actionis; secundo ostendit sponsa quod propter dignitatem sponsi debet reuerti ad laborem actionis, ibi: [2:3]*SICUT MALUM*; tertio sponsus consolando sponsam monet adolesentulas ne sponse sint moleste in statu actionis, ibi: [2,7]*ADIURO UOS FILIE*; quarto ponitur uox sponse de tali consolatione exultantis, ibi [2,8]*VOX DILECTI MEI.* In prima dicuntur duo: primo dicit sponsus quod oportet surgere a lecto contemplationis ut decoretur totus mundus predicatione sui nominis; secundo ostendit fructum predicationis, ibi: [2:1]*ET LILIUM.* Dicit ergo: [2:1]*EGO FLOS CAMPI.* Continuatur sic: [1:15]*LECTU⟨LUS⟩* etc....[116]

It will be recalled that while William on occasion substitutes *continua* or *continuat* for *dicit ergo*, he avoids employing these terms in combination. More important, after presenting a *divisio*, he does not present lemmata of preceding biblical verses. In the prior case, *lectulus* precedes the *divisio*'s initial lemma by two verses. On view in the initial *divisio* of each of *Super Canticum*'s eight chapters, this practice could well be a proper trait, or signature, of the author. We have no reason, however, to suppose that William is he.

In the *divisio*, as well as the *expositio*, spiritual expositions predominate and are generally not set apart from literal ones. Even if this may to some extent be explained by the text of the Canticle, it contrasts sharply with William's practice of consecrating the *divisio* to the literal sense and clearly delimiting spiritual exegesis within the *expositio*.

But there is still another significant departure from the typology of Group A— there is no trace of the brevity characteristic of William. To the contrary, this postill's discursiveness contrasts sharply with the concision typical of him. Transcription of several columns of text suggests that the entire postill is well over four times the length of William's *Super Threnos*, this notwithstanding the Canticle's relative shortness with respect to Lamentations.[117]

To sum up, neither the style nor the methodology of this work bears witness to William's authorship. In the absence of evidence favoring its authenticity, we refrain from listing it among his works.

16. *Super Sapientiam*; inc.: *Beati serui tui, hi qui stant.*
*Handlist* 750; *Rep. Bibl.* 2785; *Répertoire* I, 114.
Manuscript: Paris, BnF lat. 14260, f. 133ra–204vb.
Bibliography: SMALLEY, B., "Sapiential Books I," 48–50.

As was the postill *Super Ecclesiasten* (inc.: *Si annis multis uixerit homo*; no. 14), this was included by Glorieux among William of Alton's doubtful works, apparently by virtue of its association with the postill on the Canticle, *Funiculus triplex* in MS Paris, BnF lat. 14260. Though anonymous, Beryl Smalley lists this among William of Tournai's possible works, this by virtue of its association with the postill on Ecclesiastes in the same manuscript, which, as we have seen, is ascribed to him.[118]

Without passing judgment on the likelihood of William of Tournai's authorship, we may sum up the evidence for William of Alton's as follows. The prologue is based on Aristotle's four causes and is otherwise in keeping with what we would expect from William of Alton. Afterward, the vocabulary is comparable to that of the works of Group A. The *divisio* is regularly introduced by *hic*, and subdivisions by *in prima primo*, yet the latter appears less regularly than in William of Alton's known works. Rhyming of the final words of the elements resulting from the *divisio* is regular, as is the application of lemmata to all elements save the first. Neither lemmata nor citations are regularly introduced by *ibi*.

The clearest departure from the typology of Group A is the portion of text given to the *divisio*. Relative to the *expositio*, it is generally much more extensive than in William's known works. Often lengthy enough to occupy the better part of a column of text, instances of the *divisio* at times follow each other in close succession, separated by expositions of only a few lines. As a result, those elements not subdivided in a major *divisio* (introduced by *secundo, tertio, quarto,* etc.) are not regularly subjected to subdivision in a subsequent smaller scale *divisiò.* Whereas William normally employs this method so that each chapter's initial *divisio* is integrally related to each of a series of subsequent smaller scale *divisiones,* here there are successive long *divisiones* with little or no apparent connection to each other. Put simply, the *divisio* appears to be an end in itself rather than a guide to the *expositio.*[119] Finally, it will be noted that nonbiblical citations generally seem to be limited to the *Glossa Ordinaria.*

In view of the lack of evidence for William's authorship, we decline to include this postill among his authenticated works.

17. *Super Sapientiam*; inc.: *Fons sapientie uerbum Domini.*
*Handlist* 750; *Rep. Bibl.* 2786, 2938 (William of Middleton); (John of Varzy); *Répertoire* I, 115–16, 125 (John of Varzy); *SOP* I, 245b–246a; 373a.
Manuscripts: Basel, Univ. B III 20, f. 114ra–144v (inc.: *Diligite lumen sapientiae*); Univ. B IV 21, 71ra–120vb; Paris, BnF lat. 14429, f. 50ra–93ra (inc.: *Diligite lumen sapientiae*); ibid., f. 155ra–206vb; 15573, f. 156ra–189vb; Saint-Omer, Bibl. mun. 260, f. 250ra–288vb; Troyes, Bibl. Mun. 667, f. 203ra–241vb (ends incomplete at Sap 19:13).
Editions: *S. Bonaventurae Opera Omnia*, Venise, 1574, t. V, 801–933; *S. Bonaventurae Opera Omnia*, Vatican, 1588, t. I, 358–427; *S. Bonaventurae Opera Omnia*, Lyons, 1668, t. I, 341–407; *S. Bonaventurae Opera Omnia*, Vivès, 1867, t. X, 1–137; *S. Bonaventurae Opera Omnia*, Quaracchi, 1893, t. VI, 137–233.
Bibliography: BOUGEROL, J.-G., "Pecia et critique d'authenticité. Le problème du *Super Sapientiam* attribué à Bonaventure," in *La production du livre universitaire au Moyen Âge*, Paris, 1988, 205–208; "Pour des «Prolegomena Postquam» de l'édition critique de S. Bonaventure Quaracchi 1882–1902," in *The Editing of Theological and Philosophical Texts from the Middle Ages*, ed. M. Asztalos, Stockholm, 1986, 121–131; *Introduction à l'étude de Saint Bonaventure*, Tournai, 1961, 145; *Introduction à Saint Bonaventure*, Paris, 1988, 182; BRADY, I., "The Edition of the *Opera Omnia* of St. Bonaventure Revisited," in *Proceedings of the Seventh Centenary of the Death of St. Bonaventure*, ed. P. Foley, St. Bonaventure, NY, 1975, 96–97; "The Edition of the *Opera Omnia* of St. Bonaventure," *AFH* 70 (1977), 370–371; CHAPOTIN, R., *Histoire des Dominicains,* 570; DISTELBRINK, B., *Bonaventurae Scripta: Authentica dubia vel spuria critica recensita*, Rome, Instituto Storico Cappuccino, 1975, 18–19; GRABMANN, M., "Ungedruckte exegetische Shriften von Dominikanertheologen des 13. Jahrhunderts," *Angelicum* 20 (1943), 204–218 (208–209); MONTI, D., "A Reconsideration of the Authorship of the Commentary of the Book of Wisdom attributed to Bonaventure," *AFH* 79 (1986) 359–391; SMALLEY, B., "Sapiential Books I," 47–48, 66–67, 236–241; COLLEGIUM SANCTI BONAVENTURAE, "Prolegomena," *S. Bonaventurae Opera omnia,* t. VI, xiix–xxi.

This postill has been diffused with two different but closely related prologues. In one copy with the incipit listed here, it is ascribed in a posterior hand to William of Middleton, and in a correction of this ascription, to William of Alton;[120] in another, it has been ascribed in two posterior hands to John of Varzy.[121] In copies preceded by a prologue that begins *Diligite lumen sapientie*, this same postill has been ascribed in posterior hands to John of Varzy (as a bachelor)[122] and to Nicholas of Gorran[123] and has appeared in several printings under Bonaventure's name, one of which was at the Vatican, the most recent by the editors of Quaracchi. Two copies contain both prologues.[124] In none of the known copies is there a firsthand attribution to anyone. For the sake of convenience, we shall refer to this work as *Fons sapientie*. For its date of composition, we have a *terminus ad quem* of 1267 in two firsthand inscriptions (mentioned earlier in connection with the postill on Ecclesiastes *Aspexi terram*),[125] one in MS Paris, BnF lat. 14429, the other in an identical colophon after the copy in MS Basel, Univ. Bibl. B III 20.[126]

The present consideration of this conflicting evidence follows numerous precedents over the previous three centuries, of which Dominic Monti has provided an excellent survey,[127] beginning in 1722 with Casimir Oudin's affirmation of Bonaventure's authorship.[128] Without undue repetition of Monti's observations, we would do well to pause for a brief look at the main points of the more important discussions, beginning, however, a few years earlier, with the remarks of Quetif and Echard of 1719.[129] After raising the question of whether this work belongs to Bonaventure, Nicolas of Gorran, or William of Alton, they noted that Bonaventure was still alive when this postill appeared under someone else's name in 1267 among the codices of a serious man who was a master in theology, namely, Adenulph (of Anagni).[130] They added that the Roman editors (*Romani editores*) had wrongly credited Bonaventure with several works whose true authors subsequently came to be known. With respect to Nicolas of Gorran, they observed that he is credited with another postill, *Super Sapientiam*. As for William of Alton, they concluded that the evidence of ascription in a single manuscript is inconclusive and held out the hope that more curious librarians would shed light on the matter.[131]

In the prolegomena to their 1893 edition of this text, the editors of Quaracchi quoted and affirmed this reasoning and openly admitted to a lack of manuscript evidence pointing to Bonaventure.[132] The attribution to William they dismissed as lacking credibility in view of a false attribution to him of a copy of Bonaventure's postill *Super Ecclesiasten*, also in MS Paris, BnF lat. 14429. All the same, they put forward the suggestion that the term *secundum* before William's name in the two attributions could designate him as a source rather than as an author.[133] John of Varzy's candidacy they set aside in view of yet another postill *Super Sapientiam* credited to him.[134] Having disposed of each of the competing candidates, they returned to Bonaventure, whereupon they acknowledged that there was reason for suspecting that others had truncated or adulterated the work and pointed to a few internal indications to this effect. Specifically, they found unusual the frequency of the postill's borrowings from the *Glossa* (*ordinaria*) and the brevity and haphazardness of its treatment of questions.[135] None of this prevented them from attributing it to Bonaventure. In partial explanation for the postill's differences from Bonaventure's other works, they suggested that he authored it before he was a master.[136]

Writing a little more than a half century later, Beryl Smalley noted that "the (Quara-cchi) editors rely on tradition rather than on manuscript evidence in claiming it for him." She also pointed out that the work contains numerous borrowings not only from the *Glossa* (*ordinaria*) but also from Hugh of St. Cher and added that its lengthy and devel-oped *questiones* point to a master. Concluding with the remark "Chaos has resulted," she declined to decide whether Bonaventure authored it, and if so, in what form.[137]

Bonaventure's authorship was vigorously contested a few decades later in the studies of three successive Franciscan scholars: Ignatius Brady, Jacques-Guy Bougerol, and Dominic Monti.[138] While the first was content to remove it from Bonaventure, Jacques-Guy Bougerol drew attention to the ascription to John of Varzy in the manuscript at Basel and asserted that he composed two other postills (on Proverbs and the Canticle) accompanying this one in MS Troyes, Bibl. mun. 667. After stating, mistakenly, that the text is unattributed in MS Paris, BnF lat. 14429, he proposed John of Varzy as the most likely candidate.[139] Following an extensive discussion, Dominic Monti concluded that William of Alton and John of Varzy are the most likely candidates, yet remarked, "I incline towards John, if only on the strength of the Troyes MS."[140] In addition to Bonaventure, the list of possible authors for *Fons sapientie* includes William of Middle-ton, John of Varzy, Nicolas of Gorran, and William of Alton. While it lies beyond our purposes to dispel whatever chaos may surround questions concerning the writings of any of the first three, toward the end of clarifying the prospects for William's author-ship, we will consider the merits of their claims to authorship of this work.

Let us turn now to the Quaracchi editors' objections to William's authorship. First, as they would have it, the ascription to William at the incipit of the copy of MS Paris, BnF lat. 14429 (f. 155r) loses credibility in view of another attribution to him at the ex-plicit of an immediately preceding postill, *Super Ecclesiasten* (f. 154a), which they take to be Bonaventure's. Not having seen the manuscript, they took the ascriptions from Quetif and Echard and observed that the wording of the two is the same: " . . . *eisdem prorsus verbis* inscripta sit: *secundum fratrem Gulielmum de Altona ordinis Fratrum Praedicatorum* (Echard. pag. 245b)." At this, they suggested that the two are sufficiently related that their credibility stands or falls together. In fact, the two ascriptions are clearly in different hands. More to the point, as we have seen (no. 12), the former is a firsthand ascription of a postill *Super Ecclesiasten* (inc.: *Aspexi terram*) that is, in fact, William's. The Quaracchi editors mistakenly took this work to be an abridgment of Bonaventure's *Super Ecclesiasten*, which appears at the beginning of the same codex and which they printed immediately before this postill on Wisdom in the same volume.[141] It may be safely concluded that the ascription of *Aspexi terram* to William in no way argues against his authorship of the postill on Wisdom in question here.

The Quaracchi editors' second objection is less concrete. They assert, but do not show, that comparison of the two prologues indicates that the one beginning *Fons sapi-entie uerbum Domini* is derivative from the one beginning *Diligite lumen sapientie*. From this, they conclude that the author of the prologue *Fons sapientie* is someone other than the author of the postill.[142] In fact, comparison of the prologues permits no such determination. Either may be prior or posterior. More important, especially in view of the instability of the prologue material, there is no reason to assume that attribution to William or anyone else depends on the authenticity of either one. Again, in neither version are there any manuscript ascriptions to Bonaventure.

Nothing of what has been said so far allows us to eliminate any of the other contenders. Because John of Varzy was likely still a bachelor in 1267[143] and Nicolas of Gorran was never a master,[144] both would seem to be excluded on the basis of a few commonly held assumptions, specifically, that masters alone commented on the spiritual senses, that they alone entertained questions, and that they alone produced virtually all surviving commentaries.[145] The chances of either Nicolas or John are improved neither by their apparent posteriority to William nor by the ascription to them of other postills on Wisdom.[146] None of the aforesaid propositions, however, can be a matter of certainty, and the many commentaries ascribed to Nicolas[147] (at least one of which, it will be recalled, is replete with questions) present evidence to the effect that masters monopolized the production of commentaries less completely than some have supposed.[148]

However this may be, Nicolas's style, to the extent that we have been able to evaluate it, is unlike this postill's. In particular, as we have seen, when introducing subdivisions, Nicolas often employs the term *diuiditur* and seldom uses the formula *in prima primo*.[149] Later we shall see that *Fons sapientie* differs from what we know of his style in both respects.

John of Varzy presents a more difficult case because there are no commentaries for which his authorship can be a matter of confidence. As it is, we have no clear basis for comparing his style to that of *Fons sapientie*. Dominic Monti has taken note of a close correspondence between the numbers of *peciae* of three postills—on Proverbs (inc.: *Sacramentum regis*), the Canticle (inc.: *Cantabo dilecto meo*), and a copy of *Fons sapientie*—in MS Troyes, Bibl. mun. 667 and the aforesaid Paris taxation list of 1275.[150] Concluding on this basis that the three commentaries of the Troyes manuscript were copied from the exemplar indicated in the taxation list, he infers that all three were composed by the same author. What is more, because previous research had associated the postills on Proverbs and the Canticle (very tenuously) with John of Varzy,[151] he tentatively favored John's authorship of the postill on Wisdom. We have already met the postills on Proverbs and the Canticle. It will be recalled that they, as well as another, on Ecclesiastes, were included in the list of commentaries employed as a basis of comparison with William's known works. John of Varzy's authorship of each of them is highly questionable. Those on Proverbs and Ecclesiastes are anonymous and have been associated with him mainly by virtue of their inclusion in the manuscripts Paris, BnF lat. 14259 and Troyes, Bibl. mun. 667, both of which contain the third, on the Canticle, for which we have conflicting evidence—it is ascribed to William of Middleton, as well as to John of Varzy. To this, it may be added that it is consistent with William of Middleton's style.[152] However this may be, examination of these works shows that they differ markedly from one another, leaving good reason to suppose that they are from different authors.

Dominic Monti has pointed out that the explicits of *Fons sapientie* and the postill on Proverbs are alike.[153] To this, two points may be made in reply. First, the explicit to the postill on the Canticle supposedly by John, *Cantabo dilecto meo*, is wholly unlike those of the other two postills supposedly by him.[154] And second, explicits similar to the one of *Fons sapientie* close two of William's known postills, specifically, on Ecclesiastes[155] and on John's Gospel,[156] as well as one of the other postills on Wisdom (inc.: *Diligite iustitiam*) that is possibly by John of Varzy.[157] In sum, this postill's explicit presents no clear evidence pointing to anyone.

It is worth dwelling on the lack of correspondence between the style of *Fons sapientie* and that of any of the other works assigned to John of Varzy. In particular, in none of them are subdivisions indicated as frequently by *in prima primo*. While this formula is virtually absent from "John's" postill on Ecclesiastes, its purpose is regularly met by the now familiar term not used by William, *diuiditur*.[158] Though it does appear with some frequency in "John's" postill on the Canticle, its purpose is often met there by *in prima duo*,[159] a formula found neither in the postill in question nor in William's known works. And yet, one text where *in prima duo* does appear regularly is in still another postill on Wisdom in MS Paris, BnF lat. 14259, *Diligite iustitiam qui iudicatis terram*.[160] Despite its sharing much of its material with the aforementioned postill on Wisdom of the same incipit, it is a different work. On the face of it, the latter postill on Wisdom resembles more closely "John's" commentary *Super Canticum* (inc.: *Cantabo dilecto meo*) than does *Fons sapientie*. Of the works associated with John of Varzy, the one whose style is closest to that of *Fons sapientie* is the postill on Proverbs (inc.: *Sacramentum regis*). But even in this case, an important difference is conspicuous in its length. Occupying the first 150 folios, the copy of MS Troyes, Bibl. mun. 667, is nearly four times as long as the subsequent copy of *Fons sapientie* on thirty-nine folios. Given the similar lengths of the two books commented, this is remarkable; Proverbs is only slightly longer than Wisdom.[161] Put simply, while the brevity of *Fons sapientie* places it squarely in conformity with an important criterion for William's authorship, it also sharply differentiates it from a work attributed to John of Varzy. In sum, no evidence considered so far supports an attribution of the work to either Bonaventure or John of Varzy.

On the other hand, *Fons sapientie* is thoroughly in keeping with William's style. Let us consider the internal evidence in some detail. With respect to the sort of evidence that could be presented by this work's theological content, a cursory reading found no clear indications pointing either to Bonaventure or to William of Alton. There are, however, occasional hints, such as the following one at Wisdom 3:1: *Iustorum autem animae in manu Dei sunt*,[162] to which the expositor finds a parallel in John 10:28: *Et non rapiet eas quisquam de manu mea*. When in his postill *Super Iohannem* William arrives at John 10:28, he cites this same verse of Wisdom when replying to a question. Though he has taken the entire question and its response directly from Bonaventure's commentary on John,[163] the citation of Wisdom 3:1 is his own.[164] More common is the sort of case presented by a question appearing at the exposition of Wisdom 16:13: *Tu enim vitae et mortis habes potestatem*. Claiming that God cannot be the cause of death, an objector has appealed to Wisdom 1:13: *Deus mortem non fecit*. The expositor resolves the apparent contradiction by way of a distinction between efficient and deficient causality:

... dicendum quod in morte est privatio vitae, quae nihil est, et ideo causam efficientem non habet, sed magis deficientem....[165]

Anyone suspecting that is the sort of thing that Bonaventure could say will find confirmation in his commentary on John, where he raises a nearly identical question with respect to the cause of blindness when expounding John 9:39 (... *veni ut qui non vident videant et qui vident caeci fiant*). The objection that God cannot be the cause of blindness is supported by 1 Io 1:3: *Deus Lux est*. In reply, Bonaventure describes blindness as follows: ... *privatio est et non habet causam efficientem, sed deficientem*.[166] While virtually identical to the preceding solution, this case proves nothing, since in his own postill *Super Iohannem*, William has borrowed and abbreviated Bonaventure's question, as well as his reply:

> Contra: *Lux est,* ergo etc. Responsio: Excecatio potest considererari secundum illud quod est, et sic priuatio est, nec habet causam efficientem, set deficientem.[167]

This example serves to illustrate one of the difficulties lying in store for anyone attempting to establish authorship by looking for one of Bonaventure's known theological positions. William and others borrowed from him so freely that their exegesis is often not easily distinguishable from his on such grounds.

Clearer evidence of authorship is presented by the methodology and style of *Fons sapientie*. Though different from what we have seen in the works of the aforementioned authors, there is nothing about this work's style or methodology that falls outside the typology of Group A. Both of the prologues associated with it are arranged around Aristotle's four causes and are otherwise entirely typical. *Hic* methodically introduces the *divisio*, subdivisions are regularly introduced by the formula *in prima primo*, and *diuiditur* is virtually absent. As for the use of *ibi* for the introduction of either lemmata or citations, in the Quaracchi edition, it shows up more frequently than is normal in William's works. It is even more common in the copy of MS Saint-Omer 260.[168] Yet *ibi* is virtually absent from both lemmata and citations in four early copies.[169] Of these, three copies are in the two codices whose dating to 1267 we have seen—one in MS Basel, Univ. B III 20, and two in MS Paris, BnF lat. 14429. The fourth is in MS Paris, BnF lat. 15573,[170] dated to before 1272 (notable for its inclusion among the texts employed by the editors of Quaracchi to establish the printed text).[171] Further, subdivisions are generally of the first element, and subsequent elements are typically subdivided further along in the exposition. Typical of William of Alton, the following example is also typical of this work:

> *Hi sunt, quos aliquando* etc. Hic ponit *materiam* confessionis impiorum confitentium errorem proprium, primo circa *iustorum vitam*; secundo, circa *vitam propriam: Lassati* etc. In prima primo confitentur Sanctorum *contemptum*

praeteritum et irrisionem; secundo, status illorum reprobationem: *Nos insensati*
etc.; tertio, eorum tunc *praesentem exaltationem*: Ecce, *quomodo computate sunt*;
quarto, *suum errorem: Ergo erravimus.*[172]

Here as well as elsewhere, the lemmata of all elements are restated in the *expositio*, which is
brief and concentrated upon the literal sense of each line. The element left out of the sole
subdivision, indicated by *in prima primo*, is itself subjected to subdivision four verses later:
"*Lassati sumus* etc. Hic tangit. . . ."[173] To be sure, this trait is hardly proper to William—it
appears regularly in the work of Bonaventure and Nicolas of Gorran. Yet the introduction
of the *divisio* by *hic* and of subdivisions by *in prima primo* is characteristic neither of the
Franciscan master nor of Nicolas. Also in evidence here are two other traits found throughout the postill: the application of rhyming to the final words of the elements of the *divisio*
and the closing of all elements except the first with a lemma. Though typical of William,
neither trait appears systematically in Bonaventure's undisputed commentaries.[174]

As for the *expositio*, it is usually introduced by *dicit ergo*, a formula common in the
postills of many authors. More particular to William is the occasional application for
this purpose of *continuat*.[175] Perhaps the most significant trait that sets the exposition
apart from what we would expect from Bonaventure is its brevity. We have noted that
the editors of Quaracchi took this as an indication of an abridgment or corruption of
the original text. The commentary is, in fact, complete. It leaves no verse of the Wisdom
text without at least a brief literal exposition, and when placed against the background
of the postills of Group A, it has no appearance of being truncated or diminished.
Questions are closely related to the literal sense. Moreover, as the Quaracchi editors
have noticed, they are brief by comparison with Bonaventure's and are situated within
the *expositio*. The latter feature sets them apart from the questions of Nicolas of Gorran
as well as Bonaventure, who place them in clusters after each lesson.

Also worth noting is another trait identified by the Quaracchi editors, as well as
Beryl Smalley, as out of keeping with Bonaventure's manner, namely, the preponderance
of borrowings, particularly from the *Glossa ordinaria*. However odd this may have
seemed to them in their consideration of Bonaventure's authorship, it could hardly be
more typical of William, as even a cursory glance at his commentaries *Super Threnos* or
*Super Iohannem* will show. Dominic Monti has documented this postill's dependence
not only on the *Glossa ordinaria* but also on Hugh of St. Cher, "large sections being
taken almost verbatim."[176] The same could be said of any of William's known works, as
we discuss in some detail in chapter 4.

This postill, moreover, displays a notable feature that sets it apart from what we
would expect from William of Middleton, yet which is perfectly consistent with the
typology of Group A, specifically, the predominance of the literal sense. While the
commentary deals largely with the moral life, this is generally not tropology but literal
exegesis of a text that is itself primarily concerned with the moral life. Similarly, while
there is frequent discussion of Jesus Christ, especially with respect to his sufferings, this

is generally not allegory but literal exegesis of passages the author has taken as Solomon's prophecy.[177] Spiritual exegesis is brief and altogether absent from the *divisio.* Moreover, it is clearly distinguished from the literal commentary. In particular, the term *ecclesia* in its various forms is confined to remarks introduced by *allegorice.*[178]

But there is more. Again we refer to Dominic Monti, who has found evidence against Bonaventure's authorship of this work in the interest it shows in two scientific aspects of exegesis emerging at the time—literary analysis and textual criticism. With respect to the first, he provides a few examples of studies of words, notably designated by the fairly rare definite article *ly.* We have seen that this is typical of William.[179] Concerning the second, he observes that while Bonaventure is normally content to take the Vulgate text as he finds it, the author of this work is prone to offer Old Latin and Greek alternatives.[180] We have seen that this, too, is typical of William. To be sure, interests neither in literary analysis nor in textual criticism figure among the traits we have employed as criteria for William's authorship. Still, both offer evidence to that effect. Further evidence pointing to William appears in another trait that caught Monti's attention, one we have designated as a criterion for authenticity—the use of a broad range of sources, pagan and Christian, Latin and Greek, ancient and medieval.[181]

Let us sum up. Particularly clear is the evidence against the authorship of either Bonaventure or William of Middleton. If evidence against Nicolas of Gorran and John of Varzy is made somewhat less compelling by the uncertain authorship of the works used as bases for comparison, it can be said that *Fons sapientie* is markedly different from all of them and remarkably in conformity with the typology we have delineated for William of Alton. Dominic Monti has described the work as follows:

> Although not highly creative, it is a fine abridgement of the traditional sources presenting the doctrine of the Book of Wisdom, but brought to greater scholastic precision.[182]

With little more than a change of the name of the book commented, this remark could serve as an accurate description of any one of William's known works. In view of this evidence, as well as that of the ascription to William of Alton in MS Paris, BnF lat. 14429, this postill will be listed among William's works, and the attributions to Bonaventure, William of Middleton, and John of Varzy will be set aside.

As for the prologues, on the available evidence, neither of the two can be authenticated with certitude, but it will be noted that a few indications point toward the one beginning *Fons sapientie uerbum Domini.* To begin, it mentions two historical details not found in the prologue *Diligite lumen sapientie.* While both cite the *Ecclesiastical History*'s assertion that "all the chorus of ancients said the book entitled *Wisdom* was Solomon's," only *Fons sapientie* mentions the names of two members of that chorus, Hegesippus and Irenaeus. Further, only *Fons sapientie* mentions that the compilation of the book of Wisdom by Philo was similar to the compilation of Proverbs by the men of

Hezekiah (cf. Proverbs 25:2). We have seen that such historical interest is typical of William. More significant is the incipit itself. The author of the prologue *Diligite lumen sapientie* turned to Wisdom 6:23 for his introductory verse. By contrast, the author of *Fons sapientie uerbum Domini* turned to a book other than the one subject to commentary, Ecclesiasticus 1:5. As we have seen, such is also the case with all of William's known works, as well as those of his contemporaries Albert, Bonaventure, and Thomas. The practice was typical of the Parisian commentaries of the period. This is hardly insignificant, as the introductory verse provides the theme for the entire prologue and serves as the basis for the explanation of each of the book's four causes. If the preceding considerations are hardly decisive, neither are they insignificant. Of the two prologues, *Fons sapientie uerbum Domini* must be judged the more likely candidate.

18. *Super Ezechielem*; inc.: *Vidi et audiui uocem unius aquile uolantis per medium celi.*
*Handlist* 749; *SOPMA* 1435; *Rep. Bibl.* 2792; *Répertoire* I, 114; *SOP* 245a.
Manuscript: Paris, BnF lat. 573, f. 156ra–198vb.
Bibliography: DAHAN, G., *L'exégèse chrétienne*, 261, 313, 414–415.

This anonymous work is associated with William on the basis of its inclusion in MS Paris, BnF lat. 573, which, as we have seen, contains postills on Isaiah, Jeremiah, and Lamentations, each accompanied by a firsthand ascription. All four are in the hand of the same copyist. In the manuscript, a *divisio* of the entire book precedes the author's prologue whose incipit is listed above,[183] which is itself followed by a short exposition of Jerome's prologue. Explicit coherence between the apparently out-of-place opening *divisio* and the initial one of chapter 4 (as well as the absence of a *divisio* at Ez 1:1) shows that there has been no change of authorship and that it is only by an accident of copy that it precedes the two prologues.

In all respects, this postill corresponds to the typology of Group A. Specifically, though the terms *diuiditur* and *ibi* are frequent in the initial *divisio*, they are scarce afterward. The *divisio* is methodically introduced by *hic* and occasionally by *supra*. Subdivisions are usually designated by *in prima primo* and, where the last element is subdivided, by *ubi primo*. The technique of rhyming is applied regularly.

The *expositio* generally opens with *dicit ergo* and systematically restates the elements of the *divisio*. Moreover, it is concise, focused on the literal sense, and line-by-line. Spiritual interpretations follow literal ones and are explicitly designated as such.[184] Questions are brief and closely related to the literal sense.[185]

In sum, this work's methodology and style are consistent with William's throughout and provide clear evidence of his authorship. It will therefore be considered authentic.

19. *Super Danielem*; inc.: *Iustum deduxit Dominus per uias rectas et ostendit illi regnum Dei.*
*Rep. Bibl.* 2793.
Manuscript: Oxford, Bodleian, Laud. misc. 390, f. 102r–123r.
Bibliography: SMALLEY, B., "Sapiential Books I," 69.

This work is anonymous, and there is no independent evidence that William commented on Daniel. It would appear that its listing under William's name is due to its inclusion in MS Oxford, Bodleian, Laud. misc. 390, which contains a postill *Super Apocalipsin* associated with him. (Equally anonymous and also apparently listed under William's name merely by virtue of its inclusion in a manuscript containing other works attributed to him, this postill is discussed at no. 21.)

Far shorter than those accompanying William's known works (occupying about half of f. 102r), the prologue is not based on Aristotle's four causes. The terminology of neither the *divisio* nor the *expositio* corresponds to the typology of Group A. Specifically, the *divisio* is seldom introduced by the term *hic*, and subdivisions are never introduced by the formula *in prima primo*. In place of the latter, there often appear expressions not found in William's known works, such as *hic dicuntur dua/tria* and so on[186] or *hic ponitur* and the like.[187] Lemmata are applied to the elements of the *divisio* considerably less regularly than in William's known works,[188] and in such cases, they are often preceded by the term *ibi*. A survey of the text found only scarce citations of authorities and no questions at all. In sum, this postill provides no indication that it was produced by a master and no reason for including it among William's works.

20. *Super Mattheum*; inc.: *Sume tibi librum grandem et scribe in eo stilo hominis.*
*Handlist* 749–750; *SOPMA* 1436; *Rep. Bibl.* 2794, 6865 (Peter Tarentaise); *Répertoire* I, 114.
Manuscripts: Munich, Staatsbibl. Clm 7941, f. 1ra–93vb; 23620, f. 2ra–96rb; Saint-Omer, Bibl. mun. 260, f. 1ra–109va; Tours, Bibl. mun. 121, f. 1ra–91va.
Bibliography: MURANO, G., *Opere diffuse per exempla et pecia*, Turnhout, 2005, 86, 182, 475–476; SMALLEY, B., "Sapiential Books I," 64–65, 67–68.

We have seen that a postill on Matthew by William appeared on a taxation list of 1275 at Paris and in the early fourteenth century Stam's catalogue. This work, whose incipit is the same as that of Albert the Great's commentary on Matthew, is known to survive in seven copies, none of which is ascribed to William. Unattributed in the copies at Saint-Omer and Tours, as well as in two others,[189] it is ascribed by posterior hands to Nicolas of Gorran in one of the two at Munich and to Peter Tarantaise in the other.[190] The copy at Tours contains *pecia* marks on several folios, though it is impossible to determine whether their total number corresponds to the number of *peciae* indicated in the taxation list.[191] Its association with William results from its inclusion in the Saint-Omer manuscript, where it appears in the same hand as William's postill on John. As she supposed him to be a student of Thomas Aquinas, Beryl Smalley found additional evidence of William's authorship in the following contemporary rubric of a manuscript at Florence, once in the library of the Dominicans of Santa Maria Novella:[192] *Expositio sancti Thome de Aquino Ord. fratr. Pred. super Euuangelium beati Matthei per alium recollecta.* Remarking that attribution "to an unnamed pupil of

St Thomas would point to William of Alton," she classified the postill as "almost certain," despite her recognition of a lack of resemblance to the printed version of Aquinas's commentary on Matthew.[193] Apparently unknown to her was the copy at Munich ascribed to Peter Tarentaise, who just as likely was a student of Thomas,[194] since he and William became regents of the two Dominican chairs of theology at Paris at the end of Thomas's first regency there (1259).[195] More important, writing in 1950, Smalley could not have known that Thomas's lecture on Matthew in all probability belongs to his second Paris regency, between 1269 and 1272.[196] By late 1269, Peter had been elected provincial of France, and William was quite likely dead; a decade had passed since both had become masters. To the extent that it is credible, then, the rubric of the Florence manuscript points away from William, as well as Peter Tarantaise.

In its methodology and style, this postill is in several respects similar to the works of Group A. Its prologue, identical in both copies consulted, is based on Aristotle's four causes. The *divisio* is regularly introduced by *hic*, and the expositio by *dicit ergo*. Each lemma of the *divisio*, including the initial one, is restated in the *expositio*.

And yet, clear departures from the typology of Group A are recognizable, especially in the *divisio*. While usage of the formula *in prima primo* to indicate subdivisions is frequent, it is far less so than in the Group A postills. The same can be said of rhyming: while the final words of the various elements regularly rhyme one with another, they do so considerably less consistently than in William's known postills. More, they are frequently introduced by the term *ibi*.[197] More telling are a few traits of the *divisio*'s structure and function. To begin, the various elements are often closed with a reference rather than a lemma; at times, they are closed with neither.[198] In William's known works, the first trait is far less common, and the second is virtually absent. Also, the initial *divisio* of each chapter is not normally more substantial than the others and does not encompass or organize the commentary on the entire chapter, as is normally the case in William's works.[199]

As for the commentary, it is noticeably less concise than William's. As with *Super Iob* (inc.: *Surgite postquam sederitis*, no. 10), comparison with the Group A postills is facilitated by the appearance of all of them in the same scribal hand in columns of identical proportions. With respect to the biblical text as it appears in the Weber edition of the Vulgate, this postill is approximately 89 percent longer than William's *Super Ieremiam*, 40 percent longer than his *Super Threnos*, and 31 percent longer than his *Super Iohannem*.[200]

Though infrequent, questions tend to be brief, related to the literal sense, and situated within the exposition, as are William's.[201] On the other hand, the author of this postill is prone to expounding the spiritual senses before coming to the literal exposition. At Mt 2:11, for example, he begins his explanation of the Magi's gold, incense, and myrrh with a mystical interpretation (taken from the *Glossa Ordinaria*): every Christian confesses Christ as God, king, and having suffered (*quilibet Christianus Deum, regem et passum confitetur*). Only afterward does he explain that they are for Mary's poverty, the stench of the stable, and the comfort of the Christ child.[202] This is unlike William.

In sum, neither the style nor the methodology of this work provides evidence of William's authorship. In view of the absence of any other supporting evidence, we decline to include it among his authenticated works.

21. *Super Apocalipsin*; inc.: *Numquid ad preceptum tuum eleuabitur aquila.*
*Handlist* 750; *SOPMA* 1438; *Rep. Bibl.* 2796; *Répertoire* I, 114.
Manuscripts: Oxford, Bodleian, Laud. misc. 390, f. 123r–211v; Saint-Omer, Bibl. mun.
    260, f. 206 bis ra–218vb (ends incomplete at Apc 2:18).
Bibliography: SMALLEY, B., "Sapiential Books I," 66, 69–70.

To the extent that it is complete, the text of the Saint-Omer manuscript is the same as that of the Oxford manuscript. In both copies, the work is anonymous. Since there is no independent evidence that William commented on the Apocalypse, it would seem that it is only by virtue of its inclusion in MS Saint-Omer 260 (in the same hand as that of several of William's known works) that this postill has been listed in the repertories under William's name. Beryl Smalley has remarked that this postill is "probably the work of a bachelor, 'reading with the glosses,' not the work of a master."[203] The present inquiry has found no evidence to the contrary.

Though lengthy,[204] its prologue has a few lacunae with respect to Aristotle's four causes. In his known commentaries, William explicitly mentions four causes for the biblical text at hand,[205] but the author of this work names only one, the author:

> Ex iam dictis haberi possunt quod in principiis librorum queri solent, uidelicet quis auctor siue causa efficiens, que materia, quis modus agendi, quis finis.

Even if *materia*, *modus agendi*, and *finis* correspond to the material, formal, and final causes, such usage is not typical of William. The mention of the work's *modus agendi* rather than its *causa formalis* is subsequently repeated:

> Modus agendi est quia aliquando predicat ut apostolos consolando bonos et terrendo malos, aliquando ut propheta futura denuntiat.[206]

Still thinking along the lines of the earlier model of the prologue, this author appears not to have completely subscribed to the model of Aristotle's four causes.

As in the postills of Group A, the *divisio* is normally introduced by *hic*, and elements left without subdivision in larger *divisiones* (such as those at the beginnings of chapters) are subsequently subjected to subdivision further along in the exposition. Moreover, the lemmata of the *divisiones* are regularly restated in the exposition, which is regularly introduced by *dicit ergo*. In addition, questions are brief, related to the literal sense, and located within the exposition.[207] But departures from William's style are by no means limited to the prologue. Subdivisions are rarely indicated by *in prima primo*. In place of this formula, there appears another that is absent from William's known works: *in prima parte dicuntur duo* (or *tres, quatuor*, etc.). With considerable frequency, divisions and subdivisions are indicated by the term *dividitur*. The rhyming of the final words of the various elements lacks consistency. The lemmata of the *divisio* are frequently introduced by *ibi*.[208] Also worth noting is the author's manner of referring to John the Evangelist. He consistently names him *Beatus Iohannes*; in his postill *Super Iohannem*, William simply calls him *Iohannes* or *Euangelista*.[209] Since William's habit of naming John without using the form of address *beatus* has no bearing on most of the works examined by this study, it has not been listed among the criteria for authenticity. In this case, however, it seems reasonable to take it into consideration.

Given the nature of the biblical text (largely concerned with the state of the church, the Book of the Apocalypse is written in figurative language), the literal and spiritual expositions are less easily differentiated than in commentaries on other books. Still, the author in question shows no interest in setting them apart. An example appears in his handling of Revelation 8:12 (*et quartus angelus tuba cecinit et percussa est tertia pars solis et tertia pars lune et tertia pars stellarum*). Following Bede, he tells us that the striking of the sun signifies false brothers (*falsi fratri*) and adds that the moon signifies the clergy and the stars the simple people or laity.[210] Since he uses no qualifiers such as *literaliter*, *allegorice*, or *mistice*, it is for the reader to determine whether this commentary is to be taken literally or allegorically.

Put briefly, this work's style provides no evidence of William's authorship. In view of the lack of any clear evidence favoring its authenticity, we refrain from listing it among his works.

### C. CONCLUSION

Of twenty-one works of questionable authenticity, we exclude seventeen and identify one with another (Apart from its prologue, *Super Ecclesiasten*, inc.: *Vidi in omnibus uanitatem* is the same as *Super Ecclesiasten*, inc.: *Aspexi terram*). This work and two others we recognize as authentic: *Super Sapientiam* (inc.: *Fons sapientie uerbum Dei in excelsis*) and *Super Ezechielem* (inc.: *Vidi et audiui uocem unius aquile uolantis per medium celi*).

The resulting list of William's known surviving biblical commentaries is as follows:

1. *Super Ecclesiasten*, inc.: *Aspexi terram et ecce uacua erat.*
2. *Super Sapientiam*, inc.: *Fons sapientie uerbum Dei in excelsis.*
3. *Super Isaiam*; inc.: *Nemo cum prophetas* (begins incomplete at Is 5:7).
4. *Super Ieremiam*; inc.: *Direxit opera eorum in manibus prophete sancti.*
5. *Super Threnos*; inc.: *Quis dabit capite meo aquam et oculis meis fontem lacrimaraum.*
6. *Super Ezechielem*; inc.: *Vidi et audiui uocem unius aquile uolantis.*
7. *Super Iohannem*; inc.: *Acceptus est regi minister et intelligens.*

# APPENDIX II

# *Prologues*

## PRINCIPLES OF THE EDITIONS
### *General Principles*

Each of the following editions is a unique case, presenting its own set of problems. Nonetheless, each text has been established according to a common set of basic principles, specifically, those espoused by the editors of the Leonine Commission.[1] As a consequence, these editions present only the restored texts, including corrections of obvious errors. The numbers of biblical chapters are presented as they appear in the base manuscript (listed first).

### *Orthography*

Every attempt has been made to render William's text accessible to the modern reader without betraying the scribe's orthography. This study presents the transcribed text with corrections only of obvious errors, such as grammatical incoherencies and senseless readings. The spelling of the manuscript has been preserved, making exception for the following cases:

1. Because the various scribes are not consistent in their presentations of the assibilated *ci* / *ti* as either *ci* or *ti* (e.g., *cogitacio* or *cogitatio*), this form is standardized in accordance with the generally accepted orthography of the term in question (e.g., *iustitia* and *iudicium*).[2]
2. The indeterminable use of *v* / *u* is standardized as *u* in the lower case (e.g., *unde* remains *unde* and *vel* becomes *uel*) and as *V* in the upper case (e.g., *Unde* becomes *Vnde* and *Vel* remains *Vel*).
3. In view of the lack of a standard practice for the usage of *m* and *n*, wherever the letter is lost in an abbreviation, the scribe's intended spelling is surmised.

*Punctuation*

Punctuation in the manuscripts is generally light and inconsistent. The texts of the editions have therefore been punctuated with a view to William's meaning. The main function of this punctuation is to facilitate the modern reader's access to the text. Proper names are capitalized. All paragraphs are editorial. In keeping with a general medieval scribal practice of abbreviating the words of the biblical text, angular brackets [<>] enclose added text in the case of *lemmata* and biblical citations. All other editorial additions of text are indicated in the source apparatus.

*The Biblical Text*

All biblical passages are placed in italics. The key constituent of the biblical postill is the *lemma*, that is, the passage commented upon. For the sake of differentiating the lemmata from the commentary, scribes usually underlined them. For the same reason, the lemmata of the edited texts are placed in italicized small capitals, even in cases where they are not underlined in the manuscript. All lemmata are also cited by chapter and verse in boldface superscript, except where they are repeated during the course of an exposition. To the extent permitted by the commentary, punctuation of the biblical text follows D. Sabatier's edition of the Clementine Vulgate.

*The Apparatus*

Critical Apparatus

This apparatus serves to present the readings of the manuscripts wherever they diverge from the edited text. The edition of *Super Iohannem* is based on the witness of MS Saint-Omer, Bibl. mun. 260. Transmitted by a competent copyist, it is generally reliable. For this reason, we have decided to present it as faithfully as possible and to limit interventions to cases of obvious scribal errors. The only other witness to this text, the copy of ms. Assisi, Biblioteca Com. 49, is a variant. Its readings are therefore given only where there are clear reasons for supposing that the former text is defective. By contrast, each of the editions of prologues to four of William's other commentaries is based on a selection of manuscripts containing the same text, save for differences of copy. In these editions, manuscripts are cited wherever their readings diverge from the text of the edition.

Biblical Apparatus

The biblical apparatus serves mainly to present the references to the biblical citations of the commentary. It further serves to present the corresponding text from R. Weber's 1994 edition of the Vulgate (= *W*) wherever it differs from either lemmata or biblical citations. References are recorded according to the titles of books, abbreviations of titles, and numbering of chapters and verses as they appear in the Weber edition.

## Source Apparatus

The source apparatus serves to identify the sources of all nonbiblical citations, whether explicit or tacit. Patristic references are to J.-P. Migne's *Patrologia Latina* (PL) and *Patrologia Graeca* (PG) or, whenever possible, to better editions, such as those of *Corpus Christianorum*, Series Latina (CCSL) and *Corpus Scriptorum Ecclesiasticorum Latinorum* (CSEL). It is often the case that multiple sources lie behind a single section of text. In such cases, the sources explicitly cited by William are presented first; all others are presented in reverse chronological order. References to the writings of John Chrysostom indicate the column numbers of the relevant Latin translation of the PG; these are not always the same as the column numbers of the relevant Greek text. This represents no assertion that the Latin translation of the PG is the same as that of the edition.

### *Sigla Codicum*

### Codices Textus Bibliae

$\Omega^J$     BnF lat. 16722
$\Omega^s$     BnF lat. 15467

### Codices Expositionum Guillelmi

*A*     Assisi, Biblioteca Com. 49
*B*     Basel, Univ. Bibl. B III 20
*M*     Madrid, Bibl. Nac. 493
$P_1$     Paris, BnF lat. 573
$P_2$     Paris, BnF lat. 14429
$P_3$     Paris, BnF lat. 15573
$P_4$     Paris, BnF lat. 15592
*S*     Saint-Omer, Bibl. mun. 260

### Codices in Apparatu Fontium

*Ar*     Arras, Bibliothèque mun. 1083
*O*     Vaticano, Bibl. Apostolica, Ottob. lat. 227

### PROLOGUS AUCTORIS SUPER ECCLESIASTEN
(*M* f. f. 131ra–130vb [*sic*], *B* f. 93ra–93vb, $P_4$ f. 191r–191v)

*Aspexi terram et ecce uacua erat et nichili.* Hec uerba scribuntur[1] Ie. IIII,[2] que bene competunt Salomoni, inquantum fuit auctor huius libri, qui etiam per Ieremiam bene potest designari. Ieremias enim 'excelsus Domino' interpretatur.[3] Salomon uero recte excelsus dicitur. « Excelsus enim », ut dicit Ysidorus, libro VII, in principio, « quasi 'ualde celsus' dicitur;[4] 'ex' enim pro 'ualde' ponitur ».[5] Salomon autem fuit ualde celsus, quia celsus fuit multa possidendo, celsior multis presidendo, set ualde celsus omnes inimicos suos subiciendo. Nec mirum sapientia enim exaltat, Prouer. IIII: *Arripe sapientiam et exaltabit te;*[6] Eccli. XI: *Sapientia humiliati exaltabit capud illius.*[7] Set Salomon fuit sapientissimus, ut patet III Reg. III,[8] et bene sapientissimus dico,[9] quia sapiens fuit docendo in mundo, *in medio nationis praue et peruerse*[10] bene uiuere, sapientior docendo mundum contempnere, sapientissimus docendo celestia amare et in amore eorum quiescere. Primum est incipientium, secundum progredientium, tertium perfectorum. Primum pertinet ad declinationem mali, secundum ad operationem boni, tertium ad contemplationem diuini. Primum docet Salomon in Prouer., secundum in Ecclesiastice, tertium in Cantic. Canticorum. Hic triplici nomine appellatur: scilicet Salomon, id est[11] pacificus,[12] sub cuius persona docuit pacifice in mundo uiuere; Ecclesiastes, sub cuius persona fecit hunc librum;[13] Ydida, sub cuius persona fecit Cantica Canticorum.[14] Et patet ordo, quia primum disponit ad secundum; primum et secundum ad tertium. Hec est uia trium dierum, Exo. VIII.[15] Hoc est triplex Pascha: primum in Egipto, Exo. XIII;[16, 17] secundum in deserto, Numer. IX;[18] tertium Transiordanem,[19] Iosue V.[20] Hic est funiculus triplex qui difficile rumpitur, Ecclesiastes IIII.[21] Ad hoc monemur in Psalmo: *Declina a malo et fac bonum. Inquire pa&lt;cem&gt; et persequere eam.*[22]

Et ideo omnes precessit in diuitiis, III Reg. III: *Dedi tibi diuitias et gloriam, ut nemo fuerit tibi similis in regibus*[23] *cunctis retro diebus.*[24] Et infra II: *Supergressus sum*[25] *opibus omnes qui fuerunt ante me in Ierusalem.*[26] Item, omnes precessit in honore prelationis, unde III Reg. IIII: *Ipse obtinebat omnem regionem que erat trans flumen et cunctos reges*[27] *illarum regionum;*[28] Eccli. XLVII: *Inpletus est quasi flumen sapientia et terram retexit anima sua.*[29] Item, omnes precessit in subiectione inimicorum, Eccli. XLVII: *Post Dauid surrexit filius sensatus, et propter illum deiecit omnem potentiam inimicorum.*[30] Et post: *Salomon imperauit in diebus pacis, cui subiecit Deus omnes hostes.*[31] Hinc bene competit ei illud Ysaie: *Ecce intelliget seruus meus et exal&lt;tabitur&gt; et ele&lt;uabitur&gt; et sublimis erit ualde.*[32]

Supposito ergo quod per Ieremiam Salomon possit intelligi, conuenienter in istis uerbis Ieremie predictis,[33] quatuor insinuantur pertinentia ad hunc librum que solent in principiis librorum inquiri. Primo enim per hoc uerbum *Aspexi* insinuatur nobis auctor[34] huius libri et modus agendi, quantum ad causam efficientem et formalem. In sequentibus uerbis subiectum et utilitas huius libri, quantum ad materialem et finalem.[35] Primo ergo in hoc uerbo *Aspexi*, insinuatur auctor[36] operis et modus agendi. Auctor[37] uidelicet in huius uerbi supposito, modus agendi in eius[38] significato siue in aspiciendi modo. Salomon ergo, designatus per Ieremiam, fuit auctor[39] huius libri.

Set uidetur quod libri[40] huius auctor[41] esse non debuit. In hoc enim libro agitur de contemptu mundi. Set Salomon terrena non contempsit, set coaceruauit,[42] ut patet, infra II,[43] et Ioh. II dicitur:[44] *Qui de terra est de terra loquitur.*[45] Item, hic agitur de spiritualibus. Ipse autem fuit carnalis, III Reg. XIII.[46] Et, ut dicit Gregorius: « Quando carnalis spirituale predicat, potius scandalizat quam edificat ».[47] Item, ut dicitur Sap. I: *In maliuolam animam non introibit sapientia, nec habitabit in corpore &lt;subdito peccatis&gt;*[48]

etc. Set Salamon peccator fuit, igitur cum sapientiam non haberet, eam docere non potuit, Augustinus, *De agone christiano*: « Errat quisquis ueritatem se cognoscere putat, si adhuc nequiter uiuat ».[49] Item, magis creditur factis quam uerbis. Igitur cum iste doceret unum et faceret contrarium, sue doctrine non est credendum. Ad hoc posset[50] breuiter responderi, secundum Hebreos qui tradunt, ut dicitur in *Glossa*, quod iste liber est Salomonis penitentiam agentis.[51] Vel dicendum quod Spiritus sanctus non solum per bonos, set etiam per malos pluries uera et bona loqutus est, ut patet de Balaam,[52] Numer. XXIII,[53, 54] et de Chaipha, Io.[55] XI.[56] Vnde Mt. XXIII:[57] *Que dicunt facite. Que autem*[58] etc. Ad primum ergo, dicendum quod de terra est solum de terra loquitur ex se, uel quantum est de se. Spiritus tamen per os terreni bene loquitur celestia, sicut et per os carnalis spiritualia, et per os mendacis aliquando uera. Ad secundum, dicendum quod in predicatione carnali duo sunt: predicatio ipsa que frequenter edificat, et indignitas predicantis que scandalizat. Ad tertium, dicendum quod sapientia dicitur communiter et proprie: proprie secundum quod dicit diuinorum cognitionem et diuine cognitionis saporem debitum et amorem. Et sic loquitur dicta auctoritas de sapientia, non prout dicit nudam sine amore cognitionem. Ad quartum, dicendum quod magis credendum est factis quam uerbis propriis, set non quam uerbis diuinis a Spiritu Sancto inspiratis. Salomon ergo dicitur[59] auctor,[60] et recte; in hoc enim libro docentur contempni uoluptates, diuitie, honores et curiositates, de quibus iste melius docere potuit, quia expertus. Expertus enim melius rem cognoscit.[61]

Secundo, insinuatur modus agendi, siue causa formalis huius libri in significato huius uerbi *Aspexi*. Significatum enim huius dictionis causatur ex mutua rationum ad utramque partem contradictionis collatione, quia secundum Philosophum, qui bene scit dubitare, id est rationem ad utramque partem afferre, prope est uidere uerum.[62] Isto uero modo pertractat Salomon istum librum. Loquitur enim nunc in persona fatui, affluentiam mundanam[63] approbantis, nunc in persona sapientis eam[64] reprobantis.[65] Vnde concionator[66] dicitur, quia diuersorum sententias proponit.[67] Tamen secundum Ysidorem, li. IX, concionator dicitur 'multitudinis alloquitor.'[68]

Modus etiam agendi est hic, quod[69] paucus in sermone, /[**M 131rb**] multus in sententia, *scriptus est enim intus et foris*, id est sensu historico foris, et mistico et morali intus, Eze. II.[70] Set uidetur quod male procedat sic diuersorum sententias assumendo,[71] scilicet quia sententia dicta in persona fatui non est attendenda, quia Eccli. XX: *Ex ore fatui reprobabitur parabola*.[72] Item, ueritas sacre scripture omnem errorem[73] excludit, nullum admittit. Item, certitudinaliter non ambigue procedit. In tali autem processu nescitur que sit sententia fatui, que sapientis. Responsio:[74] Est loqui in persona fatui, uelut[75] eius sententia approbetur, et hoc malum est. Nec sic loquitur auctor[76] huius libri, set[77] uelut reprobetur, cum reproba ostendatur. Et sic est hic. Per hoc patet responsio ad duo prima obiecta. Ad tertium dicendum quod disputando procedere est certitudinaliter[78] procedere. Licet enim non sit certitudo in ipsa disputatione, tamen per ipsam disputationem peruenitur ad certitudinem in fine. Vnde in fine huius libri determinatur ueritas disputationis, cum dicitur: *Finem loquendi omnes pariter audiamus*[79] etc. Et ab illo fine potest cognosci certitudinaliter cui sententie sic adherendum.

Sic ergo patet de causa efficiente et formali de huius libri per hoc quod dicitur: *Aspexi.* Per sequentia[80] uero insinuatur materialis et finalis, materialis primo et principaliter, finalis secundario et ex consequenti. *Terra* enim inquantum est *uacua* per defectum boni, *et nichili* per inclinationem mali, est materia huius libri. Ostendit enim auctor[81] in hoc libro quod creature, maxime sensibiles, uane[82] sunt. Vnde uanitas proprie[83] est passio quam intendit ostendere de subiecto. Vel *terra* dicitur *uacua* per comparationem ad suum principium; dicitur *nichili* per comparationem ad suum terminum. Et stat hic *terra* non solum pro elemento terre, set pro uniuersitate corporalis creature, sicut ibi: *In principio creauit Deus celum et terram.*[84]

Secundum iam dicta, duo sunt hic querenda. Primo, qualiter creatura Dei dicatur uacua. Secundo, quomodo de uanitate possit esse scientia. Circa primum, obicitur Gen. I: *Vidit Deus cuncta que fecerat et erant u<alde> b<ona>.*[85] Ergo nulla creatura Dei est uacua. Preterea, illud solum est uanum quod ad nullum finem est ordinatum. Set omnes creature sunt ad bonum ordinate, unde Iob V: *Nichil fit in terra sine causa.*[86] Et secundum Boethium,[87] Dionysium[88] et Philosophum,[89] omnia bonum exoptant. Responsio: Vanum dicitur dupliciter: in se et in comparatione. In se, aut simpliciter, et sic priuat uerum et[90] bonum, et sic[91] nulla creatura Dei dicitur uana. Aut habito respectu ad suum principium et terminum, inquantum scilicet est de nichilo et tendit ad nichilum et est de nichilo facta, et sic dicitur uana.[92,93] Vel uanum in se dicitur dupliciter. Dicit enim priuationem iuxta essentiam et iuxta finem. Primo modo dicitur uanum quod non habet durabilitatem uel firmitatem substantie. Qualia sunt omnia sensibilia, que et si non transeant secundum substantiam, transibunt tamen secundum formam et figuram, <I> Cor. VII: *Preterit figura <huius mundi>*[94] etc. Secundo modo dicitur uanum quod caret fine utili, et sic nulla natura est uana. Item, dicitur aliquid uanum in comparatione ad utentem eo, et sic per occasionem et hominum abusionem dicuntur hec sensibilia uana, unde Sap. XIIII: *Creature Dei in odium facte sunt et in temptationem anime*[95] *hominum.*[96] Secundum istum modum possunt hec inferiora dici uana, et hoc quia carent soliditate, durabilitate, utilitate et ueritate. Cassiodorus super illud Ps.: *Preualuit in uanitate sua,*[97,98] « Vanum est quod est inane », quantum ad primum, « fragile et caducum », quantum ad secundum, « inutile », quantum ad tertium, « et ab[99] ipsa firmissima ueritate discretum »,[100] quantum ad quartum. Hec autem temporalia carent soliditate, quod patet quia non prebent fulcimentum innitentibus, Ysa. XXX: *Egiptus frustra et uane auxiliabitur;*[101] Ps.: *Vana salus hominis.*[102,103] Item, quia non prebent plenitudinem continentibus,[104] Eccl. V: *Auarus non implebitur pecunia.*[105] Hinc est quod conparantur umbre,[106] Sap. V: *Transierunt omnia uelud umbra.*[107] Item, carent durabilitate, quia transeunt a suis possessoribus, Aug., II li., *De li. ar.:* « Temporalia antequa sint non sunt, et cum fugerunt[108] non erunt »;[109] prima Io. II: *Transit mundus et concupiscentia eius.*[110] Item, carent utilitate, quia non prebent fructum diligentibus, infra V: *Qui amat diuitias fructum non ca<piet> ex eis.*[111] Item, infra II: *Quid prodest homini de uniuerso labore suo*[112] etc.; Mt. XVI: *Quid prodest homini*[113] *si uniuersum mundum lucretur*[114] etc.[115] Item, carent ueritate, quia non seruant fidem ea querentibus, unde dicuntur diuitie fallaces,

Mt. xiii.[116] Promittunt enim securitatem, secundum illud Prouer. xviii: *Substantia diuitis urbs fortitudinis eius*[117] etc. Et tamen faciunt timidum, Iob xv: *Sonitus terroris semper in auribus illius*[118] etc. Chrysostomus super Mt.: « Diuitem adulari necesse est erga[119] multos, et principes, et subiectos, et multis indigere et seruire turpiter et formidare et suspicari et tremere eorum qui emulantur », id est inuidorum, « oculos et timere calumpniatorum ora et aliorum auarorum[120] concupiscentias ».[121] Item, promittunt durationem, iuxta illud: Eccl. x: *Pecunie obediunt omnia*;[122] et Augustinus in originali super Ps.:[123] « Quantum habebis, tantus eris ».[124] Et tamen faciunt seruum, Augustinus in <De> li. <ar.>: « Vnde malum? Amore hiis inherens subditus fit eis rebus qualis ei subditus esse oportebat[125] ».[126] Iuxta illud Lu. xvi: *Non potestis Deo seruire et mammone.*[127] Item, promittunt uoluptatem, iuxta illud Ps.: *Beatum dixerunt po<pulum> cui hec sunt*;[128] et faciunt miserum, Augustinus in quarto libro *Conf.*: « Miser est omnis animus uinctus amicitia rerum mortalium, et dilaniatur cum eas amiserit ».[129]

Sunt ergo hec sensibilia uana, et ex hoc uidetur quod non possit esse de eis scientia. Omnis enim scientia est de ente uero et bono.[130] Preterea, si hec sint[131] huius scientie materia, cum ipsa sint uana, quomodo non est scientia uana,[132] sicut quando fundamentum est uanum, totum edificium est uanum? Responsio patet per predicta, cum enim uanum dicatur tripliciter: uno modo per priuationem esse simpliciter, alio modo per priuationem esse ordinati, tertio[133] modo per priuationem esse intransmutati. De primo non est scientia, nisi forte habeat esse in causa, et secundum illud esse potest doceri et cognosci, et sic non est uanum. Set quod est uanum nec per se nec per accidens est de eo scientia. De secundo modo[134] non est scientia per se, et tamen per accidens. Sicut enim[135]/[M 130vb] medicina est scientia[136] sani et egri, sani quidem per se, egri uero per accidens, ut uult Philosophus,[137] sic de peccato est scientia, set ratione uirtutis. De tertio est scientia per se, sicut patet de motu solis et orbium aliorum.[138] Ad primum ergo obiectum, dicitur[139] quod de uano potest esse scientia, set ratione ueri. Ad secundum etiam patet quod creatura non est ita uana, quin etiam habeat ueritatem et bontitatem.[140]

Sic ergo per hec uerba: *Terra uacua et nichili*,[141] que sunt materia huius libri insinuatur,[142] etiam ex consequenti, quis sit finis, scilicet contemptus huius uanitatis, iuxta illud Naum I: *Omnis qui uiderit te resiliet a te.*[143] Ad hoc monemur, prima Io. II: *Nolite diligere mundum*[144] etc., quia: *Beatus uir*[145] *cuius est nomen Domini spes eius et non respexit in uanitates et insanias.*[146] Respexit, inquam, ad appetendum uel ad amandum. *Filii enim hominum, ut quid diligitis uanitatem?*[147] Contra hoc obicitur sic: Laus operis redundat in artificem. Ergo contemptus operis. Ergo qui contempnit mundum contempnit Deum, cum maxime dicatur in Prouer. xv: *Vniuersa propter semet ipsum operatus est Dominus.*[148,149] Responsio: Hec contempnere inquantum sunt a Deo et ad Deum malum est, set in quantum elongant a Deo contempnenda sunt. Hoc autem fit aut quando plus diliguntur quam Deus, aut eque, aut quando[150] per hec minus diligitur Deus. Hinc dicit Augustinus: « Domine, qui tecum aliquid amat quod non propter te amat, minus te amat ».[151] Propter hoc dicitur, Cant. ultimo: *Si dederit homo omnem substantiam suam pro dilectione*, scilicet Dei, *quasi nichil despiciet eam.*[152]

PROLOGUS INCERTI AUCTORIS SUPER SAPIENTIAM
($P_2$ f. 155ra–156ra, $P_3$ f. 156ra–156va, $S$ f. 250ra–va)

*Fons sapientie uerbum Dei in excelsis*, Eccli. I.[1]. *Sapientiam*, ait Eccli. XXXVIII, *scribe in tempore uacuitatis*,[2] insynuans nobis in quo precipue sit studendum et qualiter et quando. Inter humana enim studia precipue est studium sapientie, nam ut ait Hugo, *De origine artium*: « Omnium expetendorum summa est sapientia, in qua perfecti boni forma consistit ».[3] Huic precipuo studio precipui inter homines, id est aliorum, uel presidentes[4] aliis existentes, uel futuri rectores, maxime debent intendere, id est firmiter retinendo.[5] *Describe eam*, ait Salomon, Prouer. III, *in tabulis cordis tui*,[6] scilicet in tribus partibus diuine ymaginis, in memoria retinendo, in[7] intelligentia recogitando, in uoluntate amando.[8] Secundum illud, Prouer. XXII: *Ecce descripsi <eam tibi tripliciter>* etc.[9] Tempus uero huic studio aptum est tempus uacuitatis, id est uacationis ab occupationibus mundanis. Tam enim tripliciter hoc est beatum otium quod reprehendit a luto et latere et[10] paleis congregandis,[11] scilicet uacando Pharao in seruis Dei, Exo. V: *Vacatis <otio> enim et idcirco dicitis: Eamus et sacrificemus Deo*[12] etc. Tale otium desiderat studium sapientie, quia: *Qui minoratur*[13] *actu in ea percipiet sapientiam*, Eccli. XXXVIII.[14] Et quia in libro Sapientie precipue agitur de studio et amore sapientie, ideo in ipso studere debent tempore uacuitatis sue amatores sapientie.

Cuius libri ut habeatur notitia oportet causas considerare. Scire namque, ait Philosophus, arbitramur unumquodque cum causas cognoscimus.[15] In uerbo igitur proposito, huius libri quatuor causas possumus designare, scilicet efficientem, formalem, materialem et finalem. Efficiens intelligitur in uerbo Dei; formalis in emanatione fontis; /[155rb] materialis in uerbo sapientie; finalis in excelsorum commemoratione.

Efficiens quidem huius libri causa triplex[16] est. Prima per modum inspirationis, scilicet Verbum Dei. Ipse enim est *Dei uirtus et Dei sapientia*, prima Corin. I.[17] A sapientia uero Dei[18] omnis causatur sapientia, sicut ab essentia Dei omnis essentia, et a ueritate ueritas, et a bonitate bonitas. Primum uero in omni genere eorum que post ipsum sunt et omne imperfectum a perfecto causatiue, secundum Boetium.[19] Ideo dicitur Eccli. I: *Omnis sapientia a Domino Deo est* etc.[20] Cum ergo liber iste sit *Sapientia*, Verbum Dei est efficiens causa prima. Secunda causa efficiens, scilicet per modum inuentionis, est Salomon. Vnde ut habetur in *Ecclesiastica Ystoria*, Hegesippus,[21] Irenaeus,[22] et omnis antiquorum ghorus[23] librum qui *Sapientia* intitulatur Salomonis esse dixerunt.[24] Vnde liber ipse *Sapientia Salomonis* inscribitur, et more ecclesiastico lectionibus de libro hoc sumptis premittitur: 'Dixit Salomon filiis Israel,' quia scilicet de eius sententiis liber iste, quamuis[25] ab alio[26] compilatus sit, sicut et liber *Prouerbiorum* pro magna parte a uiris Ezechie.[27]

Proxima causa efficiens per modum compilationis fuit Phylo, sapientissimus Iudeorum qui fuit, ut refert *Hystoria Ecclesiastica*, apostolorum temporibus, qui ab amore sapientie Phylo non inmerito nominatur.[28] Rabanus: « Ieronimus[29] hunc librum asserit non a Salomone, ut putatur, set a Phylone doctissimo quodam Iudeo[30] fuisse conscriptum »,[31] id est conpilatum. Quia « omnis causa primaria plus est influens in suum causatum quam causam secundaria »,[32] ideo efficiens causa[33] huius libri, more scripture sacre, cause prime, scilicet Verbo Dei, omissis ceteris attribuitur.

Formalis causa, id est modus agendi, in libro isto intelligitur per emanationem fontis. Aqua namque fontis de meatu[34] occulto scatitur in riuulum manifestum fluxu continuo. Habet /[155va] ergo in origine occultam profunditatem ad differentiam cisterne seu aqua celestis, Gen. II: *Fons ascendebat de terra*;[35] id est de terre occultatis uisceribus. Aqua uero cisterne descendit de celo aereo quo generatur. Habet in exitu manifestationem, ad differentiam putei, Prouer. V: *Deriuentur fontes tui foras*.[36] Habet in fluxu continuationem, ad differentiam torrentis, Cant. III: *Fons ortorum, puteus aquarum uiuentium*,[37] id est continue fluentium. Riuus[38] namque per motum continuum manifestatur. Sic liber iste habet quidem in sententiis attentam profunditatem, Iob XXVIII: *Trahitur sapientia de occultis*.[39] Habet in sermonibus claram manifestationem, Prouer. X cap.: *Argentum electum lingua iusti*.[40] Ipse stilus, secundum Ieronimum, grecam eloquentiam redolet.[41] Habet in processu rationum consequentiam et connexionem, Eccli. XXI: *Scientia sapientis tanquam inhundatio habundabit continue*, fluendo, non stillando, *et consilium illius sicut fons uite permanet*.[42]

Materialis uero causa sapientia est, de qua agit. Sapientia quidem est, secundum Augustinum, diuinarum rerum cognitio.[43] Res diuine sunt diuina attributa: potentia, sapientia et bonitas eius. Hii sunt tres digiti quibus appendit Dominus molem terre, Ysa. XL,[44] ubi soluitur questio, Iob XXXVIII: *Super quo bases illius solliditate* etc.[45]

De hiis uero hic agere intendit. Intendit enim[46] notificare Dei potentiam in punitione rebellium, ut patet primo, secundo, et tertio, et quarto, et quinto capitulis; sapientiam illuminatione humilium, ut patet sexto, septimo, octauo, nono; bonitatem[47] in collatione beneficiorum quoad utrosque, ut patet a decimo capitulo, et deinceps.[48] Quia de[49] hiis rebus diuinis copiose agit, merito intitulatur a materia liber *Sapientie*, sicut liber *De anima*. Versatur enim in laudibus increate sapientie. Ostendit utilitates sapientie create, et hortatur siue /[155vb] prouocat ad amorem utriusque.

Finalis uero causa est exhortatio principum et prelatorum ad amorem sapientie, que causa tangitur cum ait: *In excelsis*. Excelsa quidem mundi sunt[50] maiores prelati, media eorum ministri,[51] infima subditi, Eccl. V: *Excelso excelsiorum alius* etc.[52] Hos autem intendit ad studium sapientie maxime prouocare, ut patet in principio primi et sexti capituli,[53] quia a maioribus in medios diffunditur sapientia usque ad extremos, Eccli. X: *Secundum iudicem populi, sic et ministri eius, et qualis rector ciuitatis, tales inhabitantes in ea*.[54] Vbi tangit hos tres ordines: iudicum et ministrorum, subditorum. Sicut enim uidemus in illuminationibus corporeis, quod primo deriuatur[55] solaris illuminatio in loca superiora et celo uiciniora, de hinc in media, ultimo in postrema. *Sol enim tripliciter exurens montes radios exsufflat*, scilicet in ualles,[56] Ecl. XLIII.[57] Sicut enim uidemus in illuminationibus angelicis, quod diuinum radium, ut ostendit Dyonysius, primo suscipiunt illi de supprema ierarchia; secundo illi de media; ultimo illi de postrema. Lex enim, ut ait ipse, diuinitus promulgata est per prima media,[58] et per media postrema reducere.[59] Sic ergo debet esse in illuminationibus humanis, ut primo illuminentur suppremi, et per illos medii, et per illos postremi. Secundum illud, Ps.: *Suscipiant montes pacem populo.*[60] Ieromimus: « Dicebat populo Plato: Beatas fore res puplicas si eas aut sapientes regerent aut earum rectores sapientie studerent[61] ». Vt ait Boetius, lib. *Consol.*, sic enim est processus sapientie:[62] *Attingit enim a fine* supremo *usque ad finem* ultimum *fortiter et disponit omnia*, scilicet media, *suauiter*, infra capitulo VIII.[63]

Ergo actor libri primo et principaliter intendit in loca excelsa aquam sapientie diffundere, ut more fontium in excelsis erumpentium, de excelsis ad media, et de mediis ad infima, totum mundum ualeat irrigare.[64] Quia uero natura fontis est quod ad originis sue equalem /[156ra] locum possit redire, secundum illud Ecclesiastes I: *Ad locum unde exeunt flumina reuer<tuntur>*,[65] ideo sapientia de excelsis ad infima descendens, ad excelsa conatur redire: ad excelsa quidem officiorum, eleuando ad statum prelationis, Prouer. VIII: *Per me reges regnant*;[66] ad excelsa meritorum, eleuando ad statum perfectionis, infra VII: *Amicos Dei et prophetas constituit*;[67] ad excelsa premiorum, eleuando ad statum[68] regni celestis, infra VI: *Concupis<centia> sapientie deducit ad regnum perpetuum*;[69] ubi in fonte suo bibitur aqua sapientie salutaris, Aug.: « Ibi[70] beata uita in fonte suo bibitur ».[71]

---

## Prologus Auctoris Super Ieremiam
### (*M* f. 266ra, *P*₁ f. 87ra–vb)

*Direxit opera eorum in manibus prophete sancti.*[1] Hec uerba scripta sunt Sapientie X in quibus huius operis causa quadruplex insinuatur. Primo finalis: *Direxit*, ut enim due tribus a peccatis suis cessarent, et Domino seruirent, et ad celestia peruenirent, in quibus uera directio consistit. Ieremias librum istum predicendo, comminando et plangendo composuit, unde infra primo capitulo:[2] *Ecce dedi uerba mea in ore tuo*[3] etc.; et sequitur:[4] *Vt euellas et destruas et disperdas et dissipes et edifices et plantes*;[5] et Eccli. XLIX: *Male tractauerunt eum*[6] *qui de uentre matris consecratus est propheta, euertere, et eruere,*[7] *et perdere, et iterum edificare*[8] *et renouare;*[9] II Thi. III: *Omnis doctrina diuinitus*[10] *inspirata utilis est ad docendum*, et subdit docendi modum: *ad arguendum et corripiendum, ad erudiendum in iustitia: ut perfectus sit homo Dei, ad omne opus bonum instructus.*[11] De ista directione, infra XVIII: *Reuertatur unusquisque a uia sua mala et dirigite uias uestras et studia uestra.*[12]

Secundo insinuatur in hiis uerbis huius operis causa materialis, cum dicitur: *opera eorum.* De operibus enim[13] agit tripliciter: primo ea mala ostendendo, utpote quibus a Deo se auerterunt et ydolis seruierunt, et primo pro eis captiuitatem predicendo; secundo pro eis plangendo et lamentando, ut in Trenis; tertio pro eis deprecando, ut in Oratione Ieremie. Quantum ad primum dicitur Apo. VIII: *Audiui uocem unius aquile*; id est Ieremie, qui interpretatur 'excelsus,'[14] et qui admodum aquile tenerrime dilexit populum suum, *uolantis per medium celum*,[15] id est populum ad bonum excitantis in medio prophetarum. Aliqui enim prophetarum loquti sunt istam captiuitatem futuram, ut Ysaias, Osee; alii preteritam, ut Daniel, Malachias, Aggeus. Set iste simul et Ezechiel et futuram predixit, et presentem uidit, et preteritam deplorauit. Vnde Dan. xii dicitur quod uidit uirum indutum lineis super aquas fluminis, et duos alios uiros altrinsecus in ripa fluminis:[16] *Vir indutus lineis*, Ieremias, qui uirgo, qui extitit, infra xv,[17] et in utero matris[18] sanctificatus,[19] infra i,[20] *iste erat super aquas fluminis*,[21] quia in captiuitate presens, eam enim uidit propriis oculis. *Duo uiri in ripa fluminis*,[22] alii prophete, quoram quidam dictam captiuitatem precesserunt, quidam, ut dictum est, subsequti sunt.

*Dicentis uoce magna: 'ue, ue, ue.'*[23] Ter dicit propter triplicem captiuitatem. Prima fuit sub Ioachim maiore, qui primo factus est tributarius Nabuchodonosor, iiii Regum xxiiii.[24] Secunda sub Ioachim minore, qui primo ductus est in Babilonem, eodem capitulo.[25] Tertia sub Sedechia, sub quo fuit ciuitas destructa et captiuitas consummata, iiii Regum xxv.[26] Vel ideo dicitur ter, quia futuram timuit, presentem doluit, preteritam[27] deplorauit. Quantum ad secundum, dicitur in Psalmus ubi nos habemus: *Te decet hymnus Deus in Syon*, Hebraica ueritas: *Tibi s<ilens> laus Syon*;[28] ibi[29] titulus: *Canticum*, id est lamentatio Ieremie, *de uerbo peregrinationis*, uel *de populo peregrinationis, cum inciperet populus proficisci*.[30] Quantum ad tertium, ii Mach. ultimo: *Hic est fratrum amator et populi Israel*,[31] hic est qui multum orat pro populo Israel et pro uniuersa sancta ciuitate Ierusalem, Ieremias propheta Dei*.[32] Propter hec tria potest ei competere illud Ysaie xxi: *Visio dura*, Glosa: « captiuitas »;[33] *nuntiata est michi qui incredulus est infideliter agit et qui depopulator est uastat*,[34] quantum ad primum; *propterea repleti sunt lumbi mei dolore, angustia possedit me*;[35] quantum ad secundum; *corrui cum audirem*,[36] scilicet ad supplicandum, quantum ad tertium.

Tertio insinuatur causa formalis in hoc quod dicitur: *in manibus*.[37] Quod enim manuale et tangibile est, euidens est. Sic modus procedendi in isto opere facilis et manifestus, unde Ieremie potest competere quod dicitur Eccli. xxiiii: *Doctrinam quasi prophetiam effundam*.[38] Quod enim[39] effunditur, id est extra funditur manifestum est, Eccl. viii: *Sapientia hominis lucet in uultu eius*;[40] Prouer. xiiii: *Doctrina prudentium facilis*;[41] quia i Cor ix: *Nisi manifestum sermonem dederit<is>*[42] etc.[43] Fuit autem iste modus manifestus et ubi prophetat, ut in principio, et ubi texit historiam, ut in medio, et ubi lamentatur, ut in fine.

Quarto insinuatur causa efficiens: *prophete sancti*.[44,45] Ieremias fuit propheta, unde infra i: *Prophetam in gentibus dedi te*,[46] in quo apparet sublimitas sue doctrine; tum quia doctrina prophetica[47] est stabilis siue solida, Cassiodorus *Super Psalmos: Prophetia est diuina inspiratio rerum euentus immobili ueritate denuntians*; tum quia a Deo inspirata, secunda ii Pe. i: *Non enim uoluntate humana allata est aliquando prophetia, set Spiritu Sancto*[48] *inspirati loquti sunt sancti Dei homines*;[49] ii Paral. ultimo: *Non erubuit Sedechias faciem Ieremie prophete loquentis ex ore Dei*;[50] tum quia utillima,[51] Prouer. xxix: *Cum defecerit prophetia*,[52] *dissipabitur*[53] *populus*;[54] ii Thi.: *Noli negligere gratiam que data est per prophetiam*.[55,56] De hiis tribus, ii Pe. i: *Habemus firmiorem propheticum sermonem*, quantum ad primum; *cui benefacitis attendentes quasi lucerne ardenti in calig-*

*inoso loco*, quantum ad tertium; *donec dies illucescat*[57] *et lucifer oriatur*[58] *in cordibus ues-tris*,[59] per inspirationem, quantum ad secundum. Propter hoc Prima Thes. v: *Prophetias nolite spernere*,[60] quia Apo. xxii: *Beatus qui custodit uerba prophetie huius*.[61] Item, Iere-mias fuit sanctus, infra i: *Antequam exires de uulua sanctificaui te*.[62] Quod patet ex nominis interpretatione. Interpretatur enim 'excelsus.'[63] Item, ex significatione, quia sanctum, id est Christum, pre ceteris, uidetur[64] magis prefigurare.[65] Item, ex mentis et corporis castitate, infra xv: *Non sedi in consilio ludentium*.[66] Item, ex humilitate, infra i: *Nescio loqui quia puer ego sum*.[67] Item, ex malorum pro Domino perpessione, lapidatus enim fuit a Iudeis in Taphnis.[68, 69]

Huic autem operi premittit Ieronimus prologum « Ieremias propheta » etc.[70]

---

## PROLOGUS AUCTORIS SUPER THRENOS
### ($P_1$ f. 145rb–145va)

*Quis dabit capiti meo aquam et oculis meis fontem lacrimarum ut plorem die ac nocte interfectos filie populi me?*[1] Hec uerba scripta sunt Iere. ix, in quibus Trenorum causa quadruplex euidenter insinuatur.

Primo efficiens in hoc quod dicit: *dabit*; efficiens, inquam, principalis et precipua. Principalis enim efficiens Spiritus est, ii Pe. ii: *Spiritu Sancto inspirati locuti sunt sancti Dei homines*,[2] et Mt. ix: *Non uos enim*[3] *estis qui loquimini*,[4] et hic omnis doni auctor est, ut patet, Ysa. xi.[5] Vnde et luctus meritorius ab eo est, Ro. viii: *Ipse Spiritus postulat pro nobis gemitibus inenarrabilibus*,[6] id est postulare facit cum gemitu et luctu.

Causa efficiens secundaria et minus principalis Ieremias est, quod insinuatur in hoc quod dicitur: *Capiti meo et oculis meis*. Caput, quod in homine dominatur, affectus uel uoluntas intelligitur; per oculos intellectus. Hec autem duo sunt per que doctoris lin-gua[7] in scribendo uel in docendo dirigitur. Vnde in Ps.: *Os iusti meditabitur sapientiam et lingua eius loquetur iudicium*. In meditatione motus uoluntatis, in sapiencia discretio rationis intelligitur, per que lingua[8] ad iudicandum docendo[9] et scribendo excitatur; et iterum: *Eructabunt labia hominum cum docueris me iustificationes tuas*.[10] Per doctrinam informatur intellectus. Per doctrinam iustificationum affectus. Quod autem Ieremias istius lamentationis actor fuerit patet ii Par. ultimo.[11]

Causa materialis insinuatur per hoc quod dicitur, *aquam, fontem lacrimarum ut plorem interfectos*. Vehemens enim planctus quo Ieremias deplorat terre sue desolatio-nem siue deuastationem, ciuitatis et templi destructionem, populi sui et maxime regis[12] Iosie afflictionem, et interfectionem templi[13] factam per Caldeos uel tunc faciendam per Titum et Vespasianum, per Romanos secundum sensum historicum, est materia huius libri. Vnde pro primo petit Ieremias *aquam*, id est lacrimarum magnitudinem. Pro secundo *fontem lacrimarum*, id est lacrimarum multitudinem. Pro tertio *ploratum die ac nocte*, id est lacrimarum indesinentiam.

Item notandum quod secundum sensum allegoricum materia huius libri est planctus pro recessu ecclesie a statu triplici, scilicet a feruore caritatis, a luce ueritatis, a constantia soliditatis. Feruor caritatis recessit a quibuscumque malis. Lux ueritatis a Iudeis, paganis et hereticis. Constancia firmitatis ab ypocritis. De /[**145va**] tali planctu, Aggeus II: *Quis in uobis est derelictus quod uiderit domum istam in gloria sua prima et quod uos uideritis hanc nunc.*[14]

Secundum sensum moralem materia huius libri est planctus pro ruina siue lapsu anime fidelis a statu iustitie per peccatum cogitationis, locutionis, et operis, Iere. XIII: *Deducant oculi mei lacrimas quoniam contricione magna contrita est filia populi mei.*[15]Hinc est quod per ternos[16] uersus hec lamentacio texit. Vnde hec[17] lamentacio Treni dicuntur; treni grece, lamentacio latine.

Ex iam dictis patet modus agendi siue causa formalis in parte. Modus enim est triplici uersu in quadruplici alphabeto distincto dictos tres status deplangere.[18] Ad quod plenius intelligendum nota quod Ieremias quatuor lamentaciones composuit, ita quod singule habent XXII clausulas iuxta numerum litterarum alphabeti Hebreorum. Queli- bet autem clausula tres habet uersus, ita ut tres uersus prime clausule a prima littera, scilicet aleph, et uersus secunde clausule a secunda littera, scilicet beth, et sic de aliis per ordinem.[19] Quare autem in prima et secunda et quarta lamentacione ita preponantur singule littere clausulis, ita quod non singulis uersibus, in tertia uero ita singulis clausu- lis quod et singulis uersibus, sicut dicit Ysidorus libro VII *Ethimologiarum,*[20] nescio, nisi forte ad designandum quod illa tertia omnes alias includit et ita ad designandum quod ista lamentacio totalis principaliter fit pro tribus; et tamen quadruplici alphabeto repetito, secundum Ysidorum libro X,[21] distinguntur, ut quaternario hoc populum Iudaicum in quatuor mundi partes per captiuitatem Babilonicam dispersum et per Romanos dispergendum defleret. Quoad sensum allegoricum, ut hoc quaternario eccle- sie ruinam in recedentibus[22] a quatuor uirtutibus defleret. Quoad sensum moralem, ut ruinam anime fidelis per quatuor affecciones inordinatas defleret; et quia quatuor elementis corpora nostra composita aggrauantur.

Preponuntur autem clausulis littere hebrayce, non grece uel latine, quia hebraice pertinent ad significationem clausularum uersuum sequentium, quod alie littere non potuerunt.[23] Iste ergo modus agendi, dum loquimur de ternario planctus siue / de quaternario, insinuatur in illis uerbis: *aquam, fontem lacrimarum ut plorem.* Possunt enim hec sub ternario uel quaternario comprehendi. Hinc dicit Ieronimus in prologo Ieremie: «Ieremias in Iudea et Beniamin tantum prophetauit et ciuitatis sue ruinas quadruplici planxit alphabeto».[24]

Causa autem finalis insinuatur in hoc quod dicitur: *filie populi mei,* ut li *filie* sit datiui casus. Planxit *filie,* id est ad utilitatem filie, id est sinagoge, ecclesie, et fidelis anime, ut uidelicet lugeant pro bonis omissis, peccatis commissis, penis acquisitis, uel pro peccatis propriis, pro peccatis alienis, pro incolatu uel miseria presentis uite, et pro desiderio superne patrie. *Beati,* enim, *qui sic lugent quoniam ipsi consolabuntur,* Mt. V,[25] et Thobie III:[26] *Post tempestatem tranquillum facis et post lacrimacionem et fletum exul- tacionem infundis.*

Titulus: *Liber Trenorum Ieremie,* et sicut Canticum Salamonis dicitur *Canticum Canticorum,* sic ista lamentacio *Lamentacio Lamentacionum,* quia omnes excellit.[27] Cetere enim particulares: fleuerunt enim filii Iacob patrem suum, Samuel Saulem,

Dauid Saul et Ionathan et Absalonem, Ezechias mortem suam imminentem sibi predictam. Set hec fit pro omni dampno temporali et spirituali, excedit etiam alias in quantitate, ut patet, et eciam in modo plangendi. Ideo dicit in primo: *O uos omnes qui transitis per uiam* etc.

---

### Prologus Auctoris Super Ezechielem
### (*P₁* f. 156rb–va)

*Vidi, et audiui uocem unius aquile uolantis per medium celi dicentis: ue, ue, ue habitantibus in terra*, Apoc. 8.[1] In hiis uerbis tangitur quadruplex causa huius operis. Efficiens: *unius aquile.* Ezechiel fuit aquila contemplando. Aquila enim dicitur ab acumine uisus, set cum senescit uisus ebetatur donec artificio et nature beneficio reiuuenescat et sic acumen uisus resumit. Infra Ezechiel in principio sui libri et in fine uidet acute, set in medio subobscure, quia principium libri et finis sunt alte intelligentie, medium autem plane. Vnus fuit se aliis conformando[2] et idem quod alii sacre scripture scriptores intendendo, Eccl. 32: *Rectorem te posuerunt? Esto in illis quasi unus ex illis.*[3]

Causa materialis tangitur cum dicitur: *Vocem dicentis: ue, ue, ue, habitantibus in* etc. Cum enim transissent quinque anni a transmigratione Ioachim, et Ierusalem,[4] quam predixerat Ieremias destruendam, propter quam predictionem se tradidit Ioachim Nabugodonosor, cum matre sua et Ezechiele et multis aliis,[5] remaneret adhuc in gloria, murmurabant qui transmigrauerant, dicentes quod Ieremias falso prophetauerat. Ierosolimite uero transmigratis insultabant: "Alienigene eos infestabant." Vnde de hiis tribus in terris diuersis habitantibus scripsit et hoc triplex 'ue,' quia murmurantibus 'ue' iam habitantium,[6] irridentibus et infestantibus 'ue' futurum. Hinc est quod infra secundo in fine dicuntur[7] in libro expanso coram Ezechiele[8] scripta esse: *Lamentationes, carmen et ue*;[9] lamentationes deridentium, carmen murmurantium, et ue infestantium.

Spiritualis autem materia huius libri sunt duo populi, alter Dei, alter Diaboli.

Causa finalis tangitur in hoc quod dicitur: *uolantis per medium celum* uel *celi.* Celum est populus Iudaicus, Ps.: *Celi, id est Iudei, inarrant gloriam Dei.*[10] Iste populus fuit in transmigratione diuisus. In uolatu notatur eleuatio quantum ad situm, festinatio quantum ad motum. Per medium ergo celi uolare est populum Iudaicum transmigratum et derelictum ad celestia festinanter prouocare.

Item causa finalis spiritualis huius libri siue intentio fuit reuocare Ierosolimitas ab irrisione, aliengenas ab infestatione, transmigratos a murmure, per triplicem comminationem, que designatur per 'ue,' ad patientiam et consolationem, Ro.: *Quecumque scripta /*[**156va**] *sunt ad nostram doctrinam scripta sunt ut per patientiam et consolationem scripturarum*[11] etc.

Causa formalis siue modus agendi notatur in hoc quod dicitur: *Vidi et audiui.* Videre enim pertinet ad uisiones quas uidit Ezechiel que fuerunt obscure; audire ad exhortationes uel comminationes que fuerunt[12] plane. Est ergo modus agendi alicubi planus propter minus capaces et ne[13] pre sui profunditate nimis negligeretur.[14] Est etiam alicubi[15] obscurus propter prouectiores, et ne pre sui facilitate contempneretur.

## Prologus Auctoris Super Iohannem
### (*S* f. 110ra–vb, *A* f. 1ra–2rb)

*Acceptus est regi minister intelligens.* Hec uerba scripta sunt Prou. xv,[1] in quibus principaliter huius euangelii scriba commendatur, et per consequens ipsum euangelium, cum auctoris commendatio redundet in opus, secundum illud Eccli. 11: *In manu artificis opera laudabuntur.*[2] Insuper et huius operis causa quadrupliciter insinuatur.

Commendatur autem a tribus; primo quantum ad uitam: *minister*; secundo quantum ad scientiam: *intelligens*; tertio quantum ad utriusque approbationem, uel quantum ad Christi specialem familiaritatem: *Acceptus est regi.* Minister fuit non carnis, non mundi, non Dyaboli, set Christi, cum relicto patre et naui, Mt. IIII,[3] et relicta uxore, Io. 11,[4] celeriter imitando, Io. XII: *Qui mihi ministrat me sequatur.*[5] Item, uoluntatem suam uoluntati Christi conformando, Augustinus, III libro, *Conf.*: « Ille Domine minister tuus est qui non querit hoc a te audire quod uelit, set uelle quod audierit. »[6] Item, Deum et proximum excellenter diligendo, Io. XIII: *In hoc cognoscent omnes quod mei es<tis>*[7] etc. Hic ideo pre ceteris in euangelio et epistulis de dilectione pertractauit. Item, carnis desideria per abstinentiam mortificando, Gal. V: *Qui Christi sunt carnem suam*[8] etc. Item, officium sibi creditum fideliter exequendo, Mt. XXII: *Fidelis seruus et prudens*[9] etc.

Secundo commendatur quantum ad scientiam: *intelligens.* Intelligit enim utilia, sicut patet in epistulis ubi maxime caritatem, que est utilissima, predicauit. Item, secreta, ut patet in Apocalypsi, ubi maxima misteria reuelauit. Item, sublimia, ut patet in euuangelio ubi si altius intonuisset totus mundus non capere posset.[10, 11] Hic est ergo alter Daniel, cui dedit Deus intelligentiam omnium uisionum, Dan. 1.[12] Item, alter Salomon, cui dedit Deus cor sapiens et intelligens tantum ut nullus ei similis fuerit, III Regum III.[13] Origenes in omelia prima *super Iohannem*: « O beate Iohannes, non inmerito uocaris 'Iohannes'», cuius interpretatio Latine est 'cui donatum est,'[14] « quia[15] tibi donatum est uidere abdita, summi boni penetrare misteria, et ea que tibi reuelata sunt humanis mentibus intimare ».[16] Hinc comparatur aquile, que altius uolat et acutius uidet, Eze. 1;[17] *Impleuit enim eum Deus spiritum sapientie et intellectus*, Eccli. xv.[18] Vnde bene conpetit ei illud, Ysa. LII: *Ecce intelliget seruus meus, et exaltabitur*, intelligendo utilia, *et eleuabitur*, intelligendo secreta, *et sublimis erit ualde*, intelligendo sublimia.[19]

Tertio in hiis uerbis quantum ad familiaritatis cum Christo prerogatiuam: *Acceptus est regi.* Rex iste Christus est[20] ratione nominis, ratione regie uirtutis, ratione regalis dignitatis. De primo, rex secundum/[110rb] Ysidorum, libro IX, dicitur a regendo.[21] Set Christus omnibus regit melius quia uiriliter, Apoc. XII: *Mulier peperit masculum qui recturus erat omnes gentes.*[22] Item, habundanter, Ps.: *Dominus regit me et nichil michi deerit.*[23] Item, quia indesinenter, Ps.: *Ipse reget nos in secula.*[24] Item, rex dicitur a regnando, Augustinus, *de Ciuitate Dei* V: « Reges et domini a regnando et dominando apellati sunt ».[25] Christus autem regnat omnibus excellentius, quod patet ex militum multitudine, Iob xxv: *Numquid est numerus militum eius?*[26] Apoc. vii: *Vidi turbam magnam.*[27] Item, ex regni sui qualitate, cum sit omnibus aliis regnis maius in qualitate, Baruc iiii: *O Israel*[28] etc. . Item, durabilius, quia Dan. iiii: *Potestas eius potestas eterna.*[29] Item, fertilius, quia ibi nullius boni est penuria, Iud. xviii,[30] nullius mali presensia, quia Ps.: *Flagellum non appropi<nquabit> taber<naculo> t<uo>*;[31] Gregorius: « Nichil est intra quod fastiditur, nichil extra quod appetatur ».[32] Item, ex disponendi facilitate, Sap. viii: *Attingit a fine usque ad fi<nem> for<titer>, et dis<ponit> omnia suauiter.*[33] Item, « Rex », secundum Ysidorum, libro viii, « dicitur a recte operando ».[34] Christus autem omnibus operatur rectius, quia nullum malum fecit, 1 Pe. ii,[35] set: *Omnia bene fecit*, Mc. vii.[36] Item, « Rex » dicitur a sustinendo, Ysidorus, libro viiii: « Reges apud Grecos basilei uocantur, quia tanquam bases populum sustinent. Quanto enim quisque magis preponitur tanto amplius laborum pondere grauatur ».[37] Christus autem ceteris subportat amplius, He. i: *Portans omnia uerbo uirtu<tis>*;[38] scilicet et laborauit grauius, Iere. viii: *Dolor meus super dolo<rem>.*[39] Dicitur etiam Christus rex ratione regie uirtutis, que duplex est secundum Ysidorum, libro viii, scilicet iustitia et pietas.[40] Iustitia[41] pre omnibus conuenit Christo, quia pre omnibus declinauit a malum et fecit bonum, que sunt due partes iustitie, secundum Augustinum.[42] Item, secundum Senecam, due sunt partes iustitie, scilicet uelle omnibus prodesse et nulli nocere. Sic Christus. Seneca: « Amabis Deum, eumque imitaberis[43] ut omnibus prodesse, nulli nocere uelis ».[44] Item, secundum Anselmum: « Iustitia est rectitudo uoluntatis propter se seruata ».[45] Christus habuit rectissimam uoluntatem, quia nullum malum uoluit, Ps. *Non Deus uolens iniquitatem tu es.*[46] Item, quia rectissimo scilicet Patri uoluntatem suam per omnia conformauit, Mt. xxvi: *Non sicut ego uolo.*[47] Propter ipsam autem uoluntatis rectitudinem hanc seruauit, quia bonorum nostrorum non indiguit.[48] Item, hoc potest patere per opera iustitie que sunt miseris subuenire, secundum Augustinam, <de> Trin., libro xiii.[49] Item, iniqua punire, *super Gen.*, libro xii.[50] Item, bono rectissime[51]/[110 va] adherere, *Epistola* xxxiiii.[52] Item, soli Deo deseruire,[53] sexto *Musice.*[54] Item, soli amato seruire,[55] nulli equari nisi purissimis animis, nulli dominari nisi nature bestiali atque corporee,[56] *De moribus Ecclesie.*[57] Item, proximum et Deum diligere,[58] *De octoginta trium quest.*, quest. lxi.[59] Item, inferiora potioribus subdere, libro secundo, *de Lib. Arbitr.*;[60] cuicumque sua tribuere, *de Ciu.*, lib. xix.[61] Item, pietas maxime conuenit Christo, quia dare et condonare, que sunt opera misericordie,[62,63] secundum Crisostomum. Christus enim maxime dedit quia seipsum, ad Tit. i.[64] Item, maxime condonauit, quia: *Omnia delicta*, Col. iii.[65]

Huic ergo regi auctoritate fuit beatus Iohannes *acceptus*, quod patet ex hoc quod tanquam magis familiaris: *In cena super pectus eius recubuit*, Io. xiii.[66] Item, ex hoc quod thesaurum pretiosissimum sue costodie mancipauit, Io. xix: *Accepit eam in sua*[67] custodiam. Vel *sua* officia.[68] Item, ex hoc quod speciali priuilegio martirii grauissime pene sine dolore euasit. Item, per hoc quod ab hoc seculo migratus, extraneus factus est a dolore mortis, ut habetur in prologo.[69] De hiis duobus ultimis, Deuter. xxxiii: *Tinguat in oleo pedem suum. Ferrum et es cal<ciamentum> eius*, ne scilicet lederetur. *Sicut dies iuuen<tutis> t<ue>, ita et senec<tus> t<ua>*,[70] ne scilicet dolorem mortis pateretur.

Secundario notatur in hiis uerbis quadruplex causa huius operis. Materialis, per hoc quod dicit: *Regi*, quia de Christo qui est rex regum agitur in hoc libro quantum ad utrumque naturam que est in eo. Vnde Eze. VIII: *Aquila*, id est beatus Ioannes, *grandis*, per magnitudinem caritatis, *magnarum alarum*, per uolatum contemplationis, *longo membrorum ductu*, per uite durationem, *plena plumis et uarietate*, per bonorum operum multitudinem, *uenit ad Libanum*, per uirginitatis candorem, *tulit medullam cedri*.[71] Cedrus dicitur Deus, Iere. XXIIII: *Numquid regnabis quia confers te cedro?*[72] huius medulla media persona.[73] Item, cedrus Christus, Eccli. XXIIII: *Quasi cedrus*;[74] huius medulla humanitas assumpta. Vtriusque ergo cedri medullam tulit quando utrumque naturam nobis propalauit. Obiicitur, Eccli. III: *Altiora te ne quesieris*;[75] quia Prouer.: *Perscrutator maiestatis opprimetur a gloria*.[76] Responsio: Non est maiestas perscrutanda spiritu elationis uel spiritu curiositatis uel spiritu malignitatis ut heretici, set spiritu pietatis ad assertionem fidei bonum est, I Cor. II: *Spiritus scrutatur etiam profunda Dei*.[77]

Formalis: *Intelligens*, intelligendo enim diuinam naturam sine comparatione, extollere humanam et utramque esse in Christo. Prius agit de diuina, postea de humana, de/[110 **vb**] utrumque autem agit sublimiter, ut patet certitudinaliter; non tamen certitudine demonstrationis, que fidem euacuat, cum hominem uelit nolit ad assentientum agat, set certitudine auctoritatis, Augustinus: « Quod credimus debemus auctoritati ».[78] Et ideo hec scriptura procedit per modum narrationis, non ratiocinationis. Hec autem certitudo, licet in aliis scientiis sit modica, quarum inuentores sunt homines qui mentiri possunt, in hac autem est maxima quam Spiritus sanctus inspirauit,[79] Augustinus, *Super Gen.*: « Maior est huius scripture auctoritas quam omnis humani ingenii perspicacitas ».[80]

Efficiens: *Minister*.

Finalis: *Acceptus*. Ad hoc enim scribit ut in presenti simus accepti Deo per fidem, infra XX: *Hec scripta sunt ut credatis*, et in futuro per gloriam, unde sequitur: *et ut credentes uitam habeatis*.[81]

# Notes

## INTRODUCTION

1. "Est *mare* . . . sacra scriptura propter originem ex qua omnes scripture oriuntur," *Super Ecl.* 1, 7, MSS Basel, Univ. Bibl. B III 20, f. 95rb–va; Madrid, Bibl. Nac. 493, f. 134v. This commentary (*Rep. Bibl.* 2781; inc.: *Aspexi terram et ecce uacua erat*), whose authorship we shall consider, has been variously attributed to William of Middleton, Bonaventure, Thomas Aquinas, and William of Alton.

2. His recognition has improved only slightly since B. Smalley described him several generations ago as "still a shadowy figure," Sapiential Books I, 57.

3. The first printing of a complete work is my "William of Alton's Commentary on the Book of Lamentations," *AHDLMA* 73 (2006), 203–281.

4. William has been variously identified in print as *Guilelmus de Altona* (*CUP* I, 646), *Altono* (*SOP* 1, 245; J. Lelong, *Bibliotheca sacra*, Paris, 2 vols., 1723, vol. 2, 757; R. Chapotin, *Histoire des Dominicains de la province de France*, Rouen, 1898, 570), *Antona* (P. Glorieux, *Répertoire* 1, 113; W. Hinnebusch, *The Early English Friars Preachers*, Roma, 1951, 414), *Anthona* (Gérard de frachet, *Vitae Fratrum Ordinis Praedicatorum*, *MOPH* 1, 335), and *Haltona* (*Laurentii Pignon Catologi et Chronica, accedunt Catalogi Stamensis et Upsalensis Scriptorum O. P.*, ed. G. Meersseman, *MOPH* 18, 24, n. 16). In an altogether mistaken identification, he has also been named *Aulton*. Because Aulton was a barony of Perche, within the diocese of Chartres, Nicolas Lefebvre, a historian of the Dominicans of Chartres, gave this name to William and listed him as a member of the Dominican convent there; cf. R. Chapotin, *Histoire des Dominicains*, 570.

## CHAPTER I

1. Our author is to be confused neither with William of Southampton, who died in 1278 (cf. T. Kaeppeli, "Guillaume d'Alton," *DHGE*, fasc. 129–130, 836), nor with a writer describing himself as "Guillelmus Anglicus, civis Massiliensis, professione medicus, ex merito scientiae astronomus dictus," whose numerous astrological works have been dated to around 1231 (cf. P. Glorieux, *La Faculté des arts et ses maitres au XIIIe siècle*, Paris, 1971, 162–163).

2. At the time, Dominicans held two chairs at the University of Paris. It has been widely assumed that one of these was an "intern" chair, reserved for a native of the Province of France, and the other was an "extern" chair reserved for a foreign friar; cf. R. Chapotin, *Histoire des Dominicains*, 570; P. Mandonnet, "Thomas d'Aquin novice prêcheur," *RT* 8 (1925), 489–533; "Thomas Aquinas in Curia Romana lector. Chronologia suae commorationis (1259–1268)," *Xenia*

*Thomistica* 3 (1925), 9–40 (18–21); P. Glorieux, *Répertoire* I, 113; J. Destrez, "A propos d'un répertoire des maîtres en théologie de Paris," *RTAM* 3 (1931), 412–422 (413); J. Weisheipl, *Friar
Thomas d'Aquino. His Life, Thought and Works*, New York, 1974, 65; and J.-P. Torrell, *Initiation
à Saint Thomas d'Aquin. Sa personne et son œuvre*, 2nd ed., Fribourg, Suisse, Editions Universita-
ires, 2002, 110. If such was the case, it was the foreigners' chair that Thomas passed on to William. Yet S. Tugwell has argued against the dating of this practice to the thirteenth century,
remarking, "It is only in the fourteenth century that there is clear evidence for a principle of
alternating between intern and extern candidates for the two chairs"; see *Albert and Thomas,
Selected Writings* (New York, 1991), 102–103, n. 77. For documentation of the practice's codifica-
tion, see M. Mulchahey, *First the Bow Is Bent in Study. Dominican Education before 1350*,
Toronto, 1998, 374–375, nn. 89, 91.

3. J. Destrez, "A propos d'un Répertoire," 412–422 (420–422); S. Tugwell also mentions this possibility, *Albert and Thomas*, 221–222.

4. The date of Gerard of Frachet's list is uncertain, and it is possible that the names of William
and others were added after its original diffusion. Based on a copy in a Barcelona manuscript,
the edition of P. Mandonnet reads, "Anno Domini 1260: frater Petrus de Tarentasia; Guillelmus Anglicus," "Thomas Aquinas in Curia Romana lector," 9–40 (18–19). On the basis of the
copy at Barcelona, as well two others in manuscripts at the Vatican and Viterbo, B. Reichert's
edition reads, "usque ad annum domini MCCLVIII." In addition to "G(uillelmus) de Anthona,
Anglicus," it includes the names of other friars, such as Roland of Cremona, Albert the Great
(Albertus Teutonicus), Thomas Aquinas, Hugh of Metz, and Peter Tarentaise. Reichert notes
that the Vatican manuscript omits the names of William and several others; *MOPH* I, 334–335
(n. 9). Not found in any version is the name of Gerard Reveri. See S. Tugwell, *Albert and
Thomas*, 222, 313–315, nn. 212, 213, 230.

5. Gerard's list includes a large number of regent masters succeeding one another in what appears
to be a fairly limited time frame. The case of Annibald de Annibaldis is telling. By the time he
became a cardinal in 1262, he, too, had become master, very likely succeeding William; J.-P. Torrell, *Initiation*, 145; A. Weisheipl, *Frère Thomas d'Aquin*, 129.

6. In connection with a general chapter at Valenciennes in June 1259, the master of the order, Humbert of Romans, appointed five friars to a commission charged with developing proposals for
the organization of study within the order. All five were masters in theology of Paris: Albert the
Great, Thomas Aquinas, Peter Tarentaise, Bonhomme the Breton, and Florent of Hesdin, *CUP*
I, 385–386; cf. J.-P. Torrell, *Initiation*, 141–144; S. Tugwell, *Albert and Thomas*, 217, 310–311,
nn. 173, 174.

7. The date of William's death is unknown. According to Quetif and Echard, William flourished
in Paris between 1260 and 1270. R. Chapotin asserts that he died in 1265, without, however,
providing any evidence to this effect, in *Histoire des Dominicains*, 570. This date has been
repeated, without evidence, by B. Smalley, "Sapiential Books I," 41–77, 236–274 (257), and
T. Kaeppeli, "Guillaume d'Alton," *DHGE* 22 (1988), 836–837. See also W. Hinnebusch, *Early
English Friars*, 414–415; P. Glorieux, *Répertoire* I, 113–116; *CUP* I, 646; P. Mandonnet, "Thomas
Aquinas in Curia Romana lector. Chronologia suae commorationis (1259–1268)," 18–21;
J. C. Russell, *Dictionary of Writers of Thirteenth-Century England*, BIHR, Special Supplement
3, 1936, 180–181; *SOP*, I, 245.

8. Peter was regent master at Paris from 1259 to 1264 and again from 1265 to 1267. He was subsequently twice provincial of the Province of France, and in 1272 he became a cardinal and arch-
bishop of Lyons. On January 21, 1276, he was elected Pope Innocent V and died soon afterward
on June 22, 1276; cf. P. Glorieux, *Répertoire* I, 107; J.-P. Torrell, *Initiation*, 141.

9. *CUP* I, 78–79, 226–227. In his detailed survey of the statutory and manuscript evidence of theological programs at Paris and Oxford during the period, W. Courtenay observes that statutes
determining the length of lectures on Lombard's *Sentences* appeared at neither university until
the fourteenth century; see "Programs of Study and Genres of Scholastic Theological Production in the Fourteenth Century," in *Manuels, programmes de cours et techniques d'enseignement
dans les universités médiévals*, ed. J. Hamesse, Louvain-la-Neuve, 1994, 325–350 (333–334).

For a lucid discussion of what can and cannot be said about the length and content of theology courses of friars, as well as seculars, at Paris at the time, see in the same volume the study of J. Verger, "L'éxegèse, parente pauvre de la théologie scholastique?", 31–56.

10. See J.-P. Torrell, *Initiation*, 73–78, 493–494; G. Dahan, "Genres, Forms and Various Methods in Christian Exegesis of the Middle Ages," *Hebrew Bible/Old Testament: The History of Its Interpretation*, vol. 1, part 2, Göttingen, 2000, 215. For a discussion of the first of these lectures, *Rigans montes de superioribus*, see S. Tugwell, *Albert and Thomas*, 267–271, and for an English translation, ibid., 353–362.

11. Recent scholarship has assigned Thomas's *Super Isaiam* and *Super Ieremiam* to the period immediately following his arrival in Paris as a bachelor during the summer of 1251 or 1252; see A. Oliva, *Les Débuts de l'enseignement de Thomas d'Aquin et sa conception de la sacra doctrina*, Paris, 2006, 207–224; and J.-P. Torrell, *Initiation*, 41, 593 (5*). S. Tugwell dates Thomas's first arrival in Paris to 1251 and holds that the course on Isaiah belongs to this period, though he is less certain about the course on Jeremiah; cf. *Albert and Thomas*, 211, 305 n. 130. Earlier considerations may be summarized as follows: The Leonine Commission's editors of Thomas's *Super Isaiam* dated this work to his first year of teaching in Paris (for them 1252–1253), mainly because it appears to be the purely literal or cursory reading of a biblical bachelor; see "Introduction," *Exp. Sup. Isaiam Ad Lit.*, ed. Commissio Leonina, *Opera omnia*, t. XXVIII, Roma, 1974, 19–20. Writing in 1950, B. Smalley surmised that William should be expected to hold "a key position in the history of Dominican exegesis," supposing as she did that "he must have heard St. Thomas lecture on St. Matthew and on Isaias," in "Sapiential Books I," 57. Persuaded by more contemporary studies, she subsequently decided that William could not have heard Thomas lecture on Isaiah; cf. *The Study of the Bible in the Middle Ages*, 3rd ed. Oxford, 1983, 275. As is the *Lectura super Iohannem*, the *Lectura super Mattheum* is now generally placed among the numerous works belonging to Thomas's second Paris regency (1268/9–1272). Several scholars have argued that Thomas began his first teaching in Paris in 1252, not as a biblical bachelor, as once supposed, but as a bachelor of Peter Lombard's *Sentences*. On their view, Thomas's *Super Isaiam* is to be assigned to his earlier sojourn in Cologne. The same would hold for his *Super Ieremiam* and *Super Threnos* (the latter of uncertain authenticity), mainly because they, too, appear to be the works of a *cursor Biblicus*; see A. Weisheipl, *Frère Thomas d'Aquin. Sa vie, sa pensée, ses oeuvres*, French trans. C. Lotte–J. Hoffman, Paris, 1993 [*Friar Thomas de Aquino. His Life, Thought and Works*, Washington, 1974, 1983], 65–67; M. Mulchahey, *First the Bow Is Bent*, 380–382. J.-P. Torrell notices: "The scholars find themselves in difficulties when trying to identify the Biblical books that relate to this first period of teaching in Paris"; *Initiation*, 81.

12. M.-M. Dufeil, *Guillaume de Saint-Amour et la polémique universitaire parisienne 1250–1259*, Paris, 1972, 284, 316.

13. See M. Mulchahey, *First the Bow Is Bent*, 383–384. For a few discussions of Dominican education during the thirteenth century, see M. Johnson, "Aquinas's *Summa theologiae* as Pedagogy," in *Medieval Education*, ed. R. Begley and J. Koterski, New York, 2005, 133–142; S. Tugwell, *Albert and Thomas*, 211; L. Boyle, "Notes on the Education of the 'Fratres Communes' in the Dominican Order in the Thirteenth Century," *Xenia Medii Aevi historiam illustrantia oblata*, Roma, 1978, 249–267.

14. Though William is credited with *Questiones varias* by the sixteenth-century bibliographer J. Bale, to date no such questions have been identified; *Index Britaniae Scriptorum*, ed. R. Poole and M. Bateson, Oxford, 1902; repr., Woodbridge, 1990, 113.

15. *Study of the Bible*, 270–271.

16. See G. Dahan, *L'exégèse chrètienne de la Bible en Occident Medieval, XIIe–XIVe siècle*, Paris, 1999, 108–116, and "Genres, Forms and Various Methods," 213.

17. G. Murano, *Opere diffuse per exemplar e pecia*, Turnhout, 2005, 83–89 (86).

18. *Catalogus Stamsensis*, ed. G. Meersseman, *MOPH* XVIII, 60, n. 15. With the addition of "item super canctica," the same information appears in the fifteenth-century *Catalogus Upsalensis*, ed. G. Meersseman, *MOPH* XVIII, 71, n. 15. However, no postill on the Canticle appears in a listing

of the same bibliography under William's name in the anonymous *Brevis Historia Ordinis Praedicatorum*, ed. E. Martène and U. Durand O. S. B., *Veterum Scriptorum Monumentorum Historicorum, Dogmaticorum, Moralium Amplissima Collectio*, t. 6, Paris, 1729, col. 331–395 (369). Under the title, the editors indicate that the edition is based on Jean Mabillon's transcription of a manuscript, dated to 1367, at the General Archives of the Order of Preachers at Santa Sabina, Rome: "Ex ms. S. Sabina anni 1367, eruit Mabillionius." Historians have variously dated the Stams catalogue to the years from 1310 to about 1350. For an overview of these discussions and the editions cited here, see H.-D. Simonin, "Notes de la Bibliographie dominicaine," *AFP* 8 (1938), 193–214.

19. Cf. B. Smalley, "Sapiential Books I," 62.

20. N. Senocak has presented an edition of the earliest surviving inventory of the library of Todi, as well as a fine study of it: "The Earliest Library Catalogue of the Franciscan Convent of Todi (c. 1300)," *AFH* 99 (2006), 467–505. The ascription of this postill is not at all clear: *Item postilla Guillelmi super Lucam*. The specific attribution appears in a second inventory most likely compiled about forty years later: *Postilla fratris guilelmi de alona* [*sic*], ibid., 480, n. 52.

21. *Répertoire*, I, 113–116.

22. *Rep. Bibl.*, II, 392–398, n. 2771–2796.

23. *SOPMA*, 82–86, n. 1427–1438.

24. *Handlist*, 747–751.

25. Inc.: *Dimittuntur ei peccata multa*, MS Paris, BnF lat. 526, f. 241vb–242va.

26. MS Paris, BnF lat. 16482, f. 325ra–347vb. Ten are ascribed simply to "Anglicus," one sermon (*De Sancto Clemente*) is ascribed to "Magister Willelmus," f. 338rb, another (for the feast of St. Dominic) is ascribed to "Anglicus, Willelmus, frater," f. 340, rb.; *SOPMA*, 86–88, n. 1440–1452; J. Schneyer, *Repertorium der latienischen sermones des Mittelalters*, Münster, 11 vols., 1969–1980, vol. 2, 372–373.

27. The typology of university exegesis has now been well documented. See B. Smalley, *Study of the Bible*, 264–356; J. Verger, "L'exégèse de l'université," in *Le Moyen Age et la Bible*, ed. P. Riché and G. Lobrichon, Bible de tous les temps, 4, Paris, 1984, 199–232; "L'exégèse, parente pauvre de la théologie scholastique?" 31–56; G. Dahan, *L'exégèse chrétienne*, 108–116, and "Genres, Forms and Various Methods," 211–216.

28. It was by just this sort of comparative study that A. Fries identified John of La Rochelle's *In Psalmos*; see "Ein Psalmentkommentar des Johannes von La Rochelle, O.F.M.," *Franz. Studien* 34 (1952), 235–265. By a similar approach, C. Nappo ascribed to the same exegete a postill on Mark that had been subject to varying attributions and scholarly assessments; see "La Postilla in Marcum di Giovanni de Rupella e suoi riflessi nella Summa Halesiana," *AFH* 50 (1957), 332–347. For these two references, I am indebted to I. Brady, "Sacred Scripture in the Early Franciscan School," in *La Sacra Scrittura E I Franciscani*, ed. Antonianum, 1973, 65–82 (65–66).

29. *Rep. Bibl.*, 2785, 2786.

30. For example, one of the commentaries on the Canticle is attributed in various manuscripts to Thomas Aquinas, Bonaventure, and William of Middleton, as well as to William of Alton; *SOPMA* 1429. The commentary on Job is attributed, tentatively, to Simon of Hinton by B. Smalley, "Some More Exegetical Works of Simon of Hinton," *RTAM* 15 (1948), 97–106 (99–104). For a discussion of the problems of attribution presented by this text, see R. Sharpe, *Titulus*, 177–183. The commentaries on Jeremiah and Lamentations are also associated with William of Luxi and Guerric of San Quentin; *Rep. Bibl.*, 2791. For a discussion of William's authorship of the Lamentations commentary, see "William of Alton's Commentary on the Book of Lamentations," 230.

31. For a few examples, F. Stegmüller associates two different commentaries on Wisdom with William by placing a question mark after his name, *Rept. Bibl.* 2785 and 2786; T. Kaeppeli qualifies several of his entries for commentaries on Job and Proverbs with "(G. de Altona?)," on the Canticle with "(op. incertum)," and on Matthew and the Apocalypse with "(op. dubium)," *SOPMA* 1427, 1428, 1431, 1436, and 1438, respectively; R. Sharpe qualifies a series of commentaries "Genesis—Ruth" as "very doubtful," in *Handlist*, 750.

32. "Explicit Super Isaiam secundum fratrem Guillelmum de Altona de Ordine Fratrum Predicatorum, Deo gratias et beate Virgini" (f. 85vb); "Explicit Super Ieremiam secundum fratrem Guillelmum de Altona, Deo gratias" (f. 145ra); "Explicit Super Trenos secundum fratrem Guillelmum de Altona" (f. 156ra).

33. "Expliciunt postille Super Iohannem euangelistam secundum fratrem Guillelmum de Altona. Deo gratias," (MS Saint-Omer, Bibl. mun. 260, f. 177vb).

34. See note 17.

35. On the application of this method, see note 28.

36. *Super XII prophetas*; inc.: *Murus ciuitatis habens fundamenta*, MSS Paris, BnF lat. 468, f. 30ra–198ra; Oxford, Bodleian, e mus. 29, f. 247r–365v; *Super Mattheum* (begins incomplete at Mt 5:2: *Aperiens os suum docebat*), MS Bodleian, e mus. 29, f. 1r–173v. On Simon's authorship of these two commentaries, see the studies of B. Smalley, "Two Biblical Commentaries of Simon of Hinton," *RTAM* 13 (1946), 57–85 (57–60), and "Some More Exegetical Works of Simon of Hinton," *RTAM* 15 (1948), 97–106 (97–98).

37. Inc.: *Consumpta est caro eius a supliciis*, MS Paris, BnF lat. 14250, 1ra–283va.

38. Inc.: *Multorum nobis*, MS Paris, BnF lat. 15266, f. 1ra–184rb.

39. Inc.: *Stabat mare super XII boues*, MS Paris, BnF lat. 14262, f. 1ra–391vb.

40. *Opera*, t. VI.

41. Ed. Borgnet, vol. 24, Paris, 1899.

42. Borrowed at a very early date from Peter of Tarentaise to fill a lacuna in the text of Thomas Aquinas's commentary on the same book, this text has appeared in numerous printings under the latter's name. Here I have made use of *Sancti Thomae Aquinatis Opera omnia*, ed. Parma, t. XIII, 1863, 203a–233b. Cf. J.-P. Torrell, *Initiation*, 496–497.

43. Ed. Parma, 1860, t. X, 279–645.

44. MS Paris, BnF lat. 14265, f. 463va–487ra.

45. WILLIAM OF LUXI, *Postilla super Baruch, Postilla super Ionam* (ed. A. Sulavik, Turnhout, 2006, CCCM 219).

46. Inc.: *Sume tibi librum grandem*, MS Paris, BnF lat. 9418, f. 1ra–117vb.

47. Inc: *Sacramentum regis abscondere bonum est*, MSS Basel, Univ. B III 20, f.1ra–92rb; Paris, BnF lat. 14259, f. 1ra–122ra; Paris, BnF lat. 15573, f. 32ra–155va; Troyes, Bibl. mun. 667, 1ra–150v. The incipit is from the copy at Basel. Notwithstanding a difference of incipits, B. Smalley described the first two listed here as "otherwise identical," "Sapiential Books I," 237. In fact, though all four texts are alike, no two are the same.

48. Inc.: *Surge et Vade in Niniuem ciuitatem grandem*, MS BnF lat. 14259, f. 124ra–168rb.

49. Inc.: *Cantabo dilecto meo*, MSS Basel, Univ. B III 20, f.182ra–230rb; Basel, Univ. B IV 21, 71ra–120vb; Paris, BnF lat. 14259, f. 170ra–225rb; Paris, BnF lat. 15265, f. 1r–41r (inc.: *Dilectus meus candidus*); and Troyes, Bibl. mun. 667, f. 151ra–202vb.

50. Concerning Thomas's commentaries on Isaiah and Jeremiah, as well as one on Lamentations of uncertain authenticity, J.-P. Torrell observes: "Les commentaires sur Jérémie et Lamentations appartient au même genre de lecture cursive de la Bible, attachée au sens littéral, que celui sur Isaïe," in *Initiation*, 493. Of the commentary on John, he remarks that "L'exégèse théologique de l'évangile de Saint-Jean . . . compte certainement parmi les commentaires les plus achevés et les plus profonds qu'il a laisses"; *Initiation*, 496.

CHAPTER 2

1. For brief survey of the debate and a list of no fewer than nine definitions, see R. Noguchi, "Style and the Form-Meaning Link," in *The Text and Beyond: Essays in Literary Linguistics*, ed. C. Goldin Bernstein, London, 1994, 123–125.

2. Ibid., 124.

3. N. Enkvist, "On Defining Style: An Essay in Applied Linguistics," in *Linguistics and Style*, ed. J. Spencer, London, 1964, 1–56 (12), cited by R. Noguchi, ibid., 124.

4. On the general characteristics of university exegesis, see G. Dahan, "Genres, Forms and Various Methods," 211–216; *L'exégèse chrétienne*, 108–120.

5. For studies of the *divisio*, see G. Dahan, *L'exégèse chrétienne*, 271–275, and "L'Ecclésiaste contra Aristote? Les commentaires de Eccl 1, 13 et 17–18 aux XII$^e$ et XIII$^e$ siècles," in *Itenéraires de la raison. Ètudes de philosophie médievale offertes à Maria Cândida Pacheco*, ed. J. F. Meirinhos (Col. Textes et études du Moyen Age, 32), Fédération Internationale des Instituts d'Études Mediévales, Louvain-la-Neuve, 2005, 205–233 (213–216); and M. Rossi, "La 'divisio textus' nei commenti scritturistici di S. Tommaso d'Aquino: un procedimento solo esegetico?" *Angelicum*, 71 (1994), 537–548.

6. "$^1$*EGO UIR UIDENS*. Hic redit ad plorandum populi sui afflictionem, ut dictum est supra in principio libri. Et primo deplorat principaliter afflictionem que accidit post captiuitatem; secundo principaliter afflictionem populi que precessit, quarto capitulo.a. In prima primo compatitur populo proprio; secundo inprecatur penam populo aduersario: $^{60}$*VIDI⟨STI⟩ OMNEM*. In prima primo multiplicem sui et populi afflictionem commemorat; secundo Deum ad miserendum in dicta afflictione inuocat: $^{19}$*RECORDARE*; tertio ut misericordiam assequatur populum ad penitentiam inuitat: $^{40}$*SCRUTEMUR*; quarto afflictionem populi iterat ut addat: $^{43}$*OPERUISTI*. In prima primo commemorat afflictionem factam per Caldeos; secundo aliam factam per transmigrantes: $^{14}$*FACTUS SUM IN DERISUM*; tertio redit ut addat ad dolores per Caldeos illatos: $^{51}$*CONFREGIT*. In prima primo ostendit quam multipliciter penas memoratas sustinuit; secundo quod easdem euadere non$^6$ potuit: $^5$*EDIFICAUIT*. In prima primo dicit se et populum miserias suas per flagella cognouisse; secundo ostendit penas dictas ad populum flagellandum permisisse: $^2$*ME MINAUIT*; tertio hostes ad flagellandum sollicitos extitisse: $^3$*TANTUM IN ME UERTIT*; quarto ostendit in populo ex uehemencia flagelli signa apparuisse: $^4$*VETUSTAM*." Super Thren. 3:1, *AHDLMA* 73 (2006), 203–281 (260).

7. In William's commentary *Super Threnos* and in the first ten chapters of his *Super Iohannem*, every *divisio* is introduced by a *lemma*. This, in turn, is followed immediately by *hic* in 38 of 42 cases in the former work (90.48 percent) and in 249 of 258 cases in the latter (96.51 percent). In all but two of the remaining cases, *hic* appears a few words later in the initial sentence.

8. "$^{3:11}$*EGO UIR UIDENS PAUPERTATEM* etc. Supra deplorauit populi sui afflictionem et locorum habitabilium destructionem. Hic reducit ad deplorandum populi sui afflictionem. Et primo . . .," (MS BnF lat. 14265, f. 475ra).

9. It appears three times in the initial *divisio* of the first thirteen chapters of his commentary on Matthew, at the beginnings of chapters 6, 7, and 11, MS Paris, BnF lat. 9418, f. 23va, 26vb, and 41vb.

10. Critical editions have been produced for Thomas's commentaries *Super Iob* (ed. Leonina, vol. 26) and *Super Isaiam* (ed. Leonina, vol. 28). The dubious quality of the editions of his other biblical commentaries calls for caution. Thomas Aquinas, *Super Matt.*, cap 26, lec. 5; *Super Io.*, cap. 14, lec. 3 (*bis*); cap. 14, lec. 6; *Super Eph.*, cap. 1, lec. 1; *Super Tit.*, cap. 1, lec. 1.

11. E.g., *Super Os.* 1:1, MS Paris, BnF lat. 14262, f. 5vb, and *Super Ioel* 1:1, ibid., f. 85vb.

12. E.g., *Super Mt.* 1:1 and 5:1, MS Paris, BnF lat. 9418, f. 3vb and 15ra.

13. Though exceedingly rare elsewhere, exceptions are frequent in the initial *divisio* of the commentary, such as the one introducing *Super Ieremiam*: "$^{1:1}$*VERBA IEREMIE*. Iste liber diuiditur . . . ," (MS Paris, BnF lat. 573, f. 87vb).

14. For an account of the history and development of the *reportatio*, see N. Bériou, *L'avènement des maîtres de la Parole. La prédication à Paris qu xiiie siècle*, 2 vols., Paris, 1998, vol. 1, 73–131. She observes: "Toute reportation est donc un document singulier, dont on ne peut jamais préjuger de la fidélité aux paroles qu'elle prétend rapporter. Néanmoins, les conditions particulières de la production des reportations rédigées dans le milieu parisien engagent à accorder une relative confiance à ces documents, si imparfaits soient-ils," 104. In a lucid account of the manifold problems the *reportatio* presents to the study of texts, J. Hamesse remarks that "on ne peut jamais considérer les reportations comme des vestiges pleinement authentiques du texte d'un auteur" in *"Reportatio* et transmission des Textes," in *The Editing of Theological and Philosophical Texts from the Middle Ages*, Stockholm, 1986, 11–29 (17). See also, by the same author, "La méthode

de travail des reportateurs," in *Medioevo e Rinascimento* 3 (1989), 51–67; L.-J. Bataillon, "Approaches to the Study of Mediaeval Sermons," *Leeds Studies in English* 9 (1980), 1935; and B. Smalley, *Study of the Bible*, 201–207.

15. Apparently following the incipit to the commentary, R. Sharpe lists under William's name a postill on Job in MS Troyes 487, *Handlist*, 748. A cursory look at a few instances of its *divisio* may suggest that this work's terminology differs from copy to copy. Yet closer reading shows that this is a different commentary, apparently dependent upon the former. Apart from a different prologue, it consists of paraphrases of many sections of the preceding postill's *divisio* and a completely different *expositio*.

16. Application of this method for the identification of biblical commentaries may be observed in I. Brady's study of Alexander of Hales's biblical commentaries, "Sacred Scripture in the Early Franciscan School," 65–82 (72).

17. "*¹⁹RECORDARE*. Hic primo allegat propriam siue populi miseriam; secundo predicat diuinam misericordiam: *²²MISERICORDIE DOMINI*; tertio ne desperent promittit ueniam: *³¹NON REPEL-LET*; quarto ostendit quod eius est misereri qui inflixit penam: *³⁷QUIS EST ISTE*. In prima primo petit ut miseriam compaciendo reuocet; secundo ostendit quod tanta est quod nisi misereatur in aduersitate populus deficiet: *²⁰MEMORIA MEMOR*; tertio dicit quod miseriam propriam recolendo de uenia non desperat: *²¹HEC RECOLENS*. Dicit ergo: *¹⁹ZAY: RECORDARE*, ad miserendum, *PAUPERTATIS MEE*, per bonorum ablationem . . . ," *Super Thren.*, ed. cit., 263.

18. Largely absent from the *divisio* introducing the first seven chapters of his commentary on John's Gospel, clear systematic rhyming, however, appears with some frequency, such as at the outset of chapters 8, 9, 12, 13, and 17; the addition of a *lemma* to all elements except the first is also far less consistent than in William's commentaries; Albert the Great, *In Io. Com.*, ed. Borgnet, 327, 373, 466–467, 499, and 602, respectively.

19. The likeness of complexity of the *divisio* of William of Alton and William of Luxi may be illustrated by the numbers of subdivisions and resulting elements in divisions introducing each of the five chapters of their Lamentations commentaries. For William of Alton's postill, the numbers are subdivisions: 5 + 1 + 5 + 3 + 4 = 18; total elements: 15 + 8 + 17 + 10 + 11 = 61. For William of Luxi's postill, the numbers are subdivisions: 5 + 2 + 5 + 2 + 4 = 18; total elements: 15 + 10 + 17 + 8 + 11 = 61.

20. B. Smalley made the opposite judgment of one of William of Alton's near contemporaries: "William of Middleton's postills on Ecclesiasticus and Job, in fact, confirm the impression that he makes in his postill on the Twelve Prophets: he is primarily interested in the spiritual interpretation . . . ," "Sapiential Books I," 55. Indeed, a survey of the initial *divisio* of the first six chapters of his postill on Ecclesiasticus shows that the spiritual senses are predominant in each of them, MS Paris, BnF lat. 15266, f. 1va, 5vb, 8ra, 11rb, 15ra, and 17ra.

21. Here and henceforth, the term allegory corresponds to the medieval *allegoria* ("allegorically" corresponds to *allegorice*, as well as its equivalent *mistice*). For the same meaning, some modern scholars reserve the term *typology*, which they distinguish sharply from *allegory*. On their view, typology (the medieval *allegoria*) is tied to history, particularly biblical history, whereas allegory is bereft of historical moorings. Also, they generally view typology as originating in biblical thought, and allegory in pagan thought, especially Platonism. On the face of it, Paul's application of the term ἀλληγορούμενα (*allegoriam* in the Vulgate) in Gal 4:24 would appear to argue against both points. As this distinction is terra incognita for William and his contemporaries, we make no use of it. For a lucid overview of relevant discussions, including extensive bibliography, see N. T. Wright, *Rhetoric and Theory: Figural Reading of John 9*, Berlin, 2009, 59–71.

22. Notable exceptions include Aquinas's *Expositio Super Iob ad litteram* and his *Lectura Super Iohannem*. While the former is entirely literal, the latter presents highly developed spiritual exegesis throughout. The literal character of his commentaries on Isaiah and Jeremiah is generally taken as evidence that they date to his period as a biblical bachelor. A commentary on Lamentations often printed under Thomas's name is of questionable authenticity; see Chapter 4, note 96. On the commentaries on Isaiah and Jeremiah, see J.-P. Torrell, *Initiation*, 40–52, 493; on *Super Iob*, 175–178, 494, 32*; on *Super Iohannem*, 496, 33*.

23. Of 222 explicit biblical or nonbiblical references in William's *Super Threnos, illud* is never employed individually as an introduction, though it makes two appearances in combination with other terms: *iuxta illud* at Io 1:7 and *secundum illud* at Io 4:16. Of 1,250 explicit references in the prologue and first ten chapters of *Super Iohannem, illud* appears seven times, never individually: *secundum illud, Prol.; iuxta illud: In* 7:49, 8:41, and 9:15; *contra illud: In* 1:22, 8:33, and 9:22.

23. While William makes frequent use of *unde* for introducing *lemmata*, either in isolation or in the aforementioned combination *unde sequitur*, for introducing citations he normally restricts usage of it to phrases, such as: "Vnde patet sunt mentiti, Ps.: *In corde et cor⟨de⟩ lo⟨cuti⟩ sunt falsa*" (*In* Io 7:25, cf. Ps 11:3). There are only two exceptions in *Super Threnos* and three in the first ten chapters of *Super Iohannem.*

24. In *Super Threnos*, references are introduced by *simile* on twelve occasions, in *Super Iohannem* twenty-seven. The number of instances for all of Thomas Aquinas's biblical commentaries is eleven.

25. For a typology of the simple question in medieval exegesis, see G. Dahan, *L'exégèse chrétienne*, 131; for the complex question, ibid., 284–287. By the same author, see also "La méthode critique dans l'étude de la Bible (xiiᵉ–xiiiᵉ siècles)," in *La Méthode Critique au Moyen Âge*, ed. M. Chazan and G. Dahan, Turnhout, 2006, 103–128 (122–124).

26. Such grouping of questions may be observed in Bonaventure's commentaries on Ecclesiastes and John. Consultation of MS Paris, BnF lat. 14429, 1ra–49ra, for the postill on Ecclesiastes, and of MS Troyes, Bibl. Mun. 1410, f. 2r–94v, for the postill on John, shows that there is no reason to suppose that the textual arrangements of the printed editions are editorial (both appear in the Quaracchi edition *Opera omnia*, t. VI, 1893).

27. Such is the case with the first five postills of Group B, all in MS Paris, BnF lat. 526, as well as with all the postills of MSS Paris, BnF lat. 573 and Madrid, Bibl. Nac. 493.

28. See, for example, her discussion of the postill on Matthew, *Sume tibi librum grandem*. Its inclusion in MS Saint-Omer 260, which also includes William's postill on John *Acceptus est regi minister intelligens*, seems to have contributed to her qualification of its authenticity as "almost certain"; "Sapiential Books I," 67–68. The present study does not accept this work as authentic.

29. Ibid., 48.

30. A notable example is MS Paris, BnF lat. 14429, an expensive professionally written and decorated volume, which was bequeathed to St. Victor by Adenulph of Anagni (see Appendix 1, note 130). It contains two different postills on Ecclesiastes, as well as two copies of the same postill on Wisdom. Another is MS Basel Öffentliche Biblthek der Universität III. 20, once in the library of the Dominicans of that city. It contains two different postills on Wisdom.

## CHAPTER 3

1. T. Bellamah, "William of Alton's Commentary on the Book of Lamentations," *AHDLMA* 73 (2006), 203–281.

2. See the studies listed in chapter 1, note 27.

3. On these developments, see especially G. Dahan, *L'exégèse chrétienne*, 108–109, and "Genres, Forms and Various Methods," 212–213.

4. Dominicans of the thirteenth century developed their own *studia* for the organization of studies. Whereas *studia provincialia* served the needs of individual provinces, *studia generalia* served the order as a whole. On both institutions, see M. Mulchahey, *First the Bow Is Bent*, 219–396. On the close connections between biblical study and the preaching of the time, see L.-J. Bataillon, "De la *lectio* à la *praedicatio*. Commentaires Bibliques et sermons au xiiiᵉ siècle," *RSPT* 70 (1986), 559–574.

5. For studies of the development of university prologues, see A. J. Minnis, *Medieval Theory of Authorship*, 2nd ed., Aldershot, 1988, 40–72; G. Dahan, "Les prologues des commentaires Bibliques," in *Les prologues médiévaux* (Textes et études du Moyen Âge 15), Turnhout, 2000, 427–469; *L'exégèse chrétienne*, 262–271; A. Sulavik, "*Principia* and *Introitus* in Thirteenth-Century

Christian Biblical Exegesis with Related Texts," 269–287; C. Spicq, *Esquisse d'une histoire de l'exégèse latine au Moyen Âge*, Paris, 1944, 214–217.

6. Modern scholars have called these exegetes the "biblical moral school," not because they constituted an institution or even a school of thought, but because they shared a lively interest in practical moral concerns. The first to use the expression was M. Grabmann, *Die Geschichte der scholastischen Methode*, Freiburg, 1911, 467. See also B. Smalley, *The Study of the Bible*, 196–242; G. Dahan, *L'exégèse chrétienne*, 106–107.

7. Cf. A. J. Minnis and A. Scott, *Medieval Literary Theory and Criticism*, Oxford, 1988, 28–29.

8. "*Acceptus est regi minister intelligens* (Prv 14:35). Hec uerba scripta sunt Prou. xv, in quibus principaliter huius euangelii scriba commendatur, et per consequens ipsum euangelium, cum auctoris commendatio redundet in opus, secundum illud Eccli. 11: *In manu artificis opera laudabuntur* (Sir 9:24). Insuper et huius operis causa quadrupliciter insinuatur." (*Super Io.*, prol., MS Saint-Omer, Bibl. mun. 260, f. 110ra).

9. "Commendatur autem a tribus; primo quantum ad uitam: *minister*; secundo quantum ad scientiam: *intelligens*; tertio quantum ad utriusque approbationem, uel quantum ad Christi specialem familiaritatem: *Acceptus est regi*." *Super Io.*, prol., (MS Saint-Omer, Bibl. mun. 260, f. 110ra).

10. "Secundario notatur in hiis uerbis quadruplex causa huius operis. Materialis, per hoc quod dicit: *Regi*, quia de Christo qui est rex regum agitur in hoc libro quantum ad utrumque naturam que est in eo.... Formalis: *Intelligens*, intelligendo enim diuinam naturam sine comparatione, extollere humanam et utramque esse in Christo. ... Efficiens: *Minister*. Finalis: *Acceptus*. Ad hoc enim scribit ut in presenti simus accepti Deo per fidem, infra xx: *Hec scripta sunt ut credatis*, et in futuro per gloriam, unde sequitur: *et ut credentes uitam habeatis*" (Io 20:31), *Super Io.*, prol., (MS Saint-Omer, Bibl. mun. 260, f. 110va–vb).

11. "Causa materialis insinuatur per hoc quod dicitur: *aquam, fontem lacrimarum ut plorem interfectos*. Vehemens enim planctus quo Ieremias deplorat terre sue desolationem siue deuastationem, ciuitatis et templi destructionem, populi sui et maxime regis Iosie afflictionem, et interfectionem templi factam per Caldeos uel tunc faciendam per Titum et Vespasianum, per Romanos secundum sensum historicum, est materia huius libri," *Super Threnos*, prol. (ed. cit., 233–234).

12. "Item notandum quod secundum sensum allegoricum materia huius libri est planctus pro recessu ecclesie a statu triplici, scilicet a feruore caritatis, a luce ueritatis, a constantia soliditatis.... Secundum sensum moralem materia huius libri est planctus pro ruina siue lapsu anime fidelis a statu iustitie per peccatum cogitationis, locutionis, et operis..." (*Super Threnos*, prol., ed. cit., 233–234).

13. "Secundo insinuatur in hiis uerbis huius operis causa materialis, cum dicitur: *opera eorum* (Sap 11:1). De operibus enim agit tripliciter: primo ea mala ostendendo, utpote quibus a Deo se auerterunt et ydolis seruierunt, et primo pro eis captiuitatem predicendo; secundo pro eis plangendo et lamentando, ut in Trenis; tertio pro eis deprecando, ut in Oratione Ieremie" (*Super Ier.*, prol., MS Madrid, Bibl. nac. 493, f. 266ra). Reference is made here to the Book of Lamentations fifth and final chapter, often set apart in the Vulgate (e.g., the Clementine edition) as the *Oratio Ieremiae Prophetae*.

14. "Causa materialis tangitur cum dicitur: *Vocem dicentis: ue, ue, ue, habitantibus in* etc. (Apc 8, 13).... Vnde de hiis tribus in terris diuersis habitantibus scripsit, et hoc triplex 'ue,' quia murmurantibus, 'ue' iam habitantium irridentibus, et infestantibus 'ue' futurum. Hinc est quod infra secundo in fine dicuntur in libro expanso coram Ezechiele scripta esse: *Lamentationes, carmen et ue* (Ez 2:9), lamentationes deridentium, carmen murmurantium, et ue infestantium. Spiritualis autem materia huius libri sunt duo populi, alter Dei, alter Diaboli" (*Super Ezechielem*, prol., MS Paris, BnF lat. 573, f. 156rb).

15. The main source of the Latin West's account of primary and secondary causality, the *Liber de causis* is an Arabic work probably from the circle of al-Kindi of ninth-century Baghdad. Having entered medieval Europe by way of Gerard of Cremona's (d. 1187) twelfth-century Arabic-Latin translation at Toledo, it was generally attributed to Aristotle. And yet, Thomas Aquinas recognized its dependence on the *Elementatio theologica* of the fifth-century Athenian Neoplatonist Proclus, subsequent to William of Moerbeke's 1268 Greek-Latin translation of that work. See

C. D'Ancona and R. Taylor, "Le *Liber de causis*," *Dictionnaire de Philosophes Antiques. Supplément*, Richard Goulet et alii, eds., Paris, 2003, 599–647;C. D'Ancona, *Recherches sur le Liber de causis*, Paris, 2002; R. Taylor, "Remarks on the Latin Text and the Translator of the Kalam fi mahd al-khair/Liber de causis," *Bulletin de Philosophie Medievale* 31 (1989) 75–102.

16. The present discussion of the efficient cause and the roles of divine and human authors is indebted to A. J. Minnis, *Medieval Theory of Authorship*, 73–117.

17. "Titulus: *Liber Trenorum Ieremie*, et sicut Canticum Salamonis dicitur *Canticum Canticorum*, sic ista *Lamentatio Lamentationum*, quia omnes excellit. Cetere enim particulares: fleuerunt enim filii Iacob patrem suum, Samuel Saulem, Dauid Saul et Ionathan et Absalonem, Ezechias mortem suam imminentem sibi predictam. Set hec fit pro omne dampno temporali et spirituali; excedit etiam alios in quantitate ut patet, et etiam in modo plangendi. Ideo dicit 1: *O uos omnes qui transitis per uiam* etc" (*Super Threnos*, prol., ed. cit., 235).

18. "Principalis enim efficiens Spiritus est. . . . Causa efficiens secundaria et minus principalis Ieremias est" (*Super Threnos*, prol., ed. cit., 233).

19. "Efficiens quidem huius libri causa triplex est. Prima per modum inspirationis, scilicet Verbum Dei. . . . Verbum Dei est efficiens causa prima. Secunda causa efficiens, scilicet per modum inuentionis, est Salomon. . . . Proxima causa efficiens per modum compilationis fuit Phylo sapientissimus Iudeorum" (*Super Sapientiam*, prol., MS Paris, BnF lat. 14429, f. 155rb;). The equivalent text from this postill's other prologue (inc.: *Diligite lumen sapientiae*) appears in *Bonaventure Opera*, t. VI, 108a–b.

20. "Etenim multo est Philo iste, cui liber Sapientiae tamquam auctori, vel saltem interpreti tribuebatur" (Jerome, *Praefatio in libros Salomonis*, PL 28, 1242).

21. ". . . quem tamen beatus Hieronymus asserit non a Salomone, ut usus habet, sed a Philone doctissimo Iudaeo fuisse conscriptum" (Rabanus Maurus, *Comm. in Sap.*, PL 109, 671).

22. William has in mind Prv 25:1: *These also are proverbs of Solomon which the men of Hezekiah king of Judah copied.* "Vnde liber ipse *Sapientia Salomonis* inscribitur, et more ecclesiastico lectionibus de libro hoc sumptis premittitur: 'Dixit Salomon filiis Israel,' quia scilicet de eius sententiis liber iste, quamuis ab alio compilatus sit, sicut et liber *Prouerbiorum* pro magna parte a uiris Ezechie" (*Super Sapientiam*, prol., MS Paris, BnF lat. 14429, f. 155rb;). No such attribution appears in the prologue to the postill on Proverbs (inc.: *Sapiens in uerbis producet seipsum*), whose authenticity we have considered and declined to affirm. This passage has no equivalent in the other prologue to the same postill *Diligite lumen sapientiae*. William's predecessor Hugh of St. Cher also describes Proverbs as a *compilatio*, ascribing the work of compilation not only to Hezekiah's men, but to Hezekiah himself, and to Solomon, *Postillae*, in Prv., prol. (ed. Venetiis, t. III, 3vb). For a discussion of this text, see A. J. Minnis, to whom I owe the preceding reference, *Medieval Theory of Authorship*, 149–150.

23. *Medieval Theory of Authorship*, 119–133. The present discussion is largely indebted to this study. On the emergence of explicit reflections on the scientific character of theology during the thirteenth century, see M.-D. Chenu, *La Théologie comme science au XIIIᵉ siècle*, 3rd ed., Paris, 1957; G. R. Evans, *Old Arts and New Theology: The Beginnings of Theology as an Academic Discipline*, Oxford, 1980.

24. "Dicendum quod alius est modus scientiae, qui est secundum comprehensionem veritatis per humanam rationem; alius est modus scientiae secundum affectum pietatis per divinam traditionem. Primus modus definitivus debet esse, divisivus, collectivus, collectivus; et talis modus debet esse in humanis scientiis, quia apprehensio veritatis secundum humanum rationem explicatur per divisiones, definitiones et ratiocinationes. Secundus modus debet esse praeceptivus, exemplicativus, exhortativus, revelativus, orativus, quia ii modi competunt affectui pietatis; et hic modus est in sacra scriptura" (Alexander of Hales, *Summa Theologica*, Tractatus introductorius, q. 1, cap. IV, a. 3, ed. Quaracchi, *Opera omnia*, t. IV, 1948, I, 10). This text has been presented and discussed by M.-D. Chenu, *La Théologie comme science*, 40–41. For a discussion of its date and authenticity, see ibid., 38.

25. A. J. Minnis, *Medieval Theory of Authorship*, 120–127; M.-D. Chenu, *La Théologie comme science*, 37–57.

26. We shall see that William does have something to say about the usefulness of inquiry into the articles of faith, yet his remarks are not appreciably different from Bonaventure's or even Thomas's.

27. "Modus enim est triplici uersu in quadruplici alphabeto distincto dictos tres status deplangere. Ad quod plenius intelligendum, nota quod Ieremias quatuor lamentationes composuit, ita quod singule habent XXII clausulas iuxta numerum litterarum alphabeti Hebreorum . . . et tamen quadruplici alphabeto repetito, secundum Ysidorum, libro X, distinguntur, ut quaternario hoc populum Iudaicum in quatuor mundi partes per captiuitatem Babilonicam dispersum et per Romanos dispergendum defleret." (*Super Threnos*, prol., ed. cit., 234. William refers to Isidore of Seville's *Etymologiarum sive originum libri xx*, ed. W. Lindsay, 2 vols., Oxford, 1911, facsimile reprint, Oxford, 1971. As the Lindsay edition is not paginated, here and henceforth we cite J.-P. Migne's printing, *Etym.*, VI, 2, 23, PL 82, 232.)

28. "Quoad sensum allegoricum, ut hoc quaternario ecclesie ruinam in recedentibus a quatuor uirtutibus defleret. Quoad sensum moralem, ut ruinam anime fidelis per quatuor affectiones inordinatas defleret; et quia quatuor elementis corpora nostra composita aggrauantur" (*Super Threnos*, prol., ed. cit., 234).

29. The four virtues (prudence, justice, temperance, and fortitude) were stock references throughout the Middle Ages; cf. Peter Lombard, *Sent.*, III, 33, 1 (ed. Coll. S. Bonaventurae, t. II, 187–189); Gregory the Great, *Moralia in Iob*, II, 49 (ed. M. Adriaen, Turnhout, 1979, CCSL 143, 105); Augustine, *De civitate Dei*, IV, 20 (ed. B. Dombart and A. Kalb, Turnhout, 1955, CCSL 47, 114).

30. Joy, sorrow, hope, and fear; cf. Peter Lombard, *Sent.*, I, 8, 4 (ed. Coll. S. Bonaventurae, t. I, 99); Augustine, *De civ.*, XIV, 3 (CCSL 48, 417); Aristotle, *Ethic.* II (1105b23); Plato, *Phaedo* (83b).

31. Earth, fire, air, and water; cf. Augustine, *De civ.*, VIII, 15 (CCSL 47, 232–233); Aristotle, *Phys.* I, 4 (187a12); Plato, *Timaeus* (31b).

32. "Causa autem finalis insinuatur in hoc quod dicitur: *filie populi mei*, ut li *filie* sit datiui casus. Planxit *filie*, id est ad utilitatem filie, id est sinagoge, ecclesie et fidelis anime, ut uidelicet lugeant pro bonis omissis, peccatis commissis, penis acquisitis, uel pro peccatis propriis, pro peccatis alienis, pro incolatu uel miseria presentis uite, et pro desiderio superne patrie" (*Super Threnos*, prol., ed. cit., 235).

33. "Tertio insinuatur causa formalis in hoc quod dicitur: *in manibus* (Sap 11:1). Quod enim manuale et tangibile est, euidens est. Sic modus procedendi in isto opere facilis et manifestus. . . . Quod enim effunditur, id est extra funditur manifestum est. . . . Fuit autem iste modus manifestus et ubi prophetat, ut in principio, et ubi texit historiam, ut in medio, et ubi lamentatur, ut in fine" (*Super Ier.*, prol., MS Madrid, Bibl. Nac. 493, f. 266ra).

34. ". . . agit sublimiter, ut patet certitudinaliter; non tamen certitudine demonstrationis, que fidem euacuat, cum hominem uelit nolit ad assentientum agat, set certitudine auctoritatis, Augustinus: 'Quod credimus debemus auctoritati.' Et ideo hec scriptura procedit per modum narrationis, non ratiocinationis. Hec autem certitudo, licet in aliis scientiis sit modica, quarum inuentores sunt homines qui mentiri possunt, in hac autem est maxima quam Spiritus sanctus inspirauit" (*Super Io.*, prol., MS Saint-Omer, Bibl. mun. 260, f. 110vb); cf. Augustine, *De utilitate credendi*, 11: "quod intellegimus igitur, debemus rationi, quod credimus, auctoritati, quod opinamur, errori" (ed. J. Zycha, 1891, Wien, CSEL 25.1, 33). He makes a similar remark in *Retractationum libri duo*, I, 14 (ed. A. Mutzenbecher, 1984, CCSL 57, 43).

35. "Alia est certitudo auctoritatis, et haec fidem generat; unde Augustinus: 'Quod credimus debemus auctoritati' . . . oportuit habere certitudinem auctoritatis. Et haec est ratio, quare omnes libri sacrae Scripturae traduntur per modum narrationis, non ratiocinationis, quia sunt a generandam fidem, quae est per assensum liberum. . . . Dicendum est ergo, quod certitudo auctoritatis in aliis scientiis inuentis ab hominibus, qui mentiuntur saepe, parvum habet robur; sed in sacra Scriptura, quae a Spiritu sancto data est, magnam habet firmitatem, quia ipse mentiri non potest. . ." (Bonaventure, *In Io. com.*, prooemium, *Opera*, t. VI, 243b); cf. *Breviloquium.*, I (*Opera*, t. V, 210a–b).

36. Thomas Aquinas, *Super Boetium De Trinitate*, I, 2 (ed. Leonina, 1992, t. L, 77b).

37. For example: "Et sic ratio humana inducta diminuit meritum fidei: sicut etiam supra dictum est quod passio praecedens electionem in virtutibus moralibus diminuit laudem virtuosi actus. Sicut enim homo actus virtutum moralium debet exercere propter iudicium rationis, non propter passionem; ita credere debet homo ea quae sunt fidei non propter rationem humanam, sed propter auctoritatem divinam" (*ST*, II, II, q. 2, a. 10, co., ed. Leonina, vol. VIII, 38–39). On this point, see M.-D. Chenu, *Introduction*, 117.

38. The capital text here is *ST*, I, q. 1 (ed. Leonina, t. IV). For a lucid account of Thomas's thought on the matter, see M.-D. Chenu, *La Théologie comme science*, especially 67–92.

39. "Et notandum quod differunt commentator, scriptor, compilator et auctor. 'Commentator' enim est qui scribit sua et aliena, set principaliter aliena et sua tanquam annexa; 'scriptor' qui scribit tantum aliena, nichil addendo uel mutando circa ea; 'compilator' qui scribit tantum aliena, addendo tamen de dictis aliorum ad ea; 'auctor' qui scribit sua principaliter et aliena tanquam adnexa." Here I have followed the orthography of MS Madrid, Bibl. Nac. 493, f. 131V. The text, which is virtually the same in MSS Basel, Univ. Bibl. B III 20, f. 93vb and Paris, BnF lat. 15592, f. 192r, has been printed by M. Grabmann, "Ungedrukte exegetische Schriften von Dominikanertheologen des 13. Jahrhunderts," *Angelicum* 20 (1943), 204–218 (206–208), and reprinted by C. Spicq, *Esquisse*, 322. William's remarks are dependent upon Bonaventure, *In I-IV Sent.*, prooemium, q. 4, co. (*Opera*, t. I, 14b–15a).

40. "Ostendit enim auctor in hoc libro quod creature, maxime sensibiles, uane sunt. Vnde uanitas proprie est passio quam intendit ostendere de subiecto," (*Super Ecclesiasten*, prol., MS Madrid, Bibl. Nac. 493, f. 131rb).

41. A. J. Minnis has observed that the concept of *auctor* was inseparable from that of *auctoritas*: "The writings of an *auctor* contained, or possessed, *auctoritas* in the abstract sense of the term, with its strong connotations of veracity and sagacity," in *Medieval Theory of Authorship*, 10.

42. Hugh of St. Victor puts it as follows: "Expositio tria continet, litteram, sensum, sententiam. Littera est congrua ordinatio dictionum, quod etiam constructionem uocamus. Sensus est facilis quedam et aperta significatio, quam littera prima fronte prefert. Sententia est profundior intelligentia, que nisi expositione uel interpretatione non inuenitur. In his ordo est, ut primum littera, deinde sensus, deinde sententia inquiratur. Quo facto, perfecta est expositio" (*Didascalicon de studio legendi*, III, ed. C. Buttimer, Studies in Medieval and Renaissance Latin 10), Washington, 1939, 82. On the exegesis of the school of St. Victor, see B. Smalley, "L'exégèse Biblique du 12ᵉ siècle," in *Entretiens sur la renaissance du 12ᵉ siècle*, ed. M. de Gandillac and E. Jeauneau, Paris, 1968, 273–283; H. De Lubac, *Exégèse Médiévale. Les quatre sens de l'écriture*, Seconde partie, I, Paris, 1961, 288–435. On Hugh's contribution to literal exegesis, see G. Dahan, *L'exégèse chrétienne*, 240–241; D. Poirel, *Hugues de Saint-Victor*, Paris, 1998, 71–77; B. Smalley, *The Study of the Bible*, 93–95. For her observations on Andrew and his influence, ibid., 112–195; "The School of Andrew of St. Victor," *RTAM* 11 (1939), 145–167.

43. On the difference between Guerric of St. Quentin and Hugh of St. Cher on the literal sense, see M. Morard, "Hugues de Saint-Cher, commentateur des Psaumes," in *Hugues de Saint-Cher, Bibliste et théologien*, ed. L.-J. Bataillon, Gilbert Dahan, and P.-M. Gy, Turnhout, 2004, 101–153 (142).

44. The principal text here is *Sic et Non*, PL 178, 1339–1610.

45. On these developments, see M.-D. Chenu, *Introduction*, 117–131. About this, more will be said shortly.

46. As Augustine puts it: "Neque enim corpus sentit, sed anima per corpus, quo uelut nuntio utitur ad formandum in se ipsa, quod extrinsecus nuntiatur. Non potest itaque fieri uisio corporalis, nisi etiam spiritalis simul fiat; sed non discernitur, nisi cum fuerit sensus ablatus a corpore, ut id, quod per corpus uidebatur, inueniatur in spiritu. At uero spiritalis uisio etiam sine corporali fieri potest, cum absentium corporum similitudines in spiritu adparent et finguntur multae pro arbitrio uel praeter arbitrium demonstrantur. Item spiritalis uisio indiget intellectuali, ut diiudicetur, intellectualis autem ista spiritali inferiore non indiget. Ac per hoc spiritali corporalis, intellectuali autem utraque subiecta est" (*De Gen. ad lit. libri XII*, XII, ed. J. Zycha, 1894, CSEL 28.1 = BA 49, 416).

47. B. Smalley remarks: "The allegorical method captivated the Latin world. . . ." See *The Study of the Bible*, 20.

48. A. J. Minnis and A. Scott, *Medieval Literary Theory and Criticism*, 197.

49. This is certainly not a matter of the discovery of the literal sense, but of its reappraisal. Once again, B. Smalley has summed up this development well, this time in her consideration of Albert the Great's exegesis: "With St. Albert the 'literal truth' takes on a new meaning. It is not an easy preliminary but a difficult goal," in *The Study of the Bible*, 299.

50. For a study of a few key problems presented by Ecclesiastes to thirteenth-century exegetes, including Bonaventure and William, see G. Dahan, "L'Ecclésiaste contra Aristote?" 205–233.

51. *Medieval Theory of Authorship*, 116.

52. For a discussion of Bonaventure's consideration of Solomon in the prologue to his commentary on Ecclesiastes, see *Medieval Theory of Authorship*, 110–112. William's borrowing from Bonaventure in this work has been discussed by B. Smalley, "Sapiential Books I," 71–75, 272–273; "Sapiential Books II," 104.

53. Jerome, *In Ecclesiasten*, I, 12 (ed. M. Adriaen, Turnhout, 1959, CCSL 72, 258).

54. *In Ecl.*, prol. (*Opera*, t. VI, 8a–b). At issue here for Bonaventure is not whether Solomon's instruction was scandalous, but whether it was sinful. Brought into evidence against him is Ps 49:16 (*Peccatori autem dixit Deus: quare tu enarras iustitias meas?*). Bonaventure replies that Solomon, as a recipient of the gift of wisdom and as a ruler, was not merely allowed but bound to teach. That is to say, Solomon did not sin by teaching, but only by poorly disposing himself for doing so.

55. "Ad secundum, dicendum quod in predicatione carnali duo sunt: predicatio ipsa que frequenter edificat, et indignitas predicantis que scandalizat," (*Super Ecclesiasten*, prol., MS Madrid, Bibl. Nac. 493, f. 131ra).

56. "Item, ut dicitur Sap. 1: *In maliuolam animam non introibit sapientia, nec habitabit in corpore ⟨subdito peccatis⟩* etc. (Sap 1:4). Set Salamon peccator fuit, igitur cum sapientiam non haberet, eam docere non potuit, Augustinus, *De agone Christiano*: 'Errat quisquis ueritatem se cognoscere putat, si adhuc nequiter uiuat' (ed. J. Zycha, Wien, 1900, CSEL 41, 118). . . . Ad tertium, dicendum quod sapientia dicitur communiter et proprie: proprie secundum quod dicit diuinorum cognitionem et diuine cognitionis saporem debitum et amorem. Et sic loquitur dicta auctoritas de sapientia, non prout dicit nudam sine amore cognitionem" (*Super Ecl.*, prol., MS Madrid, Bibl. nac. 493, f. 131ra).

57. Bonaventure treats Solomon's sinfulness in tandem with his worldliness and disposes of both difficulties with the aforementioned appeals to his repentance and the capacity of the Holy Spirit to speak through evil people; cf. *In Ecl.*, prol. (*Opera*, t. VI, 8a–b).

58. Bon, *In Ecl. com.*, prol. (*Opera*, t. VI, 8b).

59. "Item magis creditur factis quam uerbis. Igitur cum iste doceret unum et faceret contrarium, sue doctrine non est credendum. . . . Ad quartum, dicendum quod magis credendum est factis quam uerbis propriis, set non quam uerbis diuinis a Spiritu Sancto inspiratis. Salomon ergo dicitur auctor, et recte; in hoc enim libro docentur contempni uoluptates, diuitie, honores et curiositates, de quibus iste melius docere potuit, quia expertus. Expertus enim melius rem cognoscit" (*Super Ecl.*, prol., MS Madrid, Bibl. nac. 493, f. 131ra).

60. The prologue to *Super Threnos* is discussed in the introduction to its edition, "William of Alton's Commentary on the Book of Lamentations," 216–219.

61. *Super Ier.*, prol.: "*Direxit opera eorum in manibus prophete sancti* (Sap 11:1). Hec uerba scripta sunt Sapientie x in quibus huius operis causa quadruplex insinuatur. Primo finalis: *Direxit*, ut enim due tribus a peccatis suis cessarent, et Domino seruirent, et ad celestia peruenirent, in quibus uera directio consistit. Ieremias librum istum predicendo, comminando et plangendo composuit. . . ."

62. Cf. Ier 16:2: non accipies uxorem et non erunt tibi filii et filiae in loco isto *W*.

63. *Super Ier.*, prol.: "*Vir indutus lineis*, Ieremias, qui uirgo, qui extitit, infra xv (cf. Ier 16:2), et in utero matris sanctificatus, infra I (cf. Ier 1:5), *iste erat super aquas fluminis* (Dn 12:6–7), quia in captiuitate presens, eam enim uidit propriis oculis. . . . Item, Ieremias fuit sanctus, infra I:

*Antequam exires de uulua sanctificaui te* (Ier 1:5). Quod patet ex nominis interpretatione. Interpretatur enim 'excelsus.' Item, ex significatione, quia sanctum, id est Christum, pre ceteris, uidetur magis prefigurare. Item, ex mentis et corporis castitate, infra xv: *Non sedi in consilio ludentium* (Ier 15, 17). Item, ex humilitate, infra 1: *Nescio loqui quia puer ego sum* (Ier 1, 6). Item ex malorum pro Domino perpessione, lapidatus enim fuit a Iudeis in Taphnis (cf. Heb 11:37)" (*Super Ier.*, prol., MS Madrid, Bibl. Nac. 493, f. 266ra).

64. Thomas Aquinas, *Super Ieremiam* (ed. Parma, vol. XIV, 577–667).

65. On the dating of Thomas' *Super Ieremiam*, see chapter 1, note 11.

66. "Ex quibus quatuor possunt accipi circa praesens opus quod prae manibus habetur; scilicet auctor, materia, modus, et utilitas. Circa auctorem tria designat praesens auctoritas; scilicet officium, affectum et actum. In officio ostenditur prophetalis dignitas.... In actu compassionis pietas.... Dicitur autem *propheta Dei* ad differentiam aliorum qui non sunt prophetae Dei. Sunt enim quidam prophetae caeli, quidam prophetae diaboli, quidam prophetae Dei" (Thomas Aquinas, *Super Ieremiam*, prol., ed. Parma, vol. XIV, 577a).

67. "Et haec tria, scilicet prophetalis dignitas, fraternalis caritas, et compassionis pietas, necessaria sunt prophetae" (*Super Ieremiam*, prol., ed. Parma, vol. XIV, 578a).

68. "Ex officio enim patet modus: procedit enim per similitudines et figuras, qui proprius modus prophetarum est" (*Super Ieremiam*, prol., ed. Parma, vol. XIV, 578b).

69. "Est enim finis bene vivere, et ad immortalitatis gloriam pervenire" (ibid.).

70. "Sed materia apparet ex actu: est enim materia secundum sensum historicum captivitas populi, quae compassionis orationem excitabat" (ibid.).

71. Bonaventure, William, and Albert introduce their prologues as such: "Quia commendatio auctoris redundat in in opus, et commendatio operis in auctorem . . ." (Bonaventure, *In Io. com.*, prol. (*Opera*, t. VI, 239a); "Hec uerba scripta sunt Prou. xv, in quibus principaliter huius euangelii scriba commendatur" (William of Alton, *Super Io.*, prol., MS Saint-Omer, Bibl. mun. 260, f. 110ra); "In ista auctoritate commendatur Joannes Evangelista . . ." (Albert the Great, *In Io.*, prol. (ed. Borgnet, t. XXIV, 1). Thomas employs the term toward the end, attributing it to Christ: "secreta sua huic discipulo specialiter dilecto specialiter commendavit" (Thomas Aquinas, *Super Io.*, prol., ed. Parma, t. X, 281b).

72. "*Vidi Dominum sedentem super solium excelsum et elevatum* (Is 6:1). . . . Verba proposita sunt contemplantis.... In verbis autem propositis describitur contemplatio Joannis tripliciter, secundum quod Dominum Iesum est tripliciter contemplatus. Describitur autem alta, ampla et perfecta.... Circa primum sciendum quod altitudo et sublimitas contemplationis consistit maxime in contemplatione et cognitione Dei" (Thomas Aquinas, *Super Io.*, prol., ed. Parma, t. X, 279a).

73. "Quia ergo Joannes Evangelista elevatus in contemplationem naturae divini Verbi et essentiae est . . . statim virtutem ipsius Verbi, secundum quod diffundit se ad omnia, nobis insinuat . . ." (ibid., 280a–b).

74. "quia cum Evangelistae alii tractent principaliter mysteria humanitatis Christi, Joannes specialiter et praecipue divinitatem Christi in Evangelio suo insinuat" (Thomas Aquinas, *Super Io.*, prol., ed. Parma, t. X, 280b). Cf. Albert the Great, *In Io.*, prol. (ed. Borgnet, t. XXIV, 2); Bonaventure's view is as follows: "de sublimibus *agit*, quia de Verbo incarnato secundum utrumque naturam, quae valde sublimes sunt, maxime divina" (*In Io. com.*, prol., *Opera*, t. VI, 241a). Cf. Augustine, *De consensu evangelistarum*, I, 4 (ed. F. Weihrich, Wien, 1904, CSEL 43, 6); Bede, *Homiliarum euangelii libri II*, I, 9 (ed. D. Hurst, Turnhout, 1955, CCSL 122, 62).

75. "Et ideo Ioannes Evangelista, qui veritatem divinitatis Verbi ab ipso fonte divini pectoris hauserat . . ." (Thomas Aquinas, *Super Io.*, prol., ed. Parma, t. X, 280b–281a), cf. Io 13:25.

76. For Thomas, the Book of Job's main interest is speculative—it shows that human affairs are guided by divine providence: "cuius tota intentio circa hoc versatur ut per probabiles rationes ostendatur res humanas divina providentia regi" (*Super Iob*, prol., ed. Leonina, t. XXVI, 3b). Addressing the question of whether he was an actual person (*aliquid in rerum natura*) or a fictitious character (*quaedam parabola conficta*), he concludes that the second opinion appears to run up against the authority of Scripture, yet not before remarking that with respect to the book's purpose, it makes little difference one way or the other: "Fuerunt autem aliqui quibus

visum est quod iste Iob non fuerit aliquid in rerum natura, sed quod fuerit quaedam parabola conficta ut esset quoddam thema. . . . Et quamvis ad intentionem libri non multum differat utrum sic vel aliter fuerit, refert tamen quantum ad ipsam veritatem. Videtur enim praedicta opinio auctoritati sacrae Scripturae obviare" (ibid., 4a). He finds evidence of Job's actual existence in Ez 14:14. However, questions concerning Job's historical period, origin, or even whether he was the book's author, Thomas pointedly dismisses as irrelevant to his own purposes: "Quo autem tempore fuerit vel ex quibus parentibus originem duxerit, quis etiam huius libri fuerit auctor, utrum scilicet ipse Iob hunc librum conscripserit de se quasi de alio loquens, an alius de eo ista retulerit, non est praesentis intentionis discutere" (ibid., 4b).

77. "Minister fuit non carnis, non mundi, non Dyaboli, set Christi, cum relicto patre et naui" (*Super Io.*, prol., MS Saint-Omer, Bibl. mun. 260, f. 110ra).

78. Editions of Pseudo-Jerome's prologue appear in *Nouum Testamentum Domini Nostri Iesu Christi Latine secundum editionem sancti Hieronymi*, ed. J. Wordsworth and H. J. White, Oxford, 1889–1954 (3 vols.), vol. 1, 485–487; and D. de Bruyne, *Préfaces de la Bible latine*, Namur, 1920, 173. Cf. S. Berger, "Les Préfaces jointes aux livres de la Bible," *Mémoires présentés à l'Academie des inscriptions et belles-lettres*, XI, ii, Paris, 1904.

79. *In Io. com.*, 2, 1 (*Opera*, t. VI, 272a).

80. *In Io.*, In prol. S. Jerome (*Opera*, ed. Borgnet, t. XXIV, 13a).

81. Thom. Aquin., *In Io.* 4, 35 (ed. Parma, t. X, 282a–b).

82. "et relicta uxore, Io. II, celeriter imitando, Io. XII: *Qui mihi ministrat me sequatur* (Io 12, 26). Item uoluntatem suam uoluntati Christi conformando. . . . Item Deum et proximum excellenter diligendo, Io. XIII: *In hoc cognoscent omnes quod mei es⟨tis⟩* etc. (Io 13:35). Hic ideo pre ceteris in euangelio et epistulis de dilectione pertractauit. Item carnis desideria per abstinentiam mortificando. . . . Item officium sibi creditum fideliter exequendo" (*Super Io.*, prol., MS Saint-Omer, Bibl. mun. 260, f. 110ra).

83. "commendatur quantum ad scientiam: *intelligens*. Intelligit enim utilia, sicut patet in epistulis ubi maxime caritatem, que est utilissima, predicauit. Item secreta, ut patet in Apocalypsi, ubi maxima misteria reuelauit. Item sublimia, ut patet in euuangelio ubi si altius intonuisset totus mundus non capere posset" (*Super Io.*, prol., MS Saint-Omer, Bibl. mun. 260, f. 110ra).

84. "Secundario notatur in hiis uerbis quadruplex causa huius operis: Materialis, per hoc quod dicit: *Regi*, quia de Christo qui est rex regum agitur in hoc libro quantum ad utrumque naturam que est in eo. . . . Formalis: *Intelligens*, intelligendo enim diuinam naturam sine comparatione, extollere humanam et utramque esse in Christo" (ibid., f. 110va).

85. "Huic ergo regi auctoritate fuit beatus Iohannes *acceptus*, quod patet ex hoc quod tanquam magis familiaris in cena super pectus eius recubuit, Io. XIII (cf. Io 13:25). Item, ex hoc quod thesaurum pretiosissimum sue costodie mancipauit, Io. XIX: *Accepit eam in sua* (Io 19:27) custodiam, uel *sua* officia" (ibid., f. 110va).

86. The Wedding at Cana occupied an important place in medieval preaching, especially in marriage sermons. For illustrations, see N. Bériou and D. d'Avray, "The Image of the Ideal Husband in Thirteenth Century France," in *Modern Questions about Medieval Sermons. Essays on Marriage, Death, History and Sanctity*, ed. N. Bériou and D. d'Avray, Spoleto, 1994, 31–69; and in the same volume by the same authors, "Henry of Provins, O.P.'s Comparison of the Dominican and Franciscan Orders with the Order of Matrimony," 71–76; and D. d'Avray, "The Gospel of the Marriage Feast of Cana and Marriage Preaching in France," 135–153.

87. See G. Dahan, *L'exégèse chrétienne*, 239–297.

88. See T. Bellamah, "William of Alton's Commentary on Lamentations," *AHDLMA* 73 (2006), 227–229.

89. The standard of the University of Paris, the Paris Bible belongs to the tradition of Alcuin's Carolingian recension of the Vulgate. Concerning it and the *correctoria*, see G. Dahan, "«Sorbonne II». Un correctoire Biblique de la seconde moitie du XIII^e siècle," in *La Bibbia del XIII Secolo. Storio del testo storia dell'esegesi*, ed. G. Cremascoli and F. Santi, Firenze, 2004, 113–153; "Les Textes Bibliques dans le lectionnaire du 'Prototype' de la liturgie dominicaine," in *Aux Origines de la liturgie dominicaine. Le Manuscrit Santa Sabina XIV L 1*, ed. L. Boyle and P.-M.

Gy, Paris, 2004, 159–182; "La méthode critique dans l'étude de la Bible (xiiᵉ–xiiiᵉ siècles)," 104–113; *L'exégèse chrétienne*, 175–190; "La critique textuelle dans les correctoires de la Bible du XIIIe siècle," *Langages et philosophie. Hommage à Jean Jolivet*, Paris, 1997, 365–392; "La connaissance du grec dans les correctoires de la Bible du XIIIe siècle," in *Du copiste au collectionneur: Mélanges d'histoire des textes et des Bibliothèques en l'honneur d'André Vernet*, ed. Donatella Nebiai-Dalla Guarda, Bibliologia elementa ad librorum studia pertinentia, Turnhout, 1998, 89–109; "La connaissance de l'hébreu dans les correctoires de la Bible du XIIIe siècle," *Revue théologique de Louvain* 23 (1992), 178–190; G. Lobrichon, "Les éditions de la Bible latine dans les universités du xiiiᵉ siècle," in *La Bibbia del XIII Secolo*, 15–34; B. Smalley, *The Study of the Bible*, 329–336.

90. The corruption of the Paris recension of the Vulgate is the fifth of seven principal sins of theology Roger Bacon enumerates: "Nam circa quadriginta annos [sunt] multi theologi infiniti et stationarii Parisius parum videntes hoc proposuerunt exemplar. Qui cum illiterati fuerunt et uxorati, non curantes, nec scientes cogitare de veritate Textus Sacri proposuerunt exemplaria vitiosissima et scriptores infiniti addiderunt ad corruptionem multas mutationes" (*Opus Minus*, in *Fr. Rogeri Baconi opera quaedam hactenus inedita*, ed. J. S. Brewer, London, 1859, t. 1, 333).

91. A similar use of biblical variants in the commentaries of Thomas Aquinas has been observed by E. Stump, "Biblical Commentary and Philosophy," in *The Cambridge Companion to Aquinas*, Cambridge, ed. N. Kretzmann and E. Stump, 1993, 252–268 (257–258).

92. "³:⁸*GIMEL: SET ETIAM CUM CLAMABO*, uel *CLAMAREM*, id est cum clamore orauero . . . ³:¹⁰*DELETH: URSUS INSIDIANS FACTUS EST MICHI . . . LEO IN ABSCONDITO*, uel *ABSCONDITIS*, id est magis crudelis per Vespasianum . . . ³:²²*MISERICORDIA* uel *MISERICORDIE DOMINI*. Hic primo predicat misericordiarum Dei magnitudinem" (*Super Threnos*, 3, 8.10.22, ed. cit., 262, 264).

93. "'ut sciendi desiderio collocato.' Alia littera: 'ut nescientibus inquirendi desiderium collocetur'" (*Super Io.*, Prol. Ieronimi, MS Saint-Omer, Bibl. mun. 260, f. 111va).

94. Lv 25:44: servus et ancilla sint vobis de nationibus quae in circuitu vestro sunt *W*.

95. "*Et nemini seru⟨iuimus⟩ umquam*. Mentiti sunt, quia seruierunt Babiloniis septuaginta annis, Deuter. xvi (cf. Dt 28:48). Set intellexerunt quantum ad hoc quod naturaliter liberi esse deberent, et non seruire per legem, Deuter. xxv [*sic*]: *Seruus et ancilla sint tibi* etc. Alia littera habet: *Non erit uectigal pendens in Israel*" (*Super Io.* 8:33, MS Saint-Omer, Bibl. mun. 260, f. 136ra). The Old Latin text appears in Tertullian, *De pudicitia*, IX (ed. E. Dekkers, 1954, Turnhout, CCSL 2, 1297); Jerome, *Epist.* 21 (ed. J. Labourt, t. 1, 87–88; CSEL 54, 115–116).

96. "Vnde sequitur: *GENERATIO PRETERIT*, scilicet quedam moriendo. Alia tranlatio: *UADIT AD MORTEM*. ⟨II⟩ Reg. xiiii: *Omnis morimur et quasi ⟨aque delabimur⟩* etc. (2 Sm 14:14)," (*Super Eccl.* 1:4. Here, as with other citations of this postill, I have followed the orthography of MS Madrid, Bibl. Nac. 493, f. 133r. The text is virtually the same in MS Basel, Univ. Bibl. B III 20, f. 94va and Paris, BnF lat. 15592, f. 193r. It is omitted in MS Paris, BnF lat. 14429, f. 120vb).

97. "*Iesus autem inclinans se deorsum digito scribebat in terra* (*W*) Secundum Ambrosium: *Terra, absorbe hos uiros abdicatos*, id est digne iudicandos, et sumitur de Iere. xxii secundum litteram LXX" (*Super Io.* 8:6, MS Saint-Omer, Bibl. mun. 260, f. 134rb). Cf. Ambrose Of Milan, *Epistulae*, vii, 50 (CSEL 82.2, 57–58): "Quid scribebat nisi illud propheticum: *Terra, terra, scribe hos uiros abdicatos*, quod de Iechonia lectum est in Hieremia propheta?"

98. "*VERBA IEREMIE*, supple, hec sunt; LXX: *VERBUM DOMINI*: et tunc est littera plana, *FILII ELCHIE*" (*Super Ier.* 1:1, MSS Madrid, Bibl. Nac. 493, f. 267r; Paris, BnF lat. 573, f. 88ra). For another example in the same postill: "¹:¹¹*VIRGAM VIGILANTEM*, alii: 'amigdalinam,' LXX, uigiliarum uel uigilantium. Et potest talis uirga dici grauis punitio Dei" (*Super Ier.* 1:11, MSS Madrid, Bibl. Nac. 493, f. 267v; Paris, BnF lat. 573, f. 88vb). In medieval biblical correctories, the term LXX refers only infrequently to the Septuagint; most often it designates an Old Latin text. See G. Dahan, *L'exégèse chrétienne*, 194–195.

99. "Andreas: Ex hoc perpende, scilicet ex sententia Hebreorum, eo quod in titulo prophetie nomen Elchie exprimitur, quod ipse Elchias fuerit propheta" (*Super Ier.* 1:1, MS Madrid, Bibl.

Nac. 493, f. 267r). Save for a few omissions, the text is the same in MS Paris, BnF lat. 573, f. 88ra. Another example appears in the opening of William's postill *Super Ecclesiasten*, "¹¹¹*VERBA ECCLESIASTES*. Liber iste diuiditur in tytulum siue prohemium et tractatum. Secundum Hebreos incipit ibi: ³*QUID HABET AMPLIUS*. Secundum Ieronimum, ibi: ²*VANITAS UANITATUM*, quem ad presens sequuntur" (MS Madrid, Bibl. Nac. 493, f. 132r). For an account of the meanings of various forms of reference to Hebrew texts, see G. Dahan, *L'exégèse chrétienne*, 200–204.

100. Jerome produced the Gallican Psalter c. 392 and the Hebrew Psalter c. 400. The first gained widespread acceptance in liturgical use and in most regions was never replaced by the second.

101. "... dicitur in Psalmus ubi nos habemus: *Te decet hymnus Deus in Syon*; Hebraica ueritas: *Tibi s⟨ilens⟩ laus ⟨Deus in⟩ Syon* (Ps 64, 2)" (*Super Ier.*, prol., MS Madrid, Bibl. nac. 493, f. 266ra).

102. Ps 64:2, Weber *iuxta LXX*: *te decet hymnus Deus in Sion*; Weber *iuxta Hebr.*: *Tibi silens laus Deus in Sion*. For a discussion of Hebrew biblical texts and Latin translations thereof (especially of the Psalms) in medieval libraries, see B. Smalley, *Study of the Bible*, 341–355.

103. B. Smalley remarked that William of Alton provided examples of references to the Hebrew text and to rabbinic tradition. However, the examples she cited were drawn from the postills on Genesis and Proverbs, neither of which we have authenticated. What is more, the references are indirect. The postillator borrowed them from Andrew of St. Victor and, it would seem, William of Middleton; see *Study of the Bible*, 341; "Sapiential Books I," 59–61, 76–77.

104. The Greek translation of the Old Testament produced by Symmachus (probably during the late second century) appeared in the fourth column of Origen's *Hexapla*. This elaborate edition of the Old Testament was so massive that it was probably never reproduced as a whole. The most extensive collection of fragments has been presented by F. Field, *Origenis Hexaplorum quae Supersunt*, two vols., Oxford, 1867–1875.

105. "⟨*PERGIT SPIRITUS*⟩ *ET REUERTITUR IN CIRCULOS*, id est per circulos. Symachus dicit: *PERAMBULANS UADIT UENTUS*, et de uento exponit Hugo" (*Super Eccl.* 1:6, MSS Basel, Univ. Bibl. B III 20, f. 95ra; Madrid, Bibl. Nac. 493, f. 134r).

106. Hugh of Saint Victor, *Homilae in Ecclesiasten*, II (PL 175, 136).

107. "Symmachus hunc locum ita interpretatus est: uadit ad meridiem, et circumit ad boream; perambulans uadit uentus, et per quae circumierat, reuertitur uentus," Jerome, *In Ecclesiasten*, I, 6 (CCSL 72, 255). Borrowings of Jerome's translation of Symmachus appear frequently in this postill. What follows are two examples: "*AFFLICTIO SPIRITUS*, id est malum culpe. Vnde Symachus habet *PRESUMPTIO SPIRITUS*, que sonat in culpam" (*Super Ecl.* 1:17, MSS Basel, Univ. Bibl. B III 20, f. 96rb; Madrid, Bibl. Nac. 493, f. 136r). Cf. Jerome, *In Ecclesiasten*, I, 17 (CCSL 72, 261). "Symachus habet sic: *SI POPULUS PRINCIPIS IRRUERIT TIBI, DO LOCO TUO NON RECEDAS*, et istud concordat prime littere" (*Super Eccl.* 10:4, MSS Basel, Univ. Bibl. B III 20, f. 109rb; Madrid, Bibl. Nac. 493, f. 158v). See also Jerome, *In Ecclesiasten*, x, 4 (CCSL 72, 101, 334). Jerome indicated that he had employed the original text preserved in Origen's library at Caesarea, "id quod secundo dicitur 'non sic,' in hebraeis uoluminibus non habetur, sed ne in ipsis quidem septuaginta interpretibus: nam g-hexaplous origenis in caesariensi Bibliotheca relegens semel tantum scriptum repperi" (*In Psalmos*, I, ed. G. Morin, 1959, CCSL 72, 180). On Jerome's transmission of Greek translations such as that of Symmachus into the medieval Latin West, see G. Dahan, *L'exégèse chrétienne*, 206.

108. "¹¹³⁹*DICIT EIS: UENITE ET UI⟨DETE⟩*, credendo, amando, bene operando, intelligendo, Ysa. VII: *Nisi creditis, non intelligetis*" (Is 7:9) (*Super Io.* 1:39, MS Saint-Omer, Bibl. mun. 260, f. 114vb).

109. The text is the same in the Bible of St. Jacques (= Ω^j, MS Paris, BnF lat. 16721, f. 75va) and the *Biblia sacra vulgata* of R. Weber, 4th ed., Stuttgart, 1994 (= *W*).

110. There can be no question here of a complete listing of citations, even for Augustine's corpus. What follows are a few examples: Tertullian, *Adversus Marcionem*, IV, 20. 25. 27 (ed. E. Kroymann, 1954, Turnhout, CCSL 1, 597, 611, 620); Augustine, *De doctrina christiana*, II, 12 (ed. J. Martin, 1962, Turnhout, CCSL 32, 43); *In Iohannis evangelium tractatus*, XXVII, XXXIX, XLV (ed. R. Willems, Turnhout, 1954, CCSL 36, 273, 287, 391); *Enarrationes in Psalmos*, in Ps. 8 (ed. E. Dekkers and J. Fraipont, Turnhout, 1956, CCSL 38–39–40; CCSL 38, 51); ibid., in Ps. 118 (CCSL 40, 1724); *De trinitate*, VII, 6 (ed. W. Mountain and Fr. Glorie, Turnhout, 1968, CCSL

50, 267); ibid., XV, 2 (CCSL 50, 461); Jerome, *In Hiezechielem*, XIII (ed. F. Glorie, Turnhout, 1964, CCSL 75, 605); Gregory the Great, *Moralia in Iob*, II, 46 (CCSL 143, 101); Bernard of Clairvaux, *Epistula* XVIII (*Opera*, vol. 7, 67); Peter Lombard, *Sententiae*, I, 19, 5 (ed. Coll. S. Bonaventurae, t. I, 164); Bonaventure, *Collationes de septem donis Spiritus Sancti*, VIII (ed. Quaracchi, t. V, 1891, 494b).

111. The sense intended here is that of the *rôle "négatif"* described by G. Dahan in connection with the *correctoria*, "Les Textes Bibliques dans le lectionaire du 'Prototype' de la liturgie dominicaine," 168.

112. "Dicit ergo: *ET FACTUM EST*, scilicet totum quod precessit in libro precedente; *POSTQUAM IN CAPTIUITATEM DUCTUS EST ISRAEL, IERUSALEM DESERTA EST* uel *DESTRUCTA, SEDIT IEREMIAS ... PROPHETA ... FLENS ET PLANXIT LAMENTATIONEM HANC*, uel *LAMENTATIONE HAC IN IERUSALEM*. Aliqui libri habent *AMARO ANIMO SUSPIRANS ET EIULANS*, set non est littera Ieronimi nec Paschasii; apposita / est autem ex glosis ad exaggerationem exprimendam doloris" (*Super Threnos*, Prothemata, ed. cit., 235).

113. The text is consigned to notes in *W* and the *Biblia sacra iuxta latinam vulgatam versionem* of the editors of St. Jerome (Old Testament only), vol. 14, 18 vols., Rome, 1926–1990 (= *Editio maior*). In the latter, it appears as follows: "et factum est postquam in captivitatem redactus est israel et ierusalem deserta est sedit ieremias propheta flens et planxit lamentatione hac in Ierusalem et amaro animo suspirans et eiulans dixit."

114. Paschasius Radbertus, *Expositio in Lamentationes* (ed. B. Paulus, Turnhout, 1988, CCCM 85).

115. An anonymous commentary on this passage, dating to this period, has recently been presented by A. Andrée, "'Et factum est': The Commentary to the Prologue to the Book of Lamentations in the Manuscript Paris, BnF, lat. 2578," *Revue bénédictine* 117 (2007), 129–153. Though it was included in the Rusch edition of the *Glossa ordinaria* (ed. Rusch, vol. III, 184a), it does not appear to have figured in the original text, the first chapter of which has recently appeared in a critical edition: A. Andrée, *Gilbertus Universalis Glossa ordinaria in Lamentationes Ieremie Prophete, Prothemata et Liber I*, Stockholm, 2005.

116. Toward the end of the twelfth century, Stephan Langton left its authenticity unquestioned in his commentary *Super Threnos*, MSS Paris, Arsenal 87, f. 205rb; BnF lat. 393, 177va; Maz. 172rb. An example from the subsequent generation appears in Hugh of St. Cher's *Postille*, in Threnos (ed. Venetiis, t. IV, 283ra). An instance that is probably more nearly contemporary to William is a commentary *Super Threnos* printed, questionably, under the name of Thomas Aquinas (ed. Parma, t. XIV, 669a–b, 670a). Albert The Great comments on the passage without committing himself to its authenticity: *Huic autem planctui vel Jeremias vel alius praemittit clausulam...*, *In Thren.* (ed. Borgnet, t. XXVIII, 246). In William of Luxi's slightly later postill *Super Threnos*, the entire Prothemata is qualified as inauthentic: *... non est de textu*, MS Paris, BnF lat. 14265, f. 462rb.

117. Designated in the *Editio maior* by the signs $\Omega^m$, $\Omega^s$, $\Omega^j$ (the last for the Bible of St. Jacques), the manuscripts containing the prologue are, respectively, Paris, Maz. 5, f. 211ra; Paris, BnF lat. 15467, f. 371rb; and Paris, BnF lat. 16721, f. 149ra.

118. Isidore Of Seville, *Etym.*, XVI, 24, 1 (PL 82, 590).

119. *Glossa mg.*, in Ez. 1:4 (ed. Rusch, vol. III, 223b); Jerome, *In Hiezechielem*, I, 1 (CCSL 75, 40, 9).

120. *Glossa int.*, in Ez. 1:4 (ed. Rusch, vol. III, 223b); Gregory The Great, *Homilae in Hiezechielem prophetam*, I, 2 (ed. M. Adriaen, 1971, CCSL 142, 25).

121. "*ET DE MEDIO EIUS QUASI SPECIES ELECTRI*, id est de modo ignis, id est de medio persecutionis, fulgor populi per turbationem purgati. Secundum illud ⟨*Ethimologiarum*⟩, liber 16, electrum est quoddam genus lapidis ad radium solis clarius luminis auro et argento, et est, secundum Ieromimum in *Glossa*, auro et argento pretiosius. Gregorius tamen dicit in *Glossa* quod electrum est ex auro et argento. Dum autem miscentur, argentum crescit in claritatem, aurum a fulgore suo palescit. Respondit hic quod triplex est genus electri: unum fluit ex arboribus, et est quoddam genus gummi bonum; aliud est metallum quod fit artificialiter ex tribus partibus auri et quarta argenti; tertium est quoddam genus la/pidis, quod est optimum, et de isto loquitur Ysidorus et Ieronimus, de secundo Gregorius" (*Super Ez.* 1:4, MS Paris, BnF lat. 573, f. 156vb–157ra).

Among the many other examples that could be supplied, a typical one is the following explanation of the term *infrunito*, which appears only twice in any form in the Vulgate, both in Ecclesiasticus (Sirach). What follows is William's citation of Ecclesiasticus 31:23 in his commentary on Ecclesiastes 5:12: "... Eccli. XXXI: *Colera et tortura homini infrunito*, id est sine abstinentie freno," (MSS Basel, Univ. Bibl. B III 20, f. 102va; Madrid, Bibl. Nac. 493, f. 146v).

122. For a discussion of the functioning of etymologies within medieval exegesis, including William's, see G. Dahan, *L'exégèse chrétienne*, 307–314.

123. "*QUI NUTRIEBANTUR IN CROCEIS*, id est cibis croco conditis et coloratis; crocus enim habet colorem rubeum, Ysidorus, libro XVII" (*Super Thren.* 4:5, ed. cit., 272), cf. Isidore of Seville, *Etym.*, XIX, 28, 8 (PL 82, 696).

124. E.g., *La Bible de Jerusalem*, Lam 4:5: *ceux qui étaient élevés dans la pourpre*....

125. propter–incertitudinem; cf. Bonaventure, *In Io. com.* 6, 18 (*Opera*, t. VI, 323a).

126. "*CUM REMIGASSENT ERGO QUASI STA⟨DIA⟩ UIGINTI QUINQUE AUT TRIGINTA*. Hoc dicitur propter spatii incertitudinem. Vt dicit Ysidorus, libro XV, "Stadium est octaua pars miliarii, constans ex passibus centum uigenti quinque...." (*Super Io.* 6:19, MS Saint-Omer, Bibl. mun. 260, f. 127rb. Stadium–quinque). Cf. Isidore Of Seville, *Etym.*, XV, 16, 3 (PL 82, 557); propter–incertitudinem; cf. Bonaventure, *In Io. com.* 6:19 (*Opera*, t. VI, 323a).

127. What follows are few lexicographical entries: *Thesaurus Graecae Linguae*, ed. H. Stephano, Paris, 1851, vol. VII, "Stadium, inquit, centum et vigintiquinque nostros efficit passos"; Lewis and Short: "**stadium** ... a distance of 125 paces ... it was an eighth part of a milliarium"; *Analytical Lexicon to the Greek New Testament* (ed. T. Friberg and B. Friberg, 2000): "an established measure of distance, in length around 600 feet, 200 yards, 190 meters, or one-eighth Roman mile."

128. "*ET DICIT EI: OMNIS HOMO ... PRIMUM*, aduerbialiter, id est in primis mense, *BONUM UINUM PONIT, ET CUM INEBRI⟨ATI⟩ SU⟨NT⟩, TUNC ID QUOD DETERIUS EST*. Talis fuit consuetudo tunc et nunc apud aliquos," *Super Io.* 2:10 (MS Saint-Omer, Bibl. mun. 260, f. 116rb).

129. "*DEUM TIME... ET MANDATUM EIUS OBSERUA* bona faciendo. Et subdit rationem: *HOC EST*, id est: Ad hoc est *OMNIS HOMO*, id est factus a Deo. Vel *HOC EST*, id est: ad hoc tenetur *OMNIS HOMO*. Vel *HOC*, id est: per hoc, ut sit ablatiui casus, *OMNIS HOMO*, quantum ad esse spirituale, 1 Cor. XV: *Gratia Dei sum id quod sum* (1 Cor 15:10). Item *HOC*, id est 'per hoc' *EST OMNIS HOMO*, id est perfectus homo, quia utrumque requiritur, scilicet declinatio mali et operatio boni, ad hoc ut homo sit perfectus" (*Super Eccl.* 12:13, MSS Basel, Univ. Bibl. B III 20, f. 113ra, Madrid, Bibl. Nac. 493, f. 165r). With a few omissions, this text appears in Paris, BnF lat. 14429, f. 153vb.

130. A few examples: *TOB*: "Crains Dieu et observe ses commandements, car c'est là tout l'homme"; *BJ*: "Crains Dieu et observe ses commandements, car c'est là le devoir de tout homme"; *RSV*: "Fear God, and keep his commandments; for this is the whole duty of man"; *DR*: "Fear God, and keep his commandments: for this is all man."

131. "... *IN QUO DOLUS NON EST*. Contra: Omne peccatum dolus. Responsio: 'Dolus' potest dici communiter et proprie, et sic sumitur hic" (*Super Io.* 1:47, MS Saint-Omer, Bibl. mun. 260, f. 115rb).

132. "*RESPONDIT EIS IHESUS: NONNE SCRIPTUM EST IN LEGE U⟨ESTRA⟩ QUIA: EGO DIXI: DII ESTIS?* Nota 'lex' tripliciter appellatur. Aliquando omnes libri ueteris testamenti, ut hic. Aliquando omnes preter prophetas: Mt. XI: *Lex et prophete* (Mt 11:13); et sic comprehendit psalmos sub lege. Aliquando diuidit prophetas et psalmos contra legem, Luc. ult.: *Necesse est impleri omnia que scripta sunt in lege et prophetis et psalmis de me.* (Lc 24, 44)" (*Super Io.* 10:34, MS Saint-Omer, Bibl. mun. 260, f. 142rb).

133. "Tribus enim modis dicitur Deus ... Natura ... Adoptione ... nuncapative," Hugh of St. Cher, *Postille*, in Io. 10:35 (ed. Venetiis, t. VI, 353vb); cf. Greg The Great, *Hom. in Hiez.*, I, 8 (CCSL 142, 102–103) and II, 3 (CCSL 142, 241).

134. "nunc doceamus Filium Dei Dominum nostrum Iesum Christum ab apostolis creditum non ex nuncupatione sed ex natura, neque ex adoptione sed ex natiuitate" (Hilary of Poitiers, *De Trinitate*, VI, 32, ed. P. Smulders, Turnhout, 1979, CCSL 62, 234).

135. "... cum hoc nomen deus dicatur tripliciter: natura, participatione et nuncupatione," *Bonaventure, In Io. com.* 10:35 (*Opera*, t. VI, 393b).

136. "'Deus' quandoque dicitur proprie, scilicet per naturam; quandoque large, ut per adoptionem et participationem; quandoque largissime, ut solum per nuncupationem" (*Super Io.* 10, 35, MS Saint-Omer, Bibl. mun. 260, f. 142rb).

137. On the functioning of such terminology in the thought of Thomas Aquinas, see M.-D. Chenu, *Introduction à l'étude de Saint Thomas d'Aquin*, Paris, 1950, 118–119.

138. In a fine study, M. Morard has shown that this article, of French origin, entered the Latin of the medieval schools toward the end of the first third of the thirteenth century, particularly in the context of Trinitarian theology, and eventually became a common feature of biblical and philosophical commentaries: "Le petit «li» des scolastiques : Assimilation de l'article vulgaire dans le latin des théologiens médiévaux," in *La résistible ascension des vulgaires. Contacts entre latin et langues vulgaires au bas Moyen Âge. Problèmes pour l'historien,* in *Mélanges de l'Ecole française de Rome* 117-2 (2005), 531–593.

139. "⟨RESPONDIT IHESUS NEQUE HIC PECCAUIT NEQUE PARENTES EIUS SET⟩ UT MANIFESTENTUR ⟨OPERA DEI⟩ etc., et est recta causa, quia ME OPORTET ⟨OPERARI⟩, et sic li 'ut' ponitur causatiue" (*Super Io.* 9:34, MS Saint-Omer, Bibl. mun. 260, f. 138rb).

140. "UT QUI NON ⟨UIDENT UIDEANT⟩, li 'ut' ibi est causale; set post cum subditur: ET QUI UIDENT CECI ⟨FIANT⟩, solum consecutiue" (*Super Io.* 9, 39, MS Saint-Omer, Bibl. mun. 260, f. 140ra). Another such grammatical exercise from the prologue to *Super Threnos* has been presented in note 32.

141. "SICUT ENIM PATER HABET UITAM IN SEMETIPSO, id est per essentiam, **unde li 'in' non est nota transitionis, quasi aliud sit uita, aliud Pater,** *SIC DEDIT ET FILIO* **eum gignendo** UITAM HABERE IN SEMETIPSO non per participationem" (*Super Io.* 5:26, MS Saint-Omer, Bibl. mun. 260, f. 124vb). Text independent of Bonaventure has been placed in bold. Cf. Bonaventure, *In Io. com.* 5, 26 (*Opera*, t. VI, 311b); Peter Lombard, *Sent.*, I, 20, 1–8 (ed. Coll. S. Bonaventurae, t. I, pars II, 172–174); Dionysius, *De div. nom.*, VI (ed. W. De Gruyter, vol. I, 190–193).

142. "Et uere qui manducat carnem meam habet uitam eternam, quia [56]CARO MEA UERE ⟨EST CIBUS⟩, non fantastice, sicut corporalis tantum ad tempus reficiens et cito deficiens. **Vel** UERE, **non tantum figuratiue ut manna, non tantum ibi existens ut in signo, ut quedam heretici dixerunt. Li 'uere' ergo excludit figuram, parabolam, significationem, fantasiam, defectionem**" (*Super Io.* 6:56, MS Saint-Omer, Bibl. mun. 260, f. 129vb). Text independent of Bonaventure has been placed in bold. Cf. Bonaventure, *In Io. com.* 6, 56 (*Opera*, t. VI, 333a).

143. See, for example, Thomas Of Chobham, *Summa de Arte Predicandi* (ed. F. Morenzoni, Turnhout, 1988, CCCM 82, 71–72). Berengar attracts the attention of Thomas Aquinas in several texts, *In IV Sent.*, d. 12, q. 3, a. 2c (ed. Parma, t. VII/B, 668); *ST*, III, q. 75, a. 1, co. (ed. Leonina, t. XII, 156b); q. 77, a. 7, ad 3 (ibid., 203b); *De articulis fidei et ecclesiae sacramentis ad archiepiscopum Panormitanum*, II (ed. Leonina, t. XLII, 245–257).

144. Thomas Aquinas is clear on this point, ". . . nec est litteralis sensus ipsa figura, sed id quod est figuratum. Non enim cum Scriptura nominat dei brachium, est litteralis sensus quod in deo sit membrum huiusmodi corporale, sed id quod per hoc membrum significatur, scilicet virtus operativa." *ST*, I, q. 1, a. 10, ad 3 (ed. Leonina, t. IV, 26b); cf. *Super Iob* 1:6 (ed. Leonina, t. XXVI, 7b). For discussions of this development, see G. Dahan, *L'exégèse chrétienne*, 252–262; A. J. Minnis, *Medieval Theory of Authorship*, 73–74, 131; C. Spicq, *Esquisse*, 255.

145. For a few more examples: "EST HOMO QUI DIEBUS ET NOCTIBUS OCULIS NON CAP⟨IT⟩ SOMPNUM, pre sollicitudine inuestigandi, et loquitur hyperbolice, id est parum dormit" (Super Ecl. 8:16, MSS Basel, Univ. Bibl. B III 20, f. 107rb; Madrid, Bibl. Nac. 493, f. 155r); "SUBUERSUM EST COR MEUM IN MEMETIPSO, id est motum tactu doloris in tantum quod quasi proprium locum amiserat. Et est yperbole . . ." (*Super Thren.* 1:20, ed. cit. 251).

146. For example: "ET UIDI: Methaplasmus est, scilicet immutatio persone" (Super Ez. 1:4, MS Paris, BnF lat. 573, f. 85vb). This case has been cited by G. Dahan, L'exégèse, 261, n. 6.

147. For example: "IBI MORIERIS, necdum uixeris habebis honorem qualem hic, unde subdit yronice: ET IBI⟨ERIT⟩ CURRUS GLORIE T⟨UE⟩, quasi dicat: non habebis currum quo inclite feraris sicut ante, set magis ignominiam et obprobrium" (*Super Is.* 22:18, MSS Madrid, Bibl. Nac. 493, f. 201r; Paris, BnF lat. 573, f. 31vb); "VIRGO FILIA SYDONIS. Tyrum uocat uirginem, uel yronice

propter suam uoluptatem et turpitudinem, uel propter ornatus pulcritudinem et diuitiarum splendorem" (*Super Is.* 23:12, MSS Madrid, Bibl. Nac. 493, f. 202v; Paris, BnF lat. 573, f. 33ra); "*GAUDE*, intra, *ET LETARE*, extra, *FILIA EDOM*, id est Ydumea et est yronia" (*Super Thren.* 4:21, ed. cit., 277).

148. For example: "*GAUDIO*, id est gaudenti interius, emphasys est, *DIXI: QUID FRUSTRA DECIPERIS*" (Super Ecl. 2:2, MSS Basel, Univ. Bibl. B III 20, f. 106va; Madrid, Bibl. Nac. 493, f. 133r). William's usage here is close to that of Cassiodorus in his commentary on Ps 26: "Salutari probatione completa, propheta laetus exsultat, decoram emphasim, id est exaggerationem faciens, ut si aduersus ipsum solum castrorum coeat multitudo, stabilitas mentis eius non debeat commoueri, dum soleant homines plurimorum oppugnatione terreri" (*Expositio Psalmorum* 26, CCSL 97, 236).

149. "*ET DICIT EI: VADE ET LA⟨UE⟩ IN NA⟨TATORIA⟩ SY⟨LOE⟩*. Fons erat ad radicem montis Syon cuius aque, quia non iugiter fluebant, colligebantur in quadam piscina, que erat in medio ciuitatis, que dicitur natatoria. Vel per antifrasim, quia nichil ibi natabat" (*Super Io.* 9:7, MS Saint-Omer, Bibl. mun. 260, f. 138va).

150. "*ET SERMONEM QUE⟨M⟩ AUDISTIS* ex ore meo, id est sermo, antiptosis (antithesis S A) est, casus pro casu positio, *NON EST MEUS*, quia nichil loquor preter uoluntatem Patris" (Super Io. 9:7, MS Saint-Omer, Bibl. mun. 260, f. 156ra). As the comment indicates, antiptosis is the substitution of one grammatical case for another. The present example has no equivalent in English. Its purpose is to show that the Vulgate uses the accusative *sermonem* (word) where the nominative sermo (word) would appear to be appropriate. William has borrowed the comment from Bonaventure, *In Io. com.* 14:24 (*Opera*, t. VI, 442b).

151. "*ET PORTE EIUS DESOLAMINI UEHEMENTER, DICIT DOMINUS . . .* et nota methaforam hic, quia sicut bonus homo stans in porta uideat aliquod enorme, uel retraheret se et abiret in domum suam, uel clauderet portam" (*Super Ier.* 2:12, MSS Madrid, Bibl. Nac. 493, f. 269r, Paris, BnF lat. 573, f. 89vb–90va). William identifies this device frequently. Another such case appears in *Super Thren.* 1:14, where Jeremiah laments that the yoke of his iniquity had been bound around his neck by the Lord: *vigilavit iugum iniquitatum mearum in manu eius convolutae sunt et inpositae collo meo (W)*. William explains that Jeremiah has applied to himself the metaphor of a thief caught in a noose: "*IN MANU EIUS*, id est retributione Dei, *CONUOLUTE SUNT*, uinculo insolubili, *ET INPOSITE*, ad modum grauis honeris, *COLLO MEO*. Loquitur per methaphoram furis deprehensi cum circina conuoluta et imponitur collo eius" (ed. cit., 247). All of these cases correspond to the definition given by Donatus 6, *De tropis*: "Metaphora est rerum verborumque translatio" (ed. L. Holtz, "Donat et la tradition de l'enseignement grammatical. Étude et edition critique," Paris, 1981, 667). The same definition appears in Bede's *De schematibus et tropis*, 11 (ed. C. Kendall, Turnhout, 1975, CCSL, 123A, 152).

152. "*VIDI CUNCTOS UIUENTES QUI AMBULANT SUB SOLE*, id est multos et innumerabiles, ut sit hoc dictum yperbolice. Est autem yperbole, secundum Donatum, dictio fidem excedens, augendi minuendiue causa" (*Super Ecl.* 4:15, MSS Basel, Univ. Bibl. B III 20, f. 101va, Madrid, Bibl. Nac. 493, f. 144v). William has cited Aelius Donatus: "Hyperbole est dictio fidem excedens augendi minuendi ue causa" (*De Tropis*, n. 16, ed. Holtz, 671). The same definition is given by Bede, *De schematibus et tropis*, 11 (CCSL, 123A, 161).

153. "*SATURITAS AUTEM DIUITIS NON SINIT EUM DORMIRE . . .* Ideo Boethius libro *De consolatione*, 11, yronice dicit: 'O preclara opum nobilium beatitudo, quam adeptus fueris securus esse desistis'" (*Super Ecl.* 5:11, MSS Basel, Univ. Bibl. B III 20, f. 102va, Madrid, Bibl. Nac. 493, f. 147r). Cf. Boethius, *Philosophiae consolatio*, 11, 5 (ed. L. Bieler, Turnhout, 1958, CCSL 94, 28).

154. "*NEQUE SALUABIT IMPIETAS IMPIUM*, scilicet a dampnatione inferni, set magis dampnabit. Vnde liptote est. Minus enim dicit et plus significat" (*Super Ecl.* 8:8, MSS Basel, Univ. Bibl. B III 20, f. 106va, Madrid, Bibl. Nac. 493, f. 153v). Cf. Sedulius Scotus, *In Priscianum*: "et notandum quod in hoc loco schema quod litotes dicitur emineat qua figura minus dicitur et plus significatur" (ed. B Löfstedt, Turnhout, 1977, CCCM 40C, 60).

155. "*IN PRINCIPIO* etc., id est in Patre, secundum *Glossam*. Licet principium prout imponitur creaturis dicat prioritatem, non tamen prout dicitur de diuinis personis. Vnde autem et antonomastice

conuenit Patri, quia Pater est principium Filii et Spiritus sancti et existentie creaturarum, Spiritus sanctus tantum existentie creaturarum" (*Super Io.* 1:1, MS Saint-Omer, Bibl. mun. 260, f. 111vb).

156.  Cf. *Glossa int.*, in Io. 1:1, ed. Rusch, vol. IV, 223b; Alcuin, *Commentaria in s. Ioannis Evangelium*, PL 100, 745; Augustine, *De trin.*, VI, 2, CCSL 50, 230.

157.  What follows are two other examples, one from the exposition of Pseudo-Jerome's prologue: "Talis Iohannes . . . et ultimo ubi dicitur antonomastice: *Hic est discipulus quem diligebat Ihesus*" (MS Saint-Omer, Bibl. mun. 260, f. 111ra), and another at Io 11:28, where William employs the term to describe the manner in which Martha refers to Jesus as *Magister:* "*MAGISTER*, antonomastice, *ADEST ET UOCAT TE*" (MS Saint-Omer, Bibl. mun. 260, f. 144va). His usage corresponds closely to the definition given by Donatus, *De Tropis* (ed. Holtz, 669) and Bede, *De schematibus et tropis*, II (CCSL, 123A, 155): "Antonomasia est significatio uice nominis posita."

158.  "*QUIA ADOLESCENTIA ET UOLUPTAS*, id est adolescentia uoluptuosa, ut sit endyadis, uel effectiue, *UANA SUNT* . . ." (*Super Ecl.* 11:10, MSS Basel, Univ. Bibl. B III 20, f. 111rb; Madrid, Bibl. Nac. 493, f. 162v).

159.  In medieval literature also identified as *ingeminatio*, in modern English the technique is variously called *geminatio, gemination*, and *ingemination*; in modern French, *gémination*.

160.  "*PLORANS PLO⟨RAUIT⟩*, id est multum, quia geminatio habundantiam signat" (*Super Thren.* 1:2, ed. cit., 237).

161.  "*RESPONDIT IHESUS ET DIXIT EI: AMEN, AMEN.* Geminatio firmitatis indicium est. Iohannis autem utitur in hoc euangelio tali geminatione, quia scripsit hoc euangelium ut fideles edificaret et hereticos confutaret" (*Super Io.* 3:3, MS Saint-Omer, Bibl. mun. 260, f. 117rb).

162.  "*RESPONDIT ITAQUE IHESUS ET DIXIT EIS: AMEN, AMEN*, ista geminatio dicendorum est affirmatio" (*Super Io.* 5:18–19, ibid., f. 124rb).

163.  "*MULTO ENIM MELIOR EST OBEDIENTIA . . . QUAM STULTORUM UICTIME. . . .* Nota quod hic est comparatio abusiua, quia obedientia bona est et Deo placita, set Prouer. XV: *Victime impiorum abhominabiles Domino*" (Prv 15:8) (*Super Ecl.* 4:17, MSS Basel, Univ. Bibl. B III 20, f. 101va–vb; Madrid, Bibl. Nac. 493, f. 145r).

164.  "Set Prouer. XIV: *In ore stulti uirga superbie* (Prv 14:3). Et bene dicitur, quia *MELIUS EST ⟨A SAPIENTE CORRIPI QUAM A STULTORUM ADULATIONEM DECIPI⟩*, quia abusiua comparatio est, quia illud est malum" (*Super Ecl.* 7:6, MSS Basel, Univ. Bibl. B III 20, f. 104va; Madrid, Bibl. Nac. 493, f. 150r).

165.  See the discussion of C. Spicq, who draws attention to the importance of context in the exegesis of Augustine, and later Thomas Aquinas, *Esquisse*, 250. In one of his capital texts on literal biblical interpretation, Thomas holds that the truth of an interpretation rests upon its conformity with context (litterae circumstantia): "Unde omnis veritas quae, salva litterae circumstantia, potest divinae Scripturae aptari, est eius sensus" (*De pot.*, q. 1, a. 1, co., ed. Parma, t. VIII, 79a). His source for this exegetical criterion is most likely Augustine's *De Genesi ad litteram libri XII*, XII: "Si autem contextio Scripturae hoc uoluisse intelligi scriptorem non repugnauerit, adhuc restabit quaerere, utrum et aliud non potuit" (ed. J. Zycha, 1894, Wien, CSEL 28.1 [= BA 48–49] BA 48, 136).

166.  The use of structure and rhyming as mnemonic aids in the preaching of the period has been well studied and documented. See K. Rivers, *Preaching the Memory of Virtue and Vice: Memory, Images, and Preaching in the Late Middle Ages*, Turnhout, 2010, 209–250.

167.  On Thomas Aquinas's concern for the author's intention in the *divisio textus* of his *Lectura super Ioannem*, see J. Boyle "Authorial Intention and the *Divisio Textus*," in *Reading John with St. Thomas, Theological Exegesis and Speculative Theology*, ed. M. Dauphinais and M. Levering, Washington, DC, 2005, 3–8. For general observations on the use of the *divisio* as a means of contextual analysis in thirteenth-century biblical commentary, see G. R. Evans, "Gloss or Analysis? A Crisis of Exegetical Method in the Thirteenth Century," in *La Bibbia del XIII Secolo*, 93–111.

168.  "*VIDE, DOMINE, ⟨CONSIDERA, QUONIAM FACTA SUM VILIS⟩.* Hic, ut dictum est in principio libri, introducit Ieremias plebem plangentem in persona propria; et primo propriam miseriam;

secundo ostendit eam iuste inflictam: [18]*IUSTUS ES DOMINE*; tertio plangit se spe uana decep-
tam: [19]*VOCAUI AMICOS ⟨MEOS ET IPSI DECEPERUNT ME⟩*" (*Super Thren.* 1:11, ed. cit., 245).
What follows are two further examples: "*ET DE PLENITUDINE EIUS NOS.* Hic redit Euangelista
ad testimonium sue assertionis. . ." (*Super Io.* 1:16, MS Saint-Omer, Bibl. mun. 260, f. 113va)
and "*HEC IN BETHANIA.* Hic describitur locus predictorum quem specificat Euangelista ad
significandum quod illud testimonium dabatur in publico, quia multi ad baptisma Iohannis
illuc confluxerant" (*Super Io.* 1:28, MS Saint-Omer, Bibl. mun. 260, f. 114rb). Cf. Chrysostom,
In *Io. hom.*, XLVIII (PG 59, 269).

169. "*POST HEC AMBULABAT IHESUS ⟨IN GALILEAM⟩.* Postquam narrauit Euangelista multos ex
discipulis Christi eum reliquisse propter perfectionem sue doctrine, hic narrat ex inuidia
Iudeos eum aperte persecutos fuisse. Sic continuat Crisostomus. Et primo insinuatur hic
Iudeorum persecutio per factum ipsius Christi; secundo per factum ipsorum Iudeorum:
[1]*IUDEI ERGO QUEREBANT.* Insinuat Christus hanc persecutionem, primo per eius a Iudeis
recessum; secundo per eius ad eos difficilem reditum: [2]*ERAT AUTEM IN PROXIMO ⟨DIES FESTUS
IUDEORUM SCENOPHEGIA⟩.* In prima, primo notatur recessus Christi; secundo subditur causa,
scilicet uoluntas Iudeorum in eum malignandi: [1]*NON ENIM UOLEBAT ⟨ IN IUDEAM AMBU-
LARE⟩*" (*Super Io.* 7:1, MS Saint-Omer, Bibl. mun. 260, f. 130vb).

170. Bonaventure, *In Io. com.* 7:1: "*Post haec ambulabat Iesus* etc. Ostendit Dominus supra se cura-
torem et conservatorem, hic incipit tertia pars, in qua se manifestat et ostendit directorem et
illustratorem. . ." (*Opera,* t. VI, 338a–b).

171. "*AMEN, AMEN, DICO UOBIS.* Hic ostendit Dominus eos peccatum habere, ostendens quod
nec obseruantia legis nec bona uita ualet preter eum in quem nolunt credere. Ostendit
autem per similitudinem de hostio quo intratur in ouile. Primo ergo ponitur similitudo;
secundo quod sit similitudo ponitur ab Euangelista manifestatio: [6]*HOC PROUERBIUM*; tertio notatur expositionis necessitudo: [6]*ILLI AUTEM ⟨NON COGNOUERUNT QUID LOQUERE-
TUR EIS⟩*; quarto similitudinis expositio:[7]*DIXIT ERGO EIS ITERUM ⟨DIXIT EIS IHESUS⟩.* In
prima, primo ostendit non intrantem per hostium non esse pastorem; secundo intrantem
per hostium esse pastorem: [2]*QUI AUTEM INTRAT*" (*Super Io.* 10:1, MS Saint-Omer, Bibl.
mun. 260, f. 140ra).

172. For example, 3:31–36 could plausibly be understood as spoken by John the Baptist, Jesus, or the
Evangelist; cf. R. Brown, *An Introduction to the Gospel of John,* New York, 1998, 42. H. Ridderbos sums up the alternations in authorial perspective in chapter 3 as follows: ". . . the bound-
aries between Jesus' self-testimony and the Evangelist's witness to Jesus seem to be indefinite,
at least in this chapter"; see *The Gospel of John,* Cambridge, 1997 (English translation by J.
Vriend of *Het Evangelie naar Johannes. Proeve van een theologische Exegese,* Kampen, 1991),
149. For a discussion of a few of the implications of the Evangelist's allowing Jesus to speak in
the first person, see ibid., 1–16.

173. "[18:8]*SI ERGO.* Hic ostenditur quod potuit resistere, ex Apostolorum ad solam eius iussionem
dimissione. Et primo notatur iussio; secundo ostenditur in hoc scripture adimpletio: [9]*VT
IMPLERETVR ⟨SERMO⟩.* [18:8]*SI ERGO ME QVERITIS, SINITE HOS ABIRE,* id est discipulos meos
prius fugere. Crisostomus: "Quasi dicat: Impero ut nichil ad uos cum istis sit commune. In hoc
uerbo notatur Christi maxima pietas et consummata dilectio ad Apostolos." Supra XIII: *In
finem dilexit eos.* [18:9]*VT IMPLERETVR,* quasi: per hoc implebatur *SERMO QVEM DIXIT,* supra
XVII, ⟨*QVIA*⟩ *QVOS DEDISTI MICHI, NON PERDIDI QVEMQVAM EX EIS.* Re uera, supra dixit hoc
de morte eterna; Euuanglista autem hic uult intelligere de morte corporali, et hoc uerum est.
Sciebat enim quod si, capto Domino et occiso, ipsi fuissent capti et occisi, dampnati fuissent,
quia tunc fidem non habuerunt, et sic non esset sermo Domini adimpletus. *NON PERDIDI,* quia
solus pati uoluit, Ysa. LXIII: *Torcular cal⟨caui⟩ solus.* Si obicitur de Iuda, dicendum quod per-
didit seipsum (*Super Io.* 18:8–9, MS Saint-Omer, Bibl. mun. 260, f. 165rb). Cf. Chrysostom, *In
Io. hom.,* LXXXIII (PG 59, 448).

174. Cf. Peter Lombard, *Sent.,* IV, d. 45 (ed. Coll. S. Bonaventurae, t. II, 523–529).

175. "*NOLITE MIRARI HOC,* scilicet quod Filius hominis habet potestatem iudicii, *QUIA UENIT
HORA,* in fine seculi, *IN QUA OMNES,* id est omnia corpora, modus loquendi est secundum

quem totum denominatur a parte, *QUI IN MO⟨NUMENTIS⟩ SUNT AU⟨DIENT⟩ UO⟨CEM⟩ FI⟨LII⟩ DEI*" (Super Io. 5:28, MS Saint-Omer, Bibl. mun. 260, f. 125ra).

176. "Aliqui enim prophetarum loquti sunt istam captiuitatem futuram, ut Ysaias, Osee; alii preteritam, ut Daniel, Malachias, Aggeus. Set iste simul et Ezechiel et futuram predixit, et presentem uidit, et preteritam deplorauit" (*Super Ier.*, prol., MS Madrid, Bibl. nac. 493, f. 266ra).

177. An example from a few generations earlier is Stephen Langton. In the prologue to his commentary on Lamentations (composed toward the end of the twelfth century), he makes clear that the literal or historical sense expresses Jeremiah's lament over Jerusalem's destructions at the hands of the Babylonians, and, prophetically, the Romans: "... propheta non solum loquitur hic de destructione a Babiloniis facta, set de destructione facta a Romanis." He doesn't hesitate to apply this principle throughout the commentary, such as in his exposition of Lam 4:10: "*IOTH. MANUS MULIERUM MISE⟨RICORDIUM COXERUNT FILIOS SUOS. FACTI SUNT CIBI EARUM IN CONTRITIONE FILIE POPULI MEI⟩* etc. Prophetice Ieremias plangit quod futurum erat in destructione Iudaici populi facta a Romanis, uidelicet quod mulieres fame urgente coxerunt filios suos" (MS Paris, Arsenal 87, f. 172ra and f. 218ra).

178. About the possibility of a human author's envisioning of more than one reality in one concept or word, Thomas Aquinas says, "Non est etiam inconueniens quod homo qui fuit auctor instrumentalis sacrae scripturae in uno uerbo plura intelligeret, quia prophete, ut Ieronimus dicit super Osee, ita loquebantur de factis presentibus, quod etiam intenderunt futura significare, unde non est impossibile plura intelligere in quantum unum est figura alterius" (*De quolibet* VII, q. 6, a. 1, ad 5 [ed. Leonina, t. XXV, 1, 29a–b]). A similar remark appears in *De potentia*, q. 4, a. 1, co.: "Unde non est incredibile, Moysi et aliis sacrae Scripturae auctoribus hoc diuinitus esse concessum, ut diuersa uera, quae homines possent intelligere, ipsi cognoscerent, et ea sub una serie litterae designarent, ut sic quilibet eorum sit sensus auctoris" (ed. Parma, t. VIII, 79a). A capital text whose interpretation has been particularly vexed is *ST*, I, q. 1, a.10, co.: "Quia vero sensus litteralis est, quem auctor intendit: auctor autem sacrae Scripturae Deus est, qui omnia simul suo intellectu comprehendit: non est inconueniens, ut dicit Augustinus XII *Confessionum*, si etiam secundum litteralem sensum in una littera Scripturae plures sint sensus" (ed. Leonina, t. IV, 25b); cf. *De quolibet* VII, q. 6, a. 2, co (ed. Leonina, t. XXV, 1, 30a–31a). Rejecting the possibility of multiple senses proceeding from a human author's intention, P. Synave interprets Thomas to mean here that certain senses beyond the one expressed by the human author may be called literal if their larger context allows them to be ascribed to the divine author's intention, "La doctrine de S. Thomas d'Aquin sur le sens littéral des Ecritures," *RB* 35 (1926), 40–65. Though tacitly admitting that Synave's interpretation seems a bit forced, C. Spicq accepts it and concludes: "La pluralité du sens littéral engenderait l'équivoque et la confusion," Esquisse, 276–281. For a more recent review of these discussions that arrives at much the same conclusion, see M. Aillet, *Lire la Bible avec S. Thomas*, Fribourg, Suisse, 1993, 99–128. . And yet, in a fine study, M. Johnson points out that while such a construal has often been rejected by twentieth-century commentators, a doctrine of the multiplicity of literal senses in Thomas's thought was recognized by Cajetan (*In Thomas Aquinas, ST*, I, q. 1, a.10, ed. Leonina, t. IV, 26b), Bañez (*Scholastica Commentaria in Primam Partem Summae Theologiae*, ed. L. Urbano, Madrid, 1934, 1:90–99), and John Of St. Thomas (Cursus Theologicus 1.2.12, Paris, 1931, 410. n. 19). To this list, he adds the generality of the Salamanca Thomists. The preceding references are his. By an examination of several of Thomas's relevant texts, Johnson argues, convincingly, that Thomas did in fact hold this doctrine.; see "Another Look at the Plurality of the Literal Sense," *Medieval Theology and Philosophy* 2 (1992), 117–141 (141).

179. What follows are two examples from his literal commentary on Isaiah: "*Dominorum:* Assyriorum, Chaldaeorum, Romanorum" (Thomas Aquinas, *Super Isaiam* 19, 4, ed. Leonina, t. XXVIII, 25b); "ponit promissionem: *Cum transieris per aquas*, Egyptios, *flumina*, Chaldaei, *igne*, Greci, *flamma*, Romani" (*Super Isaiam* 43, 2, Ibid., 181a–b).

180. The present remarks are indebted to the discussion in *Medieval Theory of Authorship*, 87–88.

181. "Theodorus enim Mopsuestenus dixit, quod in sacra Scriptura et prophetiis nihil expresse dicitur de Christo, sed de quibusdam aliis rebus, sed adaptaverunt Christo.... Hic autem modus damnatus est in illo concilio: et qui asserit sic exponendas Scripturas, haereticus est" (Thomas Aquinas, *Super Ps.*, prol., ed. Parma, t. XIV, 149b). Subsequently, Thomas returns to the matter: "Et in synodo Toletana quidam Theodorus Mopsuestenus, qui hunc ad litteram de David exponebat, fuit damnatus, et propter hoc et propter alia multa; et ideo de Christo exponendus est" (*Super Ps.* 21:7, ibid., 217b). Several modern scholars have argued that Theodore's views were unfairly represented at the Second Council of Constantinople. See J. M. Lera, "Theodore de Mopsueste," *Dict.* Sp. 15 (1991), 385–400; E. Amann, "Théodore de Mopsueste," *DTC* 15.1 (1946), 235–279. For a slightly less favorable appraisal of Theodore, as well as an overview of scholarly perspectives, see B. De Margerie, *Introduction à l'histoire de l'exégèse*, Paris, 1979, vol. I, 181–184.

182. "Beatus ergo Hieronymus super Ezech. tradidit nobis unam regulam quam servabimus in Psalmis: scilicet quod sic sunt exponendi de rebus gestis, ut figurantibus aliquid de Christo vel ecclesia" (Thom. Aquinas, *Super Ps.*, prol., ed. Parma, t. XIV, 149b). Several examples of this mode of interpretation appear in his commentary on John's Gospel, in the following case with reference to Theodore: "Videns ergo Isaias gloriam filii, vidit et gloriam Patris; immo totius trinitatis, quae est unus Deus sedens super solium excelsum.... Non autem ita quod Isaias essentiam Trinitatis viderit, sed imaginaria visione, cum intelligentia, quaedam signa majestatis expressit ... et Theodorum Mopsuestenum, qui dixit omnes Prophetias veteris testamenti esse de aliquo negotio dictas, per quamdam tamen appropriationem esse adductas ab Apostolis et Evangelistis ad ministerium Christi: sicut ea quae dicunt in uno facto, possunt adaptari ad aliud factum" (*Super Io.* 12:41, ed. Parma, t. X, 521b).

183. Though invoked by Thomas against Theodore, Jerome's understanding of prefiguration is not far removed from the Antiochene perspective. B. De Margerie has even referred to it as "son intelligence «antiochienne» de la *théôria*," *Introduction à l'histoire de l'exégèse*, vol. II, 175.

184. G. Dahan has identified the multiplication of alternative interpretations, at both the literal and spiritual levels, as a common feature of medieval exegesis; see "Les Pères dans l'exégèse médiévale," *RSPT* 91 (2007), 109–26 (120).

185. "*PROPTER MULTITUDINEM INIQUITATUM EIUS PARUULI EIUS DUCTI SUNT IN CAPTIUITATEM ANTE FACIEM TRIBULANTIS*, scilicet exercitus, uel populi Caldei uel Romani ..." (*Super Thren.* 1:5, ed. cit., 240); "*MANUM SUAM MISIT HOSTIS*, Caldaicus uel Romanus, *AD OMNIA DESIDERABILIA EIUS* ..." (*Super Thren.* 1:10, Ibid., 244; "*FACTI SUNT FILII MEI PERDITI*, quia interfecti, in captiuitatem ducti, a matribus deuorati, *QUONIAM INUALUIT INIMICUS*, Caldeus uel Romanus ..." (*Super Thren.* 1:16, Ibid., 248).

186. "*OMNES PORTE EIUS*, id est ciuitatis et templi, *DESTRUCTE*, per Caldeos et Romanos" (*Super Thren.* 1:4, Ibid., 239); "*VIDERUNT EAM HOSTES*, Babilonii et Romani, *ET DERISERVNT SABBATA EIUS*, id est solempnitates suas, ad litteram" (*Super Thren.* 1:7, Ibid., 242); "*TORCULAR CALCAUIT DOMINUS UIRGINI FILIE IUDA*, id est duas tribus contriuit per Caldeos et Romanos sicut uue in torculari" (*Super Thren.* 1:15, Ibid., 248).

187. "*NON EST QUI CONSO⟨LETUR⟩ EAM EX OMNIBUS CARIS EIUS* prius enim confederatis. Illud magis proprie pertinet ad captiuitatem Romanam, quando nec prophetas nec principes habuerunt consolatores; in captiuitate enim Babilonica prophetas habuerunt, scilicet Ieremiam, Ezechielem, Danielem" (*Super Thren.* 1, 2, ed. cit., 237).

188. For a typology of the simple question in medieval exegesis, see G. Dahan, *L'exégèse chrétienne*, 131, for that of the complex question, ibid., 284–287. By the same author, see also "La méthode critique dans l'étude de la Bible (XIIᵉ–XIIIᵉ siècles)," in *La Méthode Critique au Moyen Âge*, 103–128 (122–124). On the separation of the *disputatio* from the *lectio* and the differences between complex and simple questions, see B. Smalley, *The Study of the Bible*, 209–213.

189. The remarks not borrowed from Hugh of St. Cher are in bold.

190. "**Forte sitiuit, ad litteram, nec fuit qui sibi ministraret. Vnde sequitur:** [8]*DISCIPULI ENIM ⟨EIUS ABIERANT IN CIVITATEM⟩*. Set quomodo petiuit ab ea cum Iudei reputent Samaritanos inmundos? Crisostomus: "Reputabat pro indifferenci huiusmodi obseruantias custodire." **Vnde Mt. xv:** *Nichil extrincecum inquinat hominem* (Mt 15:11). Sciebat etiam quod non

daret, et tamen petiuit ut ex eius responsione haberet occasionem monendi et excitandi eam ad fidem, **ut patet ex illa Glossa: ⟨*DICIT ERGO EI MULIER*⟩, "nesciens quem potum ⟨petit ab ea⟩"** etc. Item non petiuit a discipulis, quia antequam perueniret ad illum fontem, illi precesserant in ciuitatem. **Nullum secum retinuit propter humilitatem. Vel ut daret locum mulieri loquendi secum"** (*Super Io.* 4:8, MS Saint-Omer, Bibl. mun. 260, f. 120va). Reputabat–custodire, Chrysostom, *In Io. hom.*, XXXI (PG 59, 180); Nesciens quem potum, *Glossa mg.*, in Io. 4:9 (ed. Rusch, vol. IV, 232b); Sciebat–daret . . . non petiuit–ciuitatem; cf. Hugh of St. Cher, *Postille*, in Io. 4:7 (ed. Venetiis, t. VI, 304va).

191. "*DICIT AD EUM MULIER*, secundum *Glossam*, adhuc carnaliter delectata ut amplius non sitiret; secundum Crisostomum, quodammodo spiritualiter edocta, unde dicit eam sapientiorem Nichodemo qui aquam baptismatis non petebat, supra III (Io 3:12); *DOMINE*, in hoc exhibet reuerentiam et confitetur dantis potentiam: *DA MICHI HANC AQUAM UT NON SI⟨TIAM⟩*, ecce una causa petitionis, scilicet amotio sitis siue defectus; *NEQUE UE⟨NIAM⟩ HUC HAU⟨RIRE⟩*, ecce alia, scilicet cessatio laboris. *HUC*. **Ex hoc uidetur quod non intellexerit nisi de aqua materiali, quod est contra Crisostomum. Responsio: Non ualet, quia putabat aqua illa quam promisit extingueret sitim etiam corporalem"** (*Super Io.* 4, 15, MS Saint-Omer, Bibl. mun. 260, f. 121ra).

192. "*CREDIS IN FILIUM DEI?* Quid hoc post tantum contradictionem adque ad Iudeos post tot uerba interrogans: Si credis? Non ignorans, set uolens seipsum notari et ostendens quam multum appreciatur eius fidem" (Chrysostom, *In Io. hom.*, LIX, MS Vat. Ottoblat. 227, fol. 101va; cf. PG 59, 322).

193. "*TU CREDIS IN FILIUM DEI?* Querendo excitat. Crisosotomus: 'Quomodo interrogat post tanta uerba fidei in Iudeos? Responsio: Non ignorans set laudans'" (*Super Io.* 9:35, MS Saint-Omer, Bibl. mun. 260, f. 139vb).

194. "*HOC ITERUM ⟨SECUNDUM⟩ SIGNUM FECIT IHESUS* etc. Queritur cum multa alia signa fecerit Ihesus ante mortem Iohannis in illo anno, quare solum de istis faciat mentionem. Responsio: Alii euangeliste plenius de aliis dixerunt" (*Super Io.* 4:54, MS Saint-Omer, Bibl. mun. 260, f. 123rb).

195. PL 198, 1053–1722. On the production and influence of the *Historia Scholastica*, see D. Luscombe, "Peter Comestor," *The Bible in the Medieval World. Essays in Memory of Beryl Smalley*, ed. K. Walsh and D. Wood, Oxford, 1985 (Studies in Church History, Subsidia 4), 109–129; G. Lobrichon, *La Bible au Moyen Age*, Paris, 1984, 66–67; B. Smalley, *Study of the Bible*, 178–180 and ch. 5; S. R. Daly, "Peter Comestor: Master of Histories," *Speculum* 32 (1957), 62–73; A. Landgraf, "Recherches sur les écrits de Pierre le Mangeur," *RTAM* 3 (1931), 292–306; R. M. Martin, "Notes sur l'œuvre littéraire de Pierre le Mangeur," *RTAM* 3 (1931), 54–66.

196. Cf. Chrysostom, *In Io. hom.*, XXXI (PG 59, 177).

197. "Secundum Crisostomum, hec facta fuerunt inmediate post instructionem Nichodemi, et dictam baptizationem discipulorum Christi. Magister tamen in *Historiis* interponit sanationem filii regali et socrus Petri" (*Super Io.* 4:3, MS Saint-Omer, Bibl. mun. 260, f. 120ra). Cf. Chrysostom, *In Io. hom.*, XXXI (PG 59, 177); Peter Comestor, *Hist. schol.*, In Evang., 52–53 (PL 198, 1566).

198. "Unde perpenditur hiemis tempore hoc factum" (Peter Comestor, ibid., 1568).

199. "Et secundum hoc patet Hyemis tempore hoc factum esse in Novembri, scilicet, vel Decembri, vel circa hoc, quia in Pascha offerebantur primitiae frugam maturarum. Et ex hoc perpenditur, quod hoc non fit factum immediate post illa, quae dicta sunt de ejectione ementium, & vendentium, in templo, quae facta est in Pascha" (Hugh of St. Cher, *Postille*, in Io.; ed. Venetiis, t. VI, 308vb).

200. ". . . datur intelligi quod Christus statim post captionem Joannis de Iudaea recessit . . . et transivit per Samariam; et quod hoc fuit in hieme: et Joannes similiter captus. Unde quia ibi tempastivius messes perficiuntur, quatuor menses erant ab illo tempore usque ad messem" (*Super Io.* 4:35, ed. Parma, t. X, 371b). As Albert the Great would have it, it happened around March or April: "Et hoc fuit circa Martium vel Aprilem: quia in Junio vel Julio metitur in terra promissionis, quae est medii climatis. Et hoc fuit, quia vicinum tempus hiemis ante hoc fieri impedit maturitatem" (*In Io.* 4:35, ed. Borgnet, t. XXIV, 180). There is no reason to believe that either commentary was among William's sources.

201. "Secundum litteram aestas erat propinqua" (Bonaventure, *In Io. com.* 4:35, Opera, t. VI, 297b).

202. "*Nonne uos di⟨citis⟩ quia adhuc quattuor menses*, scilicet implendi, *et messis uenit?* Ex hoc patet quod illud fuit factum ante Pascha, cum in illis regionibus sint messes tempore Pasche" (*Super Io.* 4:35, MS Saint-Omer, Bibl. mun. 260, f. 122rb).

203. Entertaining the objection that nothing in the Gospel text seems to correspond to the miraculum apparently referred to here, Thomas Aquinas (following Origen) proposes that the reference is to the cleansing of the Temple (cf. Io 2:14–16), or that it is to one of the many miracles left unmentioned by the Evangelist)*Super Io.* 4:45 (ed. Parma, t. x, 376a). For C. K. Barrett, they are the signs mentioned yet not described at 2:23; see *The Gospel According to John*, 2nd ed., Philadelphia, 1978, 244. More recently, P. Perkins described the passage as follows: "Verses 43–45 are awkward" in "The Gospel According to John," *NJBC* (61:67), 958a.

204. "*Cum ergo uenisset in Gal⟨ileam⟩ exce⟨perunt⟩ eum ⟨Galilei⟩ cum omnia uidi⟨ssent⟩ que fe⟨cerat⟩ Ierosolimis in die fe⟨sto⟩. . . . et ipsi enim ascenderant ad diem festum. . . .* Ex hoc sumpsit Magister in Historiis hoc miraculum factum circa Pascha, non quatuor mensibus ante, ut uidetur dicere littera precedens. Set non oportet, quia potuit esse aliud festum quam Pascha, scilicet festum Tabernaculorum, quod est in septembri" (*Super Io.* 4:45, MS Saint-Omer, Bibl. mun. 260, f. 122vb). Cf. Peter Comestor, *Hist. schol.*, In Evang., 37 (PL 198, 1558).

205. Many modern scholars are in broad agreement on the irreconcilability of the two accounts. See, for example, E. Haenchen, *A Commentary on the Gospel of John*, 2 vols., Philadelphia, 1984, vol. 2, 178; R. Schnackenburg, *Commentary on the Gospel of John*, 3 vols., London, 1982, vol. 3, 33–47. On the other hand, their reconcilability was given new currency by the study of A. Jaubert, *La Date de la Cène: Calendrier Biblique et liturgie chrétienne*, Paris, 1957. For more recent arguments to the same effect, see B. Smith, "The Chronology of the Last Supper," *Westminster Theological Journal* 53, no. 1 (1991), 29–45; H. Ridderbos, *The Gospel of John*, 123–124. Among the more important studies favoring the synoptic chronology, see C. K. Barret, *The Gospel According to John*, 48–51. For an extensive study favoring the Johannine chronology, see R. Brown's *Death of the Messiah, from Gethsemane to the Grave: A Commentary on the Passion Narratives in the Four Gospels*, "Appendix II, Dating the Crucifixion (Day, Monthly Date, Year)," New York, London, 1994, vol. 2, 1350–1378. As well as a thorough account of the numerous problems of dating the crucifixion, it contains a detailed discussion of various scholarly proposals in favor of the Synoptic chronology, the Johannine one, or a reconciliation of the two, the last of which he concludes is "implausible, unnecessary and misleading" (1369). Brown lists several reasons for judging the Johannine account historical (1373). Other studies favoring John's version include R. Kysar, *John*, Augsberg Commentary on the New Testament, Minneapolis, 1986, 206; P. Perkins in *NJBC* (61:171), 973a. Apart from the chronology of the Last Supper and Passover, the broader relationship between John and the Synoptic Gospels remains a matter of debate. For an overview and bibliography of scholarship on the latter issue, see R. Brown, *Introduction*, 90–114.

206. Implicit in the opening line of William's exposition, the problem of credibility is stated explicitly in the *Glossa ordinaria*: "Nec erubescunt (Greci) dicere alios evangelistas mentitos qui dicunt Dominum communiter cum aliis carnes agni comedisse. Hunc Iohannem vero illos correxisse dicunt. Set errant, quia cum omnes eodem Spiritu locutos fuisse constet. Si in uno mentirentur, in aliis eis non crederetur" (*Glossa mg.*, in Io. 13, 1, ed. Rusch, vol. IV, 255b). The statement is reprised by Bonaventure (*In Io. com.* 13:1, *Opera*, t. VI, 426b), and Thomas Aquinas (*Super Io.* 13:1 (ed. Parma, t. X, 523a–b). Both refer to the Greeks. For his part, Albert the Great affirms the Latin Church's traditional chronology without entertaining questions (*In Io.* 13:1, ed. Borgnet, t. XXIV, 499).

207. There is only fragmentary evidence concerning the use of either leavened or unleavened bread in the early medieval Latin West. Among the earliest witnesses is the mention of *panem infermentatum* by Rabanus Maurus (d. 856), *De clericorum institutione* (PL 107, 318). Less direct is an earlier remark by Alcuin, *Ad fratres Lugdunenses*, dated in Migne to 798: "Sic et panis, qui in corpus Christi consecratur, absque fermento ullius alterius infectionis, debet esse mundissimus" (*Epist.* XC, PL 100, 289). What is at issue here is the use of salt, not leaven. The use of unleavened bread, however, had become general by the mid-eleventh century. At the moment

of the Schism of 1054, the Latin and Greek churches' divergent practices were an important point of dispute. See the letters of Michael Cerularius, Patriarch of Constantinople (1043–1058) and the replies of Pope Leo IX (1048–1054), and of Cardinal Humbert (PL 143, 555, and 793; and 143, 744, 773, and 797); cf. F. Cabrol, "Azymes," *DACL*, t. I, Part 2, 1907, 3254–3260; É. Amann, "Michel Cérulaire," *DTC* II, no.2 (1929), 1677–1703.

208. Three successive popes of the period placed reunion among their priorities: Urban IV (1261–1264), Clement IV (1265–1268), and following a vacancy of three years, Gregory X (1271–1276). The last presided over the Council of Lyons of 1274, which achieved a short-lived reunion (to end in 1289) when legates of the Greek Emperor Michael VIII Paleologus declared adherence to the Roman Church. The council's remarks on the matter did not extend beyond an affirmation of the Latin Church's own practice: "Sacramentum Eucharistiae ex azymo conficit Romana Ecclesia . . ." (DS 860). William's contemporaries Bonaventure, Albert the Great, and Peter Tarentaise were present. Thomas Aquinas died on the way there.

209. All the expositions cited in note 206 defend the Latin Church's use of unleavened bread, at least implicitly, without, however, condemning the practice of the Greek Church. Apart from his commentary on this text, Thomas Aquinas discusses the use of leavened bread in several places. In sum, he affirms the Latin Church's position, yet also discusses the fittingness of the use of leavened bread among the Greeks. Cf. Thomas Aquinas, *In IV Sent.*, d. 11, q. 2, a. 2c (ed. Parma, t. VII/B, 641b–44a); *Contra errores Graecorum*, II, 39 (ed. Leonina, t. XL, 103a–104b); *SCG*, IV, c. 69 (ed. Leonina, t. XV, 218a–19b); *ST*, III, q. 73, a. 6 (ed. Leonina, t. XII, 143a–44b); *Super I ad Cor.* 5, 7 (ed. Parma, t. XIII, 190b–191a); *Super Mt.* 26, 17 (ed. Parma, t. X, 244a–b).

210. *"ANTE DIEM FESTUM PASCHE*. Ex hoc uidetur quod Dominus confecerit de fermentato, set alii euuangeliste dicunt quod comedit secundum communem morem comedendi in pascha. Responsio: Non dicitur hic dies Pasche inmolationis agni, set primus inter dies azimorum, in cuius sero precedenti inmolabatur agnus. Item, ex isto arguunt Greci quod ea que tunc facta sunt, scilicet cena et comestio agni facta sint luna quartadecima quando immolabatur agnus paschalis, sicut preceptum est, Exo. XII (Ex 12:6). Item, infra XVIII: *Non introierunt in pretorium, ut non con⟨tam⟩minarentur sed ma⟨nducarent⟩ Pascha* (Io 18:28), scilicet agnum. Ergo quartadecima luna. Set ante per unam diem fecit pascha. Ergo luna tertiadecima. Item, Iudei noluerunt eum occidere luna quintadecima, Mt. XXVI: *Non in die festo* (Mt 26:5). Ergo fuit occisus quartadecima, et ante fecit cenam. Ergo luna tertiadecima. Item, luna quartadecima agnus inmolabatur, et ueritas debuit respondere umbre. Ergo et quartadecima luna Christo occidebatur et ante fecit cenam. Ergo, ut supra. Contra, Lucas dicit expresse: *Venit dies azimorum in qua necesse erat occidi Pascha* (Lc 22:7). Set pascha occidebatur quartadecima luna. Ergo tunc comedebantur azima. Ad primum dicendum quod pascha dicitur hic solempnitas lune quintedecime. Ad aliud dicendum quod ibi dicitur pascha cibi paschales, sicut azimi panes, non ipse agnus quos non licebat edere nisi mundis. Ad aliud dicendum quod Iudei frustrati sunt propositio suo, occiderunt enim eum die quo non credebant. Ad aliud dicendum quod ueritas respondet umbre, quia luna quartadecima captus fuit et incepit sua passio. Secundum Ambrosium, pascha Grece passio Latine. Secundum hebraycam linguam dicitur Pascha illud quod transitus" (*Super Io.* 13:1, MS Saint-Omer, 260, f. 150va). Ex hoc–uidetur; cf. Bonaventure, *In Io. com.* 13:1 (*Opera*, t. VI, 426b); Hugh of St. Cher, *Postille*, in Io. (ed. Venetiis, t. VI, 364va–vb); Peter Comestor, *Hist. schol.*, In Evang. (PL 198, 1614). Secundum Ambrosium–transitus; cf. Peter Comestor, *Hist. schol.*, In Evang. (PL 198, 1614); Ambrose, *Epistulae*, I, 1 (CSEL 82.1, 7); Isidore of Seville, *De ecclesiaticis officiis*, I, 32: "Neque enim a passione (quoniam 'pascin' grece dicitur pati) sed a transitu hebreo uerbo pascha appellata est" (ed. C. Lawson, Turnhout, 1989, CCSL 113, 36); *Glossa mg.*, in Io. 13:1 (ed. Rusch, vol. IV, 255b); Jerome, *In Evangelium Matthaei*, IV: "Pascha quod hebraice dicitur phase, non a passione ut plerique arbitrantur sed a transitu nominatur, eo quod exterminator uidens sanguinem in foribus Israhelitarum pertransierit nec percusserit eos uel ipse Dominus praebens auxilium populo suo desuper ambularit" (ed. D. Hurst and M. Adriaen, Turnhout, 1969, CCSL 77, 245).

211. On the other hand, the Greek Church's practice owes nothing to the exegesis of Chrysostom, who is unequivocal on the Last Supper's character as a Passover meal celebrated with

unleavened bread; cf. *In Io. hom.*, LXXIII (PG 59, 452–453). William cites him to this effect when the question reappears in John's account of the Passion: "*IPSI*, scilicet Iudei qui duxerunt Christum, *NON INTROIERUNT IN PRETORIUM, UT NON CONTAMINAUERINTUR . . . SET MANDUCARENT*, id est manducare possent, *PASCHA*. . . . Crisostomus dicit quod Pascha stat pro agno paschali et quod Christus suo tempore comedit; pontifex tamen et Iudei occupati circa captionem Christi non potuerunt suo tempore comedere, unde expectauerunt in crastinum" (*Super Io.* 18:15, MS Saint-Omer, 260, f. 167ra).

212. On the liturgical dimensions of monastic thought and culture, see the magisterial study of J. LECLERCQ, *Initiation aux auteurs monastiques du Moyen Âge. L'Amour des lettres et le désir de Dieu*, Paris, 1957, esp. 40–41, 236–251.

213. L.-J. Bataillon, "La Bible au XIII^e siècle. Un incitation aux recherches de demain," in *La Bibbia del XIII Secolo*, 3–11 (8–9); G. Berceville, "Les commentaires évangéliques de Thomas d'Aquin et Hugues de Saint-Cher," in *Hugues de Saint-Cher, Bibliste et théologien*, ed. L.-J. Bataillon, Gilbert Dahan, and P.-M. Gy, Turnhout, 2004, 173–196. The present discussion is indebted to both studies.

214. *Homiliarum euangelii libri II*, CCSL 122, 96–97.

215. *Comm. in s. Io. Evang.*, PL 100, 766.

216. *Commentaria in euangelium sancti Iohannis*, ed. R. Haacke, Turnhout, 1969, CCCM 9, 100.

217. ". . . utraque probabilis et sustinere potest," Bonaventure, *In Io. com.* 2:1, *Opera*, t. VI, 271b–272a.

218. *In Io.* 2:1, ed. Borgnet, t. XXIV, 88b.

219. *Super Io.* 2:1, ed. Parma, t. X, 330a–b.

220. Cf. Io 1:43.

221. "*ET DIE TERTIA*, id est a die qua exiuit Ihesus in Galileam et uocauit Philippum, ut patet supra in *Glossa*: "Galilea dicitur transmigratio" etc. Secundum communem opinionem, hoc fuit dies tertia decima trecesimi primi anni Christi, quia tertia decima die a natauitate sua apparuit magis, eadem die anni trecesimi baptizatus est, eadem die anno reuoluto, hoc miraculum factum est. **Et si obiicitur quod sicut infra dicitur Dominus post istud miraculum descendit Capharnaum, et quod tunc erat proximum pascha, quod non potuit esse ista die, dicendum quod non statim descendit Capharnaum post istud miraculum, set tempore interposito.** *NUPTIE* . . ." (*Super Io.* 2:1, MS Saint-Omer, Bibl. mun. 260, f. 115vb). Cf. *Biblia Latina cum glossa ordinaria: marginalia*, vol. 4, 227a.

222. "*POST HEC*, non statim, secundum opinionem tenentium morem ecclesie, que uidetur tenere tale miraculum positum supra factum tertia decima die trecesimi primi anni Christi . . . *DESCENDIT CAPHAR⟨NAUM⟩*" (*Super Io.* 2:12, MS Saint-Omer, Bibl. mun. 260, f. 116va). The commonality of the view is attested in the widely popular general history by William's Dominican contemporary, Vincent of Beauvais, *Speculum Historiale*, ed. Douai, 1624 (reprint Graz, 1965), 224b. On this work, see M. Paulmier-Foucart, with the collaboration of M.-C. Duchenne, *Vincent de Beauvais et le Grand miroir du monde*, Turnhout, 2004 (Témoins de notre histoire 10).

223. "*ET NEMO ASCENDIT IN CELUM*, scilicet uirtute propria, *NISI QUI DESCENDIT DE CELO* per assumptionem humanitatis, *FILIUS HO⟨MINIS⟩ QUI EST IN CELO* per presensiam et inmensitatem diuinitatis. Vel *NISI FILIUS HO⟨MINIS⟩*, id est capud cum membris, Ps.: *Ascendens Christus in altum*" (*Super Io.* 3:13, MS Saint-Omer, Bibl. mun. 260, f. 117vb).

224. The Psalter of the "prototype" of the Dominican liturgy is the Gallican. The text of this verse is identical to that of the Weber edition: *Ascendisti in altum, cepisti captiuitatem, accepisti dona in hominibus* (MS Santa Sabina XIV L 1, f. 76va). In the Dominican breviary in use from the mid-thirteenth century until the reforms of Vatican II, the verse cited by William appeared as an antiphon at first vespers, and for the entire octave, it appeared as an antiphon at compline and in the responsories of the minor offices *ad sextam* and *ad nonam*. What follows are the relevant references to the breviary of the "prototype" of the Dominican liturgy (ibid., f. 107vb, 108ra, 108rb). This codex was completed in mid-1259 at Paris, at about the time William became a master there. See, among the other fine studies in the same volume, L. Boyle, "A Material Consideration of Santa Sabina MS XIV L 1," in *Aux origines de la liturgie Dominicaine: Le manuscrit Santa Sabina XIV L 1*, 19–42 (20)

and G. Dahan, "Les Textes Bibliques dans le lectionnaire du 'Prototype' de la liturgie dominicaine," ibid., 159–182. By no means confined to the Dominican liturgy, this same verse makes several appearances in the liturgy of the Ascension in a Cistercian antiphonary of the second half of the twelfth century, as well as in a breviary of Notre Dame de Paris of the late thirteenth or early fourteenth century. The relevant references, respectively, are as follows: Paris, BnF lat. 15181, f. 334v, 335r, 336v, 337r, 340r, 341 v, and Paris, BnF nouv. acq. lat. 1411, f. 108r, 109v, 111v, 112r. In the Roman Church's current breviary it appears in the responsory to lauds.

225. A. Matter has noted that the appearance of the first known commentaries on Lamentations (by Rabanus Maurus and Paschasius Radbertus) coincided with the dissemination of the *Tenebrae* liturgy, when the Roman and Gallican rites were merged under Charlemagne during the ninth century; see "The Lamentations Commentaries of Hrabanus Maurus and Paschasius Radbertus," *Traditio* 38 (1982), 137–163 (139).

226. The name *Tenebrae* most likely owes to the darkness left by the ritual of extinguishing candles, placed upon a "hearse" before the altar, which was the church's only source of light. Suggesting bereavement, the darkness of *Tenebrae* presented a stark contrast to the radiance of the Easter Vigil, which was redolent of new life and exultation. See the account of this liturgy provided by the ninth-century liturgist Amalarius of Metz (c. 780–850), "Libro de ordine antiphonarii," ed. J. M. Hanssens, *"Amalarii episcopi opera liturgica omnia III,"* *Studi e Testi* 140 (1950), 80. For parallel interpretations of this ritual from the twelfth century, see Iohannes Beleth (c. 1182), *Summa de ecclesiasticis officiis*, ed. H. Douteil, Turnhout, 1976 (CCCM 41A), 186–189; from the early thirteenth century Sicard of Cremona (d. 1215), *Mitrale*, PL 213, 298–299; and from the late thirteenth century, William Durandus, *Guillelmi Durandi Rationale Divinorum Officiorum* 5–6, ed. A. Davril and T.-M. Thibodeau, Turnhout, 1995 (CCCM 140A), 341–344. For the last two references, I am indebted to C. Vincent, *Fiat Lux. Lumière et luminaires dans la vie religieuse en Occident du XIIIe au XVIe siècle*, Paris, 2004, 258, n. 2.

227. "Moraliter. *CIUITAS*: anima; *SEDET*: spretis celestibus, terrenis inclinata; *SOLA*: bonis omnibus spiritualibus destituta; *DOMINA GENTIUM*: id est uitiorum in statu gratie; *FACTA EST QUASI UIDUA*: a uiro Christo, uel ratione separata in statu culpe" (*Super Thren.* 1:1, ed. cit., 237).

228. "Allegorice. *DOMINUS*, Pater, *REPULIT*, id est repellere uidebatur, *ALTARE*, Christum in passione, *MALEDIXIT SANCTIFICATIONI*, id est Christum malo pene addixit" (*Super Thren.* 2:7, ed. cit., 256).

229. "Moraliter.... *TEMPUS EUELLENDI*: peccatum originale per baptismum, actuale per penitentie sacramentum ... item in uerbo, opere et cogitatione omne superfluum" (*Super Ecclesiasten.* 3:2, MSS Basel, Univ. Bibl. B III 20, f. 96va; Madrid, Bibl. Nac. 493, f. 140r). The relevant line of the *Confiteor* is as follows: "Confiteor Deo omnipotenti et vobis, fratres, quia peccavi nimis cogitatione, verbo, opere et omissione."

230. On the importance of the spiritual sense in university exegesis, J. Verger sums it up as follows: "... pour ces auteurs le sens spirituel n'était pas un ornement extrinsèque ni un sens 'adapté,' de manière plus ou moins heureuse, pour illustrer telle ou telle affirmation doctrinale (ou politique). Le sens spirituel demeurait à leurs yeux *de necessitate sacrae scripturae*," in "L'Exégèse de l'Université," 208. In the preface to the third edition of her magisterial study of medieval biblical exegesis, B. Smalley identified the section titled "The Spiritual Exposition in Decline" as the faultiest part of her chapter on the friars, adding: "The spiritual senses were too integral to the faith and too useful in homiletics to be dropped or even pushed far into the margin"; see *The Study of the Bible in the Middle Ages*, xiii–xiv. In a subsequent paper, published posthumously, she studied a few of their applications, "Use of the 'Spiritual' Senses of Scripture in Persuasion and Argument by Scholars in the Middle Ages," *RTAM* 52 (1985), 44–63.

231. "... set sensus spiritualis semper fundatur super litteralem et procedit ex eo, unde ex hoc quod sacra scriptura exponitur litteraliter et spiritualiter, non est in ipsa aliqua multiplicitas" (Thomas Aquinas, *De quolibet* VII, q. 6, a. 1, ad 1, ed. Leonina, t. xxv, 1, 28b). There is nothing about William's work to suggest that he had a different view of the matter.

232. The capital text here is Augustine's *De doctrina christiana*, I, 2: "Omnis doctrina uel rerum est uel signorum, sed res per signa discuntur. Proprie autem nunc res appellaui, quae non ad significandum aliquid adhibentur, sicuti est lignum lapis pecus atque huiusmodi cetera, sed non illud lignum, quod in aquas amaras Moysen misisse legimus, ut amaritudine carerent, neque ille lapis, quem Iacob sibi ad caput posuerat, neque illud pecus, quod pro filio immolauit Abraham. Hae namque ita res sunt, ut aliarum etiam signa sint rerum. Sunt autem alia signa, quorum omnis usus in significando est, sicuti sunt uerba" (CCSL 32, 7). For a discussion of this text and the legacy to medieval exegesis of Augustine's theory of signification, see G. Dahan, *L'exégèse chrétienne*, 299–307.

233. Cf. G. Dahan, *L'exégèse chrétienne*, 299–358; B. Smalley, *The Study of the Bible*, 242–263.

234. Cf. G. Dahan, *L'exégèse chrétienne*, 314–325.

235. *Liber interpretationis hebraicorum nominum* (ed. P. de Lagarde, 1959, CCSL 72) and *Epist.* 30 (ed. Labourt, t. II, Paris, 1951, 33). Other authorities were occasionally cited, such as in the following case: "[49]*RESPONDIT IHESUS: EGO DEMONIUM NON HABEO* ... Alterum sibi impositum, scilicet quod erat Samaritanus, non negauit, quia hoc aliquo modo erat uerum quantum ad interpretationem nominis, ut dicit Gregorius" (*Super Io.* 8:49, MS Saint-Omer, Bibl. mun. 260, f. 137rb). The reference is to Gregory the Great: "Quia enim samaritanus interpretatur custos, et ipse veraciter custos est ..." (*Hom. in evang.*, I, 18, CCSL 141, 137). Gregory would also appear to be the source of an interpretation connected with the apostle Thomas: "[16]*DIXIT ERGO THOMAS, QUI DICITUR DIDIMUS*, id est geminus, uel diu dubitans" (*Super Io.* 11:16, MS Saint-Omer, Bibl. mun. 260, f. 143vb); cf. Gregory the Great, *Hom. in evang.*, II, 29 (CCSL 141, 245).

236. Pachasius Radbertus, *Expositio in Lamentationes* (ed. B. Paulus, Turnhout, 1988, CCCM 85).

237. Alcuin, *Comm. in s. Iohannem. Evangelium* (PL 100).

238. "*GIMEL, plenitudo*," Jerome, *Litterae*, Epist. 30 (ed. Labourt, t. II, 33).

239. "*GIMEL* interpretatur 'plenitudo,' quasi dicat: propter multitudinem peccatorum, ⟨*MIGRAUIT IUDAS*⟩ scilicet a terra propria in Caldeam. ... Allegorice. *IUDAS*, ecclesia confitens migrauit de afflictione in afflictionem; propter afflictionem et seruitutem et propter multitudinem affligentium eam nitentium redigere eam in seruitutem; uel propter multitudinem seruientium peccato qui eam secuntur. ... Moraliter. *IUDA* anima prius confitens; *MIGRA*⟨*UIT*⟩ de peccato in peccatum" (*Super Thren.* 1:3, ed. cit., 238. interpretatur plenitudo); cf. Glossa mg., in Thren. 1:3 (ed. Rusch, vol. III, 185a); Paschasius Radbertus, *Exp. in Lam.* (CCCM 85, 16); Jerome, *Epist.* 30 (ed. Labourt, t. II, 33); ecclesia confitens; Jerome, *Lib. interpret. hebraic. nom.* (CCSL 72, 67).

240. "*ET UNUS EX UOBIS DYABOLUS EST*, non per naturam, set per nominis interpretationem. Interpretatur enim 'deorsum fluens,' et tunc forte inclinabatur ad inferiora quia loculos habebat, infra XII (cf. Io 12, 6)" (*Super Io.* 6, 71, MS Saint-Omer, Bibl. mun. 260, f. 130vb); cf. *Glossa int.*, in Io. 6:71 (ed. Rusch, vol. IV, 241b); Jerome, *Lib. interpret. hebraic. nom.* (CCSL 72, 160).

241. On the usage of the term allegory, see chapter 2, note 21.

242. "Mistice. *ORITUR SOL*, id est Christus in natiuitate .. ⟨*ET*⟩ *OCCIDIT*, in passione ..., *ET AD LOCUM SUUM REUERTITUR*, in ascensione ... *IBIQUE*, id est in celo, *RENASCENS*, id est ad iudicium ueniens. *GIRAT PER MERIDIEM*, considerando bonos et opera eorum, qui nomine meridiei propter uirtutem et splendorem honeste conuersationis intelliguntur, *ET FLECTITUR AD AQUILONEM*, considerando malos et opera eorum, qui per aquilonem propter frigus malitie designantur" (*Super Ecl.* 1:5–6, MSS Basel, Univ. Bibl. B III 20, f. 94vb–95ra; Madrid, Bibl. Nac. 493, f. 133v).

243. "*LUSTRANS UNIUERSA IN CIRCUITU PERGIT SPIRITUS*, id est uentus, omnia perlustrando circuit; 'spiritus' enim dicitur uentus ... de hoc loco dixerunt quidam errantes quod sol et alia luminaria celi sunt spiritus. Alii nomine 'spiritus' non ipsum solem, set spiritum presidentem intelligunt. ... Mistice. *LUSTRANS UNIUERSA* ⟨*CIRCUITU PERGIT SPIRITUS*⟩ etc. Primo ostenditur Spiritus Sancti diuersa nominatio. Per 'Spiritum' hic sol, uentus, aer intelliguntur. Sol propter feruorem caritatis; sol enim fons est caloris, Gregorius, "Spiritus sanctus amor est." Vnde et ignis dicitur, Luc. XII (49) ... 'Ventus' propter uelocitatem et rapiditatem motus seu operationis, ... 'Aer' propter suauitatem, Spiritus sanctus enim suauis est ..." (*Super Ecl.* 1:6, MSS Basel, Univ. Bibl. B III 20, f. 95ra–rb; Madrid, Bibl. Nac. 493, f. 133v–134r). Cf. Greg. Mag., *Hom. in evang.*, II, 30 (CCSL 141, 256).

244. Among the most frequently cited biblical examples of such exegesis is Gal 4:22–31. Other important examples are Ro 5:14, 1 Cor 10:1–11, and Col 2:17. Prolonged allegorical reflections upon the Old Testament appear throughout the Letter to the Hebrews, much of whose language appears in the descriptions of ORIGEN (c. 185–c. 254) of a threefold typology corresponding to the levels of shadow, image, and truth. In this perspective, Old Testament realities are shadows of the image of Christ and his church, which themselves point to the truth of the heavenly Kingdom. Commenting on Jesus' instruction to the Samaritan woman at the well (Io 4:21–24), Origen has the following to say about the relation between the Old Testament and the New: "*Venit hora ut ueri adoratores neque in Hierosolymis neque in hoc monte adorent patrem. Deus spiritus est, et eos qui adorent eum, in spiritu et ueritate oportet adorare. Et uide quam consequenter ueritatem spiritui sociauit, ut ad distinctionem quidem corporum spiritum nominaret, ad distinctionem uero umbrae uel imaginis ueritatem. Qui enim adorabant in Hierosolymis, umbrae et imagini caelestium deseruientes non ueritati neque spiritui adorabant Deum; similiter autem et hi qui adorabant in monte Garizin*" (*De principiis, sec. trans. Rufini*, I, 1, 4, ed. H. Crouzel and M. Simonetti, Paris, 1978, SC 252, 96). To be sure, Origen was not the first nonbiblical author to discern Old Testament figures with New Testament correspondences. The following remark of Justin Martyr (c. 100–c. 165) is typical: "And that expression which was committed to writing by Moses, and prophesied by the patriarch Jacob, namely, 'He shall wash His garments with wine, and His vesture with the blood of the grape,' signified that He would wash those that believe in Him with His own blood." (*Dialogue with Trypho*, LIV = *Dialogue avec Tryphon*, ANF I, 423. Irenaeus of Lyons (c. 130–c. 200) expands on the typology employed by St. Paul in Ro 5:14 with the following comment on the genealogy of Lc 3:22: "Wherefore also Luke, commencing the genealogy with the Lord, carried it back to Adam, indicating that it was He who regenerated them into the Gospel of life, and not they Him. And thus also it was that the knot of Eve's disobedience was loosed by the obedience of Mary. For what the virgin Eve had bound fast through unbelief, this did the virgin Mary set free through faith." (*Against Heresies*, III, 22, 4, ANF I, 905).

245. "*HIC UENIT AD IHESUM NOCTE, Glossa*: 'Quia magister in Israel palam discere erubescat, uel pro metu.' NOCTE, forte ut quietius addiscere posset. Vel mistice, ad significandum quod tenebre ignorantie erant adhuc in eius corde" (*Super Io*. 3:2, MS Saint-Omer, Bibl. mun. 260, f. 117ra).

246. Augustine, *In Io. evang. tract.*, XI (CCSL 36, 112); Alcuin, *Comm. in s. Io. Evang.* (PL 100, 778); *Glossa mg.*, in Io. 3:2 (ed. Rusch, vol. IV, 229b). In view of the symbolism of light and darkness in John's Gospel, some modern commentators view the symbolism in this passage as intended by the human author, that is, as belonging to the literal sense; cf. R. Kysar, *John*, 52. Others refrain from doing so; cf. P. Perkins, "The Gospel According to John," *NJBC* (61:49), 955b; H. Ridderbos, *The Gospel of John*, 123–124.

247. "*NUMQUID TU MAIOR ES PATRE NOSTRO IACOB*, scilicet maius aliquid dando, *QUI DEDIT NOBIS PUTEUM?* . . . "Mistice. Puteus sacra scriptura altus, Eccl. VII: *Alta profunditas ⟨quis inueniet eam?⟩*. Hauritorium humilitas, puritas, siue uite bonitas, orationis assiduitas, asperitas. Aqua huius putei est sapientia, Eccli. XV: *Aqua sapientie salutaris ⟨potabit illum⟩*. De isto puteo bibunt *IACOB*, preliantes, ⟨*ET*⟩ *FILII* ⟨*EIUS*⟩, subditi intelligentes, *ET PECORA* ⟨*EIUS*⟩, id est simplices" (*Super Io*. 4:12, MS Saint-Omer, Bibl. mun. 260, f. 120vb).

248. "Allegorice: *PUER UNUS* ⟨*HIC*⟩, Moyses, He. III: ⟨*Et Moses quidem fidelis erat in tota domo eius*⟩ *tamquam famulus in testimonium* etc. (Hbr 3:5); ⟨*QVI HABET*⟩ *QUINQUE PANES*, quinque eius libri, secundum Ieronimum, de quibus 1 Cor. XIIII: *Volo* (malo *S A*) *loqui quinque uerba* ⟨*sensu meo*⟩ (1 Cor 14:19)" (*Super Io*. 6:9, MS Saint-Omer, Bibl. mun. 260, f. 126va).

249. Cf. Augustine, *In Io. evang. tract.*, XXIV (CCSL 36, 246); Alcuin, *Comm. in s. Io. Evang.* (PL 100, 821); *Glossa mg.*, in Io. 6:9 (ed. Rusch, vol. IV, 238a–b).

250. "*VOLUERUNT ERGO RECIPERE EUM IN NA⟨UI⟩* . . . Spiritualiter: Flatus Dyaboli cessat ad uerbum Christi, Eccli. XLIII: *In sermone eius siluit uentus* (Sir 43:25)" (*Super Io*. 6:21, MS Saint-Omer, Bibl. mun. 260, f. 127va).

251. Table 3.2  Lam 1:19: *COPH. Vocavi amicos meos, et ipsi deceperunt me. Sacerdotes mei et senes mei in urbe consumpti sunt, quia quaesierunt cibum sibi ut refocilarent animam suam.*

| Paschasius Radbertus (CCCM 85, 64–65) | *Glossa* int. (ed. Rusch, vol. 3, p. 190a) | Stephan Langton (MS Paris, Arsenal 87, f. 208rb) | William of Alton (ed. cit., 240) |
|---|---|---|---|
| Et quod peius est tunc tales contra nos crudelius seuiunt cum sacerdotes et senes quos Greci gerontas uocant in nobis fame uerbi Dei consumpti laborant. Presertim quia sectantes carnalis uitae lucra magis quaerunt cibum quo miseram refocilent uitam. . . . | Quod que peius est, tunc crudelius seuiunt cum *SACERDOTES ET SENES* fame verbi Dei *CONSUMPTI SUNT*: qui sequentes lucra carnalis vite, magis quaerunt cibum animalis vite quam celaestem. | Merito afflicta sum, quia *SACERDOTES MEI ET SENES MEI*, qui me debuerunt pascere spiritualiter, *IN URBE CONSUMPTI SUNT*, fame diuini uerbi. *Facti sunt uelud arietes non inuenientes pascua* (Lam 1:6), ut supra dictum est, *QUIA QUESIERUNT SIBI CIBUM*, non spiritualem set temporalem, *UT REFOCILLARENT ANIMAM SUAM*, id est animalitatem quod superius expositum est. | Allegorice. *AMICI* ecclesie sunt prelati, *ET IPSI DECEPERUNT ME* malis exemplis corrumpendo. *SACERDOTES MEI*, id est doctores, et *SENES*, sapientiores, *IN URBE*, id est ecclesia uel religione, *CONSUMPTI SUNT* per defectum doctrine, quia *canes ⟨muti⟩ non ualentes latrare* (Is 56:10); et hoc quia *QUESIERUNT CIBUM SIBI*, scilicet carnalem non spiritualem, set lucrum temporale, *UT REFOCILLARENT ANIMAS SUAS*, id est carnalitates. |

252. "Moraliter: [9:7]*ABIIT HOMO*, lauat penitendo, uidet contemplando" (*Super Io.* 9:7, MS Saint-Omer, Bibl. mun. 260, f. 138vb).

253. "Moraliter. *AMICI* anime dicuntur dulces affectus qui decipiunt animam sibi intentam; *SACERDOTES* sunt uirtutes ad sacerdotium pertinentes, *SENES* qui ad iudicia et consilia pertinent, *CONSUMPTI SUNT* a uitiis, *QUIA QUESIERUNT*, scilicet affectus anime, *CIBUM SIBI*, id est desideria praua" (*Super Thren.* 1:19, ed. cit., 250).

254. On the *distinctio* as a simple form or microstructure in biblical commentary, see G. Dahan, *L'exégèse chrétienne*, 134–138. On the emergence and development of collections of distinctions, see ibid., 331–338; R. H. Rouse and M. A. Rouse, "Biblical *distinctiones* in the XIII[th] Century," *AHDLMA* 41 (1974), 27–37; B. Smalley, *The Study of the Bible*, 246–248. For a study of Bonaventure's borrowing of distinctions from Hugh of St. Cher, see R. Karris, "St. Bonaventure's Use of Distinctions," *Franciscan Studies* 60 (2002) 209–244. For a few remarkable demonstrations of the usage of such collections in preaching, see L.-J. Bataillon, "Intermédiaires entre les traités de moral pratique et les sermons: les distinctiones Bibliques alphabétiques," in *Les Genres littéraires dans les sources théologiques et philosophiques médiévales*, Louvain, 1982, 213–226.

255. "Est *MARE* aqua propter congregationem, Ge. 1: *Congregationes aquarum appelauit maria* (Gn 1:10).
Item, mors propter amaritudinem, II Reg. XIIII: *Omnes morimur et quasi aque dilabimur* etc. (2 Sm 14:14).

Item, infernus propter dilationem, Abacuc II: *Ipse quasi infernus dilatauit animam suam* (Hab 2:5).

Item, mundus propter tumorem, Ps.: *Hoc mare magnum* etc. (Ps 103:25).

Item, malorum cetus propter feruorem, Ysa. LXII: *Impii quasi mare feruens* (Is 57:20).

Item, sacra scriptura propter originem ex qua omnes scripture oriuntur, Ysa. XI: *Impleta est terra scientia diuina Domini sicut aque maris operientes* (Is 11:9). Vel beata Virgo propter uirtutum plenitudinem, *Aue gratia plena,* Luc. II (Lc 1:28). De isto mare super eodem OMNIA FLUMINA ENTRANT MARE, id est omnia gratiarum fluenta, ET MARE NON REDUNDAT, id est non superbit, dixit enim: *Ecce ancilla* etc. (Lc 1:28)" (*Super Ecl.* 1:7, MSS Basel, Univ. Bibl. B III 20, f. 95rb–va; Madrid, Bibl. Nac. 493, f. 134v). Notwithstanding William's frequent borrowing from both Bonaventure and Hugh of St. Cher, he appears to be independent of both of them here.

256. The use of separate collections of distinctions for preaching has been well documented; see N. Bériou, *L'avènement des maîtres de la Parole,* vol. 1, 177–192. On the use of the biblical distinctions of postills in preaching, see M. Mulchahey, *First the Bow Is Bent,* 491–500.

257. G. Dahan has identified *nota* as a simple form or "microstructure," often employed by late-medieval exegetes to introduce a short detour from the immediate context of the literal sense, *L'exégèse chrétienne,* 129–131.

258. "Nota quod *domus luctus* est mens lugubris, lugens Dei contumelias, presentes miserias, culpas proprias et alienas.

Item, domus luctus ecclesia lugens filios suos mortuos, Iere. XXXI: *Rachel plorans filios suos.* (Mt 2, 18; cf. Ier 31, 15)

Item, incolatum huius miserie, Ps.: *Heu michi, quia incolatus m⟨eus⟩ pro⟨longatus⟩ est.* (Ps 119, 5)

Item, dilationem patrie, Ps.: *Super flumina Babilonis* etc. (Ps 136, 1)

Item, 'domus luctus' est infernus ubi *erit fletus et stridor dentium.* (cf. Mt 8, 12; 13, 42; 13, 50; 22, 13; 24, 51; 2530; 13, 28; Lc 13, 28)

Item, *domus conuiuii* est mens temere de bonis suis secura, Prouer. XV: *Secura mens quasi iuge conuiuium.* (Prv 15, 15) . . .

Item, sinagoga peccantium qui carnes aliorum conferunt ad uescendum, Mich. III: *Mordent dentibus* etc. (Mi 3, 5); Gal. V: *Si inuicem mordetis, uidete ne ab inuicem consumamini* (Gal 5, 15).

Item, mundus iste in quo mundani letantur, Ysa. XXII: *Ecce gaudium et letitia. Occidere uitulos et iugulare arietes, comedere car⟨nes⟩ et bi⟨bere⟩ ui⟨num⟩* (Is 22, 13).

Item, nota quod memoria mortis ualet ad uitanda peccata, Eccli. VII: *In omnibus operibus tuis, memorare nouissima⟨tua⟩ et in eternum non peccabis* (Sir 7, 40).

Item, ad contemnanda terrena, Ieronimus: "Facile contempnit omnia qui se semper cogitat morituri".

Item, ad domanda carnis desideria, Gregorius: "Nichil adeo ualet ad domanda carnis desideria sicut cogitare qualis sit futura mortua ad desiderandum celestia.", *Super Ecl.* 7, 3. The text is MS Madrid, Bibl. Nac. 493, f. 149v. Save for a few minor omissions, it is the same MS Basel, Univ. Bibl. B III 20, f. 104rb. In the former codex, the marginal inscription of *nota* (in this case and throughout the postill) is in the hand of the scribe; in the latter (here and throughout), it is in a posterior hand. Facile - morituri] Jerome, *Epist.* 53 (ed. Labourt, t. III, 25). Nichil - celestia] *non inuenitur apud Gregorium.*

259. "Use of the 'Spiritual' Senses of Scripture in Persuasion and Argument by Scholars in the Middle Ages", *RTAM* 52 (1985) 44–63.

260. At the outset of the prologue to his commentary on Wisdom, William clearly states such a concern, telling his students that future rectors especially ought to endeavor to study wisdom: "Inter humana enim studia precipue est studium sapientie. . . Huic precipuo studio precipui inter homines, id est aliorum, uel presidentes aliis existentes, uel futuri rectores, maxime debent intendere, id est firmiter retinendo" (*Super Sap.,* prol., MSS Paris, BnF lat. 14429, f. 155ra; 15573, f. 156ra). Elsewhere, a concern for future prelates often seems to be implied. An example appears in the following citation of Jerome, who appears to have had worldly honors in mind: "Si aliquam in mundo acciperis dignitatem, noli relinquere priora opera tua et pristina humilitatem."

(*Super Ecl.* 10, 4, MSS Basel, Univ. Bibl. B III 20, f. 109rb, Madrid, Bibl. Nac. 493, f. 158v). Cf. Jerome, *In Ecclesiasten*, x (CCSL 72, 335).

261. "*VE TIBI TERRAM ⟨CUIUS REX EST PUER ET CUIUS PRINCIPES MANE COMEDUNT⟩*. Supra dedit remedium contra inordinationem que prouenit ex prelato malo et fatuo. Hic contra inordinationem que prouenit ex prelato carnali et effeminato, ostendens talem non esse promouendum", *Super Ecl.* 10, 16, MSS Basel, Univ. Bibl. B III 20, f. 110ra, Madrid, Bibl. Nac. 493, f. 160r. Though *Super Threnos* is a fairly short commentary, it provides William the occasion to mention *prelati* no fewer than twenty–five times. These references are surveyed in the introduction to the text, ed. cit. 226.

262. Alan of Lille (d. 1203) and Peter the Chanter (d. 1197) applied the term to parish priests as well as to bishops, see N. Bériou, *L'avènement des maîtres de la Parole*, vol. I, 2, n. 4. On the other hand, R. Lerner has shown that the term was applied specifically to bishops by the team of scholars who compiled the *Postills* attributed to Hugh of St. Cher, "The Vocation of the Friars Preacher", in *Hugues de Saint-Cher, Bibliste et théologien*, ed. L.-J. Bataillon–Gilbert Dahan–P.-M. Gy, Turnhout, 2004, 218–231 (218).

263. Contemplation is often associated with preaching in thirteenth-century Dominican literature. While he was Master of the Order of Preachers, Humbert of Romans (d. 1277) took up the project of an extensive commentary on the Rule of Saint Augustine. In it he summed up the relationship between contemplation and preaching as follows: "Item, status religiosus est status contemplationis: ea vero quae praedicantur maxime colliguntur in contemplatione, juxta verbum beati Gregorii dicentis: In contemplatione hauriunt quod postmodum in praedicatione effundunt'. Probabile est ergo quod status religiosus plus habeat quod praedicari oporteat quam saecularis, quanto magis est contemplativus, et sic magis ei competit praedicatio, quia non solum per viam doctrinae, sed etiam per viam contemplationis habet quod praedicet abunde." *Expositio regulae B. Augustini*, proem., in *B. Humberti de Romanis Opera de Vita Regulari* (ed. J. Berthier, Rome, 1888, t. I, 48), cf. Gregory the Great, *Moralia in Iob*, XXVII, 24: "Aquae sunt igitur praedicatorum mentes, quae dum ad contemplanda superna se erigunt, altiori intellectu solidantur" (ed. M. Adriaen, 1981, CCSL 143B, 1363).

264. On the centrality of images to medieval preaching, see K. Rivers, *Preaching the Memory of Virtue and Vice*, esp. 73–124.

CHAPTER 4

1. See chapter 3, note 39.

2. M.-D. Chenu has called the constant recourse to *auctores* the most characteristic feature of scholasticism; *Introduction*, 106.

3. William refers to Augustine at Lm 1:22 (*Epist.* 104) and to Chrysostom at Lm 5:22, ed. cit., 252 and 281. The second borrowing is from Pseudo-Chrysostom's *Opus imperfectum in Matthaeum* (PG 56, 611–946), the authenticity of which went unquestioned at the time; cf. J. H. A. Van Banning, "Saint Thomas et l'Opus Imperfectum in Matthaeum," in *Atti dell'VIII Congresso Tomistico Internazionale* (Studi Tomistici 17), Vaticana, 1982, 73–85.

4. Ed. R. Willems, Turnhout, 1954, CCSL 36.

5. On Burgundio of Pisa's translations, see P. Classen, *Burgundio von Pisa*, Sitzungsberichte der Heidelberger Akademie der Wissenschaften, Philosophisch-historische Klasse, Jahrg. 1974, Abh. 4, Heidelberg, 1974; as well as G. Vuillemin-Diem and R. M. Rahed, "Burgundio de Pise," *Recherches de Théologie et philosophie médiévales* 64 (1997), 136–198; B. Smalley, *The Gospels in the Schools c. 1100–c. 1280*, London, 1985, I, 129–130; C. H. Haskins, *Studies in the History of Medieval Science*, 2nd ed., Cambridge, 1927, 206–209. On the history of Latin translations of Chrysostom's corpus, see J.-P. Bouhot, "Les traductions latines de Jean Chrysostome du vᵉ au xvIᵉ siècle," in *Traductions et traducteurs au Moyen Âge*, ed. G. Contamine, Paris, 1989, 31–39.

6. J. Weisheipl counted 373 citations of Augustine, 217 of Chrysostom, and 95 of Origen, in "Part I, Introduction," *Saint Thomas Aquinas, Commentary on the Gospel of St. John*, Albany, 1980, 9.

7. Though Rabanus Maurus's commentary was in all likelihood composed first, it influenced the commentatorial tradition only indirectly, by way of Paschasius's work. See A. Matter, "The Lamentations Commentaries of Hrabanus Maurus and Paschasius Radbertus," *Traditio* 38 (1982), 137–163.

8. What follows is a typical example: "*NEC HABENT ULTRA MERCEDEM*, id est locum acquirende mercedis . . . Ieronimus in originali: 'Viuentes possunt metu mortis bona opera perpetrare; mortui uero nichil ualent ad id addiscere quod semel secum tulerunt de uita'" (*Super Ecl.* 9:5, MSS Basel, Univ. Bibl. B III 20, f. 108ra; Madrid, Bibl. Nac. 493, f. 156r). Cf. Jerome, *In Ecclesiasten*, IX, 5 (CCSL 72, 323). On the history and development of this expression, see J. De Ghellinck, "Originale et originalia," in *ALMA* 16 (1939), 95–105; M.-D. Chenu, *Introduction*, 128–129.

9. Bonaventure's commentary on the Gospel of John is generally dated to his Paris regency, 1254–1257; B. Smalley, *The Gospels in the Schools*, 201–202, 205–206.

10. A case in point: "Vnde Augustinus, Ieronimus et alii sancti . . ." (*Super Ecl.* 12:12, MSS Basel, Univ. Bibl. B III 20, f. 112vb; Madrid, Bibl. Nac. 493, f. 165r).

11. E.g.: "*BETH: EDIFICAUIT IN GIRO MEO*, id est obsessio Caldeorum uel Romanorum uallauit me ne pateret fuga; *ET CIRUMDEDIT ME FELLE*, quasi dicat: in ista obsidione potatus sum aqua putrida que per fel intelligitur, Iere. IX: *Cibabo populum hunc abscinthio*; *ET LABORE*, corporis, Caldeis resistendo et etiam Romanis, ut narrat Iosephus" (*Super Threnos* 3:5, ed. cit., 261).

12. E.g.: "*DICIT EI IHESUS: MULIER CREDE MICHI*, quia discentem oportet credere, secundum Philosophum," (*Super Io.* 4:21, MS Saint-Omer, Bibl. mun. 260, f. 121rb). Cf. Aristotle, *De sophisticis elenchis*, II (165a37; trans. Boethius, *Aristoteles Latinus*, VI.1, ed. B. Dod, Bruxelles-Leiden, 1975, 7; revis. William of Moerbeke, *Aristoteles Latinus*, VI.3, ed. cit., 78).

13. For an example of Donatus appearing as an *auctoritas* on grammar, see chapter 3, note 152 .

14. C. Spicq has observed that it became common in the schools of the twelfth century for profane authors to be considered *auctoritates*, albeit inferior ones; *Esquisse*, 77.

15. "Dicit ergo *CALUMPNIA*, que scilicet est falsi criminis impositio, *CONTURBAT SAPIENTEM*, scilicet correctum. Contra, Seneca: 'Perturbatio non cadit in sapientem'; Prouer. XII: *Non contristabit iustum quicquid ei acciderit* (Prv 12:21). Responsio: Ille auctoritates loquuntur de sapiente perfecto. Hic autem loquitur de imperfecto," (*Super Ecl.* 7:8, MSS Basel, Univ. Bibl. B III 20, f. 104va; Madrid, Bibl. Nac. 493, f. 150r). Cf. Bonaventure, *In Ecl.* 7:8 (*Opera*, t. VI, 57a–b); Seneca, *Ad Lucilium*, XI, 85 (ed. F. Préchac, t. III, Paris, Les Belles Lettres, 1965, 130).

16. On the meanings of *sancti*, *magister*, and *auctoritas* and the principle of *concordia auctoritatum* for the interpretation of authoritative texts in theology and law, see M.-D. Chenu, *Introduction*, 106–118.

17. For an overview of the usage of the Fathers in medieval exegesis, see G. Dahan, "Les Pères dans l'exégèse médiévale," *RSPT* 91 (2007), 109–126; and for an account of Thomas Aquinas's conception of the authority of *doctores*, see in the same volume G. Berceville, "L'autorité des Pères selon Thomas d'Aquin," 129–143.

18. On the exegetical principle of *exponere reverenter*, with particular reference to Thomas Aquinas, see M.-D. Chenu, *Introduction*, 122–125. For a lucid criticism of his account, see the aforementioned study of G. Berceville, 138–141. In connection with an authority's "wax nose," Chenu refers to Alan of Lille, "Auctoritas cereum habet nasum, id est, diversum potest deflecti sensum," *De fide catholica*, I, 30 (PL 210, 333). See also J. De Ghellinck, *Le mouvement théologique du XIIᵉ siècle*, 2nd ed., Bruges, 1948, 233–235; J.-G. Bougerol, *Introduction à l'étude de Saint Bonaventure*, Tournai, 1961, 58–59. In his consideration of a few of the vexed questions concerning Thomas Aquinas's interpretation of Aristotle, J.-P. Torrell proposes that Thomas submitted the philosopher to an *expositio reverantialis*, which he explains as follows: "A ce

point précis Thomas se sent autorisé à se substituer à lui pour le prolonger et lui faire dire des choses à quoi il n'avait même pu penser. La reconstitution historiquement exacte de la pensée d'Aristote ne l'intéresse pas pour elle-même."See *Initiation*, 348–349. Without passing judgment on the accuracy of this remark, we will note that nothing of the sort can be said of William's handling of authoritative texts.

19. *Glossa int.*, in Io. 1:19 (ed. Rusch, vol. IV, 225a).
20. Chrysostom, *In Io. hom.*, XVI (PG 59, 103).
21. "*Tu quis es?* ut confessione ipsius Iohannis scirent quis esset, secundum *Interlin.* Vel, secundum Crisostomum, ut fateretur se esse Christum. Sciebant enim quis esset cum essent baptizati ab ipso, Luc. I (3:16)"; (*Super Io.* 1:19, MS Saint-Omer, Bibl. mun. 260, f. 113vb). Cf. *Glossa int.*, in Io. 1:19 (ed. Rusch, vol. IV, 225a); Chrysostom, *In Io. hom.*, XVI (PG 59, 103).
22. Hugh of St. Cher, *Postille*, in Io. 3:8 (ed. Venetiis, t. VI, 296va).
23. Albert the Great, *In Io.* 3:8 (ed. Borgnet, t. XXIV, 122a–b).
24. Thomas Aquinas, *Super Io.* 3:8 (ed. Parma, t. X, 346a–b).
25. Bonaventure, *In Io. com.* 3:8 (*Opera*, t. VI, 281b).
26. "*Spiritus ubi uult spirat*, Crisostomus exponit de uento qui dicitur spirare ubi uult, quia habet a natura alationem non prohibitam; uox eius dicitur sonus. Augustinus tamen huic expositioni contradicit: *Spiritus ubi uult spirat*, quia habet in potestate cuius cor illustret" (*Super Io.* 3:8, MS Saint-Omer, Bibl. mun. 260, f. 117va). Cf. Chrysostom, *In Io. hom.*, XXVI (PG 59, 155); Augustine, *In Io. evang. tract.*, XII (CCSL 36, 124).
27. "*Sequebatur autem*, inquit, *Iesum Simon Petrus, et alius discipulus*. Quisnam iste sit discipulus, non temere affirmandum est, quia tacetur. Solet autem se idem Iohannes ita significare, et addere: *quem diligebat Iesus*" (Augustine, *In Io. evang. tract.*, CXIII, CCSL 36, 636).
28. "Quis est alius discipulus? Ipse qui hec scripsit et cuius gratia enim non dixit" (Chrysostom, *In Io. hom.*, LXXXIII, MS Vat. Ottob. lat. 227, f. 146rb; cf. PG 59, 449).
29. "Quis sit iste, quia hec tacetur non temere diffiniatur. Solet tamen iste Iohannes sic se significare" (*Glossa mg.*, in Io. 18:15, ed. Rusch, vol. IV, 265a).
30. "Quis iste fuerit, Glossa non definivit. Videtur tamen fuisse Ioannes, ut dicit Victor, qui de se ut de alio loquebatur, quasi non timens" (Bonaventure, *In Io. com.* 18:15, *Opera*, t. VI, 482a). On Victor, see B. Smalley, *The Gospels in the Schools*, 155–158.
31. "*Et alius discipulus*: ut dicit Chrysostomus, Joannes, qui de se ut de alio loquitur" (Albert the Great, *In Io.* 18:15, ed. Borgnet, t. XXIV, 633b).
32. "Dicit ergo quantum ad primum: *Sequebatur autem Jesum Simon Petrus*, ex devotione, quamvis a longe propter timorem, *et alius discipulus*, scilicet Joannes, cuius nomen ipsemet occultat humilitatis gratia" (Thomas Aquinas, *Super Io.* 18:15, ed. Parma, t. X, 605b).
33. "*Et alius discipulus*. *Interlin.*, Augustinus: 'Quis iste sit non temere diffiniatur.' Dicit tamen Crisostomus aperte quod fuit Iohannes, tamen causa humilitatis nomen suum tacet" (*Super Io.* 18:15, MS Saint-Omer, Bibl. mun. 260, f. 166ra). Cf. *Glossa mg.*, in Io. 18:15 (ed. Rusch, vol. IV, 265a); Augustine, *In Io. evang. tract.*, CXIII (CCSL 36, 636); Chrysostom, *In Io. hom.*, LXXXIII (PG 59, 450).
34. Hugh of St. Cher, *Postille*, in Io. 4:20 (ed. Venetiis, t. VI, 306va).
35. Albert the Great, *In Io.* 4:20 (ed. Borgnet, t. XXIV, 168b).
36. Thomas Aquinas, *Super Io.* 4:35 (ed. Parma, t. X, 366a).
37. "*Patres Nostri*, scilicet Habraham, Ysaac et Iacob, *in monte hoc adora⟨uerunt⟩*. Secundum aliquos, quibus uidetur consentire Crisostomus, mulier ostendit montem in quo Habraham uoluit immolare filium. Set hoc falsum est, quia iste fuit mons Moria, ut patet Gen. XXII (Gn 22, 14)" (*Super Io.* 4:20, MS Saint-Omer, Bibl. mun. 260, f. 121rb). Cf. Chrysostom, *In Io. hom.*, XXXII (PG 59, 186).
38. Jerome, *Hebraicae Quaestiones in Genesim*, ed. P. de Lagarde, Turnhout, 1959, CCSL 72, 26; *In Hieremiam prophetam libri vi*, V, ed. S. Reiter, Turnhout, 1960, CCSL 74, 255.
39. Such is the understanding of *auctoritas*, which M.-D. Chenu contrasts with the sayings of masters (*dicta magistrali*), which could be set aside without scruple; *Introduction*, 115.

40. "*Maria autem erat que unxit Dominum unguent⟨o⟩ et exter⟨sit⟩ pedes eius cap⟨illis⟩ ⟨suis⟩*, infra xii (12:3) et Mt. xxvi, *cuius frater Lazarus infirmabatur*. Queritur utrum ista sit illa de qua Mt. xxvi (26:7) et Luc. vii (7:37). Crisostomus, 'Primum quidem illud necessarium est dicere quoniam non hec fuit meretrix que in Mt. xxvi, neque in Luc. vii. Ille enim plene mali. Hec studiosa et honesta.' Ergo secundum istum fuerunt tres. Ieronimus supra Mt. dicit: 'Nemo putes easdem esse que super capud effundit unguentum et que super pedes. Illa enim et lacrimis lauit et crine tersit et manifeste meretrix appellatur. De hac autem nichil tale scriptum est.' Et ita secundum Ieronimum sunt due. Item, ista de qua Luc. vii dicitur Magdalena a Magdala castro. Hec de Bethania. Contra, *Glossa*: 'Hec peccatrix iunxit' etc. Et fere idem, Mt. xxvi in *Glossa* et in *Glossa* super Luc. vii: *Maria soror* etc. Augustinus uidetur dubitare dicens: 'Ecce ipsa soror Lazari, si tamen ipsa est que pedes Domini ⟨unxit unguento⟩ et tersit capillis. . . .' Responsio: Dicendum quod sancti in talibus que pertinent ad factum bene possunt dissentire, set in hiis que pertinent ad fidem non. Ecclesia tamen tenet quod eadem fuit et quod dicunt Ieronimus et Crisostomus non esse illam, intelligendum est quantum ad ydemptitatem status, quia mutata fuit in alterum statum" (*Super Io.* 11:2, MS Saint-Omer, Bibl. mun. 260, f. 143ra). Cf. Chrysostom, *In Io. hom.*, LXII (PG 59, 342); MS Vat. ottob. lat. 227, f. 108vb: "Igitur quidem illud necessarium dicere: quoniam non hec fuit meretrix que in Matheo uel in Luca. Alia enim hec. Nam ille quidem meretrices mulieres fuerunt et multis plene malis. Hec autem honesta et studiosa"; Jerome, *In Mt.*, IV (CCSL 77, 246); *Glossa mg.*, in Io. 12:3 (ed. Rusch, vol. IV, 253a): "Maria quae olim poenitens unxit pedes"; *Glossa mg.*, in Mt 26:7 (ed. Rusch, vol. IV. 79a); *Glossa mg.*, in Lc 7:37 (ed. Rusch, vol. IV, 167b); Augustine: "ecce ipsa soror Lazari, si tamen ipsa est quae pedes Domini unxit unguento, et tersit capillis suis quos lauerat lacrymis" (*In Io. evang. tract.*, XLIX, CCSL 36, 421).

41. See chapter 3 note 222.

42. *Homiliarum euangelii libri ii*, II, 4 (CCSL 122, 209–210).

43. The conflation of the three figures stands as another example of liturgical influence upon biblical exegesis. Before William's time and during it, Mary Magdalene was identified with the "sinner" of Luke 7:36–50 and with the sister of Martha and Lazarus of Luke 10:38–42 and John 11 in preaching and the liturgy of her feast day. See N. Bériou, "La Madeleine dans les sermons parisiens du xiii^e siècle," in *La Madeleine (viii^e au xiii^e siècle)*, MEFRM 104, no. 1 (1992), 269–284 (= *Modern Questions about Medieval Sermons. Essays on Marriage, Death, History and Sanctity*, ed. N. Bériou and D. d'Avray, Spoleto, 1994, 323–399). There is an abundant literature on the development of medieval devotion to Mary Magdalene. In addition to the other collected essays in *La Madeleine*, see V. Saxer, *Le culte de Marie Madeleine en occident des origines à la fin du moyen-âge*, 2 vols. (Cahiers d'archéologie et d'histoire, 3), Auxerre-Paris, 1959; K. Jansen, *The Making of the Magdalene: Preaching and Popular Devotion in the Later Middle Ages*, Princeton, 2000. For a brief overview with extensive bibliography, see P.-M. Guillaume, "Marie-Madeleine," *Dict Sp*, 1980, 559–575.

44. "Quod autem Chrysostomus sentit contrarium, dicendum, quod non est inconveniens, expositores contraria sentire, maxime in nominibus personarum, quia non est ibi vis" (Bonaventure, *In Io. com.* 2:2, *Opera*, t. VI, 272a); cf. B. Smalley, *The Gospels in the Schools*, 210.

45. "Et hanc sententiam tota tenet occidentalis Ecclesia" (Albert the Great, *In Io.* 11:2, ed. Borgnet, t. XXIV, 436a).

46. "Secundum ergo opinionem Augustini manifestum est quod peccatrix illa de qua dicitur in Luca, est Maria ista" (Thomas Aquinas, *Super Io.* 11:2, ed. Parma, t. X, 489a). Elsewhere, Thomas often invokes the church's opinion as authoritative. What follows are a few examples drawn only from his biblical commentaries: "Manifestum est autem ex praemissis quod apud Iob et amicos eius eadem erat opinio de Daemonibus quam nunc ecclesia catholica tenet, ut scilicet ex angelica dignitate per peccatum corruerint . . ."(*Super Iob*, 40:10, ed. Leonina, t. XXVI, 215b); "Item error quorumdam dicentium, Ioseph ex alia coniuge filios

genuisse, et hos vocari fratres Domini, quod ecclesia non tenet" (*Super Io.* 2:12, ed. Parma, t. X, 336a). The following two examples concern the aforementioned dating of Jesus' baptism (see chapter 3, note 221):"Sed ista opinio non videtur vera pro tanto, quia non concordat opinioni ecclesiae: tenet enim ecclesia, quod tria miracula sint facta in die epiphaniae, scilicet de adoratione magorum, de baptismo et de conversione aquae in vinum" (*Super Mt.* 4:12, ed. Parma, t. X, 42a–b); "Sed Ecclesia tenet contrarium. Credimus enim quod eodem die quo Dominus baptizatus est, revoluto anno, factum fuerit miraculum de vino; et postea revoluto anno, prope Pascha, Joannes fuerit decollatus; et quod ab isto Paschate circa quod Joannes fuit decollatus" (*Super Io.* 2:2, ed. Parma, t. X, 336a). For the last reference, I am indebted to G. Berceville, "Les commentaires évangéliques de Thomas d'Aquin et Hugues de Saint-Cher," 189, n. 23.

47. The work is so entitled in the edition employed for this study, *Biblia Latina cum Glossa Ordinaria*, ed. A. Rusch, Strasbourg, 1480/81 (reprinted, 4 vols., Turnhout, 1992), as well as in the *Bibliae cum Glossa Ordinaria*, Anvers, 1634.

48. What follows are a few particularly valuable studies within the extensive literature on the matter: M. Zier, "The Development of the Glossa Ordinaria to the Bible in the Thirteenth Century," in *La bibbia del XIII secolo*, 155–184; G. Mazzanti, "Anselmo di Laon, Gilberto l'Universale e la Glossa ordinaria alla Bibbia," *Bullettino dell'Istituto Storico Italiano per il Medio Evo* 102 (1999), 1–18; M. Gibson, *The Bible in the Latin West*, Notre Dame, IN, 1993, 9–10, 52, 56, 60, and "The Glossed Bible," in *Biblia Latina cum Glossa Ordinaria* (facsimile reprint of the edition of A. Rusch, Strasbourg, 1480–81), Turnhout, 1992, vol. 1, 1992, vii–xi; G. Lobrichon, "Une nouveauté: les gloses de la Bible," in *Le Moyen Age et la Bible*, ed. P. Riché and G. Lobrichon (Bible de tous les temps, 4), Paris, 1984, 95–114 (= *La Bible au Moyen Age*, Paris, 1984, ch. 10, 158–172); B. Smalley, *The Study of the Bible*, 56–66; "Gilbertus Universalis, Bishop of London (1128–1134) and the Problem of the *Glossa ordinaria*," *RTAM* 8 (1936), 24–60.

49. Recent scholarship warns against differentiating too sharply between monastic and scholastic exegesis. Still, J. Leclercq's comparison of the two remains valuable, *Initiation aux auteurs monastiques*, 179–218.

50. For an overview of the sources of the *Glossa ordinaria* for the Bible's diverse books, see A. Matter, "The Church Fathers and the *Glossa Ordinaria*," in *The Reception of the Church Fathers in the West: From the Carolingians to the Maurists*, ed. Irena Backus, 2 vols., Leiden, 1997, vol. 1, 83–111. On the development of the Lamentations section of the *Glossa ordinaria*, see A. Andree, *Gilbertus Universalis: Glossa Ordinaria in Lamentationes Ieremie Prophete*, Stockholm, 2005, 18–35.

51. For my remarks on the *Glossa orindaria* on John's Gospel, as well as my references to literature concerning its sources, I am indebted to the recent study of A. Andrée, "The *Glossa ordinaria* on the Gospel of John: A Preliminary Survey of the Manuscripts with a Presentation of the Text and Its Sources" (*à suivre*), *Revue bénédictine* 118 (2008), 109–134. Responsibility for any errors in the application of his findings is entirely mine.

52. On the authority of the *Glossa ordinaria*, see G. Lobrichon, "Une nouveauté: les gloses de la Bible," 96–97 (= *La Bible au Moyen Age*, 158–160).

53. "*DICIT EI MULIER ILLA SAMARITANA*, improperando, secundum Crisostomum, quia Iudei Samaritanis erant odiosi, *QUOMODO IUDEUS CUM SIS*, cognouit eum per fimbrias uestimentorum, secundum Crisostomum, de quibus Numer. ⟨xv⟩ (15, 28), *A ME BIBERE POSCIS QUE SUM MULIER SA⟨MARITANA⟩? NON ENIM COU⟨TUNTUR⟩ IUDEI ⟨CUM⟩ SA⟨MARITANIS⟩*. Secundum Crisostomum, uerbum est mulieris. Secundum *Glossam*, uerbum Euangeliste," (*Super Io.* 4:9, MS Saint-Omer, Bibl. mun. 260, f. 120va). Cf. Chrysostom, *In Io. hom.*, XXXI (PG 59, 180); *Glossa int.*, in Io. 3:9 (ed. Rusch, vol. IV, 232b).

54. "*Non enim coutuntur Judaei cum Samaritanis*. Cui Dominus dixit . . ." (Alcuin, *Comm. in s. Io. Evang.*, PL 100, 795). Augustine does not address the question of the remark's source: "*Non enim coutuntur Iudaei Samaritanis*. Videtis alienigenas: omnino uasculis eorum Iudaei non utebantur" (*In Io. evang. tract.*, XV, CCSL 36, 154).

55. "*AMEN, AMEN, dico ⟨UOBIS⟩: QUI NON INTRAT PER HOSTIUM*, id est me . . . *IN OUILE OUIUM . . . SET ASCENDIT ALIUNDE . . . ILLE FUR EST ET LATRO* . . . Contra: Mercenarius non intrat per Christum, et tamen non est fur, quia ille est tollerandus, iste non, secundum *Glossam* infra (10, 12). Responsio: Fur sumitur large hic pro eo qui querit commodum proprium, non tamen docet peruerse. Infra dicitur fur, ubi dicitur quod non est tollerandus, qui proprium commodum querit et doctrinam peruertit," (*Super Io.* 10:1, MS Saint-Omer, Bibl. mun. 260, f. 140ra). Cf. *Glossa mg.*, in Io. 10:12 (ed. Rusch, vol. IV, 249b). The entire discussion is dependent on Augustine: "Diligendus est pastor, tolerandus est mercenarius, cauendus est latro" (*Sermones*, CXXXVII, 5, PL 38, 757).

56. The *questiones* medieval exegetes put forward were not normally "rhetorical questions" properly understood as queries to which no answers are expected in response. Here the term *rhetorical* means "expressed in terms intended to persuade or impress." This meaning has been given by the *Oxford English Dictionary*, Oxford, 2008.

57. No such gloss, either interlinear or marginal, appears in the Rusch edition, cf. *Glossa ord.*, in Is. 38:11 (ed. Rusch, vol. III, 60a).

58. "Quod autem dicit *Glossa*, infra XXXVIII, dicendum quod magistralis est" (*Super Is.* 6:1, MS Madrid, Bibl. Nac. 493, f. 179v). A similar case appears in the exegesis of Thomas Aquinas, *Super I ad Thim.* 5:9 (ed. Parma, t. XIIII, 610a), for a discussion of which, see M.-D. Chenu, *Introduction*, 115.

59. "*PRECESSI SAPIENTIA OMNES QUI FUERUNT ANTE ME IN IEROSALEM.* . . . Et intelligitur de 'sapientia' prout dicit nudam rerum cognitionem que parum prodest. Vnde Richardus super Danielem: 'Scientia sola sine sanctitatis affectum, quid aliud est quam simulacrum uanum sine motu et sensu?'" (*Super Ecl.* 1:16, MSS Basel, Univ. Bibl. B III 20, f. 96rb; Madrid, Bibl. Nac. 493, f. 135v–136r).

60. Cf. M.-D. Chenu, *Introduction*, 115.

61. Throughout the Middle Ages, exegetes referred to various *moderni*. The following example has been provided by Bede: "Obstipuerunt antiqui electi obstupescunt et moderni quoties mente simplici excipiunt. . ." (*In primam partem Samuhelis*, III, 21, ed. D. Hurst, 1962, CCSL 119, 193). Still, during William's time, the term was used to refer specifically to contemporary university masters, though not necessarily of the faculty of theology. What follows is a case in point provided by Thomas Aquinas: "Alia est opinio Aristotelis quam omnes moderni sequuntur, quod anima unitur corpori sicut forma materiae: unde anima est pars humanae naturae, et non natura quaedam per se" (*In III Sent.*, d. 5, q. 3, a. 2c, ed. Parma, t. VII/A, 73b). Cf. M.-D. Chenu, *Introduction*, 116; "*Antiqui, Moderni*. Notes de lexicographie médiévale," *RSPT* 17 (1928), 82–94.

62. Hugh of St. Cher (d. 1263) was provincial of the Province of France during the periods 1227–1230 and 1236–1244. He became the titular cardinal of Santa Sabina in 1244.

63. Bonaventure (d. 1274), born Giovanni di Fidanza, became minister general of the Franciscans in 1257. In 1271, he was instrumental in the election of Gregory X to the papacy, and in 1273, he became Cardinal Bishop of Albano.

64. Bonaventure's borrowing from Hugh of St. Cher has been well documented; see the following studies of R. Karris: "St. Bonaventure's Use of Distinctions," *Franciscan Studies* 60 (2002), 209–244; "Bonaventure's Commentary on Luke: Four Case Studies of His Creative Borrowing from Hugh of St. Cher," *Franciscan Studies* 59 (2001), 133–236; and "A Comparison of the Glossa Ordinaria, Hugh of St. Cher, and St. Bonaventure on Luke 8:26–39," *Franciscan Studies* 58 (2000), 121–236. See also B. Smalley, *The Gospels in the Schools*, 206–210; *The Study of the Bible*, 273; and C. Van Den Borne, "De fontibus Commentarii S. Bonaventurae in Ecclesiasten," *AFP* 10 (1917), 257–270. On Thomas Aquinas's borrowing from Hugh for his *Catana Aurea* and his commentaries on Matthew and John, see the aforementioned study of G. Berceville, "Les commentaires évangéliques de Thomas d'Aquin et Hugues de Saint-Cher."

65. William's use of the postills of Bonaventure and Hugh on Ecclesiastes has been shown by B. Smalley, "Sapiential Books I," 71–75.

66. On Hugh's place in the evolution of thirteenth-century exegesis, see G. Dahan, "Genres, Forms and Various Methods," 211, and "L'Exégèse de Hugues. Méthode et herméneutique," in *Hugues de Saint-Cher, Bibliste et théologien*, ed. L.-J. Bataillon, Gilbert Dahan, and P.-M. Gy, Turnhout, 2004, 65–99. For detailed accounts of the *Postille in totam Bibliam*'s manuscript tradition and editions, see in the same volume, P. Stirnemann, "Les manuscrits de la *Postille*," and B. Carra De Vaux, "La constitution du corpus exégétique," 43–63; see also *SOPMA*, vol. 2, 275, n. 1989. Still well worth consulting are the observations of B. Smalley, *The Gospels in the Schools*, 124–143; *The Study of the Bible*, 272–274; and J. Verger, "L' exégèse de l'Université," 203. On thirteenth-century efforts to supplement the *Glossa ordinaria*, see G. R. Evans, "Gloss or Analysis? A Crisis of Exegetical Method in the Thirteenth Century," in *La Bibbia del XIII Secolo*," 93–111.

67. R. Lerner, "The Vocation of the Friars Preacher," in *Hugues de Saint-Cher, Bibliste et théologien*, ed. L.-J. Bataillon, Gilbert Dahan, and P.-M. Gy, Turnhout, 2004, 215–231 (216).

68. Late in her career, B. Smalley remarked of Bonaventure's biblical exegesis, "Much has been written on his theories about the nature of Scripture and on his principles of exegesis, but very little on his actual surviving commentaries on Ecclesiastes, St. Luke and St. John"; *The Gospels in the Schools*, 203. In the same work (201–213), she provided an account of his exegesis that did much to remedy the situation. For an overview that remains valuable, see J.-G. Bougerol, *Introduction à Saint Bonaventure*, 161–185. Other important contributions appear in the aforementioned studies of R. Karris (see note 64). On Bonaventure's commentary on Ecclesiastes, see the aforementioned study of G. Dahan, "L'Ecclésiaste contre Aristote?"

69. In the event of a discovery of a postill on Luke by William, as ascribed to him in the fourteenth-century catalogue of the Franciscan convent of Todi (see chapter 1, note 20), we would expect to find in it a heavy dependence on Bonaventure's postill on this book.

70. A commentary on Lamentations (*Rep. Bibl.* 1775) was printed under Bonaventure's name in 1574 by Joannes Balainius, O.F.M. Conv., in Venice, and subsequently in the Vatican edition of his *Opera omnia* (1588–1596). It is no longer generally included among his works. For their more recent edition of his *Opera omnia* (1882–1902), the editors of Quaracchi rejected its authenticity (*Opera*, t. VII, xi–xiv), but in a nod to the printed tradition, printed it in an *Appendix duorum opusculorum saltem dubiorum* (*Opera*, t. VII, 607–651). John Peckam's authorship of this work has been established; cf. B. Distelbrink, *Bonaventurae Scripta. Authentica Dubia Vel Spuria Critice Recensita*, Roma, Cura Instituti Historici Capuccini, 1975, 169.

71. "Dicit ergo: *HANC QUOQUE SUB SOLE UIDI* per experientiam cognitionis *SAPIENTIAM*, hanc scilicet que sequitur, et *PROBAUI MAXIMAM*, **quia sapientia magna est in uincendo inimicum inferiorem, maior in uincendo equalem, maxima in uincendo fortiorem, de qua hic.** Vel magna est qua uincitur mundus; maior qua carnalis appetitus, quia propinquior est inimicus; maxima qua Diabolus"; (*Super Ecl.* 9:13, MSS Basel, Univ. Bibl. B III 20, f. 108vb; Madrid, Bibl. Nac. 493, f. 157v). Cf. Bonaventure, *In Ecl.* 9:13 (*Opera*, t. VI, 77b).

72. For an account of the provenance and development of this theme, see S. Wenzel, "The Three Enemies of Man," *MS* 29 (1967), 47–66. For discussions and examples of its use in thirteenth-century preaching, see N. Bériou, *L'avènement des maîtres de la Parole*, vol. 1, 261, 286, 323, 351, 394, 409, 428, 567. Another example in William's exegesis appears in *Super Threnos* 1:16: "Moraliter. Anima peccatrix uel penitens plorat pro malorum commissione et bonorum omissione, *QUIA LONGE FACTUS EST CONSO⟨LATOR⟩*, id est Spiritus Sanctus in statu culpe. *FACTI SUNT FILII SUI PERDITI*, id est bona opera, *QUONIAM INUALUIT INIMICUS*, id est diabolus, caro uel mundus ad peccatum attraxit" (ed. cit., 249).

73. Table 4.4  Io 1:42: *et adduxit eum ad Iesum intuitus autem eum Iesus dixit tu es Simon filius Iohanna tu vocaberis Cephas quod interpretatur Petrus.*

| Hugh of St. Cher (ed. Venetiis, t. VI, 288va) | Bonaventure (*Opera*, t. VI, 264b–65a) | William of Alton (MS Saint-Omer, Bibl. mun. 260, f. 115ra) |
|---|---|---|
| Sed quaeritur, quare Dominus isti mutat nomen potius quam Andrae, vel alicui alii? Ad quod respondendum est, quod nominis mutatio est signum mutationis quae circa ipsum Petrum futura erat. Futura enim erat Princeps Apostolorum, quod non alii. Unde et adhuc in ordinatione Papae mutatur ei nomen, quod non fit aliis Episcopis. | Item queritur: Quare Dominus imposuit nomen Petro in sui vocatione magis quam aliis? Videtur quod acceptor fuerit personae, quia dignitatem nominis contulit sine merito. . . . Ad hoc respondendum quod Deus videt non solum exteriora, sed etiam interiora; non solum quae sunt, sed quae futura sunt: in signum ergo, quod erat futurus pastor Ecclesiae, nomen ei imponitur. . . . Quare modo nomina non mutantur his qui religionem ingrediuntur, vel etiam his qui convertuntur ad Christum? Ad hoc respondet Chrysostomus, quod mutatio nominis fiebat in virtutum incitamentum. Quoniam igitur modo nomen unum habemus, quod maxime est ad virtutem incitativum; ideo illo nomine contenti esse debemus; et hoc nomen est christianitatis, quia omnes dicimur Christiani. Tamen adhuc servat mutationem nominis Romana Ecclesia in summo Pontifice. | **Queritur quare nomen eius mutauerit.** Responsio, Crisostomus: Ad significandum quod condidit uetus testamentum, in quo nomina aliquorum antiquorum mutabantur, sicut Abraham, quod fecit propter excellentiam gratie quam tales erant accepturi. **Magis autem mutauit nomen Petri quam Andree, quia excellentiam erat habiturus maiorem. Vnde adhuc nomen pape mutatur.** Non mutantur autem nomina sanctorum modo sicut in ueteri testamento, secundum Crisostomum, quia omnes unum nomen habemus excellens quo filii Dei nominamur. |

74. Table 4.5

| Bonaventure (*Opera*, t. VI, 344a–b) | William of Alton (MS Saint-Omer, Bibl. mun. 260, f. 131vb) |
|---|---|
| *Mea doctrina non est mea.* Quia removetur a se, et ideo falsa videtur. Respondet Chrysostomus, **quod doctrinam suam non esse a se inventam, sed a Patre esse; unde sensus est: mea doctrina, scilicet quam doceo, non est mea, sed a Patre est.** Et in hoc satisfacit questioni eorum, mittendo eos ad Patrem, et sedat eorum furorem per humilitatem, unde sua erat doctrina, quia est ipsa sapientia per essentiam; sed non suam esse dicebat, quia ab alio accepit. . . . Sed non erat discretive Christi solius, quia et haec eadem erat Patris, et etiam haec eadem erat a Patre. | MEA DOCTRINA NON EST MEA. Hic idem remouetur a se. Ergo locutio falsa. Responsio: Fuit sua formaliter et effectiue, set auctoritate prima non est sua, set Patris, et in hoc satisfacit questioni eorum, mittens ad Patrem, et sedat furorem per humilitatem. Dixit autem Christus quod esset ipsa sapientia Patris et quod ab alio habuit, **ostendens se esse ab alio. Item, ut ostenderet se Deo non esse contrarium. Item, ut ostenderet se hominem uerum. Item, propter imbecillitatem audientium. Item, ad docendum humilitatem. Tamen, infra viii: *Antequam Abraham* etc. (Io 8:58), loquebatur de se alta ut ostenderet nature sue altitudinem.** Vel NON EST MEA, id est ad gloriam uanam. Vel MEA, scilicet discretiue, id est mei solius. SET EIUS QUI MISIT ME, id est Patris, uel a Patre, supra v: *Non possum a meipso facere quicquam* (Io 5:30). |

75. "*Sap. 8. Attingit a fine usque ad finem fortiter, et disponit omnia suaviter*," ed. Venetiis, t. VI, 283vb.
76. "*Sap.* VII: *Attingit ubique propter sui mun⟨ditiam⟩*," (MS Saint-Omer, Bibl. mun. 260, f. 112vb).
77. "1 Joan. 5: *Omne, quod natum est ex Deo, vincit mundum*," ed. Venetiis, t. VI, 284vb.
78. "1 Io. ultimo: *Qui natus est ex Deo credit quia Ihesus est Filius Dei*," (MS Saint-Omer, Bibl. mun. 260, f. 113ra).

79. Table 4.6 Io 10:3: *huic ostiarius aperit et oves vocem eius audiunt et proprias oves vocat nominatim et educit eas.*

| Bonaventure (*Opera*, t. VI, 383b–384a) | William of Alton (MS Saint-Omer, Bibl. mun. 260, f. 140rb) |
|---|---|
| *Huic ostiarius aperit.* . . . Ostiarius iste est Christus, qui habet clavem; unde Isaiae vigesimo secundo: "Dabo clavem domus David super humerum eius; et aperiet, et non erit qui claudat; et non erit qui aperiat" (Is 22:22). *Et oves vocem eius audiunt,* quia bono pastori libenter obediunt; ad Hebraeos ultimo: "Obedite praepositis vestris et subiacete eis; ipsi enim pervigilant, quasi rationem pro animabus vestris reddituri" (Hbr 13:17). . . . *Et proprias oves vocat nominatim,* scilicet Christus; secundae ad Timotheum secundo: "Novit Dominus, qui sunt eius" (2 Tim 2:19), et *de eius imitatione;* Proverbiorum duodecimo: "Novit iustus animas iumentorum suorum" (Prv 12:10). *Et educit eas,* ad pascua, scilicet Christus; Ezechielis trigesimo quarto: "Educam eos de populis et congregabo eos de terris et inducam in terram suam" (Ez 20:38), quae scilicet erat lacte manans. Sic et *imitator Christi,* ut Moyses et Aaron; Psalmus: "Deduxisti sicut oves populum tuum in manu Moysi et Aaron" (Ps 76:21). | ³*HUIC OSTIARIUS*, id est Christus qui habet clauem, Ysa. XXII (cf. Is 22:22), *APERIT*, in curam regiminis introducendo, Heb. V: *Nemo sumit sibi honorem* (Hbr 5:4). Vel *APERIT*, sibi intelligentia scripturarum. Vel corda auditorum, ut sibi obtemperent. *ET OUES UOCEM EIUS AUDIUNT*, preceptis, monitis et consiliis eius libenter obediendo, argumentum quod non debet tacere, Exo. XXXVI, in ueste pontificis erant tintinabula, ne sine sonitu intrans tabernaculum moreretur, Eze. III: *Nisi annuntiaueris ei* etc. (Ez 3:18); II Thi. IIII: *Predica uerbum* (2 Tim 4:2). . . . ³*ET PROPRIAS OUES ⟨UOCAT⟩ NOMINATIM.* Hec uocatio nichil aliud est cognitio qua suos distinguit ab aliis per administrationem sacrementorum, predicationum, uisitationum et consilium, Prouer. XVII: *Diligenter agnosce uultum peccoris t⟨ui⟩;*(Prv 27:23); et XXI: *Nouit iustus animas iumentorum suorum* (Prv 12:10). *ET EDUC⟨IT⟩ EAS, de tenebris et umbra mortis; de tenebris ignorantie et culpe,* Exo. III: *Mittam te ut educas populum m⟨eum⟩ de Egipto* (Ex 3:10). |

80. "*OMNE QUOD DAT MICHI PATER*, per eternam electionem et temporalem uocationem, utpote **gratiam infundendo, quod dicitur de Patre, quia apud eum residet auctoritas, licet tota Trinitas gratiam infundat,** Ps.: *Dabo tibi gentes hereditatem* (Ps 2:8); *AD ME UENIET* per fidem et dilectionem. Patris est dare gratiam primam infundendo, credentium uenire gratie cooperando. Bonum opus est a Deo principaliter mouenti, a libero arbitrio tanquam ab eliciente, a gratia liberum arbitrium disponente" (*Super Io.* 6:37, MS Saint-Omer, Bibl. mun. 260, f. 128va). Cf. Bonaventure, *In Io. com.* 6:37 (*Opera*, t. VI, 328a); Hugh of St. Cher, *Postille*, in Io. 6:37 (ed. Venetiis, t. VI, 327va–vb).

81. Cf. M.-D. Chenu, *Introduction*, 115.

82. M.-D. Chenu, *Introduction*, 115. See also C. Geenen, "Saint Thomas et les Pères," *DTC* 15.1 (1946), 738–761 (744–745).

83. "*ET ERAT QUIDAM REGULUS.* . . . Secundum Crisostomum, non fuit ille centurio, ut quidam uolunt, de quo Mt. VIII (8:5) quia ille noluit ut Christus iret in domum suam. Iste (est *S*) sic. Item, iste filius, ille seruus" (*Super Io.* 4:46, MS Saint-Omer, Bibl. mun. 260, f. 123ra).

84. "Igitur quidam quidem hunc illum esse extimat que apud Mathaeum, ostenditur autem alius esse ab eo" (Chrysostom, *In Io. Hom.* XXXV, MS Vat. Ottob. lat. 227, f. 60ra; cf. PG 59, 201).

85. Cf. Augustine, *In Io. evang. tract.*, XVI (CCSL 36, 168).
86. Textual critics generally consider this verse a later addition. Though included in the Clementine edition, it is omitted by the edition of Weber, as well as by most modern translations.
87. "*ANGELUS AUTEM DOMINI SECUNDUM TEMPUS . . . DESCENDEBAT IN PISCINAM . . . ET MOUEBATUR AQUA . . . ET QUI PRIOR DESCEN⟨DISSET⟩ IN PISCINAM POST MO⟨TIONEM⟩ AQUE SANUS FIEBAT A QUA⟨CUMQUE⟩ DETI⟨NEBATUR⟩ INFIRMITATE*. Nota, quidam dicunt quod hec uirtus sic sanandi fuit per quoddam lignum unde postea facta est crux quod erat in illa aqua" (*Super Io.* 5:4, MS Saint-Omer, Bibl. mun. 260, f. 123va).
88. "Respondent quidam, quod in piscina illa erat lignum crucis, quod tunc temporis coepit apparere et supernatare. . . . Sed quia hoc de Scripturis auctoritatem non habet, eadem ratione, qua probatur, destruitur" (Bonaventure, *In Io. com.* 5:4, *Opera*, t. VI, 305a–b).
89. "Tradunt autem quidam, sed non est authenticum, quod Regina Saba vidit in spiritu. . ." (Hugh of St. Cher, *Postille*, in Io. 5:4, ed. Venetiis, t. VI, 312va–vb).
90. Apparently the source of the others, Peter's version is the most elaborate. According to it, the Queen of Sheba saw the wood of the Cross in a vision and told Solomon that someone would die on it and thus bring about the destruction of the Jews. As the story goes, Solomon buried it out of fear in a spot where a pool subsequently appeared, and as the time of Christ's Passion approached, the wood foretold the event by floating upon the waters and stirring them up: "Traditur a quibusdam. . . . Sed non est authenticum" (Peter Comestor, *Hist. schol.*, In Evang., 81, PL 198, 1579).
91. Once again, we use the adjective *rhetorical* to mean intended to persuade or impress. See note 56.
92. On *nota*, see G. Dahan, *L'exégèse chrétienne*, 129–131.
93. "*MARE AUTEM . . . FLANTE MAGNO UENTO EXURGEBAT . . . CUM REMIGASSENT ERGO QUASI STA⟨DIA⟩ UIGINTI QUINQUE AUT TRIGINTA . . . UIDE⟨N⟩T IHESUM AM⟨BULANTEM⟩ SUPRA MA⟨RE⟩. . . .* Dicunt quidam quod idem fuit istud miraculum cum illo, de quo Mt. XIIII (14:26), set Iohannes non omnia ponit. Alii dicunt quod aliud, quod ibi non cessauit tempestas nisi post uocem Christi, hic statim; ibi etiam narratur quod Petrus fere fuit submersus, hic non" (*Super Io.* 6:18–19, MS Saint-Omer, Bibl. mun. 260, f. 127rb).
94. Hugh of St. Cher, *Postille*, in Io. 6:19 (ed. Venetiis, t. VI, 325va); Peter Comestor, *Hist. schol.*, In Evang., 74–75 (PL 198, 1575–1576); Augustine, *De consensu evang.*, II, 47 (CSEL 43, 209).
95. Chrysostom, *In Io. hom.*, XLIII (PG 59, 245–246).
96. There are no early witnesses to Thomas's authorship of this work, inc.: *Ecce manus missa est ad me*. It survives in one incunable and one fourteenth-century manuscript, in which it is attributed to Augustinus de Ancona (d. 1328), *Rep. Bibl.* 8041.
97. On the dating of these commentaries, see chapter 1, note 11. William's commentary on Lamentations appears to be similarly independent of the commentary on the same book that has been attributed, questionably, to Thomas.
98. *CUP* I, 79.
99. Averröes held that the intellect, not the soul, is one for all human beings. Within the extensive literature on the reception of Averröes and "Averroism," see especially C. Burnett, "Arabic into Latin: the reception of Arabic philosophy into Western Europe," in P. Adamson and R.C. Taylor, eds., *The Cambridge Companion to Arabic Philosophy*, Cambridge, 2005, 370–404; J. Jolivet, "The Arabic Inheritance," in P. Dronke, ed., *A History of Twelfth Century Western Philosophy*, Cambridge, 1988, 113–150; J.-P. Torrell, *Initiation*, 278–281.
100. *CUP* 486–487. Specifically, proposition 7 asserted that the soul, like the body, underwent corruption upon death; proposition 8 asserted that the soul separated from the body could not be tormented by corporeal fire; and proposition 13 asserted that God could not render the body incorruptible. On these condemnations and the importance of questions about the afterlife in thirteenth-century preaching, see N. Bériou, *L'avènement des maîtres de la Parole*, vol. 1, 459–465.
101. DS 856–859. On the Council of Lyons and the contemporary concern for reunification with the Greek Church, see chapter 3, note 208. The doctrine of the particular judgment received further definition in the Latin Church, notably with respect to the beatific vision, by Pope Benedict XII in the bull "Benedictus Deus" (1336). On the particular and general judgments,

see J. Baschet, "Jugement de l'âme, jugement dernier: contradiction, complémentarité, che-
vauchement?" *Revue Mabillon* 6 (1995), 159–203. On the medieval development of the doctrine
on purgatory, see C. Carozzi, *Le Voyage de l'âme dans l'Au-Delà d'après la littérature latine
(V^e–XIII^e siècle)*, Bibliothèque de l'École française de Rome 189, Rome, 1994; A. Brodero, "Le
Moyen Âge et le purgatoire," *RHE* 78 (1983), 429–452; J. Le Goff, *La Naissanse du purgatoire*,
Paris, 1981; A. Michel, *DTC* 13 (1936), 1163–1326.

102. On suffrages for the dead, Peter Lombard, *Sent.*, IV, xlv, cap. 2 (ed. Coll. S. Bonaventurae, t. II,
523–525); Thomas Aquinas, *In IV Sent.*, d. 45, q. 2, a. 1–4 (ed. Parma, t. VII/B, 1118b–1129b); *De
quolibet* VI, q. 8, a. 1–2 (ed. Leonina, t. XXV/2, 309a–310a); VIII, q. 5, a. 2 (ed. Leonina, t.
XXV/I, 69b–71a).

103. "*NEC HABENT PARTEM IN HOC SECULO . . . ET IN OPERE QUOD SUB SOLE GERITUR* similiter
non habent partem. Hoc est certum de his qui sunt in gloria. Hi autem qui sunt in purgatorio
non habent partem rerum secularium, habent tamen partem operum que hic fiunt. Dampnati
similiter usum rerum temporalium non habent. Set utrum eis prosint suffragia questio est.
Communiter autem tenetur quod in nullo prosint. Secundum tamen illos qui dixerunt quod
prosint ad aliquam alleuiationem, non ad plenam liberationem, potest littera sic exponi: *NON
HABENT PARTEM IN HOC SECULO*, scilicet quantum ad plenam liberationem. Tenetur tamen
communiter modo quod nichil eis prosint" (*Super Ecl.* 9:6, MSS Basel, Univ. Bibl. B III 20, f.
108ra; Madrid, Bibl. Nac. 493, f. 156r–v).

104. Augustine, *Sermones*, CLXXII (PL 38, 936–937).

105. "Eadem itaque causa est cur non oretur tunc pro hominibus aeterno igne damnatis, quae nunc
etiam causa est ut non oretur pro diabolo angelis que eius aeterno supplicio deputatis" (Gregory the Great, *Moralia in Iob*, XXXIV, 19, CCSL 143B, 1760).

106. *Sent.*, IV, xlv, cap. 2 (ed. Coll. S. Bonaventurae, t. II, 524–525).

107. *Postille*, in Ecl. 9:6 (ed. Venetiis, t. III, 95rb).

108. *Breviloquium*, VII, 3 (*Opera*, t. V, 284a).

109. "Ergo suffragia damnatis in inferno non prosunt" (Thomas Aquinas, *In IV Sent.*, d. 45, q. 2, a.
2, ed. Parma, t. VII/B, 1121b–1122a).

110. On the medieval history of this text, see J.-G. Bougerol, *Introduction à Saint Bonaventure*,
61–62. He describes Bonaventure's use of it as follows: "Cet opuscule dont il est toujours
impossible de situer exactement l'auteur et la date de composition, a été cité par Bonaventure 50 fois et de manière extrêmement significative, car certaines d'entre les citations sont la
base de développements doctrinaux"; ibid., 61.

111. The following remark is typical: "Praeterea, Augustinus dicit in libro *De spiritu et anima*. . ."
(*De ver.*, q. 13, a. 1, ob. 7; a. 3, ob. 7, ed. Leonina, t. XXII/2, 416a). For other examples, see *In III
Sent.*, d. 29, q. 1, a. 3, sc. 2; d. 34, q. 3, a. 1A, sc. 2 (ed. Parma, t. VII/A, 317b); *In IV Sent.*, d. 44, q.
3, a. 3A, ob. 1; a. 3B, ob. 1, a. 3C, ob. 2 (ed. Parma, t. VII/B, 1105b.1106a.1106b); *De ver.*, q. 8, a.
3., ob. 13.15; a. 4, ob. 16; a. 15, sc. 3 (ed. Leonina, t. XXII/2, 224a.224b. 229a–230b.268a).

112. "Ad primum igitur dicendum quod liber *De spiritu et anima* non est authenticus, nec creditur
esse Augustini" (*De ver.*, q. 15, a. 1, ad 1, ed. Leonina, t. XXII/2, 481a).

113. Cf. *De ver.*, q. 18, a. 1., ob. 6.7; q. 19, a. 1., sc. 5 (ed. Leonina, t. XXII/2, 530a.564a.); q. 25, a. 2,
sc. 2; a. 3, ob. 2.3 (ed. Leonina, t. XXII/3, 732a.734a.734b).

114. Cf. *Super Boetium De Trin.*, q. 6, a. 1, sc. 1/1.2/1; a. 2, sc. 3 (ed. Leonina, t. L, 157a.159a.164b).

115. For example: ". . . dicendum quod liber *De spiritu et anima* est ypocriphus, cum euis auctor
ignoretur; et sunt ibi multa uel falsa uel improprie dicta" (*De spiritualibus creaturis*, Proemium,
a. 11, ad 2, ed. Leonina, t. XXIV/2, 120b).

116. The disputed questions *De veritate* date to 1256–1259; cf. J.-P. Torrell, *Initiation*, 87–97, 488.
The commentary *Super Boetium De Trinitate* dates to the years 1257–1258 or early 1259, ibid.,
97–99, 503.

117. "*MEMENTO CREATORIS TUI*, ut ipsum timeas a malo recedendo. . . . Augustinus, *De spiritu et
anima*: 'Miser ego homo, diligere debemus Deum meum qui me fecit cum non eram, redimit
cum perieram. Non eram, et de nichilo me fecit, non lapidem, non auem, non arborem, non
aliquid de animalibus uoluit me esse, set hominem ad ymaginem propriam'" (*Super Ecl.* 12:1,

MSS Basel, Univ. Bibl. B III 20, f. 111va; Madrid, Bibl. Nac. 493, f. 162v). Cf. *De spiritu et anima*, XVII (PL 40, 792).

118. "Sic ergo Verbum erat ab eterno in Patre, nec tamen sunt eadem persona Pater et Filius. Vnde sequitur: *ET VERBUM ERAT APUD ⟨DEUM⟩*. Cum prepositiones sint transitiue, hec prepositio 'apud' cum suo casuali importat distinctionem, quod est contra Sabellium, qui dicit quod Pater et Filius sunt una persona quia unum principium. Item, hec prepositio ratione sue specialis significationis denotat subauctoritatem in Filio respectu Patris" (*Super Io.* 1:1, MS Saint-Omer, Bibl. mun. 260, f. 111vb).

119. Bonaventure, *In Io. com.* 1:1 (*Opera*, t. VI, 246b–247a); cf. *Breviloquium*, I, 5 (*Opera*, t. V, 214b).

120. William of Auxerre, *Summa Aurea*, I, 5 (ed. J. Ribaillier, Paris-Grottaferrata, 1980, vol. XVI, 159).

121. "²⁸*DICEBAT ERGO EIS IHESUS: CUM EXALTAUERITIS*. Hic predixit eos post passionem suam pleniorem cognitionem habituros, primo quantum ad sue dignitatis imitationem; secundo quantum ad personalem distinctionem et sui respectu Patris subauctoritatem: ²⁸*ET A MEIPSO ...*" (*Super Io.* 8:28, MS Saint-Omer, Bibl. mun. 260, f. 135vb). On the other hand, Bonaventure is once again William's source for the application of *subauctoritas*, as well as a citation of Augustine, in the following remark: "²⁴*SERMONEM QUE⟨M⟩ AUDISTIS ... NON EST MEUS*, quia nichil loquor preter uoluntatem Patris. Sic exponit Crisostomus et loquitur de illo homine. Augustinus exponit de Verbo increato dicens quod solum in hoc notatur subauctoritas Filii respectu Patris" (*Super Io.* 14:24, MS Saint-Omer, Bibl. mun. 260, f. 156ra). The Franciscan master is not, however, William's source for the ascription of the term to the bishop of Hippo, which is mistaken; cf. Bonaventure, *In Io. com.* 14:24 (*Opera*, t. VI, 443b). Augustine, to the contrary, is concerned in his exposition of this passage to exclude any notion of inequality between the Father and the Son: "Recte igitur tribuit auctori quidquid facit aequalis, a quo habet hoc ipsum quod illi est indifferenter aequalis" (Augustine, *In Io. evang. tract.*, LXXVI, CCSL 36, 519), cf. Chrysostom, *In Io. hom.*, LXXV (PG 59, 407).

122. Recent scholarship has dated Thomas's lectures on the *Sentences* to 1252/53–1254/55 and his redaction of the text to 1254/55–1256, several years before William's inception as regent master in 1259. See A. Oliva, *Les Débuts de l'enseignement*, 224–253 (253); and J.-P. Torrell, *Initiation*, 58–69, 485–486, 611–612 (23*–24*), 634–635 (46*–47*).

123. "Praeterea, *sub* denotat gradum. Sed in Filio dicitur esse subauctoritas. Ergo etc. Est dicendum, quod cum gradus importet ordinem dignitatis secundum *sub* et *supra*, in divinis proprie gradus non potest concedi.... Subauctoritas autem non invenitur a sanctis in Filio posita: unde non videtur proprie esse dictum" (Thomas Aquinas, *In 1 Sent.*, d. 25, q. 1, a. 4ex, ed. Parma, t. VVI, 214b). Remarks to the same effect appear elsewhere. For example: "... sicut Hilarius, etsi concedat Patrem esse maiorem Filio propter auctoritatem originis, non tamen concedit quod Filius sit minor Patre, cui est aequale esse donatum a Patre. Et similiter non est extendendum nomen subauctoritatis vel principiati in Filio, licet nomen auctoritatis, vel principii concedatur in Patre" (*De pot.*, q. 10, a. 1, ad 9, ed. Parma, t. VIII, 202a).

124. "Quidam enim dicunt, quod ablativus ille resolvendus est in praepositionem, ut sit sensus: *Pater diligit Filium Spiritu sancto*, idest per Spiritum sanctum; et tunc quod ly *per* denotat subauctoritatem in Spiritu sancto, et auctoritatem in Patre et Filio, sicut cum dicitur, quod Pater operatur per Filium. Sed hoc non videtur conveniens; quia per praepositionem *per* designatur habitudo causae in causali cui adjungitur, quamvis non respectu operantis, sed respectu operati" (*In 1 Sent.*, d. 32, q. 1, a. 1, co., ed. Parma, t. VI, 214b).

125. "Dicendum, quod nihil impedit, quare Filius non dicatur minor Patre ratione subauctoritatis, sicut Pater maior, nisi quia nomina indignitatis in Deo non debent in usum trahi" (*In 1 Sent.*, d. 16, dub. 5, *Opera*, t. VI, 286b). Among the numerous similar texts that could be multiplied, see especially *In 1 Sent.*, d. 15, q. 1, ad 3 (ibid., 260b); d. 16, dub. 4 (ibid., 286a–b).

126. For an account of the functioning of the concept of hierarchy in Bonaventure's theology, with numerous relevant references to his works, see J.-G. Bougerol, "Saint Bonaventure et la hiérarchie dionysienne," *AHDLMA* 36 (1969) 131–167, and *Introduction à Saint Bonaventure*, 63–74. In the latter study, he sums it up as follows: "Parmi les schémas dionysiens utilisés par Bonaventure celui de la hiérarchie occupe une place privilégiée. Nous le trouvons en effet, en

théologie trinitaire, en angélologie, en ecclésiologie comme en théologie spirituelle, c'est-à-dire que saint Bonaventure n'hésite pas à universaliser la hiérarchie plus encore que n'a pu le faire Denys," 68. He points out that when discussing the Godhead, Dionysius never employed the term *hierarchy*, but *thearchy*, 69. For an overview of Bonaventure's Trinitarian theology, see C. Cullen, *Bonaventure*, Oxford, 2006, 117–127.

127. To the texts cited may be added the following: "Sed quia Filius perfecte recipit quidquid Pater habet, nulla minoratio sibi convenit: et ideo etiam nullum nomen minorationis Filio potest convenire. Et quamvis Patri attribuatur auctoritas a sanctis, tamen Filio non attribuitur subauctoritas. . ." (*In 1 Sent.*, d. 16, q. 1, a. 4ex). Without mentioning the term *subauctoritas*, G. Emery provides a lucid account of Thomas's critique of this aspect of Bonaventure's Trinitarian theology, which he sums up as follows: "Il se montre très ferme sur ce point: entre les personnes divines, il n'y a *aucune priorité*, ni de rang, ni de dignité, ni d'aucune autre manière" (emphasis in text). He includes as well an extensive list of relevant references to Thomas's works in *La théologie trinitaire de saint Thomas d'Aquin*, Paris, 2004, 195.

128. This seems to lend credence to M. Dufeil's suggestion that William succeeded Thomas as regent master without ever having been his bachelor of the Sentences, *Guillaume de Saint-Amour*, 284, 316. See chapter 1, note 12.

129. A. Minnis so describes late-medieval compilators generally, "*Nolens auctor sed compilator reputari:* The Late-Medieval Discourse of Compilation," in *La méthode critique au Moyen Âge*, ed. M. Chazan and G. Dahan, Turnhout, 2006, 47–63 (62).

130. *Libellus apologeticus* (= *Apologia totius operis*) IV, ed. A.-D. von den Brincken, "Geschichtsbetrachtung bei Vincenz von Beauvais," *Deutsches Archiv für Eforschung des Mittelalters* 34 (1978), 469–470. On this work, see S. Lusignan, *Préface au 'Speculum maius' de Vincent de Beauvais: Réfraction et diffraction*, Montréal and Paris, 1979.

131. A. Minnis, "The Late-Medieval Discourse of Compilation," 60–61. To this study I am indebted for the preceding reference to Vincent's *Libellus apologeticus.*

CHAPTER 5

1. "*APERTI SUNT CELI*, secundum interpretationem Origenis, oculis carnis, *ET UIDI*, uisione corporali, sicut Stephanus uel Paulus forte, ad litteram. Vel sicut egrotantes uident ymagines, sicut Petrus ymagines animalium in disco (cf. Act 11:5). Vel *APERTI SUNT CELI*, secundum Ieronimum, non diuisione firmamenti, set quedam secreta celata sunt ei reuelata. Vel quidam fulgor aparuit ei, ac si firmamentum esset apertum, sicut nunc aliquando in coruscatione. Origenes ergo de / corporali, Ieronimus de intellectuali intelligit uisione. *UISIONES*, pluraliter, non unam tantum, *DEI*, id est de Deo, uel a Deo ostensas omnes" (*Super Ez.* 1:1, MS Paris, BnF lat. 573, f. 156va–vb).

2. Cf. Origen, *Homélies sur Ézékiel*, I, 3 (ed. and French trans., M. Borret, Paris, 1989, SC 352, 46).

3. Jerome, *In Hiezechielem*, 1 (CCSL 75, 5–6).

4. Of the many references traditionally put forward in this connection, one of the most famous is the Lord's reply to Moses in Ex 33:20: *And again he said: Thou cannot see my face: for man shall not see me and live.*

5. Cf. Jerome, *In Esaiam*, 1 (ed. M. Adriaen, 1963, Turnhout, CCSL 73, 6).

6. "Dicit ergo *IN ANNO QUO* etc., *VIDI DOMINUM* ⟨*SEDENTEM*⟩ etc. Notatur quod secundum *Glossam* in II Co. XII, de raptu Pauli, quod est triplex uisio: Videlicet corporalis, qua uidetur Deus occulis corporalibus in subiecta creatura, et sic uidit eum Abraham, Ysaac et Iacob et Moyses, ut dicit Ieronimus in originali super istum locum. Item, ymaginaria, qua uidetur Deus occulis cordis sub figura ymaginaria, sicut uidit Ysaias hic et Daniel VII et Eze. 1. Tertia est intellectualis qua pure mentis intuitu mira Dei reuelatione Deus et creature spirituales uidentur. Sic uidit Paulus, II Co. XII. Hec uisio erit in patria perfecta, in uia

inperfecta et in paucis. Quod hic igitur dicit *Glossa* quod Ysaias uidit Deum, occulis cordis exponendum, id est uisione ymaginaria, que fuit occulis cordis, non carnis. Quod autem dicit *Glossa*, infra XXXVIII, dicendum quod magistralis est. Vel quod legere in libro prescientie, non est uidere Deum in sua substantia, set super illuminationem aut spiritus ad spiritum locutionem. Et quod dicit Crisostomus nec angelum uidere Deum in natura, intelligendum est: ita plene ut Filius" (*Super Is.* 6:1, MSS Madrid, Bibl. Nac. 493, f. 179v; Paris, BnF lat. 573 omits this text).

7. "*ET MISIT DOMINUS MANUM SUAM*, ymaginaria potuit esse uisio ista, in qua uidebat quod uisibiliter appareret quasi manus hominis descendens de celo et tangens os eius et quod manum posuerit Dominus super os eius" (*Super Ier.* 1:3, MS Madrid, Bibl. Nac. 493, f. 267v). The text is slightly different in MS Paris, BnF lat. 573, f. 88rb–88va.

8. "⁵⁶*ABRAHAM PATER UESTER EXUL⟨TAUIT⟩* . . . *UT UIDERET*, oculis cordis, *DIEM M⟨EUM⟩*, uel temporalem quo factus sum in carne, uel eternitatis in qua natus sum de Patre" (*Super Io.* 8:56, MS Saint-Omer, Bibl. mun. 260, f. 137vb).

9. Augustine, *De Gen. ad lit. libri XII*, XII, 8–12 (BA 49, 354–370). On the correspondence in Augustine's thought between these three levels of knowledge and the tripartite structure of the soul, see O. Boulnois, "Augustin et les théories de l'image au Moyen Âge," *RSPT* 91 (2007), 75–91. On the influence of Porphyry on Augustine's tripartite anthropology, see by the same author "L'image parfaite. La structure augustino-porphyrienne des théories médiévales de l'image," in *Intellect et imagination dans la Philosophie Médiévale*, ed. M. Pacheco and J. Meirinhos, Turnhout, 2006, vol. 2, 731–758.

10. *Glossa mg.*, in 2 Cor 12:2 (ed. Rusch, vol. IV, 352b); *Glossa mg.*, in Is. 6:1 (ed. Rusch, vol. III, 13a). The schema also serves as the gloss on Isaiah's opening verse, *Glossa mg.*, in Is. 1:1 (ed. Rusch, vol. III, 2a).

11. In his exposition of Io 1:18, a verse the importance of which we shall soon consider, Thomas Aquinas presents the same schema while making an important addition to the third element. He notes that intellectual vision can result from an intuition of the Creator's magnitude in the consideration of an intelligible species abstracted from sensation: "Quomodo ergo intelligendum est hoc quod dicit Evangelista: *Deum nemo vidit unquam*? Ad hujus ergo intellectum sciendum est, quod Deus dicitur videri tripliciter. Uno quidem modo per subiectam creaturam, visui corporali propositam; sicut creditur Abraham vidisse Deum, quando tres vidit, et unum adoravit, Gen. 18; unum quidem adoravit, quia tres, quos prius homines reputaverat, et postmodum Angelos credidit, recognovit mysterium Trinitatis. Alio modo per repraesentatam imaginationem; et sic Isaias vidit Dominum sedentem super solium excelsum et elevatum. Plures visiones huic similes in Scripturis reperiuntur. Alio vero modo videtur per aliquam speciem intelligibilem a sensibilibus abstractam, ab his qui per considerationem magnitudinis creaturarum, intellectu intuentur magnitudinem creatoris, ut dicitur Sap. 13:5: 'A magnitudine speciei et creaturae cognoscibiliter poterit creator horum videri,' et Rom. 1:20: 'Invisibilia Dei a creatura mundi per ea quae facta sunt, intellecta conspiciuntur.' Alio modo per aliquod spirituale lumen a Deo infusum spiritualibus mentibus in contemplatione; et hoc modo vidit Iacob Deum facie ad faciem, Gen. 32; quae visio, secundum Gregorium, facta est per altam contemplationem" (*Super Io.* 1:18, ed. Parma, t. X, 311b–312a).

12. Cf. Augustine, *Epistula 147, De videndo Deo* (ed. A. Goldbacher, 1904, CSEL 44, 304). This treatise is a prolonged reflection on John 1:18 and the problematic of human vision of God. For a discussion of its presentation of intellectual vision, see O. Boulnois, "L'image parfaite," 742. In one of his earlier discussions of the matter, Thomas Aquinas sums up the imperfection of Paul's vision by pointing out that it was not a *habitus*: "Paulus in illo raptu secundum quid participavit statum comprehensorum, non tamen tanta gloria perfectus fuit ut lumen in Angelos transfundere posset: quia, ut dicitur, factus est illius gloriae particeps miraculose quantum ad actum, et non quantum ad habitum, quod est lumen gloriae" (*In II Sent.*, d. 11, q. 2, a. 4, ad. 4, ed. Parma, t. VI, 485b). More extensive discussions *de raptu* appear in *De ver.*, 13 (ed. Leonina, t. XXII/2, 415a–33b) and *ST*, II-II, q. 175 (ed. Leonina, t. X, 402–409).

13. "Item, intellectualis, quae longe purior est, qua Deus, ceteraequae res incorporeae, non per imaginem, aut figuram, sed purae mentis intuitu mira Dei revelatione videntur. Sicut Paulus raptus ad tertium celum, 2 *Corinth*. 12. Haec tertia visio est in patria perfecte, in via imperfecte, et in paucis Sanctis" (*Postille*, in Isaiam 6, ed. Venetiis, t. IV, 17va). The scholar who has made the greatest contribution to our knowledge of this period's debate on prophetic knowledge is J.-P. Torrell. For a discussion of Hugh of St. Cher's understanding of intellectual vision in general and of Paul's vision in particular, see his *Théorie de la prophétie et philosophie de la connaissance*, Louvain, 1977, 226–230. See also the important study of S.-T. Bonino, "Le rôle de l'image dans la connsaissance prophétique d'après saint Thomas d'Aquin," *RT* 97 (1989), 533–568. On prophetic knowledge and future contingents in the thought of Bonaventure, see J.-I. Saranyana, "Conocimiento profético y futuros contingentes según san Bonaventura," in *Intellect et imagination dans la Philosophie Médiévale*, ed. M. Pacheco and J. Meirinhos, Turnhout, 2006, vol. 2, 1255–1266.

14. "Videtur tamen quod ea verba quae dixerunt in libro vitae non legissent. Cum enim Ysaias simpliciter diceret: *Morieris et non vives* (Is 38:1), et Ionas: *Ninive subvertetur* (Ion 3:4) et ista non essent futura: non videntur illa in esse in libro Dei quae non erant futura" (*Glossa mg.*, in Is 38:1, ed. Rusch, vol. III, 59b).

15. Cf. Hugh of St. Cher, *Postille*, in Isaiam 6 (ed. Venetiis, t. IV, 17va).

16. J.-P. Torrell tentatively suggests Godfrey of Poitiers, *Théorie*, 133–134. On the development of these expressions, see ibid., 188–196; and by the same author, "Hugues de Saint-Cher et Thomas d'Aquin: Contribution à l'histoire du traité de la prophétie," *RT* 74 (1974), 5–22 (12–13); "Le traité de la prophétie de S. Thomas d' Aquin et la théologie de la révélation," in *La doctrine de la révélation divine de saint Thomas d'Aquin* (Studi Thomistici 37), ed. L. Elders, Vaticana, 1990, 171–195 (180–181). These works contain extensive bibliographical references to relevant primary and secondary literature. For texts of thirteenth-century discussions of the *Glossa* on Is 38:1, see *Théorie* 9, 10, 19, 36–37.

17. On the views of these two masters, see J.-P. Torrell, *Théorie*, 61–87. The relevant texts are Philip the Chancellor, *Summa de Bono* (ed. N. Wicki, 2 vols., Berne, 1985, 489–524); and William Of Auxerre, *Summa Aurea*, II, 7 (ed. J. Ribaillier, vol. XVII, 143–144).

18. J.-P. Torrell, *Théorie*, 228.

19. Cf. J.-P. Torrell, *Théorie*, 226–230; 243–248; "Le traité de la prophétie de S. Thomas d'Aquin," 177–181; "Introduction," *Thomas d'Aquin, Questions sur la vérité. Question XII, La Prophétie (De prophetia)*, trans. S.-T. Bonino, Paris, 2006, 15. Among the numerous relevant texts in the writings of Thomas Aquinas, those anterior to William's regency include *De ver.*, 23, 3, 1 (ed. Leonina, t. XXII/2, 365–414); *Exp. super Isaiam* 1:1 (ed. Leonina, t. XXVIII, 8–9); and *Super Isaiam* 6:1 (ibid., 47–49). Particularly important among his later writings is *ST*, II-II, q. 171–178 (ed. Leonina, t. X, 367–420). The latter has recently appeared in a new edition including the French translation of P. Synave and P. Benoit, as well as an extensive introduction and notes by J.-P. Torrell, *Saint Thomas d'Aquin, Somme Théologique: La Prophetie*, Paris, 2005.

20. To this list may be added the name of Bonaventure.

21. "*VIDI DOMINUM*, scilicet in forma humana et fuit hec uisio, secundum Andream, ymaginaria, licet secundum Ieronimum dicatur intellectualis. Set potest dici quod uisio fuit ymaginaria, set significatum uidit uisione intellectuali" (*Super Is.* 6:1, MSS Madrid, Bibl. Nac. 493, f. 179v, Paris, BnF lat. 573, f. 10rb). Cf. Jerome, *In Esaiam*, VI (CCSL 73, 223).

22. For an account of the thirteenth-century evolution of this distinction, see I. Rosier-Catach, *La parole comme acte: sur la grammaire et la sémantique au XIIIe siècle*, Paris, 1994. For a discussion of its functioning in the thought of Thomas Aquinas, see G. Rocca, "The Distinction between *Res Significata and Modus Significandi* in Aquinas' Theological Epistemology," *Thomist* 55, no. 22 (1991), 173–197.

23. For discussions of this development and its aftermath, with references to the relevant texts, see O. Boulnois, "Augustin et les théories de l'image," 84–91; C. Trottmann, *La Vision Béatifique des disputes scholastiques à sa définition par Benôit XII*, BEFAR 289, Rome, 1995, 74–83; H.-F. Dondaine, "L'objet et le 'medium' de la vision béatifique chez les théologiens du XIIIe siècle,"

*RTAM* 21 (1952), 60–130. For an account of William of Middleton's attempt to reconcile the beatific vision with divine transcendence by describing the former in terms of different kinds of knowledge (*quid est, quod est, in specie* etc.), see A. Côté, "William of Middleton on Divine Beatitude," *Franciscan Studies* 60 (2002), 17–38.

24. On this translation, see chapter 4, note 5.

25. "*DEUM NULLUS UIDIT UMQUAM.* Quid igitur dicemus magniuoco Isaiae dicenti: *Vidi Dominum sedentem in throno excelso et eleuato* (Is 6:1)? Quid autem et Iohanni attestanti ei quoniam hec dixit quando uidit gloriam eius? Quid autem Ezechieli? Et enim et ipse in cherubin sedentem eum uidet (cf. Ez 10). Quid autem et Danieli? Et enim et hic ait: *Antiquus dierum sedebat* (Dn 7:9). Quid autem et ipsi Moysi dicenti: *Ostende michi gloriam tuam ut cognoscibiliter uideam te?* (Ex 33:13) Iacob autem et ab hoc nuncupationem suscepit, Israel super uocatus est (cf. Gn 35:10). Israel enim qui Deum uidet est. Set et alii eum uiderunt. Qualiter igitur Iohannes dixit: *DEUM NEMO UIDIT UMQUAM?* Ostendens quoniam illa condescensionis erant, non ipsius substantie nude uisio. Si enim ipsam uidissent naturam, nequaquam differenter eam considerassent. Simplex enim quedam est et infigurabilis hec et incomposita et incircumscriptibilis. Non sedet, neque stat, neque ambulat. Omnia enim hec corporum sunt.... Quia ipsum quodcumque est Deus, non solum prophete, set neque angeli uiderunt, neque archangeli"; Chrysostom, *In Io. hom.,* XV (PG 59, 97–98). This text has been taken from MSS Vat. Ottob. lat. 227, f. 26ra (= *O*) and Paris, BnF lat. 1782, f. 31vb (= *P₅*). The entirety of Burgundio's translation of this homily has been presented by H.-F. Dondaine, "L'objet et le 'medium' de la vision béatifique," 100–105.

26. "Divina essentia in se nec ab homine nec ab angelo videbitur," *CUP* I, 170.

27. For a detailed account of these condemnations with relevant bibliography, see C. Trottmann, *La Vision Béatifique,* ch. 2, 115–185. With H.-F. Dondaine, he notes that more solemn condemnations may have been issued in 1244 as a result of the obstinance of John Pagus, as well as that of the *frater Stephanus* named in the condemnation, now identified as the Dominican Stephen of Venisy; cf. ibid., 175–176, 178–181. Cf. H.-F. Dondaine, "L'objet et le 'medium' de la vision béatifique," 60–61, n. 4.

28. The expunging of Hugh's *Postille* has been documented by H.-F. Dondaine, "Hugues de Saint-Cher et la condamnation de 1241," *RSPT* 33 (1949), 170–174.

29. *Postille,* in Isaiam 6 (ed. Venetiis, t. IV, 17va). Concerning this exposition and the difficulty of determining the extent to which Hugh was responsible for it, see H.-F. Dondaine, "L'objet et le 'medium' de la vision béatifique," 83.

30. Advanced in the 350s and 360s by two logicians by the names of Aetius (d. c. 370) and Eunomius, bishop of Cyzicus (d. 394), Anomoean Arianism denied not only that the Son is one in being with the Father but also even that he is like Him. Primary among Eunomius's relevant writings are his first *Apologia* (ed. G.-M. De Durand and L. Doutreleau, French trans. B. Sesboüé, Paris, 1983, SC 305; PG 30, 835–868) and his treatise *Ekthesis* (PG 47, 587–590). Cf. J. Daniélou, "Eunome l'Arien et l'éxégèse néo-platonicienne du Cratyle," *Revue des Études greques* 49 (1956), 412–432; A. Benito Y Durán, "El nominalismo arriano y la philosophia cristiana: Eunomio y San Basilio," *Augustinus* 5 (1960), 207–226; E. Gilson, *La philosophie au Moyen Âge,* 2nd ed., Paris, 1999, 61–66; J. N. D. Kelly, *Early Christian Doctrines,* New York, 1978, 249; M. Spanneut, "Eunomius de Cyzique," *DHGE* 15 (1963), 1399–1405.

31. By the time Chrysostom began preaching at Antioch in 386 as a newly ordained priest, Arianism's influence in most of its strains was receding. Still, Anomoean Arianism continued to exercise considerable influence, notwithstanding an edict by the pro-Nicene Western Emperor Gratian proscribing all forms of heresy, as well as the criticisms of Basil of Caesarea and Gregory of Nyssa. The main witnesses to Basil's responses are his *Contra Eunomium,* ed. G.-M. De Durand and L. Doutreleau, French trans. B. Sesboüé, Paris, 1983, SC 305; PG 29, 497–474. Fragments of his second *Apologia* appear in Gregory Of Nyssa's *Contra Eunomium,* ed. W. Jaeger, *Gregorii Nysseni Opera,* 2 vols., Leyden, 1960. Although he never elaborated a detailed Christology of his own, and though he is not often considered a major figure in the development of Christological doctrine, much of Chrysostom's most important exegetical work took

the form of anti-Arian polemic. He took up the dispute only when challenged by them to a debate. The eventual outcome of his efforts was a series of five homilies *De incomprehensibili dei natura* preached *contra anomoeos* at Antioch about 386–387, wherein he explicitly states his purpose of opposing them. See J. N. D. Kelly, *Goldenmouth: The Story of John Chrysostom, Ascetic, Preacher, Bishop*, Ithaca, NY, 1995, 36, 59–61.

32. Within the vast literature on the Manicheans, particularly helpful among general studies are F. Decret, *Mani et la tradition manichéenne*, Paris, 2005; S. Runciman, *The Medieval Manichee*, Cambridge, 1982 (1st ed. 1947); N. Tajadod, *Mani le bouddha de lumière, catéchisme manichéen chinois*, Paris, 1991. On Christian anti-Manichean literature, see P. W. Van Der Horst and J. Mansfeld, *An Alexandrian Platonist against Dualism: Alexander of Lycopolis' Treatise "Critique of the Doctrines of Manichaeus,"* Translated with an Introduction and Notes, Leiden, 1974.

33. B. De Margerie has made this observation in connection with the anti-Manichean polemic of Augustine in *Introduction à l'histoire de l'exégèse*, 4 vols., Paris, 1980–1990, vol. 3, 116, n. 19. On the other hand, in his consideration of another very similar text of Chrysostom's, *De incomprehensibili Dei natura*, III.1 (PG 48, 722), the same scholar identifies Egyptian Christian anthropomorphists of preceding generations as the targets of Chrysostom's polemic, ibid., vol. 1, 220. More convincingly, J. N. D. Kelly points to the Manicheans (in addition to the Anomoeans), noting that by the time Chrysostom returned to Antioch from his monastic sojourn (most likely toward the end of 378), they were winning numerous converts there, particularly among the learned; see *Goldenmouth*, 59–61. On Chrysostom's encounter with Manichaeism, see also J. Quasten, *Patrology*, vol. 3, 7th ed., Westminster, 1994 (1st ed., in English, Utrecht, 1950), 435, 437. On the Manichaeism known to Augustine, see especially P. Brown, *Augustine of Hippo. A Biography*, Berkeley, 1969, 46–60. On Augustine's critique of the Manichean doctrine of creation, see E. Gilson, *Introduction à l'étude de saint Augustin*, Paris, 1943, 246.

34. C. Baur dismisses the proposition that most of Chrysostom's biblical homilies were ever delivered in spoken form; see *Johannes Chrysostomus und seine Zeit*, Munich, 1930; English translation, M. Gonzaga, *John Chrysostom and His Time*, 2 vols., London, 1959–1960, vol. 1, 222–223. Yet J. N. D. Kelly (*Goldenmouth*, 90–94) persuasively refutes Baur's reasoning and proposes 391 as the most likely date for the preaching of the course of homilies on John. See also J. Quasten, *Patrology*, vol. 3, 437–439. On the close relation between the liturgy and Chrysostom's preaching, see J.-N. Guinot, "Prédication et liturgie chez saint Jean Chrysostom," in *Prédication et liturgie au Moyen Âge*, ed. N. Bériou and F. Morenzoni, Turnhout, 2008, 53–77.

35. Rendered *condescensio* in Burgundio of Pisa's translation, the term in Chrysostom's exegesis and other Greek literature is συγκατάβασις.

36. On the functioning of condescension in Chrysostom's exegesis, see the lucid account of B. De Margerie, *Introduction à l'histoire*, vol. 1, 214–224.

37. A case in point appears at the conclusion of AESCHYLUS, *Eumenides*: "All-seeing Zeus and Fate come down (συγκατέβα) to battle fair for Pallas' town! Ring out your chant, ring out your joy's acclaim!" (trans. E. Anderson-Morshead, London, 1881).

38. E.g., Ex 3:7–8: et sciens dolorem eius descendi ut liberarem eum de manibus Aegyptiorum *W* (οἶδα γὰρ τὴν ὀδύνην αὐτῶν καὶ κατέβην ἐξελέσθαι αὐτοὺς ἐκ κειρὸς Αἰγυτίων *LXX*). For a few other examples, cf. Ex 19:11, Nm 11:17, Ps 71:6, Ps 143:5, Is 31:4, Mi 1:3.

39. Cf. B. De Margerie, *Introduction à l'histoire*, vol. 1, 221.

40. There is no clear evidence that the Cathars, also known as Albigenses, were in any way related to the Manicheans. Moreover, any attempt to describe their beliefs must remain cautious, given the fragmentary character of the surviving evidence—virtually all of it contained in the polemical literature of their adversaries. Still, it seems clear that they were radically evangelical and subscribed to a metaphysical dualism between the spiritual and material realms, the former corresponding to Good, the latter to Evil. The extent to which such dualism distinguished them from nonheterodox Christians is a matter of debate. Nonetheless, if they actually conceived of Evil as an eternal subsistent reality opposed to God, as they were said to have done, this would have represented a radical point of departure from Christian belief. The relevant

bibliography is extensive and has developed appreciably in recent years. See especially J.-L. Biget, "Héresie, politique et societé en Languedoc (~1120 – ~1320)," in *Le Pays cathare. Les religions médiévals et leurs expressions méridionales*, ed. J. Berlioz, Fanjeaux-Carcassonne, 1998; J. Duvernoy, *L'Histoire des Cathares*, Toulouse, 1979; M. Lambert, *The Cathars*, Oxford, 1998; M. Roquebert, *L'Épopée cathare*, 4 vols., Toulouse, 1970–1989; G. RottenwöHrer, *Der Katharismus*, 8 vols., Bad Honnef, 1982–1993.

41. "*OMNIA PER IPSUM FACTA SUNT*, id est omne opus creationis, siue fuerit corporale siue spirituale, contra Manicheos dicentes corpora esse a malo principio" (*Super Io.* 1, 3, MS Saint-Omer, Bibl. mun. 260, f. 112ra).

42. "*DIXIT EIS*, id est ministris, *IHESUS: IMPLETE YDRIAS AQUA* . . . ut Manicheum confunderet, dicentem omnia uisibilia a malo deo creata" (*Super Io.* 2:7, MS Saint-Omer, Bibl. mun. 260, f. 116ra).

43. "*ILLE HOMOCIDA ERAT* . . . *AB INITIO*, id est post humani generis initium, uel sui, uel mundi, *ET IN UERITATE*, scilicet naturalium et originalis innocentie . . . *NON STETIT*, quia cecidit, Ysa. XIII: *Quomodo ceci⟨disti⟩, Lu⟨cifer⟩*; *QUIA UERITAS IN EO NON EST*, post casum enim et amissionem ueritatis eam requirere noluit, Eze. XVIII: *Nichili factus es et non eris in perpe⟨tuum⟩* (Ez 28:19). Vel *UERITAS*, id est Christus, *NON EST IN EO* per gratiam, *CUM LOQUITUR MEN⟨DACIUM⟩*. Quasi dicat: Non solum ueritatem amisit, non solum non requirit, immo quod plus est: *CUM LOQUITUR MENDA⟨CIUM⟩, EX PROPRIIS LOQUITUR*, scilicet ex propriis inuentionibus, quia non habet hoc ab alio suggerente. Vnde sequitur: *QUIA MENDAX EST ET PATER EIUS*, id est mendacii pater, id est causa, et quia primo mendacium dixit: Gen. III: *Eritis sicut dii* (Gn 3:5). Non uult ergo dicere quod malum non possit esse ab alio quam a Dyabolo, set quia suum malum fuit primum" (*Super Io.* 8:44, MS Saint-Omer, Bibl. mun. 260, f. 137ra).

44. "Buzi despectus siue contemptus" (*Lib. interpret. hebraic. nom.*, CCSL 72, 130).

45. "*FILIUS BUZI*, id est spretus atque contemptus. Pater enim Christi ab hereticis contempnitur qui Vetus Testamentum non suscipiunt" (*Super Ez.* 1, 3, MS Paris, BnF lat. 573, f. 157rb).

46. "*¹⁴:⁸DICIT EI PHI⟨LIPPUS⟩: DOMINE, OSTENDE NOBIS PA⟨TREM⟩*. In hoc uidetur quod non credidit (*om. S*) eum omnino Filio similem; *ET SUFFICIT NOBIS*, in hoc innuit eum Filio maiorem, secundum Augustinum. *NOBIS*, in hoc innuit quod non ille solus esset in illo errore. Numquid ergo fuit infidelis? Secundum quosdam, credidit Patrem Filio similem, set non aduertebat raptus desiderio ad appetendum futuram gloriam. Secundum Crisostomum, corporaliter eum uidere postulabat indistincte recolens quod Ysaiah eum uidisset, Ysa. VI (1) et Micheas, III Reg. ultimo (3 Rg 22, 19)" (MS Saint-Omer, Bibl. mun. 260, f. 154va). Cf. Augustine, *In Io. evang. tract.*, LXX (CCSL 36, 504); Chrysostom, *In Io. hom.*, LXXIV (PG 59, 400).

47. "*DEUM NEMO*, id est nullus purus homo carnalibus oculis, *UIDIT UMQUQAM*. Contra, Gen. XXXI: *Vidi Deum fa⟨cie⟩ ad fa⟨ciem⟩* (Gn 32:30). Responsio: Iste uisiones et consimiles fuerunt in subiecta/ creatura. Si obiicitur de Paulo in raptu, dicendum quod illa uisio fuit supra hominem. *UNIGENITUS FILIUS QUI EST ⟨IN⟩ SINU PATRIS, IPSE ENARRAUIT*, quia: *Nemo nouit Patrem nisi Filius* etc., *uo⟨luerit⟩ Filius reue⟨lare⟩*, Mt. XI. Ipse narrat suis quid de Trinitate diuinitatis sensiendum sit, quomodo ad eam peruenendum, et ad ipsam introducit" (*Super Io.* 1, 18, MS Saint-Omer, Bibl. mun. 260, f. 113va–vb). Similar expositions appear in Hugh of St. Cher, *Postille*, in Io. 1:18 (ed. Venetiis, t. VI, 285vb); Chrysostom, *In Io. hom.*, xv (PG 59, 97–98).

48. Cf. *Glossa mg.*, in Io. 1:18 (ed. Rusch, vol. IV, 225a).

49. "*Solus igitur eum uidet Filius et Spiritus Sanctus*" (Chrysostom, *In Io. hom.*, xv, MS Vat. Ottob. lat. 227, f. 26rb; cf. PG 59, 98). The broader context of Chrysostom's remark makes clear that he has in mind the second of the Trinity.

50. The present survey has identified no explicit treatment of Jesus' human knowledge, yet in several passages, William seems to have in mind the beatific vision. What follows are two examples: "*EGO SCIO EUM*, plene et perfecte" (*Super Io.* 7:29, MS Saint-Omer, Bibl. mun. 260, f. 132va); "*VOLO UT UBI SUM EGO*, scilicet in celo, id est mox ero. Vel dicit *SUM*, quia fuit comprehensor in uia, *ET ILLI SINT MECUM* per gloriosam coheritationem" (*Super Io.* 17, 24, MS Saint-Omer, Bibl. mun. 260, f. 132va).

51. Thomas Aquinas exploits the full range of uses to which Chrysostom puts *condescensio*, yet he is often particularly explicit about its functioning in the context of anti-Manichean argument. A case in point is his exposition *Super Io.* 1:7: "*Ut testimonium perhiberet de lumine.* . . . Sed si istud lumen sufficiens est per se omnia manifestare, non solum seipsum; quid ergo indigebat ut testificaretur? Non ergo necessaria sunt testimonia Joannis et prophetarum de Christo. Respondeo dicendum, quod haec objectio est Manichaeorum, qui volunt destruere Vetus Testamentum. Unde a Sanctis contra hos multiplex ratio assignatur quare Christus testimonium prophetarum voluit habere. . . . Quarta ratio est Chrysostomi: quia scilicet homines infirmi intellectus, veritatem et cognitionem Dei seipsa capere non possunt: unde voluit Deus eis condescendere, et illuminare quosdam homines de divinis prae aliis, ut ab eis humano modo cognitionem de divinis acciperent, quorum cognitionem in seipsis attingere non valebant" (ed. Parma, t. x, 297b–298a). As does Chrysostom, Thomas describes various figures of the Old and New Testaments as condescending, as in the following remark: "Sed considerandum est quod Moyses rudi populo loquebatur, quorum imbecillitate condescendens, illa solum eis proposuit, quae manifeste sensui apparent" (*ST*, 1, q. 68, a. 3, co., ed. Leonina, t. v, 171). Still, the term is most often applied to God without further distinction or, as in the following case, to Jesus: "*Et sedens*, idest condescendens, ut ejus doctrina facilius caperetur" (*Super Io.* 8:2, ed. Parma, t. x, 441a).
52. For these comments, William is independent of Bonaventure, though the concept of *condescensio* figures in the latter's thought as well. See the discussion of H. Urs von Balthasar, *The Glory of the Lord*, ii, *Studies in Theological Style: Clerical Styles*, ed. J. Riches, San Francisco, 1982 (English trans. A. Louth, F. McDonagh, and B. McNeil, C.R.V. of *Herrlichkeit: Eine theologishe Ästhetik*, ii: *Fächer der Stile*, i: *Klerikale Stile*, Einsiedeln, 1969), 326–333.
53. "*Ego autem*, quasi: sic gratias ago, non tamen quasi dubius, quia *sciebam*, scientia certitudinis, *quia semper me audis*, non aliquando, ut alios sanctos. Vel *audis*, quasi: exaudis me hominem, Heb. v: *Exauditus est* (Hbr 5:7). **Ideo non tanquam indigens petii uel gratias egi**, secundum Crisostomum, *set propter populum qui circumstat ⟨dixi⟩, ut credat quia tu me mi⟨sisti⟩*. **Et ita non sum tibi contrarius, set per omnia concors, supra viii:** *Que placita sunt ei fa⟨cio⟩ semper* (Io 8:29). Crisostomus: '**Hoc sue sapientie est per uerba condescensionem, per res uero potestatem ostendere**'"; (*Super Io.* 11:42, MS Saint-Omer, Bibl. mun. 260, f. 145rb). Cf. Chrysostom, *In Io. hom.*, lxiv (PG 59, 357)).
54. "*Cum autem uenerit iste Spiritus ueritatis do⟨cebit⟩ uos omnem ueritatem... non enim loquetur a semetipso ... set quecumque audiet lo⟨quetur⟩*. Nota quod hec uerba condescensionis sunt, quia nichil futuritionis est in diuinis. Set audire est suum esse et sua audientia, sua essentia. Addit tamen super essentiam esse ab alio. Crisostomus: 'Per hoc nichil aliud significat nisi: nichil in fallaciam Spiritus sancti'" (*Super Io.* 16:13, MS Saint-Omer, Bibl. mun. 260, f. 160rb) cf. Chrysostom., *In Io. hom.*, lxxviii (PG 59, 423), Burgundione interprete (*O* f. 136vb): "Hoc ait quoniam nichil extra ea que Patris, nichil proprium."
55. "Nec moueat quod uerbum futuri temporis positum est. Non enim dictum est: quaecumque audiuit, aut: quaecumque audit, sed: *quaecumque audiet, loquetur*. Illa quippe audientia sempiterna est, quia sempiterna scientia. . . . Quamuis enim natura illa immutabilis et ineffabilis. . . . Quamuis enim natura illa immutabilis et ineffabilis non recipiat fuit et erit, sed tantum est, ipsa enim ueraciter est, quia mutari non potest" (Augustine, *In Io. evang. tract.*, xcix, CCSL 36, 585). In his *Contra sermonem Arianorum*, Augustine provides a very similar exposition of the same passage: "Nec moueat quod futuri temporis uerbum est, *accipiet*; quasi nondum haberet. Indifferenter quippe dicuntur temporis uerba, quamvis sine tempore manere intelligatur aeternitas" (PL 42, 700).
56. See the study of R. Schenk, "*Omnis Christi Actio Nostra Est Instructio*. The Deeds and Sayings of Jesus as Revelation in the View of Thomas Aquinas," in *La Doctrine de la revelation divine*, Studi Tomistici 37 (1990), 103–131.
57. While no consensus has resulted from any of various attempts to isolate and reconstruct a "signs source" (e.g., R. Bultmann, *Das Evangelium des Johannes*, Göttingen, 1941; R. Fortna, *The Gospel of Signs*, Cambridge, 1970), the distinctive functioning of the term

*sign* in the Fourth Gospel is generally recognized by modern exegetes; cf. R. Brown, *Introduction*, 80–81. On the other hand, some scholars have argued that "sign" designates primarily, though not exclusively, a miraculous act; cf. H. Ridderbos, *The Gospel of John*, 113; W. Nicol, *The Semeia in the Fourth Gospel: Tradition and redaction*, Leiden, 1972, 62–66, 113–116 (cited by Ridderbos).

58. "Ita ergo bonum est in me credere, *SET*, tamen, *DIXI*, supra III: *Quod uidimus testamur, et testimonium nostrum non acci⟨pitis⟩* (Io 3:11); *QUIA ET UIDISTIS ⟨ME⟩ ET NON CREDI⟨DISTIS⟩*, et ita hunc panem non accipitis. . . . Set uidetur quod male redarguat quia uiderunt et non crediderunt, cum fides sit eorum que non uiduntur (cf. Hbr 11:1). Responsio: Intelligit non de uisione humanitatis pure, que non adiuuat fidem, set de uisione uirtutis et potentie in effectum. Quod autem dicitur uisio repugnare fidei, intelligitur de uisione que est facie ad faciem, non de illa que per speculum (cf. 1 Cor 13:12)" (*Super Io.* 6:36, MS Saint-Omer, Bibl. mun. 260, f. 128rb–va).

59. Both exegetes draw attention to the ambiguity of miracles: "fidem Divinitatis . . . adiuvet" (Bonaventure, *In Io. com.* 6:36, *Opera*, t. VI, 329a); "Vidistis me per miracula ad fidem ducentia" (Hugh of St. Cher, *Postille*, in Io. 6:36, ed. Venetiis, t. VI, 327va).

60. For a discussion of Jesus' moral example in the thought and literature of the first generation of Dominicans, see R. Newhauser, "Jesus as the First Dominican? Reflections on a Sub-theme in the Exemplary Literature of Some Thirteenth-Century Preachers," in *Christ among the Medieval Dominicans*, ed. K. Emery Jr. and J. Wawrykow, Notre Dame, IN, 1998, 238–255. On Christ's moral example in the thought of Thomas Aquinas, see in the same volume, J.-P. Torrell, "Le Christ dans la spiritualité de saint Thomas," 197–219 (202–208).

61. "*RELIQUID IUDEAM.* . . . Item, propter exemplum ut ostenderet nobis, secundum Augustinum, esse licitum declinare furorem persequentium" (*Super Io.* 4:3, MS Saint-Omer, Bibl. mun. 260, f. 120ra). Cf. Augustine, *In Io. evang. tract.*, XV (CCSL 36, 151); Bonaventure, *In Io. com.* 4:3 (*Opera*, t. VI, 291a–b).

62. "*IHESUS AUTEM ABSCONDIT SE*, tanquam humiliter cedens furori, *ET EXIUIT DE TEMPLO*, in signum quod ueritas fugit quando mentem humilem non inuenit. Item, exemplum secundum Gregorium, ut quando resistere possumus, iram superbientium declinemus" (*Super Io.* 8:59, MS Saint-Omer, Bibl. mun. 260, f. 138ra). Cf. Gregory the Great, *Hom. in evang.*, I, 18 (CCSL 141, 140–141).

63. "*QUI UERO.* Hic ostendit intrantem per hostium esse pastorem uerum. Et primo hoc dicit; secundo declarat: /**[140rb]** ³*HUIC HOSTIARIUS*, ubi hoc ostenditur; primo per debitum modum et auctoritatem intrandi; secundo per debitam obedientiam gregis commissi: ³*ET OUES*; tertio per rectam executionem pastoralis officii: ³*ET PROPRIAS OUES*—primo respicit Deum, secundum subditum, tertium seipsum; quarto per hoc quod eius exemplum imitantur, subditi: ⁴*ET OUES.* . . . ³*ET PROPRIAS.* Hic ostendit esse uerum pastorem talem per pastoris officium. Et tangitur tripliciter, scilicet: oues cognoscere; a malo retrahere: ³*EDUCIT EAS*; ad bonum attrahere: ⁴*ANTE EAS UADIT.* Vbi primo notatur attractio per bonum exemplum; secundo utilitas et efficacia boni exempli quoad subditos, scilicet imitatio bonorum: ⁴*ET OUES*, et declinatio malorum: ⁵*ALIENUM AUTEM*" (*Super Io.* 10:2–4, MS Saint-Omer, Bibl. mun. 260, f. 140rb).

64. "¹⁸*SI MUNDUS.* Postquam egit ad eorum confirmationem in dilectione Dei et proximi, de ipsa dilectione multipliciter pertractando, hic contra huius dilectionis impedimentum, scilicet contra persecutiones et odium mundi armando. Et primo armat contra malum mundanorum intrinsecum, scilicet odium cordis; secundo contra malum extrinsecum, scilicet persecutiones operis: ²⁰*SI ME PERSECUTI SUNT.* In prima, primo exemplo sui ad odium mundi perferendum armat; secundo ostendit quod eius exemplum ad hoc ualere debeat: ²⁰*MEMENTO ⟨TE⟩ SERMONIS.* In prima, primo odium mundi proponitur; secundo exemplum Christi hoc odium sustinentis ad memoriam reducitur: ¹⁸*SCITOTE*; tertio causa odii manifestatur, scilicet dissimilitudo eorum a mundanis: ¹⁹*SI DE MUNDO*" (*Super Io.* 15:18–19, MS Saint-Omer, Bibl. mun. 260, f. 158va).

65. "*ALTERA DIE UIDIT IOHANNES IHESUM . . . UE⟨NIENTEM⟩ AD SE*, *Glossa*: "Non solum gressibus corporis, set interioris sue contemplationis accessibus, quia dignatus est a Iohanne cognosci

secundum diunitatem et humanitatem" (*Super Io.* 1:29, MS Saint-Omer, Bibl. mun. 260, f. 114rb). Cf. *Glossa mg.*, in Io. 1:28, ed. Rusch, vol. IV, 226a.

66. "Nec fuerunt isti fatui ita cito obtemperando, quia illuminati sunt interius" (*Super Io.* 1:49, MS Saint-Omer, Bibl. mun. 260, f. 115va). Cf. Bonaventure, *In Io. com.* 1:49, *Opera*, t. VI, 268a–b.

67. "*Amen, amen,* id est uere, *dico uobis: Venit hora et nunc est,* scilicet tempus gratie . . . *quando mortui,* per culpam, *audi⟨ent⟩ uo⟨cem⟩ Fi⟨lii⟩ Dei,* interius inspirantis ad credendum, et ad obediendum per gratiam" (*Super Io.* 5:25, MS Saint-Omer, Bibl. mun. 260, f. 124vb). Cf. Bonaventure, *In Io. com.* 5:25, *Opera*, t. VI, 311b).

68. "*Ego bap⟨tizo⟩ in aqua,* id est lauo exterius, non interius" (*Super Io.* 1:26, MS Saint-Omer, Bibl. mun. 260, f. 114ra). Cf. Bonaventure, *In Io. com.* 1:26, *Opera*, t. VI, 258b.

69. "*Quia propheta in patria sua ho⟨norem⟩ non habet.* . . . Item, obiicitur quod Galilei receperunt ipsum honorifice. Secundum Augustinum, receperunt eum honorifice non interius, set exterius" (*Super Io.* 4:44, MS Saint-Omer, Bibl. mun. 260, f. 122vb). Cf. Bonaventure, *In Io. com.* 4:43, *Opera*, t. VI, 302b–303a; Hugh of St. Cher, *Postille*, in Io. 4:45, ed. Venetiis, t. VI, 310ra; Augustine, *In Io. evang. tract.*, XVI (CCSL 36, 167).

70. "Dicit ergo: *Ego pro eis.* . . . Item, constat quod non orabat nisi pro predestinatis, set pro illis, ut uidetur, frustra orabat. Responsio, Augustinus, *De predestinatione sanctorum:* 'Pro talibus non frustra oramus, quia fortassis predestinati sunt ut nostris orationibus concedantur'" (*Super Io.* 17:9, MS Saint-Omer, Bibl. mun. 260, f. 163ra). Cf. Bonaventure, *In Io. com.* 17:9 (*Opera*, t. VI, 471b); Augustine, *De dono perseverantia*, XXII (PL 45, 1029).

71. See R. Schenk, "The Deeds and Sayings of Jesus," 112. To his study I am indebted for the following citations: "Illud praeterea debemus agnoscere firmoque animo continere, quod *oratio* quando a Domino Christo funditur, institutio est sancta fidelium, forma bonorum, sincerae humilitatis exemplum; cum a subiectis agitur, satisfactio delictorum, confessio criminum, lauacra culparum" (Cassiodorus, *Expositio psalmorum* 85, ed. M. Adriaen, 1958, CCSL 98, 780); "Christi oratio fidelium est instructio, cuius omnis actio Christiani est lectio" (*Glossa mg.*, in Ps. 85, ed. Rusch, vol. II, 565a); "Christi dicit actionem et vitam cuius omnis actio fidelium est institutio et ad Deum oratio" (*Glossa mg.*, in Heb. 5:7, ed. Rusch, vol. IV, 430b); "Christi autem oratio fidelium est instructio, cujus omnis actio Christiani est lectio" (Peter Lombard, *Magna glossatura*, in Ps. 85, PL 191, 799); "Vel preces et supplicationes Christi dicit actionem et vitam Christi, cujus omnis actio fidelium institutio et ad Deum oratio" (ibid., in Heb 5:7, PL 192, 437).

72. "Sunt autem tres species praedicationis; una quae est in verbo, de qua dicitur: *Ite, praedicate Evangelium omni creaturae,* etc. (Marc. XVI). Alia est in scripto, unde Apostolus dicit se praedicasse Corinthiis (I Cor. v), quia eis epistolas scripsit. Alia est in facto, unde dicitur: *Omnis Christi actio nostra est instructio*" (Alan of Lille, *Summa de arte praedicatoria*, PL 210, 113). J.-P. Migne's presentation of biblical references has been preserved.

73. R. Schenk points out that Thomas Aquinas, who cites the axiom on no fewer than seventeen occasions, usually juxtaposes it to an action of Christ not to be taken as a literal example; see "The Deeds and Sayings of Jesus," 112–114. For a discussion of the axiom's functioning in Franciscan theology in general and Bonaventure's sermons in particular, see J.-G. Bougerol, *St. Bonaventura, Sermones Dominicales*, Bibl. Franciscana Scholastica Medii Aevi, t. XXVII, Grottaferrata, 1977, 100.

74. "*Respondit Nathanael: Tu es Filius Dei.* Contra: Multi prophete preterita et secreta reuelabant, nec tamen fuerunt filii Dei per naturam. Responsio: Non uocat eum filium Dei per naturam set per gratie excellentiam, et hic est quod eius confessio non beatificatur, sicut Petri, Mt. xvi (16:17), secundum Crisostomum. Posset tamen dici quod confitebatur eum uerum Filium Dei, quia sciebat quod solus Deus nouit cogitationes hominum. Nec tamen beatificauit, quia non tanta firmitate confessus est sicut Petrus. Nota, cum Nathanael tantus esset, non tamen est uocatus ad apostolatum. Secundum Augustinum, quia legis peritus erat, ne sua predicatio ex subtilitate humane rationis procedere uideretur. Nec ualet oppositio de Paulo, quia fuerat apertus inimicus ante et electus a Christo iam glorificato. Et omnis Christi actio nostra sit instructio. Non sunt tamen modo ydiote eligendi, quia Christus elegit tales

ut faceret sapientes, quod nos facere non possumus" (*Super Io.* 1:49, MS Saint-Omer, Bibl. mun. 260, f. 115va).

75. Chrysostom, *In Io. Hom.* XXI (PG 59, 127–129).

76. *Glossa mg.*, in Io. 1:49 (ed. Rusch, vol. IV, 227b). In this context, Thomas Aquinas makes the same point, notably, while drawing attention to the ambiguous character of Jesus' self-manifestation: "... quod Christus virtute divinitatis conjecerat" (*Super Io.* 1:49, ed. Parma, t. X, 328b).

77. Augustine, *In Io. evang. tract.*, VII (CCSL 36, 76); cf. *Enarr. in Ps.* 65 (CCSL 39, 841).

78. On this aspect of Augustine's exegesis, see B. De Margerie, *Introduction à l'histoire*, vol. 3, 33–57.

79. "*⁴⁴ERAT AUTEM PHI⟨LIPPUS⟩ A BETHSAIDA*, quia erat in Galilea, *CIUITATE ANDREE ET PETRI*, id est in qua manebant Andreas et Petrus. Queritur quare magis uocauit Galileos quam alios. Responsio: Secundum Crisostomum, quia Galilea inter omnes prouincias habuit homines magis simplices, et ideo ne attribueretur humane sapientie, ideo etc., *Infirma mundi elegit Deus* (1 Cor 1:27)" (*Super Io.* 1:44, MS Saint-Omer, Bibl. mun. 260, f. 115rb;). Cf. Chrysostom, *In Io. hom.*, XX (PG 59, 124).

80. See chapter 3, note 83.

81. "Vnde sequitur: *ET LUX* (est *add. S*) id est Filius Dei, *IN TENEBRIS*, id est in tenebrosis hominibus per culpam et ignorantiam, *LUCET*, per predicationem et miraculorum operationem" (*Super Io.* 1:5, MS Saint-Omer, Bibl. mun. 260, f. 112rb).

82. In the introduction to his commentary H. Ridderbos emphasizes the all-embracing significance of Jesus' identity and identifies the Evangelist's motive for focusing exclusively on his person as a question of paramount importance; see *The Gospel of John*, 9.

83. "*HIC UENIT ... IN TESTIMONIUM ... UT TESTIMONIUM PERHIBERET DE LUMINE*, specificat cuius gratia uenerit. ... Nota, ut Christi ueritas declararetur, primo testificabatur per Moysen, Deuter. XXXII (cf. Dt 32:1–44); secundo per prophetas, Ysa. XLIII: *Vere uos testes mei estis* (43:10); tertio per Iohannem, qui fuit testis ex uisu et auditu; quarto per apostolos et predicatores alios, Actus I: *Eritis michi testes* (1:8); *DE LUMINE*. Christus dicitur lux in eo quod Deus, lumen in eo quod homo" (*Super Io.* 1:7, MS Saint-Omer, Bibl. mun. 260, f. 112va).

84. "Mistice. *VIE SYON*, predicatores quorum predicatio et uita ducit ad celestia, *LUGENT* pro se et aliis, pro irriguo superiori et inferiori, eo quod non sint nisi pauci qui *UENIANT* passibus fidei et morum siue pedibus affectus et intellectus, *AD SOLEMP⟨NITATEM⟩* ecclesie triumphantis; *PORTE EIUS*, patriarche et apostoli et prophete, *DESTRUCTE*, secundum eorum opinionem qui prosecuntur ecclesiam" (*Super Threnos* 1:4, ed. cit., 240).

85. "Allegorice. Pedes subportantes corpus ecclesie sunt prelati et doctores predicatores in quibus aliquando sunt *SORDES* uane glorie" (*Super Threnos* 1:9, ed. cit., 244).

86. "Allegorice. Dicit ecclesia, *DE EXCELSO*, id est celo uel Filio, *MISIT* Deus Pater *IGNEM* Spiritum Sanctum, *IN OSSIBUS MEIS*, id est apostolis, *ET ERUDIUIT ME*, Io. XVI: *Cum uenerit docebit omnem ueritatem* (Io 16:13). *EXPANDIT RETHE*, predicationis, *PEDIBUS MEIS*, predicatoribus, et *AUERTIT ME RETROR⟨SUM⟩*, ut sequerer uestigia Christi" (*Super Threnos* 1:13, ed. cit., 247).

87. "Allegorice ... *ET NON EST RECORDATUS SCAB⟨ELLI⟩ PE⟨DUM⟩ SU⟨ORUM⟩*, id est ecclesie iuxta pedes Christi, id est apostoli et predicatores sedent. Hic obliuisci uidetur cum temptari a Deo permittitur" (*Super Threnos* 2:1, ed. cit., 252–253).

88. "Item, *NUBES*, scilicet predicatores, *REUERTUNTUR*, scilicet ab actu predicationis, et hec *POST PLUUIAM*, propter obtenebrationem solis et lune etc., quando scilicet predicatio non capit in senibus, eo quod in stercore suo computruerunt (cf. Ioel 1:17)" (*Super Ecl.* 12:2, MSS Basel, Univ. Bibl. B III 20, f. 111vb; Madrid, Bibl. Nac. 493, f. 163r).

89. "Qui laborauerunt? ipse Abraham, Isaac, et Iacob. Legite labores eorum; in omnibus laboribus eorum prophetia Christi; et ideo seminatores. Moyses et ceteri patriarchae et omnes prophetae, quanta pertulerunt in illo frigore quando seminabant? Ergo iam in Iudaea messis parata erat. Merito ibi tamquam matura seges fuit, quando tot hominum millia pretia rerum suarum afferebant, et ad pedes apostolorum ponentes, expeditis humeris a sarcinis saecularibus, Christum Dominum sequebantur. ... Ad istam ergo messem non apostoli, sed angeli mittentur" (Augustine, *In Io. evang. tract.*, XV, CCSL 36, 163); cf. Alcuin, *Comm. in s. Io. Evang.* (PL 100, 799–800); Hugh of St. Cher, *Postille*, in Io. 4:36 (ed. Venetiis, t. VI, 309ra); Bonaventure, *In Io. com.* 4:37 (*Opera*, t. VI, 298a–b; 299b–300a).

90. "*VT ET QUI SEMINAT*, ut propheta, *SIMUL GAU⟨DEAT⟩ ET QUI METIT*, sicut predicatores qui sunt messores messis gratie, sicut angeli messis glorie. . . . Predicatores et prophete utroque seminant et metunt predicando, tamen ratione dicta, seminatio magis attribuitur prophetis et messio predicatoribus" (*Super Io.* 4, 36, MS Saint-Omer, Bibl. mun. 260, f. 122rb).

91. The former term's sole appearance in either the Vulgate or the Greek original is Io 13:16, where exegetes generally do not find the precise sense of a proper name for Jesus' chosen followers, as it appears for example in Mt 10:2; Mc 6:30; Lc 6:13. On the other hand, William does not employ the term *Duodecim* for this purpose, notwithstanding such usage in Io 6:67, 70, 71; 20:24.

92. For a detailed discussion of Aquinas's account in this commentary of the apostles' "special way" of believing resulting from their immediate knowledge, see S.-T. Bonino, "The Role of the Apostles in the Communication of Revelation according to the *Lectura super Iohannem* of St. Thomas Aquinas," in *Reading John with St. Thomas Aquinas, Theological Exegesis and Speculative Theology*, ed. M. Dauphinas and M. Levering, Washington, DC, 2005, 318–346.

93. "Et quidem, secundum Chrysostomum et Augustinum, seminantes semen spirituale sunt patres veteris testamenti, et Prophetae: nam ut dicitur Luc. 8, 11, 'semen est verbum Dei' quod Moyses et Prophetae seminaverunt in Iudaea; sed Apostoli messuerunt, quia ipsi quod intendebant, scilicet homines adducere ad Christum, efficere non potuerunt, quod tamen Apostoli fecerunt. . . . Prophetae seminantes sunt, quia multa de divinis tradiderunt; messores vero sunt apostoli, qui ea quae non manifestaverunt prophetae hominibus, praedicando et docendo revelaverunt. . . . Consequenter cum dicit in hoc enim est verbum verum etc., inducitur proverbium; quasi dicat, quod in hoc, idest in isto facto, verum est verbum, idest impletur vulgare proverbium, quod erat apud Iudaeos, scilicet unus seminat et alius metit" (Thomas Aquinas, *Super Io.* 4:35, ed. Parma, t. X, 372b–373a). This text has been cited by S.-T. Bonino, "The Role of the Apostles," 325–326, nn. 35, 36.

94. "*SET SCIO EUM*. Illud replicat ut addat, unde sequitur: *ET SERMONEM EIUS SERUO*, in corde per amorem, in ore per predicationem, in manu per operationem" (*Super Io.* 8:55, MS Saint-Omer, Bibl. mun. 260, f. 137vb).

95. "*ET PROPRIAS OUES ⟨UOCAT⟩ NOMINATIM*. Hec uocatio nichil aliud est cognitio qua suos distinguit ab aliis per administrationem sacramentorum, predicationum, uisitationum et consilium" (*Super Io.* 10:3, MS Saint-Omer, Bibl. mun. 260, f. 140rb).

96. Modern exegetes often take John 4:2 as evidence of a subsequent redaction of the Johannine text; cf. R. Brown, *The Gospel According to John*, 164; H. Ridderbos, *The Gospel of John*, 153 and note 145.

97. "*QUIA AUDI⟨ERUNT⟩ PHARISEI QUOD IHESUS PLURES DISCIPULOS FACIT*, scilicet baptizando, unde sequitur: *ET BAP⟨TIZAT⟩ QUAM IOHANNES. QUAMQUAM IHESUS NON BAP⟨TIZARET⟩, SET DISCIPULI EIUS*, scilicet intingendo, secundum Albinum, licet intus mundando" (*Super Io.* 4:2, MS Saint-Omer, Bibl. mun. 260, f. 120ra). Cf. Alcuin, *Comm. in s. Io. Evang.* (PL 100, 791. The same twofold agency is also at work in William's explanation for John the Baptist's description of Jesus as one who baptizes with the Holy Spirit: "*HIC EST QUI BAPTIZAT*, scilicet auctoritate, Petrus et alii ministerio, *IN SPIRITU SANCTO*" (*Super Io.* 1:33, MS Saint-Omer, Bibl. mun. 260, f. 114vb).

98. Among the numerous relevant texts that could be supplied, see especially Thomas Aquinas, *In IV Sent.*, d. 1, q. 1, a. 4, qᵃ 5 (ed. Parma, t. VII/B, 462a–463b); d. 4, a. 1, co. (ibid., 505b–506b); d. 5, q. 1, a. 2, co. (ibid., 525a–b).

99. Cf. H. Ridderbos, *The Gospel of John*, 546 and note 210.

100. Cf. R. Kysar, *John*, 254–265; P. Perkins, "The Gospel According to John," *NJBC* (61:199–206), 978a–979b.

101. "*HEC LOCUTUS EST IHESUS*. A quartodecimo capitulo usque huc, egit ad confirmationem discipulorum solicita exhortatione, hic deuota pro eis petitione. Vel primo instruxit exhortando, hic orando. Secundum Crisostomum, potest dici quod post admonitionem de habenda confidentia inter pressuras, docet hic uiam huius confidentie, scilicet confugere ad orationem. Et quia orauit non propter indigentiam, set propter nostrum exemplum, ideo primo orauit pro

se; secundo pro eis, docens in hoc orandi ordinem siue modum: [6]*MANIFESTAUI NOMEN T⟨UUM⟩*" (*Super Io.* 17:1, MS Saint-Omer, Bibl. mun. 260, f. 162ra). Cf. Chrysostom., *In Io. hom.*, LXXX (PG 59, 433).

102. "Dicit ergo *HEC*, que dicta sunt ad instructionem discipulorum . . . *LOCUTUS EST IHESUS, ET SUBLE⟨UATIS⟩ OCULIS.* In hoc etiam instruimur orare post predicationem" (*Super Io.* 17:1, MS Saint-Omer, Bibl. mun. 260, f. 162ra).

103. "*EGO TE CLARIFI⟨CAUI⟩ SUPER TERRAM* predicatione, conuersatione, miraculorum operatione, Crisostomus: "Bene dicit: *super terram* quia in celis clarificatus fuerat et ab angelis adhoratus. Gloriam ergo uocat hic culturam, que per hominem[103] fuit"; *OPUS QUOD DEDISTI MICHI UT FA⟨CIAM⟩*, quod est gentium illuminatio, Ys. XLIX: *Dedi te in lucem gentium*; *CONSU⟨MMAUI⟩*, id est cito consummabo. Vnde secundum Crisostomum, quod in ipso erat, in passione totum fecerat. Vel, ad literam, iam ordinauerat ut predicaretur. Item, dicit sub preterito ut ostenderet se fore presentem predicationi Apostolorum et conuersionem gentium" (*Super Io.* 17:4, MS Saint-Omer, Bibl. mun. 260, f. 162va). Cf. Chrysostom., *In Io. hom.*, LXXX (PG 59, 435).

104. "[17:6]*MANIFESTAUI.* Postquam orauit pro se, hic pro suis. Et primo pro suis iam credentibus; secundo pro suis per illos credituris: [17:20]*NON PRO EIS TANTUM*; tertio pro utriusque, scilicet tam istis, quam illis: [17:24]*PATER, QUOS DEDISTI MICHI UOLO*" (*Super Io.* 17:6, MS Saint-Omer, Bibl. mun. 260, f. 163va).

105. "[17:20]*NON PRO EIS AUTEM.* Postquam orauit pro suis iam existentibus discipulis, hic pro suis futuris et per illos discipulos credituris. Et primo rogat ut homo; secundo quod rogauit insinuat se daturum ut Deus: [17:22]*ET EGO CLARITATEM.* In prima, primo ostendit pro quibus rogat; secundo quid rogat: [17:21]*VT OMNES.* Continuat sic: Rogo pro illis, et [17:20]*NON PRO EIS AUTEM ROGO TANTUM*, licet primo et principaliter pro eis, *SET ⟨ET⟩ PRO EIS QUI CREDITURI SUNT PER UERBUM EORUM IN ME.* Eorum dicitur uerbum quantum ad prolationem, set Spiritus sancti per inspirationem" (*Super Io.* 17:20, MS Saint-Omer, Bibl. mun. 260, f. 163vb–164ra).

106. Bonaventure, *In Io. com.* 2:2 (*Opera*, t. VI, 475b).

107. Thomas Aquinas, *Super Io.* 4:35 (ed. Parma, t. X, 597a–599b). See the analysis of Thomas's exposition by S.-T. Bonino, "The Role of the Apostles," 324–325.

108. "[25]*HEC LOCUTUS SUM.* Hic promittit confirmationem sui dicti per missionem Spiritus sancti. Et primo reducit ad memoriam se talia dixisse; secundo promittit Spiritum sanctum uenturum et plenius docturum esse: [26]*PARACLITUS AUTEM. . . . [26]ILLE UOS DOCEBIT OMNIA*, quantum ad intellectum quem illuminabit, *ET SUGGERET UOBIS OMNIA*, quantum ad affectum quem inflammabit, *QUECUMQUE DIXERO UOBIS*, scilicet necessaria uobis ad salutem" (*Super Io.* 14:25–26, MS Saint-Omer, Bibl. mun. 260, f. 156ra).

109. William has not borrowed these comments from Bonaventure, yet he is in basic agreement with another contemporary, Thomas Aquinas, *Super Io.* 4:35, ed. Parma, t. X, 559a: "Filius ergo tradit nobis doctrinam, cum sit Verbum; sed Spiritus sanctus doctrinae ejus nos capaces facit. Dicit ergo: *ILLE UOS DOCEBIT OMNIA*; quia quaecumque homo doceat extra, nisi Spiritus sanctus interius det intelligentiam, frustra laborat: quia nisi Spiritus adsit cordi audientis, otiosus erit sermo doctoris." See S.-T. Bonino, "The Role of the Apostles," 330–331.

110. See the remarks on *theoria* in monastic exegesis offered by J. Leclercq, *Initiation aux auteurs monastiques*, 98–99.

111. "*Regressus est*: qui regressus est reductio illuminationis super audientes post egressum ab eis factum in contemplationis veritatis, et confutationem hostis. Ad haec enim duo a cura sua egreditur: ut contemplando veritatem hauriat, quam praedicando effundat" (*In Luc.* 4:14, ed. Borgnet, t. XXIV, 320b). See also the remark of Humbert of Romans, chapter 3, note 263.

112. What follows are two examples: ". . . tertio duxit contemplativos in montem liberalis communicantiae propter caritativam diffusionem gratuitae praedicationis" (*Sermones dominicales*, XVI, 7, ed. J. G. Bougerol, Bibl. Franciscana Scholastica Medii Aevi, t. XXVII , 1977, 247); "*Inclina caelos* tuos, id est contemplativos et caelestes viros ad homines terrenos per praedicationem . . ." (*Sermones dominicales*, XXVII, ibid., 325).

113. E.g., *Super Is.* 21:5 (ed. Leonina, t. XXVIII, 109a); 40:9 (ibid., 168b); *Super Io.* prol. (ed. Parma, t. X, 280b); 1:51 (ibid., 329b); 14:6 (ibid., 547a); 21:3 (ibid., 636b); *In III Sent.*, d. 35, q. 1, a. 1, ad

5 (ed. Parma, t. VII/A, 401b–402a); a. 3a, ad 3 (ibid., 404b); a. 3c, co. (ibid., 405a–b); *ST*, II-II, q. 6, a. 1, co. (ed. Leonina, t. VIII, 61a); *De viritutibus*, q. 2, a. 11, ad 6 (ed. Parma, t. VIII, 604b); *ST*, III, q. 37, a. 3, ad 4 (ed. Leonina, t. XI, 379b). Perhaps his most famous statement on the matter is *ST*, II-II, q. 188, a. 6, co.: "Unum quidem quod ex plenitudine contemplationis derivatur: sicut doctrina et praedicatio. . . . Et hoc praefertur simplici contemplationi. Sicut enim maius est illuminare quam lucere solum, ita maius est contemplata aliis tradere quam solum contemplari" (ed. Leonina, t. X, 529a).

114. "$^{115}$*ET EX MEDIO EIUS SIMILITUDO QUATUOR ANIMALIUM*, id est quatuor euuangelistorum, qui sancti non essent nisi Christi similitudinem habuissent, et ita describitur in communi, consequenter in speciali: $^{115}$*ET HIC ASPECTUS* etc. Et primo dicitur quod $^{115}$*SIMILITUDO HOMINIS* simpliciter dicta et antonomastice, id est Christi erat in eis per fidem, spem et caritatem. Secundo quod cuilibet inerat facies quadruplex. Per faciem qua quis cognoscitur, fides. $^{116}$*QUATUOR* ergo *FACIES UNI*, quia in omnibus euuangelistas una fuit notitia fidei quantum ad misterium incarnationis, passionis, ressurectionis, ascensionis (ascentionis $P_1$). Per pennam contemplatio, $^{116}$*QUATUOR* ergo *PENNE UNI*, quia eadem de diuinitate Christi contemplati sunt, scilicet unitatem essentie et trinitatem personarum. $^{117}$*PEDES EORUM RECTI* per intentionis et affectionis ordinationem, He. 12: *Gressus rectos facite* (He 12:13). $^{7}$*PLANTA PEDIS EORUM QUASI UITULI* per discretionem et maturitatem, *SCINTILLABANT* per boni exempli informationem et predicationem; $^{118}$*MANUS HOMINIS SUB PENNIS EORUM* per discretam cum contemplatione operationem *PER QUATUOR PARTES*, id est quatuor uirtutes cardinales. $^{118}$*QUATUOR FACIES ET PENNAS PER QUATUOR PARTES HABEBANT*, quia Christi humanitatem (humilitatem $P_1$) et diuinitatem per quatuor partes mundi predicabant. $^{119}$*IUNCTE ERANT PEN⟨NE⟩ EORUM ⟨ALTERIUS AD ALTERUM⟩*, quia in contemplatione habuerunt concordiam et unitatem. $^{119}$*NON REUERTABANTUR CUM AMBU⟨LERUNT⟩*, per temporalium curam et resumptionem, *SET UNUMQUODQUE ANTE FA⟨CIEM⟩ SUAM GRADI⟨EBATUR⟩*, per celestium quesitionem" (*Super Ez.* 1:5–9, MS Paris, BnF lat. 573, f. 157va).

115. Such is the sense given the term by Thomas Aquinas: "Unde et nomen contemplationis significat illum actum principalem, quo quis Deum in seipso contemplatur" (*In III Sent.*, d. 35, q. 1, a. 2c, co., ed. Parma, t. VII/A, 403b).

116. "*FACIEM BOUIS* per laborem predicationis, Ys. 11: *Conflabunt gladios suos in uo⟨meres⟩* . . . (Is 2:4); Hos. (Ios. $P_1$) x: *Arabit Iudas et sulcos* (sulcus $P_1$) *confring⟨et⟩ sibi Iacob* . . . (Os 10:11); huius sint quatuor ale, quos tangit ⟨II⟩ Thi. III: *Omnis scriptura diuinitus inspirata utilis est ad corripiendum, ad erudiendum, ad docendum, ad arguendum* (2 Tim 3:16); *FACIEM AQUILE* per contemplationem superiorum, et huius quatuor sunt ale, scilicet lectio, oratio, meditatio, diuine dulcedinis pregustatio. Lectio querit, oratio pulsat, meditatio ingreditur, pregustatio inuenit (cf. Mt 7:7; Lc 11:9)" (*Super Ez.* 1:10, MS Paris, BnF lat. 573, f. 158ra).

117. During the twelfth century, Guy the Carthusian listed them as the steps of the monk's ladder to paradise: "Cum die quadam corporali manuum labore occupatus, de spiritualis hominis exercitio cogitare cœpissem, quatuor spirituales gradus animo cogitanti se subito obtulerunt: scilicet, Lectio, Meditatio, Oratio, et Contemplatio. Hæc est Scala Claustralium, qua de terra in cœlum sublevantur" (*Scala Claustralium* 1, ed. G. El Cartujo, *Cistercium* 45 (1993), 15–35). Among the several places where the formula appears in the writings of the twelfth-century Grandmontine monk Gerard Iterius is the following: "Tempus otii est, dilectissimi, tempus quo uacare debemus lectioni, orationi, meditationi, contemplationi, et cessare a negotiis mundanae conuersationis . . ." ("Sermo de confirmatione seu enucleatione 'Speculi Granmontis'" 84, *Scriptores ordinis Grandmontensis* (ed. J. Becquet, Turnhout, 1968, CCCM 8, 411). Other writers follow a slightly different order, for example, Bernard of Clairvaux: "Hinc pretiosa illa pallia tibi explicabuntur, lectiones, meditationes, orationes, contemplationes" (*Parabolae* VII, 6, ed. J. Leclercq and H. Rochais, *Sancti Bernardi Opera*, t. VI/2, Roma, 1972, 297).

118. ". . . ad *contemplationem* non venitur nisi per meditationem perspicuam, conversationem sanctam et orationem devotam" (*Itinerarium mentis in Deum*, I, 8, *Opera*, t. V, 298a).

119. "Quattuor sunt in quibus nunc exercetur uita iustorum et, quasi per quosdam gradus ad futuram perfectionem subleuatur, uidelicet lectio siue doctrina, meditatio, oratio, et operatio. Quinta deinde sequitur, contemplatio, in qua, quasi quodam precedentium fructu, in hac uita etiam que sit boni operis merces futura pregustatur" (Hugh of Saint Victor, *Didascalicon de studio legendi*, V, ed. C. Buttimer, 109). B. Smalley observed: "The Victorines did not alter the monastic conception of *lectio divina*; they restated it, and in doing so they shifted the emphasis." She went on to mention (*The Study of the Bible*, 196), astutely, that the *Didiscalicon* sets forth an adaptation of *lectio divina* to the environment of Parisian scholarship. For discussions of this treatise, see D. Poirel, *Hugues de Saint-Victor*, 123–129; P. Sicard, *Hugues de Saint-Victor et son École*, Turnhout, 1991, 199–217; H. De Lubac, *Exegèse Médiévale*, Seconde partie, I, 288–301.

120. In a question devoted to the contemplative life, Thomas entertains an objection to the effect that these three, as well as a fourth, namely, hearing, are acts of contemplation: "Praeterea, ad vitam contemplativam pertinere dicuntur *oratio, lectio* et *meditatio.* . . ." He concludes that they are preliminary: "Haec est autem differentia inter hominem et angelum . . . quod angelus simplici apprehensione veritatem intuetur, homo autem quodam processu ex multis pertingit ad intuitum simplicis veritatis. Sic igitur vita contemplativa unum quidem actum habet in quo finaliter perficitur, scilicet contemplationem veritatis, a quo habet unitatem: habet autem multos actus quibus pervenit ad hunc actum finalem" (*ST*, II-II, q. 180, a. 3, ob. 4 et co., ed. Leonina, t. X, 426a–b, ed. Leonina, t. X, 426a–b).

121. "Hinc comparatur aquile, que altius uolat et acutius uidet, Eze. 1" (*Super Io.*, prol., MS Saint-Omer, Bibl. mun. 260, f. 110ra).

122. Origen was most likely the source of the schema of Mary and Martha as types of the contemplative and active lives; cf. *Commentarium in Canticum Canticorum, secundum translationem quam fecit Rufinus*, II (ed. W. A. Baehrens, Leipzig, 1925, GCS 33, 121. For a classic illustration of the functioning of the typology in Western exegesis, see Gregory the Great, *Moralia in Iob*, VI, 37 (CCSL 143, 331).

123. "*IHESUS ERGO UT UI⟨DIT⟩ EAM PLORANTEM ET IUDEOS* etc., ex compassione, *FREMUIT SPIRITU*, id est ueraciter doluit et se turbauit compatiendo. . . . Hic queritur quare supra quesierit (quesierunt *cod.*) de fide Marthe, non hic de fide Marie. Responsio: Quia ita fuit feruentior in fide. Item, secundum Crisostomum, nunc erant ibi multi Iudei, tunc non. Item, ad significandum quod contemplatiui clarius uident, unde *Lya lippis erat oculis* (Gn 29, 17)" (*Super Io.* 11:33, MS Saint-Omer, Bibl. mun. 260, f. 144vb).

124. William accords Martha's confession a distinct exposition, which he introduces as follows: "*AIT ILLI.* Hic exprimitur sue fidei perfectionem . . ." (*Super Io.* 11:27, MS Saint-Omer, Bibl. mun. 260, f. 144rb).

125. Bonaventure, *In Io. com.* 11:33 (*Opera*, t. VI, 402a–b). In our consideration of the manuscript witnesses to William's *Super Iohannem* in chapter 3, we observed that his synopsis of Bonaventure's comment was misunderstood either by the author, the reporter, or the copyist of the version of MS Assisi 49.

126. Chrysostom, *In Io. hom.*, LXIII (PG 59, 349).

127. For a few applications of this typology, see Gregory the Great, *Moralia in Iob*, VI, 37 (CCSL 143, 330); Gerard Iterius, "Sermo de confirmatione seu enucleatione 'Speculi Granmontis,'" 73, *Scriptores ordinis Grandmontensis* (ed. J. Becquet, 1968, CCCM 8, 398); Bernard of Claraevaux, *Sermones super Cantica Canticorum*, IX, 8 (*Opera*, ed. J. Leclercq, C. Talbot, and H. Rochais, 1972, vol. 1, 47); Thomas of Chobham, *Summa de Arte Predicandi*, Prologus (ed. F. Morenzoni, 1988, CCCM 82, 9).

128. Cf. Peter Lombard, *Sent.*, III, d. XXIII, Cap. 2: "Quid sit fides. Fides est virtus qua creduntur quae non videntur" (ed. Coll. S. Bonaventurae, t. II, 141).

129. "*⁷VADE QUOQUE* etc., usque huc exponi in bonum, ita quod primo hortatur ad iocunditatem contemplationis; secundo ad instantiam actionis: *¹⁰QUODCUMQUE POTEST.* Quantum ad primum, tangit quatuor: primo ⟨ad⟩ scripture meditationem: *⁷COMEDE IN LETITIA PA⟨NEM⟩ TUUM ET BIBE CUM GAUDIO UI⟨NUM⟩ T⟨UUM⟩*; secundo ad uite puritatem: *⁸OMNI TEMPORE*

*SINT UESTIMENTA T⟨UA⟩ CANDIDA*; tertio ad conscientie hylaritatem: [8]*ET OLEUM DE CAPITE
T⟨UO⟩*; quarto ad diuine dulcedinis gustationem: [9]*PERFRUERE UITA*; quinto quasi conclu-
dendo subiungit huius status commendationem: [9]*HEC EST ENIM PARS*. Et nota ordinem.
Primum enim generat secundum, Ieronimus: 'Ama studium litterarum et carnis uitia non
amabis.' Secundum generat tertium, ⟨II⟩ Cor. I: *Gloria nostra hec est ⟨testimonium conscientie
nostre⟩* (2 Cor 1:12). Tertium generat quartum, Prouer. XV: *Secura mens quasi iuge conuiuium*
(Prv 15:15). Quantum ad actionem, docet tria, scilicet operari utiliter: [10]*QUODCUMQUE*, quia
Iac. II: *Quicumque totam legem seruauerit, offenderit autem in uno, factus est omnium reus* (Iac
2:10); corporaliter, per se, non solum per alios: [10]*MANUS TUA*, Ps: *Manus eius in cophino seruierunt* (Ps 80:7); item, festinanter et [10]*INSTANTER OPERARE*, Gal. ultimo: *Bonum facientes non
deficiamus* (Gal 6:9)" (*Super Ecl.* 9:7–10, MSS Basel, Univ. Bibl. B III 20, f. 108rb–va; Madrid,
Bibl. Nac. 493, f. 157r). Cf. Jerome, Epist. 125 (ed. Labourt, t. VII, 123).

130. For remarks concerning spiritual sensation, there is perhaps no better place to look than in
commentaries on Ps 33:9: *gustate et videte quoniam suavis est Dominus*. An example appears in
the following remark of Cassiodorus: "Gustate non pertinet ad palatum sed ad animae suauis-
simum sensum, qui diuina contemplatione saginatur" (*Expositio psalmorum* 33, CCSL 97,
297). For a few other examples, see Augustine, *Enarr. in Ps.*, in Ps. 33 (CCSL 38, 290); in Ps. 51
(ibid., CCSL 39, 637); Bernard of Clairvaux, *Sententiae*, III, 126 (*Opera*, ed. J. Leclercq, C.
Talbot, and H. Rochais, 1972, vol. 6.2, 245); Bonaventure, *Collationes in Hexaemeron*, IIII, 1
(ed. F. Delorme, Bibl. Franciscana Scholastica Medii Aevi, t. VIII, 1934, 223). On early Christian understandings of the spiritual senses, especially of smell, see S. A. Harvey, *Scenting Salvation: Ancient Christianity and the Olfactory Imagination*, Berkeley, 2006. Among recent studies
on spiritual sensation in medieval literature, see R. Fulton, "'Taste and See that the Lord is
Sweet' (Ps. 33:9): the Flavor of God in the Monastic West," *Journal of Religion*, 86:2 (2006)
169–204; B. T. Coolman, *Knowing God by Experience: the Spiritual Senses in the Theology of
William of Auxerre*, Washington D.C., 2004; G. Rudy, *Mystical Language of Sensation in the
Later Middle Ages*, (Studies in Medieval History and Culture 14), New York, 2002; R. D. Hale,
"'Taste and See, for God is Sweet': Sensory Perception and Memory in Medieval Christian
Mystical Experience," in *Vox Mystica: Essays on Medieval Mysticism in Honor of Professor Valerie
M. Lagorio*, ed. V. M. Lagorio and A. C. Bartlett, Cambridge, 1995, 3–14.

131. "*SPIRITUM UERITATIS . . . QUEM MUNDUS*, id est mundi amatores quamdiu sunt tales, quia
pleni sunt aliunde, *NON POTEST ACCIPERE, QUIA NON UIDET EUM*, intra per fidem, *NEC SCIT
EUM*, extra per operationem" (*Super Io.* 14:17, MS Saint-Omer, Bibl. mun. 260, f. 155rb).

132. Peter Lombard, for example, explains faith as an interior vision as follows: "Quod fides nullo
capitur sensu. Sed sciendum est quod, cum uisio alia sit interior, alia exterior, non est fides de
subiectis exteriori uisioni; est tamen de his quae uisu interiori utcumque capiuntur." See *Sent.*,
III, d. XXIV, Cap. 3, ed. Coll. S. Bonaventurae, t. II, 151.

133. "*VOS AUTEM COGNOSCETIS EUM*, scilicet intra sensu interiori et quedam gustu experimentali,
et extra in signo uisibili, *QUIA APUD UOS MANEBIT*, quantum ad effectum exteriorem, et in /
*UOBIS ERIT*, quantum ad interiorem" (*Super Io.* 14:17, MS Saint-Omer, Bibl. mun. 260, f.
155rb–va).

134. On the twofold mission of the Holy Spirit, cf. Peter Lombard, *Sent.*, I, d. XVI, Cap. I, 1–2 (ed.
Coll. S. Bonaventurae, t. I, pars II, 138–139); d. XVII, Cap. I (ibid., 141–143); Augustine, *De
trin.*, II, 5 (CCSL 50, 87–93). For an account of the origins and development of the notion of
Trinitarian missions, including extensive references to relevant primary and secondary literature, see G. Emery, *La théologie trinitaire de saint Thomas d'Aquin*, 425–481 (esp. 429–465).

135. "*ET EGO UIDI* oculo corporali et spirituali *ET TESTIMONIUM PERHIBUI . . . QUIA HIC EST
FILIUS DEI*, unicus, unde potest baptizare auctoritate" (*Super Io.* 1:34, MS Saint-Omer, Bibl.
mun. 260, f. 114vb).

136. On the twofold mission of the Son, cf. Peter Lombard, *Sent.*, I, d. XV, Cap. 7–8 (ed. Coll. S.
Bonaventurae, t. I, pars II, 135–137); Augustine, *De trin.*, IV, 20 (CCSL 50, 195–202).

137. "Et nota quod dicit: [6:45]*OMNIS QUI AUDIT* / et post: [6:46]*NON QUIA PATREM UIDIT QUIS⟨QUAM⟩*,
quia licet uisus et auditus spiritualis non differant ad inuicem, tamen uisio proprie loquentem,

auditus locutionem loquentis, que dicitur hic inspiratio, respicit. Et licet inspirationem Patris percipiat quis et illam uideat sicut et audit, non tamen uidet inspirantem, quia auditus non respicit eum, set effectum" (*Super Io.* 6:45–46, MS Saint-Omer, Bibl. mun. 260, f. 129rb).

138. "*QUI UIDET ME* spiritualiter *UIDET ET EUM QUI MISIT.* Ratio est unitas essentie, infra XIIII: *Qui uidet me, uidet et Patrem* (14, 9). Et notandum quod differt uisus spiritualis a fide, quia uisus dirigitur proprie super substantiam, fides supra conditionem uel circumstantiam substantie. Vnde uisus spiritualis figitur in Deum, fides autem in hiis que de Deo" (*Super Io.* 12:45, MS Saint-Omer, Bibl. mun. 260, f. 150ra).

139. Cf. Thomas Aquinas, *In III Sent.*, d. 24, q. 1, a. 1 (ed. Parma, t. VII/A, 259b–261b); *De Ver.*, q. 14, a. 8 (ed. Leonina, t. XXII/2, 458a–461b). For later expositions of the same matter, cf. *ST*, II-I, q. 62, a. 3 (ed. Leonina, t. VI, 403); II-II, q. 1, a. 1–2 (ed. Leonina, t. VIII, 7a–11b).

140. As the printed editions of this text are faulty, the translation is based on the text of MS Vat. lat. 1030, f. 2rb: "Iohannes uero supra nebulam infirmitatis humane uelud aquila uolans, lucem incommutabilis ueritatis acutissimis atque firmissimis oculis cordis intuetur, et ipsam diuinitatem Domini nostri Ihesu Christi, qua Patri equalis est, intendens, eam in suo euangelio, quantum inter homines sufficere credidit, studuit precipue commendare. Et de hoc uolatu Iohannis dicitur Iob XXXIX: Numquid ad preceptum tuum eleuabitur aquila? id est Iohannes, et infra (ita *cod.*): *Oculi eius de longe prospiciunt,* quia scilicet ipsum Verbum Dei in sinu Patris mentis oculo intuetur" (Thomas Aquinas, *Super Iohannem,* prologue).

141. "sub imaginatione non cadit nisi corpus"; *ST* I, q. 50, a. 1, co. (ed. Leonina, t. V, 4). Thomas is unequivocal on this point and returns to it repeatedly. See, for example, *ST* I, q. 12, a. 3, co. (ed. Leonina, t. IV, 119): ". . . impossibile est Deum videri sensu visus, vel quocumque alio sensu aut potentia sensitivae partis. Omnis enim potentia huiusmodi est actus corporalis organi, ut infra dicetur. Actus autem proportionatur ei cuius est actus. Unde nulla huiusmodi potentia potest se extendere ultra corporalia. Deus autem incorporeus est, ut supra ostensum est. Unde nec sensu nec imaginatione videri potest, sed solo intellectu." For a few other examples in his systematic works, see *ST* I, q. 78, a. 1; q. 85, a. 1; I-II, q. 3, a. 3; I-II, q. 46, a. 3, ad 3; *SCG* III, 53. Among the numerous examples from his exegetical works is *Super Io.* 1:18 (ed. Parma, t. X, 312b): ". . . numquam videbit oculi corporali, vel aliquo sensu, vel imaginatione, cum per sensus non percipiantur nisi sensata corporea; Deus autem incorporeus est."

142. Here we refer to H. Urs Von Balthasar, *The Glory of the Lord: A Theological Aesthetics,* vol. 1, *Seeing the Form,* ed. J. Fessio, S.J. and J. Riches, San Francisco, 1982 (English trans. E. Leiva-Merikis of *Herrlichkeit: Eine theologishe Ästhetik,* I: *Schau der Gestalt,* Einsiedeln, 1967), 365–380. For the remarks on Balthasar and Rahner in this discussion, I am indebted to S. Fields, "Balthasar and Rahner on the Spiritual Senses," *Theological Studies* 57 (1996), 224–241.

143. Within the enormous body of the writings of Karl Rahner, we make reference to "The Doctrine of the 'Spiritual Senses' in the Middle Ages," in *Theological Investigations,* vol. 16, trans. David Morland, London, 1979, 104–134, which originally appeared as "La Doctrine des 'sens spirituels' au Moyen-Age: en particulier chez Saint Bonaventure," *RAM* 14 (1933), 263–299. This essay, which contains extensive references to other studies on the same subject, follows upon his earlier treatment of the five spiritual senses in the thought of Origen and a few of his followers, notably Evagrius of Pontus, "Le début d'une doctrine des cinq sens spirituels chez Origene," *RAM* 13 (1932), 113–145.

144. For a lucid comparison of the two theologians, see K. Kilby, "Balthasar and Karl Rahner," in *The Cambridge Companion to Hans Urs Von Balthasar,* ed. E. Oakes and D. Moss, Cambridge, 2004, 256–268.

145. *The Glory of the Lord,* I, 365–380. See O. Davies, "The Theological Aesthetics," in *The Cambridge Companion to Hans Urs Von Balthasar,* 131–142.

146. "But once the Christian has risen with Christ and ascended to the Father, then, with body and spirit, he has become a 'spiritual man' and henceforth—in so far as he is a believer—he has not only a spiritual intellect and will, but also spiritual heart, a spiritual imagination and spiritual senses" (*The Glory of the Lord,* I, 366).

147. Ibid., 150–151. Cf. S. Fields, "Balthasar and Rahner," 227.

148. "Spiritual senses, in the sense of Christian mysticism, presuppose devout bodily senses which are capable of undergoing Christian transformation by coming to resemble the sensibility of Christ and of Mary. In a Christian sense, there is something like a centre which must be accepted as a fact even before it is fully understood speculatively, The reality of this centre may be evoked above all from the cadences of the Church's greatest theologians" (*The Glory of the Lord*, I, 378–379).

149. It is unlikely that either William or Thomas was unaware of this text, wherein Augustine mentions no fewer than five senses by which he experiences God: "Quid autem amo, cum te amo? Non speciem corporis nec decus temporis, non candorem lucis ecce istis amicum oculis, non dulces melodias cantilenarum omnimodarum, non florum et ungentorum et aromatum suauiolentiam, non manna et mella, non membra acceptabilia carnis amplexibus: non haec amo, cum amo deum meum. Et tamen amo quandam lucem et quandam uocem et quendam odorem et quendam cibum et quendam amplexum, cum amo Deum meum, lucem, uocem, odorem, cibum, amplexum interioris hominis mei, ubi fulget animae meae, quod non capit locus, et ubi sonat, quod non rapit tempus, et ubi olet, quod non spargit flatus, et ubi sapit, quod non minuit edacitas, et ubi haeret, quod non diuellit satietas. Hoc est quod amo, cum Deum meum amo" (*Confessiones*, X, 6, ed. L. Verheijen, 1990, CCSL 27, 159).

150. "Postquam Apostolus posuit exhortationem suam, hic hortatur ad virtutem humilitatis, exemplo Christi: et primo inducit ad imitandum Christi exemplum: secundo ponit ejus exemplum, ibi, *Qui cum in forma in forma Dei esset, non rapinam arbitratus est esse se aequalem Deo; sed semetipsum exinaniuit*. Dicit ergo: Sitis humilis, ut dixi: ideo *hoc sentite*, idest experimento tenete, *quod* fuit *in Christo Jesu*. Notandum, quod quinque modis debemus hoc sentire, scilicet quinque sensibus. Primo videre ejus claritatem, ut ei conformemur illuminati. Isa. 33:17: 'Regem in decore suo videbunt oculi ejus.' 2 Corinth. 3:18: 'Nos autem omnes revelata facie 'gloriam Dei speculantes, in eamdem imaginem transformamur a claritate in claritatem.' Secundo audire ejus sapientiam ut beatificemur. 3 Reg. 10:8: 'Beati viri tui et beati servi tui, hi qui stant coram te, et audiunt sapientiam tuam.' Psalm. 17:45: 'In auditu auris obedivit mihi.' Tertio odorare gratias suae mansuetudinis, ut ad eum curramus. Cant. 1:3: 'Trahe me post te: curremus in odorem unguentorum tuorum.' Quarto gustare dulcedinem ejus pietatis, ut in Deo semper simus. Ps 33:9: 'Gustate et videte quoniam suavis est Dominus.' Quinto tangere ejus virtutem, ut salvemur. Mt 9:21: 'Si tetigero tantum fimbriam vestimenti ejus, salva ero'"; *Super ad Phil.* 2:2 (ed. Parma, t. XIII, 513a).

151. *The Glory of the Lord*, I, 379–380.

152. "If one assumes five different faculties which correspond analogically to the bodily powers of sensation, then one is going quite a long way beyond the empirical data" (K. Rahner, "The Doctrine of the 'Spiritual Senses' in the Middle Ages," 133).

153. S. Fields sums up Rahner's thought on the matter as follows: "The conversion to the phantasm, which links the worlds of sensate form and imagination to the intellect's preconceptual grasp of the Absolute, already baptizes sensation into the Christian order, albeit implicitly" ("Balthasar and Rahner," 232).

154. "If . . . one describes the senses as acts of intellect and will, then it is no longer obvious why there should be exactly five types of such intellectual activity. This move in fact undermines the raison d'être of the whole system, for it does not provide any fresh knowledge and does not say any more than could be said without it. This remains true even if the well-chosen metaphors are chosen from the realm of sense perception (K. Rahner, "The Doctrine of the 'Spiritual Senses' in the Middle Ages," 133).

155. "*VERBUM CARO FACTUM EST*, id est unitum carni per accessum carnis ad ipsum. Dicitur autem unitum carni magis quam / anime ad maioris humilitatis et pietatis ostensionem. Item, propter hereticos hoc negantes. Non dicit autem homo, set caro, quia homo magis sonat in personam quam caro. Dicit autem magis Verbum quam Filius ut excludat intellectum carnalem (cf. 8, 5). *ET HABITAUIT IN NOBIS*, id est in nostra natura. Vel id est inter nos (cf. Act 1:21). Vel nobiscum (cf. Mt 1:23), in nobis per fidem et gratiam" (*Super Io.* 1:14, MS Saint-Omer, Bibl. mun. 260, f. 113rb).

156. In his exposition of this verse, Thomas Aquinas similarly lists several heresies to be confuted, and similarly places this one first, ascribing it to Eutyches; see *Super Io.* 1:14 (ed. Parma, t. X, 304a). Questions remain concerning Eutyches's actual teaching; see J. N. D. Kelly, *Early Christian Doctrines*, 330–334; A. Grillmeier, *Christ in Christian Tradition*, London, 1965, 356–365; M. Jugie, "Eutychès et eutychianisme," *DTC* 15, no. 1 (1913), 1582–1609; B. Emmi, "Leone ed Eutyche," *Angelicum* 29 (1952), 3–42.

157. Here, Thomas Aquinas similarly lists this as the second heresy. Though he attributes the denial of Christ's human soul only to Arius, he subsequently associates Apollinarius with the proposition that the Word assumed a sensitive soul, though not an intellective one; see *Super Io.* 1:14 (ed. Parma, t. X, 304b–305a). Elsewhere, he ascribes the former position to both figures; cf. *SCG*, IV, c. 34 (ed. Leonina, t. XV, 118b); *ST*, III, q. 5, a. 3, co. (ed. Leonina, t. XI, 90a). On Arius's Christology, see J. N. D. Kelly, *Early Christian Doctrines*, 281–284; A. Grillmeier, *Christ in Christian Tradition*, 183–192. On the Christology of Apollinarius, see J. N. D. Kelly, ibid., 289–295; A. Grillmeier, ibid., 220–233; H. De Riedmatten, "La Christologie d'Apollinaire de Laodicée," *Studia Patristica* 2 (1957), 208–234.

158. Also listing this heresy in third place, Thomas Aquinas assigns it to the Manicheans; see *Super Io.* 1:14 (ed. Parma, t. X, 305b).

159. In this connection, Thomas Aquinas identifies Nestorius explicitly, ibid., 305a–b. Within the extensive literature on Nestorius's Christology, see especially J. Mcguckin, *St. Cyril of Alexandria: The Christological Controversy, Its History, Theology and Texts*, New York, 2004, 126–174; A. Grillmeier, *Christ in Christian Tradition*, 369–399; J. N. D. Kelly, *Early Christian Doctrines*, 310–317; E. Amann, "Nestorius. L'Église nestorienne?" *DTC* 11, no. 1 (1931), 157–323.

160. Much has been written on the development of the concept of *persona* (and its Greek counterpart πρόσωπον) in the controversies of the third, fourth, and fifth centuries surrounding Trinitarian and Christological doctrines. Particularly helpful are the discussions of A. Grillmeier, *Christ in Christian Tradition*, 124–126, 279, 338, 507–514, 551–552; and J. N. D. Kelly, *Early Christian Doctrines*, 252–279, 310–343.

161. "*RESPONDIT IHESUS ET DIXIT EI*, humiliter, non exasperando, *SI SCIRES DONUM DEI*, id est gratiam tempore isto factam mundo . . . *ET QUIS EST QUI DICIT TIBI: DA MICHI BIBERE*, id est me, per quem hec gratia facta est et Spiritus Sanctus datus, *TU FOR⟨SITAN⟩ PETISSES AB EO*, innuit libertatem arbitrii, *ET DE⟨DISSET⟩ TIBI AQUA⟨M⟩ UI⟨UAM⟩*, gratiam Spiritus sancti a peccatis abluentem et spiritualiter uiuificantem" (*Super Io.* 4:10, MS Saint-Omer, Bibl. mun. 260, f. 120va).

162. "*SET AQUA QUAM DA⟨BO⟩ EI FIET IN EO FONS AQUE SA⟨LIENTIS⟩*, id est salire facientis, *IN UITAM ETERNAM*. Gratia enim mouet liberum arbitrium ad opera meritoria per que habetur uita eterna" (*Super Io.* 4:14, MS Saint-Omer, Bibl. mun. 260, f. 121ra).

163. William does not appear to differ with Thomas Aquinas, who is clear on this point: "Omnis potentia hujusmodi est actus corporalis organi. . . . Actus autem proportionatur ei cujus est actus. Unde nulla hujusmodi potentia potest extendere ultra corporalia . . . impossibile est Deum videri sensu visus, vel quocumque alio sensu. . . . Unde nec sensu, imaginatione videri, potest, sed solo intellectu" (*ST*, I, q. 12, a. 3, co., ed. Leonina, t. IV, 119a). Similar texts could easily could be multiplied, among which see *ST*, I, q. 78, a. 1 (ed. Leonina, t. V, 250a–251b); I, q. 85, a. 1 (ibid., 330a–332b); I-II, q. 3, a. 3 (ed. Leonina, t. VI, 28a–b); *SCG*, III, c. 33 (ed. Leonina, t. XIV, 89a–b); c. 53 (ibid., 146a–147b).

164. "*CUNCTE RES DIFFICILES* ad cognoscendum, Sap. IX (16): *Difficile estimamus que in terra sunt, et que in prospectu sunt inuenimus cum labore, ⟨que in celis sunt, quis inuestigauit?⟩*. Difficile ergo sunt res corporales, difficiliores res spirituales, quia I Co. II (14): *Animalis homo non percipit que sunt Spiritus Dei*; difficilime diuine, Ro. XI (33): *O altitudo diuitiarum* etc.. Set contra: Quedam est facile cognoscere, ut hec sensibilia circa que non falluntur sensus. Responsio: Facile est ista cognoscere imperfecte quoad speciem, scilicet eorum, et figuram. Difficile autem est ea cognoscere perfecte quoad substantiam, uirtutem, operationem et causam, quia cognitio nostra incipit a sensu, a quo uirtus rei et causa remota est. Hinc Sap. IX dicitur (16): *Difficile estimamus* etc. Et quia difficiles, *NON POTEST EAS HOMO EXPLICARE SERMONE*, Eccli. XLIII

(29): *Multa dicimus et deficimus in uerbis*; Eccli. XVIII (2): *Quis sufficit enarrare opera illius?*. Loqui aliqualiter de eis contingit, set explicare ea, / id est latentes eorum rationes intus inuolutas exprimere non potest, nisi qui perfecte intelligit, que est paucorum" (*Super Ecl.* 1:8, MS Madrid 493, 134v–135r).

165. Aristot., *Metaphys.*, IV, 5 (1010b); V, 29 (1025a).

166. Aristot., *De anima*, III, 4 (430a)

167. Aristot., *Metaphys.*, I, 2 (982a).

168. A case in point is the following description of the Holy Spirit's gift of understanding, which is worth presenting at some length: "Respondeo dicendum quod nomen intellectus quandam intimam cognitionem importat: dicitur enim intelligere quasi *intus legere*. Et hoc manifeste patet considerantibus differentiam intellectus et sensus, nam cognitio sensitiva occupatur circa qualitates sensibiles exteriores; cognitio autem intellectiva penetrat usque ad essentiam rei, obiectum enim intellectus est quod quid est, ut dicitur in III *de Anima*. Sunt autem multa genera eorum quae interius latent, ad quae oportet cognitionem hominis quasi intrinsecus penetrare. Nam sub accidentibus latet natura rerum substantialis, sub verbis latent significata verborum, sub similitudinibus et figuris latet veritas figurata, res etiam intelligibiles sunt quodammodo interiores respectu rerum sensibilium quae exterius sentiuntur, et in causis latent effectus et e converso. Unde respectu horum omnium potest dici intellectus. Sed cum cognitio hominis a sensu incipiat, quasi ab exteriori, manifestum est quod quanto lumen intellectus est fortius, tanto potest magis ad intima penetrare. Lumen autem naturale nostri intellectus est finitae virtutis, unde usque ad determinatum aliquid pertingere potest. Indiget igitur homo supernaturali lumine ut ulterius penetret ad cognoscendum quaedam quae per lumen naturale cognoscere non valet. Et illud lumen supernaturale homini datum vocatur donum intellectus" (Thomas Aquinas, *ST*, II-II, q. 8, a. 1, co., ed. Leonina, t. VIII, 66a–b). For a few other examples, see *In II Sent.*, d. 11, q. 2, a. 2, ad. 5; (ed. Parma, t. VI, 483b); *In III Sent.*, d. 26, q. 1, a. 5, co. (ed. Parma, t. VII/A, 283a–b); *SCG*, IV, c. 1 (ed. Leonina, t. XV, 3a–5b); *ST*, I, q. 41, a. 1, ad 2 (ed. Leonina, t. IV, 421b–22a).

169. Cf. Bonaventure, *In Ecl.* 1:9 (*Opera*, t. VI, 16a–b).

170. At the risk of some oversimplification, this may be said to approximate the view of Bonaventure: ". . . Deus diligit praedestinatos in caritate perpetua incoarctabile donum in universarum rerum conditione quas libere condidit . . . et nobis dedit corpus cum sensibus, animam cum potentiis. . ." (*Collationes in Hexaemoron*, IV, 4, ed. F. Delorme, 267). See also *De reductione artium ad theologiam*, 8 (*Opera*, t. V, 322a–b). For an account of Bonaventure's understanding of the human soul, see A. Pegis, *St. Thomas and the Problem of the Soul in the Thirteenth Century*, Toronto, 1934, 26–76. On Bonaventure's understanding of sensation and intellection, an invaluable guide remains E. GILSON, *La philosophie de saint Bonaventure*, 2nd ed., Paris, 1943, 274–304. It should be noted, however, that Bonaventure's understanding of the structure of spiritual sensation has been the subject of sharp disagreement. Within the extensive literature on the matter, see G. LaNave, "Bonaventure," in Paul L. Gavrilyuk, ed., *The Perception of God: The Spiritual Senses in the Christian Tradition*, Cambridge, forthcoming; S. Fields, "Balthasar and Rahner," 235–241; H. Urs von Balthasar, *The Glory of the Lord*, vol. 2, 333–352; K. Rahner, "La Doctrine des 'sens spirituels,'" 268–291; J.-F. Bonnefoy, *Le Saint-Esprit et ses dons selon saint Bonaventure*, Paris, 1929, 212–215. Each of these studies provides an overview of preceding accounts, as well as extensive bibliographical references.

171. Prominent among the exponents of this view is Augustine, whose source E. Gilson identifies as PLOTINUS, *Enn.*, IV, 4, 23 (ed. E. Bréhier, t. IV, 124). Gilson paraphrases Augustine as follows, ". . . la sensation appartiendra tout entière à l'âme, sans que le corps l'éprouve en aucune façon: *sentire non est corporis sed animae per corpus*." Though the preceding is his citation of *De Gen. ad lit. libri XII*, III, 5 (BA 48, 220), he points to *De musica* VI (PL 32, 1161–1193) as Augustine's most rigorous resolution of the problem of sensation; see *Introduction à l'étude de saint Augustin*, 73–77 (76–77).

172. Such is the position of Thomas Aquinas, cf. *ST*, I, q. 75, a. 5 (ed. Leonina, t. V, 201a–202b). At issue in this article is whether the soul's various powers reside in it as their subject. Thomas

concludes that the intellect and will inhere in the soul as their principle and subject, and that the senses have the soul as their principle only, their subject being the soul-body composite. In effect, he disputes two positions. The first, which he attributes to Plato, is the view that the senses inhere immediately in the soul. The second is the aforementioned proposition that they inhere immediately in the body.

173. On Bonaventure's attempt at synthesizing the doctrines of illumination and abstraction, see the recent study of H. Nagakura, "Abstraction et illumination. Une théorie de la connaissance chez saint Bonaventure," in *Intellect et imagination dans la Philosophie Médiévale*, ed. M. Pacheco and J. Meirinhos, Turnhout, 2006, vol. 2, 1243–1254.

174. Of the several texts that could be mentioned in this connection, we present the following two: "... et ideo illarum rerum quae non habent phantasmata, cognitionem non potest accipere, nisi ex rebus quarum sibi repraesentantur phantasmata. Unde in statu viae, in qua accipit a phantasmatibus, non potest Deum immediate videre; sed oportet ut ex visibilibus, quorum phantasmata capit, in ejus cognitionem deveniat" (Thomas Aquinas, *In III Sent.*, d. 27, q. 3, a. 1, co., ed. Parma, t. VII/A, 305b); "... impossibile est intellectum nostrum, secundum praesentis vitae statum, quo passibili corpori coniungitur, aliquid intelligere in actu, nisi convertendo se ad phantasmata" (*ST*, I, q. 84, a. 7, co., ed. Leonina, t. V, 325a). On sense and imagination in Thomas's epistemology, see J. Coleman, *Ancient and Medieval Memories: Studies in the Reconstruction of the Past*, Cambridge, 1992, 422–460; E. Stump, "Aquinas on the Mechanisms of Cognition: Sense and Phantasia," in *Medieval Analyses in Language and Cognition*, ed. S. Ebbesen and R. Friedman, Copenhagen, 1999, 377–395; "Aquinas on the Veracity of the Intellect," *Journal of Philosophy* 88 (1991), 623–632. For a fine analysis of the centrality in Thomas's thought of the correlation between two human unities—of the body and soul, and of the intellect and imagination in cognition—see P. Cañas, "Intelecto e imaginación en Tomás de Aquino: La imaginación al servicio del intelecto," in *Intellect et imagination dans la Philosophie Médiévale*, ed. M. Pacheco and J. Meirinhos, Turnhout, 2006, vol. 3, 1417–1429.

175. *In Io. evang. tract.*, XXI (CCSL 36, 214–217).

176. "*ET MAIORA HIS ... DEMONSTRABIT EI OPERA.* Ergo Pater quedam successiue demonstrat Filio. Responsio: Successio non est quantum ad Patrem, set quantum ad opera quorum unum precedit aliud. Vel *EI*, id est uobis per eum, *UT UOS MIRE⟨MINI⟩*, pre magnitudine, Crisostomus: 'Admiratio est stupor de magno fantasmate'" (*Super Io.* 5:20, MS Saint-Omer, Bibl. mun. 260, f. 124va).

177. Nemesius of Emesa, *De natura hominis*, XX, for the Greek text, ed. M. Morani, Leipzig, 1987, 81; for Burgundio's Latin translation, *Traduction de Burgundio de Pise*, ed. G. Verbeke and J. Moncho, Corpus latinum commentariorum in Aristotelem graecorum, Suppl. 1, Leiden, 1975, 103. For a recent English translation with an important introduction and notes, see R. W. Sharples and P. J. van der Eijk, *Nemesius: On the Nature of Man*, Liverpool, 2008.

178. *De fide orth.*, II, 15 (PG 94, 932).

179. During the eleventh century, Nemesius's *De natura hominis* was translated into Latin by Alfanus, bishop of Salerno, but Burgundio's translation was the more widely diffused. On Burgundio's translations, see chapter 4, note 5.

180. On *theoria* in the Antiochene school, see B. de Margerie, *Introduction à l'histoire*, vol. 1, 188–213; A. Vaccari, "La *Theoria* Nella Scuola Esegetica di Antiochia," *Biblica* 1 (1920), 15–16. With respect to John Damascene, see especially A. Louth, *St John Damascene: tradition and originality Byzantine theology*, Oxford, 2002; M. Jugie, "Jean Damascène," *DTC* 8, no. 1 (1924), 693–751 (717–718); B. Studer, "S. Jean Damascène," *Dict Sp* 8 (1974), 452–466 (458–459).

181. What follows are references to a few relevant texts in the exegesis of John Chrysostom, *In Io. hom.*, XVII (PG 59, 111); XXXIV (ibid., 194); LXXXIII (ibid., 454–55).

182. "Ad tertium dicendum quod incorporea, quorum non sunt phantasmata, cognoscuntur a nobis per comparationem ad corpora sensibilia, quorum sunt phantasmata. Sicut veritatem intelligimus ex consideratione rei circa quam veritatem speculamur; Deum autem, ut Dionysius dicit, cognoscimus ut causam, et per excessum, et per remotionem" (*ST*, I, q. 84, a. 7, ad 3, ed. Leonina, t. V, 326a–b). Thomas refers here to Dionysius, *De div. nom.*, I, 5 (ed. B. Suchla,

Berlin, 1990, *Corpus Dionysiacum*, t. I = PG 3, 593. Elsewhere, he makes the same points in numerous texts, occasionally with specific reference to biblical images, e.g., *Super Boetium De Trin.*, III, q. 6, a. 2 (ed. Leonina, t. L, 163–166); *Super lib. Dionysii De div. nom.*, II, 1 (ed. Parma, t. XV, 277b).

183. See the account of theophany in the thought of Dionysius provided by O. Boulnois, "Augustin et les théories de l'image," 84–85.

184. From his early writings, cf. *De ver.*, q. 26, a 4. ad 7 (ed. Leonina, t. XXII/3, 763a); *In III Sent.*, d. 26, q. 1, a. 3, co. (ed. Parma, t. VII/A, 281a); and among his later works, *ST*, III, q. 15, a. 8, ob. 2 (ed. Leonina, t. XI, 194a); *Super II Thes.* 1:10 (ed. Parma, t. XIII, 575b). In the following variation, *admiratio* is explicitly related to contemplation: "Ad tertium dicendum quod admiratio est species timoris consequens apprehensionem alicuius rei excedentis nostram facultatem. Unde admiratio est actus consequens contemplationem sublimis veritatis." (*ST*, II-II, q. 180, a. 3, ad. 3, ed. Leonine, t. X, 427b).

185. On this dispute, the normative study remains M.-M. Dufeil's *Guillaume de Saint-Amour et la polémique universitaire parisienne 1250–1259*. See also J. Dawson, "William of Saint-Amour and the Apostolic Tradition," *MS* 40 (1978), 223–238; Y. Congar, "Aspects ecclésiologiques de la querelle entre mendiants et séculiers dans la seconde moitié du XIIIe siècle et le début du XIVe siècle," *AHDLMA* 28 (1961), 34–151. On the involvement of the Dominicans, especially Thomas Aquinas, see J.-P. Torrell, *Initiation*, 109–139; S. Tugwell, *Albert and Thomas*, 213–216; M.-D. Chenu, *Introduction*, 291–294. On the response of the Franciscans, especially Bonaventure, see M. Lambert, *Franciscan Poverty. The Doctrine of the Absolute Poverty of Christ and the Apostles in the Franciscan Order 1210–1323*, London, 1961; J.-G. Bougerol, *Introduction à Saint Bonaventure*, 209–214.

186. Bonaventure took up the challenge of William of Saint-Amour in his disputed question *De perfectione euangelica* (*Opera*, t. V, 117–198). For the precise dates of these disputations, see M. Dufeil's, *Guillaume de Saint-Amour*, 180.

187. During the spring of 1256, William of Saint-Amour published the central positions of his attack on the mendicants in his *Tractatus de periculis nouissorum temporum*, which Pope Alexander IV condemned the following October 5; cf. *CUP* I, 331–333. In the meantime, Thomas refuted the work, point by point, in his opuscule *Contra impugnantes Dei cultum et religionem* (ed. Leonina, t. XLI/A). See P. Glorieux, "Le Contra Impugnantes de s. Thomas: ses sources—son plan," in *Mélanges Mandonnet. Etudes d'histoire littéraire et doctrinale du Moyen Âge*, Bibliothèque Thomiste 13, vol. I, Paris, 1930, 51–81.

188. Before issuing the condemnation mentioned in the previous note, on June 17, 1256, Pope Alexander IV issued a letter calling for the dismissal from the University of Paris of the four secular masters most directly engaged in the conflict: William of Saint-Amour, Odon of Douai, Nicholas of Bar-sur-Aube, and Christian of Beauvais; cf. *CUP* I, 304–305, 319–323.

189. In the autumn of 1269, Bonaventure intervened with the publication of *Apologia Pauperum* (*Opera*, t. VIII, 230–330). The relevant works of Thomas belonging to this period include *De perfectione spiritualis vitae* (1270) (ed. Leonine, t. XLI/B); *Contra doctrinam retrahentium a religione* (1271–1272) (ed. Leonine, t. XLI/C); *ST*, II-II, q. 186–188 (1271–1272) (ed. Leonine, t. X, 486a–535b); *ST*, III, q. 40 (1271–1273) (ed. Leonine, t. XI, 397a–402b).

190. U. Horst, "Christ, *Exemplar Ordinis Fratrum Praedicantium*, According to Saint Thomas Aquinas," in *Christ among the Medieval Dominicans*, 256–270. On the other hand, we have no grounds for concluding that during preceding generations there were no general differences between the two orders' theological perpsectives. On the particularity of the earliest Dominicans' understanding of Jesus' moral exemplarity, specifically with respect to poverty, see in the same volume the aforementioned study of R. Newhauser, "Jesus as the First Dominican?" 238–255.

191. On the complex provenance and development of the Dominican formula of profession, see A. Thomas, "La profession religieuse des Dominicains, formule, cérémonies, histoire," *AFP* 39 (1969), 5–52. See also P.-M. Gy, "Sur le caractère consécratoire de l'acte même du voeu solonnel dans la théologie de Saint Thomas d'Aquin," *Analecta O.P.* 106 (1998), 408–410.

192. "Ad futuram vero beatitudinem ordinatur aliquis per caritatem. Et quia voluntaria paupertas est efficax exercitium perveniendi ad perfectam caritatem, ideo multum valet ad caelestem beatitudinem consequendam. . . . Divitiae autem habitae per se quidem natae sunt perfectionem caritatis impedire, principaliter alliciendo animum et distrahendo. . . . Et ideo difficile est caritatem inter divitias conservare" (*ST*, II-II, q. 186, a. 3, ad 4, ed. Leonine, t. X, 491b).

193. "Respondeo dicendum quod votum obedientiae est praecipuum inter tria vota religionis. Et hoc, triplici ratione. Primo quidem, quia per votum obedientiae aliquid maius homo offert Deo, scilicet ipsam voluntatem, quae est potior quam corpus proprium, quod offert homo Deo per continentiam; et quam res exteriores, quas offert homo Deo per votum paupertatis. . . . Secundo, quia votum obedientiae continet sub se alia vota: sed non convertitur. Nam religiosus etsi teneatur ex voto continentiam servare et paupertatem, tamen haec etiam sub obedientia cadunt, ad quam pertinent multa alia praeter continentiam et paupertatem. Tertio, quia votum obedientiae proprie se extendit ad actus propinquos fini religionis" (*ST*, II, II, q. 186, a. 8, co., ed. Leonine, t. X, 499a–b).

194. ". . . perfectio non consistit essentialiter in paupertate, sed in Christi sequela. . . . Tanto autem sollicitudo temporalium rerum magis impedit religionem, quanto sollicitudo spiritualium maior ad religionem requiritur. Manifestum est autem quod maiorem sollicitudinem spiritualium requirit religio quae est instituta ad contemplandum et contemplata aliis tradendum per doctrinam et praedicationem, quam illa quae est instituta ad contemplandum tantum. Unde talem religionem decet paupertas talis quae minimam sollicitudinem ingerat. Manifestum est autem quod minimam sollicitudinem ingerit conservare res usui hominum necessarias, tempore congruo procuratas" (*ST*, II-II, q. 188, a. 7, co., ed. Leonine, t. X, 530b–531b).

195. "*HEREDITAS . . . UERSA EST AD ALIENOS*, id est Caldeos, *DOMUS NOSTRA AD EXTRANEOS*, id est Romanos. Moraliter. De monachis per nimias expensas" (*Super Threnos* 5:2, ed. cit., 278).

196. Table 5.3   Io 6:7: *respondit ei Philippus ducentorum denariorum panes non sufficiunt eis ut unusquisque modicum quid accipiat.*

| Bonaventure (*Opera*, t. VI, 319a–b) | William of Alton (MS Saint-Omer 260, f. 131vb) | Thomas Aquinas (ed. Parma, t. X, 403a) |
|---|---|---|
| *Respondit ei Philipus: Ducentorum denariorum panes non sufficiunt eis, ut unusquisque modicum quid accipiat;* **et ita magnum pretium erat necessarium, et ipsi pauperes erant et non habebant etiam parvum**; omnia enim reliquerant. . . . | *RESPONDIT EI PHI⟨LIPPUS⟩: DU⟨CENTORUM⟩ DE⟨NARIORUM⟩ PANES,* id est: Quot possunt haberi pro ducentis denariis? *NON SUFFI⟨CIUNT⟩ EIS,* ad comedendum, *UT UNUSQUISQUE MO⟨DICUM⟩ QUID AC⟨CIPIAT⟩.* In **hoc insinuat Philippus se tot denarios non habuisse et paupertatem Christi.** | *Ducentorum denariorum panes non sufficiunt eis:* quos nos non habemus, et ideo non possumus eis dare ad manducandum. **In quo Christi paupertas insinuatur, qui nec ducentos denarios habebat.** |

197. "Si igitur quaereretur, utrum divitiae sint utiles, vel inutiles; dico, quod bene utenti utiles sunt, sed reservanti sunt inutiles, male utenti damnosae" (*In Ecl.* 5:9–10, *Opera*, t. VI, 46b, 47b).

198. "*QUI AMAT DIUITIAS* inordinate *FRUCTUS NON CAPIET EX EIS*, intellige quia nec sibi sustinet inde facere bonum, *EX EIS*, scilicet male acquisitis, male possessis, et male expensis, quia talis animam suam uenalem habet (cf. Sir 10, 10). . . . *ET HOC ERGO*, id est amare diuitias inordinate, *UANITAS EST. . . . ET QUID PRODEST POSSESSORI SUO*, scilicet multis habere diuitias . . . *NISI QUOD CERNIT DIUITIAS OCULIS SUIS*, et iste uisus non prodest cum non satiet. . . . ⟨Set⟩ infra VII: *Vtilior est sapientia cum diuitias* (Ecl 7:12) quam sine, suple. Responsio: Ista temporalia de se nec bona nec mala sunt habenti, set abusio est mala, sollicitudo peior, questus pessimus.

Male ergo utentibus male sunt, set bene utentibus sunt bone ad culpe redemptionem.... Item, ad gratie augmentationem. . . . Item, ad glorie adeptionem" (*Super Ecl.* 5:9–10, MSS Basel, Univ. Bibl. B III 20, f. 102va; Madrid, Bibl. Nac. 493, f. 146v).

199. For Thomas Aquinas's reply to this objection, see *Contra impugnantes*, cap. 6, ad 2 (ed. Leonina, t. XLI/A, 101a).

200. "*VTILIOR EST SAPIENTIA CUM DIUITIIS*, intellige quam sola sine illis, *ET MAGIS PRODEST UIDENTIBUS SOLEM*.... Contra: Esse pauperem pertinet ad statum perfectionis, Mt. XIX (21): *Si uis perfectus esse* etc., ubi simpliciter Dominus prefert paupertatem, supposita etiam utrobique sapientia. Responsio: Est quedam paupertas cum placentia, et hec bona est et melior quam diuitie; alia est cum tolerantia, que bona est, set imperfecta; tertia est cum inpatientia. Vtraque istarum melior est sapientia cum divitiis" (*Super Ecl.* 7:12, MSS Basel, Univ. Bibl. B III 20, f. 104vb; Madrid, Bibl. Nac. 493, f. 150v).

201. Cf. Bonaventure, *In Ecl.* 7:12 (*Opera*, t. VI, 59a).

202. "Christus tamquam pauper de eleemosynis vivebat . . . non derogat perfectioni, si eleemosynae in loculis reserventur" (*Super Io.* 4:35, ed. Parma, t. X, 507b). Cf. *ST*, II-II, q. 55, a. 7, ad 3 (ed. Leonine, t. VIII, 403b). In the preceding case, Thomas finds support for his position in the authority of Augustine, *De sermone Domini in monte*, II (ed. A. Mutzenbecher, 1967, Turnhout, CCSL 35, 150). Other relevant texts include *ST*, II-II, q. 188, a. 7, co. (ed. Leonine, t. X, 530a–531b).

203. We have already had the occasion to observe that in their comments on this pericope, Chrysostom, Hugh of St. Cher, and William touched on the matter of dietary laws in connection with Jesus' request for water. See chapter 3, note 190.

204. "*DISCIPULI AUTEM EIUS ABIERANT IN CIUITATEM UT CIBOS EMERE⟨N⟩T*, quia si mendicassent forte dedissent illis cibos illicitos secundum legem. Vel forte nichil dedissent quia Iudei erant eis odiosi. Item, homines inheruditi citius uerba et personam eius contempsissent. Emebant autem a gentilibus, quia necessitas compellebat. Habebat autem unde emerent, quia nondum missi erant miraculi facere et predicare. Preterea, in necessitate licebat eis argentum portare ubi non inuenissent forte qui daret" (*Super Io.* 4:8, MS Saint-Omer, Bibl. mun. 260, f. 120va). Cf. Hugh of St. Cher, *Postille*, in Io. 4:7 (ed. Venetiis, t. VI, 304va).

205. Cf. Bonaventure, *In Io. com.* 4:8 (*Opera*, t. VI, 293b). In 1279, Pope Nicholas III employed his decretal *Exiit qui seminat* to enshrine Bonaventure's position that friars ought to be permitted to use whatever should be necessary for their work. This compromise proved unacceptable to the Spirituals; cf. L. Oliger, "Spirituels," *DTC* 14 (1941), 2522–2549.

206. "Quare habuit loculos cui angeli ministrauerunt, nisi quia ecclesia ipsius loculos suos habitura erat?" (Augustine, *In Io. evang. tract.*, L, CCSL 36, 437).

207. Cf. Jerome, *In Mt.*, III (CCSL 77, 156).

208. "Dominus in extrema paupertate et praecepisset discipulis non recipere pecuniam" (Bonaventure, *In Io. com.* 12, 6, *Opera*, t. VI, 412b).

209. "*DIXIT AUTEM HOC NON QUIA DE EGENIS PERTINEBAT AD EUM*, et ita remouetur ab eo compassio. Licet enim pertineret ad eum quantum ad officii ordinationem, quia dispensator erat, non tamen quantum ad compassionem cordis et pietatem. *SET*, scilicet hoc dixit, *QUIA FUR ERAT*, ecce corruptio sue mentis! **Et bene poterat furari, quia** *LOCULOS HABENS*, Interlin.: 'Id est loculorum Domini custos.' *ET EA QUE MITTEBANTUR*, **scilicet Domino et discipulis,** *PORTABAT* **tanquam dispensator et presumitur eum habuisse et eis dedisse, Psalmus (108:9):** *Fiant filii eius orphani*. Quaeritur quare loculos uoluit habere cui angeli ministrabant? (cf. Mt 4:11; Mc 1:13) Responsio: Secundum Augustinum, ut confunderentur heretici asserentes quod ecclesia nichil debet habere. Secundum Ieronimum, habuit loculos non ad usum suum set ad usum pauperum. Vnde quando soluit dragma pro se et pro Petro, misit ad mare, Mt. XVII (26), quia nolebat ea que data erant pauperibus in usum suum conuertere. **Si opponitur illud, Mt. VI (31.34) et Luc. XII (11.22):** *Nolite solliciti ⟨esse⟩*, **dicendum quod habere non prohibet, set sollicitos esse.** Item, quomodo uoluit Dominus furi committere quod habebat? Responsio: Modicam uim faciebat in diuitiis ad nostram instructionem. Item, hoc fecit ne Iudas haberet occasionem uendendi eum propter inopiam. Item, quare

non corripuit eum? Responsio: Quia sciebat quod non melioraretur, set deterior fieret. Nec officium abstulit ne crimen proderet et ad maius inuitaret" (*Super Io.* 12:6, MSS Saint-Omer, Bibl. mun. 260, f. 146vb; Assisi 49, 53vb–54ra).

210. "Qualiter autem non peram, non uirgam, non es iubens deferre, marsupium ferebat? Ad inopium ministerium, ut discas quoniam ualde pauperem et crucifixum huius oportet partis multam facere. Multam enim ad nostram dispensans doctrinam agebat" (Chrysostom, *In Io. hom.*, LXXII, MSS Vat. Ottob. lat. 227, f. 125rb; Arras, Bibl. mun. 1083, f. 58rb; cf. PG 59, 392).

211. "... *QUIA LOCULOS HABEBAT IUDAS*, in quibus scilicet ponebatur que mittebantur. Forte Dominus eos (eos *om. S*) haberi uoluit propter sui et suorum et aliorum necessitatem. Secundum Augustinum, in exemplum, ut liceret ecclesie talia habere. Nec ipsos habuit propter cupiditatem, que prohibetur Mt. x (Mt 10:9), set propter ea que dicta sunt. Secundum Crisostomum et Ieronimum, et solum propter necessitatem pauperum eos habebant, ut dictum est plenius supra. His tamen uidetur iste textus contradicere: ⟨*QUOD DIXISSET EI IHESUS*⟩: *EME* ⟨*QUE OPUS SUNT NOBIS*⟩ etc." (*Super Io.* 13:29, MSS Saint-Omer, Bibl. mun. 260, f. 153ra; Assisi 49, 60va). Cf. Augustine., *In Io. evang. tract.*, LXII (CCSL 36, 485); Chrysostom., *In Io. hom.*, LXXII (PG 59, 392); Jerome, *Comm. in Esaiam*, IX (CCSL 73, 358); *Comm. in Mt.*, III (CCSL 77, 156).

212. On this point, see U. Horst, "Christ, *Exemplar Ordinis Fratrum Praedicantium*," 261.

213. The later William's postill *Super Threnos* is dependent upon that of our author; L.-J. Bataillon, "L'influence d'Hugues de Saint-Cher," 498–499.

214. Ed. Quaracchi, *S. Bonaventurae Opera omnia*, t. VI, 1893, 515a, note 4. The edition contains an extensive source apparatus that generally provides a good accounting for Bonaventure's explicit references. Such is not the case with the Borgnet edition of Albert the Great's commentary on John, *B. Alberti Magni Opera omnia*, t. XXIV, Paris, 1899.

215. *The Gospels in the Schools*, 244.

216. William of Auxerre's treatise *De sacramento penitentie* does not contain the discussion at hand, *Summa Aurea* IV, 8 (ed. J. Ribaillier, Grottaferrata, vol. XIX, 195–223). The same may be said of William of Auvergne's far lengthier treatises, *De sacramento poenitentiae*, ed. E. Viret, *Opera omnia*, Rouen, 1674, t. I, 451b–512b; *Tractatus novus de poenitentia*, ed. cit., t. I, 570b–592b; *Supplementum tractatus novi de poenitentia*, ed. cit., t. II, 229a–247b.

217. In a detailed discussion of the sources of Albert's Gospel commentaries, B. Smalley observed that "Albert must have had Hugh of St. Cher's *Postilla* to hand" and subsequently remarked that "there is no trace of Bonaventure on Luke or John," in *The Gospels in the Schools*, 243.

218. For a concise account of Albert's life and works, see S. Tugwell, *Albert and Thomas*, 3–38; also J. Weisheipl, "Albert the Great and Medieval Culture," *Thomist* 44 (1980), 481–501.

219. An extensive review of the evidence for this dating is given by B. Schmidt, "Prolegomena," in *Alberti Magni Super Matthaeum*, ed. Institutum Alberti Magni Coloniense, *Opera omnia*, t. XXI/1, Köln, 1987, in XIII–XVI. He concludes: "... terminum ad quem circa annum forte 1264 statuendum," ibid., XVI.

220. For evidence of the canonical ordering of Albert's Gospel commentaries, in addition to the preceding reference, see A. Fries, "Zur Enstehungszeit der Bibelkommentare Alberts des Grossen," in *Albertus Magnus, Doctor Universalis, 1280–1980*, ed. G. Meyer and A. Zimmermann, Mainz, 1980, 119–139. To the same effect, B. Smalley has discussed cross-references from Mark to Matthew, from Luke to Matthew, and from John to Luke, in *The Gospels in the Schools*, 244–245, and note 3. For remarks on the dating of Albert's works, I am indebted to the helpful comments of W. Fauser, formerly of the Institutum Alberti Magni Coloniense.

221. Having identified the text as a *reportatio*, B. Smalley found such citations in no fewer than seven places, MS Oxford, New College 40, f. 28v, 29r, 54r, 58v, 65v (2x), 66r. The references are to "Frater Hugo," which she took as an indication that they were made before Hugh became a cardinal, on May 28, 1244; "A Commentary on Isaias by Guerric of Saint-Quentin, O.P.," *Studi e Testi* 122 (1946), 383–397 (386).

222. B. Smalley found the citations in MS Schaffhausen, Ministerial-Bibliothek 84, f. 7va (2x), 33ra, 83rb. Observing that "quotations of 'Hugo' are baffling," she provided evidence pointing toward and away from Hugh of St. Cher, in *The Gospels in the Schools*, 237–238.

223. The present study has not been able to confirm often repeated statements to the effect that William of Alton died in 1265. See chapter 1, note 7.

## APPENDIX I: CONSIDERATION OF
## WORKS VARIOUSLY ATTRIBUTED TO WILLIAM

1. f. 1va–vb.
2. In both manuscripts we find *alia editio* at Is 5:7: "LXX: *5:7NOUELLA PLANTATIO DILECTISSIMA*. Alia editio: *5:7NOMEN DELECTABILE*," (MSS BnF lat 573, f. 8rb; Madrid, Bibl. Nac. 493, f. 177v). Both lemmata are Old Latin texts, presented here as variants of the Vulgate GERMEN *DELECTABILE*, which appears with commentary in the immediately preceding lines. The reference to an *alia editio* is probably to the Old Latin variant *nouellum delectabile*, mistakenly recorded in both codices as *nomen delectabile*. See *Vetus Latina. Die Reste der altlateinischen bibel*, ed. R. Gryson, vol. 12.1, *Esaias*, 157. Still, Is 5:7 would appear to be where the authentic commentary begins. Henceforth, the text thoroughly conforms to the typlogy of Group A; before, it manifestly fails to do so.
3. The prologue to *Super Isaiam* occupies exactly one column (MS Paris, BnF lat. 573, f.1ra–1rb); that to *Super Ieremiam* fills more than two (ibid, f. 87ra–va); that to *Super Threnos* three (f. 145rb–146ra); and that to *Super Iohannem*, more than three (MS Saint-Omer, Bibl. mun. 260, f. 110ra–110vb). All are in the same hand and in columns of the same length and width: 45 lines, 150 x 50 mm.
4. A *divisio* appearing at Is 5:1 is typical. After beginning with "diuiditur in duas," it presents four successive subdivisions, none of which is indicated by *in prima primo* (MS Paris, BnF lat. 573, f. 7va). The Madrid version is basically the same until the third subdivision, after which it differs (MS Madrid, Bibl. Nac. 493, f. 177r).
5. "*4:6ET TABERNACULUM*, id est ecclesia erit futura in umbraculum diei, id est sub protectione Dei, uel in refrigerio . . . *A TURBINE*, id est a suggestione demoniis, *ET A PLUUIA*, id est a temptatione carnis, quasi dicat: Dominus proteget ecclesiam a persecusione mundana, a suggestione dyabolica, et a impugnatione que est a carne propria" (MS Paris, BnF lat. 573, f. 7rb).
6. "*5:6ET NUBIBUS*, id est prophetis et predicatoribus, ne pluant imbrem doctrine. Hoc impletum est post ascensionem Domini, quando prophetas non habuerunt et apostolos repulerunt" (MS Paris, BnF lat. 573, f. 8rb).
7. "Sapiential Books I," 41–77 (62–63); "A Commentary on Isaias by Guerric of Saint-Quentin, O.P.," *Studi e Testi* 122 (1946), 383–397.
8. "L'influence d'Hugues de Saint-Cher," in *Hugues de Saint-Cher, Bibliste et théologien*, ed. L.-J. Bataillon, Gilbert Dahan, and P.-M. Gy, Turnhout, 2004, 497–502. See also A. Sulavik, "*Principia* and *Introitus* in Thirteenth-Century Christian Biblical Exegesis with Related Texts," in *La Bibbia del XIII Secolo. Storio del testo storia dell'esegesi*, ed. G. Cremascoli and F. Santi, Firenze, 2004, 269–321.
9. This has been amply documented in the studies of L.-J. Bataillon, N. Bériou, J. Hamesse, and B. Smalley, listed in chapter 2, note 14 .
10. It has long been said that many of Stephan Langton's biblical commentaries were divided into constituent parts according to the literal and spiritual senses, most likely by a subsequent redactor. For remarks on the three versions of Langton's commentary on the historical books, see G. Lacombe and B. Smalley, "Studies on the Commentaries of Cardinal Stephen Langton," *AHDLMA* 5 (1930), (Part 1), 5–151 (85), and (Part 2), 152–182 (152). On the other hand, several scholars have credited differences between versions of a few of Stephen's commentaries to his own revisions; cf. F. Stegmüller, *Rep. Bibl.*, 7704–7739; A. Saltman, *Stephen Langton: Commentary on the Book of Chronicles*, Ramat-Gan, 1978, 20; A. Sulavik, "*Principia* and *Introitus* in Thirteenth-Century Christian Biblical Exegesis," 281–282.
11. After classifying Stephen Langton's commentaries on the books of the Old Testament, B. Smalley sees evidence of just such a state of affairs—two different presentations of the same ideas (*Study of the Bible*, 205–206): "These were so unlike one another that the most careless

copying could not explain their divergences. It was impossible that they could have come from one original. . . . We found that each version made the same points, and contained the same quotations; but they used slightly different words; one would merely allude to a point which was developed in the others."

12. MS Assisi, Biblioteca Com. 49, 49ra–rb; cf. MS Saint-Omer, Bibl. mun. 260, f. 142vb.

13. Quetif and Echard take this as a first hand inscription: "Primus sic incipit eadem prima manu totius codicis: *Commentaria F. Guillelmi de Altona in Sacram Scripturam*," *SOP* 1, 244b. B. Smalley rightly recognizes the ascription as posterior, "Sapiential Books I," 57.

14. "Sapiential Books I," 57–61.

15. "Sacred Scripture in the Early Franciscan School," 65–82 (80–81, n. 34).

16. Ibid., 58.

17. Ibid., 80.

18. On the genre of the *principium Biblicum*, see G. Dahan, "Genres, Forms and Various Methods," 215; A. Sulavik, "An Unedited Principium Biblicum attributed to Petrus de Scala, O.P.," *Angelicum* 79 (2002), 87–126 (90–91).

19. MSS Paris, BnF lat. 526, f. 7ra; Vendôme 116, f. 6vb. Application of *diuiditur* for the same purpose is recognizable throughout.

20. There are three such occurrences in a *divisio* at Genesis 1:1 (MSS Paris, BnF lat. 526, f. 6vb; Vendôme 116, f. 6va–vb).

21. For example, a *divisio* opens with the lemma *DIXITQUE DEUS* (1:3) and contains the lemma *ET FACTUM EST UESPERE* (1:5), neither of which is restated in the following exposition (MSS Paris, BnF lat. 526, f. 7ra–rb; Vendôme 116, f. 6ra).

22. MSS Paris, BnF lat. 526, f. 25ra; Vendôme 116, f. 23vb.

23. MSS Paris, BnF lat. 526, f. 41vb; Vendôme 116, f. 39ra. Examples could easily be multiplied. A briefer one appears at Genesis 31:11–13, where the lemma [31:11]*DIXITQUE ANGELUS DOMINI* etc., is followed by [31:13]*EGO SUM DEUS BETHEL*, several lines further along in the biblical text (MSS Paris, BnF lat. 526, f. 38ra; Vendôme 116, f. 35va).

24. A case in point appears at Genesis 21:2 (MSS Paris, BnF lat. 526, f. 28ra; Vendôme 116, f. 26va).

25. MS Paris, BnF lat. 526, f. 50rb. The text is virtually the same in MS Vendôme 116, f. 48ra.

26. The following example is a *divisio* at Ex 1:15: "[1:15]*DIXIT AUTEM REX*. . . . In prima parte, primo tangitur malitie regis in necem puerorum occulta persecutio, ibi: [1:15]*DIXIT AUTEM REX*, et post: [1:16]*PRECIPIENS EIS*; secundo . . ., tertio . . .," (MSS Paris, BnF lat. 526, f. 51ra; Vendôme 116, f. 48va).

27. Ex 1:6: quo mortuo et universis fratribus eius omnique cognatione illa *W*.

28. MSS Paris, BnF lat. 526, f. 118ra; Vendôme 116, f. 105ra.

29. For example, none of the lemmata of a *divisio* found at Lv 27:22: [27:22]*SI AGER EMPTUS*, is restated in the following exposition (MSS Paris, BnF lat. 526, f. 165vb; Vendôme 116, f. 138rb–va).

30. Two such questions appear at Lv 8:15 and 8:24 (MSS Paris, BnF lat. 526, f. 130vb–131ra, 131rb; Vendôme 116, f. 114rb, 114vb).

31. What follows is an example from the *divisio* introducing chapter 4, "[4:18]*NOLITE PERDERE*. Et prima pars in duas diuiditur," (MSS Paris, BnF lat. 526, f. 171vb; Vendôme 116, f. 143ra).

32. E.g., a *divisio* at Nm 35:1 comprises two lemmata that are nowhere to be found in the ensuing exposition: "[35:6]*EXCEPTIS HIS*" and "[35:8]*IPSE QUOQUE URBES*," (MSS Paris, BnF lat. 526, f. 209ra; Vendôme 116, f. 138ra).

33. For example, the exposition of Nm 1:24 occupies most of an entire column and that of Nm 1:25 occupies most of the next. While a few of the intervening verses are alluded to, the next verse to be represented by a lemma is Nm 1:36 (MSS Paris, BnF lat. 526, f. 168va–vb; Vendôme 116, f. 140va–vb). A similar case appears at the lemma of Nm 2:3: *AD ORIENTEM IUDAS FUGIT*, which introduces an exposition that occupies more than half a column. The next lemma is from Nm 2:10: *IN CASTRIS (FILIORUM) RUBEN* (MSS Paris, BnF lat. 526, f. 169vb–170ra; Vendôme 116, f. 141va).

34. For example, *ibi* is employed four times to introduce lemmata in a *divisio* at Ios 6:1 (MS Paris, BnF lat. 526, f. 214ra–rb; there are six such occurrences in the copy of MS Vendôme 116, 175vb). A similar case appears earlier, in a *divisio* at Ios 1:9 (MSS Paris, BnF lat. 526, f. 212ra; Vendôme 116, f. 173vb).

35. An example is a *divisio* appearing at the *end* of the exposition of chapter 16 and only a few lines before a *divisio* introducing the next chapter: "*ET FACTUS EST TERMINUS FILIORUM EFFRAYM* etc. Hic agitur de possessione filiorum Ioseph diuisim. Et primo Effraym; secundo Manasse, infra XVII: [16:6]*EGREDIUNTURQUE CONFINIA EIUS IN MARE*," (MSS Paris, BnF lat. 526, f. 220ra; Vendôme 116, f. 181rb).

36. E.g.: "[17:14]*LOCUTI SUNT FILII IOSEPH*. Hic agitur de parte concessi filiis Ioseph propriis uiribus perquerendi. Et si obicitur . . . dicendum quod. . . . Dicit ergo. . ." (MSS Paris, BnF lat. 526, f. 220va; Vendôme 116, f. 181vb).

37. A noticeable example appears immediately after the *divisio* introducing chapter 15, where the opening exposition is moral: "[15:1]*IGITUR SORS*. Moraliter. . ." (MSS Paris, BnF lat. 526, f. 219rb; Vendôme 116, f. 180va). For a few other examples, at Ios 5:12: "[5:12]*DEFECITQUE MANNA*. Moraliter. . ." (MS Paris, BnF lat. 526, f. 214ra; Vendôme 116, f. 175va); at Ios 6:4: "[6:4]*ARCHAM*, ecclesiam in qua est manna Ihesu Christi, uel scripturam quam debent precedere bonis operibus," (MS Paris, BnF lat. 526, f. 214rb; Vendôme 116, f. 176ra).

38. Exceptions to the rule are not scarce. Examples appear at the beginnings of chapters 17, 18, and 20 (MSS Paris, BnF lat. 526, f. 236vb, 237rb, 238ra, and Vendôme 116, 196ra, 196va, 197ra).

39. Appearing nowhere in the subsequent exposition are two lemmata of the *divisio* introducing chapter 21, "[21:2]*VENERUNTQUE*" and "[21:20]*PRECEPERUNTQUE* ," (MSS Paris, BnF lat. 526, f. 238vb–239ra; Vendôme 116, 197vb).

40. In chapter 21, for example, verses 11–12 and 15–17 are left without commentary (MSS Paris, BnF lat. 526, f. 239ra; Vendôme 116, 197vb).

41. The exposition of Iud 9:1 begins with a moral interpretation, not designated as such. In the following exposition of Iud 9:1–27, several lines are given spiritual commentary before or even without literal commentary. Spiritual and literal interpretations are interspersed and are only occasionally designated by terms such as *moraliter* or *ad litteram*. Several lines are skipped altogether (MS Paris, BnF lat. 526, f. 231vb–232ra; Vendôme 116, 191vb).

42. Sir 11:3.

43. Appearing nowhere in the subsequent exposition are two lemmata of the *divisio* introducing chapter 3,"[3:13]*AC⟨TA⟩ ⟨EST SIN AUTEM⟩ ILLE* and [3:14]*DORMIUIT ITAQUE*" (MSS Paris, BnF lat. 526, f. 240vb; Vendôme 116, 199rb).

44. In chapter 3, for example, verses 4–6, 7–9, 11, and 14–18 are left without commentary, and the exposition of the entire chapter occupies considerably less than a single column (MSS Paris, BnF lat. 526, f. 240vb; Vendôme 116, f. 199rb).

45. Ez 44:2.

46. MSS Paris, BnF lat. 526, f. 241ra; Vendôme 116, f. 199rb.

47. Sap 6:10; W: ad vos ergo reges sunt hi sermones mei ut discatis sapientiam et non excidatis.

48. E.g., MS Saint-Omer, Bibl. mun. 260, f. 181vb (twice).

49. E.g., MS Saint-Omer, Bibl. mun. 260, f. 179vb, 180vb, 182ra, 183rb.

50. E.g., MS Saint-Omer, Bibl. mun. 260, f. 182rb, 189ra, 189rb.

51. Each of these three traits appears in the commentary's first *divisio* (MS Saint-Omer, Bibl. mun. 260, f. 179vb), and the first two in the second (f. 180rb).

52. Appearing nowhere in the exposition of chapter 1 Rg 3 are two lemmata of its initial *divisio*: "[3:16]*VOCAUIT ERGO*" and "[3:19]*CREUIT AUTEM*," (MS Saint-Omer, Bibl. mun. 260, f. 181va). In the exposition of chapter 4, we find none of the lemmata attached to the final three elements of the initial *divisio*: [4:3]*DIXERUNTQUE MAIORES*, [4:4]*MISIT ERGO POPULUS*, and [4:5]*CUMQUE UENISSET* (MS Saint-Omer, Bibl. mun. 260, f. 181vb).

53. The *divisio* introducing 1Rg 15 consists of one element with no divisions (MS Saint-Omer, Bibl. mun. 260, f. 186ra). Six consecutive chapters lacking any *divisio* appear at 1Rg 16–21 (MS Saint-Omer, Bibl. mun. 260, f. 186vb, 187ra, 187va, 187 vb, 188 ra, and 188 va).

54. A case in point appears at 1 Sm 6:19 (MS Saint-Omer, Bibl. mun. 260, f. 182vb).

55. Examples appear at the expositions of 1 Sm 2:3 and 1 Sm 7:15 (MS Saint-Omer, Bibl. mun. 260, f. 180va and 183ra).

56. Omitted verses include the following: 1Rg 3, verses 4–6, 9, and 16 (MS Saint-Omer, Bibl. mun. 260, f. 181va–vb; 1Rg 4, verses 2–3, 5, f. 240vb).

57. See chapter 2, note 15.

58. Though the postill *Super Iob* of MS Paris, BnF lat. 14250, f.ra–283va, has the same prologues as the work in question, it is a different commentary. Its style is altogether uncharacteristic of William.

59. Examples of the first two appear at MS Troyes 487, f. 65vb; an example of the third appears at f. 66ra.

60. All of this is on view in this postill's counterpart to the *divisio* cited in the previous note (MS Troyes 487, f. 7rb–va). Other examples appear at Iob 1:6 (f. 12ra), Iob 2:1 (f. 17va), and Iob 5:1 (f. 31va–vb).

61. Among the verses not represented by lemmata are Iob 2:12–3:3 (f. 20va–vb).

62. Comments on Iob 2:3 occupy well over a column, and those on the next verse occupy more than one and a half (MS Troyes, Bibl. mun. 487, f. 18ra–va). Examples could be multiplied easily.

63. An example appears at Iob 11:8 (MS Troyes, Bibl. mun. 487, f. 70vb).

64. This copy appears to be flawed by numerous omissions. A truncated version of a lengthy *divisio* found toward the bottom of MS Madrid, Bibl. Nac. 493, f. 13r appears in MS Paris, BnF lat. 573, f. 206va. Examples could be multiplied.

65. Ps 126:2: surgere surgere postquam sederitis qui manducatis panem doloris *W.*

66. Simon of Hinton taught at Oxford from 1248 to 1254. With respect to his authorship of this work, B. Smalley remarks: "The length and discursiveness of the exposition are also typical. Both the literal and spiritual senses are fully expounded with the help of elaborate *distinctiones*," "Some More Exegetical Works of Simon of Hinton," 102.

67. MS Basel, Univ. Bibl. B III 25, f. 5rb. This note does not appear in the manuscripts at Paris, MS BnF lat. 573, f. 204rb, and Madrid, MS Bibl. Nac. 493, f. 72v.

68. "Some More Exegetical Works of Simon of Hinton," 97–106 (99–104).

69. Concerning Hugh, G. Dahan observes: "... qui, selon toute vraisemblance, se donne pour objet, avec son équipe de Biblistes de Saint-Jacques, de remplacer la *Glossa*, mais n'y parvient pas, sa *Postille* ne connaissant qu'une diffusion relativement modeste, même à l'intérieur de l'ordre des dominicains, et les traces de son utilisation ne se repèrent pas facilement"; "La méthode critique dans l'étude de la Bible (xii$^e$–xiii$^e$ siècles)," 126.

70. *Titulus*, 180–181. R. Sharpe shows this by consulting a listing of the latter work in the 1622 catalogue of Patrick Young. His conclusion is also supported by examination of the relevant lines in the two other manuscripts consulted for this study, MSS Paris, BnF lat. 573, f. 200ra and Madrid, Bibl. Nac. 493, f. 6vb. Though B. Smalley's identification of the postill in question with one ascribed to Simon of Hinton is no longer tenable, her suggestion that the prologue as it appears in the Basel manuscript was truncated in other manuscripts, due to its considerable length, finds support in the copies at Paris and Madrid, both of which are considerably less complete.

71. The cross-reference in question appears at Iob 1:20 (*Tunc surrexit*) (MSS Paris, BnF lat. 573, f. 207va and Madrid, Bibl. Nac. 493, f. 14r). In the Paris manuscript, there is, in fact, a cross-reference indicated by an unusual sign. It refers, however, to a spiritual exposition in the lower margin, which is written in a posterior hand and overlaps with spiritual comments on the same lines in the main text. This text does not appear in the Madrid manuscript.

72. *Super Mattheum* (begins incomplete at Mt 5:2, MS Bodleian, e mus. 29, f. 1r–173v); *Super XII prophetas*; inc: *Murus ciuitatis habens fundamenta* (ibid., f. 247r–365v). B. Smalley discusses these commentaries in "Some More Exegetical Works of Simon of Hinton," 184–214.

73. Specifically, subdivisions are less regularly indicated by the formula *in prima primo*, and lemmata of the *divisio* in both copies are occasionally introduced by *ibi*. The opening *divisio* of the first chapter, for example, is not introduced by *hic*, a lemma is introduced by *ibi*, and *in prima primo* is absent from seven consecutive subdivisions: (1) *prima habet duas*, (2) *prima in duas*, (3) *prima habet tres*, (4) *prima respicit se*, (5) *ideo ista habet duas*, (6) *quia triplex est bonum . . . ideo prima habet tres*, and (7) *respectu proximi commendatur primo . . .* (MSS Paris, BnF lat. 573, f. 204ra; Madrid, Bibl. Nac. 493, f. 12rb). While *dicit ergo* generally introduces the *expositio*, *hic* less regularly introduces the *divisio* and is occasionally completely absent from it. A case in

point: "Consequenter deplorat suum et cuiuslibet hominis generaliter ingressum in uita tam periculosa, ³ᴵᴵᴵ*QUARE NON IN UULUA*, et primo. . ." (MSS Paris, BnF lat. 573, f. 211ra; Madrid, Bibl. Nac. 493, f. 16ra). Only two such examples have been found in William's works, though one of them is formally alike: "Consequenter inuitat populum ad penitentiam: ³ᴵ⁴⁰*SCRUTE-MUR UIAS N⟨OSTRAS⟩. Et primo in genere; secundo in specie. . . ."(Super Threnos*, ed. cit., 266). In the commentaries of Thomas Aquinas, *consequenter* is a commonplace introduction to the *divisio*. In addition, subdivision is occasionally of an element other than the first of the preceding series. So, for example: "Secunda pars habet tres," (MSS Paris, BnF lat. 573, f. 207va; Madrid, Bibl. Nac. 493, f. 14ra).

74. Presented here is the text of MS Basel, Univ. Bibl. B III 25, f. 4rb and 104rb. It is virtually the same in MSS Paris, BnF lat. 573, f. 204ra and f. 281vb; Madrid, Bibl. Nac. 493, 12rb and f. 72r.

75. Two such examples appear at Iob 41:24 (MSS Paris, BnF lat. 573, f. 281ra; Madrid, Bibl. Nac. 493, f. 71v). Another appears at Iob 42:12 (MSS Paris, BnF lat. 573, f. 281vb; Madrid, Bibl. Nac. 493, f. 72v).

76. Occupying two entire columns, the *divisio* at Mt 8:1, for example, contains a lengthy excursus, a question, and nonbiblical citations (MS Oxford, Bodleian, e mus. 29, 35r–36r. B. Smalley has presented the texts of a few of Simon's digressions, "Two Biblical Commentaries of Simon of Hinton," *RTAM* 13 (1946), 76–85.

77. The spiritual version survives in MS Oxford, New College 45; an incomplete copy of the literal version appears in MS Oxford, Bodleian, e mus. 29, f. 247r–365v; a complete copy appears in MS Paris, BnF lat. 468. B. Smalley, "Some More Exegetical Works of Simon of Hinton," 97; "Two Biblical Commentaries of Simon of Hinton," ibid., 57–58.

78. Both *allegorice* and *moraliter* are employed to distinguish the various senses at Iob 2:13 (MSS Paris, BnF lat. 573, f. 209vb; Madrid, Bibl. Nac. 493, f. 15v).

79. A case in point appears at the exposition of Iob 26:9 (MSS Paris, BnF lat. 573, f. 252vb; Madrid 493, f. 47r); another is at Iob 28:23 (MSS Paris, BnF lat. 573, f. 257vb, in this copy, the term *mistice* is omitted here; Madrid 493, f. 50r); and another at Iob 29:6 (MSS Paris, BnF lat. 573, f. 204va; Madrid 493, f. 50v).

80. Its relative length can be measured, since the scribe who left us this postill is the same as the one who recorded each of the works of Group A, the first three in the same manuscript, and the fourth in another of nearly identical dimensions. With respect to the biblical text as it appears in the Weber edition of the Vulgate, the commentary on Job is more than twice as long as William's *Super Ieremiam*. It is 41 percent longer than his *Super Threnos* and 39 percent longer than his *Super Iohannem*. In the Weber edition of the Vulgate, the text of Job extends from 732a to 766b, approximately thirty-four pages. Excluding the prologues, the postill under consideration occupies approximately 78¼ folios (MS Paris, BnF lat. 573, f. 204ra–282rb). A biblical text of virtually the same length as Iob 1:1–42, 16 is Ier 1:1–25, 6, Weber, 1166a–1200a. The corresponding section of William's *Super Ieremiam* occupies approximately thirty-one folios, (MS Paris, BnF lat. 573, f. 87vb–119va). At slightly less than seven pages, the biblical text of Lamentations is of about the same length as Iob 1–8. The relevant section of the postill under consideration occupies approximately 15½ folios (MS Paris, BnF lat. 573, f. 204ra–219va). William's *Super Threnos* extends to slightly more than ten folios (MS Paris, BnF lat. 573, f. 145vb–156ra). Due to the questionable authorship of its first four chapters, the commentary *Super Isaiam* has not been considered. All the same, the length of its exposition appears to be similar to that of *Super Ieremiam*. Approximately as long as the text of Job is Io 1:1–19:7, Weber, 1658a–1692b. The relevant portion of William's commentary on it occupies about 56¾ folios (MS Saint-Omer, Bibl. mun. 260, f. 111va–168rb). William's *Super Iohannem* is written in the same hand as the Paris copy of *Super Iob*, and it appears in columns of the same length and width. Physically, the manuscripts Paris, BnF lat. 573 and Saint-Omer, Bibl. mun. 260 are of virtually identical dimensions. The columns of both texts contain forty-five lines and measure 150 x 50 mm. The likelihood of this postill's authenticity is not increased by the copy in MS Basel, Univ. Bibl. B III 25. A transcription of its prologue extends to twenty printed pages, and it is generally more discursive than the version of the Basel and Paris manuscripts.

81. MSS Paris, BnF lat. 573, f. 210vb; Madrid, Bibl. Nac. 493, 16r. A variant appears in MS Basel, Univ. Bibl. B III 25, f. 11ra. Such examples appear throughout the commentary on Iob 3, where the literal remarks are rare and muddled with the predominant spiritual interpretation; terms such as *litteraliter* and *allegorice* appear only rarely.

82. "Sapiential Books I," 75.

83. Such is the case in the *divisio* introducing chapters 2, 3, 6, 7, 12, 14–17 (MSS Madrid, Bibl. Nac. 493, f. 77v, 78v, 83v, 85v, 94r, 97r, 99r 101r, 103r, 105r; Saint-Omer, Bibl. mun. 260, f. 222ra, 223rb, 227vb, 229vb, 238ra, 241va, 243rb, 245vb, 247va).

84. Of those introducing the first eighteen chapters, the *divisio* of only one begins with *hic*: "¹¹¹¹*STATERA DOLOSA*. Hic. . ."; (MSS Madrid, Bibl. Nac. 493, f. 92r, Saint-Omer, Bibl. mun. 260, f. 236vb). In twelve cases, the opening term is *supra*. On William's systematic application of *hic* for this purpose, see chapter 2, note 7ᶜ.

85. These traits appear in the *divisio* and subsequent exposition of Prv 9:1 (MSS Madrid 493, f. 89r; Saint-Omer, Bibl. mun. 260, 232vb–233ra).

86. "9¹¹*SAPIENTIA*, id est Christus, qui est Dei uirtus et Dei sapientia, ⟨1⟩ Cor 1 (24), *EDIFICAUIT*, sua operatione secundum naturam diuinam, *SIBI DOMUM*, id est corpus et animam ad habitandum. . . . Vel *DOMUS*, ecclesia in qua habitauit per gratiam. . . . Item *DOMUS*, beata Virgo"; (MSS Madrid 493, f. 89r; Saint-Omer, Bibl. mun. 260, f. 232vb).

87. "9¹³*MISIT ANCILLAS SUAS*, id est apostolos et predicatores" (MSS Madrid 493, f. 89r; Saint-Omer, Bibl. mun. 260, f. 233ra).

88. A typical case is the spiritual exposition of Prv 5:13–19, where the topics taken up under the single heading *mistice* include heresy, heretics, sound doctrine, the quest for human favor, good and evil speech, the church, Christ, prelates, and doctors (MSS Madrid 493, f. 83r; Saint-Omer, Bibl. mun. 260, f. 227va). Another interesting example appears at Prv 7:19 *(non est enim vir in domo sua abiit via longissima)*. After a brief literal comment, the term *moraliter* introduces the remark that the adulteress's absent husband may be likened to an absent rector whose servant, abandoned in the parish, replies to anyone who asks for anything that the rector has left for Paris, yet will manage to show up whenever the wine and grain are abundant. Immediately afterward we find that the husband is Christ who has gone to heaven but will return on the judgment day: "Moraliter. Ita potest respondere puer alicuius rectoris derelictus in parochia cum ab eo aliquid petitur: Non est uir, id est rector, *IN DO⟨MO⟩*, scilicet, *ABI⟨IT⟩ UIA LON⟨GISSIMA⟩*, Parisius, *IN DI⟨E⟩ PLE⟨NE⟩ LU⟨NE⟩ REUER⟨SURUS⟩ EST*, quando est habundantia uini et bladi. Item, *UIR* est Christus, *ABI⟨IT⟩ UI⟨A⟩ LONG⟨GISSIMA⟩*, in celis, *REUERSURUS*, in die iudicii quando erit tempus plenum" (MSS Madrid 493, f. 86v; Saint-Omer, Bibl. mun. 260, f. 230va). Another example appears after the literal exposition of Prv 10:1, where the term *mistice* introduces comments that are intermittently moral and allegorical, MSS Madrid 493, f. 90r; Saint-Omer, Bibl. mun. 260, f. 234rb.

89. Two such examples appear at Prv. 6:31 (MSS Madrid 493, f. 85r; Saint-Omer, Bibl. mun. 260, f. 229va).

90. MS Erfurt, Wissenschaftliche Bibliothek der Stadt Amplon. F 181, f. 47v–82v; MS Siena, Bibl. com. U. VI 7, f. 1r–39v (fifteenth century).

91. MS Paris, BnF lat. 14429, f. 119r. Stegmüller, Kaeppeli, and Sharp all note only one second-hand ascription at the incipit. None mentions a firsthand ascription to William at the explicit.

92. MS Paris, Maz. 985 (1276), 96ra–128va. Lacking an author's prologue, it was probably mistaken for *Aspexi terram* because the two postills' expositions of Jerome's prologue are similar. The attribution at the explicit is in the hand of the scribe: "Expliciunt postille fratris Bonauenture super Ecclesiasten."

93. "Postille super Ecclesiasten secundum fratrem Wilhelmum de Altona ordinis predicatorum Magistrum in theologia Parisius," (MS Basel, Univ. Bibl. B III 20, f. 93ra); "Explicit super Ecclesiasten secundum fratrem Guillelmum de Altona, Deo gratias," (MS Paris, BnF lat. 14429, f. 154ra); "Lectura ista est de fratre Guillermo de Altona. Explicit Ecclesiates," (Madrid, Bibl. Nac. 493, f. 165r); "Explicit super Ecclesiasten secundum fratrem Guillelmum de Altona, Deo gratias," (MS Tarragona, Bibl. Publ. 83, f. 76vb).

94. The manuscripts at Basel and Paris contain a commentary on Wisdom (to be discussed at no. 17), after which both of the original scribes left the following inscription: "Hic liber scriptum est ab anno ab origine mundi 6465, anno Domini 1267," (MSS Basel, Univ. Bibl. B III 20, f. 144vb; Paris, BnF lat. 14429, f. 93rb). In the Paris manuscript, the inscription is only tenuously related to the postill on Ecclesiastes now in question, since the postill on Wisdom precedes it and appears to have once belonged to another codex. A note at the top of f. 95v suggests the beginning of what was once a separate volume: "Iste liber est. . . ." In the Basel manuscript, on the other hand, the postill on Wisdom comes later than *Aspexi terram* and does not appear to have originated in a separate book.

95. Here I cite the incunables held at Munich, BSB-Ink B-33GW 3237, f. 40vb and 42va–vb; and Paris, BnF réserve D 6438, f. 40vb and 42va–vb. During the sixteenth century, Vincent's remark was cited by *Sixtus Senensis* in his *Bibliotheca sancta* (ed. Venice 1566, 377).

96. MS Madrid, Bibl. Nac. 493, f. 151v. The text is substantially the same in MSS Basel, Univ. Bibl, B III 20, f. 105rb and Paris, BnF lat. 14429, f. 140rb–va. Virtually all but the last sentence "Potuit tamen–post non" has been borrowed from Bonaventure, *In Ecl. com.* 7:21 (*Opera*, t. VI, 61b).

97. MS Madrid, Bibl. Nac. 493, f. 152v. The text is substantially the same in MSS Basel, Univ. Bibl, B III 20, f. 106ra and Paris, BnF lat. 14429, f. 141rb–va.

98. *Opera*, t. VI, xx.

99. P. Glorieux, *Répertoire* I, 115.

100. Bonaventure, *In Ecl. com.* 1:1 (*Opera*, t. VI, 9a).

101. Exceptional elsewhere, usage of *diuiditur* is not unusual at the beginning of William's postills. This incipit's usage of *diuiditur* has an identical counterpart in the incipit to *Super Ieremiam*: "$^{1:1}$*VERBA IEREMIE.* Iste liber diuiditur. . . ." (MS Paris, BnF lat. 573, f; 87vb). In both works, subsequent appearances are exceedingly rare.

102. For example: "Continua. Dixit quod omnia sunt uana, id est mutabilia, et uere, quia dignissima creatura, scilicet homo $^{1:3}$*QUID HABET ANPLIUS HOMO DE UNIUERSO LABORE SUO QUO LABORAT SUB SOLE*" (MS Madrid, Bibl. Nac. 493, f. 132v).

103. A typical example appears at Ecl 1:6, MS Madrid, Bibl. Nac. 493, f. 133v.

104. For a few examples, at Ecl 1:6: "Mistice. $^{1:6}$*LUSTRANS UNIUERSA* etc. Primo ostendit. . ." (MS Madrid, Bibl. Nac. 493, f. 134r), and at Ecl 1:7: "Moraliter. Est $^{1:7}$*MARE* aqua . . . Allegorice. $^{1:7}$*MARE* mundus. . ." (MS Madrid, Bibl. Nac. 493, f. 134v).

105. Excluding the prologue, Bonaventure's postill extends to approximately 192 columns (from the top of f. 3vb to the bottom of f. 49ra). Excluding the prologue, the postill in question extends to approximately 137 columns (from the bottom of f. 119va to the top of f. 154ra). Written in different, though similar hands, the columns of both texts are generally of thirty-seven lines.

106. "Sapiential Books I," 49.

107. A case in point appears at Ecl 1:7 (MS Paris, BnF lat. 14260, f. 65ra).

108. Each of these traits is on view in divisions at Ecl 2:1, 2:24, and 3:1 (MS Paris, BnF lat. 14260, f. 67ra, 71rb and f. 71vb–72ra).

109. "⟨ET⟩ *INUENI AMARIOREM MORTE MULIEREM*, id est concupiscentiam, que amarior est mortem, quia mors sola animam a creatore separat; set istam animam a Deo separat, conscienciam ex hoc inquietat, penam temporalem et eternam accumulat" (MS Paris, BnF lat. 14260, f. 93ra).

110. "Amen, amen, amen, dicant omnia. Explicit postilla fratris Ni. de Gorra de Ordine fratrum predicatorum" (MS Madrid 53, f. 182rb).

111. Apart from differences of copy, the explicits are virtually the same as the following: "$^{8:14}$*SUPER MONTES AROMATUM*, id est super montes fidelium. Fideles enim dicuntur esse *MONTES* per eminentiam uite, Ysa. XLIX (13): *Iubilate montes laudem.* Set *MONTES AROMATUM* dicuntur esse, quia ubique debent diffundere odorem bone opinionis, secunda Cor. II (15): *Christi bonus odor sumus in omni loco*" (MS Paris, BnF lat. 14260, 58rb).

112. William of Tournai was likely a regent from 1272 to 1274, *Répertoire*, no. 18. The four MSS are the following: Cambridge, Pembroke College 80, f. 38r–86; Cambridge, Pembroke College

97, f. 71r–176; Bordeaux 38, f. 32–56v; Siena, Bibl. com., F. V. 23, f. 38v–77; cf. B. Smalley, "Sapiential Books I," 70–71.

113. On the systematic usage of *hic* in William's postills, see chapter 2, note 7.

114. The formula *in prima dicuntur duo* or *quatuor* etc., appears in the initial *divisio* of chapters 1, 2, 3, 4, and 6 (MS BnF lat 14260, f. 1vb, 9va, 16rb, 20va, and 37vb).

115. The term *ibi* precedes biblical references four times in the prologue (MS BnF lat 14260, f. 1ra–rb). In initial *divisio* of chapter 2, it precedes lemmata four times (f. 9va); in that of chapter 3, four times (f. 16rb); in that of chapter 4, twice (f. 20va); in that of chapter 5, twice (f. 28ra); in that of chapter 6, three times (f. 37vb); in that of chapter 7, once (f. 43ra); and in that of chapter 8, twice (f. 51ra).

116. MSS Paris, BnF lat. 14260, f. 9va; Paris, BnF lat. 471, f. 38va; Paris, BnF lat. 15571, f. 29ra.

117. As printed in the Weber edition, the text of Lamentations' five chapters is more than 25 percent longer than that of the Canticle's eight. The postill in question occupies slightly more than 22 folios in MS Madrid 53, approximately 58½ in MS Paris, BnF lat. 14260, and slightly more 27 in MS Paris, BnF lat. 15592. William's *Super Threnos* fills slightly less than eleven folios of MS Paris, BnF lat. 573, f. 145rb–156ra. Comparison of transcriptions of several columns of text indicates that the text of MS Paris, BnF lat. 573 is approximately 27 percent denser than that of MS Paris, BnF lat. 14260. In other words, an average folio of the former contains about 27 percent more text than an average folio of the latter.

118. "Sapiential Books I," 48–50.

119. Examples appear at MS Paris, BnF lat. 14260, f. 154vb–155ra and f. 156va–vb.

120. MS Paris, BnF lat. 14429, f. 155r. Quetif and Echard take the ascription *de Altona* to be the prior and *de Melitona* to be the posterior, *SOP* 245b. Similarly, D. Monti has called this an ascription to William of Alton in the original hand, "A Reconsideration," 371. Such is not, in fact, the case. The inscription containing the name "Militone," in a posterior hand, has been expunctuated and "Altona Ord. fratrum predicatorum anglicum" has been written above it in another posterior hand.

121. MS Basel, Univ. Bibl. B VIII 28. This is an octavo codex containing only this work. On its front flyleaf is the inscription "Ioan. de Verdiaco super librum Sapientie." Above the incipit, f. 1r, we find: "Fratris Iohannis de Verdiaco ordinis predicatorum. Videtur esse excerptus a postilla eius." Though she mistakenly places the latter ascription at the explicit, B. Smalley has made the astute observation that it appears to be in the same posterior hand that credited John of Varzy with a different postill on wisdom, *Super Sapientiam* (inc.: *Trahitur sapientia de occultis*) in MS Basel, Univ. B III 20. Above the exposition of Jerome's prologue (which in this case precedes the author's prologue), we find "Postilla super librum sapientie secundum fratris Iohannis De Verdiaco" (f. 146r). See "Sapiential Books I," 241.

122. "Postille super librum Sapientie secundum fratrem Iohannem de Verdiaco ordinis fratrum predicatorum bachilarium in theologia" (MS Basel, Univ. Bibl. B III 20, f. 114r).

123. MS Paris, BnF lat. 14429, f. 93ra.

124. "*Fons sapientie uerbum Domini*" (MS BnF lat. 15573, f. 156ra); "*Diligite lumen sapientie*" (f. 156va). The other codex, not consulted for this study, is MS Bordeaux, Bibliothèque municipale 38.

125. See note 94.

126. "Hic liber scriptus est anno ab origine mundi 6465, anno Domini 1267" (MS Paris, BnF lat. 14429, f. 93rb); "Vnde Mt. XI (11): *Non surrexit inter natos mulierum maior Iohanne baptista. Qui autem minor est in regno celorum maior est illo.* Ad hanc magnitudinem nos perducat Ihesus Christus Dominus noster, qui est benedictus in secula seculorum. Hic liber scriptus est anno ab origine mundi 6465, anno Domini 1267" (MS Basel, Univ. B III 20, f. 145v).

127. "A Reconsideration," 359–363.

128. Oddly enough, C. Oudin cast doubt on many other works included in the Vatican edition, *Commentarius de scriptoribus ecclesiasticis*, vol. III, Leipzig, 1722, 380.

129. *SOP* I, 245b–246a.

130. Presently MS Paris, BnF lat. 14429. The provost of Saint-Omer, Adenulph of Anagni, was also the nephew of Pope Gregory IX and a canon of Notre Dame. After studying under Thomas

Aquinas, he became master of theology in Paris in 1272 and was elected bishop of Paris in 1288. Too ill to assume the charge, he entered St. Victor and died in 1289; J.-P. Torrell, *Initiation*, 289–290. On Adenulph's bequest to St. Victor, see P. Glorieux, "Essai sur les commentaires scripturaires de S. Thomas d'Aquin," *RTAM* 12 (1950), 237–266 (246); *Répertoire* I, no. 186; Delisle, L., *Cabinet des manuscrits de la Bibliothèque nationale*, Paris, 1868–1881, 210; *Inventaire des manuscrits latins de Saint-Victor conservés à la Bibliothèque impériale sous les numéros 14232–15175*, in *Bibliothèque de l'Ecole des Chartes* 30 (1869), 14.

131. *SOP* I, 245b–246a.

132. "Ingenue fatemur, deesse nobis codices, quorum auctoritate hanc postillam S. Bonaventurae vindicare possimus," "Prolegomena" (*Opera*, t. VI, xviii).

133. "Quoad *Gulielmum de Altona* primo observandum est, in eodem codice ipsi falso attributum esse etiam Commentarium Bonaventurae in *Ecclesiasten* cum inscriptione: *secundum fratrem Gulielmum de Altona*, quod auctorem postillae indicare videtur. Sed cum ea quae sequitur Postilla in *Sapientiam, eisdem prorsus verbis* inscripta sit: *secundum fratrem Gulielmum* de Altona ordinis fratrum Praedicatorum (Echard. pag. 245b); testimonium huius codicis de primo errore iam convicti perdit fidem etiam quoad alteram assertionem. Posset tamen dici, illa verba *secundum fratrem Gulielmum . . .* non significare proprie *auctorem*, sed *fontem*, ex quo alius hauserit" (italics and reference to Echard in original), *Opera*, t. VI, xx.

134. The Quaracchi editors refer to the aforementioned postill *Super Sapientiam* (inc.: *Diligite iustitiam*) that also appears in MS Basel, Univ. B III 20, f. 147rb–181vb; cf. "Prolegomena," ibid., xx.

135. "Nolumus tamen contradicere ei qui forte dixerit, originale huius Postille fuisse ab aliis aliquatenus mutatum, sive in aliquibus diminutum, sive in aliis auctum . . . suspicari licet, similem quandam mutationem ipsius Postillae accidisse. Nec desunt pro hac suspicione indicia interna non spernenda. . . . Saepius hic quam in aliis Commentariis auctor utitur Glossa. . . . Brevius solito etiam tractantur quaestiones scholasticae passim occurentes"; ibid., xx.

136. ". . . non improbabili, quod S. Bonaventura iuniore aetate et ante alios suos Commentarios librum Sapientiae in scholis explicaverit"; ibid., xxi.

137. "Sapiential Books I," 47–48.

138. Without a presentation of new evidence, Bonaventure's authorship was defended at the time by B. Distelbrink, *Bonaventurae Scripta. Authentica dubia vel spuria critica recensita*, Roma, 1975, 18–19.

139. "Je ne le sais pas encore, bien que Jean de Varzy ait pris une option probablement valable," "Pecia et critique d'authenticité," 208. In 1961, he tentatively credited the work to Bonaventure in the 1961 *Introduction à l'étude de saint Bonaventure*, 145. A few decades later, he credited it to John of Varzy without hesitation: "Il me semble que l'examen de la liste de taxation ne laisse aucun doute sur l'attribution de cette Postille à Jean de Varzy," *Introduction à Saint Bonaventure*, Paris, 1988, 182.

140. "A Reconsideration," 390.

141. "Prolegomena," *Opera*, t. VI, xvii, xix, xx.

142. "Prolegomena," *Opera*, t. VI, xix, xx.

143. Though it contains spiritual exegesis as well as questions, this postill is ascribed to John of Varzy as a bachelor; see note 122. P. Glorieux assigned John's Paris regency to 1270–1271 or slightly later, *Répertoire* I, 125. A. Walz concluded that John taught in Paris as a regent master before 1270, "Hat Johann von Freiburg in Paris studiert?" *Angelicum* 11 (1934), 245–249 (247). B. Smalley entertained both possibilities without committing herself to either one, "Sapiential Books I," 239. Even should we assume that Walz was correct, the time frame in which John could have composed *Fons sapientie* by 1267 would have been narrow.

144. Nicholas of Gorran is credited with having gained a reputation as a preacher during the period 1263–1285, *HLF* 20 (1842), 324–356. Yet B. Smalley has observed, rightly, that he "is an uncertain quantity as far as dates are concerned," "Sapiential Books I," 239. See also her remarks in *Study of the Bible*, 273; "Sapiential Books II," 106.

145. W. Courtenay, "Programs of Study and Genres," 332–333; J. Verger, "L'exégèse, parente pauvre de la théologie scholastique?" 40–41; B. Smalley, "Sapiential Books I," 47.

146. Another postill on Wisdom, inc.: *Trahitur sapientia de occultis* (MS Basel, Univ. Bibl. B III 20, f. 146ra–181vb), has been ascribed in a later hand to John of Varzy. See note 121.

147. *SOPMA* 3089; *Rep. Bibl.* 5741–5810.

148. P. Glorieux, "L'enseignement au Moyen Age. Techniques et méthodes en usage à la Faculté de Théologie de Paris, au XIII^e siècle," *AHDLMA* 35 (1968), 65–186.

149. The basis of comparison is the postill *Super Mattheum* inc.: *Sume tibi librum grandem*, (MS Paris, BnF lat. 9418, f. 1ra–117vb).

150. See G. Murano, *Opere diffuse per exemplar e pecia*, 86.

151. B. Smalley, "Sapiential Books I," 236–241.

152. Albeit with a different incipit (*Dilectus meus candidus*), the postill on the Canticle is ascribed in the first hand to William of Middleton at the explicit of a copy in MS Paris, BnF lat. 15265, f. 1–41. A firsthand ascription of this same work to John of Varzy appears in MS Paris, BnF lat. 14259, f. 225b, and secondhand ascriptions appear in MS Basel, Univ. B III 20, on the first fly-leaf and f. 182, and MS Basel, Univ. B IV 21, f. 71. Having observed that the latter two attributions are in the same hand, and having studied this work's content, B. Smalley tentatively credited it to William of Middleton, "Sapiential Books I," 55–57. The postills on Proverbs and Ecclesiastes she credited even more tentatively to John of Varzy, "Sapiential Books I," 236–240. Having examined her presentation of extracts of an anonymous postill on Proverbs (MS Cambridge, Trinity College 98), J.-G. Bougerol identified the work with a postill on Proverbs in MS Troyes, Bibl. mun. 667 and credited it to John of Varzy, "Pecia et critique d'authenticité," 207; "Pour des «Prolegomena Postquam» de l'édition critique de S. Bonaventure Quaracchi 1882–1902," 128. Yet in her presentation of the extracts, B. Smalley carefully avoided committing herself to any attribution of this work. To the contrary, she drew attention to its anonymity and remarked that "the positive evidence for John's authorship is slender" in "Sapiential Books I," 239. Examination of the commentary on the Canticle in MSS Paris, BnF lat. 14259 and Basel, Univ. B III 20, for the present study confirms her impression: it is thoroughly in keeping with what we have come to expect from William of Middleton. As they appear in MS Paris, BnF lat. 14259, the postills on Proverbs and Ecclesiastes are noticeably different from this one, though they are similar to each other.

153. "Huius gloriae tanta est magnitudo, ut illius regni minimus maior sit maximo huius mundi; unde Matthaei undecimo: 'Non surrexit inter natos mulierum maior Ioanne Baptista. Qui autem minor est in regno caelorum maior est illo.' Ad hanc magnitudinem nos perducat Iesus Christus Dominus noster, qui est benedictus in saecula saeculorum. Amen." "Ipse est finis desideriorum nostrorum, qui sine fine uidebitur. . . . Ad hoc nos perducat, qui uiuit et regnat in secula seculorum," *Super Sap.* 19:20 (*Opera*, t. VI, 233b). "Sine fastidio amabitur, sine fatigatione laudabitur, hoc munus, hic affectus, hic actus, perfectio erit omnibus sicut ipsa uita eterna communis est, ad quam nos perducat Ihesus Christus Filius Dei, qui est alpha et omega, id est principium et finis, regnans cum Patre et Spiritu sancto in secula seculorum. Amen" (*Super Prouerbiis*, MS Troyes, Bibl. mun. 667, f. 150vb).

154. "Item, secunda Cor. secundo (15): '*Christi bonus odor sumus Deo*'. Supra secundo (17): *Reuertere, dilecte mi, similis esto capre hynuloque ceruorum* etc. Laus tibi sit Christe, quoniam liber explicit iste. Amen" (MS Basel, B III 20, 220ra; the copy of MS Troyes 667 has not been cited here because it ends incomplete at Cnt 8:9).

155. "Hec sunt ergo munera illi tanto iudici premittenda, Gen. XXXII (20): *Placabo eum muneribus que precedunt et postea uidebo illum; forsitan propitiabitur michi.* Quam propitiationem nobis concedat, qui uiuit et regnat per omnia secula seculorum. Amen" (MSS Basel, Univ. Bibl. B III 20, f. 113ra; Madrid, Bibl. Nac. 493, f. 165r).

156. "Hoc contingat quod eadem scriptura in quodam loco dicit: *Cum consumauerit homo, tunc incipiet* (Ecclesiasticus 18:6). Det igitur Dominus hec uita consumasse ut alia incipiens melius possim consumare" (MS Saint-Omer, 260, f. 177va).

157. "Septimo, in gloria exaltando, Eccli. ⟨XLV⟩ (3): *Magnificauit eum in conspectu regum et dedit illi coronam glorie*, quam nobis concedat Deus, qui uiuit et regnat in secula seculorum. Amen" (MS Basel, B III 20, 181vb).

158. Examples appear in the divisions introducing chapters 3, 5 (twice), 6, 7, 8, and 9 (MS Paris, BnF lat. 14259, f. 134rb, f. 141va, f.145rb, 147ra, f. 152ra and f. 155rb).

159. The formula appears three times in the initial division of chapter 3 (MS Paris, BnF lat. 14259, f. 188ra).

160. *Super Sapientiam*; inc.: *Diligite Iustitiam qui iudicatis terram* (MS Paris, BnF lat. 14259, f. 226ra–306rb). The formula *in prima duo* appears in the initial divisions of chapters 2, 3, and 4. It makes three appearances in a division on f. 188ra.

161. In the Weber edition, Proverbs occupies about 28½ pages (extending from 958a to 986b), whereas Wisdom occupies about 25½ (extending from 1003a to 1028b).

162. In Sap 3:1, *Bonaventure Opera*, t. VI, 123a.

163. In Io 10:28, *Opera*, t. VI, 393a.

164. *Super Io.* 10:28.

165. In Sap 1:13, *Opera*, t. VI, 212b.

166. In Io 9:39, *Opera*, t. VI, 382a.

167. *Super Io.*, 9:39, 249.

168. Up until Sap 8:9 (f. 264va), the hand is other than that of the postills of Group A. Afterward, it is the same.

169. For example, in a *divisio* at Sap 2:12 *ibi* makes five appearances in the Quaracchi edition, *Opera*, t. VI, 122a; it appears three times in a truncated version of the same text in ms Saint Omer 260, 253rb. This term is altogether absent from this text as it appears in MSS Basel, Univ. B III 20, f. 117ra–rb; Paris, BnF lat. 14429, f. 54vb; ibid. f. 160rb, BnF lat. 15573, f. 160ra, and with the sole exception of a single addition of *ibi* by a posterior hand. Examples could be multiplied.

170. Cf. C. Samaran and R. Marichal, *Catalogue des MSS en écriture latine portant des indications de date, de lieu, ou de copiste*, Paris, 1974, 685; Delisle, L., *Cabinet*, t. 3, 19, 92–93; *Inventaire*, 15. This codex belonged to the library of Gerard of Abbeville and was part of his bequest to the library of the Sorbonne, where it became one of the chained reference works.

171. "Prolegomena," *Opera*, t. VI, xviii–xix.

172. In Sap 5:3, *Opera*, t. VI, 138a–b. The formatting of the Quaracchi edition has been retained.

173. In Sap 5:7, ibid, 139b. D. Monti has described the *divisio* as follows: "The text, from beginning to end, is divided and subdivided by means of a detailed logical analysis, first into broad portions, and then pericope after pericope, sentence after sentence—each with its specific function in what the commentator has determined to be the over-all plan of the inspired author." See "A Reconsideration," 382–383.

174. See, for example, the *divisio* introducing ch. 8 of his commentary on Ecclesiastes, *Opera*, t. VI, 64a–b; or the one introducing ch. 17 of his commentary on John, ibid., 467a.

175. E.g.: "Rabanus sic continuat," *Opera*, t. VI, 125a.

176. "A Reconsideration," 383.

177. See, for example, the exposition of Sap 2:12–25, *Opera*, t. VI, 122a–125b.

178. An example appears at Sap 4:6: "*Allegorice* exponit hoc Glossa de haereticis . . . qui *inutiles* sunt Ecclesiae, immo nocivi, quia eam persequuntur"(*Opera*, t. VI, 134a). Here as elsewhere, the formatting and orthography of the Quaracchi edition have been retained.

179. On William's predilection for just this sort of exercise with the use of the same term (albeit in the orthography *le* or *li*), see pages 48–50.

180. "A Reconsideration," 388–389.

181. "A Reconsideration," 385.

182. "A Reconsideration," 384.

183. MS BnF lat. 573, 156ra–va.

184. An example appears at Ez 6:7 (MS Paris, BnF lat. 573, f. 166ra).

185. Typical questions appear at Ez 1:21 and Ez 5:16 (ibid., f. 159ra and f. 165va).

186. Examples appear at Dn 1:1, Dn 3:38, and Dn 5:1 (MS Oxford, Bodleian, Laud. misc. 390, f. 102v, 107v, and 111v).

187. Instances appear at Dn 3:1 and Dn 7:1 (MS Oxford, Bodleian, Laud. misc. 390, f. 106v and 114r).

188. A case in point is the *divisio* at Dn 2:1 (MS Oxford, Bodleian, Laud. misc. 390, f. 103v).

189. MSS Napoli, Bibl. Naz. VII A 12, f. 2ra–103rb; Wien, Schottenstift 144.

190. "Nicholai de Gorram Expos. In Matth." (MS München, StaatsBibl. Clm 7941, f. 1r); "Postille fratris petri de tarentasia super Matheum sacre pagine professoris ordinis fratrum predicatorum qui papa creatus dictus est innocentius quintus" (MS München, StaatsBibl.Clm 23620, f. 1v).

191. From consulting the microfilm, I have found fifteen pecia marks: ii p$^a$, f. 4vb; iii p$^a$, f. 8va; iiii p$^a$, f. 12rb; v p$^a$, f. 16ra; vi p$^a$, f. 19va; vii p$^a$, f. 22vb; viii p$^a$, f. 26ra; ix p$^a$, f. 29rb; x p$^a$, f. 32vb; xi p$^a$, f. 36ra; xii p$^a$, f. 37vb; xiii p$^a$, 42va; xiiii p$^a$, f. 45vb; xv p$^a$, f. 49ra, MS Tours, Bibl. mun. 121. The taxation list indicates thirty-seven peciae: "Item Postille fratris Guillelmi de Altona super Matheum pec' .xxxvii."; G. Murano, *Opere diffuse per exempla et pecia*, 86.

192. MS Florence, Bibl. Laurenziana Conv. soppr. 280, f. 209r–293v.

193. "Sapiential Books I," 67–68.

194. MS München, StaatsBibl. Clm 23620, 2ra–93vb.

195. See P. Mandonnet, "Thomas Aquinas in Curia Romana lector," 18–21.

196. On the more recent scholarship concerning the dating of Thomas's *Super Mattheum*, see J.-P. Torrell, *Initiation*, 80–86, 495, and chapter 1, note 11.$^e$

197. A survey of the initial *divisio* of chapters 1 through 10 found instances of such use of the term in chapters 1, 3, and 9 (MSS Saint-Omer, Bibl. mun. 260, f. 3ra, 11ra, 35ra; Munich, StaatsBibl. Clm 7941, f. 2rb, 8va, 27ra; in MS Tours, Bibl. mun. 121, the term appears in the the initial *divisio* of chapters 1 and 9, f. 2va and 28va, though it does not appear in the *divisio* introducing chapter 3, f. 9ra).

198. Examples appear in the initial *divisio* of chapters 4, 5, and 8 (MSS Saint-Omer, Bibl. mun. 260, f. 14ra–rb, 17va, 31va; Tours, Bibl. mun. 121, f. 11va, 14va, 25vb).

199. The initial *divisio* of chapter 5 is typical. Comprising two subdivisions, it is followed shortly by another that comprises three (MSS Saint-Omer, Bibl. mun. 260, f. 17va; Tours, Bibl. mun. 121, f. 14va).

200. Excluding the prologues, *Super Mattheum* occupies approximately 105¾ folios of MS Saint-Omer, Bibl. mun. 260; *Super Iohannem* occupies approximately 67. In the Weber edition of the Vulgate, the text of Matthew occupies 48 pages, the text of John 40. The Vulgate texts of Jeremiah and Lamentations occupy approximately 48 and 7 pages, respectively. As copied in MS Paris, BnF lat. 573, excluding the prologues, William's postills *Super Ieremiam* and *Super Threnos* occupy approximately 56 folios and 10 folios, respectively.

201. Examples appear in a series of questions concerning the genealogy of Jesus at Mt 1:18 (MSS Saint-Omer, Bibl. mun. 260, f. 6va; Tours, 121, f. 5va–vb); others appear in a series of questions concerning John's baptism at Mt 3:6 (MSS Saint-Omer, Bibl. mun. 260, f. 12ra; Tours, 121, f. 10ra).

202. In Mt, 2:11 (MSS Saint-Omer, Bibl. mun. 260, f. 9va; Tours 121, f. 7vb).

203. "Sapiential Books I," 70.

204. MS Saint-Omer, f. 206(bis)ra–207ra.

205. One of the opening lines of William's *Super Iohannem* is typical: ". . . huius operis causa quadrupliciter insinuatur" (MS Saint-Omer, f. 110ra)

206. I have followed MS Oxford, Bodleian, Laud. misc. 390, f. 123v; cf. MS Saint-Omer, Bibl. mun. 260, f. 206va.

207. A case in point appears at Apc 1:4 (MSS Oxford, Bodleian, Laud. misc. 390, f. 125r; Saint-Omer, Bibl. mun. 260, f. 209ra); and another at Apc 8:7 (MS Oxford, Bodleian, Laud. misc. 390, f. 154v).

208. Examples appear at Apc 1:1; afterward, they show up regularly, e.g., in Apc 1:9, 1:10, 1:12, and 2:1 (MS Oxford, Bodleian, Laud. misc. 390, f. 124v, 126r, 126v, and 129r; MS Saint-Omer, Bibl. mun. 260, f. 207ra–rb, 210va, 210vb, 211va, and 214va–vb).

209. Throughout *Super Iohannem*, William refers to John the Evangelist thirty-six times, only twice employing the mode of address *beatus*, both in the prologue.

210. "$^{8:12}$*ET QUARTUS ANGELUS TUBA CECINIT* etc. Hec est quarta tuba que, sicut dicit Beda, significat falsorum fratri in siderum obscuratione defectum. Et primo significatur defectus in religiosis,

cum dicit: *TERTIA PARS SOLIS PERCUSSA EST*; secundo in clericis, cum dicitur: *ET TERTIA PARS LUNE*; tertio in simplicioribus, sicut in laicis, cum dicitur: *ET TERTIA PARS STELLARUM*" (MS Oxford, Bodleian, Laud. misc. 390, f. 155a).

### APPENDIX II: PRINCIPLES OF THE EDITIONS PROLOGUES

1. "Préface," in *Sententia libri Politicorum S. Thomae de Aquino*, ed. Leonina, *Opera omnia*, t. XLVIII, 1971, A63–A65.
2. L.-J. Bataillon and H.-F. Dondaine have observed that it is all but impossible to discern a general norm for the usage of *ci* and *ti*, ibid.

## PROLOGUS AUCTORIS SUPER ECCLESIASTEN
### (*M* f. f. 131ra–130vb [*sic*], *B* f. 93ra–93vb, $P_4$ f. 191r–191v)

1. leguntur] *B*.
2. Ier 4:23.
3. excelsus–interpretatur] cf. Hier., *Lib. interpret. hebraic. nom.* (CCSL 72, 127): « excelsus domini »; Isid. Hisp., *Etym.*, VII, 8, 8 (PL 82, 284).
4. ut dicit - celsus dicitur] *om. B*.
5. Excelsus–ponitur] Isid. Hisp., *Etym.*, VII, I, 9 (PL 82, 260).
6. Prv 4:8: arripe illam et exaltabit te *W*.
7. Sir 11:1.
8. Cf. 3 Rg, 3:12.
9. sapientissimus] dico *om. M*.
10. Phi 2:15.
11. id est] *om. B*.
12. Salomon - pacificus] cf. Hier, *Lib. interpret. hebraic. nom.* (CCSL 72, 138).
13. Cf. Ecl 1:1.
14. Ydida - Cantica Canticorum] cf. Hugo S. Vict., *Didascalicon*, IV (ed. C. Buttimer, 80): « tribus nominibus uocatum esse Salomonem scriptura manifestissime docet: Idida, id est dilectum Domini, quia eum dilexit Dominus, et Coeleth, id est Ecclesiasten »; Isid. Hisp., *Etym.*, VII, 6, 65 (PL 82, 279).
15. Cf. Ex 8:27.
16. 13] 31 *B*, XIII *M P*.
17. Cf. Ex 13:3.
18. Cf. Nm 9:2–5.
19. Transiordanem] Transordanem *B*.
20. Cf. Ios 5:10.
21. Cf. Ecl 4:12.
22. Ps 33:15: deverte a malo et fac bonum inquire pacem et persequere eam *W*; cf. Ps 36:27.
23. regibus] rebus *B* ^corr. a.m.^.
24. 3 Reg 3:13: dedi tibi divitias scilicet et gloriam ut nemo fuerit similis tui in regibus cunctis retro diebus *W*.
25. sum] enim *add. B*.
26. Ecl 2:9: et supergressus sum opibus omnes qui fuerunt ante me in Hierusalem.
27. reges] *add. B* ^a.m.^.
28. 3 Reg. 4:24: ipse enim obtinebat omnem regionem quae erat trans flumen quasi a Thapsa usque Gazam et cunctos reges illarum regionum et habebat pacem ex omni parte in circuitu *W*.
29. Sir 47:16: et impletus est quasi flumen sapientia et terram retexit anima tua *W*.

30. Sir 47:14: post ipsum surrexit filius sensatus et propter illum deiecit omnem potentiam inimicorum *W*.
31. Sir 47:15.
32. Is 52:13: ecce intelleget servus meus exaltabitur et elevabitur et sublimis erit valde *W*.
33. predictis] *om. B*.
34. auctor] actor *B*.
35. uerbis - finalem] *om. M*.
36. auctor] actor *B*.
37. auctor] actor *B*.
38. eius] *om. B*.
39. auctor] actor *B*.
40. libri] *add.* B *a.m.*, *om. M*.
41. auctor] libri *praem.* B *a.m.*.
42. coaceruauit] conseruauit *B*.
43. Cf. Ecl 2:4–10.
44. dicitur] *om. B*.
45. Io 3:31: qui est de terra de terra est et de terra loquitur *W*.
46. Cf. 3 Rg 11:1.
47. Quando - edificat] *non invenitur*, cf. GREG. MAG., *In librum primum Regum exp.*, II, 89 (CCSL 144, 167).
48. Sap 1:4.
49. AUG., *De agone christiano*, XIII, 14 (CSEL 41, 118).
50. posset] potest *B*.
51. Salomonis penitentiam agentis] cf. *Glossa mg.*, in Ecl. 1:1 (ed. Rusch, vol. II, 694a); ALC., *Comm. in Ecclesiasten* (PL 100, 670); HIER., *Comm. in Eccles.*, I, 12 (CCSL 72, 258): «Aiunt Hebraei hunc librum Salomonis esse, paenitentiam agentis, quod in sapientia diuitiisque confisus, per mulieres offenderit Deum.».
52. Set uidetur - Balaam] cf. BON., *In Ecl.*, prol. (*Opera*, t. VI, 7b–8b).
53. 23] 32 *B*, XXIII *M*.
54. Cf. Nm 23:5.
55. Io.] Iob B *corr. a.m.*.
56. Cf. Io 11:49–51.
57. 23] 32 *B*, XXIII *M*.
58. Mt 23:3: omnia ergo quaecumque dixerint vobis servate et facite secundum opera vero eorum nolite facere dicunt enim et non faciunt *W*.
59. dicitur] est *M*.
60. auctor] actor *B*.
61. rem cognoscit] recognoscit *M*.
62. qui bene - uerum] cf. Aristot., *Topica*, I, 2 (101a).
63. mundanam] mundanorum *M*.
64. eam] estam *M*.
65. reprobantis] detestantis *M*.
66. concionator] concionato *M*.
67. concionator dicitur] cf. Greg. Mag., *Dialogarum libri iv*, IV, 4 (SChr 265, 26); HIER, *Lib. interpret. hebraic. nom.* (CCSL 72, 155).
68. Cf. ISID. HISP., *Etym.*, VII, 6, 65 (PL 82, 279).
69. quod] est *add.* B *a.m.*.
70. Ez 2:9: erat scriptus intus et foris *W*.
71. assumendo] sumendo *B*.
72. Sir 20:22.
73. errorem] ueritatem M, B, errorem $P_4$.
74. Responsio] Respondendum est *B*.

75. uelut] ule *praem. exp. B.*
76. auctor] actor *B.*
77. set] om. *M.*
78. certitudinaliter] conditionaliter *B.*
79. Ecl 12:13–14: ¹³finem loquendi omnes pariter audiamus Deum time et mandata eius observa hoc est enim omnis homo ¹⁴et cuncta quae fiunt adducet Deus in iudicium pro omni errato sive bonum sive malum sit *W.*
80. sequentia] consequentia *B.*
81. auctor] actor *B.*
82. uane] *add. B* ᵃ·ᵐ·.
83. proprie] proprie *B* ᵃ·ᶜ·, propria *B* ᵖ·ᶜ·.
84. Gn 1:1.
85. Gn 1:31: viditque Deus cuncta quae fecit et erant valde bona *W.*
86. Iob 5:6: nihil in terra sine causa fit *W.*
87. Cf. Boethius, *Philosophia consolatio*, III (CCSL 94, 55).
88. Cf. Dion., *De diu. nom.*, sec. Iohannem Scotum (*Dionysiaca. Recueil donnant l'ensemble des trad. latines des ouvrages attribués au Denys de l'Aréopage*, ed. P. Chevalier, Bruges and Paris, 1937–1951, 199, col. 3).
89. Cf. Aristot., *Ethic.* I (1094a4).
90. et] *om. M B.*
91. sic] *bis M.*
92. et sic dicitur uana] *om. M.*
93. qualiter creatura - dicitur uana] cf. Bon., *In Ecl.*, prol. (*Opera*, t. VI, 6b–7a).
94. 1 Co 7:31: praeterit enim figura huius mundi *W.*
95. anime] uel animis *add. B* ᵃ·ᵐ·.
96. Sap 14:11: creaturae Dei in odium factae sunt et in temptationem animis hominum *W.*
97. Ps 51:9.
98. sua] dicit *add. B* ᵃ·ᵐ·.
99. ab] c *add. exp. M.*
100. Vanum est–ueritate discretum] Cassiod., *Expositio psalmorum* 51 (CCSL 97, 476): «Vanum enim dicitur, quod est inane, fragile uel caducum et ab ipsa firmissima ueritate discretum. ».
101. Is 30:7: Aegyptus enim frustra et vane auxiliabitur *W.*
102. hominis] hominum *B.*
103. Ps 59:13 et 107, 13.
104. contenentibus] continentibus *B.*
105. Ecl 5:9.
106. umbre] unbre *M.*
107. Sap 5:9: transierunt omnia illa tamquam umbra *W.*
108. fugerunt] fuerint *B.*
109. Temporalia–non erunt] Aug., *De lib. arbit.*, III, 7 (CCSL 29, 287): «quae temporalia et antequam sint non sunt, et cum sunt fugiunt, et cum fugerint non erunt».
110. 1 Io 2:17.
111. Ecl 5:9: qui amat divitias fructus non capiet ex eis et hoc ergo vanitas *W.*
112. Ecl 2:22: quid enim proderit homini de universo labore suo *W.*
113. de uniuerso - homini] *om. hom. B.*
114. Mt 16:26: quid enim prodest homini si mundum universum lucretur animae vero suae detrimentum patiatur *W.*
115. etc] *om. M.*
116. Cf. Mt 13:22.
117. Prv 10:15.
118. Iob 15:21: sonitus terroris semper in auribus illius *W.*
119. erga] *om. M, add. B* ᵃ·ᵐ·.

120. auarorum] auatorum *B.*
121. Diuitem–concupiscentias] Chrys., *In Mt. hom.*, XC (PG 58, 791), Burgundione interprete (ms. Vat lat. 383, f. 278vb): « . . . diuitem enim adulari necesse est multos, et principes, et subiectos, et multis indigere, et turpiter seruire, et formidare, et suspicari, et tremere eorum qui emulantur oculos, et timere calumpniatorum ora, et aliorum auarorum concupiscentias. ».
122. Ecl 10:19.
123. Ps.] *scripsi,* Prouer. *B M.*
124. Quantum–eris] Aug., *Enarr. in Ps.* 51 (CCSL 39, 633).
125. Augustinus - oportebat] *om. B.*
126. Vnde malum –esse oportebat] Aug., *De lib. arbit.* I, 15 (CCSL 29, 234).
127. Lc 16:13.
128. Ps 143:15.
129. Miser–amiserit] Aug., *Confessiones,* IIII, 6 (CCSL 27, 45).
130. scientia - bono] cf. Aristot., *Poster.*, I, 2 (71b).
131. sint] sunt *B.*
132. quomodo non est sciencia uana] quoniam non est scientia uana *B* $^{a.c.}$, uidetur quoniam est scientia uana *B* $^{p.c. a.m.}$.
133. tertio] alio *B.*
134. modo] *om. B.*
135. enim] *bis M.*
136. scientia] *om. B.*
137. medicina - Philosophus] cf. Aristot., *De soph. elench.* (181b).
138. aliorum] et *praem. M.*
139. dicitur] dicendum *B.*
140. Sunt ergo - et bonitatem] cf. Bon., *In Ecl.*, prol. (*Opera*, t. VI, 6b–7b).
141. Gn 1:2: terra autem erat inanis et vacua *W.*
142. insinuatur] *sic B M.*
143. Na 3:7.
144. 1 Io 2:15.
145. beatus uir] uir beatus *B.*
146. Ps 39:5.
147. Ps 4:3: filii hominum usquequo gravi corde ut quid diligitis vanitatem et quaeritis mendacium diapsalma *W.*
148. Dominus] Deus *B.*
149. Prv 16:4.
150. quando] quoniam *B.*
151. Domine–te amat] Aug., *Conf.*, X, 29 (CCSL 27, 176).
152. Cnt 8:7: si dederit homo omnem substantiam domus suae pro dilectione quasi nihil despicient eum *W.*

## PROLOGUS INCERTI AUCTORIS SUPER SAPIENTIAM
### ($P_2$ f. 155ra–156ra, $P_3$ f. 156ra–156va, *S* f. 250ra–va)

1. Sir 1:5.
2. Sir 38:25.
3. Omnium - consistit] Hugo S. Vict., *Didascalicon,* I (ed. C. Buttimer, 4).
4. presidentes] possidentes $P_2$.
5. retinendo] retinende $P_2$ $P_3$.
6. Prv 3:3: misericordia et veritas non te deserant circumda eas gutturi tuo et describe in tabulis cordis tui *W.*
7. in] *om.* $P_2$.
8. in tribus - uoluntate amando] cf. Aug., *De trin.*, XIV, 7 (CCSL 50A, 434–435)

9. Prv 22:20.
10. et] id est $P_3$.
11. Cf. Ex 5:7.
12. Ex 5:17: vacatis otio et idcirco dicitis eamus et sacrificemus Domino $W$.
13. minoratur] inmoratur $P_2$ $P_3$.
14. Sir 38:25: qui minoratur actu sapientiam percipiet $W$.
15. Scire - cognoscimus] cf. Aristot., *Poster.*, I, 2 (71b); *Phys.*, I, 4 (184a); *Metaphys.* II, 2 (994b).
16. triplex] triplicitum $P_2$.
17. 1 Cor 1:24.
18. Dei] deicitur *corr.* $P_2$.
19. Primum – causatiue] cf. Pseudo-Boethius (= Jacobus de Venetia), *Interpretatio posteriorum analyticorum Aristotelis*, xx (PL 64, 737): « cui enim per se inest aliquid, hoc idem ipsi causa est: universale autem primum, causa ergo universale est. »; cf. Aristot., *Poster.*, I, 2 (85b).
20. Sir 1:1.
21. Hegesippus] egippus $P_2$, egiptus $P_3$.
22. Irenaeus] phirenus $P_2$, phitenus $P_3$.
23. ghorus] *sic* $P_2$ $P_3$.
24. Egiptus - dixerunt] cf. Eusebius Caesariensis sec. trans. quam fecit Rufinum *Historia ecclesiastica*, lib. IV, cap. 22 (ed. T. Mommsen, 373): « verum et hic ipse et Irenaeus et omnis antiquorum chorus librum, qui adtitulatur Sapientia, Salomonis dixerunt, sicut et Proverbia et cetera »; cf. Pet. Com., *Hist. schol.*, VIII (PL 198, 1502).
25. quamuis] quamuix $P_2$.
26. alio] alioquo *corr.* $P_2$.
27. Cf. Prv 25:1.
28. apostolorum - nominatur] cf. Eusebius Caesariensis sec. trans. quam fecit Rufinum *Historia ecclesiastica* , lib. II, 16 (ed. Mommsen, 141).
29. Ieronimus] *om.* $P_2$.
30. quodam Iudeo] quodammodo $P_3$.
31. Ieronimus – conscriptum] Rab. Maur., *Comm. in Sap.* (PL 109, 671): « . . . quem tamen beatus Hieronymus asserit non a Salomone, ut usus habet, sed a Philone doctissimo Judaeo fuisse conscriptum »; cf. *Glossa mg.*, in Sap. 1:1 (ed. Rusch, vol. II, 724a); HIER., *Praefatio in libros Salomonis, Biblia Sacra Vulgata* (ed. Weber, 957): «Etenim multo est Philo iste, cui liber Sapientiae tamquam auctori, vel saltem interpreti tribuebatur.»
32. Omnis causa - causam secundaria] *Liber de causis*, I, 1 (ed. Pattin, 46).
33. efficiens causa] efficientia *corr.* $P_2$.
34. meatu] futuro *corr.* $P_2$.
35. Gen 2:6: sed fons ascendebat e terra inrigans universam superficiem terrae $W$.
36. Prv 5:16.
37. Can 4:15.
38. Riuus] Vicos *corr.* $P_2$.
39. Iob 28:18: trahitur autem sapientia de occultis $W$.
40. Prv 10:20.
41. Ipse stilus - redolet] Hier., *Praefatio in libros Salomonis, Biblia Sacra Vulgata* (ed. Weber, 957); cf. Hugo S. Vict., *Didascalicon*, IV (ed. C. Buttimer, 82).
42. Sir 21:16: scientia sapientis tamquam inundatio abundabit et consilium illius sicut fons vitae permanet $W$.
43. Sapiencia - cognitio] cf. Aug., *De trin.*, XIV, 1 (CCSL 50A, 423).
44. Cf. Is 40:12.
45. Iob 38:6: super quo bases illius solidatae sunt $W$.
46. enim] *om.* $P_2$.
47. bonitatem] bonitate $P_2$ $P_3$.
48. deinceps] dicitur inceps $P_2$ $P_3$.
49. de] *bis corr.* $P_2$.

50. sunt] *om. P₂*.
51. ministri] manifestum *P₂ P₃*.
52. Ecl 5:7: excelso alius excelsior est et super hos quoque eminentiores sunt alii *W*.
53. Cf. Sap 1:1; 6:1–10.
54. Sir 10:2: secundum iudicem populi sic et ministri eius et qualis rector est civitatis tales et inhabitantes *W*.
55. deriuatur] *conieci*.
56. in ualles] *om. P₂*.
57. Sir 43:4: tripliciter sol exurens montes radios igneos exsuflans et refulgens radiis suis obcaecat oculos *W*.
58. ultimo illi de postrema. Lex enim, ut ait ipse, diuinitus promulgata est per prima media] *om. hom. P₂ P₃*.
59. diuinum - reducere] Dion., *De cael. hier.*, IV, 3 (ed. G. Heil, 22); *De ecclesiast. hier.*, V, 4 (ed. G. Heil, 106–107).
60. Ps 71:3.
61. Dicebat - studerunt] Hier., *Comm. in Ionam*, III (CCSL 76, 408): «Vnde et Plato dicit: Felices fore respublicas, si aut philosophi regnent, aut reges philosophentur.»; cf. Boethius, *Philosophia consolatio*, I, 4 (CCSL 94, 7): «atqui tu hanc sententiam platonis ore sanxisti beatas fore res publicas si eas uel studiosi sapientiae regerent uel earum rectores studere sapientiae contigisset»; Plato, *Res Pub.*, 5, 18 (473d).
62. sic - processus] cf. Boethius, *Philosophia consolatio*, IV, 6 (CCSL 94, 80).
63. Sap 8:1.
64. irrigare] irragare *P₂*, irrogare *P₃*.
65. Ecl 1:7.
66. Prv 8:15.
67. Sap 7:27.
68. perfectionis - statum] *om. P₂ P₃ hom.*
69. Sap 6:21.
70. Ibi] in *P₂*.
71. Ibi - bibitur] Aug., *De Gen. ad lit.*, XII (CSEL 28.1, 419).

## PROLOGUS AUCTORIS SUPER IEREMIAM
### (*M* f. 266ra, *P₁* f. 87ra–vb)

1. Sap 11:1: direxit opera illorum in manibus prophetae sancti *W*.
2. primo capitulo] capitulo primo *P₁*.
3. Ier 1:9.
4. sequitur] post *P₁*.
5. Ier 1:10.
6. eum] Ieremiam prophetam *P₁*.
7. et eruere] *om. M*.
8. edificare] reedificare *P₁*.
9. Sir 49:9: male tractaverunt illum qui a ventre matris consecratus est propheta evertere et eruere et perdere et iterum aedificare et renovare *W*.
10. diuinitus] diuinitut *corr. M^{eo. ma.}*.
11. 2 Tim 3:16: omnis scriptura divinitus inspirata et utilis ad docendum ad arguendum ad corrigendum ad erudiendum in iustitia *W*.
12. Ier 18:11.
13. enim] enim eorum *P₁*.
14. Interpretatur–excelsus] cf. Isid. Hisp., *Etym.*, VII, 8, 8 (PL 82, 284); HIER, *Lib. interpret. hebraic. nom.* (CCSL 72, 136).
15. Apc 8:13.

16. Dn 12:5.
17. Cf. Ier 16:2: non accipies uxorem et non erunt tibi filii et filiae in loco isto *W*.
18. matris] *om. P₁*.
19. sanctificatus] fuit *add. P₁*.
20. Cf. Ier 1:5.
21. Dn 12:6–7: et dixi viro qui indutus erat lineis qui stabat super aquas fluminis usquequo finis horum mirabilium et audivi virum qui indutus erat lineis qui stabat super aquas fluminis cum levasset dexteram et sinistram suam in caelum et iurasset per viventem in aeternum *W*; cf. Ez 9:11.
22. Dn 12:5: et vidi ego Danihel et ecce quasi duo alii stabant unus hinc super ripam fluminis et alius inde ex altera ripa fluminis *W*.
23. Cf. Apc 8:13: et vidi et audivi vocem unius aquilae volantis per medium caelum dicentis voce magna vae vae vae habitantibus in terra *W*.
24. Cf. 4 Rg 24:1.
25. Cf. 4 Rg 24:15.
26. Cf. 4 Rg 25:1–17.
27. preteritam] et *praem. P₁*.
28. Ps 64:2: te decet hymnus Deus in Sion *W iuxta LXX*; Tibi silens laus Deus in Sion *W iuxta Hebr.*
29. ibi] tibi *M*.
30. Ps 64:1: in finem psalmus David canticum Hieremiae et Aggei de verbo peregrinationis quando incipiebant proficisci *W*.
31. Israel] *om. P₁*.
32. 2 Mcc 15:14.
33. *Glossa interlin.*, in. Ier. (ed. Rusch, t. 3, 35b).
34. Is 21:2: visio dura nuntiata est mihi qui incredulus est infideliter agit et qui depopulator est vastat *W*.
35. Is 21:3.
36. Is 21:3.
37. Sap 11:1.
38. Sir 24:46.
39. enim] *om. P₁*.
40. Ecl 8:1.
41. Prv 14:6: doctrina prudentium facilis *W*.
42. 1 Cor 14:9: nisi manifestum sermonem dederitis quomodo scietur id quod dicitur eritis enim in aera loquentes *W*.
43. etc.] quomodo scient id quod dicitur *P₁*.
44. prophete sancti] *bis M*.
45. Sap 11:1.
46. Ier 1:5: te prophetam gentibus dedi te *W*.
47. prophetica] prophetia *P₁*.
48. Sancto] Sancti *M*.
49. 2 Pt 1:21.
50. 2 Par 36:12: nec erubuit faciem Hieremiae prophetae loquentis ad se ex ore Domini *W*.
51. utillima] utilissima *P₁*.
52. defecerit prophetia] prophetia defecerit *P₁*.
53. dissipabitur] discipabitur *P₁*.
54. Prv. 29:18.
55. II Thi … prophetiam] *om. M*.
56. 1 Tim 4:14: noli neglegere gratiam quae in te est quae data est tibi per prophetiam *W*.
57. illucescat] lucescat *P₁*.
58. lucifer oriatur] oriatur lucifer *P₁*.

59. 2 Pt 1:19: habemus firmiorem propheticum sermonem cui bene facitis adtendentes quasi lucernae lucenti in caliginoso loco donec dies inlucescat et lucifer oriatur in cordibus vestris *W*.
60. 1 Th 5:20.
61. Apc 22:7: beatus qui custodit verba prophetiae libri huius *W*.
62. Ier 1:5.
63. Interpretatur enim excelsus] cf. Isid. Hisp., *Etym.*, VII, 8, 8 (PL 82, 284); HIER, *Lib. interpret. hebraic. nom.* (CCSL 72, 136).
64. uidetur] ut *praem. P*₁.
65. prefigurare] prefigurat *P*₁.
66. Ier 15:17.
67. Ier 1:6: nescio loqui quia puer ego sum *W*.
68. Cf. Heb 11:37.
69. lapidatus] cf. Tertul., *Scorpiace* (CCSL 2, 1083).
70. Huic - etc.] *om. P*₁.


## PROLOGUS AUCTORIS SUPER THRENOS (*P*₁ f. 145rb–145va)

1. Ier 9:1: quis dabit capiti meo aquam et oculis meis fontem lacrimarum et plorabo die et nocte interfectos filiae populi mei *W*.
2. 2 Pet 1:21.
3. uos enim] uost *P*₁.
4. Mt 10:20: non enim vos estis qui loquimini *W*.
5. Cf. Is 11:2–3.
6. Rm 8:26.
7. lingua] ligua *P*₁.
8. lingua] ligua *P*₁.
9. docendo] docen duo *P*₁.
10. Ps 118:171: eructabunt labia mea hymnum cum docueris me iustificationes tuas *W*.
11. Cf. 2 Par 36:20.
12. regis] reges *P*₁.
13. templi] tem *P*₁.
14. Agg 2:4: quis in vobis est derelictus qui vidit domum istam in gloria sua prima et quid vos videtis hanc nunc *W*.
15. Ier 14:17: deducant oculi mei lacrimam per noctem et diem et non taceant quoniam contritione magna contrita est virgo filia populi mei *W*.
16. ternos] trenos *P*₁.
17. hec] hic *P*₁.
18. triplici - deplangere] cf. *Glossa mg.*, in Thren. 1, Prothemata (ed. Rusch, vol. 1, 183a); Pasch. Radb., *Exp. in Lam.*, 1 (CCCM 85, 7); Hier., *Litterae*, Epist. 30 (ed. J. Labourt, t. II, 33).
19. aleph - ordinem] cf. *Glossa mg.*, in Thren. 1, Prothemata (ed. Rusch, vol. 1, 183b); PASCH. RADB., *Exp. in Lam.*, 1 (CCCM 85, 7); Hier., *Litterae*, Epist. 30 (ed. J. Labourt, t. II, 33).
20. clausulis - uersibus] Isid. Hisp., *Etym.*, 1, 39 (PL 82, 120): «Clausulas autem lyrici appellant, quasi praecisos versus integris subjectos, ut est apud Horatium».
21. tamen quadruplici alphabeto repetito] Isid. Hisp., *Etym.*, VI, 2 (PL 82, 232): «Jeremias similiter edidit librum suum cum threnis ejus, quos nos *lamenta* uocamus, eo quod in tristioribus rebus funeribus que adhibeantur, in quibus quadruplicem diverso metro composuit alphabetum, quorum duo prima quasi Sapphico metro scripta sunt, quia tres uersiculos, qui sibi nexi sunt et ab una tantum littera incipiunt, heroicum comma concludit».
22. recedentibus] recentibus *P*₁.
23. littere - potuerunt] cf. *Glossa mg.*, in Thren. 1, Prothemata (ed. Rusch, vol. 1, 183b); Pasch. Radb., *Exp. in Lam.*, 1 (CCCM 85, 11); Hier., *Litterae*, Epist. 30 (ed. J. Labourt, t. II, 33).

24. Ieremias - alphabeto] Hier., *Praefatio in libro Hieremiae prophetae* (*Biblia sacra iuxta uulgatam uersionem*, ed. R. Weber, 4th ed., Stuttgart, 1994, 1166): « Weber: Unde in Iuda tantum et Beniamin prophetavit et civitatis suae ruinas quadraplici planxit alfabeto. ».
25. Mt 5:5.
26. Tb 3:22.
27. Canticum - excellit] cf. *Glossa mg.*, in Thren. 1, Prothemata (ed. Rusch, vol. 1, 183a); Pasch. Radb., *Exp. in Lam.*, 1 (CCCM 85, 8).


## PROLOGUS AUCTORIS SUPER EZECHIELEM ($P_1$ f. 156rb–va)

1. Apc 8:13: et vidi et audivi vocem unius aquilae volantis per medium caelum dicentis voce magna vae vae vae habitantibus in terra *W*.
2. conformando] confirmando $P_1$.
3. Sir 32:1: rectorem te posuerunt noli extolli esto in illis quasi unus ex ipsis *W*.
4. Ierusalem] Israhelem $P_1$.
5. Cf. 4 Rg 24:12.
6. habitantium] *conieci.*
7. dicuntur] in *praem. exp. $P_1$.*
8. Ezechiele] Ezechile $P_1$.
9. Ez 2:9.
10. Ps 18:2.
11. Rm 15:4: quaecumque enim scripta sunt ad nostram doctrinam scripta sunt ut per patientiam et consolationem scripturarum spem habeamus *W*.
12. fuerunt] *om. $P_1$.*
13. ne] *om. $P_1$.*
14. negligeretur] neggligeretur $P_1$.
15. alicubi] alicubii $P_1$.


## PROLOGUS AUCTORIS SUPER IOHANNEM
### (*S* f. 110ra–vb, *A* f. 1ra–2rb)

1. Prv 14, 35.
2. Sir 9:24: in manus artificum opera laudabitur *W*.
3. Cf. Mt 4:22.
4. Cf. Io 2:11–12.
5. Io 12:26: si quis mihi ministrat me sequatur *W*.
6. Ille - audierit] Aug., *Conf.*, x, 26 (CCSL 27, 175).
7. Io 13:35: in hoc cognoscent omnes quia mei discipuli estis *W*.
8. Gal 5:24: qui autem sunt Christi carnem crucifixerunt cum vitiis et concupiscentiis *W*.
9. Mt 24:45.
10. Cf. Io 21:25.
11. si altius - posset ] cf. Bon., *In Io. com.*, prooemium (*Opera*, t. VI, 241a); IOHANNES BELETH, *Summa de ecclesicis officiis*, 70 (CCCM 41A, 132).
12. Cf. Dn 1:17.
13. Cf. 3 Rg 3:12.
14. cui donatum est] cf. Hier., *Lib. interpret. hebraic. nom.* (CCSL 72, 155).
15. quia] quid *S*.
16. O beate - uocaris Iohannes . . . quia - intimare] cf. Orig., *In Io.* 1 (ed. Brooke, vol. 1, 11; PG 14, 36).
17. Cf. Ez 1:10.
18. Sir 15:5: adimplebit illum spiritu sapientiae et intellectus *W*.

19. Is 52:13: ecce intelleget servus meus exaltabitur et elevabitur et sublimis erit valde *W*.

20. est] *om. S.*

21. rex - regendo] cf. Isid. Hisp., *Etym.*, IX, 3 (ed. Lindsay , n 4).

22. Apc 12:5: et peperit filium masculum qui recturus erit omnes gentes *W*.

23. Ps 22:1.

24. Ps 47:15.

25. Reges - sunt] Aug., *De civ.*, V, 12 (CCSL 47, 143): «hinc est quod regalem dominationem non ferentes "annua imperia binos que imperatores sibi fecerunt, qui consules appellati sunt a consulendo, non reges aut domini a regnando atque dominando"; cum et reges utique a regendo dicti melius uideantur, ut regnum a regibus, reges autem, ut dictum est, a regendo».

26. Iob 25:3.

27. Apc 7:9.

28. Bar 3:24: o Israhel quam magna est domus Dei et ingens locus possessionis eius *W*.

29. Dn 7:14.

30. Cf. Idc 18:10.

31. Ps 90:10.

32. Nichil - appetatur] *non inuenitur apud Gregorium Magnum*; cf. Aelred. Rieval., *De speculo caritatis*, III, 31 (CCCM 1, l41): «nihil erit exterius quod appetamus, nihil interius, quod fastidiamus».

33. Sap 8:1: adtingit enim a fine usque ad finem fortiter et disponit omnia suaviter *W*.

34. Rex . . . dicitur a recte operando] Isid. Hisp., *Etym.*, IX, 3 (ed. Lindsay , n° 4).

35. Cf. 1 Pt 2:22: qui peccatum non fecit nec inventus est dolus in ore ipsius *W*; cf. Is 53:9; Lc 23:41.

36. Mc 7:37: bene omnia fecit *W*.

37. Reges - grauatur] Isid. Hisp., *Etym.*, IX, 3 (ed. Lindsay , n° 18).

38. Hbr 1:3: portansque omnia verbo virtutis *W*.

39. Ier 8:18.

40. regie - pietas] cf. Isid. Hisp., *Etym.*, IX, 3 (ed. Lindsay, n° 4).

41. Iustitia] Iustia *S*.

42. declinauit - partes iustitie] cf. AUG., *Enarr. in Ps.* 98 (CCSL 39, 1384).

43. imitaberis] imitabis *S*.

44. Amabis - uelis] cf. Seneca, *Ad Lucilium*, XV, 95 (ed. Prechac, t. IV, 104).

45. Iustitia – seruata] cf. Ansel. Cant., *De veritate*, XII (ed. Schmitt, vol. I, 194); *De conceptu virginali et originali peccato*, III (ed. Schmitt, vol. II, 143).

46. Ps 5:5.

47. Mt 26:39.

48. Cf. Ps 15:2.

49. iustitie - subuenire] cf. Aug., *De trinitate*, XIV, 9 (CCSL 50A, 439).

50. iniqua punire] cf. Aug., *De Genesi ad litteram libri XII*, XII (CSEL 28.1, 419).

51. rectissime] rectissimo *S*, rectissime *A*.

52. bono rectissime adherere] cf. Aug., *Epist.* 155 (CSEL 44, 443): « . . . et iustitia, quia rectissime adhaerebit bono, cui merito subiciatur ».

53. soli Deo deseruire] cf. Aug., *De musica*, VI (PL 32, 1189).

54. Item soli Deo deseruire, sexto *Musice*] *bis S*.

55. soli amato seruire] cf. Aug., *De moribus ecclesiae catholicae et de moribus Manichaeorum*, XV (PL 32, 1322): «justitia, amor soli amato serviens».

56. corporee] cor *S*, corpori *A*.

57. nulli equari - corporee] cf. Aug., *De musica*, VI (PL 32, 1189): «Jamvero ipsa ejus ordinatio qua nulli servit nisi uni Deo, nulli coaequari nisi purissimis animis, nulli dominari appetit nisi naturae bestiali atque corporeae».

58. Cf. Lv 19:18, Mc 12:30–33, Lc 10:27.

59. proximum et Deum diligere] cf. Aug., *De div. quaest. octoginta tribus lib.*, XXXVI (CCSL 44A, 58).

60. inferiora – subdere] cf. Aug., *De lib. arbit.*, II, 10 (CCSL 29, 257).
61. cuicumque sua tribuere] cf. Aug., *De civ.*, XIX, 4 (CCSL 48, 666).
62. que sunt opera misericordie secundum Crisostomum] que secundum Crisostomum sunt opera misericordie *A*.
63. dare - misericordie] cf. Chrys., *Opus Imperfectum in Matthaeum*, IX (PG 56, 682).
64. Tit 2:14: qui dedit semet ipsum *W*.
65. Col 2:13
66. Io 21:20: recubuit in cena super pectus eius *W*; cf. Io 13:25.
67. Io 19:27: accepit eam discipulus in sua *W*.
68. officia] cf. Aug., *In Io. evang. tract.*, CXIX (CCSL 36, 659).
69. prologo] cf. *Bibliorum Sacrorum, Vulg. nova* (ed. Sabatier, 383).
70. Dt 33:24–25.
71. Ez 17:3: aquila grandis magnarum alarum longo membrorum ductu plena plumis et varietate venit ad Libanum et tulit medullam cedri *W*.
72. Ier 22:15: numquid regnabis quo            niam confers te cedro *W*.
73. media persona] cf. Bon., *Breviloquium*, prol. (*Opera*, t. V, 205a).
74. Sir 24:17.
75. Sir 3:22: altiora te ne scrutaveris et fortiora te ne exquisieris sed quae praecepit tibi Deus *W*.
76. Pro 25:27: qui scrutator est maiestatis opprimitur gloria *W*.
77. 1 Cor 2:10: Spiritus enim omnia scrutatur etiam profunda Dei *W*.
78. Quod credimus - auctoritati] Aug., *Retract.*, I, 14 (CCSL 57, 43): «quod intellegimus igitur, debemus rationi, quod credimus, auctoritati, quod opinamur, errori»; cf. *De utilitate credendi*, II (CSEL 25.1, 33); Bon., *In Io. com.*, prooemium (*Opera*, t. VI, 243b).
79. sublimiter - certitudine auctoritatis . . . modum narrationis- inspirauit] cf. BON., *In Io. com.*, prooemium (*Opera*, t. VI, 242a, 243b).
80. Maior - perspicacitas] Aug., *De Genesi ad litteram libri XII*, II (CSEL 28.1, 39).
81. Io 20:31: haec autem scripta sunt ut credatis quia Iesus est Christus Filius Dei et ut credentes vitam habeatis *W*.

# Bibliography

## MANUSCRIPT SOURCES

### Authors

Bonaventure, *Commentarius in Ecclesiasten.*

Paris, BnF lat. 14429, f. 1ra–49ra.

——, *Commentarius in Evangelium S. Ioannis.*

Troyes, Bibliothèque mun. 1410.

Guerric of St. Quentin, *Super Isaiam;* inc.: *Spiritu magno uidit ultima et consolatus est lugentes in Sion.*

Oxford, New College 40, f. 2r–153r.

John Chrysostom, *In Ioannem homiliae.*

Arras, Bibliothèque mun. 1083.
Bibl. Apostolica, Ottob. lat. 227.

——, *In Mattheum homiliae.*

Vat. lat. 383.

John of Varzy, *Super Canticum Canticorum;* inc.: *Cantabo dilecto meo* (see William of Middleton).

Basel, Univ. B III 20, f.182ra–230rb.
Basel, Univ. B IV 21, 71ra–120vb.
Paris, BnF lat. 14259, f. 170ra–225rb.
Paris, BnF lat. 15265, f. 1r–41r (inc.: *Dilectus meus candidus*).
Troyes, Bibl. mun. 667, f. 151ra–202vb (ends incomplete at Cnt 8, 9).

——, *Super Ecclesiasten;* inc.: *Surge et Vade in Niniuem ciuitatem grandem.*

Paris, BnF lat. 14259, f. 124ra–168rb.

---

*Uncertain authorship.

————, ˙*Super Prouerbiis;* inc: *Sacramentum regis abscondere bonum est.* (The incipit is from the copy at Basel. All four have been listed together because they are very close to one another, yet no two are the same.)

Basel, Univ. B III 20, f.1ra–91va.

Cambridge, Trinity College 98.

Paris, BnF lat. 14259, f. 1ra–122ra (inc.: *Ipse mittet tanquam imbres*).

Paris, BnF lat. 15573, f. 32ra–155va.

Troyes, Bibl. mun. 667, 1ra–150vb.

————, ˙*Super Sapientiam;* inc.: *Trahitur sapientia de occultis.*

Basel, Univ. B III 20, f.146ra–181vb.

————, ˙*Super Sapientiam;* inc.: *Diligite iustitiam qui iudicatis terram.*

Paris, BnF lat. 14259, f. 226ra–306rb.

Nicholas of Gorran, *Super Mattheum;* inc.: *Sume tibi librum grandem.*

Paris, BnF lat. 9418, f. 1ra–117vb.

Simon of Hinton, *Super Mattheum* (begins incomplete at Mt 5:2: *Aperiens os suum docebat*).

Oxford, Bodleian, e mus. 29, f. 1r–173v.

————, *Super XII prophetas;* inc: *Murus ciuitatis habens fundamenta.*

Oxford, Bodleian, e mus. 29, f. 247r–365v.

Stephan Langton, *Super Threnos;* inc.: *Aspexi terram et ecce uacua erat.*

Paris, Arsenal 87, f. 205ra–221rb.

Paris, BnF lat. 393, f. 177rb–185va.

Paris, Mazarine 177, f. 172ra–182rb.

William of Alton, *Sermones.*

Paris, BnF lat. 16482, f. 325ra–347vb.

————, *Super Ecclesiasten;* inc.: *Aspexi terram et ecce uacua erat.*

Basel, Univ. Bibl. B III 20, f. 93ra–113ra.

Erfurt, Wissenschaftliche Bibliothek der Stadt Amplon. F 181, f. 47v–82v.

Paris, BnF lat. 14429, f. 119ra–154ra.

Paris, BnF lat. 15592, f. 191ra–213rb.

Madrid, Bibl. Nac. 493, f. 131r–165r.

Siena, Bibl. com. U. VI 7, f. 1r–39v.

Tarragona, Bibl. Publ. 83, f. 47ra–76vb (inc.: *Vidi in omnibus uanitatem et afflictionem*).

————, *Super Ezechielem;* inc.: *Vidi et audiui uocem unius aquile uolantis per medium celi.*

Paris, BnF lat. 573, f. 156ra–198vb.

————, *Super Ieremiam;* inc.: *Direxit opera eorum in manibus prophete sancti.*

Paris, BnF lat. 573, f. 87ra–145ra.

Madrid, Bibl. nac. 493, f. 266r–381v.

————, *Super Iohannem;* inc.: *Acceptus est regi minister et intelligens.*

Assisi, Biblioteca Com. 49, f. 1ra–88rb.

Saint-Omer, Bibliothèque mun. 260, f. 110ra–177vb.

————, *Super Isaiam;* inc.: *Nemo cum prophetas.*

Paris, BnF lat. 573, f. 1ra–85vb.

Madrid, Bibl. Nac. 493, f. 170r–265v.

Saint-Omer, Bibl. mun. 155, f. 76r–120v.

————, *Super Sapientiam;* inc.: *Fons sapientie uerbum Domini.*

Basel, Univ. B III 20, f. 114ra–144vb (inc.: *Diligite lumen sapientiae*).

Basel, Univ. B VIII 28.

Paris, BnF lat. 14429, f. 50ra–93ra (inc.: *Diligite lumen sapientiae*).

Ibid., f. 155ra–206vb.

Paris, BnF lat. 15573, f. 156ra–189vb.

Saint-Omer, Bibl. mun. 260, f. 250ra–288vb.

Troyes, Bibl. Mun. 667, f. 203ra–241vb (ends incomplete at Sap 19:13).

————, *Super Threnos;* inc.: *Quis dabit capiti mei aquam.*

Paris, BnF lat. 573, f. 145rb–156ra.

William of Alton (works of unverified or doubtful attribution), *Sermo de Maria Magdalena;* inc.: *Dimittuntur ei peccata multa.*

Paris, BnF lat. 526, f. 241vb.

————, *Super Apocalipsin;* inc.: *Numquid ad preceptum tuum eleuabitur aquila.*

Oxford, Bodleian, Laud. misc. 390, f. 123r–211v.

Saint-Omer, Bibl. mun. 260, f. 206 bis ra–218vb (ends incomplete at Apc 2:18).

————, *Super Canticum Canticorum;* inc.: *Funiculus triplex difficile rumpitur.*

Bordeaux 38, f. 32–56v.

Cambridge, Pembroke College 80, f. 38r–86.

Cambridge, Pembroke College 97, f. 71r–176.

Madrid, Bibl. Nac. 53; f. 160ra–182rb.

Paris, BnF lat. 472, f. 34ra–69vb.

Paris, BnF lat. 14260, 1ra–58rb.

Paris, BnF lat. 15571, f. 27ra–38rb.

Paris, BnF lat. 15592, f. 214ra–251rb.

Paris, BnF lat. 15960, f. 166ra–240ra.

Siena, Biblioteca Com. F. v 23.

Troyes, Bibl. mun. 1861, 171ra–219va.

————, *Super Danielem;* inc.: *Iustum deduxit Dominus per uias rectas et ostendit illi regnum Dei.*

Oxford, Bodleian, Laud. misc. 390, f. 102r–123r.

————, *Super Ecclesiasten;* inc.: *Si annis multis uixerit homo.*

Paris, BnF lat. 14260, f. 59–126v ("Expliciunt scripta fratris Guillelmi de Tornay super Ecclesiasten").

————, *Super Exodum;* inc.: *Hec sunt nomina.*

Paris, BnF lat. 526, f. 50rb–117va.

Vendôme, 116, f. 48ra–104va.

———, *Super Genesim;* inc.: *Transite ad me omnes.*

Paris, BnF lat. 526, f. 1ra–50ra.

Vendôme 116, f. 1ra–46vb.

———, *Super Iob;* inc.: *Consumpta est caro eius a suppliciis.*

Troyes, Bibl. mun. 487.

———, *Super Iob;* inc.: *Surgite postquam sederitis.*

Basel, Univ. Bibl. B III 25, f. 1ra–105rb.

Madrid, Bibl. Nac. 493, f. 6v–73r.

Paris, BnF lat. 573, f. 199ra–282rb.

Roma, Bibl. Casanatensis 454.

Toledo, Bibl. Capitular 5–5.

———, *Super Iosue;* inc.: *Fortis in bello.*

Paris, BnF lat. 526, f. 210ra–224ra.

Vendôme 116, f. 172ra–184vb.

———, *Super lib. Iudicum;* inc.: *Iudicabit Dominus populum suum.*

Paris, BnF lat. 526, f. 224rb–239rb.

Vendôme 116, f. 185ra–198ra.

———, *Super Leviticum;* inc.: *Vocavit autem.*

Paris, BnF lat. 526 , f. 117va–166rb.

Vendôme, 116, f. 104va–139ra.

———, *Super Mattheum;* inc.: *Sume tibi librum grandem et scribe in eo stilo hominis.*

Munich, BSB Clm 7941.

Munich, BSB Clm 23620.

Saint-Omer, Bibl. mun. 260, f. 1ra–109va.

Tours, Bibl. mun. 121, f. 1ra–91va.

———, *Super Numeros;* inc.: *Locutus est Dominus.*

Paris, BnF lat. 526, f. 166va–209vb.

Vendôme 116, f. 139ra–170vb.

———, *Super Prouerbiis;* inc.: *Sapiens in uerbis producet seipsum.*

Madrid, Bibl. Nac. 493, f. 73v–130v (ends incomplete at the end of Prv 17).

Saint-Omer 260, f. 219ra–249rb (ends incomplete at the end of Prv 17).

———, *Super I–IV Regum;* inc.: *Ad uos ergo o reges.*

Saint-Omer, Bibl. mun. 260, f. 178ra–206ra (ends incomplete at 3 Rg 2:27).

———, *Super Ruth;* inc.: *Breuis in uolatilibus.*

Paris, BnF lat. 526, f. 239rb–241va.

Vendôme 116, f. 198ra–199vb.

———, *Super Sapientiam;* inc.: *Beati serui tui, hi qui stant.*

Paris, BnF lat. 14260, f. 133ra–204vb.

William of Luxi, *Super Threnos;* inc.: *Quis dabit capiti meo aquam et oculis meis fontem lacrimarum?*

Paris, BnF lat. 14265, f. 463va–487ra.

William of Middleton, *Super Canticum Canticorum;* inc.: *Cantabo dilecto meo*
(see John of Varzy).

> Basel, Univ. B III 20, f. 182ra–230rb.
>
> Basel, Univ. B IV 21, 71ra–120vb.
>
> Paris, BnF lat. 14259, f. 170ra–225rb.
>
> Paris, BnF lat. 15265, f. 1r–41r (inc.: *Dilectus meus candidus*).
>
> Troyes, Bibl. mun. 667, f. 151ra–202vb (ends incomplete at Cnt 8:9).

———, *Super Ecclesiasticum;* inc.: *Multorum nobis.*

> Paris, BnF lat. 15266, f. 1ra–184rb.

———, *Super Iob;* inc.: *Consumpta est caro eius a supliciis.*

> Paris, BnF lat. 14250, 1ra–283va.

———, *Super XII prophetas;* inc.: *Stabat mare super XII boues.*

> Paris, BnF lat. 14262, f. 1ra–391vb.

### Bibles

> Paris, BnF lat. 15467.
>
> Paris, BnF lat. 16721, 16722.
>
> Paris, Mazarine 5.

### Liturgical Texts

> Paris, BnF lat. 15181.
>
> Paris, BnF nouv. acq. lat. 1411.
>
> Roma, Santa Sabina XIV L 1.

## PRINTED SOURCES

### Latin Texts of the Bible

*Biblia Sacra iuxta latinam Vulgatam versionem ad codicum fidem.* Cura et studio
Monachorum Abbatiae pontificiae Sancti Hieronymi in Urbe Ordinis sancti Bene-
dicti edita, Roma, 1926 et sqq. = *Editio maior.*

*Bibliorum Sacrorum Latinae Versiones Antiquae seu uetus Italica,* ed. D. Sabatier, Paris,
3 vols., 1751.

*Biblia sacra iuxta uulgatam Clementinam,* ed. A. Colunga and L. Turrado, Madrid,
4th ed., 2002 = Clementine.

*Biblia sacra iuxta uulgatam uersionem,* ed. R. Weber, 4th ed., Stuttgart, 1994 = *Editio
minor.*

*Biblia Latina cum Glossa Ordinaria,* ed. A. Rusch, Strasbourg, 1480/81 (reprinted,
4 volumes, Turnhout, 1992).

*Vetus Latina. Die Reste der altlateinischen bibel,* ed. R. Gryson, Freiburg, currently being published.

## Bibliographical Sources

*Catalogue général des manuscrits des bibliothèques publiques de France. Départements* 3, Paris, 1861.

*Catologus Stamsensis,* ed. G. Meersseman, *Laurentii Pignon Catalogi et chronica,* Monumenta ordinis fratrum praedicatorum historica 18, Roma, 1936, 1–33.

*Chartularium Universitatis Parisiensis,* 2 vols., ed. H. Denifle and É. Chatelain, 1889–1891.

*Clavis Scriptorum Latinorum Medii Aevi,* ed. M.-H. Jullien and F. Perelman, 2 vols., Turnhout, 1994–1999.

*Inventario General de Manuscritos de la Biblioteca Nacional,* vol. 1, Madrid, 1953.

Alessandri, L., *Inventario dell'antica biblioteca del S. Convento di S. Francesco in Assisi compilato nel 1381,* Assisi, 1906, 61.

Bale, J., *Index Brittaniae Scriptorum,* ed. R. Poole and Mary Bateson, Oxford, 1902 (reprinted with additional material, C. Brett and J. P. Carley, Woodbridge, 1990).

Cenci, C., *Bibliotheca manuscripta ad sacrum conventum assisiensem,* 2 vols., Assisi, 1981.

Delisle, L., *Cabinet des manuscrits de la Bibliothèque nationale,* 3 vols., Paris, 1868–1881.

––––––, *Inventaire des manuscrits latins de la Sorbonne conservés à la Bibliothèque Impériale sous les numéros 15176–16718 du fonds latin,* in *Bibliothèque de l'Ecole des Chartes* 31 (1870).

––––––, *Inventaire des manuscrits latins de Saint-Victor conservés à la Bibliothèque impériale sous les numéros 14232–15175,* in *Bibliothèque de l'Ecole des Chartes* 30 (1869).

Glorieux, P., *La Faculté des arts et ses maitres à Paris au XIIIe siècle,* Paris, 1971.

––––––, *Réportoire des maîtres en théologie de Paris au XIIIe siècle,* Paris, 1933–1934.

Kaeppeli, T., *Scriptores Ordinis Praedicatorum Medii Aevi,* 4 vols., Roma, 1970–1993 (vol. 4: T. Kaeppeli and E. Panella).

Lauer, P., *Bibliothèque nationale. Catalogue générale des manuscrits latins,* t. 1, Paris, 1939.

Meyer, G., and Burckhardt, M., *Die mittelalterlichen Handschriften der Universitätsbibliotek Basel,* Abteilung B: *Theologische Pergamenthandschriften,* Band 1, Basel, 1960.

Murano, G., *Opere diffuse per exemplar e pecia,* Turnhout, 2005.

Quétif, J., and Echard, J., *Scriptores Ordinis Praedicatorum,* 2 vols., Paris, 1719–1721 (reprinted Th. Bonnet, R. Coulon, and A. Papillon, Lyon, Paris, and Roma, 1885–1934).

Russell, J. C., *Dictionary of Writers of Thirteenth-Century England,* BIHR, Special Supplement 3, 1936.

Samaran, C., and Marichal, R., *Catalogue des mss. en écriture latine portant des indications de date, de lieu, ou de copiste,* vol. 3, Paris, 1974.

Schmidt, P., "Die Bibliothek des chermaligen Dominikanerkloster in Basel," in *Basler Zeitschrift für Geschichte und Altestumskunde* 18 (1919), 183–244.

Schneyer, J.-B., *Repertorium der latienischen sermones des Mittelalter,* 11 vols., Münster, 1969–1980.

Sharpe, R., *A Handlist of the Latin Writers of Great Britain and Ireland before 1540,* Turnhout, 1997.

Stegmüller, F., *Repertorium Biblicum Medii Aevi,* Madrid-Barcelona, 11 vols., 1–7, Madrid, 1950–1961; completed with the assistance of N. Reinhardt, 8–11, Madrid, 1976–1980.

Torre, M. dela, and Longas, P., *Catálogo de códices latinos,* Madrid, 1935.

*Ancient and Medieval Authors*

Aelius Donatus, see Donatus.

Aelred of Rievaulx, *De speculo caritatis,* ed. C. Talbot, Turnhout, 1971, CCCM 1.

Aeschylus, *Eumenides,* trans. E. Anderson-Morshead, London, 1881.

Alan of Lille, *De fide catholica,* PL 210, 305–430.

———, *Summa de arte praedicatoria,* PL 210, 111–198.

Albert the Great, *In Evangelium secundum Ioannem,* ed. Borgnet, *Opera omnia,* t. XXIV, Paris, 1899.

———, *In Evangelium secundum Lucam,* ed. Borgnet, *Opera omnia,* t. XXII–XXIII, Paris, 1894–1895.

Alcuin, *Commentaria in s. Ioannis Evangelium,* PL 100, 733–1007.

———, *Epistola* XC, PL 100, 287–294.

Alexander of Hales, *Summa Theologica seu sic ab origine dicta "Summa fratris Alexandri,"* ed. P. Collegii S. Bonaventurae, Ad Claras Aquas (Quaracchi), 4 vols., 1924–1948.

Amalarius of Metz, "Libro de ordine antiphonarii," ed. J.-M. Hanssens, "*Amalarii episcopi opera liturgica omnia III,*" *Studi e Testi* 140 (1950).

Ambrose of Milan, *Epistulae,* VII, Epistula 50, ed. M. Zelzer, Wien, 1990, CSEL 82.2, 56–59.

———, *Explanatio Psalmorum XII,* ed. M. Petschenig, Wien, 1919, CSEL 64.

Andrew of Saint Victor, *Expositiones historicae in libros Salomonis,* ed. R. Berndt, Turnhout, 1991, CCCM 53B.

Anselm of Canturbery, *De conceptu virginali et originali peccato,* ed. F. Schmitt, *Opera omnia,* 6 vols., vol. 2, Edinburgh, 1946.

———, *De veritate,* ed. F. Schmitt, *Opera omnia,* vol. 1, Edinburgh, 1946.

Aristotle, *Analytica Posteriora,* Translatio Iacobi, ed. L. Minio-Paluello and B. Dod, Bruges and Paris, 1968, *Aristoteles Latinus,* IV; Recensio Guillelmi de Moerbeke, ibid., IV.4.

———, *De sophisticis elenchis*, Translatio Boethii, ed. B. Dod, Leiden and Bruxelles, 1975, *Aristoteles Latinus*, VI.1; Recensio Guillelmi de Moerbeke, ibid., VI.3.

———, *Physica*, Translatio Vetus, ed. F. Bossier and J. Brams, Leiden and New York, 1990, *Aristoteles Latinus*, VII.1.

———, *Topica*, Translatio Boethii, ed. L. Minio-Paluello, adiuv. B. Dod, Bruxelles and Paris, 1969, *Aristoteles Latinus*, V.1.

Pseudo-Aristotle, *Liber de causis*, ed. A. Pattin, Louvain, 1966; French trans. P. Magnard, O. Boulnois, B. Pinchard, and J.-L. Solère, *La demeure de l'être*, Paris, 1990.

Augustine of Hippo, *Adnotationes in Iob*, ed. J. Zycha, Wien, 1895, CSEL 28.2.

———, *Confessiones*, ed. L. Verheijen, Turnhout, 1981, CCSL 27.

———, *Contra sermonem Arianorum*, PL 42, 683–708.

———, *De agone christiano*, ed. J. Zycha, Wien, 1900, CSEL 41.

———, *De civitate Dei*, ed. B. Dombart and A. Kalb, Turnhout, 1955, CCSL 47–48.

———, *De consensu evangelistarum*, ed. F. Weihrich, Wien, 1904, CSEL 43.

———, *De diversis quaestionibus octoginta tribus liber*, ed. A. Mutzenbecher, Turnhout, 1975, CCSL 44A, 11–249.

———, *De doctrina christiana*, ed. J. Martin, 1962, Turnhout, CCSL 32, 1–167.

———, *De dono perseverantiae*, PL 45, 993–1034.

———, *De Genesi ad litteram libri XII*, ed. J. Zycha, 1894, Wien, CSEL 28.1 = BA 48–49).

———, *De libero arbitrio*, ed. W. Green, 1970, Turnhout, CCSL 29, 211–321.

———, *De moribus ecclesiae catholicae et de moribus Manichaeorum*, PL 32, 1309–1378.

———, *De musica*, PL 32, 1081–1094.

———, *De natura boni*, ed. J. Zycha, Wien, 1892, CSEL 25.2, 855–889.

———, *De peccatorum meritis et remissione et de baptismo paruulorum*, ed. C. Urba and J. Zycha, Wien, 1913, CSEL 60, 3–151.

———, *De praedestinatione sanctorum*, PL 44, col. 968.

———, *De sancta virginitate*, ed. J. Zycha, Wien, 1900, CSEL 41, 235–302.

———, *De sermone Domini in monte*, CCSL 35.

———, *De trinitate*, ed. W. Mountain and Fr. Glorie, Turnhout, 1968, CCSL 50–50A.

———, *De utilitate credendi*, ed. J. Zycha, 1891, Wien, CSEL 25.1.

———, *Enarrationes in Psalmos*, ed. E. Dekkers and J. Fraipont, Turnhout, 1956, CCSL 38–39–40.

———, *Enchiridion de fide, spe et caritate*, ed. E. Evans, Turnhout, 1969, CCSL 46, 49–114.

———, *Epistulae*, ed. A. Goldbacher, 1885–1898, Wien, CSEL 34,1; 34,2; 44; 57; 58.

———, *In Iohannis epistulam ad Parthos tractatus x*, v, 7 (PL 35, 2016).

———, *In Iohannis evangelium tractatus*, ed. R.Willems, Turnhout, 1954, CCSL 36.

———, *Regula tertia uel Praeceptum* (ed. L. Verheijen, *La Règle de saint Augustin*, I, Études Augustiniennes, Paris, 1967, 417–437).

———, *Retractationum libri duo*, ed. A. Mutzenbecher, Turnhout, 1984, CCSL 57.

———, *Sermones de Vetere Testamento,* IX, ed. C. Lambot, 1961, Turnhout, CCSL 41.

———, *Sermones,* LXVI, CXXXVII, CCLXII, PL 38, 430–433, 754–763, 1207–1209.

———, *Sermones,* CXXXIIA, ed. G. Morin, *Sancti Augustini Sermones post Maurinos reperti,* MiAg, 1, Rome, 1930.

Pseudo-Augustine of Hippo, *De spiritu et anima,* IX, PL 40, 779–832.

Basil the Great, *Hom.* XII, *In principium Proverbiorum,* PG 31, 385–424.

Bede, *De schematibus et tropis,* ed. C. Kendall, Turnhout, 1975, CCSL, 123A, 142–171.

———, *Homiliarum euangelii libri II,* ed. D. Hurst, Turnhout, 1955, CCSL 122.

———, *In Lucae euangelium expositio,* ed. D. Hurst, Turnhout, 1960, CCSL 120, 5–425.

———, *In Marci euangelium expositio,* ed. D. Hurst, Turnhout, 1960, CCSL 120, 431–648.

———, *In primam partem Samuhelis libri IV. Nomina locorum,* ed. D. Hurst, Turnhout, 1962, CCSL 119, 5–287.

Bernard of Clairvaux, *De consideratione ad Eugenium papam,* ed. J. Leclercq and H. Rochais, *Sancti Bernardi Opera,* t. III, Roma, 1963, 393–493.

———, *De gradibus humilitatis et superbiae,* ed. J. Leclercq and H. Rochais, *Sancti Bernardi Opera,* t. III, Roma, 1963, 15–59.

———, *Epistolae,* XII, XVIII, ed. J. Leclercq and H. Rochais, *Sancti Bernardi Opera,* t. VII, 61–62, 66–69.

———, *Parabolae,* ed. J. Leclercq and H. Rochais, *Sancti Bernardi Opera,* t. VI/2, Roma, 1972, 261–303.

———. *Sententiae,* ed. J. Leclercq and H. Rochais, *Sancti Bernardi Opera,* t. VI/2, Roma, 1972, 7–255.

———, *Sermo in dominica infra octauam assumptionis beatae Mariae Virginis,* ed. J. Leclercq and H. Rochais, *Sancti Bernardi Opera,* t. V, Roma, 1968, 262–274.

———, *Sermones super Cantica Canticorum,* ed. J. Leclercq, C. Talbot, and H. Rochais, *Sancti Bernardi Opera,* t. I, Roma, 1957.

Boethius, *Philosophiae consolatio,* ed. L. Bieler, Turnhout, 1958, CCSL 94.

Bonaventure, *Apologia Pauperum,* ed. Quaracchi, *Opera omnia,* t. VIII, 230–330.

———, *Breviloquium,* ed. Quaracchi, *Opera omnia,* t. V, 1891.

———, *Collationes de septem donis Spiritus Sancti,* ed. Quaracchi, *Opera omnia,* t. V, 1891, 457–503.

———, *Collationes in Hexaemoron,* ed. F. Delorme, Bibl. Franciscana Scholastica Medii Aevi, t. VIII, 1934.

———, *Commentarius in Ecclesiasten,* ed. Quaracchi, *Opera omnia,* t. VI, 1891, 201–291.

———, *Commentarius in Evangelium S. Ioannis,* ed. Quaracchi, *Opera omnia,* t. VI, 1893.

———, *Itinerarium mentis in Deum,* ed. Quaracchi, *Opera omnia,* t. V, 1891, 295–313.

———, *De reductione artium ad theologiam,* ed. Quaracchi, *Opera omnia,* t. V, 1891, 319–325.

———, *In 1 Sent.*, d. 15, q. 1, ad 3, ed. Quaracchi, *Opera omnia*, t. VI, 1889.

———, *Sermones dominicales*, ed. J. G. Bougerol, Bibl. Franciscana Scholastica Medii Aevi, t. XXVII, 1977.

Cassiodorus, *Expositio psalmorum*, ed. M. Adriaen, Turnhout, 1958, CCSL 97–98.

Christian of Stavelot, *Expositio in Lucam*, PL 106, 1503–1514.

———, *Expositio in Matthaeum*, PL 106, 1261–1504.

Chromatius of Aquileia., *Sermones*, ed. R. Etaix and J. Lemarié, 1974, CCSL 9A, 3–182.

(Pseudo) Dionysius the Areopagite, *De caelesti hierarchia*, eds. G. Heil, Berlin, 1991, *Corpus Dionysiacum*, t. II.

———, *De divinis nominibus*, ed. B. Suchla, Berlin, 1990, *Corpus Dionysiacum*, t. I; *Dionysiaca. Recueil donnant l'ensemble des trad. latines des ouvrages attribués au Denys de l'Aréopage*, ed. P. Chevalier, Bruges and Paris, 1937–1951.

———, *De ecclesiastica hierarchia*, eds. G. Heil and A. Ritter, Berlin, 1991, *Corpus Dionysiacum*, t. II.

Donatus, *Ars grammatica*, ed. L. Holtz, "Donat et la tradition de l'enseignement grammatical. Étude et edition critique," Paris, 1981.

Eunomius, *Apologia*, ed. G.-M. de Durand and L. Doutreleau, French trans. B. Sesboüé, Paris, 1983, SC 305; PG 30, 835–868.

Eusebius of Caesarea, *Ecclessiastical History = Historia ecclesiastica* sec. trans. quam fecit Rufinus, ed. T. Mommsen, 2 vols., Leipzig, 1903–1908, GCS 9.

Flavius Josephus, *De bello Judaico*, ed. and French trans. A. Pelletier, 3 vols. (Les Belles Lettres), Paris, 1975–1982.

Fulgentius Ruspensis, *De dispensatoribus Domini*, ed. J. Fraipont, Turnhout, 1968, CCSL 91A, 889–896.

Gennadius Massiliensis, *De ecclesiaticis dogmatibus*, PL 58, 979–1000.

Gerard Iterius, "Sermo de confirmatione seu enucleatione 'Speculi Granmontis,'" *Scriptores ordinis Grandmontensis*, ed. J. Becquet, Turnhout, 1968, CCCM 8, 411.

Gerard of Frachet, *Vitae Fratrum Ordinis Praedicatorum*, MOPH I.

Gregory of Nyssa, *Contra Eunomium*, ed. W. Jaeger, *Gregorii Nysseni Opera*, 2 vols., Leyden, 1960.

———, *Ekthesis*, PG 47, 587–590.

Gregory the Great, *Homilae in Hiezechielem prophetam*, I, II, ed. M. Adriaen, 1971, CCSL 142.

———, *Homiliarum in evangelia libri duo*, ed. R. Etaix, Turnhout, 1999, CCSL 141.

———, *Moralia in Iob*, ed. M. Adriaen, Turnhout, 1979–1981, CCSL 143, 143A, 143B.

———, *Regula Pastoralis*, ed. F. Rommel, Paris, 1992, SC 381–382.

Guy the Carthusian, *Scala Claustralium*, ed. G. El Cartujo, *Cistercium* 45 (1993), 15–35.

Heiricus Autissiodorensis, *Homiliae per circulum anni*, ed. R. Quadri, Turnhout, 1992–1994, CCCM 116, 116A, 116B.

Herman of Runa, *Sermones festivales*, ed. E. Mikkers, I. Theuws, and R. Demeulenaere, Turnhout, 1986, CCCM 64.

Pseudo-Hilary of Arles, *Tractatus in septem epistulas catholicas,* ed. R. E. McNally, Turnhout, 1973, CCSL 108B, 53–124.

Hilary of Poitiers, *De Trinitate,* ed. P. Smulders, Turnhout, 1979–1980, CCSL 62–62A.

Hugh of St. Cher, *Postille in totam Bibliam,* ed. Venetiis, 1754.

Hugh of St. Victor, *De sacramentis christiane fidei,* PL 176, 173–618.

*Didascalicon de studio legendi,* ed. C. Buttimer (*Studies in Medieval and Renaissance Latin* 10), Washington, 1939, French trans. M. Lemoine (*Sagesses chrétiennes*), *Hugues de Saint-Victor. L'Art de lire, Didascalicon,* Paris, 1991.

——, *In Salomonis Ecclesiasten Homile,* PL 175, 113–256.

——, *Sententiae de divinitate,* ed. A. Piazzoni, *Ugo di San Vittore "auctor" delle "Sententie de diuinitate,"* in *Studi Medievali,* 3rd series, 23, 1982, 861–955.

Humbert of Romans, *Opera de Vita Regulari,* ed. J. J. Berthier, 2 vols., Rome, 1888–1889.

Innocent iii, pope, *Sermones de Tempore,* XIV, PL 217, 375–382.

Irenaeus of Lyons, *Contre les Hérésies,* ed. and French trans. F. Sagnard, Paris, 1952, SC 210.

Isaac of Stella, *Sermones,* 15, ed. A. Hoste, French trans. G. Salet, Paris, 1967, SC 130, 282–292.

Isidore of Seville, *De ecclesiaticis officiis,* ed. C. Lawson, Turnhout, 1989, CCSL 113.

——, *Etymologiarum sive originum libri xx,* ed. W. Lindsay, 2 vols., Oxford, 1911 (facsimile reprint, Oxford, 1971) = PL 82.

Jacob of Venice (= Pseudo-Boethius), *Interpretatio posteriorum analyticorum Aristotelis,* PL 64, 711–762.

Jerome, *Adversus Helvidium de Mariae virginitate perpetua,* PL 23, 193–216.

——, *Commentariorum in Matheum,* ed. D. Hurst and M. Adriaen, Turnhout, 1969, CCSL 77.

——, *De situ et nominibus locorum Hebraicum,* PL 23, 859–928.

——, *Dialogus aduersus Pelagianos,* ed. C. Moreschini, Turnhout, 1990, CCSL 80.

——, *Hebraicae Quaestiones in Genesim,* ed. P. de Lagarde, Turnhout, 1959, CCSL 72, 1–56.

——, *Homilia in euangelium secundum Matthaeum,* ed. G. Morin, Turnhout, 1958, CCSL 78, 503–506.

——, *Homilia in Iohannem euangelistam,* ed. G. Morin, Turnhout, 1958, CCSL 78, 517–523.

——, *In Ecclesiasten,* ed. M. Adriaen, Turnhout, 1959, CCSL 72, 249–361.

——, *In Epistulam ad Galatas,* PL 26, 307–438.

——, *In Esaiam,* ed. M. Adriaen, 1963, Turnhout, CCSL 73–73A.

——, *In Evangelium Matthaei,* ed. D. Hurst–M. Adriaen, Turnhout, 1969, CCSL 77.

——, *In Hieremiam prophetam libri vi,* ed. S. Reiter, 1960, Turnhout, CCSL 74.

——, *In Hiezechielem,* ed. F. Glorie, Turnhout, 1964, CCSL 75.

——, *In libro Hieremiae prophetae Praefatio (Biblia sacra iuxta uulgatam uersionem,* ed. R. Weber, 4th ed., Stuttgart, 1994, 1166).

——, *In prophetas minores,* ed. M. Adriaen, Turnhout, 1969–1970, CCSL 76–76A.

——, *In Psalmos,* ed. G. Morin, 1959, CCSL 72, 177–245.

——, *Liber interpretationis hebraicorum nominum,* ed. P. de Lagarde, Turnhout, 1959, CCSL 72, 59–161.

——, *Litterae,* ed. J. Labourt, 8 vols. (Les Belles Lettres), Paris, 1949–1963.

——, *Praefatio in libros Salomonis,* PL 28, 1242.

——, "Prologus in Hieremiam Prophetam," *Biblia Sacra Vulgata,* ed. R. Weber, Stuttgart, 1994, 1266.

——, *Tractatus in Marci euangelium,* ed. G. Morin, Turnhout, 1958, CCSL 78, 451–500.

John Beleth, *Summa de ecclesiasticis officiis,* ed. H. Douteil, Turnhout, 1976, CCCM 41A, 186–189.

John Chrysostom, *In Ioannem homiliae,* PG 59, 23–482.

——, *In Mattheum homiliae,* PG 57–58.

Pseudo-John Chrysostom, *Opus imperfectum in Matthaeum,* PG 56, 611–946.

John Damascene, *De fide orthodoxa,* PG 94, 789–1228.

John Peckam (= Pseudo-Bonaventure), *Postilla in Threnos, Appendix duorum opusculorum saltem dubiorum,* ed. Quaracchi, *S. Bonaventurae Opera omnia,* VII, 1895, 607–651.

John Scot Eriugena, *Commentaire sur l'Évangile de Jean. Introduction, texte critique, traduction, notes et index,* ed. and French trans. E. Jeauneau, 2nd ed., Paris, 1999, SC 180.

——, *Homélie sur le prologue de Jean,* ed. and French trans. E. Jeauneau, Paris, 1969, SC 151.

Josephus, see Flavius Josephus.

Justin Martyr, *Dialogue avec Tryphon,* ed. and French trans. G. Archambault, t. I, Paris, 1909.

Maximus of Tours, *Collectio sermonum antiqua nonnullis sermonibus extrauagantibus adiectis,* LXVI, ed. A. Mutzenbecher, Turnhout, 1962, CCSL 23, 276–278.

Nemesius of emessa, ed. M. Morani, Leipzig, 1987, 81; *De natura hominis,* "Traduction de Burgundio de Pise," ed. G. Verbeke and J. Moncho, Corpus latinum commentariorum in Aristotelem graecorum, Suppl. 1, Leiden, 1975; *Nemesius: On the Nature of Man,* English trans., intro., and notes, R. W. Sharples and P. J., van der Eijk, Liverpool, 2008.

Origen, *Commentarium in Canticum Canticorum, secundum translationem quam fecit Rufinus,* ed. W. A. Baehrens, Leipzig, 1925, GCS 33, 61–241.

——, *Commentary on the Gospel of John,* ed. A. E. Brooke, Cambridge, 1896.

——, *De principiis, secundum translationem quam fecit Rufinus,* ed. P. Koetschau, Leipzig, 1913, GCS 22, 7–364.

——, *Hexapla* = *Origenis Hexaplorum quae supersunt,* ed. F. Field, 2 vols., Oxford, 1867–1875.

——, *Homélies sur Ézékiel,* ed. M. Borret, Paris, 1989, SC 352, 47.

——, *In Exodum homiliae, secundum translationem quam fecit Rufinus,* ed. W. A. Baehrens, Leipzig, 1920, GCS 29, 145–279.

————, *In Hiezechielem homiliae, secundum translationem quam fecit Rufinus*, 1, 3, ed. W. A. Baehrens, Leipzig, 1925, GCS 33, 61–241.

Ovid, *Fasta*, ed. R. Schilling, 2 vols. (Les Belles Lettres), Paris, 1992–1993.

Paschasius Radbertus, *Expositio in Lamentationes*, ed. B. Paulus, Turnhout, 1988, CCCM 85.

*Passio sanctorum apostolorum Petri et Pauli*, ed. R. A. Lipsius, M. Bonnet, *Acta apostolorum apocrypha* post Constantinum Tischendorf, Hildesheim, 1959, pars prior, 119–177.

Peter Abelard, *Sic et Non*, PL 178, 1339–1610.

Peter Comestor, *Historia Scholastica*, PL 198, 1053–1722.

Peter Lombard, *Commentarius in Psalmos in Psalmos Davidicos* (= *Magna glossatura*), PL 191, 61–1296.

————, *Sententiae*, ed. Coll. S. Bonaventurae, 2 vols., Grottaferrata, 1971–1981.

Peter of Tarantaise, *Super I Epistolam ad Corinthios*, ch. 7, 10–10, 33, *Sancti Thomae Aquinatis Opera omnia*, ed. Parma, t. XIII, 1863, 203a–233b.

Philip the Chancellor, *Summa de Bono*, ed. N. Wicki, 2 vols., Berne, 1985.

Plotinus, *Enneads*, ed. and French trans. E. Bréhier, 6 vols. (Les Belles Lettres), Paris, 1924–1938.

*Polythecon*, ed. A. Orban, Turnhout, 1990, CCCM 93.

Prosper of Aquitane, *Expositio psalmorum a centesimo usque ad centesimum quinquagesimum*, ed. P. Callens, Turnhout, 1972, CCSL 68A, 3–211.

————, *Liber sententiarum*, ed. M. Gastaldo, Turnhout, 1972, CCSL 68A, 257–365.

Rabanus Maurus, *Commentariorum in librum Sapientiae*, PL 109, 671–762.

————, *De clericorum institutione*, PL 107, 293–420.

Rupert of Deutz, *Commentaria in euangelium sancti Iohannis*, ed. R. Haacke, Turnhout, 1969, CCCM 9.

————, *De gloria et honore filii hominis super Matthaeum*, ed. R. Haacke, Turnhout, 1979, CCCM 29, 3–421.

Sedulius Scotus, *In Priscianum*, ed. B Löfstedt, Turnhout, 1977, CCCM 40C, 57–84.

Seneca, *Ad Lucilium*, ed. F. Préchac, 5 vols. (Les Belles Lettres), Paris, 1945–1971.

Sicard of Cremona, *Mitrale seu De officiis ecclesiasticis summa*, PL 213, 13–434.

Tertullian, *Adversus Marcionem*, ed. E. Kroymann, 1954, Turnhout, CCSL 1, 441–726.

————, *De pudicitia*, ed. E. Dekkers, 1954, Turnhout, CCSL 2, 1281–1330.

————, *Scorpiace*, ed. A. Reifferscheid and G. Wissowa, 1954, Turnhout, CCSL 2, 1069–1097.

Thomas Aquinas, *Contra errores Graecorum*, ed. Leonina, *Opera omnia*, t. XL, 1969, 71a–105b.

————, *Contra impugnantes Dei cultum et religionem*, ed. Leonina, *Opera omnia*, t. XLI/A, 1970.

————, *De articulis fidei et ecclesiae sacramentis ad archiepiscopum Panormitanum*, ed. Leonina, *Opera omnia*, t. XLII, 1979, 245–257.

————, *De perfectione spiritualis vitae,* ed. Leonina, *Opera omnia,* t. XLI/B, 1970.

————, *Expositio super Epistolas Pauli Apostoli,* ed. Parma, *Opera omnia,* t. XIII, 1863.

————, *Expositio super Ieremiam Prophetam,* ed. Parma, *Opera omnia,* t. XIV, 1863, 577–667.

————, *Expositio super Iob ad litteram,* ed. Leonina, *Opera omnia,* t. XXVI, 1965.

————, *Expositio super Isaiam ad litteram,* ed. Leonina, *Opera omnia,* t. XXVIII, 1974.

————, *Expositio super Psalmos,* ed. Parma, t. XIV, *Opera omnia,* 1860, 148–553.

————, *In libros Sententiarum,* ed. Parma, *Opera omnia,* t. VI–VII 1/2, 1856–1858.

————, *Lectura super Iohannem,* ed. Parma, *Opera omnia,* t. X, 1860, 279–645.

————, *Lectura super Matthaeum,* ed. Parma, *Opera omnia,* t. X, 1860, 1–278.

————, *Quaestio disputata De spiritualibus creaturis, Opera omnia,* ed. Leonina, t. XXIV/2, 2000.

————, *Quaestiones de quolibet,* ed. Leonina, *Opera omnia,* t. XXV 1/2, 1996.

————, *Quaestiones disputatae De potentia,* ed. Parma, *Opera omnia,* t. VIII, 1856, 1–218.

————, *Quaestiones disputatae De veritate,* ed. Leonina, *Opera omnia,* t. XXII 1/2, 1972–1975.

————, *Quaestiones disputatae De virtutibus,* ed. Parma, *Opera omnia,* t. VIII, 1856, 545–568.

————, *Summa contra Gentiles,* ed. Leonina, *Opera omnia,* t. XIII–XV, 1918, 1926, and 1930.

————, *Summa theologiae,* ed. Leonina, *Opera omnia,* t. IV–XII, 1888–1906.

————, *Super Boetium De Trinitate,* ed. Leonina, *Opera omnia,* t. L, 1992.

————, *Super librum Dionysii De divinis nominibus,* ed. Parma, *Opera omnia,* t. XV, 1864, 259–405.

Thomas of Chobham, *Summa de Arte Predicandi,* ed. F. Morenzoni, Turnhout, 1988, CCCM 82.

Vincent Bandellus, *De veritate conceptionis Beatae Virginis Mariae* (incunable, Munich, BSB-Ink B-33GW 3237; Paris, BnF réserve D 6438), 1475.

Vincent of Beauvais, *Libellus apologeticus* (= *Apologia totius operis*) IV, ed. A.-D. von den Brincken, "Geschichtsbetrachtung bei Vincenz von Beauvais," *Deutsches Archiv für Eforschung des Mittelalters* 34 (1978) 469–70.

————, *Speculum Historiale,* ed. Douai (reprint Graz, 1965).

William Durandus, *Guillelmi Durandi Rationale Divinorum Officiorum* 5–6, ed. A. Davril and T.-M. Thibodeau, Turnhout, 1995, CCCM 140A.

William of Alton, *Super Threnos;* inc.: *Quis dabit capiti meo aquam et oculis meis fontem lacrimarum,* "William of Alton's Commentary on the Book of Lamentations," *AHDLMA* 73 (2006), 233–281.

William of Auvergne, *De sacramento poenitentiae,* ed. E. Viret, *Opera omnia,* t. I, Rouen, 1674, 451b–512b.

————, *Supplementum tractatus novi de poenitentia,* ed. E. Viret, *Opera omnia,* t. II, Rouen, 1674, 229a–247b.

————, *Tractatus novus de poenitentia,* ed. E. Viret, *Opera omnia,* t. I, Rouen, 1674, 570b–592b.

William of Auxerre, *Summa Aurea,* ed. J. Ribaillier (Spicilegium Bonaventurianum, XVI–XIX), Paris–Grottaferrata, 1980–1986.

William of Luxi, *Postilla super Baruch, Postilla super Ionam,* ed. A. Sulavik, Turnhout, 2006, CCCM 219.

## Modern Authors

Aillet, M., *Lire la Bible avec S. Thomas,* Fribourg, Suisse, 1993.

Amann, É, "Michel Cérulaire," *DTC* 11, no. 2 (1929), 1677–1703.

———, "Nestorius. L'Église nestorienne?" *DTC* 11, no. 1 (1931), 157–323.

———, "Théodore de Mopsueste," *DTC* 15, no. 1 (1946), 235–279.

Andrée, A., "'Et factum est': The Commentary to the Prologue to the Book of Lamentations in the Manuscript Paris, BnF, lat. 2578," *Revue bénédictine* 117 (2007), 129–153.

———, *Gilbertus Universalis: Glossa Ordinaria in Lamentationes Ieremie Prophete, Prothemata et Liber I,* Stockholm, 2005.

———, "The *Glossa ordinaria* on the Gospel of John: A Preliminary Survey of the Manuscripts with a Presentation of the Text and Its Sources" (*à suivre*), *Revue bénédictine* 118 (2008), 109–134; (*suite et fin*), in print.

Barrett, C. K., *The Gospel According to John,* 2nd ed., Philadelphia, 1978, 244.

Baschet, J., "Jugement de l'âme, jugement dernier: contradiction, complémentarité, chevauchement?" *Revue Mabillon* 6 (1995), 159–203.

Bataillon, L.-J., "Approaches to the Study of Medieval Sermons," *Leeds Studies in English* 9 (1980), 1935.

———, "Bulletin des d'histoire des doctrines," *RSPT* 64 (1980), 101–132.

———, "De la *lectio* à la *praedicatio*. Commentaires bibliques et sermons au XIIIᵉ siècle," *RSPT* 70 (1986), 559–574.

———, "Intermédiaires entre les traités de moral pratique et les sermons: les distinctiones bibliques alphabétiques" in *Les Genres littéraires dans les sources théologiques et philosophiques médiévales. Définition, critique et exploitation,* Louvain-la-Neuve, 1982 (Publications de l'Institute d'études mediévales. Textes, Études, Congrés, 5), 213–226.

———, "La Bible au XIIIᵉ siècle. Un incitation aux recherches de demain," in *La Bibbia del XIII Secolo. Storio del testo storia dell'esegesi,* ed. G. Cremascoli and F. Santi, Firenze, 2004, 3–11.

———, "L'influence d'Hugues de Saint-Cher," in *Hugues de Saint-Cher, bibliste et théologien,* ed. L.-J. Bataillon, G. Dahan, and P.-M. Gy, Turnhout, 2004, 497–502.

Bataillon, L.-J. and Dondaine, H.-F., "Préface," in *Sententia libri Politicorum S. Thomae de Aquino,* ed. Leonina, *Opera omnia,* t. XLVIII, 1971, A63–A65.

Baur, C., *John Chrysostom and His Time,* 2 vols., London, 1959–1960 (English trans. M. Gonzaga of *Johannes Chrysostomus und seine Zeit,* Munich, 1930).

Benito y Durán, A., "El nominalismo arriano y la philosophia cristiana: Eunomio y San Basilio," *Augustinus* 5 (1960), 207–226.

Berceville, G., "L'autorité des Pères selon Thomas d'Aquin," *RSPT* 91 (2007), 129–143.

——, "Les commentaires évangéliques de Thomas d'Aquin et Hugues de Saint-Cher," in *Hugues de Saint-Cher, bibliste et théologien*, ed. L.-J. Bataillon, Gilbert Dahan, and P.-M. Gy, Turnhout, 2004, 173–196.

Berger, S., "Les Préfaces jointes aux livres de la Bible," *Mémoires présentés à l'Academie des inscriptions et belles-lettres*, XI, ii, Paris, 1904.

Bériou, N., *L'avènement des maîtres de la Parole. La prédication à Paris qu xiiie siècle*, 2 vols., Paris, 1998.

——, "La Madeleine dans les sermons parisiens du XIII<sup>e</sup> siècle," *MEFRM* 104, no. 1 (1992), 269–284 (= *Modern Questions about Medieval Sermons. Essays on Marriage, Death, History and Sanctity*, ed. N. Bériou and D. d'Avray, Spoleto, 1994, 323–399).

Bériou, N., and d'Avray, D., "Henry of Provins, O.P.'s Comparison of the Dominican and Franciscan Order's with the Order of Matrimony," in *Modern Questions about Medieval Sermons. Essays on Marriage, Death, History and Sanctity*, ed. N. Bériou and D. d'Avray, Spoleto, 1994, 71–76.

——, "The Image of the Ideal Husband in Thirteenth Century France," in *Modern Questions about Medieval Sermons. Essays on Marriage, Death, History and Sanctity*, ed. N. Bériou and D. d'Avray, Spoleto, 1994, 31–69.

Biget, J.-L, "Héresie, politique et societé en Languedoc (∼ 1120—∼ 1320)," in *Le Pays cathare. Les religions médiévals et leurs expressions méridionales*, ed. J. Berlioz, Fanjeaux-Carcassonne, 1998.

Bischoff, B., "Wendepunkte in der Geschichte der lateinischen Exegese im Frühmittelalter," *Sacris eruditi*, 6 (1954), 189–279; English trans. Colm O'Grady, "Turning-Points in the History of Latin Exegesis in the Early Middle Ages," in *Biblical Studies: The Medieval Irish Contribution*, ed. M. McNamara, Dublin (Proceedings of the Irish Biblical Association 1), 1976, 73–160.

Bogaert, P.M., "La tradition des oracles et du livre de Jérémie, des origines au Moyen Âge," *Revue Théologique de Louvain* 8 (1977), 305–328.

Bonino, S.-T., "Le rôle de l'image dans la connsaissance prophétique d'après saint Thomas d'Aquin," *Revue thomiste* 97 (1989), 533–568.

——, "The Role of the Apostles in the Communication of Revelation according to the *Lectura super Iohannem* of St. Thomas Aquinas," in *Reading John with St. Thomas Aquinas, Theological Exegesis and Speculative Theology*, ed. M. Dauphinas and M. Levering, Washington, DC, 2005, 318–346.

Bonnefoy, J.-F., *Le Saint-Esprit et ses dons selon saint Bonaventure*, Paris, 1929.

Bonniwell, W., *A History of the Dominican Liturgy*, New York, 1945.

Bougerol, J.-G., *Introduction à l'étude de saint Bonaventure*, Tournai, 1961.

——, *Introduction à Saint Bonaventure*, Paris, 1988.

————, "Pecia et critique d'authenticité. Le problème du *Super Sapientiam* attribué à Bonaventure," in *La production du livre universitaire au Moyen Âge*, Paris, 1988, 205–208.

————, "Pour des «Prolegomena Postquam» de l'édition critique de S. Bonaventure Quaracchi 1882–1902," in *The Editing of Theological and Philosophical Texts from the Middle Ages*, ed. M. Asztalos, Stockholm, 1986, 121–131.

————, "Saint Bonaventure et la hiérarchie dionysienne," *AHDLMA* 36 (1969), 131–167.

————, *St. Bonaventura, Sermones Dominicales*, Bibl. Franciscana Scholastica Medii Aevi, t. XXVII, Grottaferrata, 1977.

Boulnois, O., "Augustin et les théories de l'image au Moyen Âge," *RSPT* 91 (2007), 75–91.

————, "L'image parfaite. La structure augustino-porphyrienne des théories médiévales de l'image," in *Intellect et imagination dans la Philosophie Médiévale*, ed. M. Pacheco and J. Meirinhos, vol. 2, Turnhout, 2006, 731–758.

Boyle, J., "Authorial Intention and the *Divisio textus*," in *Reading John with St. Thomas, Theological Exegesis and Speculative Theology*, ed. M. Dauphinais and M. Levering, Washington, DC, 2005, 3–8.

Boyle, L., "A Material Consideration of Santa Sabina ms. XIV L 1," in *Aux origines de la liturgie Dominicaine: Le manuscrit Santa Sabina XIV L 1*, ed. L. Boyle and P.-M. Gy, Paris, 2004, 19–42.

————, "Notes on the Education of the 'Fratres Communes' in the Dominican Order in the Thirteenth Century," *Xenia Medii Aevi historiam illustrantia oblata*, Roma, 1978, 249–267.

Brady, I., "Sacred Sripture in the Early Franciscan School," in *La Sacra Scrittura E I Franciscani*, ed. Antonianum, 1973, 65–82.

Brodero, A., "Le Moyen Âge et le purgatoire," *RHE* 78 (1983), 429–452.

Brown, P., *Augustine of Hippo. A Biography*, Berkeley and Los Angeles, 1969.

Brown, R., *Death of the Messiah, from Gethsemane to the Grave: A Commentary on the Passion Narratives in the Four Gospels*, 2 vols., vol. 2, New York, London, 1994, 1350–1378.

————, *An Introduction to the Gospel of John*, New York, 1998.

————, *The Gospel According to John*, New York, 1970.

Bruyne, D. de, *Préfaces de la Bible latine*, Namur, 1920,

Bultmann, R., *Das Evangelium des Johannes*, Göttingen, 1941.

Burnett, C., "Arabic into Latin: the reception of Arabic philosophy into Western Europe," in P. Adamson and R.C. Taylor, eds, *The Cambridge Companion to Arabic Philosophy*, Cambridge, 2005, 370–404.

Cabrol, F., "Azymes," *DACL*, t. 1, Part 2, 1907, 3254–3260.

Cañas, P., "Intelecto e imaginación en Tomás de Aquino: La imaginación al servicio del intelecto," in *Intellect et imagination dans la Philosophie Médiévale*, ed. M. Pacheco and J. Meirinhos, vol. 3, Turnhout, 2006, 1417–1429.

Cantelli Berarducci, S., "La genesi redazionale del commentario di Alcuino di York al Vangelo di Giovanni e il codice Sankt Gallen, Stiftsbibliothek 258," in *Immagini del Medioevo. Saggi di cultura mediolatina*, Centro italiano di studi sull' alto medievo, 13, Spoleto, 1994.

Cappuyns, M., *Jean Scot Érigène, sa vie, son œuvre, sa pensée*, Paris and Louvain, 1933.

Carozzi, C., *Le Voyage de l'âme dans l'Au-Delà d'apres la littérature latine (V^e-XIII^e siècle)*, Bibliothèque de l'École française de Rome 189, Rome, 1994.

Carra de Vaux, B., "La constitution du corpus exégétique," in *Hugues de Saint-Cher, bibliste et théologien*, ed. L.-J. Bataillon, G. Dahan, and P.-M. Gy, Turnhout, 2004, 43–63.

Chapotin, R., *Histoire des Dominicains de la province de France*, Rouen, 1898.

Chenu, M.-D., "*Antiqui, Moderni*. Notes de lexicographie médiévale," *RSPT* 17 (1928), 82–94.

———, *Introduction à l'étude de Saint Thomas d'Aquin*, Montreal and Paris, 1950, 117.

———, *La Théologie comme science au XIII^e siècle*, 3rd ed., Paris, 1957.

Coleman, J., *Ancient and Medieval Memories: Studies in the Reconstruction of the Past*, Cambridge, 1992.

Collegium Sancti Bonaventurae, "Prolegomena," *S. Bonaventurae Opera omnia*, t. VI, xix–xxi.

Coolman, B. T., *Knowing God by Experience: the Spiritual Senses in the Theology of William of Auxerre*, Washington D.C., 2004. Congar, Y., "Aspects ecclésiologiques de la querelle entre mendiants et séculiers dans la seconde moitié du XIIIe siècle et le début du XIVe siècle," *AHDLMA* 28 (1961), 34–151.

Côté, A., "William of Middleton on Divine Beatitude," *Franciscan Studies* 60 (2002), 17–38.

Courtenay, W., "Programs of Study and Genres of Scholastic Theological Production in the Fourteenth Century," in *Manuels, programmes de cours et techniques d'enseignement dans les universités médiévals*, ed. J. Hamesse, Louvain-la-Neuve, 1994, 325–350.

Cullen, C., *Bonaventure*, Oxford, 2006.

Dahan, G., "Genres, Forms and Various Methods in Christian Exegesis of the Middle Ages," *Hebrew Bible/Old Testament: The History of Its Interpretation*, vol. 1, Part 2, Göttingen, 2000, 215.

———, "Guilliame de Flay et son Commentaire du Livre des Juges. Étude et edition," *Recherches Augustiniennes* 13 (1978), 37–104 (48–50)

———, "Histoire de l'Exégèse Chétienne au Moyen Âge," *Annuaire*. École Practique des Hautes Études, Section des Sciences Religeuses, t. 110, 2001–2002, 377–383 (380–383).

———, "La connaissance du grec dans les correctoires de la Bible du XIIIe siècle," in *Du copiste au collectionneur: Mélanges d'histoire des textes et des bibliothèques en l'honneur d'André Vernet*, ed. Donatella Nebiai and Dalla Guarda, Bibliologia elementa ad librorum studia pertinentia, Turnhout, 1998, 89–109.

————, "La connaissance de l'hébreu dans les correctoires de la Bible du XIIIe siècle," *Revue théologique de Louvain* 23 (1992), 178–190.

————, "La critique textuelle dans les correctoires de la Bible du XIIIe siècle," *Langages et philosophie. Hommage à Jean Jolivet,* Paris, 1997, 365–392.

————, "La méthode critique dans l'étude de la Bible (xii<sup>e</sup>–xiii<sup>e</sup> siècles)," in *La Méthode Critique au Moyen Âge,* ed. M. Chazan and G. Dahan, Turnhout, 2006, 103–128.

————, "L'Ecclésiaste contra Aristote? Les commentaires de Eccl 1, 13 et 17–18 aux xii<sup>e</sup> et xiii<sup>e</sup> siècles," in *Itenéraires de la raison. Ètudes de philosophie médiévale offertes à Maria Cândida Pacheco,* ed. J. F. Meirinhos (Col. Textes et études du Moyen Age, 32), Fédération Internationale desInstituts d'Études Mediévales, Louvain-la-Neuve, 2005, 205–233.

————, *Les Intellectuels Chrétiens et les Juifs au Moyen Âge,* Paris, 1990, 242–249.

————, "Les Pères dans l'exégèse médiévale," *RSPT* 91 (2007), 109–126.

————, "Les prologues des commentaires bibliques," in *Les prologues médiévaux,* ed. J. Hamesse, Turnhout, 2000 ("Textes et études du Moyen Âge," 15), 427–469.

————, "Les Textes bibliques dans le lectionnaire du 'Prototype' de la liturgie dominicaine," in *Aux Origines de la liturgie dominicaine. Le Manuscrit Santa Sabina XIV L 1,* ed. L. Boyle and P.-M. Gy, Paris, 2004, 159–182.

————, *L'exégèse chrétienne de la Bible en Occident Medieval, XIIe-XIVe siècle,* Paris, 1999.

————, "L'Exégèse de Hugues. Méthode et herméneutique," in *Hugues de Saint-Cher, bibliste et théologien,* ed. L.-J. Bataillon, Gilbert Dahan, and P.-M. Gy, Turnhout, 2004, 65–99.

————, "L'Exégèse de l'Histoire de Cain et Abel Du XIIe au XIVe Siècle en Occident," *RTAM* 50 (1983), 38–43.

————, "Lexiques hébreu/latin? Les recueils d'interpretations des noms Hébraïques," in *Les Manuscrits des lexiques et glossaires de l'antiquité tardive à la fin du moyen âge,* ed. J. Hamesse, Louvain-la-Neuve, 1996, 481–526.

————, "Nommer les êtres: exégèse et théories du langage dans les commentaires médiévaux de Gen. 2, 19–20," in *Sprachtheorien in Spätantike und Mittelalter,* ed. S. Ebbesen, Tübingen, 1995, 55–74 (55–56).

————, "Samson et Dalila: le chapitre 16 des Juges dans l'exégèse chrétienne du XIIe et du XIIIe siècle," in *Samson et Dalila = Graphè* 13 (2004), 97–118 (113).

————, " «Sorbonne II». Un correctoire biblique de la seconde moitie du xiii<sup>e</sup> siècle," in *La Bibbia del XIII Secolo. Storio del testo storia dell'esegesi,* ed. G. Cremascoli and F. Santi, Firenze, 2004, 113–153.

Daly, S. R., "Peter Comestor: Master of Histories," *Speculum* 32 (1957), 62–73.

Daniélou, J., "Eunome l'Arien et l'éxégèse néo-platonicienne du Cratyle," *Revue des Études greques* 49 (1956), 412–432.

Davies, O., "The Theological Aesthetics," in *The Cambridge Companion to Hans Urs Von Balthasar,* ed. E. Oakes and D. Moss, Cambridge, 2004, 131–142.

d'Avray, D., "The Gospel of the Marriage Feast of Cana and Marriage Preaching in France," in *Modern Questions about Medieval Sermons. Essays on Marriage, Death, History and Sanctity,* ed. N. Bériou and D. d'Avray, Spoleto, 1994, 135–153.

Dawson, J., "William of Saint-Amour and the Apostolic Tradition," *MS* 40 (1978), 223–238.

Decret, F., *Mani et la tradition manichéenne,* Paris, 2005.

Destrez, J., "A propos d'un répertoire des maîtres en théologie de Paris," *RTAM* 3 (1931), 412–422.

Distelbrink, B., *Bonaventurae Scripta. Authentica Dubia Vel Spuria Critice Recensita,* Roma, 1975.

Dondaine, H.-F., "Hugues de Saint-Cher et la condamnation de 1241," *RSPT* 33, 1949, 170–174.

———, "L'objet et le 'medium' de la vision béatifique chez les théologiens du XIII$^e$ siècle," *RTAM* 21 (1952), 60–130.

Dufeil, M.-M., *Guillaume de Saint-Amour et la Polémique Universitaire,* Paris, 1972.

Duvernoy, J., *L'Histoire des Cathares,* Toulouse, 1979.

Emery, G., *La théologie trinitaire de saint Thomas d'Aquin,* Paris, 2004.

Emmi, B., "Leone ed Eutyche," *Angelicum* 29 (1952), 3–42.

Enkvist, N., "On Defining Style: An Essay in Applied Linguistics," in *Linguistics and Style,* ed. J. Spencer, London, 1964.

Evans, G. R., "Gloss or Analysis? A Crisis of Exegetical Method in the Thirteenth Century," in *La Bibbia del XIII Secolo. Storio del testo storia dell'esegesi,* ed. G. Cremascoli and F. Santi, Firenze, 2004, 93–111.

———, *Old Arts and New Theology: The Beginnings of Theology as an Academic Discipline,* Oxford, 1980.

Fauser, W. *Die Werke Des Albertus Magnus in Ihrer Handshcriftlichen Überlieferung. Teil die Echten Werke,* Westf., 1982.

Fields, S., "Balthasar and Rahner on the Spiritual Senses," *Theological Studies* 57 (1996), 224–241.

Fortna, R., *The Gospel of Signs,* Cambridge, 1970.

Fries, A., "Ein Psalmentkommentar des Johannes von La Rochelle, O.F.M.," *Franz. Studien* 34 (1952), 235–265.

———, "Zur Enstehungszeit der Bibelkommentare Alberts des Grossen," in *Albertus Magnus, Doctor Universalis, 1280–1980,* ed. G. Meyer and A. Zimmermann, Mainz, 1980, 119–139.

Fulton, R., "'Taste and See that the Lord is Sweet' (Ps. 33:9): the Flavor of God in the Monastic West," *Journal of Religion,* 86:2 (2006) 169–204.

Geenen, C., "Saint Thomas et les Pères," *DTC* 15, no. 1 (1946), 738–761.

Ghellinck, J. de, "Originale et originalia," *ALMA* 16 (1939), 95–105.

Gibson, M., *The Bible in the Latin West,* Notre Dame, IN, 1993.

———, "The Glossed Bible," in *Biblia Latina cum Glossa Ordinaria* (facsimile reprint of the edition of A. Rusch, Strasbourg, 1480–1481), vol. 1, Turnhout, 1992, vii–xi.

Gilson, E., *Introduction à l'étude de saint Augustin,* Paris, 1943.

———, *La philosophie au Moyen Âge,* 2nd ed., Paris, 1999.

———, *La philosophie de saint Bonaventure,* 2nd ed., Paris, 1943.

Glorieux, P., "Le Contra Impugnantes de s. Thomas: ses sources—son plan," in *Mélanges Mandonnet. Etudes d'histoire littéraire et doctrinale du Moyen Âge,* Bibliothèque Thomiste, 13, vol. 1, Paris, 1930, 51–81.

———, "Essai sur les commentaires scripturaires de S. Thomas d'Aquin," *RTAM* 12 (1950), 237–266.

———, "L'enseignement au Moyen Age. Techniques et méthodes en usage à la Faculté de Théologie de Paris, au XIIIᵉ siècle," *AHDLMA* 35 (1968), 65–186.

———, *Réportoire des maîtres en théologie de Paris au XIIIe siècle,* Paris, 1933, 107, 113–116.

Grabmann, M., *Die Geschichte der Scholastischen Methode,* Freiburg, 1911.

———, "Ungedruckte exegetische Shriften von Dominikanertheologen des 13. Jahrhunderts," *Angelicum* 20 (1943), 204–218.

Grillmeier, A., *Christ in Christian Tradition,* trans. J. S. Bowden, London, 1965.

Guillaume, P.-M., "Marie-Madeleine," *Dict Sp* 10 (1980), 559–575.

Guinot, J.-N., "Prédication et liturgie chez saint Jean Chrysostom," in *Prédication et liturgie au Moyen Âge,* ed. N. Bériou and F. Morenzoni, Turnhout, 2008, 53–77.

Gy, P.-M., "La Bible dans la liturgie du Moyen Âge," in *Le Moyen Age et la Bible,* ed. P. Riché and G. Lobrichon (Bible de tous les temps, 4), Paris, 1984, 537–552.

———, "Sur le caractère consécratoire de l'acte même du voeu solonnel dans la théologie de Saint Thomas d'Aquin," *Analecta O.P.* 106 (1998), 408–410.

Haenchen, E., *A Commentary on the Gospel of John,* 2 vols., Philadelphia, 1984.

Hale, R. D., "'Taste and See, for God is Sweet': Sensory Perception and Memory in Medieval Christian Mystical Experience," in *Vox Mystica: Essays on Medieval Mysticism in Honor of Professor Valerie M. Lagorio,* ed. V. M. Lagorio and A. C. Bartlett, Cambridge, 1995, 3–14.

Hamesse, J., "La méthode de travail des reportateurs," in *Medioevo e Rinascimento* 3 (1989), 51–67.

———, "*Reportatio* et transmission des Textes," in *The Editing of Theological and Philosophical Texts from the Middle Ages,* Stockholm, 1986, 11–29.

Harvey, S. A., *Scenting Salvation: Ancient Christianity and the Olfactory Imagination,* Berkeley, 2006.

Haskins, C. H., *Studies in the History of Medieval Science,* 2nd ed., Cambridge, 1927.

Hinnebusch, W., *The Early English Friars Preachers,* Roma, 1951.

Horst, U., "Christ, *Exemplar Ordinis Fratrum Praedicantium,* According to Saint Thomas Aquinas," in *Christ among the Medieval Dominicans,* ed. K. Emery Jr. and J. Wawrykow, Notre Dame, IN, 1998, 256–270.

Jansen, K., *The Making of the Magdalene: Preaching and Popular Devotion in the Later Middle Ages,* Princeton, 2000.

Jaubert, A., *La Date de la Cène: Calendrier biblique et liturgie chrétienne,* Paris, 1957.

Jeauneau, J., *Jean Scot: Commentaire sur l'Évangile de Jean. Introduction, texte critique, traduction, notes et index,* ed. and intro., SC 180, 2nd ed., Paris, 1999.

Johnson, M., "Another Look at the Plurality of the Literal Sense," *Medieval Theology and Philosophy* 2 (1992), 117–141.

Jolivet, J. "The Arabic Inheritance," in P. Dronke, ed., *A History of Twelfth Century Western Philosophy,* Cambridge, 1988, 113–150.

Jugie, M., "Eutychès et eutychianisme," *DTC* 15, no. 1 (1913), 1582–1609.

———, "Jean Damascène," *DTC* 8, no. 1 (1924), 693–751.

Kaeppeli, T., "Guillaume d'Alton," *DHGE,* fasc. 129–130, Paris, 1987.

Karris, R., "Bonaventure's Commentary on Luke: Four Case Studies of His Creative Borrowing from Hugh of St. Cher," *Franciscan Studies* 59 (2001), 133–236.

———, "A Comparison of the Glossa Ordinaria, Hugh of St. Cher, and St. Bonaventure on Luke 8:26–39," *Franciscan Studies* 58 (2000), 121–236.

———, "St. Bonaventure's Use of Distinctions," *Franciscan Studies* 60 (2002), 209–244.

Kelly, J. N. D., *Early Christian Doctrines,* New York, 1978.

———, *Goldenmouth: The Story of John Chrysostom, Ascetic, Preacher, Bishop,* Ithaca, NY, 1995.

Kilby, K., "Balthasar and Karl Rahner," in *The Cambridge Companion to Hans Urs Von Balthasar,* ed. E. Oakes and D. Moss, Cambridge, 2004, 256–268.

Kysar, R., *John,* Minneapolis, 1986.

Lacombe, G., "Studies on the Commentaries of Cardinal Stephen Langton" (Part 1), *AHDLMA* 5 (1930), 5–151.

Lambert, M., *The Cathars,* Oxford, 1998.

———, *Franciscan Poverty. The Doctrine of the Absolute Poverty of Christ and the Apostles in the Franciscan Order 1210–1323,* London, 1961.

LaNave, G., "Bonaventure," in Paul L. Gavrilyuk, ed., *The Perception of God: The Spiritual Senses in the Christian Tradition,* Cambridge, forthcoming.

Landgraf, A., "Recherches sur les écrits de Pierre le Mangeur," *RTAM* 3 (1931), 292–306.

Leclercq, J., *Initiation aux auteurs monastiques du Moyen Âge. L'Amour des lettres et le désir de Dieu,* Paris, 1957.

Le Goff, J., *La Naissanse du purgatoire,* Paris, 1981.

Lelong, J., *Bibliotheca sacra,* 2 vols., vol. 2, Paris, 1723, 757.

Lera, J. M., "Theodore de Mopsueste," *Dict Sp.* 15 (1991), 385–400.

Lerner, R., "The Vocation of the Friars Preacher," in *Hugues de Saint-Cher, bibliste et théologien,* ed. L.-J. Bataillon, G. Dahan, and P.-M. Gy, Turnhout, 2004, 215–231.

Lobrichon, G., *La Bible au Moyen Age,* Paris, 2003.

———, "Les éditions de la bible latine dans les universités du XIIIᵉ siècle," in *La Bibbia del XIII Secolo. Storio del testo storia dell'esegesi,* ed. G. Cremascoli and F. Santi, Firenze, 2004, 15–34.

———, "Une nouveauté: les gloses de la Bible," in *Le Moyen Age et la Bible,* ed. P. Riché and G. Lobrichon (Bible de tous les temps, 4), Paris, 1984, 95–114 (= *La Bible au Moyen Age,* ch. 10, 158–172).

Louth, A., *St John Damascene: tradition and originality Byzantine theology,* Oxford, 2002.

Lubac, H. de, *Exegèse Médiévale. Les quatre sens de l'écriture,* Seconde partie, 1, Paris, 1961.

Luscombe, D., "Peter Comestor," in *The Bible in the Medieval World. Essays in Memory of Beryl Smalley,* ed. K. Walsh and D. Wood, Oxford, 1985 (Studies in Church History, Subsidia 4), 109–129.

Lusignan, S., *Préface au "Speculum maius" de Vincent de Beauvais: Réfraction et diffraction,* Montréal and Paris, 1979.

Mandonnet, P., "Chronologie des écrits scripturaires," *RSPT* 11 (1928); 12 (1929).

———, "Thomas Aquinas in Curia Romana lector. Chronologia suae commorationis (1259–1268)," *Xenia Thomistica* 3 (1925), 9–40.

———, "Thomas d'Aquin novice prêcheur," *RT* 8 (1925), 489–533.

Margerie, B. de, *Introduction à l'histoire de l'exégèse,* 4 vols., Paris, 1980–1990.

Martimort, A. G., *Les lectures liturgiques et leurs livres.* Typologie des sources du Moyen Âge occidental, Fasc. 64. Brepols, 1992, 74–75.

Martin, R. M., "Notes sur l'œuvre littéraire de Pierre le Mangeur," *RTAM* 3 (1931), 54–66.

Matter, E. A., "The Church Fathers and the *Glossa Ordinaria,*" in *The Reception of the Church Fathers in the West: From the Carolingians to the Maurists,* ed. Irena Backus, 2 vols., Leiden, 1997.

———, "The Lamentations Commentaries of Hrabanus Maurus and Paschasius Radbertus," *Traditio* 38 (1982), 137–163.

Mazzanti, G., "Anselmo di Laon, Gilberto l'Universale e la Glossa ordinaria alla Biblia," *Bullettino Dell'Istituto Storico Italiano per Il Medio Evo* 102 (1999), 1–18.

McGuckin, J., *St. Cyril of Alexandria: The Christological Controversy, Its History, Theology and Texts,* New York, 2004.

Merlette, B., "Écoles et bibliothèques à Laon, du déclin de l'antiquité au développement de l'université," in *Enseignement et vie culturelle (IXe–XVIe siècle),* Paris, 1975, 31–53.

Michel, A., Purgatoire, *DTC* 13 (1936), 1163–1326.

Minnis, A. J., "*Nolens auctor sed compilator reputari:* The Late-Medival Discourse of Compilation," in *La méthode critique au Moyen Âge,* ed. M. Chazan and G. Dahan, Turnhout, 2006, 47–63.

———, *Medieval Theory of Authorship,* 2nd ed., Aldershot, 1988.

Minnis, A. J. and A. B. Scott. *Medieval Literary Theory and Criticism,* Oxford, 1988.

Monti, D., "A Reconsideration of the Authorship of the Commentary of the Book of Wisdom Attributed to Bonaventure," *AFH* 79 (1986), 359–391.

Morard, M., "Hugues de Saint-Cher, commentateur des Psaumes," in *Hugues de Saint-Cher, bibliste et théologien,* ed. L.-J. Bataillon, G. Dahan, and P.-M. Gy, Turnhout, 2004, 101–153.

Mulchahey, M., *First the Bow Is Bent in Study. Dominican Education before 1350.* Toronto, 1998.

Nagakura, H., "Abstraction et illumination. Une théorie de la connaissance chez saint Bonaventure," in *Intellect et imagination dans la Philosophie Médiévale,* ed. M. Pacheco and J. Meirinhos, vol. 2, Turnhout, 2006, 1243–1254.

Nappo, C., "La Postilla in Marcum di Giovanni de Rupella e suoi riflessi nella Summa Halesiana," *AFH* 50 (1957), 332–347.

Newhauser, R., "Jesus as the First Dominican? Reflections on a Sub-Theme in the Exemplary Literature of Some Thirteenth-Century Preachers," in *Christ among the Medieval Dominicans,* ed. K. Emery Jr. and J. Wawrykow, Notre Dame, IN, 1998, 238–255.

Nicol, W., *The Semeia in the Fourth Gospel: Tradition and redaction,* Leiden, 1972.

Noguchi, R. "Style and the Form-Meaning Link," in *The Text and Beyond: Essays in Literary Linguistics,* ed. C. Goldin Bernstein, London, 1994.

Oliger, L., "Spirituels," *DTC* 14 (1941), 2522–2549.

Oliva, A., *Les Débuts de l'enseignement de Thomas d'Aquin et sa conception de la sacra doctrina,* Paris, 2006.

O'Meara, J., *Eriugena,* Oxford, 1988.

Oudin, C., *Commentarius de scriptoribus ecclesiasticis,* vol. 3, Leipzig, 1722, 380.

Palazzo, É., *Histoire de livres liturgiques. Le Moyen Âge. Des origines au XIIIe siècle.* Paris, 1993.

Paulmier-Foucart, M., with the collaboration of M.-C. Duchenne, *Vincent de Beauvais et le Grand miroir du monde,* Turnhout, 2004 (Témoins de notre histoire 10).

Pegis, A., *St. Thomas and the Problem of the Soul in the Thirteenth Century,* Toronto, 1934, 26–76.

Perkins, P., "The Gospel According to John," *NJBC* 61 (1990), 942–985.

Poirel, D., *Hugues de Saint-Victor,* Paris, 1998.

Quasten, J., *Patrology,* vol. 3, 7th ed., Westminster, 1994 (1st ed., Utrecht, 1950).

Rahner, K., "Le debut d'une doctrine des cinq sens spirituels chez Origene," *RAM* 13 (1932), 113–145.

———, "The Doctrine of the 'Spiritual Senses' in the Middle Ages," in *Theological Investigations,* vol. 16, trans. David Morland, London, 1979, 104–134, originally "La Doctrine des 'sens spirituels' au Moyen-Age: en particulier chez Saint Bonaventure," *RAM* 14 (1933), 263–299.

Ray, R., "What Do We Know about Bede's Commentaries?" *RTAM* 49 (1982), 1–20.

Ridderbos, H., *The Gospel of John,* Cambridge, 1997 (English translation by J. Vriend of *Het Evangelie naar Johannes. Proeve van een theologische Exegese,* Kampen, 1991).

Riedlinger, H., *Die Makellosigkeit der Kirche in Den Lateinischen Hoheliedkommentaren Des Mittelalters,* Munster, 1958.

Riedmatten, H. de, "La Christologie d'Apollinaire de Laodicée," *Studia Patristica* 2 (1957), 208–234.

Rivers, K., *Preaching the Memory of Virtue and Vice: Memory, Images, and Preaching in the Late Middle Ages,* Turnhout, 2010.

Rocca., G., "The Distinction between *Res Significata and Modus Significandi* in Aquinas' Theological Epistemology," *Thomist* 55, no. 22 (1991), 173–197.

Roquebert, M., *L'Épopée cathare,* 4 vols., Toulouse, 1970–1989.

Rosier-Catach, I., *La parole comme acte: sur la grammaire et la sémantique au XIIIe siècle,* Paris, 1994.

Rossi, M., "La 'divisio textus' nei commenti scritturistici di S. Tommaso d'Aquino: un procedimento solo esegetico?" *Angelicum* 71 (1994), 537–548.

Rottenwöhrer, G., *Der Katharismus,* 8 vols., Bad Honnef, 1982–1993.

Rouse, R. H., and M. A., "Biblical *distnctiones* in the XIII[th] Century," *AHDLMA* 41 (1974), 27–37.

Rudy, G., *Mystical Language of Sensation in the Later Middle Ages,* (Studies in Medieval History and Culture 14), New York, 2002.

Runciman, S., *The Medieval Manichee,* Cambridge, 1982 (1st ed. 1947).

Russell, J., "Dictionary of English Writers of the XIII Century," *Bulletin of the Institute of Historical Research,* 1936, Special Supplement, III, 180–181.

Saltman, A., *Stephen Langton: Commentary on the Book of Chroni cles,* Ramat-Gan, 1978.

Saranyana, J.-I., "Conocimiento profético y futuros contingentes según san Bonaventura," in *Intellect et imagination dans la Philosophie Médiévale,* ed. M. Pacheco and J. Meirinhos, vol. 2, Turnhout, 2006, 1255–1266.

Saxer, V., *Le culte de Marie Madeleine en occident des origines à la fin du moyen-âge,* 2 vols. (*Cahiers d'archéologie et d'histoire,* 3), Auxerre and Paris, 1959.

Schenk, R., "*Omnis Christi Actio Nostra Est Instructio.* The Deeds and Sayings of Jesus as Revelation in the View of Thomas Aquinas," in *La Doctrine de la revelation divine, Studi Tomistici* 37 (1990), 103–131.

Schmidt, B., "Prolegomena," in *Alberti Magni Super Matthaeum,* ed. Institutum Alberti Magni Coloniense, *Opera omnia,* t. XXI/1, Köln, 1987, VII–LXVII.

Schnackenburg, R., *Commentary on the Gospel of John,* 3 vols., London, 1982.

Senocak, N., "The Earliest Library Catalogue of the Franciscan Convent of Todi (c. 1300)," *AFH* 99 (2006), 467–505.

Sharpe, R., *Titulus,* Turnhout, 2003.

Sharples, R. W. and van der Eijk, P. J., *Nemesius: On the Nature of Man,* Liverpool, 2008.

Sicard, P., *Hugues de Saint-Victor et son École,* Turnhout, 1991.

Smalley, B., "A Commentary on Isaias by Guerric of Saint-Quentin, O.P.," *Studi e Testi* 122 (1946), 383–397.

———, "Gilbertus Universalis Bishop of London and the Problem of the Glossa Ordinaria," *RTAM* 7 (1935), 235–262.

———, *The Gospels in the Schools c. 1100–c. 1280,* London, 1985.

———, "The School of Andrew of St. Victor," *RTAM* 11 (1939), 145–167.

———, "Some Latin Commentaries on the Sapiential Books in the Late Thirteenth and Early Fourteenth Centuries," *AHDLMA* 18 (1950), 103–128 = Sapiential Books II.

———, "Some More Exegetical Works of Simon of Hinton," *RTAM* 15 (1948), 97–106.

———, "Some Thirteenth-Century Commentaries on the Sapiential Books," *Dominican Studies* 2 (1949), 318–355; 3 (1950), 41–77, 236–274 = Sapiential Books I.

———, "Studies on the Commentaries of Cardinal Stephen Langton" (Part 2), *AHDLMA* 5 (1930), 152–182.

———, *The Study of the Bible in the Middle Ages,* 3rd ed., Oxford, 1983.

———, "Two Biblical Commentaries of Simon of Hinton," *RTAM* 13 (1946), 57–85 (57–60).

———, "Use of the 'Spiritual' Senses of Scripture in Persuasion and Argument by Scholars in the Middle Ages," *RTAM* 52 (1985).

———, "William of Middleton and Guibert of Nogent," *RTAM* 16 (1949), 281–291.

Smith, B., "The Chronology of the Last Supper," *Westminster Theological Journal* 53, no. 1 (1991), 29–45.

Spanneut, M., "Eunomius de Cyzique," *DHGE* 15 (1963), 1399–1405.

Spicq, C., *Esquisse d'une histoire de l'exégèse latine au Moyen Âge,* Paris, 1944.

Stegmüller, F., *Repertorium biblicum medii aevi,* I-VII Matriti 1950–1961; VIII-XI, cura Reinhardt, 1976–1980, II, 392–398.

Stirnemann, P., "Les manuscrits de la *Postille,*" in *Hugues de Saint-Cher, bibliste et théologien,* ed. L.-J. Bataillon, G. Dahan, and P.-M. Gy, Turnhout, 2004, 31–42.

Studer, B., "S. Jean Damascène," *Dict Sp.* 8 (1974), 452–466.

Stump, E., "Aquinas on the Mechanisms of Cognition: Sense and Phantasia," in *Medieval Analyses in Language and Cognition,* ed. S. Ebbesen and R. Friedman, Copenhagen, 1999, 377–395.

———, "Aquinas on the Veracity of the Intellect," *Journal of Philosophy* 88 (1991), 623–632.

———, "Biblical Commentary and Philosophy," in *The Cambridge Companion to Aquinas,* ed. N. Kretzmann and E. Stump, Cambridge, 1993, 252–268.

Sulavik, A., "*Principia* and *Introitus* in Thirteenth-Century Christian Biblical Exegesis with Related Texts," in *La Bibbia del XIII Secolo. Storio del testo storia dell'esegesi,* ed. G. Cremascoli and F. Santi, Firenze, 2004, 269–321.

———, "An Unedited Principium Biblicum attributed to Petrus de Scala, O.P.," *Angelicum* 79 (2002), 87–126.

Synave, P., "La doctrine de S. Thomas d'Aquin sur le sens littéral des Ecritures," *RB* 35 (1926), 40–65.

Tajadod, N., *Mani le bouddha de lumière, catéchisme manichéen chinois,* Paris, 1991.

Thomas, A., "La profession religieuse des Dominicains, formule, cérémonies, histoire," *AFP* 39 (1969) 5–52.

Tischler, M., "Dal Bec a San Vittore: L'aspetto delle Bibbie *neomonastiche* e *vittorine*," in *Forme e modelli della tradizione manoscritta della Bibbia*, ed. Paolo Cherubini, Littera Antiqua, 13, Città del Vaticano, 2005, 373–405.

Torrell, J.-P., "Le Christ dans la spiritualité de saint Thomas," in *Christ among the Medieval Dominicans*, ed. K. Emery Jr. and J. Wawrykow, Notre Dame, IN, 1998, 197–219.

———,"Hugues de Saint-Cher et Thomas d'Aquin: Contribution à l'historie du traité de la prophétie," *RT* 74 (1974), 5–22.

———, *Initiation à Saint Thomas d'Aquin. Sa personne et son œuvre*, 2nd ed., Fribourg, Suisse, 2002, 110.

———, "Introduction," *Saint Thomas d'Aquin, Somme Théologique: La Prophetie*, Paris, 2005.

———, "Introduction," *Thomas d'Aquin, Questions sur la vérité. Question XII, La Prophetie (De prophetia)*, Paris, 2006.

———, *Théorie de la prophétie et philosophie de la connaissance*, Louvain, 1977.

———, "Le traité de la prophétie de S. Thomas d'Aquin et la théologie de la révélation," in *La doctrine de la révélation divine de saint Thomas d'Aquin* (Studi Thomistici 37), ed. L. Elders, Vaticana, 1990, 171–195.

Trottmann, C., *La Vision Béatifique des disputes scholastiques à sa définition par Benôit XII* (BEFAR 289), Roma, 1995, 74–83.

Tugwell, S., *Albert and Thomas, Selected Writings*, New York, 1991.

Urs von Balthasar, H., *The Glory of the Lord: A Theological Aesthetics*, I, *Seeing the Form*, ed. J. Fessio, S.J. and J. Riches, San Francisco, 1982 (English trans. E. Leiva-Merikis of *Herrlichkeit: Eine theologishe Ästhetik*, I: *Schau der Gestalt*, Einsiedeln, 1967).

———, *The Glory of the Lord*, II, *Studies in Theological Style: Clerical Styles*, ed. J. Riches, San Francisco, 1982 (English trans. A. Louth, F. McDonagh, and B.McNeil, C.R.V. of *Herrlichkeit: Eine theologishe Ästhetik*, II: *Fächer der Stile*, I: *Klerikale Stile*, Einsiedeln, 1969).

Vaccari, A., "La *Theoria* Nella Scuola Esegetica di Antiochia," *Biblica* I (1920), 15–16.

Van Banning, J. H. A., "Saint Thomas et l'Opus Imperfectum in Matthaeum," *Atti dell'VIII Congresso Tomistico Internazionale* (*Studi Tomistici* 17), Vaticana, 1982, 73–85.

Van den Borne, C., "De fontibus Commentarii S. Bonaventurae in Ecclesiasten," *AFP* 10 (1917), 257–270.

van der Horst, P. W., and J. Mansfeld, An Alexandrian Platonist against Dualism: Alexander of Lycopolis' Treatise "Critique of the Doctrines of Manichaeus," *Translated with an Introduction and Notes*, Leiden, 1974.

Verger, J., "L'Exégèse de l'Université," in *Le Moyen Age et la Bible*, ed. P. Riché and G. Lobrichon (Bible de tous les temps, 4), Paris, 1984.

———, "L'exégèse, parente pauvre de la théologie scholastique?" in *Manuels, programmes de cours et techniques d'enseignement dans les universités médiévals*, ed. J. Hamesse, Louvain-la-Neuve, 1994, 31–56.

Vincent, C., *Fiat Lux. Lumière et luminaires dans la vie religieuse en Occident du XIIIe au XVIe siècle,* Paris, 2004.

Vosté, I.-M., *S. Albertus Magnus sacrae paginae magister.* Opuscula Biblica Pontificii Colegii Angelici, vol. 1, Roma, 1932–1933, 22.

Vuillemin-Diem, G., and Rahed, R. M., "Burgundio de Pise," *RSPT* 64 (1997), 136–198.

Walz, A., "Hat Johann von Freiburg in Paris studiert?" *Angelicum* 11 (1934), 245–249.

Weisheipl, J., "Albert the Great and Medieval Culture," *Thomist* 44 (1980), 481–501.

———, *Friar Thomas d'Aquino. His Life, Thought and Works,* New York, 1974.

Wielockx, R. "Autour de la *Glossa Ordinaria,*" *RTAM* 49 (1982), 222–228.

Wright, N. T., *Rhetoric and Theory: Figural Reading of John 9,* Berlin, 2009.

Zier, M., "The Development of the *Glossa Ordinaria* to the Bible in the 13th Century: The Evidence of the Bibliothèque Nationale, Paris," in *La Bibbia del XIII Secolo. Storio del testo storia dell'esegesi,* ed. G. Cremascoli and F. Santi, Firenze, 2004, 155–184.

# Index

book

   *108*, 251*n204*, 256*n245*, 260*n6*, 272*nn1*,
   *2*, 285*n122*, 287*n143*, 316*n16*

Paris Bible, 40, 240*nn89–90*
Paschasius Radbertus, 44, 70, 74–75, 81–82,
   89, 242*nn113*, *115*, 254*n226*, 255*n240*,
   257*n252*, 260*n7*
Peter the Chanter, 27, 259*n263*
Peter Comestor, 62–65, 82, 91, 99–101, 165,
   250*nn196*, *198*, *199*, 251*n205*, 252*n211*,
   269*nn90*, *93*
Peter Lombard, 8, 9, 91, 103, 104, 123, 129,
   226*n9*, 227*n11*, 235*nn29*, *30*, 242*n111*,
   244*n142*, 248*n175*, 270*n102*, 280*n71*,
   285*n128*, 286*nn132*, *134*, *136*
Peter of Tarantaise, 4, 202–203
Philip the Chancellor, 110, 274*n17*
Plato, Platonism, and Neoplatonism, 33, 34,
   48, 141, 142–144, 148, 216, 231*n21*,
   233*n15*, *30*, *31*, 290–291*n172*, 313*n61*
Plotinus, 290*n171*
poverty, evangelical, 149–157, 203, 292*nn185–191*,
   293*nn192–198*, 294*nn199–209*,
   295*nn210–211*
preaching, 5–7, 19, 26, 35–36, 39, 41, 66, 75,
   77–80, 89, 90, 94, 98, 100, 107, 113,
   123–124, 125–132, 133, 151, 154–155,
   158, 164, 168, 186, 191, 204, 210–211,
   221, 231*n16*, 232*n4*, 237*n55*, 239*nn84*,
   *87*, 240*n93*, 246*n167*, 255, 258*n257*,
   259*nn264*, *265*, 262*n43*, 265*n72*,
   268*n79*, 269*n100*, 275*n31*, 276*n34*,
   280*n74*, 281*nn81*, *83–89*, 282*nn90*,
   *94*, *95*, 283*nn102*, *103*, 284*nn114*, *116*,
   294*n204*, 296*n6*, 301*n87*, 304*n143*
Proclus, 233*n15*
prologues, to biblical commentaries, 4, 15–16,
   26–40, 42, 53, 57, 62, 83, 84, 140–141,
   168–205, 209–223, 231*n15*, 232*n23*,
   232*n5*, 234*nn16–25*, 235*nn26–35*,
   236*nn37–46*, 237*nn47–62*, 238*nn63–75*,
   239*nn76–86*, 248*n178*, 258*n261*,
   287*n140*, 296*n3*, 299*nn58*, *70*, 300*n80*,
   303*nn115*, *121*, 307*n209*

prophecy, 5–7, 21, 32–37, 56–59, 107–119,
   124, 126–129, 133, 140, 158, 165–166,
   199–200, 217–220, 235*n33*, 238*nn67–75*,
   248*nn177–179*, 249*nn180–188*,
   256*n245*, 272*nn1–6*, 273*nn7–12*,
   274*nn13–23*, 275*nn25–29*, 276*nn35–38*,
   277*nn41–50*, 278*nn51–55*, 281*nn83–84*,
   *89*, 282*nn90*, *93*, 296*n6*, 313*n9*
Psalter, 42, 68, 241*n101*, 253*n225*
purgatory, 56, 101, 102, 269*n101*, 270*nn102*,
   *103*

questio, 4, 6, 22–23, 48, 59–61, 62–67, 80,
   83–88, 90–91, 94–96, 99–103,
   123–124, 135–136, 153–162, 173–174,
   177, 178, 179, 181, 183–186, 188–190,
   194–199, 201, 203, 204, 235, 227*n14*,
   232*nn25–26*, 239*n77*, 243*n132*,
   249*n189*, 250*nn192*, *194*, *195*, 252*n11*,
   253*n212*, 260*n15*, 262*n40* 263*n46*,
   264*nn55*, *56*, *58*, *59*, 266*n73*, 267*n74*,
   270*nn103*, *112*, *115*, 273*n11*, 277*n47*,
   279*n58*, 280*nn70*, *74*, 281*n79*,
   285*n123*, 289*n164*, 291*n176*, 293*nn192*,
   *198*, 294*nn200*, *209*, 295*nn210*, *211*,
   297*n30*, 300*n76*, 304*n143*, 306*n185*,
   306*n291*

Rabanus Maurus, 22, 30, 82, 214, 234*n21*,
   252*n208*, 254*n226*, 260*n7*, 306*n175*
rapture, 108–110*nn6*, *10–13*, *18*, 116–117,
   272*n6*, 273*n12*, 274*nn13*, *18*, 277*nn46*,
   *47*
revelation, 7, 31, 34, 38, 80, 107–149, 158,
   165–166, 272*nn1–6*, 273*nn7–12*,
   274*nn13–23*, 275*nn24–31*, 276*nn32–40*,
   277*nn41–50*, 278*nn51–57*, 279*nn58–*
   *65*, 280*nn66–74*, 281*nn75–89*,
   282*nn90–101*, 283*nn102–113*, *114–118*,
   *119–127*, 286*nn130–137*, 187*nn138–145*,
   288*nn148–155*, 289*nn156–164*,
   290*nn165–172*, 229*nn173–182*,
   292*nn183–184*
reverential exposition (*expositio reverentialis*),
   35, 80–88, 165, 260*n18*

DISCARDED
CONCORDIA UNIV. LIBRARY

CONCORDIA UNIVERSITY LIBRARIES
MONTREAL